REBELLIONS AND REFORMATIONS

ENGLAND C.1450-1603

ANDREW

HISTORY, HERITAGE AND ARCHAEOLOGY PRESS

Copyright © 2015 Andrew Pickering

All rights reserved. No part of this publication may be reproduced or transmitted in any form or by any means, electronic or mechanical including photocopying, recording or any information storage or retrieval system, without prior permission in writing from the publishers.

The right of Andrew Pickering to be identified as the author of this work has been asserted by him in accordance with the Copyright, Designs and patents Act 1988.

Published in 2015 by the History, Heritage and Archaeology Press, an imprint of Ape or Eden Books.
apeoredenbooks@gmail.com

Table of Contents

PART ONE: REBELLIONS 13
Timeline of significant events 14
The Mortimer Claim 19
The House of Lancaster 20
The House of York 21

CHAPTER 1: SOCIETY AND CIVIL WAR 22
Change and continuity 22
Industry, commerce and agriculture 29
The Church 34
Civil war, culture and society 40
Warfare 48
Sources 51
Livery and maintenance, 1472 51
Regulations for the woollen cloth industry, 1465 52
Enclosure, c.1460 53
Lord Chancellor John Russell's speech on enclosures, 1483 55
Act against vagabonds and beggars, 1495 56
The burning of a heretic, 1494 57
A sumptuary law, 1483 58

CHAPTER 2: THE REIGN OF HENRY VI 60
The government of England 60
Plantagenets and Lancastrians 63
The reign of Henry VI 66
Losses in France 67
Rebellion and civil war 73
The causes of the Wars of the Roses 87
Sources 90
The murders of the Bishops of Chichester and Salisbury, 1450 90
The recovery of Normandy by France, 1450 90
The murder of the Duke of Suffolk, 1450 92

*Charges, found to be true in 1451, brought against John and
William Merfeld, 1450* 93
Jack Cade's manifesto, 1450 94
Jack Cade's rebellion, 1450 95
Jack Cade's posthumous attainder, 1451 97
Tension and provocation in London, 1450 98
The Duke of York's justification for marching on London, 1452 99
The struggle over the regency, 1454 100
The release of the Duke of Somerset, 1455 103
The First Battle of St Albans, 1455 103
The death of the Duke of Somerset 104
A royal pardon and an oath of allegiance, 1455 106
The Duke of York's second protectorship, 1455 107
The Battle of Blore Heath, 1459 108
The attainder of the Yorkists, Coventry, 1459 109
The return of the Duke of York, 1460 110
The flight of Queen Margaret, 1460 111
The Battle of Wakefield, 1460 112
The Battle of Mortimer's Cross, 1461 113
The Second Battle of St Albans, 1461 114
The accession of Edward IV, 1461 115
The Battle of Towton, 1461 116

CHAPTER 3: THE REIGN OF EDWARD IV **118**
   THE FIRST REIGN OF EDWARD IV 118
   THE READEPTION OF HENRY VI 128
   THE SECOND REIGN OF EDWARD IV 133
   GEORGE, DUKE OF CLARENCE 134
   FOREIGN POLICY 135
   FINANCIAL POLICY 140
   THE 'NEW MONARCHY' DEBATE 143
   SOURCES 148
      The battles of Hedgeley Moor and Hexham, 1464 148
      The marriage of Edward IV, 1464 150

    The capture of Henry VI, 1465 .... *150*
    Warwick's alliance with Clarence, 1467 .... *151*
    Edward IV's plans for an invasion of France, 1468 .... *153*
    The marriage of Charles Duke of Burgundy and Margaret of York,
    1468 .... *155*
    The capture of Edward IV, 1469 .... *157*
    The Lincolnshire rebellion and the confession of Sir Robert Welles,
    1470 .... *158*
    The alliance between Margaret of Anjou and the Earl of Warwick,
    1470 .... *159*
    War between England and Burgundy, 1471 .... *162*
    The Battle of Barnet, 1471 .... *162*
    The death of the Earl of Warwick, 1471 .... *165*
    The Battle of Tewkesbury, 1471 .... *166*
    Thomas Neville's attack on London, May 1471 .... *170*
    The death of Henry VI, 1471 .... *171*
    The murder of Henry VI, 1471 .... *171*
    Preparations for the marriage of Anne Neville and Richard Duke of
    Gloucester, 1472 .... *172*
    The Anglo-Burgundian treaty, 1474 .... *173*
    Funding the invasion of France, 1475 .... *174*
    The discomposure of Louis XI, 1475 .... *175*
    The Treaty of Picquigny, 1475 .... *176*

CHAPTER 4: THE REIGN OF RICHARD III **178**
    RICHARD, DUKE OF GLOUCESTER 178
    THE USURPATION OF THE THRONE OF EDWARD V 179
    THE DUKE OF BUCKINGHAM'S REBELLION 182
    THE GOVERNMENT OF RICHARD III 185
    THE HISTORICAL REPUTATION OF RICHARD III 191
    THE OVERTHROW OF RICHARD III 198
    SOURCES 203
    The Richard III's usurpation of the throne, 1483 .... *203*
    The execution of Lord Hastings, 1483 .... *206*

The Bishop of St David's comments on the popularity of Richard III, 1483 .... *207*
The Duke of Buckingham's rebellion, 1483 .... *208*
Act of parliament settling the crown upon Richard III, 1484 .... *210*
Richard III's declaration regarding rumours following the death of the Queen, 1485 .... *211*
The supposed crimes of Richard III *212*
The battle of Bosworth, 1485 .... *212*

CHAPTER 5: THE REIGN OF HENRY VII 216
HENRY, EARL OF RICHMOND 216
THE CONSOLIDATION OF POWER 217
REBELLIONS AND PRETENDERS TO THE THRONE 220
THE CORNISH REBELLION, 1497 228
FOREIGN POLICY 230
OPPOSITION IN IRELAND AND POYNINGS' LAW 235
GOVERNMENT 239
THE KING AND THE NOBILITY 243
ACTS OF ATTAINDER, BONDS AND RECOGNISANCES 245
THE KING'S COUNCIL 246
PARLIAMENT 249
THE CHURCH 250
EARLY TUDOR KINGSHIP 252
SOURCES 256
Henry VII's policy after the battle of Bosworth *256*
Lambert Simnel's rebellion, 1487 .... *257*
Lord Lovell's invasion *259*
The battle of Stoke *260*
The Treaty of Medina del Campo, 1489 .... *260*
A letter from Perkin Warbeck to Isabella of Castile, 1493 .... *261*
Perkin Warbeck and Margaret, duchess of Burgundy *261*
Warbeck's invasion of Kent, 1495 .... *264*
Perkin Warbeck's assault on Exeter, 1497 .... *265*
Perkin Warbeck's confession, 1496 .... *267*

 The Cornish rebellion, 1497 269
 The defeat of the Cornish rebels, 1495 270
 War and diplomacy 271
 Ralph Wulford's pretence, 1499 273
 A description of Henry VII 274
 The kingdom of Henry VII 275
 An Act of Attainder, 1491 275
 Bonds and recognisances 276
 A licence to retain 276
 The king's bodyguards 277
 Tonnage and poundage, 1485 277
 Benevolences 278

PART TWO: REFORMATIONS 279
 TIMELINE OF SIGNIFICANT EVENTS 280
 THE HOUSE OF TUDOR 288

CHAPTER 6: THE REIGN OF HENRY VIII 289
 THE NEW KING 289
 THE RISE OF CARDINAL WOLSEY 292
 THE FALL OF CARDINAL WOLSEY 297
 HERESY AND POPULAR PROTESTANTISM 301
 KING HENRY'S 'GREAT MATTER' 302
 THE BREAK WITH ROME 304
 THOMAS CROMWELL AND THE BREAK WITH ROME 307
 THE DISSOLUTION OF THE MONASTERIES 309
 THE LAST DECADE 312
 FOREIGN AFFAIRS, FORTRESS-ENGLAND 316
 SCOTLAND, IRELAND AND WALES 320
 THE DEATH OF KING HARRY 323
 SOURCES 327
  Resistance to the Amicable Grant, 1525 327
  In defence of Wolsey 327
  Anne Boleyn – victim of faction 328
  The Lutheran heresy, 1526 328

Henry to Anne, 1527 329
Anne to Henry, 1527 329
The Act in Restraint of Appeals, 1533 330
The Act of Supremacy, 1534 330
Sir Thomas More, 1535 331
Report on a visitation, 1535 331
The Ten Articles, 1536 332
The Pilgrim's oath, 1536 332
The Pilgrims' ballad, 1536 333
The Pontefract Articles, 1536 333
Hugh Latimer on the Pilgrimage of Grace, 1536 334
Robert Aske's defence, 1537 335
Retribution, 1537 336
A royal injunction concerning the Great Bible, 1538 336
The Bishops' Book, 1537 336
The Act of Six Articles, 1539 337
War with France, 1527 337
Solway Moss and the Treaties of Greenwich, 1543 338

CHAPTER 7: THE REIGN OF EDWARD VI 339
EDWARD VI AND PROTECTOR SOMERSET, 1547-49 339
EDWARD SOMERSET, EARL OF HERTFORD, THE DUKE OF SOMERSET
.... 339
REFORM AND COMPROMISE: SOMERSET'S RELIGIOUS POLICIES 343
FOREIGN AFFAIRS 1547-49 344
THE DUKE OF NORTHUMBERLAND, KING EDWARD AND QUEEN JANE
.... 346
GOVERNMENT AND RELIGION UNDER THE DUKE OF NORTHUMBERLAND 348
THE 'DEVICE FOR THE SUCCESSION': JANE GREY, THE NINE DAY QUEEN 351
SOURCES 354
The 'Good Duke' 354
Rebellion in Somerset, 1549 354

    The Prayer Book Rebellion, 1549 .... *354*
    Kett's Rebellion, 1549 .... *355*
    England and Scotland 1547-49 .... *356*
    The usurpation of Mary Tudor, 1553 .... *357*
    The Nine Day Queen, 1553 .... *357*
    Jane Grey and the Duke of Norfolk *358*

CHAPTER 8: THE REIGN OF MARY I, 1553-58 359
    QUEEN MARY 359
    A SPANISH MARRIAGE AND AN ENGLISH REBELLION 360
    THE ENGLISH COUNTER-REFORMATION... 365
    REFORMATION AND PROPAGANDA.. 366
    COLONIAL RULE AND THE COUNTER-REFORMATION IN IRELAND ... 371
    SOURCES 373
        Queen Mary's proclamation in York, 1553 .... *373*
        Celebrations in London, 1553 .... *373*
        Treason Act, 1553 .... *373*
        The legitimisation of Mary I, 1553 .... *374*
        The Queen to her subjects, 1554 .... *374*
        Wyatt's Rebellion, 1554 .... *374*
        Wyatt's proclamation, 1554 .... *375*
        Foxe's martyrs, 1557 .... *375*
        War with France, 1557 .... *376*
        The fall of Calais, 1558 .... *377*

CHAPTER 9: THE REIGN OF ELIZABETH I 378
    PRINCESS ELIZABETH 378
    THE RELIGIOUS SETTLEMENT, 1559 379
    THE PURITAN MOVEMENT.. 382
    THE DECLINE OF THE 'OLD RELIGION' 385
    THE 'AULD ALLIANCE' 388
    MARY, MURDER AND MAYHEM: SCOTLAND C.1565-70 391
    THE REBELLION OF THE NORTHERN EARLS, 1569 393
    THE STRUGGLE WITH SPAIN 395
    THE NETHERLANDS, ENGLAND AND SPAIN 396

SPAIN AND SPANISH ARMADAS 397
FOREIGN AFFAIRS AFTER 1588 401
PRIVATEERING AND PIRACY 402
MARRIAGE AND DIPLOMACY 404
THE FRENCH DUKES 406
THE COURT 408
THE QUEEN'S COUNCIL 411
THE EARL OF ESSEX 413
ELIZABETHAN PARLIAMENTS 415
GLORIANA 417
THE VIRGIN QUEEN 418
SOURCES 422
   Princess Elizabeth, c.1550 .... *422*
   Queen Elizabeth, 1558 .... *422*
   Elizabeth I and Edmund Grindal, 1576 .... *423*
   Via Media, 1564 .... *424*
   Mary, Queen of Scots, and the succession, 1559 .... *424*
   The rebellion of the northern earls, 1569 .... *425*
   Causes of rebellion, 1569 .... *426*
   The confession of the Earl of Northumberland, 1572 .... *426*
   The excommunication of Elizabeth I, 1570 .... *427*
   The Genoese Bullion Crisis, 1568-9 .... *427*
   Spain: 'that wicked nation', 1568 .... *428*
   Retaliation in Antwerp, 1568 .... *428*
   The 'Enterprise of England', 1587 .... *429*
   Spanish landing craft, 1588 .... *429*
   Spanish troops, 1588 .... *430*
   English artillery, 1588 .... *430*
   Spain and the Earl of Tyrone's Rebellion, 1595 .... *430*
   Spanish aspirations, 1596 .... *430*
   Ireland, Spain and England, 1598 .... *431*
   Privateers, 1603 .... *431*
   Elizabeth I on marriage, 1565 .... *432*
   Elizabeth I's early suitors *432*

The court of Queen Elizabeth, 1598 .... *433*
Faction, c.1598 .... *434*
The rebellion of the Earl of Essex, 1601 .... *434*
Peter Wentworth, 1576 .... *434*
Queen of the Amazons, 1695 .... *435*

CHAPTER 10: SOCIETY AND THE STATE 436
ANTI- CLERICALISM AND THE AUTHORITY OF THE CHURCH. 436
FAMINE, HUNGER AND REBELLION 438
POPULATION 440
WORK 442
ENCLOSURES 444
THE WOOLLEN CLOTH TRADE 447
OTHER INDUSTRIES 449
FAMILIES, SEX AND MARRIAGE 451
A 'WANT OF AFFECTION'? CHILDREN'S LIVES IN TUDOR TIMES 454
THE SIXTEENTH CENTURY PRICE RISE 458
MORTALITY AND ECONOMIC STRESS 459
POVERTY AND THE ELIZABETHAN POOR LAW 461
ELEMENTARY EDUCATION 463
UNIVERSITIES AND INNS OF COURT 464
THE FLOWERING OF THE ARTS 466
POPULAR CULTURE 469
THE LAW 471
CRIME AND PUNISHMENT 473
WITCHCRAFT 475
POPULAR PROTEST 477
OVERSEAS TRADE 479
EXPLORATION 481
TUDOR GOVERNMENT – COURT, COUNCIL AND PARLIAMENT 484
THE TUDOR AGE 491
SOURCES 494
Luther's sect *494*
Scripture in the mother tongue *494*

A Supplication for the Beggars, 1528 .... *495*
Poverty and the dissolution of the monasteries, 1546 .... *495*
The Statute for Artificers, 1563 .... *496*
Vagabonds, 1567 .... *496*
Plague, 1574 .... *497*
Sickness and mortality, Plymouth, 1588 .... *497*
Thomas More on enclosure, 1516 .... *498*
Robert Kett on enclosure, 1549 .... *499*
Good husbandry, 1557 .... *499*
Act against vagabonds and beggars, 1495 .... *500*
Poverty in Somerset, 1596 .... *500*
Gypsies, 1597 .... *501*
Bear baiting, 1599 .... *501*
On arranged marriages, c.1562 .... *502*
Star Chamber, 1565 .... *502*
Star Chamber, c.1600 .... *503*
A bill in Star Chamber, 1500 .... *503*
War and trade, 1586 .... *504*
The start of England's trade in African slaves, 1564 .... *505*
Raleigh's Search for El Dorado *506*
The court of Henry VIII *508*
Royal patronage *509*
Henry VIII's Privy Council, 1540 .... *509*

HISTORICAL SOURCES **511**

INDEX **515**

PART ONE: REBELLIONS

Timeline of significant events

1421 Henry VI born

1422 Henry V died; Henry VI became king

1437 Henry VI's minority ended

1444 Treaty of Tours made with France; Henry VI betrothed to Margaret of Anjou

1445 Henry VI married to Margaret of Anjou

1450 Normandy lost to the French; Suffolk murdered and Cade's rebellion broke out

1452 *February to March* the Duke of York's first insurrection; Richard III born at Fotheringay castle - a frail child considered unlikely to survive infancy

1453 Henry VI became insane; Henry VI's son and heir, Edward, Prince of Wales, born

1454 York's first protectorate began

1455 Henry VI recovered and York's protectorate ended; the Wars of the Roses began: *May* The First Battle of St Albans; *November* York's second protectorate began

1456 Mobs attacked foreigners in London

1457 Further riots against foreigners broke out in London; Bishop Pecock condemned for heresy

1459 *September* The Battle of Blore Heath; York fled to Ireland

REBELLIONS: TIMELINE

1460 *July* The Battle of Northampton; *December* York killed at the Battle of Wakefield

1461 *February* The Battle of Mortimer's Cross; Edward IV's first reign began; Queen Margaret defeated the Yorkists at the second Battle of St Albans; *March* Edward IV defeated the Lancastrians at the Battle of Towton; Edward IV's brother, Richard, made Duke of Gloucester

1462 Queen Margaret, with French support, attacked the north of England from Scotland.

1463 A Sumptuary Law was passed; Edward IV secured a truce with France; the French promised to withdraw support from the Lancastrians

1464 Edward IV married Elizabeth Woodville; the Battle of Hexham

1465 Henry VI captured

1466 Elizabeth Woodville's father, Earl Rivers, made Treasurer of England

1468 A naval war broke out with the Hanseatic League

1469 Thomas Malory completed *Le Morte d'Arthur*; rebellion led by Robin of Redesdale; the Battle of Edgecote; Edward IV held prisoner by Warwick

1470 *February* The Lincolnshire rising; *March* Warwick defeated at the Battle of Empingham; *September* Warwick invaded England and Edward IV fled; *October* The readeption (restoration) of Henry VI; Edward IV and Richard, Duke of Gloucester, went into exile

1471 Start of the second reign of Edward IV; *March* Edward IV returned to England; *April* Warwick defeated and killed at the Battle of Barnet; *May* Prince Edward killed at the Battle of Tewkesbury; Queen Margaret captured; Henry VI put to death in the Tower of London

1474 The Treaty of Utrecht

1475 Edward IV invaded France in alliance with Burgundy and Brittany, but failed to secure the French crown; the Treaty of Picquigny

1476 William Caxton set up England's first printing press

1477 Louis XI invaded Burgundy

1478 George Plantagenet, Duke of Clarence, put to death in the Tower of London

1480 Edward pledged support to the Burgundian cause, now taken up by Maximilian of Austria, married to Mary of Burgundy; the Scots, perhaps encouraged by the French king, began making raids on English border territory

1482 England invaded Scotland; Berwick upon Tweed regained; Burgundian conflict ended with the Treaty of Arras

1483 *April* Edward IV died; *June* Edward V usurped as King of England by the Duke of Gloucester, now Richard III; the two young princes in the Tower disappeared; *October to November* Buckingham's rebellion; Alexander, Duke of Albany, brother of James III of Scotland, launched an abortive, English-sponsored, attack on Scotland; Henry Tudor attempted an invasion of England, supported by the Duke of Brittany

1484 Richard III's only legitimate son died; papal bull condemned witchcraft; three-year truce between England and Scotland, backed by a marriage alliance, signed

1485 *March* Anne Neville, Richard III's wife, died; *August* Henry Tudor defeated and killed Richard III at Bosworth; start of Henry VII's reign; truce signed between England and Scotland; first Navigation Act

1486 Commercial Treaty made with France

1487 The pretender, Lambert Simnel, invaded England, supported by German mercenaries; Simnel defeated at the Battle of Stoke

1488 Henry VII's famous ship, *Great Harry*, constructed

REBELLIONS: TIMELINE

1489 Treaty of Redon signed by Brittany and England; Treaty of Medina del Campo between England and Spain, which included a marriage alliance between Prince Arthur Tudor and Catherine of Aragon; second Navigation Act; temporary truce with France made during conflict over English and French claims to Brittany came to an end

1490 Commercial treaty with Denmark renewed; commercial treaty is made with Florence

1491 Perkin Warbeck arrived in Cork, Ireland claiming to be Richard, Duke of York

1492 Warbeck made welcome in the court of Charles VIII and joined in Paris by around 100 English Yorkists; *October* English invaded France and laid siege to Boulogne; *November* Treaty of Étaples made between Henry and Charles; Warbeck fled to the court of his 'aunt', Margaret of Burgundy, in Flanders

1493 The Austrian Emperor, Maximilian, supported Warbeck's claim and gave him protection; Henry VII ended English trade with Antwerp and the Low Countries in retaliation

1494 The Irish parliament passed Poynings' Law

1495 A new Statute of Treasons; Sir William Stanley (chamberlain of the kings household) and Lord Fitzwalter (royal steward) executed for alleged conspiracy; *July* Warbeck lands with supporters at Deal, Kent - lack of local support resulted in his fleeing to Ireland; Warbeck besieged Waterford without success; failed Scottish invasion of England; James IV signed lasting truce with Henry

1496 Trade treaty signed with Burgundy, Warbeck's native country; Henry VII commissioned John Cabot to find a new trade route to Asia; weights and measures standardised

1497 Cornish rebellion; Warbeck returned to Ireland before sailing to Cornwall in search of support; the Anglo-Scottish truce prevented a simultaneous invasion in the north; Warbeck surrendered to Henry VII

1498 Warbeck escaped, was captured, publicly humiliated in the stocks, and sent to the Tower

1499 Allegations of further conspiratorial behaviour surfaced, which resulted in Warbeck's execution by hanging; the Earl of Warwick, nephew of Edward IV and imprisoned in the Tower since the beginning of Henry's reign, was implicated in the conspiracy and beheaded; commercial treaty made with Riga

1501 Marriage between Prince Arthur and Catherine of Aragon; Henry VII declined the pope's request to lead a crusade against the Turks

1502 Treaty of Perpetual Peace made between England and Scotland; death of Prince Arthur

1503 Henry VII began to build his chapel in Westminster Abbey; James IV of Scotland and Henry VII's daughter, Margaret, were married

1504 Henry VII placed an embargo on Anglo-Flemish trade; guilds and trade companies placed under supervision of the crown

1505 Christ's College, Cambridge, founded

1506 Trade and defence treaty signed with Burgundy

1508 Princess Mary Tudor betrothed to Prince Charles, son of the Duke of Burgundy and grandson of Emperor Maximilian

1509 Death of Henry VII

The Mortimer Claim

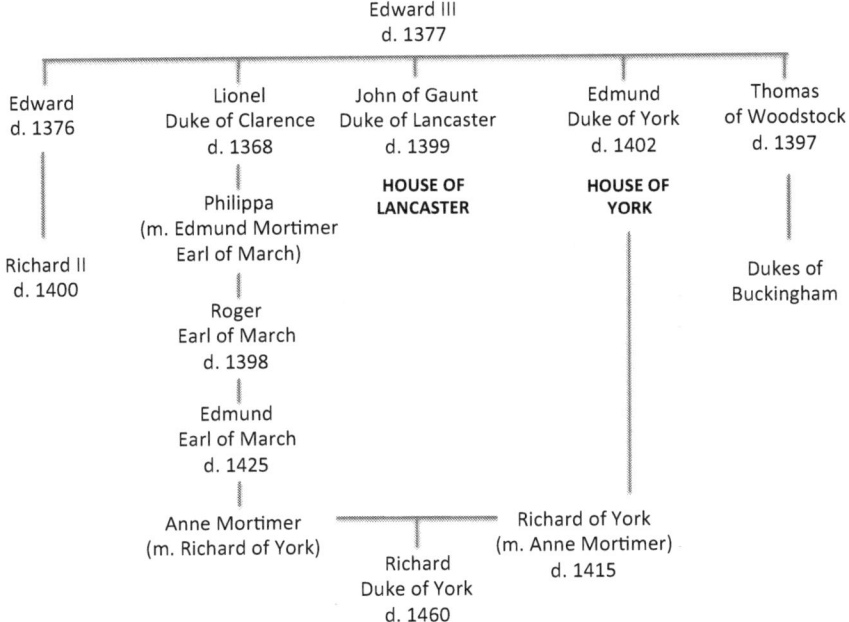

The House of Lancaster

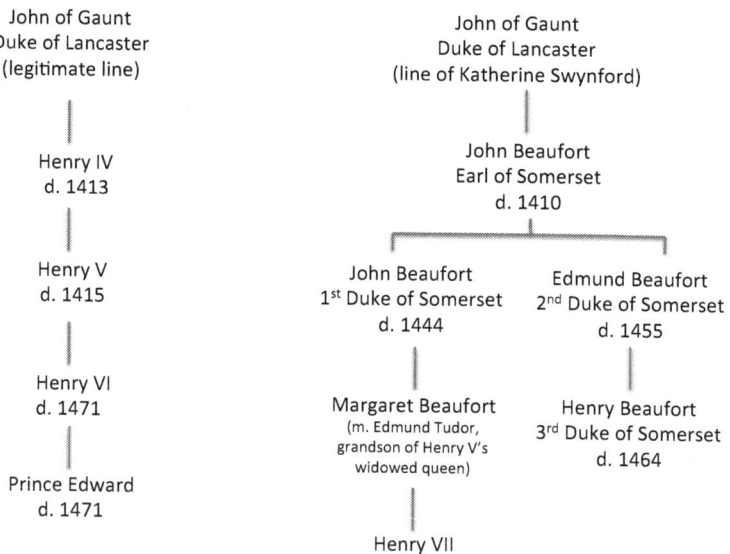

The House of York

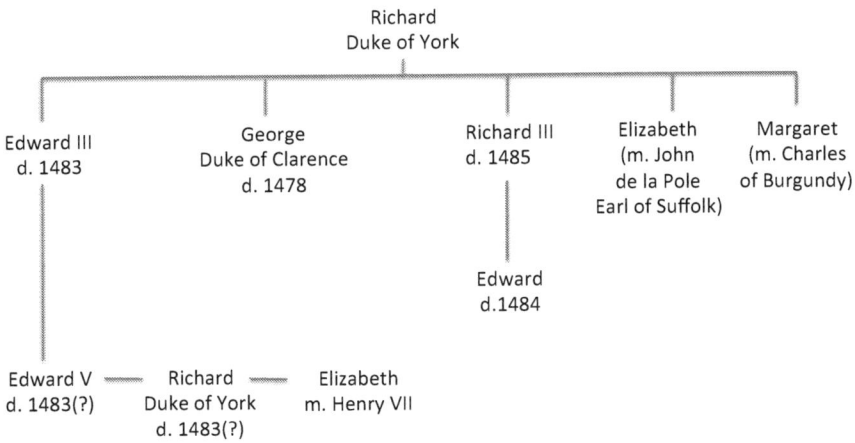

Chapter 1: Society and Civil War

Change and continuity

'England hath long been mad, and scarred herself;
The brother blindly shed the brother's blood,
The father rashly slaughtered his own son,
The son, compelled, been butcher to the sire:
All this divided York and Lancaster.'

(William Shakespeare, *Richard III* Act V Scene V)

The second half of the fifteenth century was an era of civil war but not a time of cultural or economic stagnation. It was an epoch of change. In all spheres developments can be identified. The social order, with the decline of medieval feudalism and an expansion of the 'middle classes', was acquiring a 'modern' hue; the growth of education and greater levels of literacy among the laity provided new opportunities; in religion, even before the Reformation, the pope was becoming a more remote figure; in warfare the cannon had begun to have a role; finished cloth began to dominate the export trade in place of the traditional raw wool; explorers were starting to reshape the world-picture; professional bureaucrats, appointed on merit not birth, were beginning to take the helm of an ever more sophisticated ship of state.

Much of the old survived too. The legacy of the Black Death of the mid-fourteenth century was still felt. Bubonic plague remained one of many fearsome diseases that could decimate populations and bring a sudden and un-forewarned death. The medieval vision of the hereafter, of Paradise and Hell, was as real and terrifying in the later-fifteenth century as it had ever been. The illiterate masses, property-less and having no political power, struggled to survive on the land. They led short, harsh lives that were only a little better than those of their fourteenth century predecessors.

'The choice of the year 1485 as marking the division between medieval and modern England is nowhere more patently absurd than in the matter of religion', commented A. R. Myers in *England in the late Middle Ages* (1978). The church in the reign of Henry VII continued to provide men for some of the highest secular posts in the land, it retained its internationalism as a part of the pope's spiritual kingdom, 'Christendom'. Although monasticism, perhaps, was in decline, the church continued to attract the unquestioning loyalty of the masses. It also attracted the money of those who were able to buy silver and gold plate and build chantries where prayers were offered for the dead. If anything, the church, which owned at least a fifth of all the land in England, was getting richer. Although people might criticise the church as an institution - its wealth and worldliness, for example - the teachings of the greatest English heretic of the fourteenth century, Wycliffe, were the interest of a tiny minority. Ecclesiastical buildings were still the focal point of every community, the church dominated education, and religious observances were part and parcel of secular, economic and domestic activity.

Taking centre-stage in the political history of the period was the nobility:

> 'The nobility, who are endowed with great honours, possessions and riches, can be compared to the firm ground while the lower people, who lack such endowments, can be likened to the unstable, running water [...] the reason why the nobles need to agree and listen to each other is that the well-ordered government of every region depends on the nobility [...]'[1]

In 1436 the nobility were required to pay an income tax. The surviving record of how much they were worth in terms of the amount of land they held provides the historian with a useful profile of the peerage in the middle of the fifteenth century, before the upheaval of the Wars of the Roses. Of the fifty or so lords, three, the Earls of Warwick and Buckingham, and the Duke of York, were much larger landowners than the rest. Even before the Wars of the Roses, England's nobility was divided by the struggle for royal patronage and arguments over the ownership of land. Old rivalries between the great families helped make possible civil wars fought, by and large, by noblemen's retainers.

Fifteenth-century kings were challenged by the threat of

---

[1] John Russell, Bishop of Lincoln and Chancellor of England, 1484.

'overmighty nobles'. On the one hand, they relied on the might of the nobility to protect their interests, and fight with and for them if necessary, on the other, they felt the need to curb the power of those that could find reason to oppose them. In an era of civil war, the allegiance of the great magnates was of supreme importance. Edward IV was remarkably lenient and forgiving in his dealings with former enemies. During, his reign a clique of nobles acquired enormous power and virtual independence in the areas they administered - his brother, Richard, Duke of Gloucester, for example, in the north, the Stanleys in Cheshire and Lancashire, the Woodvilles in Wales. The accumulation of power in the hands of a favoured few instilled resentment in families less fortunate. When one of the lucky families happened to be one that previously was ignoble, as in the case of the Woodvilles, resentment turned to anger.

The Wars of the Roses did not diminish the nobility at large but they did help undermine the phenomenon of the 'super-noble'. The deaths of heads of houses leaving estates in the hands of minors and royal wards, the acquisition by the crown of attainted nobles' territory, and shrewd marital arrangements for members of the king's family, all reduced the potential for successful rebellion in the reign of Henry VII. Henry was far less willing than his immediate predecessors (although similar to Henry V and the earlier Lancastrian kings) to court popularity by awarding titles. The growth of the nobility, seen in the years of Yorkist rule, slowed down. He further controlled the nobility by imposing 'recognisances' on many aristocrats, by which agreed fines would be payable in the event of their failing to fulfil their obligations to the king, such as the collecting of taxes.

The ownership of land and titles changed dramatically during the civil-war years. Lands forfeited through defeat in Edward IV's reign provided the means for the creation of a new Yorkist nobility. The leading beneficiaries were the king's brothers, the Duke of Clarence and Richard, Duke of Gloucester (later Richard III). Edward, however, created far fewer peerages in his second reign than his first, a principle to which Henry VII also adhered. The reign of Edward IV witnessed the meteoric rise of certain gentry families, most notably that of his wife, the Woodvilles, and also the Herberts from Wales. His growing reliance on these 'new' nobles proved disastrous in 1469 when Warwick rebelled. Their rise eclipsed Warwick and the previously dominant Neville clan. The final straw was the marriage of William Herbert's heir to the queen's sister, Mary Woodville. Such an alliance was intolerable to Warwick.

The success of his rebellion, making the king his effective prisoner and being able to purge the court of the Woodville clique, was testimony to the unpopularity of the new nobility, and it demonstrated the danger of a reliance on magnates who lacked well-established gentry loyalties.

The Yorkist kings failed to maintain a dynasty, in part because they invested too much power in too few hands. Richard III died defeated on Bosworth Field because he lacked the grassroots loyalty of his subjects. Although Henry VII did not create many new peers he was skillful in the handling of patronage. While he was careful to contain the custom of retaining among his wealthier subjects, he established his own vast retinue, awarding countless, sometimes redundant, offices, each of which brought with it a fee and certain privileges. With the duchies of both Lancaster and York in his possession, Henry VII had the means, as well as the wisdom, to build dependency upon, and hence support for, his house.

Of all sections of society, the nobility had been the one that was most affected by years of dynastic struggle. Fortunes had been won and lost, new noble families had emerged and some older ones had disappeared. Numerically little had changed and the peerage at the turn of the century numbered just 55. The era of the 'super-noble' had, perhaps, passed, and government was more assured and centralised. The nobility, nevertheless, remained enormously important in local politics and constitutional affairs. The landowning elite would continue for a further couple of centuries to wield pretty much the whole of the political, economic and social power. By the end of Henry VII's reign, the divisions between the great families, to a degree, had been removed and the conditions for civil war eradicated.

The Sumptuary Law of 1463 sought to clarify distinctions within an increasingly complex order of social classes. The gentry by this time included classifications, in descending order of rank, of knights, esquires and gentlemen. By the end of the century, there were 500 knights, 800 esquires and 5,000 gentlemen. The fifteenth century largely predated the era of the 'pseudo-gentry' whose status would rely on wealth. The gentry almost certainly still had status by virtue of their ownership of land. With the aristocracy still secure, the church unreformed (and its monasteries undissolved), and a 'pre-industrial' economy, the greatest age of expansion of the gentry class was yet to occur.

If the ownership of land distinguished the nobility and gentry from other 'classes', their political status separated them. Peers were called to parliament on the personal invitation of the king and their first-born sons according to the principle of primogeniture inherited this privilege, along with their estate. Like ennoblement, knighthoods were awarded as a royal prerogative. Although traditionally these were earned through military service, wealth in land (income worth £100 a year or more) had become a benchmark for the distribution of knighthoods in the emerging post-feudal, capitalist society.

The gentry relied heavily on the patronage of the nobility. Lords could provide opportunities of advancement for knights and esquires and their sons. Nobles still needed retainers and, in an era of 'bastard feudalism', when the old feudal system was breaking down, the bond between lord and retainer was frequently a cash arrangement. The retainer, in return for services and the wearing of the lord's livery, would receive a cash fee.

Although it would be wrong to detect any intent to drive a wedge between the gentry and the old noble elite, Henry VII's inclination for rewarding merit, together with an increasing bureaucratisation of government, helped raise members of the gentry to posts of considerable political importance. The elevation of whole gentry families into the peerage, however, remained extremely unusual. The spectacular rise of the Woodvilles and, indeed, a marriage between peer and gentlewoman (Edward IV and Elizabeth Woodville) were not typical of the age.

It was difficult, too, for those who had made money through trade and commerce in the towns to buy into the landed rural gentry elite. The fifteenth and early-sixteenth-century gentry jealously held on to their land. Moreover, before the Reformation, as the population began to recover after the ravages of the Black Death, land was in short supply and rarely for sale. There was no significant shift in the size and structure of the landowning gentry until the middle years of the sixteenth century.

The great mass of the people owned no land and can be described in a single broad term as 'peasants'. During the fourteenth and fifteenth centuries the character of the English peasantry underwent huge changes. The principal reason for this was the dramatic reduction in the size of the population in the aftermath of the Black Death, which arrived in England, on the back of plague-infested, flea-bearing rats, in 1348. Geoffrey le Baker, a contemporary Oxfordshire cleric and chronicler, wrote:

'And at first it carried off almost all the inhabitants of the seaports in Dorset, and then those living inland and from there it raged so dreadfully through Devon and Somerset as far as Bristol and then men of Gloucester refused those of Bristol entrance to their country, everyone thinking that the breath of those who lived amongst people who died of plague was infectious. But at last it attacked Gloucester, yea and Oxford and London, and finally the whole country of England so violently that scarcely one in ten of either sex was left alive. As the graveyards did not suffice, fields were chosen for the burial of the dead [...] A countless number of common people and a host of monks and nuns and clerics as well, known to God alone, passed away. It was the young and strong that the plague chiefly attacked [...] This great pestilence [...] raged for a whole year in England so terribly that it cleared many country villages entirely of every human being.'

By the time of its passing, England's population was reduced by at least a third, perhaps even a half. Further major outbreaks followed in 1360, 1369 and 1375 - on average every four years until 1480. By the middle of the fifteenth century, the population, already in decline before the arrival of the Black Death, had fallen from around 5 or 6 million in 1300 to 2.5 million or less.

The frequent recurrence of the plague and other epidemics, such as the sweating sickness, a virulent influenza, was a main factor in the general 'malaise' that has been identified as a fundamental characteristic of the period. Many considered this new disease, the 'English sweat', like others, a natural punishment for sin, confirming the inherent corruptness and degradation of human society. Dr Perne, Vice Chancellor of Cambridge University, wrote in 1574:

> 'Although we must confess that our sins are the principal cause of this and all other plagues sent by almighty God, the secondary cause [...] so far as I understand, is not the corruption of the air as the Physicians presently claim, but partly by the apparel of one that carne from London to the Midsummer fair and died of the plague in Barnwell, where the plague has been and is now most vehement.'

The 'miasma' theory, of airborne disease, however, prevailed until the nineteenth century. In any case, there could be little hope in relying upon natural contrivances to cure plagues of supernatural origin.

From such afflictions none was immune. In the *Registrum Annalium Collegii Mertonensis* for 1485 it was noted that:

> 'In the same year, about the end of August and the beginning of September, a marvellous and unprecedented sickness broke out in the University which beginning suddenly with an unexpected sweat, deprived many of their lives. By the end of September this mortality was spread abroad almost without warning through the whole country. In the city of London three mayors died within ten days; and so borne on the breeze from east to west it struck down with extraordinary slaughter almost all the nobility, except however the lords spiritual and temporal. All either died or escaped within the twenty-four hours: but so great and cruel a massacre of wise and prudent men has not been heard of in our history for many centuries. This mortality did not last for more than a month or six weeks, at any rate with the exception of a few cases.'

The condition of the English economy in a labour-intensive, agrarian age was largely shaped by factors to do with population. The Black Death had ravaged Europe and economic recovery was chiefly reliant on the recovery of population. The population of England continued to decline for a century after the Black Death, falling to barely 2 million by the middle of the fifteenth century. Recovery did not begin until the 1480s. Even by the end of the sixteenth century, the population of England was only around 4.1 million.

For those who survived, epidemics could bring economic advantages. With a population of maybe as much as 6 million in 1300 England faced a crisis in which the total demand for food began to outstrip the supply, and people starved. Malnutrition was rife and the people prone to fall victim to plague and famine. By the end of the century, however, land and employment in many areas were in abundant supply. Rents were reduced, or even abandoned entirely, ancient feudal labour duties were commuted into services for cash payments (a process that in some areas predated 1348), wages went up while food prices came down. The era of the Lancastrian kings was one of economic prosperity for the peasantry at large and of depression for the great landlords. Although the Ordinance and Statute of Labourers in 1349 and 1351 was designed to fix maximum wage rates, many employers from the start were inclined to pay more than regulations allowed. In some places peasants, for the first time in their history, were sufficiently well off to start building their own stone houses. Old feudal structures began to break down as the peasantry prospered and began to acquire greater economic independence. The buying and selling of land between peasants, or for that matter the changing of the old feudal dues to cash payments, was not unheard of before the Black Death, but the rate of change in the structure of rural society became much more rapid in the later fourteenth and fifteenth centuries. By 1500 differences in wealth among the peasantry were more marked than ever before: some had become prosperous independent farmers, while others remained landless peasants. Many left the land completely, attracted by the high wages offered to craftsmen and labourers in England's 700 or so towns. Marxist historians, interested in the emergence of the modern industrial working class, consider this a major development in the creation of the capitalist economy. The growth of the cash economy stimulated a growing number of bakers, tailors, shoemakers, carpenters, smiths, butchers and other artisans. Many of these divided their labour between their specialised craft and land husbandry, investing the cash gains of the one in the expansion of the other. Landowners, of course, were less likely to benefit. Low prices for their wheat and wool, coupled with their labourers' demands for higher wages, resulted in severely reduced profits.

In addition to a high mortality rate, the birth rate for the fifteenth century was significantly lower than it had been in the fourteenth. Women in the late fourteenth century tended to marry in their mid or late teens. During the fifteenth century, couples typically married in their mid twenties and a much higher proportion did not marry at all. According to the evidence of wills for the period 1430-80, 24.2 per cent of males died unmarried.

Industry, commerce and agriculture

England's main industries in the fifteenth century were the same as those of the early Middle Ages. These were cloth, mining, salt production, fishing at sea, metalworking, and building. Although fulling mills were now used in the process in preparing wool for weaving, few technological advances had been made. Compared to the highly capitalised Flemish cloth industry, the industry in England was unsophisticated. Traditionally, most wool was exported in a raw state to be worked by the weavers of Antwerp and the Low Countries. Wool was so central to medieval England's prosperity that the chancellor in parliament sat on a symbolic woolsack. During the closing decades of the century significant changes occurred, with a 60 per cent increase in the export of cloth and a 30 per cent decrease in the export of wool. During Henry VII's reign, there was a corresponding increase in total imports of around 50 per cent.

Increased trade promoted an expansion of the merchant class. Business was conducted through the various trade companies, each specialising in a particular commodity. The Mercers were associated with silk, the Grocers with spices, the Merchant Adventurers with woollen cloth, and the Merchant Staplers with raw wool. The merchants' status was asserted through the building of magnificent town houses and the wearing of fine clothes. The most successful traders invested in land and joined the ranks of the gentry, distinguished from others by the wearing of a sword and the bearing of a coat of arms.

A great deal of England's trade was conducted through the Hanseatic League, an organisation of German merchants which had secured special trading privileges in Germany, Scandinavia and Russia and monopolies in the purchase and carriage of certain goods. The merchants brought fish, furs, softwoods and other commodities to England in return for English wool and cloth, coal, tin and other valuable raw materials. In England they too had a privileged position: they were exempt from customs duties, much to the chagrin of English merchants. They operated all along England's east coast with a main base in London - an autonomous community on the Thames called the Steelyard. Venetian merchants had a similar control over trade between England and the eastern Mediterranean.

Fifteenth-century English kings, particularly Edward IV and Henry VII, tried to secure equivalent privileges for English merchants abroad and to undermine the activities of monopolists like the Hanse merchants. In 1485 and 1489, for example, Navigation Acts were passed in order to try to prevent the carriage of certain imported goods in foreign ships.

The 1450s marked the low-point in fifteenth-century English trade, culminating in civil war from 1459 to 1461. Henry VI's struggles with Charles VII of France brought the prosperous trade with Gascony to a virtual halt, worsening the effect of the loss of Henry V's French kingdom. Piracy at the time was rife in the waters around Europe and English privateers, sanctioned by the government, had seized goods belonging to the Hanseatic League from a great merchant fleet of Flemish and Dutch ships in 1449. In retaliation the Hanse merchants took English possessions abroad and, worse still, forbade the passage of English cloth to the east. Riots against foreigners in London in 1456 and 1457, which undermined the activities of foreign merchants in the capital, further damaged international relations, particularly since the English government proved incapable of quelling the disturbances. English merchants, in turn, were further alienated from their government when, by way of compensation, Italian merchants were issued with letters of pardon for past trading offences. Such misfortunes and malpractice led A. R. Myers to the following conclusion:

> 'At the crisis of its fate the Lancastrian regime had therefore not only lost the support of the English merchants but had alienated every commercial power in Europe. No wonder English merchants looked for better things from Yorkist rule.'[2]

Relations with Burgundy improved after 1467 and the new French king, Louis XI, did not share his father's opinion that political hostilities should necessarily impact upon trade. This led to the beginnings of a recovery in the 1460s. The old squabble with the Hanseatic League, however, continued and, by the end of the decade, English and Hanse merchants were engaged in open warfare at sea. The cutting-short of Edward IV's first reign in 1470 brought the quarrel to an end, to the advantage of the Hanseatics. In 1471 Edward returned to England in a flotilla which included fourteen Hanseatic ships and, in return, by the Treaty of Utrecht of 1474, their privileges, which hindered England's direct trade to the east, were fully restored. The new relationship with the League reopened markets abroad and was an important factor in the comparative commercial prosperity of the second half of the fifteenth century.

---

[2] A. R. Myers, *England in the Late Middle Ages* (1978).

The kingdom's 3,000 market places, all authorised by royal charter, fell to just about a thousand as the population declined in the wake of the Black Death. The greatest commercial centres were all ports and included Bristol, Hull, Plymouth, Southampton and, of course, London. Here the streets were said to be paved with gold and people flocked to the city, expanding its population from around 50,000 at the start of Henry VII's reign (1485) to an estimated 120,000 by the end of Henry VIII's (1547).

The growth of the cloth industry and international trade during the second half of the fifteenth century might seem surprising considering the fact that for thirty-two years (1455-87) Englishmen, Yorkists and Lancastrians were at war with one another. The number of woollen cloths exported trebled between 1470 and 1500: a crucial development for the crown since customs duties were its greatest source of revenue. In the same period, the value of land increased, largely because of the cloth trade and also because the population began to grow. Great landowners, notably the king himself, could therefore charge higher rents. The industry also stimulated the growth of an entrepreneurial class of capitalist clothiers, who organised the work of spinners, fullers, weavers and dyers, keeping the ownership of the raw materials in their own hands throughout. They took the lion's share of the profit when the finished product finally arrived at the market place. Eventually the activities of the clothiers became so large-scale and widespread, that historians enquiring into the eighteenth-century 'industrial revolution' have coined a phrase, 'proto-industry', to acknowledge the sophistication of the industry in its pre-factory age.

Agriculture was still the main economic activity. Different environments resulted in different types of land exploitation. In the mid-nineteenth century an agricultural enthusiast, James Caird, divided the country into two 'zones' - the 'highland' and 'lowland'. The moorland and mountainous regions of the highland zone encouraged a pastoral economy, while the lowland zone was better suited to arable farming. The lowland zone continued to be more densely populated and richer. Its great open fields, farmed in strips, supported numerous small, concentrated, 'nuclear' villages. In the highland zone the settlements were more dispersed and farms frequently isolated. In both zones the vast majority of the population was settled in the countryside and worked on the land. Incomes were supplemented by a huge variety of other jobs, such as spinning and weaving. Spinning was such an integral part of a female's working life that unmarried women came to be known as spinsters. Increasingly, cloth manufacture was located in the countryside. This was partly because the restrictive practice of craft guilds that had taken root in the towns kept new entrants out of the industry, but mainly because of the growing need for water power to turn the fulling mills. These began to increase in numbers after the twelfth century.

Population pressure in the thirteenth century had stimulated more intensive use of the land and more sophisticated farming techniques. In some areas, particularly on the big monastic estates, specialisation was developing. The Cistercian monks at Rievaulx and Fountains Abbeys, for example, raised vast flocks of sheep for the wool trade. The scarcity of labour led to a decline in arable farming, as more lords turned their land over to cattle and sheep-rearing, which was less labour intensive. Although self-sufficiency was still the order of the day for some isolated hamlets, particularly in the highland zone, most villages produced a surplus for sale at nearby or even distant markets. This, of course, stimulated the growth of towns during the period, towns which, in turn, represented the principal market places in any locality.

The dramatic decline in population during the fourteenth century resulted, in part, in the decline of the feudal system for the reasons outlined above. The old arrangement whereby work was an obligation to one's overlord and benefactor was fast disappearing in the fifteenth century, as services were commuted to money payments. As early as the late 1200s, kings were relying on paid soldiers, in addition to their feudal vassals, to fight their campaigns.

Despite bouts of civil war, the late-fifteenth-century economy was relatively stable. Agricultural wages in southern England for routine work stood at around four pence a day until the 1540s, and wheat prices, despite considerable fluctuations from year to year, on average rose scarcely at all until the reign of Henry VIII. Overall, the unskilled agricultural labourer of the late fifteenth century was likely to be considerably better off than his late sixteenth-century counterpart, with a wage that could well command at least twice as much purchasing power.

The most prosperous of English towns was London, which thrived on the wool and cloth trades with the Netherlands. Unlike other eastern ports such as Newcastle which specialised in coal, London had a 'diverse trade which made her less susceptible to economic fluctuations. London's merchants lent money to the government which, usually, sat in their town. Great merchant families, such as the Boleyns, joined the gentry as they acquired the status of country seats and official titles. In 1334, just 2 per cent of England's taxable lay wealth was located in London, by 1515 it was 9 per cent. The most powerful merchants formed the Merchant Adventurers Company, which dominated all trade, except that in wool, with the Low Countries. Resentment, particularly among traders based outside London, of the Adventurers' virtual monopoly prompted Henry VII, in 1505, to lower the cost of entry into the company. Very rapidly, as evidenced by Anne Boleyn's marriage to Henry VIII in 1533, the families of London merchants were learning to aspire to the highest places in English society.

The Church

The condition of the Church in the decades before its reformation under Henry VIII in the 1530s is a controversial subject. In the 1960s A. G. Dickens identified a church in trouble. Clerics were criticised for abusing their positions, their secular and ecclesiastical authority was in decline, and the church, it was widely believed, was in need of reformation.

According to Dickens, the power and influence of the church in England was more apparent than real. The church no longer inspired, and lacked the unity and intellectual supremacy it needed to be the truly 'supranational' body it once represented. More recently, historians have painted a very different picture of the pre-Reformation church. J. J. Scarisbrick, for example, studied about 2,500 wills dating from the first half of the sixteenth century and covering most parts of England. He found that the majority left bequests to the Church, an indication, he presumed, of its continuing popularity. Most experts in the field would now agree with Christopher Haigh, who has claimed that Catholic Christianity was flourishing and that the Reformations of the 1500s in themselves do not prove otherwise.

The scores of beautiful Perpendicular churches built in the fifteenth century, particularly in areas associated with the wool and cloth trades, give some indication of the wealth of the Church and its benefactors during the last century of Roman Catholic England. Church income was derived from a variety of sources. Bequests to the parish church might take the form of property that could be rented out. Church land (the glebe) was farmed for profit, flocks of sheep being the mainstay for many of the greatest monasteries and the humblest parishes. Of great importance, too, was the tithe, the obligatory payment of a tenth of each man's income collected in cash or kind. Traditionally, in agrarian communities, this would be a portion of the harvest, stored by the church in a great barn known as the 'tithe barn'. These can still be seen in many parts of England, particularly in the south and west. Although people sometimes resented having to pay the tithe, just as people in more recent times might resent paying income tax, the comparative rarity of tithe suits brought to court during the period suggests that, in principle, the payment of tithes was generally accepted. Although there were prolonged and bitter disputes, sometimes involving large numbers of parishioners arrayed against their priest, as at Barfreston in Kent in 1511, it has been the mistake of some historians to see these really exceptional cases as evidence of general hostility.

Complaints against tithe payments were frequently concerned with the 'mortuary', theoretically the exaction of tithes unpaid during the lifetime of the recently deceased, in practice a death duty. Again, the principle seems to have been accepted and disputes were most likely to arise when a cleric was seen to break with tradition concerning such payments. This was the complaint of the bailiffs of Kingston-upon-Thames in 1509 who accused their vicar of 'taking mortuaries otherwise than hath been taken and used since time out of mind'.

Other traditional payments were voluntary, collections for the Paschal candle at Easter, for example, and money raised at the 'gatherings' of men on Hock Monday and women on Hock Tuesday. Such revenue might buy the church's sacramental silver plate, a new bell, candles or new vestments for the priest. Further petty cash was raised from the sale of church ale, special brews sold to parishioners in association with the various church holidays. For major projects such as the building of a steeple, the church wardens might impose an obligatory rate known as a 'cess' but most parishes appear to have managed without resorting to additional and unpopular impositions.

The greatest patron of the Church was the Crown. In this era of usurpers and pretenders, the king had every reason to secure the ecclesiastical, and better still, papal blessing. Henry VI and Henry VII were renowned for their great piety. Henry VI wrought a triumph of architecture in the Perpendicular style when he commissioned the building of King's College Chapel in Cambridge, and Henry VII constructed the wonderful chapel in Westminster Abbey, originally intended as a shrine for Henry VI, but which became his own mausoleum.

For the illiterate masses of the fifteenth century, the church was a focus for a deep-seated belief in the supernatural, pagan as well as Christian. Superstition and myth were a part of daily life. Fairies and pixies were real phenomena; spells and charms were thought to have magical effect. Many pre-Christian festivals and rituals associated with pagan sites, such as holy wells and standing stones, had survived a thousand years or more of institutionalised Christianity. The Devil, too, was a very real entity, although, as the ultimate shape-changer, he might appear in many guises. The witches with whom he communed were acquiring a higher profile in Western Europe in anticipation of the witchcraft mania of the sixteenth and seventeenth centuries. A papal bull of 1484 provided official condemnation of witchcraft, confirmed its existence, described its practices, and ordered its suppression:

> '[...] many persons of both sexes unmindful of their own salvation [...] have abandoned themselves to devils [...] and by their incantations, spells, conjurations, and other accursed charms [...] have slain infants yet in the mother's womb, as also the offspring of cattle, have blasted the produce of the earth, the grapes of the vine, the fruit of the trees [...] The witches, furthermore, afflict and torment men and women [...] they blasphemously renounce the faith which is theirs by the Sacrament of Baptism, and at the instigation of the enemy of mankind they also shrink not from committing and perpetrating the foulest abominations and the filthiest excesses to the deadly peril of their own souls.'

The medieval Christian church created an imaginary landscape which could be as terrifying as that of any pagan culture. Damnation, which awaited every unrepenting and unforgiven sinner, was a truly terrible prospect. According to one early-fifteenth-century preacher, Richard Alkerton, the wicked would be 'boiled in fire and brimstone without end. Venomous worms [...] shall gnaw all their members unceasingly, and the worm of conscience shall gnaw the soul [...] This fire that tormenteth you shall never be quenched, and they that tormenteth you shall never be weary neither die.' And he was not speaking metaphorically.

Various devices existed for reducing the chances of this dread fate. Pilgrimage to the shrines of saints for example might be a requirement of penitents, as well as those who sought the miraculous healing properties of the array of sacred relics that awaited them at their journey's end. Even after death the rich could speed their passage through purgatory to salvation by leaving money to chantry priests to say masses on their behalf.

Criticism of certain clerical assumptions and practices came from the humanists, inspired particularly by the ideas of the great Dutch humanist, Desiderius Erasmus. Humanism challenged the orthodox theology that man was born sinful and only through divine intervention was he capable of virtue. The humanists placed destiny in human hands with their belief that each individual has the potential to choose a virtuous path through life. Erasmus, encouraged by the example of the English theologian, John Colet, whom he met at Oxford in 1499, adopted a scientific approach to the study of sacred texts. In place of a theology based upon traditional interpretations of ecclesiastical texts, humanists studied the scriptures in their earliest existing form. To this end, Erasmus studied Greek and produced his much-celebrated Greek New Testament. The historical approach to the Bible, as adopted by scholars such as Colet, revealed to humanists the disparity between religious traditions and the original sources, as well as the potential for interpreting a single text in radically different ways. At their most optimistic, humanists believed their methods could help resolve religious differences by revealing the common inspiration for different beliefs. While advocating tolerance for different traditions and interpretations, humanism also promoted a simpler, less ritualistic approach to religion. In Colet's opinion '[...] rites and ceremonies neither purify the spirit nor justify the man.'

The humanists have been seen as a crucial link in the transition from English Catholicism to Protestantism. As well as challenging certain deeply held theological beliefs they highlighted clerical abuses. Colet, for example, was critical of excessive tithes, 'money extorted by bitter exactions under the name of tithes and obligations'. In a sermon delivered in 1510, he found the clergy guilty of 'lust of the flesh', 'covetousness', 'pride of life', and 'worldly occupation'. A friend of Bishop Colet, William Melton, chancellor of York Minster, in a sermon to the ordinands in the diocese of York delivered in about 1510, argued:

> 'We must avoid and keep far from ourselves that grasping, deadly plague of avarice for which practically every priest is accused and held in disrepute before the people, when it is said that we are greedy for rich promotions, or harsh and grasping in retaining or amassing money, and spend but little or nothing on works of piety. For shame! How notorious are we for cunning in making contracts! How absorbed we are in careful purchases or profitable sales! These men take up the fields, the richest pastures, so that their herds of cattle and flocks of sheep may enjoy the finest grazing, but they take neither thought nor care for the tending of their own souls. Because of such people is the honour of the holy priesthood profaned and defiled.'

Colet called for a 'reformation of ecclesiastical affairs'. However he continued to believe in transubstantiation – the miracle of the mass – and accepted the divinely given supremacy of the pope. Some historians have challenged the view that humanism was a radical departure from clerical tradition; in Christopher Haigh's opinion:

> 'Colet's cry for reform was not provoked by a decline in the morals or commitment of priests; rather it stood in a long tradition of Christian protest against the contamination of God's priests by man's ambition. Before Colet there had been Gascoigne in the fifteenth century, Langland in the fourteenth, Grosseteste in the thirteenth, and Bernard of Clairvaux in the twelfth; all critics of clergy who followed the ways of Mammon rather than the path of Christ. The cry for moral reform is a constant theme in Christian history, not the precursor of crisis, and it is unwise to read realities from the claims of crusaders. Colet was not a proto-Protestant, disgusted with the ecclesiastical structure and the sacramental system; he was a high clericalist, anxious to maintain the privileges of priests by raising their prestige.'[3]

Colet himself declared to the Canterbury Convocation in 1510 that 'the diseases which are now in the church were the same in former

---

[3] Christopher Haigh, *English Reformations* (1993).

ages [...] The need, therefore, is not for the enactment of new laws and constitutions, but the observance of those already enacted.'

More radical than Colet and Melton were the Lollards. Lollards were the followers of the remarkably outspoken Yorkshireman, John Wycliffe, an Oxford don who was condemning clerical abuses in the early 1380s. He denied certain fundamental sacramental beliefs, including that of transubstantiation; those in holy orders he likened to 'ravening wolves' and 'fat cows'; his description of the pope as 'a limb of Lucifer' made him a marked man, saved from papal arrest only through the intervention of his powerful patron, John of Gaunt, son of Edward III. He utterly rejected the notion that clerics, by definition, were virtuous, and considered that priests devoid of 'grace' were worthless. Most importantly he stressed the authority of the Bible and, with his Oxford disciples, produced the first English translation since the Norman Conquest. This challenged the privilege of clerics by enabling men other than Latin scholars to read and interpret the scriptures independently.

By the early years of the fifteenth century, the Lollard movement was losing momentum and was widely viewed as heretical. Known Lollards were obliged to wear on their clothing a badge showing a faggot, a symbol of the bundles of sticks used to burn condemned heretics. The movement was driven underground, its followers meeting secretly and the token of their belief, the English Bible, being carefully hidden from the prying eyes of servants and visitors. Over 70 people were put on trial for heresy in Henry VII's reign, of which three were probably burned. By the early sixteenth century Lollards were to be found only in a number of enclaves scattered around southern England, particularly in small towns and villages. Determined bishops effectively purged some traditional centres of the heresy; Archbishop Warham for example persecuted Lollardy in Kent and five public burnings helped eliminate Lollard activity in the county. A vigorous campaign against the movement in Buckinghamshire, perpetrated by Bishop Longland in 1521 and 1522, led to further burnings, public penances and the economic ruin of many identified with the heresy. The focus of this attack was the town of Amersham in which it is estimated around twenty-five per cent of taxpayers were Lollards and around ten per cent of the total population. Nevertheless the Lollard heresy should not be entirely ignored in explaining England's sixteenth century Protestant Reformation.

The Lollard movement spawned the most important theological works written in England and, uniquely since Anglo-Saxon times, in

English in the late Middle Ages. Bishop Reginald Pecock, convinced Lollardy was on the increase, produced many books designed to convert Lollards. His was an intellectual approach to the heresy, which supported the notion that discussion and education were more effective forms of combat than the threat of burning. By doing so, he offended both religious reactionaries and reformers alike. On the one hand, he appealed to reason and arbitration to resolve the dispute with Lollards, in treatises that extended participation in theological discussion beyond the reach of only those who could read Latin, while, on the other hand, he defended the church and certain of its 'abuses' including the non-residence of bishops who had other duties to attend to. He ended up being condemned for heresy himself in 1457, his critics having taken his words out of context and contrived to misinterpret them. His cause was championed by Pope Calixtus III but Rome abandoned him when Pius II became pope in 1458. He spent the rest of his life, in some comfort, imprisoned by the church authorities. This stifling of intellectual and philosophical enquiry into religion, which combined reason and faith, would make the church all the less attractive to educated men of the sixteenth century as the European Renaissance unfolded and took root in England.

The Lollards championed learning. Back in 1384 a group of them even petitioned parliament for the disendowment of the church with a view to using its wealth in the founding of new universities. Lollardy had its origins in the learned discussions of Oxford academics before gaining popularity among poorly educated artisans. They recognised that a growth of education, together with making the scriptures more accessible by having them translated into the vernacular, would have a profound effect upon religious practices and popular beliefs.

Civil war, culture and society

One of the most interesting questions about the period concerns the extent to which the Wars of the Roses impaired the development of English society and culture. The conclusion most historians draw is that the general impact of civil war has, in the past, been exaggerated, and important positive developments in political, economic and religious spheres can be identified for the period 1450 to 1509, some, perhaps, even accelerated by war. Even in the short term, the immediate effects of war were mild when compared to those of the Hundred Years' War fought across the scorched earth of mainland Western Europe in preceding decades.

The wars did impinge upon civilian life, with ordinary men pressed into service and with the land in the path of the armies exploited for provisions. War, however, was not continuous nor was it large scale. Some battles were over in a few hours or less, leaving just a few hundred dead on the battlefield. Any damage sustained by English merchants and other tradesmen in the period was far more likely to be the result of international diplomacy than the immediate consequences of dynastic war fought on English soil. In fact, while the fortunes of the great magnates were both won and lost, the gentry and merchant classes continued to prosper. Royal investment in magnificent ecclesiastical buildings at times languished, but many parishes continued to raise the capital necessary to create the beautiful churches for which the age is renowned.

Nineteenth-century historians assumed the civil wars were catastrophic in every respect: a period of virtual anarchy, dislocation, social and economic collapse. Modern historians are less convinced: 'to argue that the Wars came close to destroying the economic life of the country, or left devastated villages in their wake, or irreparably damaged the relationship between noble and monarch, is simply inaccurate.'[4]

Such opinions were confirmed by the accounts of the wars' contemporaries. Philippe de Commynes, Louis XI's councillor, commented 'England enjoyed this peculiar mercy above all other kingdoms, that neither the country nor the people, nor the houses were wasted, destroyed or demolished; but the calamities and misfortunes of the war fell only upon the soldiers, and especially on the nobility.'

Compared to the savagery of the French wars of the fifteenth century the civil wars in England must have seemed tame to a French observer. To those on the receiving end, however, if we accept this account of the prior of Crowland writing about the aftermath of the Battle of Wakefield (1460), the violence off the battlefield was real enough:

> '[...] fancying that every thing tended to insure them freedom from molestation, paupers and beggars flocked forth from those

---

[4] John Warren, *The Wars of the Roses and the Yorkist Kings* (1995).

quarters in infinite numbers, just like so many mice rushing forth from their holes, and universally devoted themselves to spoil and rapine, without regard of place or person [they] rushed, in their unbridled and frantic rage, into churches and other sanctuaries of God, and most nefariously plundered them of their chalices, books, and vestments [...] When the priests and the other faithful of Christ in any way offered to make resistance, like so many abandoned wretches as they were, they cruelly slaughtered them in the very churches or churchyards. Thus did they proceed with impunity, spreading in vast multitudes over a space of thirty miles [50 kilometres] in breadth and, covering the whole surface of the earth just like so many locusts, made their way almost to the very walls of London [...]'

Although the security of London, as on this occasion, was threatened during the wars, towns and cities were remarkably unscathed by, and uninvolved in, the fighting. Few towns, and certainly no major towns; were sacked, and their trading activities, by and large, remained intact.

Townspeople, following the lead of their city fathers, endeavoured to maintain a neutral, non-participatory role; the Wars of the Roses were fought, in the main, by countrymen. The conduct of Margaret of Anjou's army after Wakefield seems to have been the exception and not the rule - she and the other figureheads had no desire to turn public opinion against the cause, and the logic of civil war dictated the desirability of preserving the prosperity of the territory across which the battles were fought. J. R. Lander's conclusion that the wars 'had little or no effect upon agrarian and commercial life'[5] is, in the broadest terms, true, although quite serious localised disruption at different stages must also have occurred.

A period of thirty years of sporadic campaigning amounted to just a few months of actual 'warfare'. J. R. Lander, writing in 1965, estimated that the campaigns lasted as little as thirteen weeks while A. J. Pollard, writing in 1983, estimated that they lasted almost two years. Many parts of the country were untouched. While kings struggled to raise the capital to complete grand-scale architectural projects, lesser lords, bishops and wealthy merchants continued to build great new

---

[5] J. R. Lander, *The Wars of the Roses* (1965).

homes with comfort and aesthetics, and not war, in mind. Beautifully proportioned Perpendicular ecclesiastical buildings, utterly lacking in the defensive measures associated with contemporary European architecture, mushroomed in town and country alike. Conversely, the number of grants for improving town defences were little higher in the era of the wars than in preceding decades. This implies that there was little heightened sense of insecurity for those who might reasonably have considered themselves a likely target of the belligerents (as they certainly were during the Civil War of the 1640s). The slump in high status building activity during the 1450s and 1460s can be explained by a general economic malaise rather than any sudden outburst of violence.

This was, by modern standards; a violent and, at times, a lawless age. Chaos afflicted war zones during the crises of 1459-1461 and 1469-1471 but there was no general breakdown of law and order. Before and between the civil wars men in high places, and elsewhere, literally got away with murder. Charles Ross related the remarkable, but unexceptional, case of Sir Thomas Malory, author of the greatest Arthurian romance, *Le Morte d'Arthur*:

> 'Although he sat in parliament on no less than three occasions, Malory was also a flagrant law-breaker. In late 1449 or early 1450, with a gang of twenty-six men, he tried to ambush and murder the Duke of Buckingham; in May 1450 he committed rape and extortion, and again in August. The next year he stole several hundred head of livestock, terrorised the monks of Monks Kirby, stole deer from the Duke of Buckingham's park at Caludon, broke into Combe Abbey to steal money and ornaments, and came back the next day with a hundred men to insult the monks and steal more money.'[6]

His further offences included two successful gaol-breaks. The example amplifies Ross's point that 'The high level of violence which characterised late-medieval society, and the difficulties of obtaining justice, were [...] not products of the civil war.' Indeed the soldiery at large appears to have been remarkably well-behaved according to J. R. Lander 'Looting was not unknown'[7] but complaints of it were singularly

---

[6] Charles Ross, *The Wars of the Roses* (1976).

[7] J. R. Lander, *The Wars of the Roses* (1965).

rare: Where, in a continental campaign, 'scorched earth' and requisitioning policies might have been the order of the day, pillaging in the Wars of the Roses was likely to carry the death penalty.

Tradition once had it that the wars all but destroyed the political power and autonomy of the old feudal lords. Certainly many peers died on the battlefield or in the subsequent bouts of retribution. Even so, this rarely extinguished noble families; the failure to produce male heirs was far more likely to cause extinction. Henry VI and Edward IV each more than compensated for the loss in the nobility's numbers by their inclination to create new peers. The new nobility, however, did not entirely take the place of the old. In any case, the male line in such families typically died out every three or four generations; the creation of new nobility was no novelty and the 'old' nobility was not necessarily very old. Kings continued to rely on the nobility and governed trusting to the loyalty of a handful of mighty magnates. If any significant change in the period occurred at all in the political involvement of the English nobility, it lay in the beginnings of a new reluctance among the great families to participate in the deadly conflicts of kings and kingmakers.

The era of the Wars of the Roses was not a great period in terms of the written and visual arts. In previous and at contemporary courts in more settled parts of Europe the arts were stimulated by royal and noble patronage. While little formal courtly poetry of particular merit was produced, this was an age in which less elitist verse flourished in the form of carols, religious songs and narrative ballads. It is likely, for example, that it was during the fifteenth century that many of those particularly English tales of the struggle for justice in unruly and dangerous times - the adventures of Robin Hood and his merry men - were first composed in ballad form.

Portraiture in the fifteenth century was developing a more realistic style and, by the end of the century, portraits of kings and their courtiers were pictures of actual people rather than mere generalisations. The tradition of profile portraiture had also given way to the more informative 'three-quarter face' portrait with the sitter's face painted at an angle, revealing aspects of both the right and left.

The early part of the century, encouraged particularly by the patronage of Henry IV, had been a rich one for courtly and devotional music. During Henry V's reign, English music was a powerful influence on the development of music elsewhere in Europe, as English musicians and composers mingled with their continental counterparts in Henry's

French provinces. The civil wars, however, stifled this art like others during the 1450s and 1460s, when music continued to flourish only in its popular forms.

Perhaps the greatest architectural statement of the age was King's College Chapel, Cambridge. Henry VI laid its foundation stone in 1446 and proceeded to fund the finest piece of fifteenth-century building in the Perpendicular Gothic style. It was unfinished and had already cost £16,000 when Henry was deposed in 1461. Work on it was not resumed until 1480, not to be finished until after the reign of Henry VII. Edward IV spent over £1,000 each year between 1477 and 1483 developing St George's Chapel, also in the Perpendicular style, for the glorification of his dynasty. Similar work was continued during the period at Gloucester Abbey, completed around the time of the accession of Henry VII.

Building on such a grand scale during this period, however, was rare. Other examples include the nave of Winchester Cathedral and the west front of Beverley Minster. Many less grandiose parish churches were built during these turbulent years. This shows, in part, that the 'middle classes', engaged in the wool and cloth trades, continued to prosper while the fortunes of the aristocracy fluctuated. Many were adorned with spectacular woodwork, shaping their roofs, rood screens and misericord seats. Many churches were sumptuously decorated, too, with wall paintings created by local firms of commercial artists. Typically they might reflect society's preoccupation with mortality by depicting the Last Judgement or a picture of St Christopher: a talisman against death, for he who gazed on his image would be spared for the rest of that day.

No new universities were established in England in the fifteenth century, although three were founded in parts of France still under English rule in the 1430s and 1440s (Poitiers, Caen and Bordeaux). New colleges were founded at Oxford (Lincoln in 1429, All Souls in 1438 and Magdalen in 1448) and Cambridge (King's in 1441 and Queens' in 1448). Many new grammar schools were also established during the period. In 1441 Henry VI founded Eton College. Richly endowed by the royal purse, Eton and King's, Cambridge, each soon housing seventy scholars, became two of the greatest centres of learning in pre-Reformation England. While Cambridge University grew in size and reputation, Oxford was in decline and had no more than 600 students by the mid-fifteenth century. Parents began to choose Cambridge over Oxford because of the latter's association with John Wycliffe and the disgraced

Bishop Pecock.

It is not possible to measure accurately the level of literacy in late-medieval Britain. Detailed statistical data from the period does not exist and what constitutes 'literacy', in any case, is open to question. A measure of literacy for more recent times is the frequency with which marriages are confirmed in parish registers with signatures as opposed to crosses. This, of course, helps identify levels of absolute illiteracy but is unhelpful as a device for measuring the *extent* of any individual's literacy.

The historian of the fifteenth century must use a wide variety of sources in order to estimate literacy levels. Customs accounts reveal the numbers of books imported, while private papers and business records reveal the relative importance of documentation. The records of ecclesiastical courts can be used in much the same way as later parish registers, and wills sometimes contained specific reference to valuable manuscripts and devotional books. The careful analysis of such evidence reveals certain facts:

- Literacy was increasing.
- Literacy was no longer restricted and largely confined to the clergy.
- Reading and writing skills extended beyond the nobility and clergy to merchants and skilled artisans. Terms of apprenticeship for some craft guilds required minimum levels of literacy.
- More commercial, legal and government business was conducted through the written word than before.
- English, as opposed to French or Latin, was becoming more common as the language in which even officialdom communicated.
- Literary interests (establishing personal libraries, reading and writing verse, going to plays) became increasingly popular leisure pursuits.

All of these developments would be greatly enhanced by the arrival of the printing press, first introduced to England by William Caxton in 1476. Caxton printed over 18,000 pages on a hand press which was, essentially, a modified wine press. This technology was invented by his fellow printers in the Rhine Valley in the 1440s. His enterprise made nearly a hundred affordable books available between 1476 and 1491, covering a wide range of topics. The print-runs were small, numbering tens or, at best, hundreds, but, like modern periodicals, their circulation among the purchaser's acquaintances was usually wide. Caxton was typical of the new 'literate class'; not a cleric but a rich, educated wool merchant. Besides the clergy, he catered for the tastes of kings, aristocrats, and middle-class landowners and businessmen. The diversity of his output is revealed in the titles of his first publications: *The Recuyell of the Historyes of Troye* (1475), *The Game and Playe of the Chesse* (1476) and *Dictes and Sayenges of the Phylosophers* (1477). He printed most existing English literature, including Sir Thomas Malory's *Le Morte d'Arthur* and Geoffrey Chaucer's *Canterbury Tales*.

Such volumes were instrumental in helping to forge a common English language. England at this time abounded in dialects. In some extreme cases, like that of Northumbrian and Cornish, for example, dialects were virtually different languages. Without a dictionary to guide him, in an age that had no rules regarding accurate spelling and grammatical structure, the printer faced a dilemma. As William Caxton put it in his *Preface* to Virgil's *Aeneid*:

> 'Certayn marchauntes were in a shippe in Tamyse and for lacke of wynde thei taryed atte Forlond and wente to lande for to refreshe them; And one of theym [...] cam in-to an hows and axed for mete; and specyally he axyed after eggys; and the goode wyf answerde that she coude speke no Frenshe [...] And theene at laste another sayd that he wolde haue 'eyren' then the goode wyf sayd that she vnderstod hym wel. Loo, what sholde a man in thyse dates now wryte, 'egges' or 'eyren'?'

That we say these days 'eggs' is in part due to Caxton's books. The language Caxton selected was that in common use in London among the well-to-do circles in which he moved. This language in turn was derived largely from the dialects of the Midlands, reflecting a migration of many Midlanders to the capital during the fourteenth and fifteenth centuries. Thus the English language came to be standardised in Caxton's work according to his own principle of writing 'English not over rude, nor curious, but in such terms as shall be understood by God's grace.'

Warfare

The military historian trying to investigate the Wars of the Roses has little detailed, reliable evidence from which to draw conclusions. Few accounts of the conflicts were ever written down: of the thirteen battles fought, a total of just four provide eye-witness versions of these momentous events that determined dynastic history. Unreliable and often conflicting chronicles, written some time after the events described, provide the 'history' of the rest.

The nature of warfare in the middle years of the fifteenth century was quite unlike that of earlier times. The outcome of the fighting was more likely to be determined by unarmoured foot soldiers rather than mounted knights; artillery, particularly in siege scenarios, began to play a crucial role. On the other hand, the traditional long bow retained, for the time being, its importance as the preferred projectile weapon of English commanders. The primitive handguns familiar to German mercenaries were virtually absent on England's fifteenth-century battlefields, although Edward IV brought with him a contingent of Flemish hand-gunners when he returned from Burgundy in 1471. The infantry were armed with billhooks and bows. The long bow forced cavalrymen to dismount and fight on foot to preserve their horses. For their own protection they wore heavy fluted armour, capable of deflecting arrows and blades. Quality mid-fifteenth-century armour was more vulnerable to bludgeoning, and maces and flails (spiked iron balls on chains) were widely employed. A popular weapon among men of rank, such as the Duke of Gloucester (later Richard III) at Barnet, was the poleaxe: an axe mounted on a metal-studded, five-foot long pole, designed to crush and rip open armour. The weight of their arms and armour, perhaps as much as 50 kilograms, rapidly exhausted the combatants and thus most engagements were of no more than a couple of hours' duration. The unmounted men-at-arms and infantry determined the outcome in battles that, after an initial exchange of arrows and cannon fire, dissolved into a melee of ferocious hand-to-hand fighting, in which the long bow no longer played a decisive part. Under such circumstances, skill, weaponry and armour were critical, and the extent of participation by the nobility, their retainers and hired professional mercenaries was all-important. Lords and kings, with the exception of Henry VI, fought, and sometimes fell, in the thickest of the fighting; twelve noblemen were killed in the fighting between 1459 and 1461 and ten between 1469 and 1471. Such 'leadership from the front' virtually eliminated the chance of tactical warfare once the enemy was engaged at close quarters. The survival of the leaders would help determine whether or not their followers fought on.

In their defence against an attacker, armies used caltraps and pavises. The caltrap was made up of a number of small metal spikes forged together, each pointing in a different direction. A precursor of twentieth-century tank traps, it was designed to bring down the heavy cavalryman whose mount had the misfortune to tread on one of the caltraps littering the ground. The pavise was a wooden screen protecting an archer, with windows cut into it through which he could shoot. This, too, might be spiked with nails protruding from one side so it could be laid on the ground to further hinder the enemy as the archer withdrew.

The number of soldiers involved in any of these pitched battles can only be guessed at. Certainly the figures provided by the chroniclers and eyewitnesses are notoriously inaccurate. William Gregory claimed for example that 200,000 fought for the Yorkists against an even larger Lancastrian force at Towton. This simply does not tally with modern demographers' calculations of a total of just 600,000 men of fighting age living in the whole of England at that time. In most cases the soldiers were local men fighting as an obligation to their lords. Paid professionals could be relied upon to undertake extensive campaigns over considerable distances, but not the unpaid amateurs who had fields to tend and more peaceful trades to pursue. Only the biggest engagements, such as Towton (1461) and the Second Battle of St Albans (1461), were anything more than local conflicts grounded in local feuds and loyalties. At Towton, however, no less than seventy five per cent of the surviving adult peers participated and this exceptional battle probably involved over 50,000 less than the 500,000 or so implied by William Gregory but still a colossal encounter by contemporary standards. This was far and away the greatest battle in numerical terms; even the decisive Battle of Bosworth in 1485 was fought out by fewer than 25,000 men. Many were a good deal smaller still. There were, for example, just 5,000 or so men at the First Battle of St Albans.

Overgenerous estimates for the numbers involved inevitably mean the casualty totals were exaggerated. Towton was an unusually large battle, of uniquely long duration, and exceptionally bloody. Thousands were killed: contemporary sources range from almost 40,000 to a more credible 9,000.

The high proportion of nobility killed in the wars reflects both the number involved and their personal contribution in hand-to-hand combat. Participation, and every great family in England participated, provided opportunities for reward and the chance to defeat a rival in some private vendetta. Old rivalries polarised allegiances: as one family sided with York or Lancaster another supported the opposition. Gentry retainers, however, were not always willing to follow the example of their turn-coat lords, as the Duke of Clarence found in 1469.

Self-interest motivated many of those involved and determined the sides on which they fought, which might well change between battles. For others, honour and kinship were the decisive factors and some pursued lost causes to their own ruination. The Duke of Exeter lost everything in 1461 and went into exile in France where he was reduced to walking barefoot, begging for food from house to house while taking care not to reveal his identity.

SOURCES

Livery and maintenance, 1472

(*The Coventry Leet Book*)

The 19th day of February the mayor received a privy seal from our sovereign lord, the king [Edward IV], directed to him and to the sheriffs in these words as hereafter follows:

By the king
Trusty and well-beloved, we greet you well. Calling to our remembrance and consideration the great tempests, divisions, and troubles that in recent days have occurred in this our realm, the great wildness [...] also that has followed by occasion whereof, and hence by embracery [corrupting a jury], corruption, might, and maintenance that has been, and daily is, used through this our land, both by giving of tokens, liveries, signs, making of retainers and otherwise, we have understood the course and order of our laws have been hindered [...] whereof great extortions, robberies, murders, and other great exorbitances and mischiefs have ensued, to the great displeasure of God and to the great hurt of us, of all our subjects, and the common weal and advantage of all this realm. And we, intending by all means possible to ordain and provide for the pacification, defence, and surety of the same our land and subjects [...] and that the administration of justice may be evenly [...] done as well to poor as to rich [...] have had a ripe communication herein with the lords of this our realm, who one and all have agreed and also promised ' [...] that they will do their true duty [...] that the administration of justice should have due place, and be put into due execution according to our laws [...] and that they shall do nothing [...] nor suffer to be done [...] in favour of any cause or person [...] whereby the due order and course of our laws or the administration and execution of justice may in any way be hindered. Wherefore we report to you these things to the intent that amongst yourselves you should also ordain and see that all things that have been and are used contrary to our said laws be corrected [...] And also that no retainers, liveries, signs, or tokens of clothing be taken, had, nor used by the inhabitants of our city of Coventry, contrary to our laws and statutes ordained and provided in this

matter. And if anyone should presume or take upon him to do or attempt the contrary and will not be reformed, we will and charge you that without any excuse or delay you will expel and put him out of the same our city [...] certifying us in all possible haste what he is, whose livery he uses, and who supports him, not sparing any person, whoever he is. And moreover whereas there are many vagabonds, and ungodly and ill-disposed persons [...] run through the same our land sowing seeds of discord and division in making and telling of tidings, false lying and tales, to the intent abovesaid, we will and strictly charge you that when and as often [blank] person or persons within our said city or jurisdiction, you [blank] in all haste certify us thereof [...] Given under our privy seal at Westminster the 11th day of February.

Regulations for the woollen cloth industry, 1465

Our lord King Edward the Fourth [...] by the advice and assent of the lords spiritual and temporal, and at the special request of his commons in the said parliament, has ordained [...] certain statutes [...] First, whereas many years past, and now at this day, the workmanship of cloth, and things requisite to the same, is and has been of such fraud, deceit and falsity that the said cloths in other lands and countries are had in small reputation, to the great shame of this land; and by reason thereof a great quantity of cloths of other strange lands are brought into this realm, and there sold at a high and excessive price, evidently showing the offence, default, and falsehood of the making of woollen cloths of this land; our said lord the king [...] has ordained certain statutes.

    First, that every whole woollen cloth called broad cloth [...] after the full watering, racking, straining or tentering [stretching, hence the phrase 'on tenterhooks'] of the same ready to sale, shall hold and contain in length 24 yards, and to every yard an inch, containing the breadth of a man's thumb, to be measured by the crest of the same cloth, and in breadth 2 yards, or 7 quarters at the least, within the lists [...]

    Also whereas before this time in the occupations of cloth-making the labourers thereof have been driven to take a great part of their wages in pins, girdles, and other unprofitable wares, under such price as did not stretch to the amount of their lawful wages, and also have delivered to them wools to be wrought by very excessive weight, whereby both men and women have been discouraged; therefore it is ordained and established by the authority aforesaid that every man and woman being doth-makers [...] shall pay to the carders, spinners, and all such other labourers in any part of the said trade lawful money for all their lawful wages [...] and also shall deliver wools to be wrought according to the faithful delivery and due weight thereof.

Also it is ordained [...] that every carder, spinster, weaver, fuller, shearman, and dyer, shall duly perform his duty in his occupation [...] and that every fuller [...] shall exercise and use teasels and not cards, deceitfully impairing the same cloth.

Also it is ordained [...] that all manner of woollen cloth made in any other region brought into this realm and set to sale within any part of this realm [...] shall be forfeit to our said sovereign lord the king; except cloths made in Wales and Ireland, and cloths taken by any of the king's liege people upon the sea, without fraud or collusion.

Enclosure, c.1460

(J. Rous, *Historia Regum Angliae*)

[...] hearing the clamour and murmurings of the people about the pulling down and destruction of towns by great enemies of the commonwealth, I was incited by many to rise against them by speech and pen; and to strive against them as effectively as I could. And they were the more insistent because they knew that long before I had collected against these spoliators many objections, which I set down in certain articles in a certain petition, presented in the Parliament of Coventry after the field of Ludlow in 1459 in Michaelmas term. My labour then was quite in vain, and so I presented petitions in several parliaments afterwards about the aforesaid matter, but to no effect. Therefore in this little work I will expound this matter, so that frequent reading of it by the nobility may stir their hearts to the praise of God and the great profit of the commonwealth [...] And so these internal enemies of the kingdom triumph over the lord king, collecting together a great part of his realm, towns and hamlets, from which they have ignominiously and violently driven out the inhabitants. They are all lovers or inducers of avarice [...] murderers of the poor, destroyers of human sustenance [...] and so they cause a dearth on account of the unusual scarcity [...] of grain, and in this dearth the poor cannot find the price of grain, and so they often die of hunger. Trade is also destroyed by reason of the fewness of men, for the fugitives had been wont to be purchasers from craftsmen and sellers of grain and nutritious animals and other articles. [...] And so the destruction of villages and hamlets destroys trade, cities, stewards, and craftsmen, and hence the whole realm if their avarice should continue and a remedy is not found. We may see the number of villages now destroyed in the southern part of Warwickshire, and if only the inhabitants of these were to come to market, as they used to do, a large market place would be needed for them, In my countryside near Warwick where I was born, within 12 miles or so, the following villages and hamlets have been destroyed [he names sixty-two]. All these villages mentioned here are either destroyed ' or shrunken, which is to be deplored. And as I saw in a record about certain of these villages in the 7th and 8th year of King Edward the first since the Conquest how many tenures they then had, I will set it down here. Upper Woodcote had 13, and Lower Woodcote 14, Charlcote had 57, now it has only 6 or 7 with the rectory and the manor-house. Compton Verney now has only a manor-house and a church, but once it had 27 holdings of freemen and bondmen, in addition to a good rectory with its house. Kington or Lower Chesterton Parva once had 11 holdings, Compton Scorpion once had 63; now they have none, and the chapel is destroyed and despoiled. Chesterton Magna manor still survives, but it had anciently 79 tenures, of which scarcely three remain. Also by another record Hurst once had 19 tenures, now there is only one house [...] Crulfield once had twelve tenants, now there is only a grange. [...] At Billesley Trussell only the manor house remains, and all the tenants have been driven away, which is deplorable. Canston above Dunsmore in the parish of Dunchurch was once a village, but now it is only a grange of die abbot of Pipewell in the gift of the Earls of Warwick, and it has become a den of thieves and robbers. The monks rejoice in the gain which results from the enclosure, but those who have been despoiled are saddened by the thefts committed there. [...] Fulbrook was once a rectory, but the church is destroyed, the villagers have fled, only the manor house remains, and the rest was imparked by John, Duke of Bedford, brother of King Henry V, who built there a noble village equivalent to a town, but now there is almost nothing left [...] If there should have been as much destruction of villages in other provinces of the realm as there has in Warwickshire and its neighbourhood, it would be grievous news to all lovers of the commonwealth [...] Now instead of buyers and sellers in cities and market towns there are swarms of beggars, driven out by the destroyers of villages from their houses and lands. [...] These destroyers of villages sin grievously [...] for the lord king cannot resist enemy invaders without the help of the realm [...] but what can [lords and noblemen] do without the common people?; for the common folk carry the burden, even though lords provide the leaders. And in these days, the number of the common folk is much reduced, with the destruction of villages, hamlets, and houses, and countless unhappy men and women. For men who are turned out with their families [...] do not attend any longer to the procreation of children, but all their care is on how they are to live. Many do so by begging, and many, driven by necessity, resort to theft and robbery, and their wives and daughters exist by harlotry, and most of their days are spent in idleness. Those who resort to theft are finally hanged, and those who resort to idleness and begging live miserably, and are no use to either king or commonwealth, but their villages everywhere are desolate. And whereas the lord king once had strong men for his warlike affairs, now instead of men nothing alive is found in some places but horses and mares and in other places sheep and oxen and cows. In other places you will find wolves, badgers, rabbits and hares, stags, goats, deer, pigs, and other wild beasts, but neither men nor women, nor children, except shepherds, swineherds, and suchlike [...] To thee, Oh noble king, is entrusted the duty of enforcing justice under heavy penalties, and to rule this noble realm which has been committed to thee, and to defend it with all thy might from external foes and internal enemies, like these destroyers of villages [...] Study therefore, Oh most noble king, as a soldier of Christ, to resist the adversaries of God, of thyself. and of the realm. And so when thou departest from this world, Christ will meet thee on thy arrival, and graciously invite thee to his supper with the words: "Friend, go up higher." [...] May God grant that it be so. Amen.

Lord Chancellor John Russell's speech on enclosures, 1483

Would to God that our people of England, where every man now severally studies to his own singular avail, and to the accomplishment of his own particular affection, would think upon his own body, the common and public body of the realm, where of right a great person is often but a small member. And yet, be he never so great, if by his doing his body falls into decay, as we see daily it does by enclosures and emparking, by driving away of tenants and letting down of tenantries, and yet, what is most to be lamented, by unlawful assemblies and insurrections [...] such a one [...] is but as it were a rotten member of the body, having neither the ability nor might to save it from falling.

[This speech, intended for Edward V's doomed first parliament, was not delivered.]

Act against vagabonds and beggars, 1495

Forasmuch as the King's Grace most entirely desireth amongst all earthly things the prosperity and restfulness of this his land and his subjects of the same to live quietly and surefully to the pleasure of God and according to his laws, willing and always of his pity intending to reduce them thereunto by softer means than by such extreme rigour [...] considering also the great charges that should grow to his subjects for the bringing of vagabonds to the gaols [...] and the long abiding of them therein [...] His Highness will by the authority of this present Parliament it be ordained and enacted, that where such misdoers should be by examination committed to the common gaol [...] that the sheriff, mayors, bailiffs, high constables, and petty constables [...] within three days after this Act proclaimed, make due search, and take or cause to be taken all such vagabonds, idle and suspect persons, living suspiciously, and them so taken to be set in stocks, there to remain by the space of three days and three nights and there to have none other sustenance but bread and water; and after the said three days and three nights to be had out and set at large and then to be commanded to avoid the town; And if eftsoons he be taken in such default in the same town or township, then he to be set in the like wise in stocks by the space of six days with like diet as is before rehearsed; and if any person or persons give any form of meat or drink to the said misdoers being in stocks in the form aforesaid [...] that then they forfeit for every time so doing 12d.

    And it is also ordained [...] that all manner of beggars not able to work [...] go, rest, and abide in his hundred where he last dwelled, or there where he is best known or born, there to remain [...] without begging out of the said hundred, upon pain to be punished as is beforesaid.

Where in all places throughout this realm of England vagabonds and beggars have of long time increased and daily do increase [...] by the occasion of idleness, mother and root of all vices, whereby hath insurged and sprung [...] continual thefts, murders, and other heinous offences [...] to the great displeasure of God, the inquietation and damage of the King's people, and to the marvellous disturbance of the common weal of this realm [...] Be it therefore enacted [...] that the Justices of the Peace [...] shall make diligent search and enquiry of all aged, poor, and impotent persons which live or be compelled to live by alms of the charity of the people that be or shall be hereafter abiding [...] within the limits of their division [...] and the said Justices of Peace [...] shall have the power and authority by their discretions to enable to beg, within such [...] limits as they shall appoint, such of the said impotent persons which they shall find and think most convenient within the limits of their division to live of the charity and alms of the people, and to give in commandment to every such aged and impotent beggar that none of them shall beg without the limits to them so appointed, and shall also register and write the names of every such impotent beggar in a bill or roll indented, the one part to remain with themselves and the other part by them to be certified before the Justices of Peace at the next Sessions after such search [...] And if any such impotent person so authorised to beg do beg in any other place than within such limits that he shall be assigned unto, that then the Justices of Peace shall [...] punish all such persons by imprisonment in the stocks by the space of two days and two nights, giving them but only bread and water, and after that cause every such impotent person to be sworn to return again [...] where they be authorised to beg in.

The burning of a heretic, 1494

(Robert Fabyan, *Great Chronicle of London*)

Upon the xxviii day of April was an old cankered heretic, weak-minded for age, named Joan Boughton, widow, and mother unto the wife of Sir John Young, which daughter, as some reported, had a great smell of an heretic after the mother, burnt in Smithfield, This woman was four score years of age or more, and held eight opinions of heresy which I pass over, for the hearing of them is neither pleasant nor fruitful. She was a disciple of Wyclif, whom she accounted for a saint, and held so fast and firmly seven of his twelve opinions that all the doctors of London could not turn her from one of them. When it was told to her that she should be burnt for her obstinacy and false belief, she set nought at their words but defied them, for she said she was so beloved with God and His holy angels that all the fire in London should not hurt her. But on the morrow a bundle of faggots and a few reeds consumed her in a little while; and while she might cry she spake often of God and Our Lady, but no man could cause her to name Jesus, and so she died, But it appeared that she left some of her disciples behind her, for the night following, the more part of the ashes of that fire that she was burnt in were had away and kept for a precious relic in an earthen pot.

A sumptuary law, 1483

Because our sovereign lord the king has understood, by a petition made to him by his commons, that divers statutes and ordinances touching the restraint of the excessive apparel of the people of his realm were made and ordained, and that for the lack of execution of the same statutes his said realm was fallen into great misery and poverty, and likely to fall into greater, unless the better remedy be provided, [he] has ordained [...] that no manner of person of whatever estate, degree, or condition he may be, shall wear any cloth of gold or silk of purple colour, except the king, the queen, the king's mother, the king's children, his brothers and sisters, upon pain of forfeiture for every default, £20. And that no one under the estate of a duke shall wear any cloth of gold of tissue, on pain of forfeiture for every default 20 marks. And that no man under the estate of a lord shall wear plain doth of gold, upon pain of forfeiture for every default, 10 marks. And that no man under the degree of a knight shall wear any velvet in their doublets or gowns. And that no man under the same degree wear any damasks or satin in their gowns but only esquires for the king's body, upon pain of forfeiting for every default, 40s. And that no yeoman of the crown or any other men under the degree of an esquire or a gentleman shall wear in their doublets damask or satin, or gowns of chamlet [very fine woolen cloth], upon pain to forfeit for every default, 40s. And that no man under the estate of a lord shall wear any kind of woollen cloth made outside this realm of England, Ireland, Wales, and Calais, nor wear any furs of sables, upon pain to forfeit for every default £10. And also it is ordained and established by the same authority that no servant of husbandry or any common labourer, nor servant to any artificer outside a city or borough shall wear in their clothing any cloth, of which the broad yard exceeds the price of two shillings; nor that any of the servants or labourers shall suffer their wives to wear any clothing that is of higher price than is allowed to their husbands; and they shall not allow their wives to wear any piece of cloth called a kerchief, of which the price exceeds 20d; and none of the servants or labourers shall wear any hose, of which the pair exceeds in price 18d; upon pain of forfeiting for every default, 40d.

Chapter 2: The Reign of Henry VI

The government of England

Kingship by the fifteenth century had acquired a mystical quality; kings were not like other men: their touch alone could cure scrofula and it had become customary to approach them on bended knee and address them as 'Majesty'. It was assumed that kings ruled by 'divine right', that is that they were appointed by God - a belief emphasised by the fact that they were anointed with holy oil at their coronation. There was a general acceptance of the concept of the 'royal prerogative', the monarch's right to rule, in such areas as foreign policy, by issuing proclamations which had the force of law. However, it was generally accepted that the king should consult a parliament before making new statute laws or imposing new taxes.

The king's strength in the fifteenth century lay in the combination of traditional respect for his authority with the fact that the nobility depended on royal patronage. The traditional feudal bonds between king and subject were largely broken down by the later Middle Ages. Loyalty was only likely when it was in each party's mutual interest. As the king was the richest man in the kingdom and had power to bestow positions and other gifts on those he chose to patronise, he was well equipped to gain the service and support of the nobility.

The mystique of monarchy was reinforced by the stories associated with its lineage. English kings claimed an ancestry that included King Arthur, the Emperor Constantine and the great-grandson of Aeneas of Troy. These enduring legends were written down as 'history' in about 1130 by Geoffrey of Monmouth in his *History of the Kings of Britain*.

The kingdom that the later-fifteenth-century monarchs ruled, in effect, was made up of England, Wales and a part of Ireland - Dublin and the area around it known as the Pale. Assumptions were made regarding the ancient allegiance owed to the English crown by the Welsh, Irish and Scottish, but these were not really enough to unite all the peoples of the British Isles. Much of Ireland and all of Scotland were fiercely independent and frequently in conflict with England. Despite its 'conquest' in the twelfth century, most of Ireland was not subdued and certainly not Anglicised despite the influence of certain Anglo-Irish families. Here the English king's title was that merely of 'Lord of Ireland'. The Welsh Marcher lords and the northern earls enjoyed a good deal of autonomy too, having secured privileges, 'liberties', in return for their loyalty and willingness to defend the king's most vulnerable borders.

Henry V had won a second kingdom for English kings after defeating the French at Agincourt in 1415. This kingdom comprised half of France, but all except Calais and its Pale was lost by 1453. The war in which it was lost, the Hundred Years' War, probably encouraged a sense of national identity and encouraged a cultural cohesion within the realm. French, a language long cultivated by the English nobility, went into decline in England as English fortress towns in France were recaptured by French armies. Until Calais was lost in 1558, English kings were active in asserting their French dynastic claims. Calais was an immensely important outpost during the period since it provided the main port through which English cloth entered continental Europe.

The king's council was the body on which the monarch was most reliant for advice. Traditionally it comprised some of the greatest magnates, but stronger medieval kings also surrounded themselves with advisers who were capable, yet could claim no 'natural' right to enjoy the privilege of joining the king's inner sanctum. A strong council was necessary during the minorities of both Richard II and Henry VI until they came of age. The turbulent years of the second half of the fifteenth century, moreover, encouraged a less informal relationship between king and council, as monarchs with a fragile power base tried to strengthen their position. Thus the king's council became more of a permanent institution during the fifteenth century.

In medieval England, parliament was already divided into two chambers: the Lords (the upper house) and the Commons (the lower house). Those sitting in the latter were representatives of the shires and boroughs, elected from 1429 by freeholders worth 40 shillings a year in land. Two knights were selected for each shire and two burgesses for each borough, in all totalling around 300. The members of the upper house were the heads of the great landowning families. By the fifteenth century, the two houses had evolved into vitally important elements in the process of England's government. Parliament acted as an advisory body to the monarch, administered and could act as a court of law. The Commons was valuable to the crown for its ability to approve and give its consent to taxation proposals. The Commons, in return, presented petitions to the crown regarding issues considered to be of common interest. Monarchs had the right to accept or reject petitions but they could not alter them.

By the middle of the fifteenth century, the struggle between king and parliament for the authority to govern was an old one. In the 1380s, parliament for a time triumphed over King Richard II, by calling for the arrest, trial and punishment of those royal favourites thought to be responsible for a despotic approach to government which- neglected the traditional involvement of the council and Commons. Led by the 'Lords Appellant' - so called because they 'appealed' (accused) five of the king's closest advisers of treason, the 'Merciless Parliament' of 1388 initiated a full-scale purge of the royal household.

Time-honoured customs were the substance of common law - a law based on precedent in the form of written or reported statements of judges. Some laws (statutes) were always written down and usually came from parliament. Common law and statute law were enforced by the king's courts, King's Bench and Common Pleas, both of which usually sat at Westminster. Their work in the counties was carried out by itinerant judges through such institutions as courts of assize. In some areas lords of manors still held their own private 'manorial' courts for the handling of their tenants' minor misdemeanours, and many towns had the equivalent by which the town corporation could try cases involving such matters as weights and measures in the market place, the pollution of waterways, the maintenance of fences and ditches, and the creation of dunghills. All over the country there were 'liberties' - places where the king had handed over full judicial authority to a local magnate. Cases involving issues like divorce and the reading of wills were still the province of the church and its courts. Cases that could not be resolved by common law or statute law were heard in Chancery. The system was, therefore, complex to say the least and corruption was rife.

The single most important legal and administrative post in the provinces during the fifteenth century was that of justice of the peace (JP). These JPs were nominated and unpaid. From 1363 they were required to hold sessions four times a year. At these quarter sessions, minor cases were resolved and more serious ones were brought to trial, perhaps at the county court presided over by the sheriff. Details of the sessions were recorded by the JP's 'clerk of the peace'. JPs also had the right to arrest people accused of a breach of the peace.

Plantagenets and Lancastrians

The origins of the Wars of the Roses, the struggles between the Plantagenet houses of York and Lancaster and between York and Tudor during the second half of the fifteenth century, have been traced by some historians to the reign of Edward III. In 1328 Edward laid claim to the French throne when Charles IV died. Edward's mother was the sister of Charles but, according to French custom, which did not recognise inheritance through the female line, the throne had been granted to Edward's cousin, Philip of Valois. In the continuing wars against France, which Edward had begun in 1337, England was victorious at Sluys (1340), Crécy (1346) and Poitiers (1356). Although much of the territory won was subsequently lost, England held five French towns and the Calais Pale on Edward's death. As well as providing his kingdom with a claim to the French throne Edward also produced thirteen children, some of whose descendants, ultimately, would wage war with one another in pursuit of the crown. Five of his sons were married to rich heiresses and became some of the most powerful magnates in the kingdom.

Edward's eldest son, Edward, the Black Prince, died before his father and the throne was inherited by his nine-year-old son, Richard II. Unlike his prolific grandfather, Richard died in 1400 without children. Richard II's choice of unpopular and incompetent advisers, the fact that he sometimes ignored parliamentary decrees and his unspectacular foreign policy turned powerful members of the nobility against his regime. In 1387 the Lords Appellant rose against the king's favourite, Robert de Vere, Earl of Oxford, and defeated him at the Battle of Radcot Bridge in Oxfordshire. The earl escaped and fled abroad, to die a few years later after being gored by a boar while out hunting. His estates were confiscated and he was condemned to death by the so-called 'Merciless Parliament' of 1388.

Cowed by the actions of the Lords Appellant in 1387, Richard ruled for a time with restraint and he was fairer in his patronage of the aristocracy. By the late 1390s, however, he had reverted to his former practice and worse. He determined to rule without parliament, considered himself the font of law, promoted a new and unpopular favourite, his cousin Edward, Earl of Rutland, and began plotting his revenge upon the Lords Appellant. Murders, arrests and executions followed. His cousin, Henry Bolingbroke, the son of John of Gaunt - the mightiest of England's magnates - was banished for ten years in 1398. When his father died the next year, Bolingbroke's vast estate was confiscated and distributed to the king's favourites.

On 4 July 1399, Bolingbroke, the new Duke of Lancaster, returned to England with a few hundred supporters, determined to win back his inheritance. Richard II was abroad in Ireland and Bolingbroke met no resistance as he began to gather an army around him. When Richard returned, arriving in south Wales in late July, he found himself deserted by his uncle, Gaunt's brother, the Duke of York. Even Rutland now abandoned him and pledged his support to Lancaster. In despair Richard fled to Conway Castle, Persuaded to surrender he was then taken to London and placed in the Tower. Here he was forced to abdicate and, on 29 September 1399, he gave up his throne. This was now to be occupied by Henry Bolingbroke. Thus began the reign of Henry IV: the first king of the House of Lancaster.

A plot to rescue Richard II from the Tower prompted Henry IV to have him murdered in February 1400. His dubious claim to the throne, financial difficulties and Owen Glendower's nationalist revolt in Wales made for a perilous start to Henry's reign. In 1403 he was almost dethroned by the mighty Percy family, rebelling in alliance with Glendower. Although they had helped Henry snatch the crown from Richard II in 1399, they now claimed they had supported him in his recovery of his Lancastrian inheritance but never intended to promote his seizure of the throne or the killing of the king. In fact it is more likely that they sought revenge on Henry, who had failed to provide them with the rich rewards they expected in return for their support. Lack of organisation among the rebels' leaders saved Henry, who defeated them in battles at Shrewsbury (1403) and Bramham Moor (1408).

The last years of Henry's reign saw peace which, by reducing his financial demands, improved his relationship with parliament, but during this time he suffered from chronic ill-health. He died in 1413 at the age of forty-six, to be succeeded by his eldest son, Henry.

Within a few months of his accession, Henry V faced a rising led by Sir John Oldcastle. Although a personal friend of the new king, Oldcastle had run into trouble, having been revealed as a closet Lollard.

His desperate endeavour to save himself by engineering a coup against the king was unsuccessful and he went into hiding, a wanted man for the combined crimes of blasphemy and treason. After three years he was captured, hanged and burned in 1417.

In 1415 a second attempted coup, designed to replace Henry with Edmund Mortimer, Earl of March, was thwarted when Edmund himself betrayed the conspirators to the king. The plot was uncovered just as Henry was about to embark for France in order to re-assert the ancient claim of English kings to the throne of France. In October he and the English archers achieved heroic status by pulling off a staggering victory at Agincourt against a larger and more heavily armed French force. With the full support of a delighted parliament and people, he was able to continue his campaign and bring large areas of northern and a greater part of South-West France under English control. The Treaty of Troyes in 1420 was the crowning glory for, by its terms, the French king, Charles VI, betrothed his daughter, Catherine of Valois, to Henry and made him his heir. He would not live to inherit, however, for he died a short time later of dysentery while still campaigning in France, leaving behind a baby son - the new king, Henry VI. His legacy was a partly recovered French kingdom that was proving disastrously expensive to hold onto as indicated in the closing lines of Adam of Usk's *Chronicle*:

> '[...] our lord the king [...] designs to return again to France in full strength. But, woe is me! mighty men and treasure of the realm will be most miserably fordone about this business. And in truth the grievous taxation of the people to this end being unbearable, accompanied with murmurs and with smothered curses among them from hatred of the burden, I pray that my liege lord become not in the end a partaker [...] of the sword of wrath of the Lord!'[8]

---

[8] Adam of Usk, *Chronicle*, 1421, edited and translated by E. Maunde Thompson, quoted in J. R. Lander, *The Wars of the Roses* (1965).

The reign of Henry VI

'The reign of Henry VI has strong claims to be considered the most calamitous in the whole of English history.'

(B. P. Wolffe, 'The personal rule of Henry VI', in S. B. Chrimes, C. D. Ross and R. A. Griffiths (eds.), *Fifteenth-century England 1399-1509*, Stroud, 1972)

Henry VI (1421-71) was the third and last of the Lancastrian monarchs, King of England and, for a time, France. The first, Henry IV, had been the Duke of Lancaster - hence the adjective 'Lancastrian' which is used to describe his dynasty and its supporters.

The first misfortune of Henry VI's reign was that it began in 1422 in his early infancy, although his formal coronation was delayed until 1429, shortly before his eighth birthday. A strong council of seventeen nevertheless governed effectively during Henry's minority in spite of 'protector' Duke of Gloucester's attempts to extend his own authority. On coming of age in 1437, however, Henry proved inept. He was too forgiving towards high-profile offenders, showed too much favouritism to the ruling elite and he imposed high levels of taxation. All these faults were listed among the king's shortcomings by his contemporaries.

The contrast between the stability of Henry's minority and the disasters of the reign after he came of age is striking. From 1437 to 1450 he played the central role in creating a situation in which once-loyal subjects were driven to contemplating that most terrible of crimes - the deposition of their anointed king. Worst of all, perhaps, Henry VI was blamed for undoing Henry V's greatest achievement by losing almost all of the huge French empire his father had gained after his victory at Agincourt in 1415.

Henry VI became King of France on the death of his maternal grandfather, Charles VI of France, whose daughter, Catherine, had married Henry V in accordance with the terms of the Treaty of Troyes of 1420. He only made one single boyhood visit to this troubled second kingdom in which, from about 1429, the spirit of French nationalism threatened to cast out the English presence. In May 1430, both Henry and the recently captured Joan of Arc were in English-held Rouen. Henry made his way to Paris and Notre Dame Cathedral to be crowned King of France while Joan of Arc, convicted as a witch, stayed in Rouen to face execution by burning at the stake. Henry's formal coronation was an attempt to counter the crowning of a French claimant to the throne, Charles VII, in the previous year. For fifteen years, Charles VII was accepted only in the south and centre while the English king retained Paris, Aquitaine and much of the north.

Two humiliating defeats, Formigny in 1450 and Castillon in 1453, helped push the English out of Aquitaine and Normandy. By 1461 a single outpost, Calais and its Pale, remained. It was finally relinquished in 1558 during the reign of Mary I, although English monarchs continued to claim a title to the French throne until 1802.

Careless in his use of the royal patronage, Henry showed particular favour to the dukes of Somerset and Suffolk, giving them titles, land and favours, while denying the same to other great and powerful families. Among these was Richard, Duke of York, a descendant of Edward III, who, before the birth of Henry's son in 1453, was regarded by many as the legitimate heir to the throne.

The fact that Richard of York was ignored in this way, together with the king's general misfortunes and personal weaknesses, resulted in rebellion. Thus began the first of the Wars of the Roses - thirty years of intermittent warfare which, in 1461, ended the, reign of Henry VI and, finally, in 1485, destroyed the Lancastrian dynasty.

Losses in France

'[...] the conduct of the war in France and the problems of government at home were quite inseparable to contemporaries and cannot be considered separately by historians.'

(B. P. Wolffe, 'The personal rule of Henry VI', in S. B, Chrimes, C. D, Ross and R. A. Griffiths (eds.), *Fifteenth-century England 1399-1509*, Stroud, 1972)

Chief among Henry VI's concerns at the beginning of his personal rule was the war with France. England was desperately engaged in a struggle to hold on to the territories captured by Henry V and the regency government of Henry VI's minority, and was beginning to lose the contest. The situation deteriorated further, as relations with England's most important ally, Burgundy, worsened, and its duke, Philip, gravitated towards a truce with France. When Philip finally broke his alliance with England in 1434 there were riots in London, and Flemish settlers, whose homeland was subject to Burgundy, were lynched in the streets. In September 1435 the Treaty of Arras bound together the interests of France and Burgundy.

In April 1436 the French recaptured Paris and, by 1442, Pontoise was surrendered too, despite five attempts to relieve the besieged English garrison. By 1444, after years of expensive and largely futile campaigning, some of the most powerful men in England wished to relieve England of the full burden of Henry V's French ambitions. These included Edmund Beaufort, Duke of Somerset, and William de la Pole, Duke of Suffolk, who was rapidly emerging as the leader of the dominant faction in Henry's court. The king shared their disenchantment with the French war. Suffolk negotiated a two-year truce with France at Tours in 1444 which included arrangements for Henry's marriage to Margaret of Anjou, the fifteen-year-old niece of Charles VII. In order to secure this valuable marriage alliance Henry promised to surrender Maine to Charles, to expect no dowry from his bride (much to the disgust of the Duke of Gloucester) and to foot the bill for the cost of the wedding. Knowing how unpopular the abandonment of such hard-won territory would be, care was taken to keep this part of the proposal a carefully guarded secret until such time as the truce could be converted into a lasting peace.

In April 1445, 23-year-old Henry married his beautiful bride, Margaret of Anjou. Of this marriage one of his chaplains, a Carthusian monk, would later remark:

> '[...] King Henry was chaste and pure from the beginning of his days. He eschewed all licentiousness in deed or word while he was young; until he was of marriageable age, when he espoused the most noble lady, Lady Margaret, daughter of the King of Sicily, by whom he begat one only son, the most noble and virtuous Prince Edward; and with her and toward her he kept his marriage vow wholly and Sincerely, even in the absences of the lady, which were sometimes very long: never dealing unchastely with any other woman. Neither when they lived together did he

use his wife unseemly, but with all honesty and gravity.'[9]

Represented at the time as a triumph of diplomacy by the Beauforts and their supporters, who wanted peace with France, the marriage would soon be associated with national humiliation by those of Gloucester's inclination. Not surprisingly, Margaret sought allies in the Beaufort faction and her preferential treatment of the Beauforts further alienated their opponents.

Henry had yet to fulfil his part of the bargain - the surrender of Maine - and as the end of the two-year truce approached so too did the day of reckoning. Henry vacillated while Charles sent envoys to pressure England's king into an early settlement. Meanwhile Queen Margaret nagged him incessantly on behalf of her uncle. As news leaked out regarding Henry's intent, Gloucester and other magnates, particularly those with personal interests in France, raged. Henry's correspondence with Charles V at the time of these discussions was compliant:

> 'To the most high and powerful prince, our very dear uncle of France [Charles VII] [...] Most high and powerful prince, our very dear uncle, knowing that you would be very glad that we should make deliverance of the city, town and castle of Le Mans, and all that we have and hold within the comté of Maine, to [...] the King of Sicily and Charles of Anjou, his brother [...] who have most affectionately upon your part required us so to do, and moreover informed us that it. appeared to you that this was one of the best and aptest means to arrive at the blessing of a peace between us and you [...] favouring also our most dear and well-beloved companion the queen, who has requested us to do this many times [...]'[10]

Maine was finally surrendered in March 1448 but only after the French had threatened the English garrisons with a massive army.

---

[9] in J. R. Lander, *The Wars of the Roses* (1965), pp. 26-27.

[10] Henry VI to Charles VII of France, 22 December 1445 *Annales Rerum Anglicarum,* May 1451, in Stephenson. J. (ed.), *Letters and papers illustrative of the wars of the English in France during the reign of Henry VI,* 2 vols., Rolls Series, 1861.

Between 1445 and 1449 an uneasy peace was maintained until Charles VII brought this phase of the Hundred Years' War to a conclusion when he launched the assault on Normandy that smashed the English forces at Rouen and Formigny in 1450.

English aggression provoked the French attack - an ill-conceived and foolhardy decision in 1449 to capture Fougères on Brittany's border. By 1453 Henry had lost virtually all of the remaining French territories.

Events in France in the 1440s contributed a great deal to the deepening rivalries between the most powerful of the English families which eventually led to civil war. Humphrey, Duke of Gloucester, Henry V's surviving brother and Henry VI's uncle, was the most influential advocate of the policy of conquest during the period. This brought him into conflict with the then dominant Suffolk faction which, by and large, endorsed the king's policy of appeasement. In 1447, as tensions between England and France increased over the fate of Maine, Suffolk had Gloucester arrested, together with almost 30 of his associates, on treason charges. He was accused of planning to usurp the throne and smearing the queen's reputation by spreading rumours of an alleged affair with Suffolk. Five days later, the fifty-seven-year-old prisoner was dead. He probably died of a stroke after years of debauchery but rapidly the 'Good Duke' became a martyr for those despairing of the present government and many believed Suffolk had engineered his murder.

Gloucester's death left Richard, Duke of York, heir to the throne. York owned vast estates in England, Wales and Ireland and held several castles, including his stronghold at Ludlow in the heart of his Welsh Borders domain. Not only was Richard the wealthiest of Henry's subjects but some maintained his claim to the throne was even greater than that of the king's. Hard-featured and arrogant, York extended his influence through marriage to Cecily Neville, the twenty-second child of Ralph Neville, Earl of Westmorland. In all, York sired twelve children. Thus he, like his sons after him (Edward IV and Richard III), was at the centre of a great web of aristocratic relations and a powerful force to be reckoned with by those who crossed him.

York served as Henry's lieutenant in France in 1436-37 and then as governor of France and Normandy from 1440 to 1445. He had worked hard to save Henry V's crumbling French kingdom (and his own Norman estates) and shared Gloucester's dislike of appeasement. After two years of prevarication, his command in France was not renewed but, in 1447, granted to Suffolk's ally, Edmund Beaufort, the Duke of Somerset. This was portrayed by the chronicler Jean de Waurin as the culmination of Somerset's personal campaign to oust York:

> 'the Duke of Somerset, who despised the Duke of York [...] found a way to harm him. He was well liked by the queen of England, Margaret of Anjou, daughter of René, Duke of Anjou, and the King of France's niece. She worked on King Henry, her husband; on the advice and support of the Duke of Somerset and other lords and barons of his following, such that the Duke of York was recalled from France to England. There he was totally stripped of his authority to govern Normandy, which he had done well and for some time, and despite his having acted commendably throughout the whole English conquest of France. In York's place, the Duke of Somerset was appointed due to the solicitation and exhortation of the said queen and of some barons who, at that time, were in positions of power in the kingdom.'

In the same year, York was made lieutenant of Ireland - a post he was reluctant to fill. He doubtless regarded his appointment as banishment; designed to keep him away from the king and a court dominated by Suffolk He was further annoyed by the crown's failure to pay him monies owed for his services in France. He reluctantly pawned his most precious possession - a heavy jewel-studded golden collar, decorated with the white roses of York: next to the crown jewels, the most valuable treasure in the kingdom. By the time he finally left England for Ireland in 1449, his financial difficulties had forced him to sell some of his manors. Meanwhile Somerset faced no such problems and his requests for outstanding payments, much to York's chagrin, were usually met with alacrity. To add insult to injury, in 1449, York lost further assets as Normandy fell to Charles VII, for which the duke, and the country at large, blamed Somerset and Suffolk.

Jean de Waurin, summarised the dangerous factional conflict that had developed during the 1440s:

> 'At the time we are talking about, there were, in the kingdom of England, two parties contending for the government and administration of the king and his people. In one of these parties there was Humphrey, Duke of Gloucester, King Henry's uncle, Richard, Duke of York, and several other princes and notable

barons; the other was an alliance between the Dukes of Somerset and Suffolk, Lord Say, the Bishop of Salisbury and several others not named here [...]

William, Duke of Suffolk [...] was the principal advisor to the king, and also well loved by the queen. It was through her and Edmund, Duke of Somerset, and other men of his party that they managed to talk to the king in private, and point out to him that Normandy was costing him a lot to maintain, in wages to the soldiers he was keeping there under the Duke of York and in other sundry daily expenses. So they recommended to him that the country of Normandy should be handed back to the French [...]'

Somerset shared York's descent from Edward III but, unlike York, he was also descended, like the king himself, from John of Gaunt, the Duke of Lancaster. When, early in 1450, Suffolk made arrangements for his son to marry Somerset's niece, Margaret Beaufort, it must have seemed likely to York that, in the event of Henry dying without issue, his claim to the throne would be challenged by Suffolk and his 'Lancastrian' allies.

Suffolk's days, however, were numbered for, identified as a prime mover in the plans to seize Fougères in 1449, he was blamed for the loss of Normandy. Made the scapegoat for a humiliating foreign policy, the crown's bankruptcy and an embargo placed on English cloth exports by the Duke of Burgundy, parliament sent him to the Tower in 1450 on a treason charge. Among other things, he was accused of planning to place his son on the throne, having arranged his betrothal to Margaret Beaufort, the direct descendant of John of Gaunt. Henry declared him innocent of the treason charge but, nevertheless, banished him for five years to save him from further condemnation. Having escaped a lynching in London, he set sail from England with a small entourage but his ship was intercepted off Dover by his enemies. They forced him aboard one of their own boats and after a few days on board, having been found guilty by an impromptu kangaroo-court, he was sentenced to death and beheaded with half-a-dozen strokes of a rusty sword.

Rebellion and civil war

The fear of reprisals against the people of Kent for the murder of Suffolk, together with general disaffection with the regime, high taxes, and the shock of the military disasters in France, precipitated Jack Cade's revolt in Kent in 1450. The rebels' demands, as described in their 'Complaint of the Commons of Kent', were for greater political equity among the aristocratic elite, the bringing to justice of Gloucester's 'murderers', an inquiry into the losses in France, and for financial efficiency - the king should live of his own. By 1450 the government was in debt to the tune of £372,000 and the sum was increasing at the rate of around £20,000 per annum. However, the rebels declared that they had no desire to depose their sovereign – they aimed instead to persuade him to form a new council:

> 'The king should take about his noble person men of true blood from his royal realm, that is to say, the high and mighty prince, the Duke of York, exiled from our sovereign lord's person by the suggestions of those false traitors the Duke of Suffolk and his affinity.'[11]

Cade's army was substantial (one contemporary source estimated it at 16,000) and it included many gentry. Among them were two members of parliament and three sheriffs. Henry VI, convinced the rebellion was a dynastic coup masterminded by York in Dublin, donned armour and marched a substantial army from Leicester towards London to meet the rebels. Half of the king's army confronted the rebels at Sevenoaks in Kent and was routed after a short but bloody fight. As mutiny spread through his army and Cade's popularity grew, Henry decided to withdraw to Kenilworth Castle in Warwickshire, leaving the archbishop and most of the council sheltering in the Tower. For a few days in July London fell into rebel hands. A number of courtiers, including Lord Say, the treasurer of England, were captured and executed but Cade's inability to keep control of his undisciplined army,

---

[11] Jack Cade's Manifesto, quoted in Sarah Newman, *Yorkists and Tudors, 1450-1603*, (1989), p. 42.

together with the resentment of Londoners, soon forced him, after a bloody fight against the retinue in the Tower of London, to disperse his troops and abandon the cause. Though promised a free pardon, Cade was then pursued into Sussex and killed by the sheriff of Kent at Heathfield on 12 July. His body was brought back to London where it was beheaded and quartered. His head was boiled and its fleshless skull replaced those of his own victims, impaled on spikes on London Bridge. Alison Weir has illuminated the significance of these events:

> 'The rebellion had achieved nothing [...] However, what had been made strikingly manifest by Cade's uprising was the inability of king and council to cope with such a crisis. A king was supposed to lead his armies, protect his people and enforce justice, but this king had fled, and in his absence the government of the realm had all but broken down. What had also been made alarmingly clear was how easy it had been for the insurgents to occupy the capital.'[12]

The troubles were not confined to London and the south-east. Simultaneous risings and riots occurred in the Midlands, the south and west. In June the congregation of Edington Church in Wiltshire hacked to death the Bishop of Salisbury, Suffolk's friend and the king's chaplain, after he had said mass.

The revolt had not been an attempt to depose Henry, although Cade had claimed connections with the house of York and declared his opposition to the dominant Beaufort faction. Absent in Ireland during these events, Richard of York was not directly implicated but he soon returned to England, probably with a view to declaring his loyalty as well as hoping to win political favour from a king scared by Yorkist supporters. His return was greeted with enormous public support and he soon rallied around him an 'army' several thousands strong. He marched on London and demanded to see the king, to whom he pledged his loyalty but also harangued for the misgovernment of the country. Shortly afterwards, he presented the king with a list of personal demands regarding payment of monies owed and recognition of his position as heir presumptive, together with a list of more general grievances echoing those contained in Cade's manifesto. A frightened king now admitted

---

[12] Alison Weir, *Lancaster and York* (1995).

him onto the council but refused to abandon York's deadly enemy, Somerset. Returning to London, now that he had been admitted to the 'inner sanctum', York brought with him 3,000 armed retainers. However, while York's supporters dominated parliament, Somerset maintained his supremacy within the council. He was confident of the king's approval, which was confirmed in early 1451 by his appointment as captain of Calais.

Despite attempts to impeach Somerset through parliament and the submission of a petition concerning York's position as heir apparent, it soon became clear that Henry would not be budged by protest and public demand alone. Indeed, those that championed his cause were likely to run into trouble:

> 'In the same parliament Thomas Yonge of Bristol, apprentice in law, moved that because the king had no offspring, it would be for the security of the kingdom that it should be openly known who should be heir apparent. And he named the Duke of York. For which cause the same Thomas was afterwards committed to the Tower of London.'[13]

York began to prepare for an armed confrontation, certain that if he could not shift Somerset he stood to lose all. A London chronicler recorded York's actions and grievances:

> 'The king heard that the Duke of York, the Earl of Devonshire and Lord Cobham were marching towards London [from Ludlow], with twenty thousand men, so he rode to Northampton and sent the Bishop of Winchester, the count of Eu and Lord Stourton to the Duke of York, to tell him not to rise up in arms.
>
> The duke replied, commending himself to the king's good grace and saying that he had never rebelled against the king and would obey him always. He asserted that his uprising had been directed against those who betrayed the king and the kingdom of England and that he was not against the king and desired nothing but the good of England. He wished to tell the

---

[13] *Annales Rerum Anglicarum*, May 1451, in J. Stephenson (ed.), *Letters and papers illustrative of the wars of the English in France during the reign of Henry VI*, 2 vols., Rolls Series, 1861-64.

king of those who were encompassing the destruction of his two kingdoms, that is to say, of England and France. And these men were Edmund, Duke of Somerset, who had been responsible for the shameful loss of all Normandy, and John Kemp, the Archbishop of York, who was a cardinal and the Chancellor of England.'[14]

York met with the king at Dartford, on March 2, 1452, but submitted in the face of a stronger royal force – the figure of 20,000 for the size of York's army mentioned above is most probably an exaggeration typical of contemporary sources. In return York was given an assurance from the king that he would arrest Somerset. In a remarkable scene that followed, York, having dispersed his army, rode into the king's camp with just 40 of his retainers, and stumbled upon a row in the royal tent between the king and queen concerning the fate of the newly arrested Somerset, who was also present. The tables rapidly turned on York, who now found himself a virtual prisoner, while Somerset regained his liberty. York's popularity saved him and, after making a solemn vow in St Paul's Cathedral never to rebel against the king, he retired to his castle at Ludlow under what amounted to a suspended sentence of attainder should he offend the king. Without a blow being struck, the first engagement in the 'Wars of the Roses' was over.

The crisis was made worse in August 1453 when, a few days after receiving news of an English defeat at Castillon and Charles VII's capture of Bordeaux, which marked England's final defeat in the Hundred Years' War and the loss of all territories except Calais, Henry, according to his contemporaries, 'went mad'. For a year-and-a-half he would be completely incapacitated and his eventual recovery was only a partial one, leaving him, it seems, a schizophrenic and, in the historian Charles Ross's memorable phrase, a 'useful political vegetable'. Then, in October 1453, Henry's queen, Margaret of Anjou, bore a son. Immediately rumours spread regarding the child's supposed illegitimacy, some of which maintained he was Somerset's bastard. The fact that Henry, in his illness, did not (because he could not) acknowledge the

---

[14] *Annales Rerum Anglicarum*, in J. Stephenson (ed.), *Letters and papers illustrative of the wars of the English in Prance during the reign of Henry VI*, 2 vols., Rolls Series, 1861-64.

baby as his son merely heightened speculation:

> 'at the prince's coming to Windsor, the Duke of Buckingham took him in his arms and presented him to the king in goodly wise, beseeching the king to bless him; and the king gave no answer [...] the queen came in, and took the prince in her arms and presented him in like form as the duke had done, desiring that he should bless it; but all their labour was in vain, for they departed thence without any answer or countenance saving only once that he looked on the prince and cast down his eyes again [...]'[15]

Whether Henry survived his illness or not, the kingdom needed a regent and to this Richard of York, the king's nearest adult blood relation, promptly laid claim. His eventual success was the result of a swing in the political allegiances of the biggest and most powerful of the great families in fifteenth century England, the Nevilles.

Richard Neville, the Earl of Warwick, and a close relative to York by marriage, disputed the right to the lordship of Glamorgan granted to the Duke of Somerset by Henry in 1453, even though Warwick had held it and administered it well for three years. Sharing York's sense of having been wronged by Somerset and the king himself, Warwick began to support York and abandoned the family's old loyalty to the house of Lancaster. The new alliance vastly improved York's position for, some said, Warwick was as rich as, maybe richer than, York himself. Moreover, his power was apparent in his massive fortresses and great armies of retainers, all of who wore his livery of red jackets embellished with the insignia of a white bear and ragged staff. A considerable number of peers in the House of Lords were closely connected to him by blood or marriage. He was popular in both the north and at London. At his residence in the capital, six oxen were boiled and roasted for breakfast each day and members of his 600-strong retinue were endowed with the right to share with their friends as much meat as they could carry away on the blade of a dagger.

As the regency was being debated in parliament and at court, York and Warwick sought support and demonstrated their strength and determination by bringing with them to London a couple of thousand

---

[15] *The Paston Letters.*

armed retainers. In March 1454 York was made protector of the realm at the request of the king's council. In the likely event of Henry failing to recover his sanity, York seemed set to rule the kingdom for the next 14 years. Somerset had been vanquished. He was sent to the Tower and the queen banished to Windsor to tend her ailing husband. She had failed in the struggle for the regency and it was clear York intended to deny her further participation in courtly intrigues. It is likely that at this point Margaret saw a future, perhaps imminent, Yorkist bid for the throne and the disinheritance of her baby son.

When Henry recovered at the end of 1454, the tables once again were turned on York. Edmund Clere remarked on the king's recovery in a letter to John Paston dated 9 January 1455:

> 'And on that Monday afternoon the queen came to him, and brought my lord prince with her. And then he asked what the prince's name was, and the queen told him Edward; and then he held up his hands and thanked God thereof. And he said he never knew till that time, nor wist not what was said to him, nor wist not where he had been whilst he hath been sick till now.'[16]

The king, remembering nothing of the past 16 months, recognised his son and had Somerset released. He was reinstated as captain of Calais, a position of considerable military strength recently usurped by York. York and Warwick retired to the north. John Benet recorded his views on this reinstatement, shared by many others, in his *Chronicle*:

> 'On 6 February, the Duke of Somerset was released from the Tower of London on bail. Very shortly afterwards the Duke of York resigned his office to the king at Greenwich, after he had governed England most excellently for a whole year, miraculously calming rebels and villains, according to the laws and without unnecessary violence; and he reigned his office much honoured and much loved.
>
> Then the king, in response to the' intercession of the Archbishop of Canterbury and the Duke of Buckingham, pardoned all those who had entered into recognisances for the

---

[16] *The Paston Letters.*

Duke of Somerset. Once more, the Duke of Somerset became head of the government under the king, although in the past he had almost ruined the whole of England with his misrule.'

Formally deposed as protector in February 1455, York once more raised an army in order to march on London and persuade the king to abandon Somerset - a pre-emptive strike designed to defeat his rival before he found some means of destroying York himself. John Benet described the events leading to the ensuing battle in his chronicle:

> 'Soon after Easter [1455], another dispute arose between the noble Duke of York, on the one hand, and the evil Duke of Somerset and the Duke of Buckingham, on the other. For Somerset was plotting the destruction of the noble Duke of York. He offered advice to the king, saying that the Duke of York wished to depose the king and rule England himself - which was manifestly false.
> Because of this, around the middle of May, the Duke of York and with him the Earls of Shrewsbury and Warwick, approached London, with seven thousand armed men. When the Duke of Somerset heard this news, he suggested to the king that York had come to usurp the throne. For this reason, the king sided with the Duke of Somerset.'

The king and Somerset learned too late of York's preparations and only managed to put around 2,500 men in the field to confront, according to Benet, York's 7,000. They met at St Albans on 22 May 1455. The battle was preceded by prolonged negotiations, which failed due to the king's absolute refusal to hand over Somerset and York's refusal to back down. An account, written within five days of the events described, survives, probably by a foreigner resident in England:

> 'When the Duke of Somerset and those who were of his party then being in the City of London, heard that the Duke of York and many other lords, in his company were advancing against them with a force of five thousand men and when he considered what he had done against the said Duke of York and that he was also in very bad odour with the people of London, he came to the conclusion that he should not remain in the City of London for

> fear that the people would fall upon him the moment he [the Duke of York] arrived. For which cause he persuaded the king to sally forth against the said, Duke of York [...] the king sent a herald to the Duke of York to know the cause for which he had come there with so many men and that it seemed to the king something quite new that he, the duke, should be rising against him, the king. The reply made was that he was not coming against him thus, [he] was always ready to do him obedience but he well intended in one way or another to have the traitors who were about him so that they should be punished, and that in case' he could not have them with good will and fair consent, he intended in any case to have them by force. The reply that was made from the king's side to the said Duke of York was that he [the king] was unaware that there were any traitors about him were it not for the Duke of York himself who had risen against his crown. And even before this reply came to the Duke of York there begun the skirmish before the village by one side and the other. And thus when the Duke of York had the aforesaid reply the battle became more violent and both sides with banners displayed began to fight.'[17]

After just half an hour of ferocious fighting, the royalist army began to flee; the king fell into York's hands and was placed in the abbey for safety and Somerset took refuge with the Duke of Buckingham in an inn. A contemporary account, found in the archives in Dijon, France, described what happened next:

> 'after the doors were broken down the Duke of Somerset, seeing that he had no other remedy, took counsel with his men about coming out and did so, as a result of which he and all his people were surrounded by the Duke of York's men. And after some were stricken down and the Duke of Somerset had killed four of them with his own hand, so it is said, he was felled to the ground with an axe and being so wounded in several places there he ended his life.'

---

[17] Quoted by C. A. J. Armstrong in 'Politics of the Battle of St Albans, 1455', in *Bulletin of the Institute of Historical Research*, XXXIII, 1960.

Meanwhile, the king, wounded in the neck by an arrow, was met by Richard of York in the abbey. Here the duke pledged his loyalty and begged forgiveness for endangering the king's life. The king, needless to say, forgave all and accepted York as his unrivalled first minister. Warwick replaced Somerset as captain of Calais - a role in which he was to distinguish himself and become a hero of the southern ports for his success in clearing the Channel of privateers and destroying a Spanish fleet.

St Albans was the first battle of the Wars of the Roses, so called because of the badges worn by the two sides, the Lancastrian red rose and the Yorkist white rose, at the Battle of Bosworth thirty years later.

For four years an uneasy peace was maintained. Henry, prone to insanity and seemingly anxious to end the feuding, was easily contained by the new regime. Margaret of Anjou, the Yorkists' most bitter enemy now that Somerset was dead, was more of a threat. She established a rival court in the Midlands, made up of members of families hostile to York and vengeful for the defeat at St Albans. As the niece of Charles VII of France, she was blamed by some, undeservedly, for the losses in France. Some believed it was the Frenchwoman's loyalty to her kin that had shaped the disastrous half-hearted and pacifist foreign policy of her weak, easily influenced husband. What was certainly true, however, was the fact that she had needed to cultivate friendships among the leading noble families. The patronage and favouritism by which this need was fulfilled contributed to the formation of factions and the feuds between them.

In February 1456 Henry felt sufficiently confident and well enough (it is likely he suffered a relapse in 1455) to remove York from office, although he retained his dominant position within the council. As a pay-off York was granted over £1,800 arrears from his first protectorate and the promise of more to come for expenses incurred during the second. Of even greater value to the Yorkist cause was Henry's appointment of Warwick to the captaincy of Calais, the military base from which he would later launch his invasion of England. Peace continued for the next three years, propped up in 1458 by a public show of reconciliation engineered by the king, the 'Loveday' of 24 March, when members of the rival factions walked into St Paul's Cathedral arm-in-arm. In reality, the rift was anything but healed. While York was away carrying out his duties in Dublin, the feud between York and Lancaster revolved mainly around Warwick and Margaret of Anjou, who tried to have Warwick arrested for alleged crimes of piracy and inciting a riot at court.

The general mood of the people at around this time is conveyed in the words of an anonymous chronicler:

> 'In this same time, the realm of England was out of all good governance, as it had been many days before, for the king was simple and led by a covetous counsel, and owed more than he was worth. His debts increased daily, but payment was there none; all the possessions and lordships that pertained to the crown the king had given away, some to lords and some to other lesser persons, so that he had almost nothing left to own. And such impositions as were put to the people, as taxes and tallages [taxes like tolls or customs duties], all that came from them was spent in vain, for he held no household nor maintained any wars [...] The queen with such as were of her affinity ruled the realm as she liked, gathering innumerable riches [...] The queen was defamed and slandered, that he that was called prince, was not her son, but a bastard gotten in adultery; wherefore she, dreading that he should not succeed his father as King of England, allied unto her all the knights and squires of Cheshire [...]'[18]

By 1459 Margaret of Anjou and the Duke of Buckingham appear to have convinced the king that Richard, and his ally, the Earl of Warwick, intended to seize the throne. In June 1459 the Lancastrians decided the time had come to crush the Yorkist opposition by force. Indicted for treason, York and his supporters mobilised their forces once again. A small Yorkist army led by the Earl of Salisbury defeated a larger Lancastrian force in September at Blore Heath in Shropshire, A game of cat and mouse followed as the bulk of the king's army, together with the king, pursued York to his base at Ludlow. The subsequent desertion of Yorkist troops, however, following the king's promise of a pardon, put paid, for the time being, to the Yorkist cause. Duke Richard, leaving his remaining commanders arrayed for battle in the field, fled to Ireland while Salisbury and Warwick fled to Calais. York left his wife, his two young sons and thirteen-year-old daughter behind at Ludlow.

---

[18] Davies, J. S. (ed.), *An English Chronicle of the Reigns of Richard II, Henry IV; Henry V and Henry VI*, c. 1465 (Camden Society, 1856).

The duchess was taken into captivity and Ludlow was ransacked by the Lancastrian soldiers.

From this point on, the position of the Yorkists, and other malcontents, was markedly different. The leaders of the Yorkist party were declared rebels at the so-called 'Parliament of Devils' in Coventry in November 1459 and their lands and goods forfeited to the crown. The harsh treatment of the rebels and the disinheritance of their innocent heirs shocked other members of the nobility, who otherwise might have stayed loyal to Henry. Meanwhile, Warwick and Salisbury in Calais prepared for their next campaign, Warwick funding it through piracy against the French, which had the added value of making good nationalist propaganda for the Yorkist cause.

In June 1460 Warwick and York's son, Edward, the Earl of March, returned to England, landing with 2,000 men at Sandwich. Declaring his intent to relieve the king of evil counsellors, Warwick was admitted into Canterbury with the blessing of the archbishop and then marched towards London, gathering support as he went. The lord mayor of London was persuaded by popular feeling and the Yorkist sympathies of certain resident magnates to open the capital's gates to Warwick's now vast army of around 40,000. A number of Lancastrian nobles meanwhile took refuge in the Tower of London.

The inevitable engagement between the Yorkists and King Henry took place at Northampton on 10 July 1460. Outnumbered, the Lancastrians were soundly defeated in the space of half-an-hour. Between 300 and 400 soldiers were killed out of 50,000 or so involved and, among them, lay the Duke of Buckingham. The king, on Warwick's orders, was taken alive. The day was a wet one, so wet that the king's army was unable to fire its batteries of guns on Warwick's soldiers as they marched towards Northampton along the London road. Lord Grey turned his private army against the king at a critical moment, probably in the hope of receiving Yorkist support in a property dispute in which he was presently engaged and, very likely, in return for the promise of a position – he became Treasurer in 1463. The hero of the day was York's son, Edward, soon to become Edward IV. Richard himself was still in Ireland.

A parliament was called with a view to revoking the Parliament of Devils' attainder of 1459. Only when York returned in September was a Yorkist claim made to the throne of England. This appears to have been on York's own initiative, unexpected by his supporters and resisted by his ally, Warwick, who feared the fury such a claim would unleash. A fifteenth-century chronicler, Whethamstede, recorded York's arrogant behaviour when he arrived at Westminster in October 1460:

> 'On entering the palace he marched straight through the great hall until he came to the solemn chamber where the king is wont to hold his parliament with his Commons. And when he came there he walked up to the king's throne and putting his hand 'on the cushion, as a man taking possession of his own, and kept it there for a short space. At length withdrawing it he turned his face towards the people and, standing quietly under the royal' cloth of state, awaited the applause of the onlookers. While he stood, Master Thomas Bourchier, Archbishop of Canterbury, approached him, and with due reverence asked him whether he wished to come and see the lord king. To which he answered thus: 'I mind me of no one in this kingdom to whom it is not more fitting that he should come to see me than I to him.' Then the duke withdrew to the principal chambers in the whole palace (as the king occupied the queen's apartment), and the bolts having been broken and the doors forcibly opened, he took up his abode there for some time in the manner of a king rather than of a duke.'

York did not succeed in persuading the lords to depose the king in his favour but they did agree that York and his heirs should inherit on Henry's death. An Act of Settlement, the 'Act of Accord', was drawn up to this effect on 24 October 1460, becoming law by regal and parliamentary agreement four days later. In the same month the attainders against York and his followers were reversed. Charles Ross has described the years 1460 to 1487 as 'the first truly revolutionary period in English history'.[19] As often as not, after 1460 the king himself, in addition to his 'evil counsellors', became the target of opposition bent on overthrowing the governments of the day. As a result, the crown changed hands six times in just twenty-five years.

Incensed by the Act of Accord, which had turned a struggle for governmental reform into a dynastic one, the Lancastrians rallied under Queen Margaret at Hull. In November 1460 they marched south,

---

[19] Charles Ross, *The Wars of the Roses* (1976).

determined to free the king in London from his captors. The speed with which the Lancastrians responded to recent developments and their decision to wage war so late in the campaigning season appear to have taken York by surprise. Leaving Warwick to safeguard London, York marched north with a small army of around 4,000 to meet the 20,000 or so Lancastrians. Although he recruited as he marched, York finally confronted Queen Margaret with no more than about 12,000 soldiers. York's final battle was fought outside his castle at Sandal, near Wakefield, on 30 December. His army, depleted while soldiers were out foraging for provisions, was overwhelmed by the larger Lancastrian force and both he and his second son, the young Earl of Rutland, were killed. Their heads, the duke's adorned with a paper crown, were impaled on Micklegate, an entrance into the city of York.

Margaret then marched south, her forces ravaging the towns and villages through which they passed, 'just like so many locusts' according to one contemporary chronicler. The disreputable and the impoverished joined them for no better reason than seizing booty from the villages, manor houses and monasteries that were plundered as they passed. Whole towns, including Coventry, switched allegiances from Lancaster to York as news of the northerners' atrocities reached them. Queen Margaret enjoyed a second victory at St Albans on 17 February 1461, when Warwick's army was overwhelmed. Warwick had taken Henry VI with him, who, it is said, passed the battle a mile away, sitting under an oak tree, laughing and singing. Warwick fled and Henry was reunited with his wife.

Margaret now looked set to recapture London but the reputation of her army went before it. The city prepared to defend itself against Lancastrian butchery, by now perceiving the Wars of the Roses as a struggle between the north and the south. According to some historians, it was her genuine desire to protect the interests of Londoners that inspired Margaret to withdraw and so allow the Yorkists under Edward, Earl of March, to enter the capital on 27 February.

Fresh from his victory against a Lancastrian army at the Battle of Mortimer's Cross, fought in Herfordshire a few weeks earlier, eighteen-year-old Edward now proclaimed himself king. The Lords in Parliament declared his claim superior to that of Henry VI and he received the rapturous support of crowds of ordinary Londoners.

The greatest and bloodiest battle of the Wars of the Roses was fought days later at Towton in Yorkshire where, on 29 March, Palm

Sunday, Edward IV caught up with the Lancastrians who had regrouped around the city of York with a view to organising a decisive strike on the south. Between 60,000 and 100,000 men met at Towton, around 2 per cent of the total population. The Lancastrian army was made up of mainly northerners, the Yorkist army of southerners. The battle was exceptionally long, lasting from 11 a.m. to about 9 p.m. in an era when most battles were over within three or four hours. The weather was vile, the wind driving snow into the soldiers' faces. The fight had started badly for Edward when, on the previous day, an advance force was ambushed by a contingent of cavalry led by Lord Clifford and massacred.

The Yorkists won the day and the enemy force was shattered with the killing of six Lancastrian peers and more than forty knights. Thousands more died, many drowned in the river or were cut down as they fled the battlefield. It is likely as many as 9,000 perished during and directly after the battle. One contemporary commented: 'so many dead bodies were seen as to cover an area six miles long by three broad', and modern historians, like Alison Weir in *Lancaster and York* (1995), consider it 'probably the bloodiest battle ever to take place on English soil'. At York, Queen Margaret and Henry VI received news of the defeat and promptly fled to Scotland, narrowly avoiding capture by those in pursuit. In the opinion of the fifteenth-century chronicler, Waurin, the house of Lancaster had received its just deserts:

> 'King Henry and his wife Queen Margaret were overthrown and lost that crown which his grandfather Henry IV had violently usurped and taken from King Richard II, his first cousin, whom he caused to be wretchedly murdered [...] Men say that ill-gotten gains cannot last.'

Edward entered York in triumph. Passing through Micklegate he was greeted by the dismal sight of the rotting heads of his father and brother. These he had removed and buried with the other remains at Pontefract. In their place were now impaled the heads of the Earl of Devon and two other leading Lancastrians who had also taken refuge in York.

The causes of the Wars of the Roses

It can be argued that the struggle between two dynasties that partly gave rise to the wars stemmed from at least as early as the unfortunate reign of Richard II. This was ended by his cousin, Henry Bolingbroke, the dispossessed Duke of Lancaster. However justified Bolingbroke, now Henry IV, had been in usurping his vengeful, profligate and predatory cousin, the doubtful claim of the Lancastrians to rule would trouble the closing years of the reign of Henry's grandson, Henry VI. From the earliest Tudor times, historians held that Henry VI merely reaped the sins of his fathers.

Some historians, however, view the causes of the civil wars in the shorter term. According to one, 'it is unnecessary to look back beyond the period of Henry VI's personal rule.'[20] Just as Richard II had been the author of his own downfall, it is claimed by Henry's latest biographers that his incompetence alone explains the conflict that led to his overthrow. Wolffe even frees the government of the 'protector' during Henry's minority, from all blame. Indeed, most authorities now consider England was ruled well until Henry VI was old enough to take over.

Both perspectives are equally credible. Alison Weir has combined the short-term and long-term causes of conflict:

> 'At the centre of this bloody faction fight was the pathetic figure of the mentally unstable Henry VI, whose ineptitude in government and mental incapacity gave rise to political instability, public discontent, and dissensions between the great landed magnates that in turn led ultimately to war and a bitter battle over the throne itself. Henry's chief rival was Richard Plantagenet, Duke of York, the man who should have been king, according to the law of primogeniture as it was then understood.'[21]

---

[20] B. P. Wolffe in 'The personal rule of Henry VI', in S. B. Chrimes, C. D. Ross and R. A. Griffiths (eds.), *Fifteenth-century England 1399-1509* (1972).

[21] Alison Weir, *Lancaster and York: the Wars of the Roses* (1995).

Furthermore, she takes the roots of the conflict back even further to the reign of the prolific Edward III (1327-77), who helped establish a history of rivalry among those of royal blood by producing a brood of thirteen princes and princesses:

> 'The kingdom of England was not an island in the first half of the fourteenth century. The claim of English kings to territories in France and the wars they fought, first to seize and then to protect them, have a place in any explanation of the origins of the Wars of the Roses. Henry V, victorious at Agincourt, immortalised by Shakespeare, has long been held to be the greatest of the English kings of the Middle Ages. However, his enthusiasm for campaigning resulted in his early death and, therefore, the first potential disaster of Henry VI's reign: accession at the age of nine months. Furthermore, as Charles Ross has observed in *The Wars of the Roses* (1976), while beacons, lit on English hilltops to celebrate and spread the news of victory over the French, made good royal propaganda at the time, the French wars saddled the English crown with a heavy burden of debt. This debt was to increase steadily 'under the crippling strain of another 22 years of campaigning; and Henry's preoccupation with France effectively prevented him from tackling the urgent problems of lawlessness and disorder which afflicted his realm of England.'

Thus the debate, in part, revolves around the controversial issue of how far Henry VI really was to blame for the misfortunes of his reign and how far he was the victim of his inheritance and other circumstances beyond his control. In his account of Henry VI's rule John Watts reached the conclusion that those who were behind the conflicts that eventually erupted into civil war were themselves 'victims, driven by the hideous logic of a dysfunctional system to the fruitless creation and defence of an authority which could not be exercised'[22]. According to Watts, the fault lay not with any over-mighty subject or dynastic faction, defeat in foreign wars or the misapplication of patronage, but a constitution which relied too much on the personality of the king. In the hands of a Henry V or an Edward IV, the monarchy was relatively secure, but with a man

---

[22] John Watts, *Henry VI and the Politics of Kingship* (1996).

like Henry VI at the helm, the system was almost bound to fail.

SOURCES

The murders of the Bishops of Chichester and Salisbury, 1450

(*An English Chronicle of the Reigns of Richard II, Henry IV, Henry V and Henry VI*)

And this year, the 9th day of January, Master Adam Moleyns, Bishop of Chichester and keeper of the king's privy seal, the king sent to Portsmouth, to make payment of money to certain soldiers and shipmen for their wages: and so it happened that with boisterous language, and also for curtailment of their wages, he fell at variance with them, and they fell on him, and cruelly killed him there.

And this same year, in the feast of Saint Peter arid Paul after midsummer, that is to say, the last day of June save one, Master William Aiscough, Bishop of Salisbury, was slain by his own parishioners and people of Edington after he had said mass, and was drawn from the altar and led up to a hill nearby, in his alb, and his stole about his neck; and there they slew him horribly, their father and their bishop, and despoiled him unto the naked skin, and rent his bloody shirt in pieces and bore them away with them, and made boast of their wickedness; and the day before his death his chariot was robbed by men of the same country of a huge store of treasure, to the value of 10,000 marks, as those who knew it said. These two bishops were amazingly covetous men, and badly liked among the common people, and were held suspect of many faults, and were assenting and willing to the death of the Duke of Gloucester, as it was said.

The recovery of Normandy by France, 1450

(J. Chartier, *Chronique Française du Roi de France Charles VII*)

Whoever might wish to make mention of all the valiant men and of their deeds which have been done during the recovery of the said duchy of Normandy would find it too long for recital or writing. But nevertheless one must make some mention and record of the matter for those who in time to come may wish to read or hear the method and means of the miraculous recovery of this duchy.

First of all, the King of France imposed such good order on the conduct of his men-at-arms that it was a fine thing. For he has caused all those men-at-arms to be equipped with good and sure armour and weapons; that is to say; the men-at-arms were all armed with good cuirasses, armour for their limbs, swords, salets, and most of the salets were adorned with silver; also with lances carried by pages of the men-at-arms, each of whom had three good horses, for himself, his page, and his varlet, being armed with a salet, jacket, dirk, hauberk or brigandine, axe or bill. And each of the said men-at-arms had two mounted archers, armed mostly with brigandines, leg harness, and salets, of which the majority were also adorned with silver, or at least had jacks and hauberks.

And these men at arms were paid each month, so that they did not dare nor venture during this war and conquest of Normandy to take any of the people of that countryside prisoners, nor to take or ransom any beast whatever it was, whether they were in the obedience of the English or of their own side; nor to seize any victuals wherever they were, without paying for them, except only from the English or their adherents, in which case they could take the victuals lawfully.

The said war was conducted in masterly fashion, valiantly and honourably, by the said Count of Dunois, lieutenant general of the king [twenty more names follow] with many other men at arms, great lords, knights, and squires, who all notably, each one according to his duty, subjected themselves to great labours, travails, dangers, discomforts, pains and perils of their bodies.

Just as important was the provision that the king had made in his artillery for warfare and [...] he had a very great number of great bombards, great canons, veuglaires, serpentines, crapaudins, culverins, and ribaudquins, so that never in the memory of man did a Christian king have such a numerous artillery at one time, nor so well furnished with powder, shot, and all other things necessary to approach and take towns and castles, nor had more carriages to drag them nor gunners more experienced to handle them, which gunners were paid from day to day. And the organizers of this artillery were Master Jehan Bureau, treasurer of France, and Jaspart or Gaspard Bureau, his brother, master of the said artillery; who during these wars have suffered great pains and were found in many perils, for they have done well their best and have acquitted themselves well of their duty, with satisfaction to all.

It was a marvellous thing to see the bulwarks, mounds, ditches, moats, and mines that the Bureau brothers caused to be made before all the towns and castles that were besieged during the war; for indeed there was not a town taken by composition or otherwise which could not have been taken by assault and by force of arms, if one had wished, because of the great valour and subtlety of the men at arms who were there. But always when the places were hard pressed and ready to be taken by assault, the king, of his kindness, always wished to take them by composition, to avoid the shedding of human blood, and the destruction of his own country, and of the people who were besieged in the fortresses.

The murder of the Duke of Suffolk, 1450

(*The Paston Letters*)

William Lomnor to John Paston.

To my right worshipful sir, I recommend me to you, and am right sorry of what I shall say, and have so washed this little bill with sorrowful tears that you shall scarcely read it.

As on Monday next after May Day [4 May] there came tidings to London, that on Thursday before the Duke of Suffolk came unto the coasts of Kent very near Dover with his two ships and a little pinnace; the which pinnace he sent with certain letters to certain of his trusted men towards Calais, to know how he would be received; and with him met a ship called the *Nicholas of the Tower*, with other ships waiting on him, and from those who were in the pinnace the master of the Nicholas had knowledge of the duke's coming. And when he espied the duke's ships, he sent forth his boat to know what they were, and the duke himself spoke to them and said that he was by the king's commandment sent to Calais. And they said he must speak with their master; and so he with two or three of his men went forth with them in their boat to the *Nicholas*. And when he came, the master bade him "Welcome traitor!" as men say; and after this the master desired to know if the shipmen wished to support the duke, and they sent word that they would not in any way; and so he was in the Nicholas until the following Saturday.

Some say he wrote many thanks to be delivered to the king, but that is not truly known. He had his confessor with him. And some say that he was arraigned in the ship, in their way, upon the impeachments, and found guilty.

Also he asked the name of the ship, and when he knew it he remembered Stacy, who had said that if he could escape the danger of the Tower, he should be safe; and then his heart failed him, for he thought he was deceived. And in the sight of all his men he was drawn out of the great ship into the boat, and there was an axe and a block; and one of the most ignorant of the ship bade him lay down his head, and he should be fairly treated, and die by a sword; and the man took a rusty sword, and smote off his head with half a dozen strokes, and took away his gown of russet, and his doublet of velvet sewn with metal rings, and laid his body on the sands of Dover. And some say that his head was set on a pole by it, and his men were disembarked with great ceremony and deference. And the sheriff of Kent watches the body and has sent his under sheriff to the judges to know what to do, and also to the king. What shall be done further I do not know, but this is what has happened so far; if the process be erroneous, let his council reverse it.

Charges, found to be true in 1451, brought against John and William Merfeld, 1450

It is to be inquired for our sovereign lord the king whether John Merfeld of Brightling in the shire of Sussex, husbandman, and William Merfeld of Brightling in the shire aforesaid, husbandman, at Brightling in the open market the Sunday in the feast of Saint Anne, the 28th year of our sovereign lord [26 July 1450], falsely said that the king was a natural fool and would often hold a staff in his hands with a bird on the end, playing therewith as a fool, and that another king must be ordained to rule the land, saying that the king was no person able to rule the land.

Also the said John at Brightling the Sunday next before St Luke's Day, the 29th year of our said sovereign lord in the open alehouse falsely said to William Burford (senior) that the charter that our said sovereign lord made for the first insurrection was false and he also.

Also the said John at Brightling on St James's eve, the 28th year above said [24 July], falsely said that he and his fellowship would rise again and when they were up, they would leave no gentleman alive but such as they pleased to have.

Jack Cade's manifesto, 1450

These are the points, causes, and mischiefs of gathering and assembling of us the king's liege men of Kent the 4th day of June [1450]

[...] We, considering that the king our sovereign lord, by the insatiable covetous malicious pomps of [...] certain persons [who] daily and nightly are about his person and daily inform him that good is evil and evil is good [...]

Also they say that our sovereign lord is above his laws to his pleasure, and he may make them and break them as he will, without any distinction.

Also they say that the commons of England would first destroy the king's friends and afterwards himself, and then bring the Duke of York to be king, so that by their false means and lies they make him to hate and to destroy his friends, and cherish his false traitors.

Also they say that the king should live upon his commons, and that their bodies and goods are the king's [...]

Also they say that it would be a great reproof to the king to take again [through the Act of Resumption of 1450] what he has given, so that they will not suffer him to have his own goods, lands, or forfeiture [...]

Also it is to be remedied that the false traitors will suffer no man to come to the king's person for any cause 'Without bribes where none ought to be had [...]

Also, it is a heavy thing that the good Duke of Gloucester was impeached to treason by one false traitor alone and was murdered so soon that he might never come to his answer; but the false traitor Pole was impeached by all the commons of England [...]

Also the law serves for nought else in these days but to do wrong, for nothing is sped almost but false matters by colour of the law for bribery, dread, and favour, and so no remedy is obtainable in the court of conscience in any way. Also we say our sovereign lord may understand that his false council has lost his law, his merchandise is lost, his common people is destroyed, the sea is lost, France is lost, the king himself is so beset that he may not pay for his meat and drink, and he owes more than ever any King of England ought, for daily his traitors about him, when any thing should come to him by his laws, at once ask it from him [...]

Also we will that it be known we will not rob nor levy nor steal, but that these faults be amended and then we will go home [...]

Also his true commons desire that he will dismiss from him all the false progeny and affinity of the Duke of Suffolk, who are openly known, and that they be punished according to the law of the land, and to take about his noble person his true blood of his royal realm, that is to say, the high and mighty prince the Duke of York, exiled from our sovereign lord's person by the noising of the false traitor the Duke of Suffolk and his affinity. Also to take about his person the mighty prince the Duke of Exeter, the Duke of Buckingham, the Duke of Norfolk, and his true earls and barons of this land, and he shall be the richest Christian king.

Also, the taking of wheat and other grains, beef, mutton, and other victuals, which is an insupportable hurt to the commons, without provision of our sovereign lord and his true council, for his commons may no longer bear it.

Also, the state upon the labourers and the great extortioners of Kent, that is to say, Slegge, Crowmer, Isle, and Robert Est.

Also, we move and desire that some true justice with certain true lords and knights may be sent in to Kent to enquire of all such traitors and bribers, and that the justice may do upon them true judgement, whoever they may be.

Jack Cade's rebellion, 1450

(An English Chronicle of the Reigns of Richard II, Henry I, Henry V and Henry VI)

And this same year, in the month of May, arose the men of Kent and made themselves a captain, a ribald, an Irishman, called John Cade, who at the beginning took upon him the name of a gentleman and called himself Mortimer for to have the favour of the people. And he called himself John Amend-All, for as much as then and long before the realm of England had been ruled by untrue counsel, wherefore the common profit was sore hurt and decreased; so that the common people, what with taxes and tallages and other oppressions, might not live by their handiwork and husbandry, wherefore they grudged sore against those who had the governance of the land.

Then came the said captain and the Kentishmen to Blackheath, and there kept the field a month and more, pillaging the country round about; to whom the city of London at that time was very favourable and friendly, but it did not last long afterwards. In the mean time the king sent notable men to the captain and his fellowship, to know their purpose and the cause of their insurrection. The captain was a subtle man and [...] showed unto them the articles of his petitions concerning and touching the mischiefs and misgovernment of the realm, wherein was contained but what was right and reasonable, whereof a copy was sent to the parliament held at that time at Westminster: wherefore the said captain desired that such grievances should be amended and reformed by the parliament and that he should have answer thereof again, but he had none.

Soon afterwards the king removed from Westminster to Greenwich; and while he was there he would have sent certain lords with a force to have distressed the Kentishmen, but their men who should have gone with them answered their lords and said that they would not fight against those who laboured to amend and reform the common profit; and when the lords heard this, they gave up their purpose.

[...] The king then returned to London, and sent out a squire called William Stafford, and Sir Humphrey Stafford, knight, his cousin, to espy where the Kentishmen were; and when they knew that they were at Sevenoaks, they rode thither hastily with a few men, thinking to have gained a special respect and praise; but they were within danger of them before they knew it, and were both slain there, with most of their men who were with them.

When this happened, the king dissolved parliament and retired to Kenilworth. And when the Kentishmen heard that the king was gone from London, they came again to Southwark, and their captain was lodging at the [White] Hart. And the Thursday afterwards by favour of some of the men of London, he came into the city, but soon after they repented, for they were divided among themselves [...] And when he had entered the city at once he and his men fell to robbery, and robbed certain worthy men of the city and put some of them into prison till they had paid notable sums of money to save their lives. And the said captain rode about the city bearing a naked sword in his hand, armed in a pair of brigandines, wearing a pair of gilt spurs, and a gilt salat [helmet] and a gown of blue velvet, as if he had been a lord or a knight, and yet he was but a knave, and had his sword borne before him.

[...] On the Sunday next the men of London who had seen the tyranny and robbery of the said cursed captain and his men, laid hands when it was night on those who were dispersed about the city and beat them and drove them out of the city and shut the gates. And when the captain who was in Southwark saw this, at once with his men he made an assault on London Bridge, and would have come in, and despoiled the city; and the lord Scales with his own men and men of the city fought with them from 9 o'clock in the evening to 10 o'clock on the morrow; and many men were slain on both sides; and there were killed Matthew Goghe [Gough], a squire of Wales and John Sutton, an alderman of London. And this skirmish lasted until the wooden bridge was set on fire and then those of Kent withdrew little by little. And their captain put all his pillage in a barge and sent it to Rochester by water; and he went by land and would have gone into the castle of Queenborough with a few men that were left with him but he was prevented from achieving his purpose. And at once he fled into the wooded country near Lewes and the sheriff of Kent pursued him and there he was wounded to the death, and taken and carried in a cart towards London, and on the way he died. And then his head was smitten off and set on London Bridge and his body quartered and sent to divers towns of England; whose tyranny endured from Trinity Sunday to the eve of St Thomas of Canterbury's day. And thus ended this captain of mischief.

Jack Cade's posthumous attainder, 1451

Pray your commons of this present parliament that whereas the false traitor John Cade, naming himself John Mortimer, lately called captain of Kent, the 8th day of July, the 28th year of your reign, at Southwark in the shire of Surrey, and on the 9th day of July of the aforesaid year at Dartford and Rochester in the shire of Kent, also at Rochester aforesaid and elsewhere the 10th and 11th day of July then next following, within this your noble realm of England, falsely and traitorously plotted your death, destruction, and subversion of this your said realm, in gathering and raising a great number of your people, and stirring them to rise against you falsely and traitorously in the places aforesaid, and the times afore rehearsed, against your royalty, crown, and dignity, and there and then made and levied war falsely and traitorously against you and your highness, and although he is dead and beheaded, yet by the law of your said land not punished.

To consider the premises and to put such traitors in doubt so to do in time to come, and for the salvation of your self and your said realm, by advice of your said lords spiritual and temporal in this your present parliament assembled, to ordain by authority of the said parliament that he be attainted of these treasons, and by authority aforesaid forfeit to you all his goods, lands, tenements, rents, and possessions, which he had the said 8th day of July or after, and his blood corrupted and disabled for ever, and to be called within your said realm false traitor for evermore.

Reply: The king consents.

Tension and provocation in London, 1450

(Robert Bale's chronicle)

Also the 6th day of November began the parliament at Westminster. And the commons chose Sir William Oldhall, knight with the Duke of York, as speaker of the parliament [...]

Also the same time was ordained in various places of the city that chains should be drawn across the ways to keep the city safe; for people stood in great dread and doubt, for the variance between the lords. And a cry was made the said sixth day in the city that no one should speak or meddle with my matter done in the parliament nor of the lords.

Also the same time was levied a great sum of money to convey and set towards Bordeaux the soldiers and such people as were driven out of France and Normandy and had not the means wherewith to live but robbed, and so to have occupied them in the wars, to save and keep the king's right there. But there were so many false peculations and restraints of the money that the said soldiers should have had that they therefore did not leave the country, and so became thieves and murderers in various places of this land. And the eight day of November the commons of the parliament presented to the king a bill desiring the said Duke of Gloucester might be proclaimed a true knight. [No evidence of this supposed petition has been found on the parliamentary rolls.]

Also the 23rd day of November the said Duke of York with 3,000 men and more came riding through the city his sword borne before him and went to the parliament and the king. And on the following morning came riding through the city the Duke of Norfolk with a great crowd of men in brigandines, and six clarions blowing before him.

Also on the following morning came the Earl of Warwick through the city with a great company of men arrayed for war, and the Monday the last day of November there was a marvellous and dreadful storming and noise of the commons and of lords' men at Westminster crying and saying to the lords: "Do justice upon the false traitors or let us be avenged." And upon the morning, which was the first day of December, the lords' men made assault upon the Duke of Somerset's house at Blackfriars in London, and there despoiled much of his goods. The mayor and the commons of the city gathered a power together and remedied it at once; otherwise the duke would have been taken or slain.

The Duke of York's justification for marching on London, 1452

Right worshipful friends, I recommend me unto you, and I suppose it is well known unto you [...] what laud, what worship [...] was ascribed of all nations unto the people of this realm, whilst the kingdom's sovereign lord stood possessed of his lordship in the realm of France and duchy of Normandy; and what derogation, loss of merchandize, lesion of honour, and villainy, is [...] reported generally unto the English nation, for loss of the same; namely unto the Duke of Somerset, when he had the command and charge thereof; the which loss has caused and encouraged the king's enemies to conquer [...] Gascony and Guienne, and now daily they make their advance to lay siege to Calais and to other places in the marches there [...] to come into the land with great power, to the final destruction thereof if they might prevail, and to put the land in their subjection, which God defend. And on the other hand it is to be supposed it is not unknown to you how that after my coming out of Ireland, I, as the king's true liege man, and servant, (and shall ever be to my life's end) [...] advised his royal majesty of certain articles concerning the well-being and safeguard, both of his most royal person, and of the tranquility and conservation of all this his realm; the which terms of advice, though they were thought fully necessary, were laid apart, and to be of no effect, through the envy, malice, and untruth of the Duke of Somerset; who [...] labours continually about the king's highness for my undoing [...] and to disinherit me and my heirs [...] without any desert or cause done or attempted on my part or theirs, I make Our Lord the judge. Wherefore, worshipful friends, to the intent that every man shall know my purpose […] I signify unto you that with the help and support of Almighty God, and of Our Lady, and of all the company of Heaven, I […] seeing that the said Duke ever prevails and rules about the king's person, that by this means the land is likely to be destroyed, am fully determined to proceed in all haste against him, with the help of my kinsmen and friends; in such a way, that it shall prove to promote ease, peace, tranquility, and the safeguard of this land; and more, keeping me within the bounds of my liegeance as it pertains to my duty, praying and exhorting you, to strengthen, enforce, and assist me, and to come to me with all diligence, wheresoever I shall be, or draw, with as many goodly and likely men as you may muster to execute the intent abovesaid. Written under my signet at my castle of Ludlow, the 3rd day of February. Furthermore, I pray you that such strait appointment […] be made, that the people which shall […] be sent to me by your agreement […] behave in such a manner, on the way, that they do no offence, robbery, or oppression upon the people, in injury of justice. Written as above, Your good friend, R. York. To my right worshipful friends, the bailiffs, burgesses, and commons of the good town of Shrewsbury.

The struggle over the regency, 1454

(*The Paston Letters*)

John Stodeley, agent of the Duke of Norfolk, to his master, 19 January 1454.

As touching tidings, may it please you to know that at the prince's coming to Windsor the Duke of Buckingham took him in his arms and presented him to the king in goodly fashion, beseeching the king to bless him; but the king gave no answer. Nevertheless the duke still stayed with the prince by the king; and when he could have no kind of answer, the queen came in and took the prince in her arms and presented him in like form as the duke had done, desiring that the king should bless him; but all their labour was in vain, for they departed thence without any answer or look from the king, saving only that once he looked on the prince and cast his eyes down, without any more.
      Also, the Cardinal [John Kempe, Archbishop of Canterbury] has

charged and commanded all his servants to be ready with bows and arrows, swords and bucklers, crossbows, and all other weapons of war, such as they can use, to wait on the safeguard of his person [...]

Also, the Earl of Wiltshire, the Lords Beaumont, Poynings, Clifford, Egremont, and Bonville, make all the power they can and may to come hither with them [...]

Also the Duke of Buckingham has caused to be made 2,000 bands with knots, to what entent men may construe as their wits will give them.

Also, the Duke of Somerset's harbinger has taken up all the lodging that may be gained near the Tower, in Thames Street, Mart [Mark] Lane, St Katherine's, Tower Hill, and thereabouts.

Also, the queen has made a bill of five articles [...] whereof the first is that she desires to have the whole rule of this land; the second is that she may make the chancellor, the treasurer, the [keeper of the] privy seal, and all other officers of this land, with sheriffs and all other officers that the king should make; the third is that she may give all the bishoprics of this land, and all other benefices belonging to the king's gift; the fourth is that she may have sufficient livelihood assigned to her for the king and the prince and herself. But as for the fifth article, I cannot yet find out what it is.

Also the Duke of York will be at London definitely on Friday next coming at night, as his own men tell for certain, and he will come with his household train, cleanly set up and likely men. And the Earl of March comes with him, but he will have another fellowship of good men that shall be at London before him [...] and such jacks [dense quilted jackets, sometimes lined with metal plates], salets [type of helmet] and other harness as his followers shall have, shall come to London with them, or before them in carts. The Earl of Salisbury will be at London on Monday or Tuesday next coming with seven score knights and squires, besides other followers.

The Earls of Warwick, Richmond, and Pembroke come with the Duke of York, as it is said, each of them with a goodly fellowship. And nevertheless the Earl of Warwick will have 1,000 men awaiting on him besides the fellowship that comes with him, as far as I can tell. And as Geoffrey Poole says, the king's brothers [Edmund and Jasper Tudor, Earls of Richmond and Pembroke – his half-brothers] are likely to be arrested at their coming to London, if they come. Wherefore it is thought by my lord's servants and well-wishers here that my lord, at his coming hither, should come with a good and able company, such as is suitable and according to his estate to have about him; and their harness to come in carts, as my lord of York's harness did the last term, and shall at this time also. And moreover, that my lord have another goodly fellowship to wait on him and to be here before him, or else soon after him, in like manner as other lords of his blood will have.

And so that such a fellowship will be ready all the sooner, let my lord send responsible and wise messengers to his servants and tenants in Sussex and elsewhere, that they be ready at London for his coming, to wait on my lord. But let my lord beware of writing letters for them, lest the letters be delivered to the cardinal and lords, as one of my Lord's letters was now lately […] for that letter has done much harm and no good.

And as for such tidings as are contained in the letter sent home by John Sumpterman, I cannot so far hear the contrary of any of them, but that every man that is of the opinion of the Duke of Somerset makes himself ready to be as strong as he can. Wherefore it is necessary that my lord look well to himself and keep himself among his followers and depart not from them, for it is to be feared lest ambushes should be laid for him. And if that happened, and my lord came this way as he has been used to come, he might easily be ensnared and trapped, which God forbid. And therefore let my lord make good watch and be sure.

The Duke of Somerset has spies about in every lord's house of this land; some pose as friars, some as shipmen taken on the sea, and some as other kinds of men; they report to him all that they can see or hear touching the said duke. And therefore make good watch and beware of such spies.

And as regards the [letter of] privy seal and my lord's safety, my lord must be advised that if the chancellor [Cardinal Kempe] or any other make any question to my lord about his coming contrary to the tenor of the said privy seal [letter], my lord should by his wisdom make answer that he was credibly informed that both the Duke of Somerset, who is in prison, and others, who are still at large and support his views against the welfare of the king and of the land, made great assemblies and gatherings of the people, to maintain the views of the said Duke of Somerset and to distress my lord; and that the coming of my lord in such form as he shall come is only for the safeguard of his own person, and to no other intent, as my lord himself can say much better than anyone here can advise him […]

Written at London, the 19th day of January.

The release of the Duke of Somerset, 1455

(*An English Chronicle of the Reigns of Richard II, Henry IV, Henry V and Henry VI*)

Then there was a mortal debate and variance between Richard Duke of York, Richard Earl of Salisbury, Richard Earl of Warwick and Edmund Duke of Somerset, by whom at that time the king was principally guided and governed, as he had been before by the Duke of Suffolk. And this said duke always kept near to the king, and dared not depart from his presence, dreading always the power of the said Duke of York and of the aforesaid earls, and constantly excited and stirred the king against them; notwithstanding that the commons of this land hated this Duke Edmund and loved the Duke of York, because he loved the commons and preserved the common profit of this land.

    The said Duke Richard and the earls abovesaid, seeing that they might not prevail against nor withstand the malice of the aforesaid Duke Edmund [...] gathered privily a power of people and kept them [...] about the town of St Albans.

The First Battle of St Albans, 1455

(*The Paston Letters*)

Be it known [...] that the 21st May, 33 Henry VI, our sovereign lord took his journey from Westminster towards St Albans and rested at Watford all night; and on the morrow betimes he came to St Albans, and with him [...] the Duke of Buckingham, the Duke of Somerset, the Earls of Pembroke, Northumberland, Devon, Stafford, Dorset, Wiltshire, Lords Clifford, Dudley, Barners, and Roos, with other divers [...] gentlemen and yeomen to the number of 2,000 and more. And upon the 22nd day of the said month [...] assembled the Duke of York and with him came in company the Earls of Salisbury and Warwick with divers knights and squires to [...] the Key Field, beside St Albans. Furthermore our said sovereign lord the king, hearing and knowing of the said duke's coming [...] put his banner at the place called Butt's Lane in St Peter's Street, which place was called earlier Sandford, and commanded the ward and barriers to be kept in strong wise; the aforesaid Duke of York abiding in the field aforesaid from 7 of the clock in the morning till it was almost 10 without any stroke smitten on either side. [During which time York's request for the deliverance into his custody of Somerset was rejected.]

And when this was said the Duke of York and the said Earls of Salisbury and Warwick between 11 and 12 of the clock at noon broke into the town in three different places, and several places of the aforesaid street. [...] This done, the aforesaid Lord Clifford kept strongly the barriers that the Duke of York might not in any wise [...] enter nor break into the town. The Earl of Warwick, knowing thereof, took and gathered his men together and ferociously broke in by the garden side between the sign of the Key and the sign of the Chequer in Hollowell Street; and as soon as they were in the town they blew trumpets and shouted with a great voice: "A Warwick! A Warwick!" [...] and at once forthwith after the breaking in, they set on them manfully. [The Duke of Somerset, the Earl of Northumberland, Lord Clifford and about 50 more of the king's followers were killed] This done, the said lords, that is, the Duke of York, the Earl of Salisbury, the Earl of Warwick, came to the, our sovereign lord, and on their knees besought him of grace and forgiveness for what they had done in his presence, and besought him of his highness to take them as his true liege men, saying that they never intended hurt to his own person. And therefore the king our sovereign lord took them to grace, and desired them to stop their followers, and see that no more harm should be done. And they obeyed his command and caused a cry to be made in the king's name that everybody should stop fighting and not be so bold as to strike one stroke more after the proclamations of the cry; and so ceased the said battle, thanks be to God.

And on the morrow the king and the said duke, with other certain lords, came to the Bishop of London's palace, and there kept residence with joy and solemnity, deciding to hold parliament at London the 9th of July next coming.

The death of the Duke of Somerset

[Written in England by a correspondent on behalf of the Duke of

Burgundy.]

When the Duke of Somerset and those who were of his party then in the town of London heard that the Duke of York and several other lords [...] were coming against him with a power of 5,000 men, and when he considered what he had done against the said Duke of York and how also he was in very bad odour with the people of London, he came to the conclusion that he would not await them in the town of London [...] When these foes knew of the king's approach they at once drew near and on the 22nd May early in the morning the king sent a herald to the Duke of York to know the cause why he had come with so many people [...] The duke replied that he had by no means come against the king and was always ready to do him obedience, but he intended in all ways to have the traitors who were with the king so that they could be punished, and that if he could not have them by friendly and voluntary means he intended in any event to have them by force. Reply was made on the king's behalf to the said Duke of York that he did not have any traitors near him except the Duke of York himself who had risen against his crown. But before this reply came to the Duke of York a skirmish had already started between the men of both sides, before the town [...] And first the people of the Duke of York approached the town and placed good guards on all the roads around it, and entered the town so vigorously that soon they took and barred the market-place, where [...] the real fighting began. The battle started just on 10 o'clock but because the place was small few combatants could fight there; and matters became so critical that four of those who were of the king's bodyguard were killed in his presence by arrows, and even the king was wounded in the shoulder by an arrow, but it only grazed the skin. At last when they had fought for three hours the king's party saw that they had the worst and broke away on one side and began to flee; and the Duke of Somerset retreated into a house to save himself by hiding. but he was seen by the men of the Duke of York, who at once surrounded the house. And the Duke of York ordered that the king should be taken out of the press and led into the abbey for safety and this was done. And into this abbey retreated with him the Duke of Buckingham who was wounded by three arrows. And at once York's men began to fight Somerset and his men who were in the house, which they defended valiantly. And at last after the doors were broken, Somerset saw that there was nothing for it but to come out with his men [...] And after [...] the Duke of Somerset had killed four men with his own hand, he was, it is said, felled with an axe, and was at once wounded in so many places that he died. And while Somerset was making his defence [...] others of his party fought those of York so that three lords of Somerset's party were slain, that is, the Earl of Northumberland, Lord Clifford, and Sir Richard Harrington (controller of the king's household) [...] The battle lasted until half past two in the afternoon, and when it was over, the Duke of York's men went to the abbey to kill the Duke of Buckingham and the treasurer whom they call the Earl of Wiltshire [...] so the king willingly agreed to let York arrest the two lords; Buckingham was taken but the treasurer could not be found for he had already fled in a monk's habit, and still until today, May 27th, no one knows whither he has gone. And when all these things were done the Duke of York entered the abbey and knelt before the king [...] protesting that he had not opposed him but had been against the traitors to his crown. And before York left, the king pardoned him and received him into grace. And that day the king, York, and all the other lords went to London, where they have been received with great joy and solemn procession.

A royal pardon and an oath of allegiance, 1455

We therefore considering the premises, declare [...] our said cousins and all those persons who came with them in their fellowship to the said town of St Albans, the said 22nd day, and all other persons who [...] helped them, our true and faithful liegemen. [...] And that none of our said cousins, the Duke of York, and the Earls of Warwick and Salisbury, nor any of the said persons coming or being with them, nor any of their [...] helpers [...] be impeached, sued, vexed, grieved, hurt or molested in any wise in their bodies, lands, or goods, for any thing supposed or claimed to have been done to or against our persons, crown, or dignity.

    The 24th day of July, the 33rd year of our sovereign lord King Henry VI, at Westminster, in the great council chamber, in the time of parliament, in the presence of our said sovereign lord, the lords spiritual and temporal in showing their troth, faith and love that they have and bear to his highness, every lord spiritual laying his hand upon his breast, and every temporal lord taking our said sovereign lord, by the hand, freely swore and promised in manner and form as follows:

    I promise unto your highness by the faith and troth that I owe to

God and to you that I shall truly and faithfully keep the allegiance that I owe unto you my most sovereign lord., and to put me in my duty to do all that may be to the welfare, honour, and safeguard of your most noble person, and royal estate, pre-eminence, and prerogative; and I shall at no time will or consent to anything which might be or sound to the hurt or prejudice of your said most noble person, dignity, crown, or estate. And moreover I shall with all my power resist and withstand all those who would in any wise presume to attempt the contrary. So God help me and his saints.

[This oath was taken 33 lords spiritual and 27 lords temporal.]

The Duke of York's second protectorship, 1455

The king to all, etc. Greeting.

Know that as the commons of our realm of England, assembled in the present parliament, have frequently and humbly petitioned us and urgently implored us that in order to put down the disturbances, rebellions, murders, and riots, which are attempted and committed in various parts of the realm and to preserve the public good, the defence of our realm and of our peace, and the tranquility of our subjects, we should be pleased to agree and consent to constitute and ordain some powerful and suitable person as protector and defender of the realm. [...]

    We, considering the petition of the commons and the infirmity with which it has pleased the Most High Saviour to visit our person, an affliction which hinders us from the actual execution of the protection and defence of the realm and of the church of England, and considering that if we are troubled with numerous matters of business, the speed of our recovery will be impaired, and reposing full confidence in the circumspection and industry of our most dear cousin Richard Duke of York.

    By the advice and assent of the lords spiritual and temporal and the assent of the commons of our realm of England, assembled in our present parliament, ordain and constitute our cousin to be protector and defender and our principal councillor of our realm of England and of the church of England.

    The authority of the duke in occupying and exercising the burden of protector and defender to cease entirely when Edward our eldest son shall come to years of discretion.

Witnessed by the king at Westminster, 19th November, 1455.

The Battle of Blore Heath, 1459

(An English Chronicle of the Reigns of Richard II, Henry IV, Henry V and Henry VI)

In this same time the realm of England was out of all good governance as it had been many days before, for the king was simple and led by covetous counsel, and owed more than he was worth. His debts increased daily but payment there was none. All the possessions and lordships that pertained to the crown the king had given away, some to lords and some to other simple persons, so that he had almost nothing to live on. And the impositions that were imposed on the people, such as taxes, tallages, and fifteenths, all that came from them was spent in vain, for he maintained no household and waged no wars. Because of these misgovernances and many others the hearts of the people were turned away from those who governed the land, and their blessing was turned into cursing.

  The queen with such as were of her affinity ruled the realm as she liked, gathering riches innumerable. The officers of the realm, especially the Earl of Wiltshire, treasurer of England, to enrich himself, fleeced the poor people, and disinherited rightful heirs and did many wrongs. The queen was defamed and denounced., that he who was called prince was not her son but a bastard gotten in adultery; wherefore she, dreading that he should not succeed his father in the crown of England, sought the alliance of all the knights and squires of Cheshire, to have their goodwill, and held open household among them. And she made her son, called the prince, give a livery of swans to all the gentlemen of the countryside and to many others throughout the land, trusting through their strength to make her son king, and making secret approaches to some of the lords of England to stir the king that he should resign the crown to her son; but she could not bring her purpose about.

  The 28th year of King Harry, in the month of September, the year of Our Lord 1459, on the Sunday in the feast of St Matthew [23 September], Richard Earl of Salisbury, having with him 7,000 well arrayed men, dreading the malice of his enemies and especially of the queen and her company, which hated him mortally, and the Duke of York, and the Earl of Warwick too, took his way towards Ludlow where the Duke of York lay at that time, so that they both together could have ridden to the king at Coleshill in Staffordshire, to have cleared themselves of certain articles and false accusations touching their allegiance laid against them maliciously by their enemies. When the king heard of their coming, those who were about him counselled him to gather a power to withstand them, and informed him that they came to destroy him. The queen lay then at Eccleshall, and at once by her stirring the king assembled a great power, whereof Lord Audley was the chief and had the leading of them, and went forth to a field called Blore Heath, by which the said Duke of York and the Earl must needs pass. And there both hosts met and encountered and fought a deadly battle. And there was Lord Audley slain, and many of the notable knights and squires of Cheshire that had received the livery of the swans. And there were taken prisoners the Earl of Salisbury's two sons, Thomas and John, and Sir Thomas Harington, and imprisoned in the castle of Chester; but soon afterwards they were delivered. After this discomfiture the earl went on to Duke Richard at Ludlow, and thither came to them from Calais the Earl of Warwick.

The attainder of the Yorkists, Coventry, 1459

Wherefore may it please your highness [...] by the advice and assent of your lords spiritual and temporal and of your commons assembled in this your present parliament, and by the authority of the same to ordain, establish, and enact, that the said [...] Richard Duke of York, Edward Earl of March, Richard Earl of Salisbury, Edmund Earl of Rutland, etc. [...] for their said traitorous levying of war against your said most noble person, at Ludford specified above in the fields of the same, in the way explained above, be declared [...] attainted of high treason, as false traitors and enemies against your most noble person high majesty, crown, and dignity. [...]

Reply: The king agrees to this act: so that by virtue thereof he be not put from his prerogative, to show such mercy and grace as shall please his highness, according to his regality and dignity, to any person or persons whose names are expressed in this act, or to any other who might be hurt by the same [...]

The return of the Duke of York, 1460

(*Registrum Abbatiae Johannis Whethamstede*)

When the Duke of York returned from Ireland to the realm of England, landing at Red Bank near the town of Chester, there were varied and contrary rumours amongst the people about his return. Some said that his arrival was peaceful, and that he intended nothing else than to restore harmony among the quarrelling peers of the realm, and bring peace by his authority everywhere throughout the realm, and reform it. But others, amongst whom were the older and wiser in mind, suspected that he was going to be litigious and act litigiously against the lord king for the right of the royal crown and claim that crown by the title of hereditary right.

While the people were wavering thus in doubt, and the lord king was assembled with the prelates, peers, and commons in parliament at Westminster, for the good government of the realm, soon, almost at the beginning of the parliament, the Duke of York, with the pomp of a great following, arrived in no small exultation of spirit; for he came with horns and trumpets and men at arms, and very many other servants. And entering the palace there, he marched straight through the great hall until he came to that solemn room where the king was accustomed to hold parliament with his commons. And when he arrived there, he advanced with determined step until he reached the royal throne, and there he laid his hand on the cushion or bolster, like a man about to take possession of his right, and kept his hand there for a short while. At last, drawing it back, he turned his face towards the people, and standing still under the cloth of state, he looked attentively at the gazing assembly.

And while he stood there, looking down at the people, and awaiting their applause, Master Thomas Bourgchier, the Archbishop of Canterbury, came up, and, after a suitable greeting, asked him whether he wished to come and see the lord king. At this request the duke seemed to be irritated, and replied curtly in this way: "I know of no person in this realm whom it does not behove to come to me and see my person rather than that I should go and visit him."

When the archbishop had heard this reply, he retired in haste and told the king of the reply which he had from the mouth of the duke. When the archbishop had left, Richard retired also and went to the principal chamber of the whole palace and broke the locks (for the king was at that time staying in the queen's apartments); and when the doors had been opened, he stayed there for some time in the manner of a king rather than of a duke. And when the news of the duke's high-handedness was published among the people, and they heard how he had entered thus of his own ill-considered presumption without any weighty discussion, everyone, of whatever estate, rank, age, sex, order, or condition, at once began to murmur against him and say that he had acted in a rash manner.

The flight of Queen Margaret, 1460

(Gregory's chronicle)

And that same night the king removed to London against his will, to the bishop's palace of London, and the Duke of York came to him that same night by the torchlight and took upon himself as king, and said in many places that "this is ours by very right". And then the queen, hearing this, went away into Wales, but she was encountered beside the castle of Malpas, and a servant of her own that she had made both yeoman and gentleman, and afterwards appointed to be in office with her son the prince, despoiled her and robbed her, and put her so in doubt of her life and her son's life also. And then she came to the castle of Harlech in Wales, and she had many great gifts and was greatly comforted, for she had need thereof [...] And most commonly she rode behind a young poor gentleman of fourteen years of age, named John Coombe, born at Amesbury in Wiltshire. And thence she moved very secretly to Jasper, Earl of Pembroke, for she dared not abide in any place that was open, but in secret. The reason was that counterfeit tokens were sent to her as though they had come from her most dread lord King Henry VI; but it was not of his sending [...] but forged things, for they that brought the tokens were of the king's house, and some of the prince's house, and some of her own house, and bade her beware of the tokens, that she gave no credence thereto. For at the king's departing from Coventry towards the field of Northampton, he kissed her and blessed the prince and commanded her not to come to him till he should send her a special token that no man knew but the king and she. For the lords would have liked to have had her to London, for they well knew that all the arts that were done were encouraged by her, for she was more intelligent than the king. [...]

Then the queen, having knowledge of this, in a short while sent to the Duke of Somerset, at that time in Dorset at the castle of Corfe, and for the Earl of Devon, and for Alexander Hody, and prayed them to come to her as hastily as they could with their tenants as strong in their armour as men of war, for the Lord Roos, the Lord Clifford, Baron Grestock, Lord Neville, Lord Latimer were waiting upon the Duke of Exeter to meet with her at Hull. And this matter was not delayed but very secretly done; and she sent letters to all her chief officers that they would do the same, and that they should warn all those servants that loved her or meant to preserve and encourage her royal office, to wait upon her at Hull by the day that she appointed. All these people were gathered and conveyed so secretly that they were assembled to the number of 15,000 before any man would believe it; so that if any man said, or told, or talked of such a gathering, he would be disgraced; and some were in great danger, for the common people said to those who told the truth "You talk just as if you wished it were so" [...] And the 9th day of December next following set out the Duke of York, the Earl of Salisbury, the Earl of Rutland (he was the Duke of York's second son, one of the best disposed lords in this land) and Sir Thomas Harington, with many more knights and squires and great people with them, and so departed out of London towards York.

The Battle of Wakefield, 1460

(Attributed to William of Worcester, *Annales Rerum Anglicarum*)

On 21st December [1460] the Duke of York and the Earl of Salisbury, with 6,000 soldiers came to Sandal Castle, where they spent Christmas, the Duke of Somerset and the Earl of Northumberland with the opposite party lying meanwhile at Pontefract. King Henry with the Earl of Warwick and others spent Christmas in the palace of the Bishop of London at St Paul's. Edward Earl of March spent Christmas in the town of Shrewsbury at the Friary. On December 29th at Wakefield when the Duke of York's men were roaming through the countryside for victuals, a horrible battle took place between them and the Duke of Somerset, Earl of Northumberland and Lord Neville with a great army; and there were killed in the field the Duke of York, Thomas Neville, son of the Earl of Salisbury, Thomas Haryngtone, Thomas Parre, Edward Boucher [Bourgchier], James Pykeryng, and Henry Rathforde, many other knights and squires, and common soldiers to the number of 2,000. And after the battle Lord de Clyfforde [Clifford] killed Lord Edmund, Earl of Rutland, son of the Duke of York, on the bridge at Wakefield as he fled. And the same night the Earl of Salisbury was captured by a servant of Andrew Trolloppe. And on the morrow at Pontefract the Bastard of Exeter killed the Earl of Salisbury, and there by the counsel of the lords they beheaded the bodies of the Duke of York, the Earls of Salisbury and Rutland, Thomas Nevyle, Edward Boucher, Thomas Haryngton, Thomas Parre, James Pykeryng, and John Harrowe of London, mercer, and placed their heads on various gateways of York. The head of the Duke of York they also in contempt crowned with a paper crown.

When the battle was over, Queen Margaret came from Scotland to York where it was decided by the counsel of the lords to march in force to London, and to rescue King Henry from the hands of his enemies [...]

The Battle of Mortimer's Cross, 1461

(Gregory's chronicle)

Also Edward, Earl of March, the Duke of York's son and heir, had a great victory at Mortimer's Cross in Wales the 2nd day of February next following, and there he put to flight the Earl of Pembroke and the Earl of Wiltshire. And there he took and slew knights and squires and others to the number of 3,000.

And in that conflict Owen Tudor was taken and brought to Haverford-West and he was beheaded at the market place, and his head was set on the highest pinnacle of the market cross, and a mad woman combed his hair, and washed away the blood off his face, and got candles, and set about him burning, more than a hundred. This Owen Tudor was father to the Earl of Pembroke and had wedded Queen Katherine, mother to King Henry VI. He thought and trusted all along that he would not be beheaded until he saw the axe and block, and when he was in his doublet he trusted on pardon and grace until the collar of his red velvet doublet was ripped off. Then he said: "That head shall lie on the stock that was wont to lie on Queen Katherine's lap," and put his heart and mind wholly on God, and very meekly took his death.

Also the same day, that the Earl of March should take his journey towards Mortimer's Cross from Haverford-West [...] over him men saw three suns shining.

The Second Battle of St Albans, 1461

(Gregory's chronicle)

The lords in King Henry's party pitched a field and fortified it very strongly, and like unwise men broke their array and field and took another, and before they were prepared for battle the queen's party was at hand with them in the town of St Albans, and then everything was to seek and out of order, for their scouts came not back to them to bring tidings how near the queen was, save one who came and said that she was nine miles away. And before the gunners and Burgundians could level their guns they were busily fighting, and many a gun of war was provided that was of little avail or none at all; for the Burgundians had such instruments that would shoot both pellets of lead and arrows of an ell in length with six feathers, three in the middle, and three at one end, with a very big head of iron at the other end, and wild fire, all together [...] In time of need they could not shoot one of them, for the fire turned back on those who would shoot these three things. Also they had nets made of great cords of four fathoms long and four feet wide, like a hedge, and at every second knot there was a nail standing upright. so that no man could pass over it without a strong chance of getting hurt. Also they had a pavise borne as a door, made with a staff folding up and down to set the pavise where they like, and loop holes with shooting windows to shoot out at. [...] And when their, shot was spent and finished, they cast the pavise before them; then no man might come over the pavise because of the nails that stood upright, unless he wished to do himself a mischief Also they had a thing made like a lattice full of nails as the net was, but it could be moved as a man would: a man might squeeze it together so that the length would be more than two yards long, and if he wished, he might pull it wide, so that it would be four square. And that served to be at gaps where horsemen would enter [...] And as the real opinion of worthy men who will not dissemble or curry favour for any bias, they could not understand that all these devices did any good or harm, except on our side with. King Henry. Therefore they are much neglected, and men betake themselves to mallets of lead, bows, swords, glaives, and axes. As for spearmen, they are only good to ride before the footmen and eat and drink up their victuals, and many more such fine things they do. You must hold me excused for these expressions, but I say the best; for in foot soldiers is all the trust.

The accession of Edward IV, 1461

(Attributed to William of Worcester, *Annales Rerum Anglicarum*)

On Shrove Tuesday [...] took place the Battle of St Albans, where the Duke of Norfolk and the Earls of Warwick and Arundel and many others fled from the field. And King Henry was captured on the field along with Lord Montagu, his chamberlain. And the prince came to the king in the field, where the king, his father, dubbed him knight. And in the battle were killed 2,000 men, not only in the field but in divers crofts. [...] And on Ash Wednesday William Bonville and Thomas Kyriell, knight, were taken and beheaded in the presence of the prince at St Albans. When the battle was ended, the aldermen of London sent the Duchesses of Bedford and Buckingham to sue to the queen for grace and the peace of the city, and other ambassadors were sent to the king and queen at Barnet.

The Archbishop of Canterbury, Lord Thomas Bourgchier, and the Bishop of Exeter, George Neville, then the chancellor of England, were then in Canterbury, awaiting better news. On the following Thursday the king and queen turned back from St Albans to Dunstable with their army for fear that if their men had entered London, they would have sacked the city. And this was the downfall of King Henry and his queen; for if they had entered the city of London, they would have had all at their will.

On Friday morning at Newgate the commons of the city destroyed the cart with victuals ordered by the aldermen to go to Barnet for the queen's ambassadors. And on the same day Baldwin Foulforthe, knight, of Devonshire, and Alexander Hody, knight, with a great crowd of armed men, came to Westminster on the queen's behalf, because the commons of London rose against them.

When he heard this news, Edward, the new Duke of York, who was then near Gloucester, hastened towards London, and at Chipping Norton, in Oxfordshire, met the Earl of Warwick. And then there were in the army of the Duke Edward, Walter Devereux, William Herbert, John Wenlock, William Hastings, and many others of the Welsh Marches, with 8,000 armed men, and entered London with him [...] And Edward stayed at his house at Barnard's Castle.

On the Sunday following [March 1], after midday, in the big field at Clerkenwell the populace of the city congregated together with the army of the duke to the number of 3,000 or 4,000, whom the said reverend father George Neville, then the chancellor of England, ordered to stand in the field. And he caused to be proclaimed the title by which the said Edward could claim the crown of England and France, and at once all the people shouted that Edward was and should be king. I was there and heard this, and I went down with them at once into the city.

On the third day of March the Archbishop of Canterbury, the Bishops of Salisbury and Exeter, and John, Duke of Norfolk:, Richard, Earl of Warwick, Fethwater [Fitzwalter], William Herbert, Lord Freers [Ferrers] of Chartley, and many others held a council at Baynard's Castle, where they agreed and decided that Edward. Duke of York, should be King of England. And on the fourth of March the Lord Edward, Duke of York, went publicly to Westminster with the lords and was received with a procession. After the declaration of his title, he took the crown and sceptre of St Edward, and caused himself to be proclaimed King Edward IV.

The Battle of Towton, 1461

(Hearne's Fragment, in *Thomae Sprotti Chronica*, ed, T. Hearne, Oxford, 1719)

The journey was determined by the newly elected King Edward, the fourth of that name, to follow his enemies King Harry the sixth and his queen northward. First on the morrow John Duke of Norfolk went in to his countryside with all diligence to prepare for the war on the part of King Edward. And on the next Saturday, the Earl of Warwick with a great band of men departed out of London northward, followed on the next Wednesday by the king's footmen in a great number, of whom most were Welshmen and Kentishmen. Then on the Friday ensuing King Edward issued out of the city in goodly order at Bishopsgate, on the ninth day of March, and held on his journey, following those others. And when the foreprickers [scouts] came to Ferrybridge, there was a great skirmish in which John Ratcliff then Lord Fitzwalter was slain. And thereupon they advanced themselves until they came to Towton eight miles out of York upon a Friday at night, awaiting the residue of their company, which were assembled in good order on the Saturday, the eve of Palm Sunday [28 March 1461]. And about four of the clock at night the two battles joined and fought all night till on the morrow in the afternoon. About noon the aforesaid John, Duke of Norfolk, with a fresh band of good men of war came to the aid of the newly elected King Edward. This field was sore fought; for there were slain on both sides 24,000 men, and all the time it snowed. There were slain the Earls of Northumberland and Westmoreland with Sir Andrew Trolloppe and others, and the Earls of Devonshire and Wiltshire were taken and beheaded there. And the deposed King Henry and his queen with Harry, Duke of Somerset, and others, in great haste fled to Scotland. When this victory had been obtained, King Edward followed the chase for a little while, but shortly he returned to York where he kept his Easter.

Chapter 3: The Reign of Edward IV

The first reign of Edward IV

Edward IV was a very different kind of king from the pious, schizophrenic and generally unheroic Henry VI. The new king was eighteen and handsome, unusually tall, lean and athletic. Edward was usually good-natured and approachable; his appetite for food and women was excessive: he was known to make himself vomit in order to enjoy the pleasure of filling his stomach again, and he seduced women of all rank, married and unmarried. He spent considerable sums of money on a luxurious lifestyle and he loved hunting. This king made every effort to look the part, wearing his crown whenever making a public appearance, enforcing strict rules of etiquette on his courtiers, dressing in fine and lavish costumes. A visiting dignitary from Bohemia described his as 'the most splendid court that one could find in all Christendom'. The Crowland chronicler was similarly upbeat in his reflections on the king and his family:

> 'In those days you would have seen a royal court worthy of a leading kingdom, full of riches and men from almost every nation, and above all with fine looking and most delightful children, the offspring of his marriage to Elizabeth Woodville. They had ten children, of whom three had died and seven were living at the time [1482]. Of these latter, the two boys, Edward, Prince of Wales, and Richard, Duke of York and Norfolk, [the 'Princes in the Tower'] had not yet reached manhood. There were five beautiful girls [...] Although in earlier years solemn embassies and pledges of faith in the words of princes had been despatched, with letters of agreement drawn up in due form, concerning the marriage of each of the daughters, it was not now thought that anyone of the marriages would materialise, for everything was susceptible to change given the unstable relations between England and France, Scotland, Burgundy and Spain.

> [...] This prince, although at the time [1483] it was thought that he indulged his desires and passions to excess, was a Catholic of the truest faith and a most stern enemy of heretics, a most benevolent patron of learned men, scholars and clerics, a most devoted observer of the sacraments of the church and most penitent of sinners.'

Edward IV took a personal interest in the details of government and he worked hard at establishing a personal rapport with the mightiest of his subjects:

> 'Edward was of a gentle nature and cheerful aspect: nevertheless should he assume an angry countenance he could appear very terrible to beholders. He was easy of access to his friends and to others, even the least notable ... he seized any opportunity that the occasion offered of revealing his fine stature more protractedly and more evidently to on-lookers. He was so genial in his greeting, that if he saw a newcomer bewildered at his appearance and royal magnificence, he would give him courage to speak by laying a kindly hand upon his shoulder [...] He was more favourable than other princes to foreigners, who visited his realm for trade or any other reason. He very seldom showed munificence, and then only in moderation, still he was very grateful to those from whom he had received a favour. Though not rapacious of other men's goods, he was yet so eager for money, that in pursuing it he acquired a reputation for avarice.'[23]

Furthermore, although he had no interest in promoting an imperialist foreign policy, Edward had proved himself to be dynamic and relentless in war. He was victorious in his first command at the Battle of Mortimer's Cross and it was he who had steered the Yorkists into the triumph at Towton. In the propagandist *Historie of the Arrivall of King Edward in England,* celebrating his further victories in 1470 and 1471 at the start of his second reign, he was portrayed as a heroic warrior:

> '[...] the king, trusting verily in God's help, our blessed Lady's

---
[23] Dominico Mancini.

and St George [...] with the faithful, well-beloved and mighty assistance of his fellowship that in great number dissevered not from his person, and were as well assured unto him as to them was possible [...] he manly, vigorously and valiantly assailed them in the midst of the strongest of their battle, where he, with great violence, beat and bore down before him all that stood in his way, and then turned to the range, first on that one hand, and then on that other hand, so beat and bear them down that nothing might stand in the sight of him and that well-assured fellowship that attended truly upon him.'

The decade of Edward's first reign was a turbulent one which saw further civil war, betrayal by his closest friends and relatives, capture, defeat and flight. His success in holding on to power for so long, given the circumstances of his accession, is as remarkable as the speed with which he regained it in 1471.

For a long time it was assumed that the battles Edward fought for the throne were disastrous for the people and economy at large. This view was most forcibly put by the early Tudor chronicler, Polydore Vergil, in his *Anglica Historia*, completed in 1537:

'while one [faction] sought by any manner to subdue the other, and raged in revenge upon the subdued, many men were utterly destroyed, and the whole realm brought to ruin and decay.'

In more recent times, however, historians, as discussed in the opening chapter, have questioned the extent to which the wars represented catastrophe and widespread anarchy.

Edward IV's position in 1461 was tenuous to say the least. Many families in the north, secure in their great fortress castles, remained staunchly loyal to the Lancastrian cause. The house of Lancaster had two figureheads with which rebels in England or invaders from abroad might find common cause: King Henry in the north and young Prince Edward in Scotland.

Warwick, to whom Edward IV gave full responsibility for military affairs, was successful in the first months of the reign in taking rebel fortresses in the north of England, which included the castles of Bamburgh, Alnwick and Dunstanburgh. After the slaughter of Towton, Edward was remarkably lenient during the 1460s in his dealings with the leaders of pro-Lancastrian families and Henry Beaufort, Duke of Somerset, and Sir Ralph Percy were both forgiven and their castles restored to them. Such generosity did not payoff: by 1462 Percy was back in league with the rebels, and was eventually killed on the battlefield of Hedgeley Moor in 1464. The Duke of Somerset, despite being shown real friendship by Edward, which included the rare privilege of occasionally sharing his bed, led the resistance of 1464 which ended in defeat at Hexham in May.

In November 1462 Queen Margaret reopened hostilities by invading the north from Scotland with the support of a small army provided, with the French king's approval, by the grand seneschal of Normandy. Her reliance on French support made her cause all the more unpopular in England. Worse still, she had promised Louis XI Calais in return for his help. Although the castles of Alnwick, Bamburgh and Dunstanburgh admitted her, she was unable to raise a force capable of withstanding the massive army Edward launched against her. She fled by sea, having narrowly escaped capture, further north.

In October 1463, Edward secured a truce with the French King Louis XI by which it was agreed that France would cease funding the Lancastrian cause. Warwick began to seek a suitable French bride for Edward in order to strengthen the new Anglo-French rapport. In December a similar agreement was reached with the Scottish government and Henry VI was obliged to leave Edinburgh and seek the refuge of Bamburgh Castle from which to rule his small kingdom. This was now made up of only a handful of Northumbrian castles.

In the spring of 1464 the Duke of Somerset launched one last desperate attempt to revive the house of Lancaster by trying to inspire rebellion in Wales, Cheshire and Lancashire. The Lancastrians were defeated at the skirmish of Hedgeley Moor and, decisively, at the Battle of Hexham by Warwick's brother, John Neville. Although Henry VI escaped, the most prominent Lancastrian leaders, including Somerset, were either killed in the fighting or executed shortly afterwards. A few pockets of resistance remained but the Lancastrian cause as a whole was shattered. Henry spent over a year in Yorkshire, Lancashire and the Lake District on the run with a single companion, his chamberlain, Sir Richard Tunstall. He was finally captured in July 1465 and brought to London, lashed to his horse and wearing an undignified straw hat. As he rode through the streets on his way to the Tower, he was abused and even pelted with rubbish by onlookers as he passed.

Having suppressed the Northumbrian revolt in 1464 and finally taken Henry into captivity, Edward's position was relatively secure so long as his Yorkist sympathisers stayed loyal. The next crisis of the reign would come from an unexpected quarter - the rebellion of his former ally, the, Earl of Warwick.

Warwick has been labelled by tradition with the epithet 'Kingmaker' for his part in championing and fighting for the Yorkist cause. In fact, it was an even alliance and the victories were Edward's own, Warwick proving less skillful in battle. Edward was neither 'made' by Warwick nor controlled by him. Warwick was rewarded for his support with territories and titles such as captain of Calais, admiral of England and constable of Dover Castle. This mightiest of subjects, however, was denied a complete monopoly of power as royal patronage extended to other faithful pro-Yorkists. This was particularly true in the case of Lord Hastings, who was given Warwick's stewardship of the duchy of Lancaster, and Sir William Herbert, who was elevated to the lieutenancy of South Wales in place of the earl. To add insult to injury, Edward secretly married Elizabeth Woodville just as Warwick was close to concluding a political marriage alliance with the French royal family. A chronicler, John Warkworth, described the circumstances in which the marriage took place:

> 'In that year, the Earl of Warwick was sent into France to look for a wife for the king. The fair lady in question was the niece of the King of France, and the Earl of Warwick managed to arrange this wedding. However, while the Earl of Warwick was away in France, the king was married to Elizabeth Woodville, a widow, whose husband Sir John Grey had been slain in battle on King Henry's side, and whose father was Lord Rivers. The wedding took place in great secrecy, on the first day of May 1464.'

Edward's marriage appears to have been a purely romantic affair - unlike other women moving in court circles, the beautiful and manipulative Elizabeth refused to let the king sleep with her unless wed. Politically, the marriage, and Edward knew it, was utterly irresponsible at a time when the young king's hand could have been used to great national advantage. Edward was the first English monarch to marry a commoner since before the Norman Conquest. Furthermore, their union went against royal marital convention because she could not protest her virginity - she had had two sons by a previous marriage to Sir John Grey. He had died at the Second Battle of St Albans in 1461, fighting with Edward's enemies, the Lancastrians.

The Italian chronicler, Dominico Mancini, writing in December 1481, recalled the deep offence caused by this unfortunate marriage:

> 'Edward IV, though he was then King of England, allowed himself to be ruled by his appetites in all things. In his choice of his wife too he was governed by lust. For he married a woman of low stock, called Elizabeth, against the wishes of the magnates. They would not stoop to show regal honour in accordance with her exalted rank to a woman of such humble origins, who was, moreover, a widow with two sons.
>
> [...] The marriage caused the nobles to turn against Edward - later, indeed, he was even obliged to make war on them - while the members of Edward's own house were bitterly offended. His mother was furious and offered to submit to a public enquiry, asserting that Edward was not the child of her husband, the Duke of York, but was conceived in adultery. For this reason, she claimed, he had no right to be king.'

The anger felt by his brother, George, Duke of Clarence, was remembered by Mancini:

> 'Edward had two brothers then living and they, for their part, were sorely displeased at Edward's marriage. The Duke of Clarence, who was closest in age to Edward, showed his anger more openly. He criticised Elizabeth's humble origins bitterly and in public and asserted that the king ought to marry a virgin, not a widow, which was contrary to established custom.
>
> The other brother, however, Richard, Duke of Gloucester, was better able to dissemble his thoughts and was in any case, because of his youth, less influential. He said and did nothing that might have been used against him.'

On 14 September 1464, while under pressure from Warwick to conclude a French marriage alliance, Edward confessed to the council he was already wed. The assembled magnates were horrified as the Woodville family was thus suddenly and unexpectedly raised to the upper echelons of the English aristocracy. The further marriages in quick succession of Elizabeth's several siblings linked the family to some of the greatest houses in the kingdom. Warwick's own daughters were usurped as Elizabeth's sisters secured the most eligible bachelors in the kingdom, including the heir of Lord Herbert and the eleven-year-old Duke of Buckingham. Her brother John, at the age of nineteen, was married off to a rich heiress, Katherine Neville, the Dowager Duchess of Norfolk, who was approaching her seventieth birthday. Members of the Woodville clan acquired some of the highest positions in the land: one of Elizabeth's brothers was made Bishop of Salisbury, another admiral of the fleet. In 1466 Earl Rivers, her father, became Treasurer of England in place of Lord Mountjoy, Warwick's uncle.

Edward's marriage provoked an ultimately fatal rift in the house of York. Warwick and other magnates were alienated by this elevation of a 'low' family with previous Lancastrian sympathies (Elizabeth's father, brother and first husband had fought on 'the other side'). Edward's two brothers and mother were equally outraged.

As the Woodvilles rose, Warwick's influence over the king declined. His family remained powerful, indeed his brother, George Neville, was enthroned as Archbishop of York in September 1465 but, increasingly, Edward failed to act on his advice. Family matters aside, the king and his hitherto first minister were divided over foreign policy. Edward moved towards Burgundy, while Warwick believed that England's best interests lay in permanent alliance with the traditional enemy of England, and present enemy of Burgundy, France. As early as 1467, Louis was contemplating the possibility of bringing Queen Margaret and the Earl of Warwick together in an attempt to overthrow the increasingly pro-Burgundian English king.

At much the same time, Warwick began to engineer the marriage, against the king's wishes, of his daughter, Isabel, to the king's ambitious brother and heir presumptive, George, Duke of Clarence. When Edward became aware of Warwick's overtures, he was furious and regarded the earl's plans as a blatant attempt to make himself more powerful and to challenge the Woodvilles. Then, in June 1467, he heard that George Neville, Archbishop of York, was seeking dispensation from the pope to marry his niece to Clarence. Edward dismissed him from his office as Lord Chancellor, to the approval of the Woodvilles. This last insult seems to have determined the final collapse in the once close friendship between Warwick and Edward. The ensuing alliance with

Burgundy, applauded by London's merchants and consolidated by Edward's sister's marriage to the Duke of Burgundy's eldest son in 1468, marked the beginning of Warwick's personal alliance with King Louis of France. Jean de Waurin, a contemporary chronicler, wrote:

> 'He [Louis XI] had done his utmost to make an alliance with the English in order to destroy the Duke of Burgundy, so it was generally said, and he had succeeded in winning over the Earl of Warwick to his side, and with him almost the whole commons of England.'

According to the chronicler of the abbey of Crowland, this marriage, rather than that of Edward to Elizabeth Woodville, was the principal reason for the conflict between the king and the Earl of Warwick:

> 'At this marriage [that of Margaret of York, Edward IV's sister, and the Duke of Burgundy], Richard Neville, Earl of Warwick, who had for some years appeared to favour the party of the French against the Burgundians, conceived great indignation. For he would greatly have preferred to have sought an alliance for the said Lady Margaret in the kingdom of France, by means of which a favourable understanding might have arisen between the monarchs of those two kingdoms; it being much against his wish, that the views of Charles, now Duke of Burgundy, should be in anyway promoted by means of an alliance with England. The fact is, that he pursued that man with a most deadly hatred.
>
> This, in my opinion, was really the cause of the dissensions between the king and the earl, and not the one which has previously been mentioned - the marriage of the king with Queen Elizabeth.'

Deeply alarmed by the resurrection of the Anglo-Burgundian alliance, Louis cultivated the rift between Edward and Warwick and even offered the earl a principality forged out of Holland and Zeeland as an incentive for dismantling the Edward-Woodville regime.

By the spring of 1469 Warwick was in league with Clarence in seeking to undermine the Woodvilles, the one with a view to controlling the king himself, the other contemplating taking his brother's place on the throne. Clarence encouraged Warwick to turn against the king and helped spread the rumour that his brother was not Duke Richard's son but the bastard of an archer called Blaybourne.

In July 1469 at Calais, Clarence defied his brother by marrying Warwick's daughter, Isabel. The marriage coincided with a pro-Warwick rebellion in the north led by Robin of Redesdale, almost certainly instigated by the earl himself. Edward commanded Warwick, who was part of the wedding party in Calais, to return to England and lend his support but Warwick refused. Instead, on 12 July, he issued a manifesto declaring his intent to relieve England from the tyranny of poor government, high taxes and lawlessness by petitioning the king to dispense with his corrupt and inept councillors. If he failed to do so he would deserve deposition, like unreliable kings before him.

Warwick invited his supporters to meet him in three days at Canterbury, while his ally, Sir John Conyers, marched a large army from Yorkshire towards the Midlands. Warwick arrived at Canterbury on 16 July. With an army made up of men of Kent and soldiers from the Calais garrison he then rode north to join the northern army and do battle with the loyalists, led by the Earl of Pembroke. They met and fought a ferocious battle at Edgecote Hill, ten kilometres north of Banbury, on 26 July. Pembroke was defeated and, without justification, beheaded for treason on Warwick's orders.

Edward IV received news of Pembroke's defeat three days later while camped a few kilometres away at the village of Olney near Coventry. Knowing he was now at Warwick's mercy with his main army shattered, he allowed his supporters to disperse and remained at Olney, awaiting the arrival of Warwick's soldiers.

With Edward held in custody, first in Warwick Castle and then Middleham, Warwick, with Clarence's support, attempted to rule in his name. The Woodville dynasty now suffered the retribution of the Nevilles: following their capture in the Forest of Dean, Earl Rivers and Sir John Woodville were beheaded on 12 August and Rivers' wife shortly after was accused of witchcraft and arrested, though later released.

Anarchy in parts of the realm, including London, and a Lancastrian rising in the north, forced Warwick to release the king in mid-September, for, without him, Warwick was unable to gain the support of the lords or command the loyalty of Yorkist soldiers. Warwick gave Edward his liberty in return for the support of the loyal northern magnates, who provided him with an army which rapidly suppressed the rebellion.

Edward, reinstated, returned to London where, in December, he was publicly reconciled with his brother and Warwick. Despite their recent antics, neither was punished and those who had fought for them in the summer were pardoned - Edward could ill afford to maintain old enmities but, equally, Warwick no longer could expect any further royal favour.

A rebellion in Lincolnshire in the spring of 1470, largely engineered by Clarence, presented Warwick with another chance to achieve his objectives, this time throwing in his lot with the king's brother in a bid for the crown. The swift defeat of the Lincolnshire rebels, crushed by Edward at the Battle of Empingham (Lose-Cote Field) before Warwick could provide reinforcements, put paid to their attempts to extend rebellion into the north and west. The traitors fled to France and the protection of Louis XI. Men seized from ships at Southampton belonging to the earl, one of which had been destined to carry Warwick and Clarence to safety, were less fortunate. According to Dr John Warkworth of Cambridge University, a contemporary chronicler, writing about 12 years later in his *Chronicle of the First Thirteen Years of the Reign of King Edward the Fourth*, they received the full force of Edward's violent retribution:

King Edward then came to Southampton and commanded the Earl of Worcester to sit in judgement of the men who had been captured in the ships: and so 20 gentlemen and yeomen were hanged, drawn and quartered, and then beheaded, after which they were hung up by their legs and a stake was sharpened at both ends; one end of this stake was pushed in between their buttocks, and their heads were stuck on the other. This angered the people of the land and, forever afterwards, the Earl of Worcester was greatly hated by them, for the irregular and unlawful manner of execution he had inflicted upon his captives.

In France, Warwick enacted a startling change of heart in seeking the forgiveness of Margaret of Anjou and promising to support the Lancastrian cause in the hope of redeeming his position in England. In this grand project, Warwick had the full support of the French king, who promised to aid their cause with money, ships and soldiers. In return, Louis would receive English support in the campaign he planned to launch against Burgundy. After lengthy talks with King Louis and uncomfortable audiences with her old enemy, Warwick, Queen Margaret was eventually persuaded to accept the earl as her ally. The alliance was sealed by the marriage of Prince Edward to Warwick's daughter, Anne Neville, but only after Warwick had agreed to withdraw all allegations he had previously made regarding his new, son-in-law's paternity. Margaret meanwhile accepted the fact that her husband was incapable of ever ruling his kingdom alone again, and promised to make Warwick Henry's regent and governor of England. Clarence was not entirely neglected in these proceedings: he was promised the crown in the event of Prince Edward dying without issue.

As other members of the Neville family rose in the north, distracting the king from possible invasion in the south, Warwick and Clarence returned in force. They landed in Devon, a Lancastrian stronghold, in September 1470 when King Edward was away in Yorkshire concerned with the northern rebels. Warwick marched north to do battle with Edward and the king headed south. However, while Warwick gathered support along the way from his own admirers and supporters of the house of Lancaster, Edward's followers began to desert him, most crucially the Marquess of Montague, who had raised an army ostensibly intended for the suppression of the northern rebels but was now urging his troops to join Warwick. Edward was obliged to abandon thoughts of defeating Warwick in a last heroic battle in the Midlands and instead fled east with a small entourage, boarded a ship at King's Lynn on 2 October and sailed for Holland and the protection of Burgundy.

The readeption of Henry VI

On 3 October 1470 Henry VI was released from captivity in the Tower of London and formally readepted (restored) to the English throne:

> 'in the beginning of the month of October [...] 1470, the Bishop of Winchester, by the assent of the Duke of Clarence and the Earl of Warwick, went to the Tower of London where King Henry was in prison [...] and brought him to the Palace of Westminster, and so he was restored to the crown again [...]'[24]

---

[24] Warkworth's chronicle.

Warwick, who had played such an important part in his overthrow, now made him king once again and carried his train in St Paul's Cathedral in a formal thanksgiving ceremony. The contemporary chronicler, John Warkworth, explained the reasons why Edward failed to keep his throne in 1470 in his *Chronicle of the First Thirteen Years of the Reign of King Edward the Fourth*:

> 'They [Edward's supporters] had expected prosperity and peace from Edward IV, but it was not to be. One battle followed another, and there was widespread disorder, and the common people lost much of their money and goods. Firstly, a tax of a fifteenth part of all their property was levied, and then another fifteenth to pay for the fighting. These and many other factors had reduced England to the direst poverty. Many people thought, moreover, that King Edward was to blame for harming the reputation and esteem of the merchants for, at that time, both in England and abroad, these were not as great as they had been before.'

The readeption of Henry brought with it war with Burgundy: the condition on which Louis XI of France had supported Warwick's campaign of 1470. France opened the hostilities in December of the same year and England followed suit in February. England's merchant community was horrified as the loss of the wool trade's chief markets loomed. For Warwick, the support of France was a political disaster for it pushed Duke Charles of Burgundy into close alliance with England's fugitive King Edward. With 50,000 crowns donated by Duke Charles, Edward IV was able to start planning his own restoration. Once again, the attitude and involvement of foreign powers would determine English history.

England had entered the war without the consent of parliament and against the wishes of the London merchants. When Edward set sail for England in March at the head of a tiny army, Warwick could no longer rely on widespread public support.

Edward landed at Ravenspur in Yorkshire on 14 March 1471. Although he expressed his determination to succeed by giving orders for the ship he had sailed in to be burned, there was no certainty that the country at large would rise in his support. While Edward made his way to York, Warwick desperately tried to assemble an army to defeat him.

Initially neither party was particularly successful in its recruiting drive: Hull barred its gates to Edward and a number of magnates ignored Warwick's pleas for help. Defiantly, Edward headed south with a couple of thousand men preparing to challenge the might of Warwick's much larger conscript army (according to one contemporary chronicle his soldiers were enlisted 'on pain of death'). By the time he confronted Warwick, camped behind Coventry's city walls with perhaps as many as 7,000 men, Edward's army was at least 5,000 strong and led by a king who had never yet lost a battle. According to the chroniclers, some of those who lent him their support did so because he owed them money, others because their wives, with whom he had been secretly acquainted, urged them into the field! Warwick wisely stayed put and awaited reinforcements while Edward occupied the earl's castle at nearby Warwick.

At Banbury, on 3 April, Clarence, with, allegedly, a host of 12,000, joined forces with his brother, Edward, who forgave him and promised the full restoration of his estates, Together they now marched on London, taking care to guard their rear with seasoned troops against an attack from Warwick. Meanwhile Warwick's brother, Archbishop of York, George Neville, prepared to defend London, parading his liege, Henry VI, through London's streets in the hope of securing public support and confidence. He gained neither, for when the mayor and aldermen of the capital were made aware of the size of the army descending upon them they decided not to resist. Even Neville himself abandoned his brother at this point and sent messages to Edward declaring his readiness to open London's gates. On 11 April Edward and Clarence entered the city, received by cheering crowds and formal greetings from its mayor and other dignitaries. Having confined Henry VI to the Tower, Edward was reunited with his wife, Elizabeth, and their two daughters. Here too Edward met, for the first time, his five-month-old son - the hope and future of the Yorkist dynasty.

Rather than await Warwick's arrival, Edward next decided to ride out of London and meet the earl's pursuing force some distance away from the capital. They met at Barnet, sixteen kilometres out of London, and fought a fierce battle on Easter Sunday, 14 April. Warwick had the larger force - possibly twice the size of Edward's, which numbered around 10,000. Both Edward and Warwick were engaged in the thickest of the fighting, choosing, as was then the custom, to lead their armies from the front. Confusion in Warwick's ranks, which began when a body of archers mistook some of their own for the enemy and fired on them, gave Edward a hard-earned victory. The Yorkists lost 500 men and around 1,000 of Warwick's men were slain. The earl himself was killed as he tried to escape from the battlefield. His body was brought to London and displayed for three days in St Paul's Cathedral for public viewing, in order to scotch any rumours that he had survived.

The day before the battle, Henry's queen, Margaret of Anjou, and son, Prince Edward, had sailed into Weymouth to raise an army in the south and west against Edward. Margaret heard the news of Warwick's defeat while resident at Cerne Abbey in Dorset. Initially she abandoned all hope of defeating her husband's usurper but, as her army swelled with Lancastrian supporters from the southern counties joining her at Cerne, her resolve strengthened. A plan of campaign was developed in which Jasper Tudor would ride ahead and set about raising an army in Wales and she would follow, heading north to Lancashire via Bristol, Gloucester and Chester.

On 23 April, a week after hearing of Margaret's landing, Edward left London, at the head of a small army, in an attempt to engage Margaret before she was able to join forces with Jasper Tudor. As Margaret headed north through Exeter, Glastonbury and Wells, recruiting as she marched, Edward moved west to Cirencester and then went south to Malmesbury, hoping to block her advance. However, Margaret was already in Bath and, instead of veering north-east towards Edward's waiting army, she chose to go further west to Bristol, arriving there on May Day. With Edward in pursuit, Margaret continued north and rested at Berkeley Castle, a little way south of Gloucester, with Edward camped some miles behind at Chipping Sodbury.

The Lancastrian army then continued to Tewkesbury, intending to cross the Severn, but here Edward finally caught up with Queen Margaret and the prince. Margaret's army outnumbered Edward IV's but his was more experienced and better equipped. The Battle of Tewkesbury was fought on 3 May 1471 and, for the second time in three weeks, Edward was victorious. In the carnage Prince Edward, together with many other Lancastrian magnates, was killed and, a few days later, Queen Margaret was captured. Although Warwick's cousin, the Bastard of Fauconberg, launched an unsuccessful assault on London, Edward was triumphant and arrived back in the capital on 21 May to great public acclaim. Towards midnight on the same day the fifty-year-old King Henry VI was put to death in the Tower, presumably on Edward's orders.

This monumental event was recounted by John Warkworth about twelve years later, in his *Chronicle of the First Thirteen Years of the Reign of King Edward the Fourth*:

> 'And the same night that King Edward came to London, King Harry, being in ward in prison in the Tower of London was put to death the 21st day of May on a Tuesday night between eleven and twelve of the clock, being then at the Tower the Duke of Gloucester, brother to King Edward, and many other; and on the morrow he was chested and brought to Paul's and his face was open there that every man might see him. And in his lying he bled on the pavement there; and afterwards at the Black Friars was brought, and there he bled new and fresh; and from thence he was carried to Chertsey Abbey in a boat and buried there in Our Lady's Chapel.'

It is interesting to note that in this account, which almost certainly predates his reign, Richard III (the Duke of Gloucester) is implicated in the martyred king's murder. His queen, Margaret, was spared and, after some years of benevolent captivity in England, she was permitted to return to France where she died in poverty in 1482. Jasper Tudor, with whom, fatally, she had failed to meet in May 1471, fled to France, eventually to return with his nephew, Henry Tudor, the future Henry VII, in 1485.

Most of the lords, in fact, remained loyal to their feeble king, Henry VI, until his defeat at Towton in 1461. Edward IV effectively created a new Yorkist nobility by reviving old titles and making new ones. In twenty-two years he added to their ranks thirty-five 'new' peers. For the remainder of the conflict between York and Lancaster, therefore, the peerage was more evenly divided between the two sides. Lands forfeited to the king by the vanquished provided endowments for some of these additional lords. Edward's growing reliance on these jumped-up gentry, to the detriment of established peers, has been shown as a political blunder by historians, and the main cause of Warwick's change of allegiance and rebellion in 1469.

Some historians have depicted the elevation of such peers as Rivers and Stafford as too radical a break with tradition for the longer-established magnate families to tolerate. Furthermore, Warwick's defeat of this new aristocracy proved how unsubstantial this power could be;

the Woodvilles and their allies lacked the loyalties that, after generations of service, bound together the older lords and the gentry.

The greatest magnates, such as Warwick, had a substantial retinue made up of retainers who held their estates as the feudal tenants of their lord. In 1448 the Duke of Buckingham, for example, numbered among his retinue ten knights and twenty-seven esquires, many in receipt of valuable annuities, and numerous paid servants and officials managing his estates across twenty-two counties. Consequently, Buckingham probably had the capacity for creating the largest private army in England. His decision to abandon a neutral stance in 1459, and to support Margaret of Anjou's cause, provided her with the resources to challenge the Yorkist protectorate and so provoke further civil war. The initial rout of the enemy after Blore Heath brought rewards for Buckingham in the form of forfeited Yorkist lands and goods. A few months later he was killed when Warwick and the future Edward IV defeated the Lancastrians at Northampton. Typical of his caste, he had been driven by a combination of loyalty to his anointed king and the prospect of material gain.

The second reign of Edward IV

After the drama of the first, the second decade of Edward IV's reign might seem a little dull. There were no further crises after 1471 to compare with Warwick's rebellion. Moreover, the campaigns Edward launched against France and Scotland lack the drama of the string of bloody 'all or nothing' battles fought on English soil in 1460 and 1461, when he first secured the throne. Nevertheless, the second reign was not uneventful: he was threatened by a rebellious brother, his invasion of France brought to mind Henry V's empire-building and, on the eve of his death in 1483, English armies ravaged the lowlands of Scotland. For a time, Scotland's king and his seat of Edinburgh were held captive. Edward was barely forty when he died of an illness allegedly brought on as a result of a dissolute lifestyle. His early death, leaving a child as heir, was the one great disaster of his reign. Had he lived long enough to see his son grow into adulthood, the history of the turbulent 1480s would have been very different indeed.

George, Duke of Clarence

George Plantagenet (1449-78) had much in common with his older brother, Edward IV; he was tall and good looking, charming and crafty, but also fatally ambitious and jealous of power. In 1467 he was just 17 when he became embroiled in the rift between the Earl of Warwick and Edward IV following the king's ill-advised marriage to Elizabeth Woodville. Warwick at this had made overtures to both Clarence and his younger brother, Richard, Duke of Gloucester, regarding their marriage to his daughters, Isabel and Anne. Edward, when he realised what was being hatched, was furious. He summoned his brothers and commanded them to abandon the scheme; a York-Neville marriage would greatly strengthen Warwick and possibly inspire treason. Warwick, however, continued to work towards a marriage alliance and found in Clarence a willing participant. Clarence was a headstrong youth who did not like being told what to do by his older brother. Furthermore, like Warwick, he believed his right to a position of real power had been eclipsed by the rise of the Woodvilles. Easily led, he married Isabel in 1469 and joined Warwick in the coup, which resulted in the readeption of Henry VI.

By 1471 Edward IV had recovered the throne, Warwick, Henry VI and his son were all dead and Clarence was reconciled to his brother. That Clarence should then contemplate treason a second time around the year 1477, this time from a much weaker position, is remarkable, perhaps an act of insanity. Once again rumours began to circulate, as they had in 1470, regarding Edward IV's legitimacy. Clarence, who may have initiated the current notion that his brother was born out of wedlock, rarely visited the court and when he did so refused to eat or drink anything, the implication being that he feared his brother wished to have him poisoned. Worse still, he accused the queen of witchcraft! Even after two of his associates, Dr John Stacey and John Burdett, were executed for treason - a final warning to Clarence - he remained outspoken and critical of the king. On 18 February he was put to death in the Tower of London.

His mother protested against a public execution and, according to legend, he was 'drowned in a butt of malmsey' - a barrel of wine. Various explanations have been provided for this unusual fate: it has been suggested that Clarence, as a joke, requested it himself; one intriguing theory proposes he was drowned in his bath, for baths commonly were made from sawn-down wine butts. Some historians have rejected it outright as a colourful fiction while others accept it as a literal, and telling, truth.

The Italian chronicler, Dominico Mancini, was convinced that Queen Elizabeth instigated Clarence's execution:

> 'The queen remembered the insults to her family and the calumnies with which she was reproached, namely that according to established usage she was not the legitimate wife of the king. Thus she concluded that her offspring by the king would never come to the throne, unless the Duke of Clarence were removed; and of this she easily persuaded the king. The queen's alarm was intensified by the comeliness of the Duke of Clarence, which would make him appear worthy of the crown: besides he possessed such mastery of popular eloquence that nothing upon which he set his heart seemed difficult for him to achieve. Accordingly whether the charge was fabricated, or a real plot revealed, the Duke of Clarence was accused of conspiring the king's death by means of spells and magicians. When the charge had been considered before a court, he was condemned and put to death. The mode of execution preferred in this case was, that he should die by being plunged into a jar of sweet wine.'

Foreign policy

Edward IV's foreign policy was characteristic of kings throughout the fifteenth century. He was preoccupied with French relations, France being the 'traditional enemy' of England and the natural ally of an independent Scotland (in what was known as the 'Auld Alliance'). Like his predecessors, Edward laid claim to the French crown. Although he probably believed it was beyond his grasp, this was the ultimate objective of his invasion of France in 1475. Such ventures were hugely expensive and Edward relied heavily upon benevolences to fund them as Robert Fabyan, a London draper, commented in 1471:

'This year this king, intending to make a voyage over sea to France, called before him his lords [...] to know their good minds, what of their free wills they would aid and depart with him toward the said voyage. And after he had known their good disposition towards him, he sent for the Mayor of London and his brethren, the aldermen, assessed each one and exhorted [them] to aid and assist him toward the great journey, of which the mayor for his part granted £30, and the aldermen some 20 marks, and the least £10. And that done, he sent for all the trusty commoners within the said city, and them exhorted in like manner, of whom most granted to him the wages of half a man for a year [...] And after that he rode about [the kingdom] and raised thereby notable sums of money, the which way of the levying of this money was after named a benevolence.'

Obviously Edward had enough to occupy him in securing his position at home without becoming entangled in dynastic struggles abroad. In fact, foreign policy was intimately wrapped up in domestic matters since the French king, Louis XI, was likely to do all he could to undermine the English crown and to keep England at bay while he pursued his own continental objectives. Furthermore, Louis was sympathetic to the Lancastrian cause, as he was related to Margaret of Anjou, Henry VI's queen. Louis' obvious ally in this was Scotland, who was fiercely determined to remain independent of England, while Edward's continental allies, who wished to be independent of France, were the duchies of Burgundy and Brittany.

Edward organised two major campaigns abroad - one in France, the other in Scotland. A huge army was landed in France in July 1475, partly paid for by a benevolence. The Duke of Burgundy failed to provide much support, however, and, within weeks of landing, the campaign was terminated by the Treaty of Picquigny in August 1475.

This temporary restoration of good relations would be wrecked by England's involvement in the French-Burgundian conflict that erupted in 1477. With the guarantee from Burgundy's ally, Maximilian of Austria, that he would pay the Picquigny pension in the event of war between England and France, in 1480 Edward prepared to launch a further campaign.

Any plans Edward laid were stalled by Scottish incursions into English territory in the same year. The resulting English invasion of

Scotland started well with the capture of Edinburgh and James III, but bad planning and poor leadership left just Berwick upon Tweed in English hands.

Meanwhile Louis had greatly diminished the independent status of Burgundy and, in the Treaty of Arras (1482), Maximilian was forced to concede territory, and his daughter was promised to the dauphin, Louis' son. By the time Edward died, he had lost his French pension and the alliances upon which the successful outcome of his continental policy depended.

Edward had been restored to the throne at least in part because of the support of Burgundy. Drawn together by a mutual and traditional antipathy for France, some form of retaliation for French interference in English affairs would have seemed likely after Edward's victory in 1471. The young king had earned for himself a formidable reputation as a warrior and might reasonably have been considered a new Henry V, destined to rebuild his great predecessor's French kingdom, so ignominiously lost during the reign of Henry VI. At the very least, Edward could be expected to commit England to the defence of Calais, the obvious target of French aggression. In fact, although not necessarily by intent, Edward's second reign saw no major continental campaign. The absence of such a campaign greatly contributed to Edward's success in financial terms: despite the cost of winning the throne and the general turbulence of civil war, helping to provoke the economic crisis he inherited in 1471, he was the first King of England in two hundred years to leave the crown solvent on his death.

Edward, born in Normandy, certainly envisaged war with France and inherited the traditional ambition of English kings to wear the French crown. He was sufficiently the realist to know that a full reconquest was out of the question but he relished the prospect of glory abroad and limited territorial gains. At the very least, he could hope to prevent Louis XI of France from lending further support to the Lancastrians. In this he had the support of parliament. Lengthy negotiations with potential allies in a continental campaign resulted in 1475 in a tripartite alliance between England, Burgundy and Brittany. A large army, consisting of 12,000 troops and almost the entire English nobility, was raised, paid for by additional taxes and a benevolence. In the summer of 1475, Edward invaded France. One chronicler on the French side, Philippe de Commynes, later wrote in his *Memoires*:

> '[...] this army was the largest that a king of England had ever brought over, and all the men were mounted and were better armed than any that had ever come to France, and nearly all the lords of England were there [...]'

This, however, did not mark the beginning of a glorious campaign and within a few weeks it was over, concluded by the terms of the Treaty of Picquigny of August 1475. An Anglo-French war would have been cripplingly expensive and unlikely to achieve the ultimate objective. Charles Ross was of the opinion that Edward was inadvertently saved from his own misadventure by the actions of the Duke of Burgundy: 'It is hard to say exactly what Edward's plans entailed but it is fairly certain he hoped to achieve something more glorious, and probably less bloodless, than the final outcome.'[25] Ross argued that his invasion of France was not an impromptu decision but a scheme for which Edward had been preparing, diplomatically and militarily, during the preceding three-and-a-half years.

If, in fact, Edward merely intended to intimidate France and wrest from the French king some compensation for his interference in recent English affairs then the campaign was a great success. By the terms of the treaty, Edward secured an immediate 'tribute' of around £15,000, on condition he withdraw his army, and a further annual 'pension' of £10,000 to prevent his returning. This arrangement, designed to last for seven years, was to be reinforced by the intended marriage of Edward's daughter to the French dauphin. The English king and his whole army had been lavishly feted by the French at Amiens as a satisfactory settlement was being agreed. After Edward had departed from Calais, Louis is said to have joked, 'I chased the English out of France far more easily than my father did - he had to do so by force of arms, but I simply used meat pies and good wine.'

The *Crowland Chronicle* provides fascinating details of the aftermath of the 1475 campaign and Edward's personal engagement in maritime trade:

> 'When they [some soldiers after the French campaign of 1475] got back home they gave themselves up to theft and pillage to the extent that no road in all England was safe for merchants or

---

[25] Charles Ross in *Fifteenth Century England 1399-1509* (1995).

pilgrims.

The king was thus compelled to travel through his own kingdom with his justices, sparing no one, not even from his own household, from being hanged if they were arrested for theft or murder. Wherever it was enforced, this severe justice eliminated highway robbery for a long time to come [...] [The king] was aware that he had reached a position where he no longer dared demand subsidies from the English people [...] Accordingly he devoted all his attention to how he might in future gather funds commensurate with his position as king from his own resources and by his own endeavour.

When parliament had been summoned, he took back almost all the royal patrimony from all those, whoever they were, on whom it had been conferred and devoted it entirely to bearing the crown's costs. He appointed as overseers of tolls at every port of the kingdom hand-picked men who were reputedly excessively hard on the merchants.

The king himself fitted out cargo ships and loaded them with fine wool, cloth, tin and other commodities of the kingdom and, like any other merchant, he traded for goods [...] He studied the Chancery registers and rolls and from those persons discovered to have trespassed on inheritances without observing due legal procedure he demanded heavy fines [...] the income from these and similar snares - more than could be devised by someone inexperienced - made the king very rich over the next few years. Indeed, in the collecting of gold and silver vessels, tapestries, valuable ornaments, both regal and religious, in the building of castles, colleges and other important places, in the acquisition of lands and estates, none of his predecessors could equal his outstanding achievements.'

Despite continued tension between the two countries and the implicit support that Louis XI gave to the troublesome James III of Scotland, the truce ran its course and Edward continued to receive his valuable French pension until Burgundy and France made their own truce - the Treaty of Arras in December 1482.

In the same year, Edward launched a punitive invasion of Scotland against James who, encouraged by Louis, continued to condone border raids on the north of England. Supporting James's brother's claim to the Scottish throne, Edward's army, led by Richard of Gloucester, seized Edinburgh and captured the king. When his brother, the Duke of Albany, suddenly renounced his claim, there was no longer any reason for the invasion and Gloucester withdrew, retaining for England the border fortress town of Berwick-upon-Tweed. The exercise had been very costly, provoking riots in southern England, and could be said to have been quite unnecessary. It is true that, for a short while, Gloucester's exploits made good royal and English nationalist propaganda: celebratory bonfires were lit and cannons fired all over England when the duke entered Edinburgh. The string of minor victories on land against the Scots, and the devastation of James III's fleet in the Firth of Forth in May 1482, was some consolation for the lack-lustre campaign in France seven years earlier.

Edward's foreign policy was unspectacular during his second reign and doubtless he did not live up to the expectations of those contemporaries who had seen him triumphant in 1471. The Treaty of Arras was a bitter blow that, it has been suggested, hastened his death in 1483. It might have been prevented had he concentrated on preserving the old animosity between France and Burgundy instead of undertaking the venture in Scotland. Some historians have painted a very negative picture of Edward IV's foreign undertakings. The Treaty of Arras is highlighted as his greatest failure. He was, it is claimed, out-manoeuvred by Louis XI and he failed, through lack of resources, to take full advantage of the rivalry between France and Burgundy.

A more sympathetic assessment might highlight the huge financial burden a more 'heroic' policy would have represented, and point to the peace with France, the payment of the French pension, the humiliation of James III and the acquisition of Berwick as modest successes.

Financial policy

It is likely that Edward IV's personal excesses contributed to his early death. This was the result of a stroke, brought on in the opinion of Charles Ross by excessive, relentless gluttony. He was renowned for his splendid costume and once impressive figure, but infamous for his overindulgence. In the words of the chronicler, Dominico Mancini, an

Italian cleric resident in London in 1482-83:

> 'In food and drink he was most immoderate: it was his habit, so I have learned, to take an emetic for the delight of gorging his stomach once more. For this reason and for the ease, which was especially dear to him after his recovery of the crown, he had grown fat in the loins, whereas previously he had been not only tall but rather lean and active.'

Although Edward IV had added the wealth of the estates of Henry VI and other defeated Lancastrians to his own in 1461, he was still short of money. Edward's luxurious court, the lavish gifts to his favourites and kin, as well as the cost of maintaining the royal castles, conducting foreign campaigns and paying the salaries of certain officials, placed a substantial financial burden upon the royal shoulders. His ordinary income derived from the crown lands (spectacularly increased by the attainders of 113 of his enemies after 1461), feudal dues (including wardships involving the juvenile heirs of nobility killed in the wars), customs duties and fines. Any 'extraordinary' income to meet extraordinary expenditure, that associated with a military campaign for example, could be raised as a tax introduced by parliamentary consent. Corruption, reluctance to pay additional taxes and general bureaucratic inefficiency obliged Edward to rely in part upon the 'voluntary' payment of benevolences, and loans from London merchants and foreign bankers. His need for cash in order to fund his invasion of France in 1475 led him into one of his many 'perambulations' around the kingdom, as he cajoled nobles, mayors, aldermen and rich widows into making donations. 'And thus', reads *The Great Chronicle of London*, 'by his own labour and other solicitors [...] he gathered notable sums of money with the which all provision was made in all goodly haste for the said voyage.' The campaign provided Edward with a welcome additional income by the terms of the Treaty of Picquigny. By such means Edward was able to 'live of his own' without having to rely too heavily upon unpopular taxation. Claims that he promoted a more lucrative, reformed management of the crown estates have, however, been challenged by some historians who have identified many estates in which there was no significant increase in yield across the years of Edward's second reign.

Under Edward the handling of royal finances became more efficient, with the king himself at the centre of affairs. Many of the financial responsibilities of the heavily bureaucratised Westminster-based Exchequer were transferred to the Chamber; royal funds were now housed in the king's personal apartments and he scrutinised spending. The Chamber clerks thus held some of the highest posts in the kingdom. The lord chamberlain had to be a most trusted servant.

His debasement of the coinage in 1464 was a further source of revenue:

> '[In the year] 1464, Edward IV changed the coinage of England, which proved most profitable to him. He made an old noble a royal, the value of which was declared to be ten shillings; but the new coins contained some alloy, which reduced their value and made them weigh more; and he changed the design. He also made a groat worth threepence and an Angle noble worth six shillings and eightpence, and with all these changes caused great harm to the common people.'[26]

Although Edward, by 1478, was solvent and, unusually among England's medieval kings, he died solvent, it would be inappropriate to consider him as financially astute as the greatest royal economist of the fifteenth century, Henry VII. Inheritance, attainders and luck, as much as, perhaps more than, careful financial administration, accounted for his success in this particular area.

The monk, Ingulf, wrote in the *Chronicle of the Abbey of Crowland*:

> 'He dared not from now on demand subsidies from the English people [...] he bent all his thoughts towards gathering together a treasure worthy of his royal estate from his own substance and by his own industry [...] He appointed surveyors of the customs in every port of the kingdom, the most prying of men, and, by all accounts, excessively hard on the merchants. The king himself procured merchants' ships, loaded them with the finest wool, cloths, tin and other commodities of the kingdom and, just like any man living by trade, exchanged merchandise for merchandise [...] He would only part with the revenues of vacant prelacies [bishoprics], which according to Magna Carta

---

[26] Dominico Mancini.

cannot be sold, for sums which he had determined on, and on no other terms. He scrutinised the registers and the rolls of Chancery and exacted heavy fines from those heirs whom he found to have intruded themselves without due process of law, as recompense for the issues which they had enjoyed in the meantime [...] Within a few years he had made himself into a most opulent prince so that none of his predecessors could have equalled him in collecting vessels of gold and silver, tapestries and precious ornaments for his palaces and churches, in building castles, colleges and other fine places and in acquiring new lands and possessions.'

The 'new monarchy' debate

Edward has been more admired for the strength of his rule in England than for his foreign policy. Claims that he reduced the autonomy of the nobles, that he centralised power and made the process of government more efficient, have inspired historians, notably J. R. Green (1837-83), to describe Edward's as a 'new monarchy', the model his successors would fashion into Tudor 'despotism'. Such commentators regarded the civil and dynastic wars as the principal means by which fifteenth-century monarchs broke the might of 'over-powerful' noble families. One advocate of this view is S. B. Chrimes:

> 'He [Edward IV] did much to consolidate the monarchy, to rehabilitate its finances, and to restore its prestige. He stopped the process of decay in monarchy and government [...] The foundations of what has commonly been called the 'new monarchy' were laid not by Henry VII, but by Edward IV.'[27]

Recent examinations of the relationship between the crown and nobility conclude that, in fact, there was no significant change under Edward IV, reign, spending in the royal household was more carefully monitored, he acquired the wealth of a number of estates confiscated from defeated

---

[27] S. B. Chrimes, *Lancastrians, Yorkists and Henry VII* (1964), pp.124-25.

Lancastrians and the officials running his estates were made more accountable. In 1465 parliament was persuaded to grant him, for life, the monies raised by customs duties at England's ports. His wealthier subjects were required to offer benevolences -'gifts' of money to their monarch from time to time as a gesture of loyalty. Unlike Henry VI, he was careful to repay loans, thus making the crown more creditworthy. This helped whenever he needed to borrow money. Furthermore, his reign coincided with a general improvement in trade with continental Europe as the economic depression lifted in the later 1460s.

Although he just about managed to keep control over them during his second reign, Edward continued the tradition of allowing great magnates to rule more or less independently, on his behalf, in peripheral regions. David Grossel has observed:

> 'The king's council retained its importance and its functions changed little. There is no doubt that many of Edward's personal servants were capable and effective, but he did lack a strong personal following in the provinces, such as that built up by Richard of Gloucester in the north, and there was always suspicion and jealousy of the Woodvilles. Edward made no consistent effort to restrain the power of the aristocracy. He still relied on the support of the great families in the shires, such as the Stanleys in Lancashire and Cheshire. His failure to restrain aristocratic power can be contrasted unfavourably with the far more assertive Henry VII. If the country was not as lawless as in the reign of Henry VI, this simply reflected Edward's more powerful personality.'[28]

Charles Ross is among those historians who have argued that Edward's was very much a medieval style of kingship:

> 'The crux of the problem [maintaining law and order] lay in the immunity of the powerful offender, especially those who had the king's support. There was an inherent conflict between repeated demands for impartial justice and the king's committed support of the great men to whom he had given rule of the shires. Bitter complaints against their excesses run through the reign. The

---

[28] David Grossel, in John Lotherington (ed.), *The Tudor Years* (1994), p. 21.

Commons in 1467 were particularly outspoken in linking a rising crime rate with the 'heavy lordship' of men in standing with the king, against whom redress could not be obtained [...] Edward was extraordinarily lavish in delegating local power and influence to his supporters. No man had ever enjoyed the power in south Wales wielded by Lord Herbert in the 1460s. The same is true of Richard of Gloucester in the north in the 1470s. Professor Chrimes would have us believe that by 14S3 'there was no over-mighty subject left in England.' But was not Gloucester [later Richard III] the mightiest of overmighty subjects? And was not his great north-country connection, built up with active royal encouragement, a major factor in enabling him to consolidate his hold on the throne? This was part of the price that Edward IV paid for effective political control during his lifetime.'[29]

However, in this second reign Edward IV proved less tolerant of those who might seek to usurp him a second time; Henry VI was murdered on 21 April 1471, and Edward's brother, Clarence, who had conspired with Warwick in 1469, was finally arrested in 1477 and placed in the Tower, accused of further treasonable activities. He was killed there in February 1478. This in the opinion of some contemporaries and some historians was an act of despotism:

> 'Rather than centralising power, he [Edward] took the traditional course of relying on the nobility as his agent in the localities. The great nobles retained their independence and freedom of manoeuvre. It was Henry VII who succeeded in making service at court, rather than extensive lands and local authority, the benchmark of status for a noble. Edward IV made no such attempt. Granted, he did choose to exploit the increasing education of the lesser nobility by employing them in such roles as receivers: granted also that he elevated others to the dignity of magnate. But this does not amount to a policy of supplanting the old nobility with 'new men' of markedly lower social status. Nor does it mean that the power of the king increased at the expense

---

[29] C. D. Ross, 'The reign of Edward IV', in S. B. Chrimes, C. D. Ross and R. A. Griffiths (eds.), *Fifteenth-century England 1399-1509* (1972, 1995), pp. 62-63.

of the nobility - another supposed characteristic of new monarchy. [...] When J. R. Green wrote *A short history of the English people* in the 1870s, he not only argued that Edward IV was the founder of the new monarchy, but also that he was despotic: in fact, despotism, or the exercise of an unconstrained, absolute authority, was supposed to be part and parcel of new monarchy itself. Was Edward IV a despot? Some contemporary chroniclers clearly thought that he had that tendency and intention. The judicial execution of his dangerous brother, the Duke of Clarence, in 1478 was cited as an example [...] Also, Edward's use of benevolences - in effect, 'gifts' extracted from the nobility, supposedly as an alternative to military service - might be taken as further proof of creeping despotism. But the overall case is not a strong one. The benevolences were never intended as a permanent system of taxation [...] And it could be argued that Clarence brought about his own doom.'[30]

On the other hand, the king was a generous patron of his supporters and allowed some particularly close family members, notably his brother, the Duke of Gloucester, the future Richard III, to become very powerful indeed. He permitted them to retain their private armies of retainers, relying on mutual interests to curb any inclination to use them against him. Old opponents were given the opportunity to redeem themselves and, between 1472 and 1475, thirty attainders were reversed. Meanwhile old feuds between great families, such as the one between the Harringtons and Stanleys, continued unabated. Full-scale civil war was temporarily ended, but regular bouts of localised provincial lawlessness, violence and bloodshed remained as one contemporary complained:

'in divers parts of this realm great abominable murders, robberies, extortions, oppression and other manifold maintainences, forcible entries [...] affrays, assaults be committed and done by such persons as either be of great might, or else favoured under persons of great power [...] yet remain unpunished [...] a number of people have been slain, some in Southwark [...] and some here at Westminster Gate, regardless of your presence here at your Palace of Westminster, or that your

---

[30] John Warren, *The Wars of the Roses and the Yorkist Kings* (1995), pp.141-42.

high court of Parliament is in session [showing] contempt of your highness [...] to the great emboldening of all rioters and misgoverned persons.'[31]

---

[31] Sarah Newman, *Yorkists and Tudors 1450-1603* (1989), p. 67.

SOURCES

The battles of Hedgeley Moor and Hexham, 1464

(Gregory's chronicle)

This year Queen Margaret came out of France with 52 ships, with Frenchmen and some English men in the ships. And they landed in Northumberland; it was seven days before All Hallows-tide. And there she took the castle of Alnwick and put it full of Frenchmen. And then she returned to Scotland by water. And there arose such a tempest upon her that she forsook her ship and escaped with the boat of the ship. And the ship was sunk with much of her stuff and three great ships as well. And 406 Frenchmen were taken in the church of Holy Island. Then King Edward heard tell of this and made himself ready towards the North with many lords, gentles, and commons with him. And there he laid siege to Alnwick Castle and the castles of Bamborough, and Dunstanborough [...] And Bamborough and Dunstanborough were surrendered by Sir Ralph Percy and Sir Harry Beaufort, late Duke of Somerset, to the king's will, With the condition that the said Ralph Percy should have the keeping of the two castles, Bamborough and Dunstanborough. The said Sir Ralph Percy and Sir Harry Beaufort, late Duke of Somerset, were sworn to be true and faithful as true liege men to our king and sovereign lord Edward IV. And they came to Durham, and there they were sworn before our king [...] And then the aforesaid Ralph Percy returned again to Northumberland and had the keeping of the said two castles according to the agreement. And the said Sir Harry Beaufort abode still with the king, and rode with him to London. And the king made much of him; so much so that he slept with the king in his own bed many nights, and some times rode hunting behind the king, the king having about him not more than six horsemen at the most, and yet three were men of the Duke of Somerset, The king loved him well, but the duke thought treason under fair cheer and words, as it appeared [...] But within a short time afterwards Sir Ralph Percy by false collusion and treason allowed the Frenchmen to take the castle of Bamborough from him [...] And then King Edward made Sir John Ashley [...] captain of the castle [of Alnwick], and Sir Ralph Gray constable of the said castle of Alnwick. And within three or four months afterwards that false knight and traitor,

Sir Ralph Gray, by false treason took the said Sir John Ashley prisoner and delivered him to Queen Margaret and then delivered the castle to the Lord Hungerford and unto the Frenchmen who accompanied him; and by this means he put the king our sovereign lord out of possession. And then after King Harry that was, and the Queen had come to the King of Scots, Sir Pierre de Brezé, with 80,000 Scots, laid a siege unto the castle of Norham, and lay there 18 days. And then my lord of Warwick and his brother the lord Montague laboured to rescue the said castle of Norham, and so they did, and put both King Harry and the King of Scots to flight. And Queen Margaret with all their counsel, and Sir Pierre de Brett with the French men, fled away by water with four balingers [small seaworthy boats] and they landed at Sluys in Flanders, and left King Harry that was behind them, and all their horse and harness, they were so hastily pursued by my lord of Warwick and his lord of Montague, and those who accompanied them [...]

And this same year about Christmas that false Duke of Somerset, without leave of the king, stole out of Wales with a private following towards Newcastle, for he and his men were leagued to have betrayed the said Newcastle. And in the way thither he was noticed and was nearly taken beside Durham in his bed. But he escaped away in his shirt and barefoot and two of his men were taken [...] And when his men knew that he had escaped, and his false treason was discovered, his men stole from Newcastle as very false traitors, and some of them were taken and lost their heads for their labour. And then the king [...] had knowledge of the false disposition of this false Duke Harry of Somerset. The king sent a great fellowship of his household men to keep the town of Newcastle, and made Lord Scrope of Bolton captain of the town; and so they kept it surely all that winter. And about Easter next after [1464] the Scots sued unto our sovereign lord the king for peace. And the king ordained commissioners to meet with the Scots [...] And then the Lord Montague [...] gathered a great fellowship and went to Newcastle and so took his journey towards Norham. And on the way thither they met that false Duke of Somerset, Sir Ralph Percy, Lord Hungerford, and Lord Roos, with all their company, to the number of 5,000 men at arms. And this meeting was upon St Mark's Day [25 April, the Battle of Hedgeley Moor], and that same day Sir Ralph Percy was slain. And when he was dead all the party was discomforted and put to rebuke; and every man fled [...] And then my lord of Montague took his horse and rode to Norham, and fetched in the Scots, and brought them unto the Lords

Commissioners. And there was concluded a peace for 25 years with the Scots [...] And the 14th day of May next afterwards, my lord of Montague took his journey towards Hexham from Newcastle. And there he took that false Duke Harry Beaufort of Somerset, Lord Roos, Lord Hungerford, Sir Philip Wentworth, Sir Thomas Findern, with others. [All subsequently beheaded.]

The marriage of Edward IV, 1464

(Warkworth's chronicle)

Also the fourth year of King Edward the Earl of Warwick was sent into France I for a marriage for the King, for one fair lady, sister-daughter [Bona of Savoy, sister of the Queen and ward of Louis XI] to the King of France, which was concluded by the Earl of Warwick. And while the said Earl of Warwick was in France, the king was wedded to Elizabeth Gray, widow, the which Sir John Gray that was her husband was slain at York field [Towton] in King Harry's party; and the same Elizabeth was daughter to the Lord Rivers; and the wedding was privily in a secret place, the first day of May, the year above said. And when the Earl of Warwick came home and heard this, then was he greatly displeased with the king; and after that great dissension rose ever more and more between the king and him, for that and other causes. And then the king put out of the chancellorship the Bishop of Exeter, brother to the Earl of Warwick, and made the Bishop of Bath chancellor of England. After that the Earl of Warwick took to him in fee as many knights, squires, and gentlemen as he might, to be strong; and King Edward did what he could to enfeeble the earl's power. And yet they were reconciled several times; but they never loved each other afterwards.

The capture of Henry VI, 1465

(Warkworth's chronicle)

Also the same year King Harry was taken near a house of religion in Lancashire, by the means of a black monk of Abingdon, in a wood called Clitherwood, near Bungerly stepping-stones, by Thomas Talbot, son and heir to Sir Edmund Talbot of Bashall, and John Talbot his cousin of Colebury with others besides. He was betrayed, being at his dinner at Waddington Hall, and was carried to London on horse back, with his legs bound to the stirrups, and so was brought through London to the Tower, where he was kept a long time by two squires and two yeomen of the crown, and their men; and every man was suffered to come and speak with him, by licence of the keepers.

Edward IV's treaty with Burgundy, 1467-8

Extracts from the treaty:

First, that all merchants, as well of the realm of England, Ireland, and of Calais, as the merchants of the duchy, country, and district of Brabant, Flanders, the town and lordship of Malines, and other regions of our said cousin the duke, whether they be merchants of wools, leathers, victuals, or other merchandise, their factors and servants, may go safely by land, on foot, on horseback, or otherwise, passing on and over the water of Gravelines, from Calais into Brabant, Flanders, Malines, and the other above-mentioned regions (and vice-versa) [...] keeping their road between the sea and the castles of Mark and Oye, to trade with each other in all manner of merchandise, victuals, and other things [...] except armour, artillery, cannon, powder, and other similar and warlike goods.

Also, that all the merchants of England, Ireland, and Calais [...] may go by sea, pass, return, converse, come, be, and abide safely in the said duchy, county, and district of Brabant, Flanders, the lordship and town of Malines, and the other regions, and in the ports and harbours of the same with all their goods, merchandise, and ships, and trade with all merchants of Brabant, Flanders, and Malines [...] and all other merchants whatsoever.

Warwick's alliance with Clarence, 1467

(Waurin, *Recueil des croniques*)

On St John the Baptist's Day [24 June] Monsieur Anthony Bastard of Burgundy, having taken leave of the King of England and the lords and ladies of the court, came to Dover, where he crossed the sea. And the same day the Earl of Warwick arrived at Sandwich returning from France where he had achieved part of his desires; but on his return he found that his brother the Archbishop of York, had been deprived of the seal which he used as chancellor of England. This troubled the earl very much, but he did not show his anger, for he was especially astute and cunning. The carl had brought with him an embassy from King Louis [...] When these ambassadors had arrived in London and were all lodged, the earl went to Westminster to the king to tell him about his visit and to know when it would please the king to receive the French embassy [...] When on the morrow the Earl of Warwick knew that the ambassadors of King Louis were ready to go to King Edward, he announced the fact to the council of England, and then went to tell the French that the king and his council awaited them. They had caused two richly dressed barges to be ready to carry them up the Thames to Westminster. When the king· learnt of their arrival he sent down from his chamber his brother of Clarence, accompanied by Lord Hastings, chamberlain to the king, Lord Scales, and his brother Lord Woodville, who carne to them on the stage where they landed from their barge. When [he Earl of Warwick saw the Duke of Clarence he greeted him warmly, for he wanted to talk to him [...] When the king had heard the ambassadors, he went away and caned his council to have advice, so that he could reply to their proposals, and soon afterwards he told them that they were very welcome and that he would appoint men to communicate with them, touching their proposals, for he could not do it himself because of other matters that had come to him. After this reply Lord Rivers caused wine and spices to be brought, then after taking leave of the king they returned to London; but as they returned in their barges they had many discussions, and the Earl of Warwick was so angry that he could not refrain from saying to the Admiral of France: "Have you not seen the traitors who surround the king?" To which the admiral replied: "Sire, will you not be revenged on them?" And the earl said. "Know that these are the men by whom my brother has "been deprived of the office of chancellor and of the seal."

After this embassy had left the king [...] the king and queen left by water [...] and went to Windsor, where they stayed fully six weeks, chiefly because the king did not wish to communicate with the French. This troubled Warwick greatly, and the ambassadors knew well that the king did not regard them highly, nor was he prepared to entertain them, as they had entertained the English in Normandy; though the Earl of Warwick saved his honour, for he feasted them greatly.

While the king was at Windsor, and the French were in London, there came to London the Duke of Clarence, and had a talk with the Earl of Warwick, on the matter of the embassy, and how the ambassadors were grumbling because the king had shown them so little welcome. Then the Duke of Clarence replied that it was not his fault, and the earl said he knew that very well. Then they spoke of the circle round the king, saying that he had scarcely any of the blood royal at court, and that Lord Rivers and his family dominated everything. And when they had discussed this matter, the duke asked the earl how they could remedy this. Then the Earl of Warwick replied that if the duke would trust him, he would make him King of England, or governor of the whole realm, and he need be in no doubt that most of the country would support him. When the Duke of Clarence, who was young and trusting, heard the earl promise so much to him, together with the hand of the earl's elder daughter in marriage, he agreed, on these promises that the earl made to him, to take her as his wife.

Edward IV's plans for an invasion of France, 1468

Be it remembered that the 17th day of May, the 8th year of the king's noble reign abovesaid, the king sitting in his royal seat in this present parliament, then being present the lords spiritual and temporal, and also the commons come for the commonalty of this land: it was shown by the king's commandment, and in his name, by the mouth of the right reverend father in God the Bishop of Bath and Wells, chancellor of England, to the said lords and commons, that justice was the true ground and root of all the prosperity, peace and politic rule of every realm [...] Wherefore first he asked, what is justice? Justice is, every person to do his office that he is put in according to his estate or degree; and as for this land, it is understood that it stands by three estates, and above that one principal; that is to say, lords spiritual, lords temporal, and commons, and besides that, the royal state above, as our sovereign lord the king, who had given to him in commandment to say to them that his final intention was to minister law and justice, and to plant, fix, and set peace through all this his realm, by the advice of his lords spiritual and temporal, and he also intended to provide an outward peace for the defence and surety of this realm. But first they must remember the state and condition of this realm, very different from what it was at the time of the king's entry to use and take upon him his right and title, as true and rightful King of England; for at that time this land was quite naked and barren of justice, the peace not kept, nor laws duly administered in the same, and was also spoiled of the crown of France, the duchies of Normandy, Gascony, and Guienne, and also with enmity surrounded and laid about on every side, as with Denmark, Spain, Scotland, Brittany, and other countries, and also with our old and ancient enemies of France [...] And what the king has done to the performing of his said intention, he declared how first his said highness had laboured to establish peace in his own realm, and also he had concluded with the King of Spain a league and perpetual peace, with intercourse of merchandise, also a peace and a league with the King of Denmark and intercourse of merchandise, also an amity and intercourse of merchandise with his old friends of Almayn, also a peace with Scotland for 50 winters, also an amity and a league with intercourse of merchandise taken with the King of Naples, and also that negotiations were well under way for a league and amity with intercourse to be taken with the King of Aragon [...] And moreover he had made an amity and confederation with that high and mighty prince, the Duke of Burgundy, who is to wed the Lady Margaret, the king's sister, and also an amity and confederation with the Duke of Brittany, which two dukes are the mightiest princes that hold of the crown of France. All these labours, confederations and conclusions he had laboured and borne at his great cost and charge, as well by sending out of ambassadors as in receiving ambassadors for the same [...] and all these labours and matters he had used and done at his own charge as means to a principal intent, that is to diminish and lessen the power of his old and ancient adversary of France, the French king, whereby his said highness should the more easily recover his right and title to the crown and land of France, and possession of the same. Wherefore his said highness was fully set and purposed, with the might and help of almighty God, and with the advice and assistance of his lords spiritual and temporal, and also of the commons of this land, to proceed and perform his said principal intention, for the defence of this land, that is to say, to go over the sea into France, and to subdue his great rebel and adversary Louis, usurping the same, and to recover and enjoy the title and possession of the said realm of France [...]

The marriage of Charles Duke of Burgundy and Margaret of York, 1468

(Waurin, *Recueil des croniques*)

The last day but one of June in 1468 there arrived at the port of Sluys in Flanders Margaret, sister of King Edward of England, whose marriage to Duke Charles of Burgundy took place notwithstanding the hindrances and impediments which the King of France had wished to put in the way. For he had striven with all his might to make alliances with the English to try to destroy this Duke of Burgundy, as it was commonly said; and the king had so conducted his business that he had on his side the Earl of Warwick, who had the support of almost all the commons of England. And he made them believe that if the Duke of Burgundy had not made this alliance with King Edward's sister, he would have had against him, both at once, the kingdoms of France and England. And so, in order to avoid such great perils, the duke had condescended to make this marriage.

The manifesto of Warwick, Clarence and Archbishop Neville, 1469

Right trusty and well-beloved, we greet you well. And well you know that the king our sovereign lord's true subjects of diverse parts of this his realm of England have delivered to us certain bills of articles [...] remembering in the same the deceitful covetous rule and guiding of certain seditious persons, that is to say, the Lord Rivers, the Duchess of Bedford his wife, Sir William Herbert, Earl of Pembroke, Humphrey Stafford, Earl of Devonshire, the Lords Scales and Audley, Sir John Woodville and his brothers, Sir John Fogge, and others of their mischievous rule, opinion and assent, which have caused our said sovereign lord and his said realm to fall in great poverty of misery disturbing the administration of the laws, only tending to their own promotion and enrichment. The said true subjects with piteous lamentation calling upon us and other lords to be means to our said sovereign lord for a remedy and reformation; wherefore we, thinking the petition comprised in the said articles reasonable and profitable for the honour and profit of our said sovereign lord and the common weal of all this his realm, fully purposed, with other lords, to show the same to his good grace, (desiring and praying you to dispose and prepare yourself to accompany us thither) with as many persons defensibly arrayed as you can make, letting you know that by God's grace we intend to be at Canterbury upon Sunday next coming. Written under our signets and sign manual the 12th day of July, 1469.

In the three next articles underwritten are comprised and specified the occasions and true causes of the great inconveniences and mischiefs that befell in this land in the days of King Edward II, King Richard II, and King Henry VI, to the destruction of them, and to the great hurt and impoverishment of this land.

First, where the said kings estranged the great lords of their blood from their secret council, and were not advised by them, and taking about them others not of their blood, and inclining only to their counsel, rule and advice, which persons took no respect or consideration to the welfare of the said princes, nor to the commonwealth of this land, but only to their singular honour and enriching of themselves and their blood [...] by which the said princes were so impoverished that they had not sufficient livelihood or goods whereby they might keep and maintain their honourable estate and ordinary charges within this realm [...]

These underwritten are the petitions of us true and faithful subjects and commons of this land for the great welfare and surety of the king our sovereign lord and his heirs and the commonweal of this land, ever to be continued. [...]

First, that the said malicious persons above named, which by their subtle and malicious means have caused our said sovereign lord to estrange his good grace from the counsel of the noble and true lords of his blood, moved him to break laws and statutes, diminished his livelihood and household, changing his richest coinage, and charging this land with such great and inordinate impositions, as is above expressed [...] only to the enriching of themselves, may be punished according to their works and untruths, so that all others hereafter shall take warning from this.

Also to avoid the occasions and causes of the great inconveniences and mischiefs that by the same have fallen in the king's days, above expressed, both upon himself and upon this land [...] We, the king's true and faithful commons and subjects of this land, meekly beseech him [...] to appoint, ordain, and establish for ever to be had such a sufficiency of livelihood and possessions by which he and all his heirs after him may maintain and keep their most honourable estate, with all other ordinary charges needed in this land. So that neither he nor any of his heirs [...] need charge and lay upon his true commons and subjects such great impositions as is expressed earlier, except for the great and urgent causes concerning our welfare and that of our said sovereign lord, according to the promise that he made in his last parliament, openly with his own mouth to us.

(Any person thereafter presuming to ask or take royal estates of land, except the king's issue or brothers, shall be regarded as trying to diminish and impair the royal estate of the lord, and to be punished accordingly. The revenue of tunnage and poundage to be reserved for the keeping of the sea as it was granted. The laws and statutes made in King Edward III's day for the keeping of the land in good peace, as well in Wales as in England, be duly observed.)

The capture of Edward IV, 1469

(Waurin, *Recueil des croniques*)

About midnight there came to the king the Archbishop of York, accompanied by many men of war, and thrust himself into the king's lodgings, saying to the king's bodyguard that he must speak to the king [...] but the king sent answer that he was resting, and would come in the morning, when he would gladly hear him. But the archbishop was not satisfied with this reply, and sent renewed messages to say that it was essential for him to speak to the king [...] and then the king commanded them to let him come [to] him to hear what he said, for he had no suspicion of him. When the archbishop came into the room, where he found the king in bed, he said to him brusquely: "Sire, get up!", whereupon the king asked to be excused, saying that he had not yet had any rest: but the archbishop, false and disloyal as he was, said to him the second time: "You must get up and come to my brother Warwick, for you cannot oppose this." And then the king, for fear that worse might befall, dressed himself and the archbishop brought him quietly to the place where the said earl and Clarence were between Warwick and Coventry, where he presented to them his king and sovereign lord, taken by him in the manner aforesaid. The Earl of Warwick greeted the king courteously without doing him any bodily harm; but to keep his person safe Edward was sent to Warwick Castle, and they provided him there with guards, who led him every day to take exercise where he wished, to the limit of one league or two.

The Lincolnshire rebellion and the confession of Sir Robert Welles, 1470

About last Candlemas a chaplain of my lord of Clarence called master John Barnby and with him John Clare, priests, came to my lord my father and me at Hellow with letters of credence given to the said master John which he revealed in this way. My lord of Warwick was at London with the king, whereupon for the safety of both of them he prayed us in both their names to be ready with all the fellowship that we could or might make and assemble of the commons whensoever my said lord of Clarence should send us word. Nevertheless he willed us to tarry and not stir until such time as my lord of Warwick should come again from London, for fear of his destruction. And. soon afterwards my lord of Clarence sent me a patent of the stewardship of Cawlesby in Lincolnshire by the said John Clare.

The cause of our great rising at this time was grounded upon this report raised amongst the people that the king was coming down with great power into Lincolnshire, where the king's judges would sit and hang and draw a great number of the commons. Wherefore with as many as we might collect by all possible means we came to Lincoln upon the Tuesday; and upon the Wednesday a servant of my lord of Clarence [...] a yeoman of his chamber, by his commandment told us the same, and that the gentlemen of the countryside would judge us in such a way that necessarily a great multitude of the commons must die, thereupon desiring us to rise and proceed in our purpose, as we loved ourselves. And as my father was in London and perhaps would be endangered there, which he did not wish, he would go himself to London to help excuse my said lord my father and to delay the king's coming forth.

The [...] servant of my lord of Clarence, went with me to the field, and took a great share in guiding our host, not departing from the same to the end. And before that, as soon as I came to Lincoln, I sent Sir John Clare to my lord of Warwick, to learn from him how he would have us guided forwards; but as he seemed to us to tarry long, we sent hastily after him one John Wright, of Lincoln, for the same cause; and thereupon

I departed with our host towards Grantham. And in the way, about Temple Brewer, Sir John Clare met me, saying on my lord of Warwick's behalf, that he greeted us well, and bade us be of good comfort, for he and my said lord of Clarence would raise all the people they could in all haste, and come towards us [...]

The following Sunday John Wright came to Grantham and brought me a ring from my said lord of Warwick, and desired me to go forward, bidding me and us all to be of good comfort, for he was raising all that he could persuade, and would be at Leicester on Monday night with 20,000 men, and join with us [...]

Also when my lord my father went to London, he charged me that if I understood him to be in jeopardy at any time I should come to his help with all the might that I could muster.

Also, my lord of Clarence's servant [...] that came to us at Lincoln, exhorted and urged our host many times and in many places, that when the matter should come near the point of battle they should call upon my lord of Clarence to be king, and to destroy the king who was thus about to destroy them and all the realm; to such an extent, that when the king was before us in the field, he took a spear in his hand, and said that he would run with it as freely against the king as against the mortal enemy of himself and his master.

Also, I have well understood by many messages, as well from my lord of Clarence as of Warwick, that they intended to make great risings, to such a degree as ever I could understand, that they intended to make the Duke of Clarence king; and so it was often and loudly reported in our host.

The alliance between Margaret of Anjou and the Earl of Warwick, 1470

(*Calendar of State Papers of Milan*, I)

Sforza de Bettini of Florence, Milanese Ambassador in France, to Galeazzo Maria Sforza, Duke of Milan.

Amboise June 2nd, 1470.

His Majesty left here today for Angers, about eight leagues from Tours, where he is to meet the Earl of Warwick, who comes to make him reverence. It is considered certain that they will arrange a marriage between a daughter of the earl and the Prince of Wales, King Henry's son, and by thus raising up once more the party of that king and earl will return forthwith to England. It is thought that in this way his affairs will prosper. His Majesty assists him with money and men, nothing being omitted to render him victorious, and he is very hopeful.

The Duke of Burgundy is in his country of Holland, and we hear he is making great preparations of ships and men to go to the assistance of King Edward.

Amboise, June 12th, 1470.

The Duke of Clarence and the Earl of Warwick arrived in this place on the 8th inst., and were received by the Most Christian King in the most honourable and distinguished manner possible [...] And so every day his Majesty has gone to visit them in their rooms, and has remained with them in long discussions, while he honours and feasts them, giving them tournaments and dancing, and everything else of distinction.

Today they have left and gone away, the Duke of Clarence to Normandy [...] and the Earl of Warwick to Angers [...] until the arrival of the queen, wife of King Henry, and the Prince of Wales, her son, who will be here or at Tours in six or eight days. The Earl of Warwick does not want to be here when that queen first arrives, but wishes to allow his Majesty to shape matters a little with her and induce her to agree to an alliance between the prince, her son, and a daughter of Warwick, and to put aside all past injuries and enmities. That done, Warwick will return here to give the finishing touches to everything, and immediately afterwards, according to all accounts, he will return to England with a great fleet, taking with him the prince, in order to raise up the party of King Henry, and to see if his plan will prove successful this way. Many are very hopeful about it, and his Majesty the king more than all.

Amboise, 29th June 1470.

The Queen of England, wife of King Henry, and the prince, her son, arrived in this place on the 25th inst. and were received in a very friendly and honourable manner by his Majesty the king and the queen. His Majesty has spent and still spends every day in long discussions with that queen to induce her to make the alliance with Warwick and to let the prince, her son, go with the earl to the enterprise of England. Up to the present the queen has shown herself very hard and difficult, and although his Majesty offers her many assurances, it seems that on no account whatever will she agree to send her son with Warwick, as she mistrusts him. Nevertheless it is thought that in the end she will let herself be persuaded to do what his Majesty wishes.

Angers, 24th July, 1470.

The Queen of England and the Prince of Wales, her son, arrived here the day before yesterday, and on the same day the Earl of Warwick also arrived. The same evening the king presented him to the queen. With great reverence Warwick went on his knees and asked her pardon for the injuries and wrongs done to her in the past. She graciously forgave him and he afterwards did homage and fealty there, swearing to be a faithful and loyal subject of the king, queen, and prince as his liege lords unto death. They have not yet spoken of the marriage alliance, though it is considered as good as accomplished, and it is argued that they are only waiting for the arrival of King René, who may come any day, to announce it.

Angers, 28th July, 1470.

The marriage of Warwick's daughter to the Prince of Wales is settled and announced. His Majesty has sent for the lady to Amboise, where the marriage will be consummated. In two days Warwick will leave for his fleet.

Angers, 7th August 1470.

The Earl of Warwick departed, as your Excellency has heard. He did not wish to lose time in waiting for his daughter's marriage. The ceremony will take place at Amboise, according to what they say. The earl has not yet gone on board, but we expect to hear, at any moment, that he has sailed in the name of St George [...] We shall wait to hear how matters progress in England, before any movement is made against the Duke of Burgundy, and if things go prosperously for Warwick, fire will be immediately applied.

Omans, 14th September, 1470.

The Earl of Warwick, in the name of St George, left the port of La Ogha with all his fleet and with the fleet of Queen Margaret on the 9th inst., and sailed towards England. We are anxiously waiting to hear of their victorious progress. The fleet of the Duke of Burgundy has not since put in an appearance. It is thought to have gone to the English coast to prevent Warwick from landing [...] Warwick has taken the Duke of Clarence with him for more favour.

War between England and Burgundy, 1471

(British Museum, Add. MS. 48988 (1), letter from Richard Neville, Earl of Warwick, to Louis XI, 12 February 1471)

Sir, I commend myself to your good grace in the humblest possible way. And may it please you to know that I have received your letters by this messenger, by which I have learnt that now war has begun between you, your adversary, and ours, wherefore I pray to Almighty God to give you the victory. In the matter of beginning the war at Calais, I have sent instructions to start it, and have today had certain news that the garrison of Calais has already begun and has advanced from Ardes, and has killed two of the garrison of Gravelines. As soon as I possibly can, I will come to you to serve you against this accursed Burgundian without any default, please God, to whom I pray to grant you all that your high heart desires. Written at London the 13th day of February.

[Signed] Your very humble servant,

R Warrewyk.

The Battle of Barnet, 1471

(Warkworth's chronicle)

And in the second week of March, the 49th year of the reign of King Harry the IVth, and in the 10th year of the reign of King Edward the IVth, the same King Edward took his shipping in Flanders, and had with him the Lord Hastings and the Lord Say, and 900 Englishmen and 300 Flemings with hand-guns, and sailed towards England. And they had great trouble upon the sea with storms, and lost a ship with horses. And they purposed to have landed in Norfolk, but one of the brothers of the

Earl of Oxford with the commons of the country rose up together, and put him back to the sea again. And after that, he was so troubled in the sea that he was fain to land in Yorkshire at Ravenspur. And there rose against him all the country of Holderness, whose captain was a priest, and a parson in the same country called Sir John Westerdale, who afterwards for his hostile disposition was cast into prison in the Marshalsea at London by the same King Edward. For the same priest met King Edward and asked the cause of his landing; and he answered that he came thither by the Earl of Northumberland's advice, and showed the earl's letter sent to him under his seal, and also he came to claim the Duchy of York, which was his inheritance of right. And so he passed on to the city of York, where Thomas Clifford let him in, and there he was examined again. And he said to the mayor and aldermen and to all the commons of the city the same as he had done in Holderness at his landing; that was to say, that he would never claim any title, nor take upon him to be King of England, and that he would not have done so before that time, but for the incitement and stirring of the Earl of Warwick. And thereupon before all the people he cried "Hurrah! King Harry! Hurrah! King and Prince Edward!" and wore an ostrich feather, Prince Edward's livery. And after this he was suffered to pass the city, and so held his way southwards, and no man hindered him nor hurt him.

After that he came to Nottingham, and there Sir William Stanley came to him with 300 men and Sir William Norris, and various other men and tenants of Lord Hastings, so that he had 2,000 men and more; and immediately after this he made his proclamation and called himself King of England and France. Then he took his way to Leicester, where were the Earl of Warwick and the lord marquis his brother, with 4,000 men or more. And King Edward sent a messenger to them that if they would come out, he would fight with them. But the Earl of Warwick had a letter from the Duke of Clarence that he should not fight with the king until the duke came himself; and all was to the destruction of the Earl of Warwick, as it happened afterwards. Yet so the Earl of Warwick kept still the gates of the town shut, and suffered King Edward to pass towards London, and a little way out of Warwick the Duke of Clarence met with King Edward, with 7,000 men, and there they were reconciled, and made a proclamation forthwith in King Edward's name. And so all covenants of fidelity, made between the Duke of Clarence, and the Earl of Warwick, Queen Margaret, and Prince Edward her son, both in England and in France, were clearly broken and forsaken of the said

Duke of Clarence; which, in the end, brought destruction both to him and them, for perjury shall never have a better end, without the grace of God.

King Harry was then in London, and the Archbishop of York, in the palace of the Bishop of London. And on the Wednesday next before Easter Day King Harry and the Archbishop of York with him rode about London, and desired the people to be true to him; and every man said they would. Nevertheless, Christopher Urswick, Recorder of London, and divers aldermen, who had the government of the city, commanded all the people who were in arms, protecting the city and King Harry, to go home to dinner; and during the dinner time King Edward was let in, and so went to the palace of the Bishop of London and there took King Harry and the Archbishop of York and put them in ward, the Thursday next before Easter Day. And the Archbishop of Canterbury, the Earl of Essex, Lord Berners, and such others as bore towards King Edward good will, as well in London as in other places, produced as many men as they could to strengthen the said King Edward; so then he had 7,000 men and there they refreshed themselves well all that day and Good Friday [12 April 1471].

And upon Easter Eve he and all his host went towards Barnet and he took King Harry with him; for he understood that the Earl of Warwick and the Duke of Exeter, the Marquis Montagu, the Earl of Oxford, and many other knights, squires, and commons, to the number of 20,000 men, were gathered together to fight against King Edward. But it happened that he with his host entered the town of Barnet before the Earl of Warwick and his host. And so the Earl of Warwick and his host lay outside the town all night, and each of them fired guns at the other all night. And on Easter Day in the morning, the 14th April, right early, each of them came upon the other; and there was such a thick mist that neither of them might see the other perfectly. There they fought, from 4 o'clock in the morning unto 10 o'clock of the forenoon. And at various times the Earl of Warwick's party had the victory, and supposed that they had won the field. But it happened so that the Earl of Oxford's men had upon them their lord's livery, both in front and behind, which was a star with streams, which was much like King Edward's livery, a sun with streams. And the mist was so thick that a man might not properly judge one thing from another; so the Earl of Warwick's men shot and fought against the Earl of Oxford's men, thinking and supposing that they had been King Edward's men. And at once the Earl of Oxford and his men cried "Treason! Treason!" and fled away from the field with 800 men. The lord

Marquis Montagu had an agreement and understanding with King Edward and put upon him King Edward's livery; and a man of the Earl of Warwick saw that and fell upon him and killed him. And when the Earl of Warwick saw his brother dead, and the Earl of Oxford fled, he leapt upon his horse, and fled to a wood by the field of Barnet, from which there was no road. And one of King Edward's men had espied him and came upon him and killed him and despoiled him naked. And so King Edward won that field.

And there were slain of the Earl of Warwick's party the Earl himself, Marquis Montagu, Sir William Tyrell, knight, and many others. The Duke of Exeter fought manfully there that day, and was greatly despoiled and wounded, and left naked for dead on the field, and so lay there from 7 o'clock until 4 in the afternoon; but he was taken up and brought to a house by a man of his own, and a physician was brought to him, and so afterwards he was brought Into sanctuary at Westminster. And on King Edward's side were slain the Lord Cromwell, son and heir to the Earl of Essex, Lord Berners's son and heir, Lord Say, and various others, to the number (of both sides) of 4,000. And after the battle was over, King Edward commanded both the Earl of Warwick's body and the marquis's body to be put in a cart, and he returned with all his host again to London. And there he commanded the said two bodies to be laid in the church of St Paul's, on the pavement, that every man might see them. And so they lay three or four days, and afterwards were buried. And King Harry, being in the van during the battle, was not hurt, but he was brought again to the Tower of London, there to be kept.

The death of the Earl of Warwick, 1471

(*Memoirs*, ed. B. de Mandret, Bk 3, ch. 7)

The Earl of Warwick was never accustomed to want to dismount, but he had the habit of mounting his horse when he had ordered his men to engage in fight. If the struggle went well for him, he was in the thick of it; and if it went badly, he fled in good time. On this occasion, however, he was constrained by his brother, the Marquis of Montagu, who was a very valiant knight, to dismount and to send away his horses. But this battle turned out in such a way that the earl died, and his brother the marquis, and a great number of high rank. And the slaughter was very great, for Edward had resolved, on his departure from Flanders, to call out no more, as he had been wont to do, that they should spare the common people and kill only the men of rank, as he had done in former battles. For he had conceived a very great hatred against the people of England, because of the great favour which he had seen them bear towards the Earl of Warwick and also for other reasons; wherefore this time they were not spared.

The Battle of Tewkesbury, 1471

(*Historie of the Arrivall of Edward IV in England*)

After all these things had thus befallen, the Tuesday in Easter week, the 16th day of April, came certain tidings to the king how that Queen Margaret, her son called Prince of Wales, the Countess of Warwick, the Prior of St John, at that time called treasurer of England, Lord Wenlock and many other knights, squires, and others of their party, who long had been out of the land with them [...] had arrived and landed in the west-country, upon Easter Day, at Weymouth, after long awaiting passage, and being on the sea, and landing again for default of good wind and weather [...] And so at divers times they took the sea, and forsook it again, till it was the 13th day of April, Easter Even. That day they passed [...] The queen Margaret, and her son went from where she landed to an abbey near by, called Seern [Cerne] and all the lords, and the remnant of the fellowship with them. Thither came unto them Edmund, called Duke of Somerset, Thomas Courteney, called the Earl of Devonshire, with them, and welcomed them into England, comforted them, and put them in good hope that, although they had lost one field, whereof the queen had knowledge the same day, Monday, the 15th day of April, and was therefore right heavy and sorry, yet it was to be thought that they should have right good speed, and that, for that loss, their party was never the feebler, but rather the stronger, and that they doubted nothing but that they should assemble so great a power of people in divers parts of England, truly assured unto their party, that it would not lie in the king's power to resist them; and in that country they would begin. And so, forthwith, they sent all about in Somerset, Dorset, and part of Wiltshire, for to get ready and raise the people by a certain day [...] and they raised the whole might of Cornwall and Devon, and so, with great numbers of people they departed out of Exeter and took the right way to Glastonbury and thence to the city of Bath [...] and as they went they gathered the able men of all those parts [...]

The king being at London and having knowledge of all this their movements from time to time, at once provided for the relief of his sick and hurt men, who had been with him at Barnet field, which were right many in number [...] and sent to all parts to get him fresh men and at once prepared all things that were thought necessary for a new field of battle [...] so he provided artillery, and ordnance, guns, and other things for the field, in great plenty [...] And for as much as they (Edward's enemies) at that season were in an angle of the land, and needs must take one of two ways (one way, to London, via Salisbury or via Sussex and Kent) [...] or else they, not thinking themselves powerful enough to have an encounter with the king and therefore, perhaps, would draw northward into Lancashire and Cheshire, trusting also to have in their way the assistance of Welshmen; for which considerations, the king caused great diligence to be done by means of scouts [...] If they had taken their way eastwards, his intention was to have encountered them as soon as he could [...] but for as much as he understood well they took the other way, towards the northwest, he hastened with his host as fast as he could, upon the purpose that he had taken to stop them. They (his enemies) [...] therefore endeavoured greatly to deceive the king's party in that matter, for which cause and purpose they sent their advance riders straight from Exeter to Shaftesbury, and afterwards to Salisbury, and took the straight way to Taunton, and to Glastonbury, to Wells, and thereabouts [...] whence, another time, they sent advance riders to a town called Yeovil and to a town called Bruton, to make men understand that they would have drawn towards Reading and [...] London [...] Such manner of riding nevertheless served them of two things; one was, to call and raise the people to make towards them for their help out of all those parts; another was to have deceived the king in his approach towards them, but, thanked be God, he was not unaware of it, but by good and serious advice, provided for every way, as may appear in telling forth his progress from Windsor towards them. [Edward went from Windsor, to Abingdon, Cirencester, Bath, and Malmesbury] And there he had knowledge that they, understanding his approaching and marching near to them, had left their purpose of giving battle, and turned aside, and went to Bristol, a good and strong walled town, where they were greatly refreshed and relieved, by such as were the king's rebels in that town, of money, men, and artillery. They therefore decided to meet Edward in battle at Sudbury; but when they heard of the king's approach, they fled to Berkeley, then to Gloucester. The king sent a message to Richard Beauchamp, who was in charge of the defence of Gloucester, that the Lancastrians were not to be admitted to the city, and that Edward was coming to the relief as quickly as possible. The Lancastrians found themselves unable to gain admittance to Gloucester, and so, in order to cross the Severn into Wales, they had to go on to Tewkesbury [...] Therefore they shortly took their decision to go the next way to Tewkesbury, whither they came the same day, about four after noon, by which time they had so travelled with their host the previous night and day that they were right weary with their travelling. For by that time they had travelled 36 long miles, in a foul country, all in lanes and stony ways between woods, without any good refreshment. And for as much as the greater part of their hosts were footmen, the other part of the host, when they were come to Tewkesbury, could not have laboured any further unless they had wilfully forsaken and left their footmen behind them, and those who were horsemen were right weary of that journey, as were their horses [...] They therefore determined to abide there the chance that God would send them in the adventure they had taken in hand. And for that reason the same night they pitched camp in a field, in a close just at the town's end with the town and the abbey at their backs; before them, and upon every side of them, foul lanes, and deep ditches, and many hedges, hills and valleys, a right evil place to approach [...]

The king, the same morning, Friday, early advanced his banners, and divided his whole host into three battles, and sent before him his forerunners, and scouts on every side of him, and so, in fair array and order, he took his way through the open country called Cotswold, making all his people, of whom there were more than 3,000 footmen, travel that Friday, which was a right hot day, thirty miles and more. His troops could not find, anywhere along the way, horsemeat or man's meat, or so much as drink for their horses, save in one little brook, where there was very little relief, it was as soon muddied with the carriages that had passed through it. And all that day the king's host was within five or six miles of his enemies; he in open country and they among woods, having always good reconnoitering of their position. So continuing that journey he came, with all his host, to a village called Cheltenham, only five miles from Tewkesbury, where the king had certain knowledge that, only a little before his coming thither, his enemies had come to Tewkesbury and there were taking a field. [...] Whereupon the king did not tarry long, but comforted himself a little and his people with such meat and drink as he had caused to be carried with him for the victualing of his host; and at once set forth towards his enemies, and took the field, and lodged himself and all his host within three miles of them.

Upon the morrow following, Saturday, the 4th day of May the king appareled himself, and set all his host in good array, displayed his banners, did blow up the trumpets, committed his cause and quarrel to God, and advanced directly upon his enemies [...] who were pitched strongly in a marvellously strong ground, very difficult to assail. [...] In front of their field were such evil lanes and deep dikes, so many hedges, trees, and bushes, that it was very hard to approach near and come 'to hand fighting. But Edmund, called Duke of Somerset, having that day the vanguard [...] advanced with his troops somewhat on one side of the king's vanguard, and by certain paths and ways previously surveyed, and unknown to the king's party, he departed out of the field, passed a lane, and came to [...] a close, just in front of the king [...] and from the hill that was in one of the closes, he set right fiercely on the end of the king's division. The king, in manly fashion, at once set upon them [...] won the dike and hedge and with great violence pushed them back up the hill, assisted by [...] the Duke of Gloucester.

Here it is to be remembered that when the king had come to the field, before he attacked, he considered that, upon the right hand of the field was a park, with many trees. He, thinking to provide a remedy in case his said enemies had laid any ambush of horsemen in that wood, he chose, out of his troops, 200 spears and set them in a group together, about a quarter of a mile from the battlefield, charging them to keep a close watch on that part of the wood, and to do what was necessary if the need should arise, and if they saw no such need [...] to employ themselves in the best way they could [...] This provision came as well to the point at this time of the battle as could well have been devised, for the said spears of the king's party, seeing no likelihood of any ambush in the said corner of the wood, and seeing also a good opportunity to employ themselves well, all at once burst out upon the Duke of Somerset and his vanguard from one side, unexpectedly. Upon this his men, seeing that the king gave them enough to do before them, were greatly dismayed and abashed, and so took to flight in the park, and into the meadow that was near, and into lanes and dikes where they best hoped to escape the danger. Nevertheless, many were distressed, taken, and slain;

and even at this point in their flight the king courageously set upon that other part of the field, where was Edward, called prince, and in a short while put him to discomforture and flight. And so it befell in the chase of them that many of them 'were slain, and at a mill, in the meadow by the town, many 'of them were drowned. Many ran towards the town, many to the church, to the abbey, and elsewhere, as best they might.

In the winning of the field such as endured hand-strokes were slain at once. Edward, called prince, was taken, fleeing towards the town, and slain in the field. There were also slain, Thomas, called the Earl of Devonshire, John of Somerset; called Marquis Dorset; Lord Wenlock; with many others in great numbers.

When this was done, and achieved with God's might, the king took the direct way to the abbey there to give unto Almighty God praise and thanks for the victory that of his mercy he had that day granted and given him.

Thomas Neville's attack on London, May 1471

(Journal 8, f. 1, of the City of London, printed in R. R. Sharpe, *London and the Kingdom* (1895), III, 391)

Be it remembered that the mayor and aldermen with the assent of the common council fortified the banks of the river Thames from Castle Baynard as far as the Tower of London with men at arms, bombards, and other implements of war to prevent an attack by the seamen who had brought a large fleet of ships near the Tower, and the bank was held by the aldermen and the rest of the citizens in great numbers. Be it remembered also that on Sunday, viz. the 12th day of May in the 11th year of Edward IV, Kentish men and others, rebels of the lord the king, made an attack on London Bridge and on the new gate there and set fire to divers houses called "berehouses" near the hospital of St Katharine; and afterwards on the 14th day of May being Tuesday the 11th year aforesaid, about 11 o'clock in the morning, the Kentish seamen and other rebels made an attack with great force and set fire to 13 tenements on London Bridge. The Kentish seamen and others to the number of 3,000 persons also made an attack from the Thames upon the gates of Aldgate and Bishopsgate and set fire to divers tenements. The citizens, however, sallied out of the gates and made a stout resistance and put them to flight besides those who were drowned in endeavouring to get on board their ships at Blackwall, etc. And afterwards, viz. on the eve of the Ascension the eleventh year our lord King came with a great multitude of armed men to the city of London and there to the honour of the city created knights John Stockton the mayor, Thomas Urswyk, the recorder [and 10 aldermen], And the lord king conferred on them knight's badges.

The death of Henry VI, 1471

(*Historie of the Arrivall of Edward IV*)

The king this season, well accompanied and mightily with great lords and [...] many other able men, well arrayed for the war [...] came to the city of London [...] the 21st day of May, the Tuesday; where he was honourably received of all the people, the mayor, aldermen, and many other worshipful men, citizens of the said city. [...] Here it is to be remembered that, from the time of Tewkesbury field, where Edward, called prince, was slain [...] all the noblemen that came from beyond the sea with the said Edward, called prince, were taken and slain [...] and Queen Margaret herself was taken and brought to the king; and in every part of England where any commotion was begun for King Henry's party, at once they were rebuked, so that it appeared to every man at a glance that the said party was extinct and repressed for ever, without any kind of hope of revival [...] The certainty of all this came to the knowledge of the said Henry, lately called king, being in the Tower of London; not having, before that, knowledge of the said matters, he took it to such great hatred, anger, and indignation, that of pure displeasure and melancholy he died the 23rd day of the month of May. The king caused his body to be brought to the Friars Preachers of London, and there his funeral service was sung. Then the body was carried by water to an abbey called Chertsey by the Thames, 16 miles from London, and there it was honourably interred.

    The King, immediately after coming to London, tarried there only one day, and went with his whole army after his said traitors into Kent, to repress them in case they were assembled in any place.

The murder of Henry VI, 1471

(Warkworth's chronicle)

And the same night that King Edward came to London, King Harry being imprisoned on the Tower of London, was put to death, the 21st May, on a Tuesday night, between 11 and 12 o'clock, being then at the Tower the Duke of Gloucester, brother to King Edward, and many others. And on the morrow he was put in a coffin and brought to St Paul's, and his face was open so that every man might see him; and in his lying he bled on the pavement there, and afterwards he was brought to the Blackfriars and there he bled new and fresh; and thence he was carried to Chertsey Abbey by boat, and was buried there in the chapel of Our Lady.

Preparations for the marriage of Anne Neville and Richard Duke of Gloucester, 1472

(The Crowland chronicle)

It is my intention here to insert an account of the dissensions which arose during this Michaelmas Term [1472] between the two brothers of the king, and which were with difficulty quieted. After [...] the son of King Henry, to whom the lady Anne, the youngest daughter of the Earl of Warwick, had been married, was slain at the Battle of Tewkesbury, Richard, Duke of Gloucester, sought Anne in marriage. This proposal did not suit the views of his brother, the Duke of Clarence, who had previously married the elder daughter of the earl. Such being the case, he caused the damsel to be concealed, in order that it might not be known by his brother where she was; as he was afraid of a division of the earl's property, which he wished to come to himself alone in right of his wife, and not to be obliged to share it with any other person. Still, however, the astuteness of the Duke of Gloucester so far prevailed that he discovered the young lady in the city of London disguised in the habit of a cookmaid; upon which he had her removed to the sanctuary of St Martin's. In consequence of this, such violent dissensions arose between the brothers and so many arguments were, with the greatest acuteness, put forward on either side, in the king's presence, who sat in judgement in the council chamber, that all present, and the lawyers even, were quite surprised that these princes should find arguments in such abundance by means of which to support their respective causes [...] At last their most loving brother, King Edward, agreed to act as mediator between them; and in order that the discord between princes of such high rank might not cause any hindrance to the carrying out of his royal intentions in relation to the affairs of France, the whole misunderstanding was at last set at rest, upon the following terms. The marriage of the Duke of Gloucester with Anne was to take place, and he was to have such and so much of the earl's lands as should be agreed upon between them through the mediation of arbitrators; while all the rest were to remain in the possession of the Duke of Clarence. The consequence was that little or nothing was left at the disposal of the true lady and heiress, the Countess of Warwick, to whom for the whole of her life the most noble inheritance of the Warwicks and the de Spencers properly belonged.

The Anglo-Burgundian treaty, 1474

As the most famous realm of France is at present, alas! oppressed by intolerable tyranny, so that no place is left for piety, right, justice or religion, but everywhere in that land appears robbery, violence, slaughter, treason, poisonings [...] which all take their origin nom Louis, usurper of the realm [...] and since it also greatly concerns us that that kingdom should be well and justly governed in the fear of the Lord, especially by him to whom it belongs by hereditary right, that is, by the most excellent and powerful prince, our lord and brother the honourable brother Edward, King of France and England, since he abounds in all these virtues which are required to govern rightly and devoutly.

We make it known that we, desiring to help the people oppressed by the aforesaid Louis, and to exalt justice in that realm of France, whence it is exiled [...] have made an agreement with our brother [...] according to the following chapters and articles:

In the first place the most serene lord Edward, King of France and England, for the recovery of his duchies of Normandy and Aquitaine, and also of his kingdom of France, shall magnificently and fittingly equip and prepare himself and his army to the number of over 10,000, to be transported and taken into Normandy or other parts of France, before the first day of the month of July next coming, so far as sea and wind allow, and if Almighty God should of his benevolence permit.

Also that the most illustrious Charles, Duke of Burgundy and Brabant, etc. should take the King's part in person and with his power and assist him ... until he achieves his right and title, which the lord king claims and has in the realm and crown of France [...]

[...] Since our illustrious and very dear brother Charles, Duke of Burgundy has decided to employ his great strength for the recovery of our realm of France and we desire to show our gratitude to him from whom we have received and expect so many benefits that we may appear to have acted in equity and honesty.

We, after mature deliberation of our council, have given, ceded, and handed over for ever to our brother Duke Charles the principalities, lands, dominions, and rights which are written below [...]

In the first place, the Barrisien Duchy, commonly called the Duchy of Bar; the County of Champagne; the Nivernensen county, called in French the County of Nevers; the county of Rethell; the county of Eu; the county of Guise; the barony of Douai; the city of Tournai, with the bailiwick, territory and district of Tournai; the city of Langres, with the county, bailiwick, and appurtenances; the castle and town of Picquigny; the towns and dominions on both sides of the river Somme formally pledged to our brother [...] And moreover all the lands and dominions which Louis of Luxembourg, called the Count of St Pol, at present possesses; provided that they are not of the ancient demesne and patrimony of the duchies of Normandy and Aquitaine or the crown of France.

Funding the invasion of France, 1475

(*Calendar of State Papers and Manuscripts of Milan*)

Battesu Oldovini de Brugnato to Antonio de Bracellis, 17 March 1475, London.

Since I reached England I have written by every post save one, when I had to write for my masters and had no time for even the shortest letter except to your father-in-law. Now, though I am still very pressed with business, I have decided to snatch this little time to tell you about some of the events that have taken place here. You must have heard that some time ago this most serene king constantly said that he wanted to cross to the continent to conquer France. Especially for the last four months he has been very ardent in the matter, and has discovered an excellent device for raising money. He has plucked the feathers from the magpies without making them cry out. This autumn the king went about the country from town to town, and he made a note of how much each man from that town could pay. He sent for them all one by one and told them how he wished to cross to France to conquer it, with other words that ensnared their minds. Finally he worked to such a conclusion that there is nobody whatsoever who has not contributed money to the value of £40 sterling and more. Everyone seemed to give willingly. I have many times seen our neighbours here who were called before the king; when they went they looked as if they were going to the gallows; when they returned they were dated, saying that they had talked with the king; and because he had spoken to them so many kind words, they did not regret the money they had paid. From what some have told me, the king adopted this method. Whenever any person appeared before him, he gave him a very great welcome as though he had always known him. After some conversation he asked him what he could pay of his own free will towards this expedition. If the man made an honest offer, the king had his clerk ready, who noted the name and the sum. If, the king thought otherwise, he said: "Such a man, who is poorer than you, has paid so much; you who are richer can easily pay more" and by such means he brought him with fair words up to the mark; and in this way it is agreed that he has extracted a very large quantity of money.

Now he has had everything put in order and every day he inspects all his artillery, and he has assembled it all in the castle of St Catherine here in London; and although he has a large number of bombards, he has fresh ones made every day. And now he has given money to a great part of his captains, who are to be ready on 26th May with their men, and to make a muster of them. And indeed, everyone is putting his harness in order and everything else that is needed for a campaign [...]

The discomposure of Louis XI, 1475

(Calendar of State Papers of Milan)

Christofforo de Bollato, Milanese Ambassador at the French court, to Galeazzo Maria Sforza, Duke of Milan.

I think your lordship will have taken note of the words spoken by the very lips of the King of France, which I enclose herewith. I inform your lordship that his Majesty has had positive information that the English are preparing a large force to invade Normandy at once, and the King of England is coming in person with a good number of men.

His Majesty is more discomposed than words can describe, and has almost lost his wits.

[...] All this is due to the coming of the English, which is confirmed every day by letters and messengers, whom I have seen and heard speak to his Majesty. It is always to the effect that the King of England will cross to Calais with 30,000 persons, to join the Duke of Burgundy and 10,000 others in Normandy and 6,000 in Gascony, and he has had proclaimed at Calais a league, peace, and good accord between the Kings of Castile, England, Aragon, Scotland, Denmark, Portugal, Naples, and Sicily, and open war declared against the French [...]

The king has been advised that the King of England and the Duke of Burgundy requested the pope to grant them leave to exact a fifth of ecclesiastical revenue in their dominions for the expenses of their wars, and his Holiness gives them hope of his consent.

The Treaty of Picquigny, 1475

Also we [Edward IV] wish, promise, agree, and conclude that after we have received from our aforesaid cousin of France 75,000 gold crowns [...] the army and arms which we now have with us we will withdraw into England without any deception, ceasing entirely from war against our cousin and his subjects, and refraining from taking in hostile manner any city, town, or castle of the realm of France during our retreat.

[...] these truces shall be neither broken nor terminated but last until the end of seven years [...]

[...] the most illustrious prince of France shall help and assist the King of England against any of his subjects who shall invade with arms and make rebellion in the realm of England.

Also, that neither of the princes of England and France shall in any way give aid and help to subjects of the other to invade the other's realm with arms and make open war against their lord in his lands and dominions [...]

[...] a marriage shall be contracted between the most illustrious Prince Charles, son of the most powerful prince of France, and the most serene lady Elizabeth, daughter of the most invincible King of England, when they shall reach marriageable years [...]

We make it known that we [Louis XI] have conceded, promised, and bound ourselves to pay [to Edward IV] each year, during the life of either of us, fifty thousand gold crowns [...]

Given in our city of Amiens, 29th August. 1475.

Chapter 4: The Reign of Richard III

Richard, Duke of Gloucester

'Richard III has divided opinion for five hundred years. To many he has always been a villain, a bloody tyrant and detestable child-murderer deservedly overthrown. To others he was and remains a hero, a noble prince and enlightened statesman tragically slain.'

(A. J. Pollard, *Richard III and the Princes in the Tower*, Stroud, 1991, p.1)

Richard, Duke of Gloucester, was Richard of York's son and the youngest brother of Edward IV. When Edward died in 1483 he was the only surviving brother - four of York's sons died in childhood, Edmund, Earl of Rutland, was killed with his father almost a quarter of a century earlier at the Battle of Wakefield and George, Duke of Clarence, was put to death in the Tower of London in 1478. Unlike Clarence, Richard had been entirely loyal to his brother and was rewarded accordingly. His marriage to the widowed Anne Neville, Warwick's daughter, resulted in his inheriting the earl's great northern estates. Clarence, as recounted in the *Crowland Chronicle,* had protested against the proposed marriage from the start and did everything in his power to prevent it:

'It is my intention here to insert an account of the dissensions which arose [...] between the two brothers of the king [...] After the son of King Henry, to whom the Lady Anne, the youngest daughter of the Earl of Warwick, had been married, was slain at the Battle of Tewkesbury, Richard, Duke of Gloucester, sought the said Anne in marriage. This proposal, however, did not suit the views of his brother, the Duke of Clarence, who had previously married the eldest daughter of the same earl [...] as he was afraid of a division of the earl's property, which he wished to come to himself alone in right of his wife, and not be obliged to share it with any other person [...] In consequence of this, such violent dissensions arose between the brothers, and so many arguments were, with the greatest acuteness, put forward on either side, in the king's presence, who sat in judgement in the council chamber, that all present, and the lawyers even, were quite surprised that these princes should find arguments in such abundance by means of which to support their respective causes. In fact, these three brothers, the king and the two dukes, were possessed of such surpassing talents, that, if they had been able to live without dissensions, such a threefold cord could never have been broken without the utmost difficulty [...]'[32]

Gloucester was entrusted by his brother with the defence of the realm in the north, with full authority to cede to his territories anything he could conquer across the border in Scotland.

When Edward died, his thirteen-year-old son became Edward V. Before his coronation, however, Richard took the boy into custody, first declaring himself protector and then the rightful King of England. The prince and his younger brother disappeared some time in the summer of 1483, probably murdered in the Tower, and members of the Woodville faction were put to death. His enemies now rallied around the hitherto insignificant figure of the exiled Henry Tudor, who, in 1485 at the Battle of Bosworth Field, defeated and killed the usurper and made himself King Henry VII, the first of the mighty Tudor dynasty.

The usurpation of the throne of Edward V

'Every tale condemns me for a villain'

(William Shakespeare, Richard III, Act I, Scene i)

Richard, Duke of Gloucester, was greatly empowered by his

---

[32] N. Pronay, and J. Cox (eds.), *The Crowland Chronicle Continuations 1459-86* (1986).

marriage to Anne Neville, heir to much of Warwick's estate, and had been rewarded with Scottish territory by his brother, Edward IV, for the recapture of Berwick from the Scots in 1483. He, in what one of his recent biographers, Desmond Seward, has described as 'one of the most brilliant double coup d'états in history', seized the throne shortly after his brother's untimely death at the age of forty-two, in April 1483.

Edward IV's immediate successor was his twelve-year-old son, who reigned until June as Edward V. In a battle for survival, Richard found himself, after years of loyalty to his brother, facing a desperate struggle against the ambitions of the Woodville family, elevated to greatness by Edward IV's irresponsible marriage to Elizabeth Woodville. Indeed, his defenders cite a Woodville attempt to usurp Richard from his rightful place (according to the terms of Edward IV's will) as regent as the fundamental cause of his determination to shatter Woodville aspirations and, ultimately, to remove Elizabeth Woodville's son, the uncrowned Edward V, from the scene altogether.

Initially, at least, Richard could count on the support of those courtiers who considered themselves undermined by the Woodvilles' meteoric rise. Most importantly he had the backing of William, Lord Hastings, and Henry Stafford, Duke of Buckingham, the greatest magnate among the old nobility.

Three weeks after his father's death, his uncle, Richard of, Gloucester, took Edward V into his custody and made himself protector for the duration of the boy king's minority. Meanwhile, Richard's supporter, Henry Stafford, Duke of Buckingham, challenged the legitimacy of Edward V's reign by claiming that Edward IV was already contracted to marry Lady Eleanor Butler when he married Elizabeth Woodville. Richard and his faction doubtless feared the consequences of Woodville revenge in the event of Edward V coming of age and reinstating his mother's family. Furthermore, Richard's supporters wished for rewards that only a king could grant. Some historians, therefore, consider his removal of Edward V as a historical inevitability.

On 26 June Edward was dethroned and the Duke of Gloucester became King Richard III. Edward and his younger brother, Richard, were held in the Tower of London. By the autumn of 1483, they had disappeared from public view, almost certainly murdered, very likely on their uncle's instruction. Richard's ostentatious coronation in mid-July was followed by an extensive royal progress around his kingdom, reaching York in triumphant procession in August. By September, however, he was on his way back to London as discontent swelled in the southern and western counties.

Prince Edward, Edward IV's son and heir, was twelve years old when his father died in April 1483. Immediately the Woodville-dominated royal council began preparations for the boy's coronation. Earl Rivers made preparations to bring the child from Ludlow to London. The royal party was intercepted by Richard, Duke of Gloucester, the boy's uncle, at Stony Stratford in May and taken into Gloucester's custody. According to the Italian chronicler, Mancini, Gloucester, in so doing, was safeguarding the terms of Edward's will, which declared his brother should become protector during the child's minority. This cannot be corroborated since the will has not survived. As protector, Gloucester would be far more powerful than as the mere figurehead of a royal council.

Gloucester now entered London as protector and the coronation was postponed until the end of June. By the beginning of that month, it is clear that Richard of Gloucester was already making arrangements for the purge of the council which began with the execution of Lord Hastings, a loyal servant of Edward IV and, hitherto, Gloucester's friend, but one certain to resist any attempts on Gloucester's behalf to depose the heir. In the same year, 1483, the Italian Dominic Mancini reported Hastings' destruction:

> 'Having got into his power all the royal blood in the land, yet he [Richard, Duke of Gloucester] considered that his prospects were not sufficiently secure, without the removal or imprisonment of those who had been the closest friends of his brother, and were expected to be loyal to his brother's offspring. In this class he thought to include Hastings, the king's chamberlain; Thomas Rotherham, whom shortly before had been relieved of his office; and the Bishop of Ely [...] Therefore the protector [Richard] rushed headlong into crime [...] One day these three and several others came to the Tower about ten o'clock to salute the protector, as was their custom. When they had been admitted to the innermost quarters, the protector, as prearranged, cried out that an ambush had been prepared for him [...] Thereupon the soldiers, who had been stationed there by their lord, rushed in with the Duke of Buckingham, and cut down Hastings on the false pretext of treason; they arrested the others, whose life, it

was presumed, was spared out of respect for religion and holy orders.'

Gloucester again raised the spectre of Edward IV's supposed illegitimacy, and introduced a new notion that his marriage to Elizabeth Woodville was illegitimate, because he had been pre contracted to Lady Eleanor Butler (hence bastardising all of their children). Justifying his actions in this way, he had himself crowned king on 26 June.

By the end of the summer, rumours were spreading that the children had been done away with in the Tower and Richard III made no effort to quell them. Edward V had been king in name only, although until 16 June government was carried out in his name. A contemporary illustration of a fair-haired boy, the subject of numerous later romantic paintings, has survived, but little is known of his personality or potential. John Russell, the Crowland chronicle continuator, wrote a brief sketch, probably designed to highlight for his readers the iniquity of Richard III's conduct:

> 'To King Edward IV succeeded, but for a lamentably short time, his son King Edward V, who was residing at Ludlow at the time of his father's death; the boy was thirteen and a half, or thereabouts. He was brought up virtuously by virtuous men, remarkably gifted, and very well advanced in learning for his years.'

The Duke of Buckingham's rebellion

One of the most enigmatic characters of the period, Buckingham was instrumental in Richard Ill's usurpation of power and yet gave his name a few weeks later to the futile rebellion that cost him his life. This was despite having been massively rewarded by Richard with offices in Wales and the Marches. Buckingham had served Edward IV faithfully and, as steward at the time, pronounced the Duke of Clarence's death sentence in 1478. His support for Edward IV's remaining brother, Richard, immediately after the former's death is indisputable - he promoted the idea of Edward V's bastardy, and some maintained that he initiated, even carried out, the murder of the princes in the Tower. His loyalty to Richard, according to one contemporary, the Italian, Dominic Mancini, was important in persuading other magnates to support the usurper:

> '[...] the lords were mindful of the fate which had befallen Hastings and were well aware that the alliance of these two dukes, of Gloucester and Buckingham, who had such vast armed forces at their disposal, would be difficult and dangerous to resist. Fearing for their own safety, they decided to declare Richard king and request him to assume the duties of government.'

Buckingham had been Richard's greatest ally in the usurpation, but now, like Warwick the Kingmaker before him, enacted a startling turn around, quite possibly inspired by the Woodville faction, to save the princes before it was too late. Rumour at the time had it that he was making a bid for the throne himself, to which he had a very remote claim. Buckingham and the countess of Richmond were: the only peers involved. The other leaders were gentlemen loyal to Edward IV and his sons.

According to the Crowland chronicler, Buckingham's change of heart, which led him into rebellion, was a matter of personal conscience:

> 'It was publicly proclaimed that Henry, Duke of Buckingham, who had supported Richard III and was then living in Wales at Brecon, was repentant of what had happened and was to lead the enterprise against the king. After this, it was widely believed that Edward's two sons must have met their fate by some unspecified act of violence.'

The contemporary chronicler and Warwickshire antiquary, John Rous, accredits Buckingham with hatching the plot to put forward Henry Tudor, hitherto floundering in exile abroad and the political backwater, as the new candidate for the throne. According to Rous it was also Buckingham's idea to wed Henry Tudor to Elizabeth of York, Edward IV's daughter, in order to make his claim more credible. Buckingham, it seems, was quite as much the 'kingmaker' as the Earl of Warwick in the reign of Henry VI.

As rumours of the murder of the princes spread, the rebels began to champion the doubtful regal claim of Henry Tudor, grandson of Henry V's queen, Catherine of Valois, by her second marriage, to Owen Tudor. Buckingham invited Henry back to England from exile in Brittany and a plan was hatched to reinforce his claim by marrying him to Elizabeth, Edward IV's eldest daughter. Richard's royal progress through central England immediately after his coronation probably helped him secure the loyalty of the Midlands when his tour was interrupted by the rebellion in October.

Richard raised an impressive army and marched south to Exeter. The revolt was suppressed without a fight following the arrest or flight of its perpetrators. Buckingham was tracked down in hiding having sought refuge in the hut of a 'poor man' and was given away by 'the unusually abundant supply of food that had been brought there'. The estates of Buckingham and other 'traitors' were seized by the king and given to his supporters even before such actions could be legalised by parliamentary Acts of Attainder. A wave of these followed in the parliamentary sittings of January 1484. This intrusion of newly rewarded loyal nobility from the north and elsewhere into the lives of the southern gentry was deeply resented. Two years later, and shortly after Richard's defeat at Bosworth, the Crowland chronicler made the following remarks:

> 'What great numbers of estates and inheritances were amassed in the king's treasury in consequence! He distributed all these amongst his northerners whom he planted in every part of his dominions, to the shame of all the southern people who murmured ceaselessly and longed more each day for the return of their old lords in place of the tyranny of the present ones.'

More than ever before, the conflicts of the second half of the fifteenth century had taken on a regional character - the north versus the south. Buckingham was executed without trial in the market place at Salisbury on 2 November. Meanwhile, Henry Tudor, who had sailed to the south-west on Buckingham's invitation but not participated, retreated back into exile, followed to Brittany by a number of rebel members of the southern gentry.

The victory over Buckingham, however, had not come cheaply, as the Crowland chronicler a while later recorded:

> 'After these events, the king gradually reduced the size of his

army, discharging those whom he had summoned to the expedition from the distant northern Marches, and came to London having triumphed over his enemies without going to war, though at no less cost than if the two armies had fought it out hand-to-hand. In this way all that very great treasure and wealth which King Edward had thought he was leaving behind him for very different purposes began rapidly to be used up.'

The government of Richard III

In stark contrast to his overindulgent brother, Richard III cultivated his image as a pious, God-fearing and just monarch. Legislation was passed by parliament outlawing benevolences - the much-despised obligatory 'gifts' upon which Edward IV had relied; another new law protected accused felons from losing their goods before conviction. Despite this, his unpopularity, even before posterity turned history into legend, cannot be denied. An early disaster in Richard's reign was the death, in 1484, of his only son, Prince Edward, perceived by some it would seem as an omen:

'One afternoon in February almost all the lords spiritual and temporal of the realm and the most powerful knights and esquires of the king's household foregathered, at the king's specific command, in a downstairs room off the corridor leading to the queen's quarters. Each man put his name to a new oath [...] pledging their allegiance to Edward, King Richard III's only son, as their supreme lord, if anything should happen to his father. Soon afterwards, however, it was made plain how fruitless are the plans of men when they wish to arrange their own affairs without God.

The following April, on a day close to the anniversary of King Edward IV's death, this only son on whom rested all hope of the royal succession, expressed in so many oaths, died in Middleham Castle after a brief illness. Then you would have seen both the father and the mother, when they received the news in Nottingham where they were staying, go almost out of their minds for a time with sudden grief.'³³

The death of his son in was followed by the death of his wife in March 1485. Richard now made known his plan to marry Edward's daughter, Elizabeth, himself. Not only did this expose him to accusations of incest but also it alienated the enemies of the Woodvilles and those who had benefited from their recent fall; inevitably there would have been some restoration of Woodville influence if the king married his niece, the daughter of Elizabeth Woodville. Malicious rumours were spread through London that Richard had his wife poisoned because of, in the words of a contemporary chronicler, his 'incestuous passion'. In a scene reminiscent of impeachment proceedings against certain modern heads of state, Richard felt obliged to make a public statement of denial before a special congregation of lords, aldermen and the mayor of London. This extraordinary announcement was recorded in the annals of the London-based Mercers' Company:

> 'Slander and rumour, spread among the people by evil disposed individuals to the very great displeasure of the king, claims that the queen, by the consent and will of the king, was poisoned so that he might marry Lady Elizabeth, eldest daughter of his brother, the late King of England [...]
> [...] the king sent for and had before him at St John's yesterday the mayor and aldermen [...] in the great hall there, in the presence of many of his lords and many other people, he showed his grief and displeasure and said it never came to his thought or mind to marry in such manner, nor did he wish the death of his queen but was sorry and in heart as heavy as a man might be [...]'³⁴

Of this unhappy set of events the Crowland chronicler wrote:

> 'It was said by many that [by the beginning of 1485] the king was concentrating all his attention on contracting marriage with

---

[33] The Crowland chronicle.

[34] L. Lyell and F. D. Watney (eds.), *Acts of Court of the Mercers' Company, 1453-1537*, (1936).

Elizabeth [of York, daughter of Edward IV], either after the death of the queen - for which he was waiting - or through a divorce for which he considered he had sufficient grounds. He could see no other way of confirming his position as king nor of depriving his rival of hope. A few days later, the queen fell seriously ill and died and her weakness was considered to have worsened because the king entirely forsook his consort's bed [...] Towards the middle of March 1485, on a day when a major eclipse of the sun took place, Queen Anne died [...]

The king's intention and plan to marry his niece, Elizabeth of York, was finally reported to certain people who did not favour it and, after he had summoned the council, the king was compelled to make a lengthy denial to the effect that this idea had never entered his head. There were those in the council who were quite aware that this was not true. Those who objected most strongly to this marriage, and whose opinion the king himself rarely dared oppose, were Sir Richard Ratcliffe and William Catesby, a member of the royal bodyguard. They told the king to his face that if he did not repudiate this plan [...] the northerners, on whom he principally relied, would rise up against him, accusing him of the death of the queen, the daughter and one of the heirs of the Earl of Warwick, through whom he had obtained his first honour, in order to satisfy his incestuous desire for his close relative, in defiance of God. Furthermore they brought forward more than twelve doctors of theology to state that the pope could not grant a dispensation covering that degree of consanguinity.'

The growing unpopularity and insecurity of the regime, even before the humiliating outcome of Richard's advances on his niece, is evident in the brutal suppression of those that dared speak out against it:

'In these days [1484] the king's chief advisers were Lord Lovell, and two gentlemen named Mr Ratcliffe and Mr Catesby of the whom a seditious rhyme was made and fastened upon the Cross in Cheap and other places of the city which went as follows: 'The cat, the rat, and Lovell our dog, rule all England under a hog.' This was to mean that these three ruled England under the king who had a white boar as his symbol. A great search was made for the devisers of this rhyme and finally two gentlemen named Turberville and Collingbourne were charged for that and other offences, arrested and cast into prison [...] Collingbourne was convicted [...] he was drawn into Tower Hill and there full cruelly put to death, at first hanged and straight after cut down and ripped open, and his bowels cast into a fire. The punishment was so speedily carried out that when the butcher pulled out his heart he spoke and said 'JESUS JESUS'.[35]

Meanwhile the removal of benevolences forced the king to resort to the equally unpopular device of forced loans to pay for his preparations against the anticipated invasion of Henry Tudor.

The history of Richard's usurpation and the popular assumption that he had done away with the princes in the Tower tarnished his reputation forever. He tried to undermine the authority of the mighty, but unreliable, Earl of Northumberland by instituting a Council of the North under his supporter, John Howard, Duke of Norfolk. Even so, when Henry Tudor launched his assault in 1485, the extent of Richard's authority proved fatally inadequate. Unable to secure the loans from his greater subjects necessary to protect his realm, he died defeated on Bosworth Field in 1485.

Richard III's short reign was plagued by the consequences of his usurpation and he never had much of an opportunity to demonstrate fully his capacity for kingship. Had he survived the first few years, as had the usurpers Henry IV and Edward IV before him, history might have remembered him rather differently. After a brief respite of three and a half weeks following a spectacular coronation, his troubles began. The first and only parliament of his reign had to be postponed in the autumn of 1483 because of risings in the south and west. When finally it met in December, its main business concerned the forming of legislation designed to confirm Richard's right to the throne. The Act which followed, the *Titulus Regius*, was designed for public consumption; it proclaimed his nephews' illegitimacy and contrasted the corruption of the previous reign with the glorious epoch now looming as England's rightful heir to the throne took the stage. In February most of the lords were requested to take an oath of loyalty to Richard's son, Edward - a safeguard against the possibility of the king's early death.

---

[35] *The Great Chronicle of London.*

Despite his difficulties, perhaps because of them, during the reign there were several economic and legal reforms. These included protection of English producers and traders against foreign imports, a commitment to the principle of bail for suspected felons, and the abolition of benevolences. It is difficult to determine the extent to which these were initiated by parliament and how much by the king himself. Where he does appear to have played a central role in promoting justice, the principle to which he had committed himself on making his coronation oath, it is hard to tell how far this was prompted by a sense of social responsibility and how far by a self-interested desire to cultivate personal popularity.

In a reign that lasted just twenty-six months, Richard III was in London for only six. He undertook a great progress of central England following his coronation in the summer of 1483, which was followed by the campaign against Buckingham and his fellow rebels in the autumn. He spent much of 1484 in the north visiting his estates and planning a major invasion of Scotland, although this was abandoned because of the cost and the threat of Henry Tudor. After returning to London a final royal progress was made eastwards to Canterbury. In the summer of 1485 the king marched north for the last time - a journey that terminated at Bosworth Field.

The confiscation of rebel estates after the October 1483 rebellion enabled him to expand his power base by rewarding his followers. Much of the property and the titles taken from the hundred or so attainted rebels fell into the hands of Richard's supporters, several of whom came from the north of England - a fact of course which contributed nothing to promoting his popularity in the south. But not all beneficiaries of the rebellion were from the north, and some of the rebels themselves were forgiven and welcomed into Richard's fold. Nevertheless, Richard's own household was dominated by northerners.

Richard had been the archetypal 'over-mighty noble' who had relied on his power-base in the north as the means of asserting his claim to the throne in 1483. It is not surprising, therefore, that he took measures to try to prevent anyone magnate from becoming too powerful in his own reign. Instead of handing over authority in the north to his principal advocates in 1483, the Earls of Northumberland and Westmorland, he established a new Council of the North, a number of northern peers ruling directly on his behalf.

The rebellion of 1483, war with Scotland in 1484 and

preparations for facing Tudor's invasion in 1485 made huge demands on the royal purse. Sir Thomas More's later allegations of extravagance and excessive generosity to his friends and supporters were unfounded. Even so he had to rely on loans once again in 1485 and what reputation he had cultivated for 'living of his own' was moribund by the time of his destruction at Bosworth. According to the Crowland chronicler, these loans were not freely given:

> 'He resorted to the demands of King Edward IV which he had condemned in parliament - although he spurned entirely the use of his brother's word 'benevolence' - sending out hand-picked men to extract the greatest possible sums of money from the coffers of almost all the estates of the kingdom by pleas and threats, by fair means or foul.'

Richard III's foreign policy, like that of his brother, was determined by relations with France and Brittany, and concern to prevent an alternative claimant to the throne gaining foreign support. In this he was clearly, and fatally, unsuccessful. He appears, however, to have came close to removing the threat of Henry Tudor by eventually persuading the Bretons, after they had attempted to invade England in support of Henry in 1483, that they had more to gain by backing him. In return for handing over Henry, it was promised that Duke Francis of Brittany would receive the earldom of Richmond, English ships would cease to harass Breton merchants, and that England might support the duchy in another campaign against France. A timely flight to France, advised by fellow exile, John Morton, Bishop of Ely, saved Henry and paved the way for his victory in 1485.

Richard's decision to continue the campaign against Scotland, which had begun in the previous reign, was probably motivated by his wish to be revealed as a conquering hero and worthy King of England. That the planned assault largely fizzled out in the early summer of 1484 is explained perhaps by the fact of his son and heir's death in April, an event which, declare the chronicles, traumatised both parents. The less ambitious programme which followed was inglorious, culminating in the defeat of a small English army at Lochmaben in July and a three-year truce concluded in September. By this time, the border struggle had paled into insignificance in the face of the greater threat of invasion from Brittany or France by Henry Tudor.

In addition to diplomacy Richard used propaganda widely in his struggle with Henry. He took the controversial decision to associate himself with the Woodville clan, posing as their friend and benefactor so that, in the public imagination, they might seem reconciled to the new regime rather than allied to Tudor's cause. The Crowland chronicler commented on the exchange of clothes, during the Christmas festivities of 1484 to 1485, by Queen Anne and Queen Elizabeth Woodville's daughter, Elizabeth. According to the chronicler, Richard was already planning to marry Princess Elizabeth:

> '[…] after the death of the queen - for which he was waiting - or through a divorce for which he considered he had sufficient grounds. He could see no other way of confirming his position nor of depriving his rival of hope.'

Another propagandist device was the promotion by Richard's regime of the cult of King Henry VI. In August 1484 Henry VI's remains were exhumed from Chertsey Abbey and reburied in St George's Chapel, Windsor, and Richard began, publicly, to patronise Henry's foundation of King's College, Cambridge. By such means he endeavoured to make his claim to the Lancastrian inheritance stronger than that of Henry Tudor.

By the time Henry was ready to invade England in the summer of 1485, Richard III was still far from secure within his realm. Powerful forces were arrayed against him as the usurper, a supposed child-killer, an ungenerous friend to those who had helped him, a Woodville-sympathiser, possibly a wife-killer, and an insolvent. Propaganda and reformism had proved inadequate foes of history and circumstance.

The historical reputation of Richard III

> 'But I, that am not shap'd for sportive tricks,
> Nor made to court an amorous looking-glass,
> I, that am rudely stamp'd, and want love's majesty
> To strut before a wanton ambling nymph;
> I, that am curtail'd of this fair proportion,
> Cheated of feature by dissembling nature,
> Deform'd, unfinish'd, sent before my time

> Into this breathing world scarce half made up,
> And that so lamely and unfashionable,
> That dogs bark at me as I halt by them;
> Why, I, in this weak piping time of peace,
> Have no delight to pass away the time,
> Unless to spy my shadow in the sun,
> And descant on mine own deformity:
> And therefore, since I cannot prove a lover,
> To entertain these fair well-spoken days,
> I am determined to prove a villain [...]'
>
> (William Shakespeare, *Richard III*, Act I, Scene ii)

Shakespeare's portrayal of Richard III as a deformed, scheming, cold-hearted murderer shattered any reputation for good his acolytes once tried to establish. Just as his former supporters changed sides in the rebellion of 1483 and, later, at Bosworth, so too did the chronicler of his reign. The contemporary chronicler, John Rous, in his *History of the Earls of Warwick*, originally described Richard as a model king, 'most mighty', appointed 'by the grace of God', a selfless and just king loved by his subjects and admired by 'the people of all other lands about him'. Once Henry Tudor was king, however, Rous rewrote his version of the history, now describing Richard as some kind of freak, 'retained within his mother's womb for two years and emerging with teeth and hair to his shoulder', a cruel master of deception, 'like a scorpion he combined a smooth front with a stinging tail'. He, not Edward IV, was now found guilty of causing the murder of the deposed Lancastrian, Henry VI, after his final defeat at the Battle of Tewkesbury in 1471. He also had on his hands the blood of the princes in the Tower and his own wife, Queen Anne, whom, allegedly he had poisoned. John Rous also helped establish the tradition, so central to Shakespeare's characterisation, that Richard III was a hunchback: 'He was small of stature, with a short face and unequal shoulders, the right higher and the left lower.' This tradition was developed in earlier Tudor writings, notably in the remarks of Polydore Vergil:

> 'He reigned two years and so many months, and one day over. He was little of stature, deformed of body, the one shoulder

being higher than the other, a short and sour countenance, which seemed to savour of mischief, and utter evidently craft and deceit. The while he was thinking of any matter, he did continually bite his nether lip, as though the cruel nature of his did rage against itself in that little carcase [...] his courage [...] failed him not in the very death, which, when his men forsook him, he rather yielded to take with the sword, than by foul flight to prolong his life [...]'

The recent discovery of Richard III's remains, exhumed by from the site of a car park in Leicester in 2012 by archaeologists from the University of Leicester, supports the claims that he was 'deformed' by a severely curved spine.

Richard has his defenders too, notably members of the Richard III Society, who seek the restoration of Richard's reputation. Attempts have been made to portray him as a deeply religious man driven to usurpation by the shock discovery of the illegitimacy of Edward V's claim to the throne, and the case for his innocence in the princes in the Tower affair has often been proclaimed. Either way, by anyone's criteria, his reign was a failure, the disastrous outcome of a desperate coup that resulted in the accession of the Tudors.

Much of what we know, or might think we know, of the personality and deeds of Richard III comes from Thomas More's *History of King Richard the Third*, which first appeared in the 1540s, although he started work on it many years earlier, probably in 1513. In this Richard is damned as:

'close and secret, a deep dissembler, lowly of countenance, arrogant of heart, outwardly companionable where he inwardly hated, not hesitating to kiss whom he thought to kill, pitiless and cruel, not for evil will always but oftener for ambition and either for the surety or increase of his position.'

The work is written on the epic scale and it has been criticised as both propagandist and melodramatic. On the other hand, More probably based his narrative, in part at least, on the accounts of those who had been witnesses to the events it describes. As Desmond Seward, in *Richard III: England's Black Legend* (1997), has pointed out, More was 'a man famous for plain dealing and love of truth - he paid for it with his life' when he ran into trouble with his master, Henry VIII, concerning the latter's claim to supremacy over the church in England. More's assumption that Richard III was a murderer was certainly one shared by many who lived during his reign. Some historians, however, regard More's work as a political treatise, designed on the one hand to gratify the Tudors, and on the other to illustrate the horrors of *realpolitik*, the 'ends justifies the means' approach to politics, which was taking root in parts of Europe at the time. The later Tudor historian, Edward Hall, who provided Shakespeare with his version of the legend, painted More's picture of the king even blacker.

It has been said many times that history is written by the victors and, for Richard III's apologists, this is an essential consideration in forming any verdict on his reign. The remarkable evidence of John Rous, who attempted, but failed, to destroy his first, pro-Richard, account of the reign, stands testimony to the unreliability of the early chronicles. In this he had written:

> 'The most mighty Prince Richard, by the grace of God King of England and of France and lord of Ireland [...] all avarice set aside, ruled his subjects in his realm full commendably, punishing offenders of his laws, especially extortioners and oppressors of his Commons, and cherishing those that were virtuous, by the which discreet guiding he got the great thanks of God and the love of all his subjects rich and poor and the great praise of the people of all other lands about him.'

At worst, Richard's supporters portray him as a man of his times, at best he is seen as a well-meaning and capable, even great, king who was cruelly betrayed and prevented from fulfilling his potential.

Students of history are taught to question the evidence and perceived truths. The highly influential and highly controversial English historian, A. J. P. Taylor, carved a reputation for himself by questioning the received wisdom on such sensitive issues as the origins of the Second World War. This principle of 'playing the Devil's advocate' in order to reopen the debate and shake other, more conservative, historians out of their complacency was nothing new when Taylor was rocking the boat in the 1960s. The first great historian-iconoclast was Horace Walpole (1717-97). Walpole wrote a book entitled *Historic Doubts* (1768) in which he refuted tradition by trying to prove that Richard did not kill

Henry VI or the princes. This was the first, and one of the least convincing, of many books and papers defending Richard III. Even so, to the dismay of Richard's supporters, the version of the story popularised by More, Hall and Shakespeare continues to dominate. In the opinion of Paul Murray Kendall in *Richard the Third* (1955): 'What a tribute this is to art; what a misfortune this is for history.'

Much near-contemporary comment indicted Richard III for the murder of his nephews and this tradition, despite brave attempts to detract from it, has endured. The assumption that they had been killed appears in contemporary records by the end of the summer of 1483. For example, Robert Ricard wrote in his *Kalendar* for 1483 'in this year the two sons of King Edward were put to death in the Tower of London'. Another source, that of a citizen of London, declared at the time:

> 'Item: this year King Edward V, late called Prince of Wales, and Richard, Duke of York, his brother, King Edward IV's sons, were put to death in the Tower of London on the instruction of the Duke of Buckingham.'[36]

The birth of the legend of Richard as murderer coincided with the disappearance of the princes who, in the early stages of their captivity, it appears, were seen frequently at play about the Tower. The most influential account of their alleged murder by Richard III is that of Sir Thomas More who recorded their fate about thirty years after the events described:

> 'I shall rehearse you the dolorous end of those babes [Edward and Richard: 'the princes in the Tower'], not after every way I have heard, but after that way that I have so heard by such men and such means me thinketh it were hard but it should be true [...]
>
> King Richard, after his coronation, taking his way to Gloucester [...] devised as he rode to fulfil that thing which he before had intended. And for as much as his mind gave him that, his nephews living, men would not reckon that he could have right to the realm, he thought therefore without delay to rid them,

---

[36] R. F. Green (ed.), 'Historical notes of a London citizen', 1483-88, in *English Historical Review*, vol. 96, 1981.

> as though the killing of his kinsmen could amend his cause and make him a kindly king.
> [...] Sir James Tyrell devised that they should be murdered in their beds. To the execution whereof, he appointed Miles Forest, one of the four that kept them, a fellow fleshed in murder before-time. To him he joined one John Dighton, his own horse-keeper, a big broad, square, strong knave. Then, all the others being removed from them, this Miles Forest and John Dighton, about midnight (the silly lie innocent] children lying in their beds) came into the chamber and suddenly lapped them up among the clothes, so bewrapped them and entangled them, keeping down by force the feather bed and pillows hard unto their mouths, that within a while, smothered and stifled, their breath failing, they gave up to God their innocent souls into the joys of heaven, leaving to the tormentors their bodies dead in bed. Which after that the wretches perceived, first by the struggling with the pains of death, and after long lying still, to be thoroughly dead: they laid their bodies naked out upon the bed, and fetched Sir James to see them. Which, upon the sight of them, caused those murderers to bury them at the stair foot, meetly deep in the ground, under a great heap of stones.'

Writing in the year of the princes' disappearance, 1483, the Italian observer, Dominico Mancini, heard the gossip but had arrived at no firm conclusion regarding their fate:

> 'Richard's actions up until now had given reason to think he was aiming for the crown. Yet some hope remained that this might not be his intention, for he had not yet gone so far as to lay claim to the throne itself. Indeed, he declared that he acted as he did only so that treason might be avenged and past wrongs righted. Moreover, all private deeds and official documents continued to bear the titles and name of Edward V. However, after the removal of Hastings, the attendants who had previously ministered to the young king's needs were all kept from him. He and his brother were transferred to the inner chambers of the Tower. Every day their appearances behind the windows grew less frequent and eventually they ceased to appear altogether. The doctor, Argentine, was the only one of Edward's former

retinue who still attended him. He told how the young king, like a victim prepared for sacrifice, sought remission for his sins by daily confession and penance, believing that death was close at hand [...] And after he disappeared I saw many men moved to weeping and lamentation at the mention of his name. However, I have not yet been able to establish whether he was done away with and, if so, by what means.'

Certainly the assumption that they had been murdered was shared by many by the early years of Henry VII's reign and, in 1488, in *Historical notes of a London citizen*, Richard's henchman, the exceptionally powerful Duke of Buckingham, was implicated:

'Item: this year King Edward V, late called Prince of Wales, and Richard, Duke of York, his brother, King Edward IV's sons, were put to death in the Tower of London on the instruction of the Duke of Buckingham.'

Attempts have been made in recent times to find Buckingham the initiator of, rather than an accessory to, the supposed crime. The most popular alternative solution, however, to the disappearance of the princes which absolves Richard from any blame, is that 'the other side' was guilty, that Henry VII, not Richard III, was the murderer. It has been suggested, most colourfully perhaps in Josephine Tey's detective 'docu-novel', *The Daughter of Time* (1951), that the princes survived Richard's reign but were dispatched at the start of Henry's. The evidence is flimsy to say the least. The only 'proof' that the children enjoyed Richard's protection are a couple of contemporary records regarding provision for children in the king's household in 1484 and 1485 but very likely they refer to other children, possibly including Richard's own illegitimate son, John. It is quite reasonable to assume that, had they been found alive, Henry VII would have done away with the boys for the very same reasons that Richard probably had them murdered.

A more popular, and politically charged, third explanation at the time for the fate of the children was that they survived both Richard's reign and Henry Tudor's usurpation. Thus Henry VII was plagued by pretenders during the first half of his reign. However, the shift of the opposition's focus away from the princes and towards Henry Tudor, even by the end of 1483, implies that, long before the invention of new identities for the pretenders Lambert Simnel and Perkin Warbeck, Richard's enemies had abandoned hope of ever again seeing Edward V and his brother alive. The fact that Richard III made no real attempt to deny his guilt, or to give them any sign that the children lived still, would have confirmed their suspicions.

Without doubt, Richard's reputation was damaged as a result of the disappearance of the princes and it was a factor in the continued opposition to his reign. The killing of innocent children, and one's own flesh and blood, was then, as now, regarded as the most loathsome of acts. His 'northerness' and 'plantation' of northerners into the great estates of the south and high offices (half his council were northerners), however, was a greater cause of discontent. If indeed he did arrange for their murder, it was a measured step and one that he would have considered a necessary, if distasteful, political expedient. He was not the first, nor would he be the last, to consolidate his position by such means.

The overthrow of Richard III

Henry Tudor's exile began in 1471 when he fled from England with his Lancastrian uncle and guardian, Jasper Tudor, following the collapse of Henry VI's regime. His mother, Margaret Beaufort, is accredited with being a prime mover in promoting his claim after the disappearance of the princes in the Tower. In 1472, Margaret Beaufort had married Edward IV's councillor and steward, Thomas, Lord Stanley, Richard III's constable of England. The wife of one of the most powerful men in England, Margaret was in a strong position to shape peoples' loyalties, not least her husband's. The possibility of a Stanley-backed rebellion did not pass Richard III by - when he marched to Bosworth he took with him, effectively as a hostage, Stanley's son and heir, Lord Strange.

Having promised to marry Princess Elizabeth on securing the throne, Henry Tudor's credibility was further strengthened when he won the financial and military backing and general hospitality of the government of Charles VIII, France's child king, late in 1484. Henry Tudor had spent most of his exile in Brittany but, by 1484, his position there had become extremely insecure. This was because Richard III negotiated a deal with his hosts whereby England would supply the

Bretons with a company of archers, for their struggle for independence against France, in return for Henry's arrest. In the nick of time, Tudor learned of the plan and, in September, escaped to France. The French were now only too willing to strike back at an English king prepared to ally with rebel Bretons.

In the summer of 1485, Henry began to assemble an army and invasion fleet at the port of Le Havre. Richard had been preparing for the now inevitable invasion since December 1484. In June he established his headquarters at Nottingham, a central position from which he could respond equally fast to an invasion at any port in the kingdom.

On 7 August Henry Tudor with a French army and other English exiles landed at Milford Haven in south Wales and marched north through Wales and into Shropshire. The king knew of his arrival by 11 August and began mobilising his army and summoning further support. Henry now headed east towards London and Richard left Leicester to intercept him. They met just outside Market Bosworth on 22 August. As he had feared, Stanley proved unfaithful to Richard and his assault at the rear of the king's army helps account for his stepson Henry's swift victory. Although Richard's army outnumbered Tudor's, he was further let down by the failure of the Earl of Northumberland to engage his force, which was large and well equipped. The lack of support at the critical hour reflected his mismanagement of patronage earlier in the reign. His favouritism towards the few when it came to distributing offices and attainted lands resulted in his having to rely on a small powerful clique of nobles. Had he spread the fruits of his usurpation wider, he might have enjoyed broader-based support. These factors, combined with a reckless charge led by the king, resulted in Richard's defeat and death in the fighting. As Rous reported:

> 'King Richard, after receiving many mortal wounds, died a fearless and most courageous death, fighting on the battlefield, not in flight. His body [...] after suffering many humiliations [...] was taken to Leicester in an inhuman manner, with a rope around its neck, while the new king also was proceeded to Leicester wearing the crown he had so conspicuously won.'

Richard III, killed at the age of thirty-two after a brief but dramatic reign, was buried with little ceremony in the choir of a Franciscan friary in Leicester. Rous concludes that 'Although Richard

III's days were short, they were ended with no lamentation from his groaning subjects.' In truth there were those who regretted his passing, particularly in the north where he had established himself so effectively in Edward IV's reign. The records of the York City Council in the immediate aftermath of the battle of Bosworth observed:

> 'King Richard, late mercifully reigning upon us, [...] with many other lords and nobility of these northern parts, was piteously slain and murdered, to the great heaviness of this city.'[37]

The support of the Stanleys at Bosworth was a, probably the, decisive factor in Henry Tudor's victory. From the start, Richard III had relied on the support of four overmighty magnates: the Duke of Buckingham, Lord Stanley, the Earl of Northumberland and the Duke of Norfolk. Only the last mentioned remained true to his cause. Buckingham gave his name to the revolt of 1483 and Stanley and Northumberland abandoned Richard at the critical hour in 1485. After Buckingham's death, the power base was contracted, with Buckingham's lands and titles being shared out among his remaining supporters. The fact that Stanley's wife, Margaret Beaufort, mother of Henry Tudor, had helped instigate the conspiracy should perhaps have given Richard III sufficient cause to restrict the power of her husband. Instead, having proclaimed his loyalty, Stanley replaced Buckingham as Lord Great Chamberlain of England.

As Henry Tudor's invasion loomed in 1485, it is clear Richard III had no doubts regarding the danger of relying upon the loyalty of Lord Stanley and his brother, Sir William. Consequently the king had Stanley's son in his custody as he marched to Bosworth:

> 'Shortly before these men landed [Henry Tudor's invasion force], Thomas Stanley, steward to the king's household, had received permission to cross into his native Lancashire to see his home and family from whom he had been absent for a long time; but he was not permitted to stay there unless he sent his eldest son, George, Lord Lestrange, to the king at Nottingham in his place. This he did.

---

[37] R. Davies (ed.), *York records: extracts from the municipal records of the City of York* (1843), p.218.

> After the landing at Milford Haven in Wales [...] the rebels advanced along difficult and out-of-the-way routes in the northern part of the province where William Stanley, brother of the steward, had sole command as chamberlain of north Wales.
>
> The king sent word to Thomas, Lord Stanley, that he should appear before him at Nottingham without delay. The king was afraid that the mother of the Earl of Richmond [Henry Tudor], who in fact was married to Thomas Stanley, would persuade her husband to support her son's faction. However, Lord Stanley was unable to come, claiming the sweating sickness from which he was suffering was his excuse.
>
> Meanwhile his son, George, who had secretly prepared his escape from the king, was discovered and taken in an ambush. After revealing a conspiracy to support the cause of the Earl of Richmond involving himself, William Stanley, his uncle, and Sir John Savage, he asked for mercy and promised that his father, Thomas, would come to the king's aid as quickly as possible with all his forces. In addition he wrote to his father informing him of the danger he was in, and of his wish that this help should be forthcoming.'[38]

Although Stanley's support of Henry Tudor by this stage is indisputable, he was held back from fully committing himself to his stepson by the precarious situation of his son, particularly after the latter's failed attempt to escape from his captivity at Nottingham Castle, where the royal army was encamped in August. Richard could at least feel reasonably assured of Stanley's neutrality and Henry, without the earl's support, faced almost certain defeat.

At Bosworth both Richard and Henry sent messages to the Stanleys, who had brought their vast army to the field, imploring them to lend their support.

> '[...] though he [Henry Tudor] were of noble courage [...] yet he was in great fear, because he thought that he could not assure himself of Thomas Stanley, who, as I have shown, feared the danger that King Richard might do his son [effectively held hostage in the king's entourage], did incline as yet to neither

---

[38] John Rous.

party [...] Moreover he heard that King Richard, with an host innumerable, was at hand [...] After that he went privily to Atherstone, where Thomas Stanley and William lay encamped. Here Henry did meet with Thomas and William, where taking each other by the hand, and yielding mutual salutation, each man was glad for the state of the others, and all their minds were moved to great joy. After that they discussed tactics should they come to blows with King Richard, whom they heard to be not far off.'[39]

Richard's army numbered around 12,000, Henry's 5,000 and the Stanleys' 3,000-8,000. They remained undecided, even when Richard ordered the immediate execution of Stanley's son, Lord Strange, (which his captains refused to carry out). Only when Richard launched and led a foolhardy charge against Henry and his bodyguard, resulting in a melee in which quite possibly he exchanged blows with Tudor himself, did William Stanley act, seizing the moment to take advantage of the king's rash and impetuous move to enter the fray. The chronicler John Rous provided an evocative description of Richard III's demise:

'This King Richard, who was excessively cruel in his days, reigned for three years and a little more, in the way that Antichrist is to reign. And like the Antichrist to come, he was confounded at his moment of greatest pride. For having with him the crown itself, together with great quantities of treasure, he was unexpectedly destroyed in the midst of his army by an invading army, small by comparison, but furious in impetus, like a wretched creature.

For all that, let me say the truth to his credit: that he bore himself like a soldier and despite his little body and feeble strength, honourably defended himself to his last breath, shouting again and again that he was betrayed, and crying 'Treason! Treason! Treason!''[40]

---

[39] Polydor Vergil.

[40] John Rous.

SOURCES

The Richard III's usurpation of the throne, 1483

(Mancini, *The Usurpation of Richard the Third*)

In claiming the throne Richard was actuated not only by ambition and lust for power, for he also proclaimed that he was goaded by the ignoble family of the queen and the affronts of Edward's relatives by marriage [...] At that time [of Clarence's execution] Richard Duke of Gloucester was so overcome with grief for his brother, that [...] he was overheard to say that he would one day avenge his brother's death. Thenceforth he came very rarely to court. He kept himself within his own lands and set out to acquire the loyalty of his people through favours and justice. The good reputation of his private life and public activities powerfully attracted the esteem of strangers. Such was his renown in warfare, that whenever a difficult and dangerous policy had to be undertaken, it would be entrusted to his discretion and his generalship. By these arts Richard acquired the favour of the people and avoided the jealousy of the queen, from whom he lived far separated [...]

Two opinions were propounded [in the council following Edward IV's death]. One was that the Duke of Gloucester should govern because Edward in his will had so directed, and because by law the government ought to devolve on him. But this was the losing resolution; the winning was that the government should be carried on by many persons among whom the duke, far from being excluded, should be accounted the chief [...] All who favoured the queen's family voted for this proposal, as they were afraid that, if Richard took unto himself the crown or even governed alone, they, who bore the blame of Clarence's death, would suffer death or at least be ejected from their high estate [...]

While in London these events were happening, in the country the Duke of Gloucester allied himself with the Duke of Buckingham, complaining to the latter of the insult done him by the ignoble family of the queen. Buckingham, since he was of the highest nobility, was disposed to sympathize with another noble, more especially because he had his own reasons for detesting the queen's kin, for, when he was younger, he had been forced to marry the queen's sister, whom he scorned to wed on account of her humble origin. Therefore, having exchanged views and united their resources, both dukes wrote to the young king in Wales, to ascertain from him on what day and by what route he intended to enter the capital, so that, coming from the country, they could alter their course and join him, that in their company his entry to the city might be more magnificent.

[...] When this news [of the arrest of Lord Rivers and Sir Richard Grey by Gloucester] was announced in London the unexpectedness of the event horrified every one. The queen and the Marquis [of Dorset], who held the royal treasure, began collecting an army, to defend themselves, and to set free the young king from the clutches of the dukes. But when they had exhorted certain nobles who had come to the city, and others, to take up arms, they perceived that men's minds were not only irresolute, but altogether hostile to themselves. Some even said openly that it was more just and profitable that the youthful sovereign should be with his paternal uncle than with his maternal uncles and uterine brothers. Comprehending this, the queen and marquis withdrew to the place of refuge at Westminster Abbey standing close to the royal palace and called by the English a sanctuary.

[...] Edward [Woodville], whom we spoke of as the queen's other brother, appointed by the council captain of a fleet of twenty ships, had put out to sea the day before. For no sooner had the death of King Edward IV become known, than the French not only made the seas unsafe, but even bore off prizes from the English shores. [...] Therefore in the face of threatening hostilities, a council, held in the absence of the Duke of Gloucester, had appointed Edward Woodville; and it was commonly believed that the late king's treasure, which had taken such years and such pains to gather, was divided between the queen, the marquess, and Edward. As there was current in the capital a sinister rumour that the duke had brought his nephew not under his care, but into his power, so as to gain for himself the crown, the Duke of Gloucester amidst these doings wrote to the council and to the head of the city, whom they call mayor.

[...] After these letters had been read aloud in the council chamber and to the populace, all praised the Duke of Gloucester for his dutifulness toward his nephews and for his intention to punish their enemies. Some, however, who understood his ambition and deceit, always suspected whither his enterprises would lead. After a few days when he had ascertained the attitude of every one, and with the help of friends in the capital had provided against all eventualities, he and the young king entered the dry, accompanied by no more than 500 soldiers drawn partly from his own and partly from the Duke of Buckingham's estates. The latter was always at hand ready to assist Gloucester with his advice and resources. By turns they guarded the king, for they were afraid lest he should escape or be forcibly delivered from their hands, since the Welsh could not bear to think that owing to their stupidity their prince had been carried off. As these dukes were seeking at every turn to arouse hatred against the queen's kin, and to estrange public opinion from her relatives, they took special pains to do so on the day they entered the city. For ahead of the procession they sent four wagons loaded with weapons bearing the devices of the queen's brothers and sons, besides criers to make generally known, throughout the crowded places by whatsoever way they passed, that these arms had been collected by the duke's enemies and stored at convenient spots outside the capital, so as to attack and slay the Duke of Gloucester coming from the country. Since many knew these charges to be false, because the arms in question had been placed there long before the late king's death for an altogether different purpose, when war was being waged against the Scots, mistrust both of his accusation and designs upon the throne was exceedingly augmented. Having entered the city, the first thing he saw to was to have himself proclaimed, by authority of the council and all the lords, protector or regent of the king and the realm. Then he set his thoughts on removing, or at least undermining, everything that might stand in the way of his mastering the throne.

[...] Thus far, though all the evidence looked as if he coveted the crown, yet there remained some hope, because he was not yet claiming the throne, inasmuch as he still professed to do all these things as an avenger of treason and old wrongs, and because all private deeds and official documents bore the title and name of King Edward V. But after Hastings was removed, all the attendants who had waited upon the king were debarred access to him. He and his brother were withdrawn into the inner apartments of the Tower proper, and day by day began to be seen more rarely behind the bars and windows, till at length they ceased to appear altogether. Dr. Argentine, the last of his attendants whose service the king enjoyed, reported that the young king, like a victim prepared for sacrifice, sought remission of his sins by daily confession and penance, because he believed that death was facing him. [...] In word and deed he gave so many proofs of his liberal education, of polite, nay rather scholarly attainments far beyond his age; all of these should be recounted, but require such labour, that I shall lawfully excuse myself the effort. There is one thing I shall not omit, and that is, his special knowledge of literature which enabled him to discourse elegantly, to understand fully, and to declaim most excellently from any work whether in verse or prose that came into his hands, unless it were from among the more abstruse authors. He had such dignity in his whole person, and in his face such charm, that however much they might gaze he never wearied the eyes of beholders. I have seen many men burst forth into tears and lamentations when mention was made of him after his removal from men's sight; and already there was a suspicion that he had been done away with. Whether, however, he has been done away with, and by what manner of death, so far I have not at all discovered.

The execution of Lord Hastings, 1483

(*The Great Chronicle of London*)

And all this season the Lord Hastings was had in great favour with the said protector and received of him many great benefits and gifts, as many other noble men did, and all to bring his evil purpose about. And thus driving and delaying the time till he had compassed his mind, upon the 13th day of June he appointed a council to be held within the Tower, to the which were invited the Earl of Derby, the Lord Hastings with many others, but most of such as he knew would favour his cause. And upon the same day dined the said Lord Hastings with him and after dinner rode behind him or behind the Duke of Buckingham to the Tower, where when they with the other lords were entered into the council chamber, and had communed for a while of such matters as he had previously proposed, suddenly one made an outcry at the said council chamber door, "Treason, treason!" and forthwith the usher opened the door and then pressed in such men as were before appointed and straightway laid hands upon the Earl of Derby and the Lord Hastings; and at once without any process of law or lawful examination led the said Lord Hastings out unto the green beside the chapel and there, upon an end of a squared piece of timber, without any long confession or other space of repentance, struck off his head. And thus was this noble man murdered for his truth and fidelity which he firmly bare unto his master, upon whose soul and those of all Christians may Jesus have mercy, Amen! And in like manner the

Earl of Derby would have been dealt with, as rumour would have it, saving that the protector feared the Lord Strange, the said earl's son who was then in Lancashire, wherefore he was immediately set at his liberty without hurt, except that his face was grazed a little with some weapon when the tyrants first entered the chamber. Then were the Archbishop of York, Doctor Rotherham, and the Bishop of Ely, Doctor Morton, set in surety for a time, and forthwith a crew of men was arrayed in the north and the protector commanded them to speed towards London. After this the Prince and the Duke of York were held more straitly and then there was whispering in London that the lord protector should be king. Accordingly upon the Sunday next following the day of execution of the Lord Hastings, at Paul's Cross, in the presence of the said Lord Protector and the Duke of Buckingham, with a huge audience of lords spiritual and temporal, it was declared by Dr Ralph Shaa brother to this mayor and proved by such reasons as he made there and then, that the children of King Edward were not rightful inheritors of the Crown, and that King Edward was not the legitimate son of the Duke of York as the lord protector was. By this declaration and many other allegations and opprobrious reports he then alleged that the lord protector was most worthy to be king and no other [...]

The Bishop of St David's comments on the popularity of Richard III, 1483

(Letter to the Prior of Christ Church, *Christ Church Letters,* ed. J. B. Sheppard, Camden Society, 1877)

I trust to God soon, by Michaelmas, the king shall be at London. He contents the people wherever he goes better than ever did any prince; for many a poor man that has suffered wrong many days has been relieved and helped by him and his commands in his progress. And in many great cities and towns were given to him great sums of money which he has refused. Upon my word I never liked the qualities of any prince so well as his; God has sent him to us for the welfare of us all.

The Duke of Buckingham's rebellion, 1483

(The Continuation of the Crowland Chronicle)

In the meantime, and while these things were going on, the two sons of king Edward before-named remained in the Tower of London, in the custody of certain persons appointed for that purpose. In order to deliver them from this captivity, the people of the southern and western parts of the kingdom began to murmur greatly, and to form meetings and confederacies. It soon became known that many things were going on in secret, and some in the face of all the world, for the purpose of promoting this object, especially on the part of those who, through fear, had availed themselves of the privileges of sanctuary and franchise. There was also a report that it had been recommended by those men who had taken refuge in the sanctuaries, that some of the king's daughters should leave Westminster, and go in disguise to the parts beyond sea; in order that, if any fatal mishap should befall the said male children of the late king in the Tower, the kingdom might still, in consequence of the safety of the daughters, some day fall again into the hands of the rightful heirs. On this being discovered, the noble church of the monks at Westminster, and all the neighbouring parts, assumed the appearance of a castle and fortress, while men of the greatest austerity were appointed by king Richard to act as the keepers thereof. The captain and head of these was one John Nesfeld, Esquire, who set a watch upon all the inlets and outlets of the monastery, so that not one of the persons there shut up could go forth, and no, one could enter, without his permission.

    At last, it was determined by the people in the vicinity of the city of London, throughout the counties of Kent, Essex, Sussex, Hampshire, Dorsetshire, Devonshire, Somersetshire, Wiltshire, and Berkshire, as well as some others of the southern counties of the kingdom, to avenge their grievances before-stated; upon which, public proclamation was made that Henry, Duke of Buckingham, who at this time was living at Brecknock [Brecon] in Wales, had repented of his former conduct, and would be the chief mover in this attempt, while a rumour was spread that the sons of King Edward before-named had died a violent death, but it was uncertain how. Accordingly, all those, who had set on foot this insurrection, seeing that if they could find no one to take the lead in their designs, the ruin of all would speedily ensue, turned their thought to Henry, Earl of Richmond, who had been for many years living in exile in

Brittany. To him a message was, accordingly, sent, by the Duke of Buckingham, by advice of the lord Bishop of Ely, who was then his prisoner at Brecknock, requesting him to hasten over to England as soon as he possibly could, for the purpose of marrying Elizabeth, the eldest daughter of the late king, and, at the same time, together with her, taking possession of the throne.

The whole design of this plot, however, by means of spies, became perfectly well known to King Richard, who, as he exerted himself in the promotion of all his views in no drowsy manner, but with the greatest activity and vigilance, contrived that, throughout Wales, as well as in all parts of the marches thereof, armed men should be set in readiness around the said duke, as soon as ever he had set a foot from his home, to pounce upon all his property; who, accordingly, encouraged by the prospect of the duke's wealth, which the king had, for that purpose, bestowed upon them, were in every way to obstruct his progress. The result was, that, on the side of the castle of Brecknock, which looks towards the interior of Wales, Thomas, the son of the late Sir Roger Vaughan, with the aid of his brethren and kinsmen, most carefully watched the whole of the surrounding country; while Humphrey Stafford partly destroyed the bridges and passes by which England was entered, and kept the other part closed by means of a strong force set there to guard the same.

In the meantime, the duke was staying at Weobley, the house of Walter Devereux, Lord Ferrers, together with the Bishop of Ely and his other advisers. Finding that he was placed in a position of extreme difficulty, and that he could in no direction find a safe mode of escape, he first changed his dress, and then secretly left his people; but was at last discovered in the cottage of a poor man, in consequence of a greater quantity of provisions than usual being carried thither. Upon this, he was led to the city of Salisbury, to which place the king had come with a very large army, on the day of the commemoration of All Souls (2 November); and, notwithstanding the fact that it was the Lord's day, the duke suffered capital punishment in the public market-place of that city.

On the following day, the king proceeded with all his army towards the western parts of the kingdom, where all his enemies had made a stand, with the exception of those who had come from Kent, and were at Guildford, awaiting the issue of events. Proceeding onwards, he arrived at the city of Exeter; upon which, being struck with extreme terror at his approach, Peter Courteney, Bishop of Exeter, as well as Thomas,

Marquis of Dorset, and various other nobles of the adjacent country, who had taken part in the rebellion, repaired to the sea-side; and those among them who could find ships in readiness, embarked, and at length arrived at the wished-for shores of Brittany. Others, for a time trusting to the fidelity of friends, and concealing themselves in secret spots, afterwards betook themselves to the protection of holy places. One most noble knight of that city perished, Thomas Saint Leger by name; to save whose life very large sums of money were offered; but all in vain, for he underwent his sentence of capital punishment.

While the matters which have been mentioned above were going on here and there in the western parts, and the king was still in the said city of Exeter, Henry, Earl of Richmond, being unaware of these disturbances, had set sail with certain ships, and arrived with his adherents from Brittany, at the mouth of Plymouth harbour, where he came to anchor, in order to ascertain the real state of affairs. On news being at last brought him of the events which had happened, the death of the Duke of Buckingham, and the flight of his own supporters, he at once hoisted sail, and again put to sea.

Act of parliament settling the crown upon Richard III, 1484

And here also we consider how that the said pretended marriage between the above-named King Edward and Elizabeth Grey was made of great presumption, without the knowledge and assent of the lords of this land, and also by sorcery and witchcraft, committed by the said Elizabeth and her mother Jacquetta Duchess of Bedford, as the common opinion of the people and the public voice and fame is through all this land. [...] And here also we consider how that the said pretended marriage was made privily and secretly, without the giving out of banns, in a private chamber, a profane place, and not openly in the face of the church, according to the law of God's church, but contrary to it, and to the laudable custom of the Church of England. And how also that at the time of contract of the same pretended marriage, and before and long after, the said King Edward was and stood married and troth plighted to one Dame Eleanor Butler, daughter of the old Earl of Shrewsbury, with whom the same King Edward had made a precontract of marriage, a long time before he made the said pretended marriage. [Wherefore] it appears and follows evidently that the said King Edward during his life and the said

Elizabeth lived together sinfully and damnably in adultery [...] Also it appears evidently and follows, that all the issue and children of the said King Edward are bastards, and unable to inherit or to claim anything by inheritance, by the law and custom of England.

Moreover we consider how that afterwards by the three estates of this realm assembled in a parliament held at Westminster, the 17th year of the reign of the said King Edward IV [...] George, Duke of Clarence, brother to the said King Edward now deceased, was convicted and attainted of high treason [...] by reason whereof all the issue of the said George was and is disabled and barred of all right and claim which in any wise they might have or challenge by inheritance to the crown and dignity royal of this realm, by the ancient law and custom of this same realm.

Richard III's declaration regarding rumours following the death of the Queen, 1485

(Acts of the Court of the Mercers' Company, 1453-1527, ed. L. Lyell and F. D. Witney, Cambridge, 1936)

Whereas as there have been long discussions and much uninformed talk among the people by evil-disposed persons, who have [...] sown these rumours to the very great displeasure of the king, showing how the queen was poisoned by consent and will of the king, so that he might marry and have to wife the Lady Elizabeth, eldest daughter of his brother, late King of England, deceased, whom God pardon [...] the king sent for and had before him at St John's Day, yesterday, the mayor and aldermen. And in the great hall, in the presence of many of his lords and many other people he shewed his grief and displeasure, and said it never came into his thought or mind to marry in such manner, nor was he pleased or glad at the death of his queen but as sorry and heavy in heart as a man would be [...] And he then admonished and charged every person to cease from such untrue talking, on peril of his indignation. And any person who henceforward tells or repeats any of these aforesaid untrue rumours, is to be put in prison until the author be produced from whom the said person heard the said untrue rumour. And in this way the king has given command and charge to the mayor to punish, and to call before him the wardens of all crafts, constables, and others, and to show to them the matter of his displeasure.

The supposed crimes of Richard III

(Rous, *Historia Regum Angliae*)

And in short he [Richard of Gloucester] imprisoned King Edward V, king in deed but not crowned, with his brother Richard, taken from Westminster under promise of safety, so that it was afterwards known to very few by what death they were martyred. Then he ascended the throne of the dead princes, whose protector he had been in their minority, this tyrant King Richard, who was born at Fotheringhay in the county of Northampton: retained for two years in his mother's womb and issuing forth with teeth and hair down to his shoulders [...] At his birth Scorpio was in the ascendant, whose sign is the house of Mars. And as Scorpio was smooth in countenance but deadly with his tail, so Richard showed himself He received his lord King Edward V blandly with embraces and kisses, and yet within about three months or little more he had killed him with his brother, and he poisoned the lady Anne, his queen, daughter of the Earl of Warwick. He imprisoned during his lifetime his mother-in-law Anne, the dowager countess, lady and just heir of that noble lordship [...] And what was most detestable to God and to all the English, indeed to all nations who shall hear of it, he killed that most holy man king Henry VI, either by others or, as many believe, by his own hands.

The battle of Bosworth, 1485

(Vergil, *Anglica Historia*)

In the mean time King Richard, hearing that the enemy drew near, came first to the place of fight, a little beyond Leicester (the name of that village is Bosworth), and there, pitching his tents, refreshed his soldiers that night from their travails, and with many words exhorted them to the fight to come. It is reported that King Richard had that night a terrible dream; for he thought in his sleep that he saw horrible images as it were of evil spirits hovering clearly about him, as it were before his eyes, and that they would not let him rest [...] his heart told him upon this that the result of the following battle would be grievous, and he did not buckle himself to the conflict with such liveliness of courage and countenance as before [...] But I believe it was no dream but a conscience guilty of heinous offences [...] The next day afterwards King Richard, furnished thoroughly with all manner of things, drew his whole host out of their tents, and arrayed his vanguard, stretching it forth of a wondrous length [...] and in the front were placed his archers [...] of these archers he made John Duke of Norfolk the leader. After this long vanguard followed the king himself with a choice force of soldiers. In the mean time Henry, having returned from the conference with his friends, began to take better heart, and without any delay encamped himself near his enemies, where he rested all night, and early in the morning commanded the soldiers to arm themselves, sending as well to Thomas Stanley, who had now approached the place of fight, as in the mid-way between the two battles, that he would come with his forces [...] He made a slender vanguard for the small number of his people; before the same he placed archers, of whom he made captain John, Earl of Oxford; in the right wing of the vanguard he placed Gilbert Talbot to defend the same; on the left truly he set John Savage; and himself trusting to the aid of Thomas Stanley, did follow with one troop of horsemen, and a few footmen; for the number of all his soldiers, altogether, was scarcely 5,000, besides the Stanleyans, of whom about 3,000 were at the battle, under the conduct of William. The king's forces were twice as many and more. [...] There was a marsh between both hosts, which Henry purposely left on the right hand, that it might serve his men instead of a fortress; by doing this he left the sun upon his back; but when the king saw the enemies past the marsh, he commended his soldiers to charge against them. They made suddenly great shouts and assaulted the enemy first with arrows; their foes were not at all loath to fight and began also to shoot fiercely; but when they came to hand strokes the matter then was dealt with by blades [...] While the battle continued thus hot on both sides between the vanguards, King Richard understood [...] when Earl Henry was afar off with a small force of soldiers about him; then after drawing nearer he knew it perfectly by evident signs and tokens that it was Henry. Wherefore, all inflamed with ire, he struck his horse with the spurs, and ran against him out of his own army ahead of the vanguard. [...] King Richard at the first brunt killed some men, overthrew Henry's standard, together with William Brandon the standard bearer. Then he matched himself against John Cheney, a man of much strength, far exceeding the common sort, who strove with him as he came; but the king with great force drove him to the ground, making way with his weapon on every side. But yet Henry abode the brunt longer than even his own soldiers would have thought, who were now almost out of hope of victory, when suddenly William Stanley with 3,000 men came to the rescue. Then truly in a moment the remainder all fled, and King Richard was killed fighting manfully in the thickest press of his enemies. In the mean time also the Earl of Oxford after a little skirmishing put to flight those who fought in the van, whereof a great company were killed in the chase. But many more forbore to fight, who came to the field with King Richard for awe, and for no goodwill, and departed without any danger, as men who desired not the safety but destruction of that prince whom they hated. There were about 1,000 men killed [...] As for the number of captives it was very great [...] amongst them the chief were Henry, Earl of Northumberland, and Thomas, Earl of Surrey. The latter was committed to prison, where he long remained; the former as a friend at heart was received unto favour. Henry lost in that battle scarcely a hundred soldiers, amongst whom there was one principal man, William Brandon, who bore Earl Henry's standard [...]

The report is that King Richard might have sought to save himself by flight; but he [...] is said to have answered that that very day he would make an end either of war or of life, such great fierceness and such huge force of mind he had; wherefore, knowing certainly that that day would either yield him a peaceable and quiet reign thenceforth or else perpetually bereave him of the same, he came to the field with a crown upon his head, that thereby he might either make a beginning or end of his reign.

After the victory was obtained, Henry gave forthwith thanks unto Almighty God for the same; then afterwards [...] the soldiers cried "God save King Henry, God save King Henry" and with heart and hand uttered all the show of joy that might be; which, when Thomas Stanley did see, he at once set King Richard's crown, which was found among the spoil in the field, upon his head. [...] After that [...] Henry with his victorious army proceeded in the evening to Leicester where, for refreshing of his soldiers from their travail and pains, and to prepare for going to London he tarried two days.

In the mean time the body of King Richard, naked of all clothing, and laid upon a horse's back, with the arms and legs hanging down on both sides, was brought to the abbey of Franciscan monks at Leicester [sic – Leicester Abbey was an Augustinian foundation], a miserable spectacle in good truth, but not unworthy for the man's life, and was buried there two days afterwards without any pomp or solemn funeral. He reigned two years and so many months and one day over. He was little of suture, deformed of body, the one shoulder being higher than the other, with a curt and sour countenance, which seemed to savour of mischief, and manifested clearly craft and deceit. While he was thinking of any matter, he did continually bite his nether lip, as though that cruel nature of his did so rage against itself in that little carcase. Also he was wont to be ever with his right hand pulling out of the sheath to the middle, and putting in again, the dagger which he did always wear. Truly he had a sharp wit, cautious and subtle, apt both to counterfeit and dissemble; his courage also high and fierce, which failed him not in the very death. When his men forsook him, he preferred rather to take death with the sword, than by foul flight to prolong his life, uncertain what death perchance soon afterwards to suffer by sickness or other violence.

Chapter 5: The Reign of Henry VII

Henry, Earl of Richmond

The year 1485 is one of the great landmarks in British dynastic and constitutional history. In that year Richard III was defeated in the field at Bosworth, Henry VII's reign began, and a new dynasty, which would last for more than a century, was founded. Its longevity alone contrasts markedly with the turbulent decades before Henry's accession, as the houses of York and Lancaster wrestled over possession of the throne, which changed hands no less than five times between 1461 and 1485.

History has treated Henry VII well. He has been celebrated as the individual who, after years of disorder, secured the peace and stability that would continue until the outbreak of a new civil war in 1642. This led his biographers into an assumption that Henry brought to the throne a unique and 'modern' approach to government and in so doing played a leading role in hauling England out of its 'middle ages'. Modern historians, however, wary of the dangers of oversimplifying the past, are less inclined to see the year of his accession, 1485, as such a watershed.

The son of Edmund Tudor, half-brother of Henry VI, Henry Tudor, the Earl of Richmond, became head of the house of Lancaster in 1471 after Henry VI was put to death following his defeat by Edward IV at the Battle of Tewkesbury. With the crown back in the hands of the Yorkists, Henry's own life was in jeopardy and a childhood that had begun in Pembroke, Wales, in 1457 was now continued in exile in Brittany with his uncle, and guardian, Jasper Tudor. King Edward was eager to lay hands on 'the only imp now left of Henry VI's brood' and nearly succeeded when he almost lured Henry back to England in the mid-1470s with the offer of his daughter's hand in marriage. Henry was warned of Edward IV's true intention and stayed in Brittany under the protection of Francis II. However, it was only after Richard III's usurpation and the supposed murder of Edward IV's sons that Henry

Tudor became a credible contender for the crown.

His triumphant return in 1485 was the result of many factors, including the support of the French king, the efforts of his mother, Margaret Beaufort, to steer the champions of the princes in the Tower in his direction, the aid of the Stanleys, and a measure of good fortune. He displayed that remarkable capacity of late-fifteenth-century kings, kingmakers and pretenders alike, of gambling all in desperate bids for power which had anything but a certain outcome.

When, at the age of twenty-eight, he became king he had little familiarity with his new kingdom and none of the grounding in, or experience of, the world of government that a young prince growing up at court would have received.

Despite such inauspicious beginnings, Henry proved both an able administrator and a shrewd politician. His reputation for austerity might be deserved in some respects but he could be indulgent, establishing a lavish court, investing in exotic wild animals, housed in the Tower, and patronising fools, jesters and troupes of actors. He had a passion for hunting, he commissioned several major palatial building works, added considerably to the stock of the royal library, and promoted all kinds of artistic enterprise. Assessments of his reign, in part, revolve around the question whether this energetic and talented prince was the archetypal Renaissance man, establishing a 'new monarchy', or a king in the more traditional medieval mould.

The consolidation of power

When Henry became king he was faced with a number of potential challenges to his authority. The danger of a Yorkist uprising was considerable, other claimants to the throne might (and did) appear, and some form of foreign invasion was always a possibility. This insecurity, in fact, was a feature of most of Henry's reign, at least until the early years of the sixteenth century.

Just over a fortnight after defeating Richard at the battle of Bosworth, Henry was proclaimed king on 7 September 1485, and subsequently crowned at the end of October. His coronation was further strengthened by a parliamentary bill in November, designed to uphold Henry's authority in the courts and to ensure he had full possession of crown lands. This read:

> 'To the pleasure of almighty God, the wealth, prosperity and surety of this realm of England, to the singular comfort of all the king's subjects of the same, and in avoiding all ambiguities and questions, be it ordained, established and enacted by authority of this present parliament that the inheritance of the crowns of the realms of England and of France [...] be, rest, remain and abide in the most royal person of our now sovereign lord King Harry the VIIth and in the heirs of his body lawfully coming, perpetually with the grace of God so to endure, and in no other.'

By having his coronation before parliament sat in November, Henry made sure that parliament could never claim to have made him king, a claim which would have set a very dangerous precedent for the present and future rulers. The Tudor dynasty was careful to maintain the ancient assumption that God made kings, that theirs was a monarchy established by divine and ancestral right. As Henry VIII's chronicler, Edward Hall, wrote:

> 'King Henry obtained and enjoyed the kingdom as a thing elected and provided by God, and encompassed and achieved by his special favour and gracious aspect. For men commonly report that 797 years ago it was revealed by a heavenly voice to Cadwallader, last king of the Britons, that his stock and progeny should reign and have dominion in this land again. Most men were convinced that by this heavenly voice Henry VII was provided and ordained long ago to enjoy and obtain this kingdom, which Henry VI also claimed. Wherefore Henry VII was by right and just title of inheritance, and by divine providence, thus crowned and proclaimed king.'

Officially the reign was said to have begun on 21 August 1485, the day before Bosworth. Thus Richard and his supporters were declared traitors and their lives and property forfeit. In one fell swoop Henry was now able to rid himself of potential opponents and strengthen his position by seizing their lands or encourage their loyalty with the threat of such retribution.

Henry proved decisive in the opening weeks of his reign, though more inclined to forgive than condemn. True, certain powerful individuals who had survived the wars were promptly gaoled until such time as they ceased to pose a threat; these included the Earl of Surrey and the Duke of Northumberland. The strongest claimant to the throne by blood lineage on Richard's side, his ten-year-old nephew, the Earl of Warwick, was confined, in some comfort, in the Tower of London. Another nephew, however, the Earl of Lincoln, was asked to join the king's council, having declared his loyalty to Henry despite being Richard's chosen heir. Freedom was granted to other Yorkist magnates in return for their promises of good and loyal behaviour. His supporters, needless to say, were rewarded: Jasper Tudor, his uncle, was made Duke of Bedford and Thomas Stanley received the earldom of Derby. Other followers, such as Bishop Morton and Richard Fox, were awarded high offices in his council.

The new king's approach to the consolidation of his position is summarised in this contemporary letter to Rome from John de Giglis, one of the pope's ambassadors and the papal collector of taxes in England. It is dated 6 December 1485.

> 'Most blessed father, after most humble commendation and kisses of thy most blessed feet. Since the last letters which I wrote to you, most Holy Father, little or nothing new has occurred in the state of these affairs. Certainly a new public assembly of the kingdom, which they call parliament, is being held for the information of the kingdom, and in this some Acts have been passed, the chief of which is a general pardon of all offence committed against the king. The Earl of Northumberland, who has been captured and imprisoned, has been set at liberty, but on security from all the prelates, temporal lords, and also the Commons. The Earl of Surrey is still kept in prison: but I hear that he will be released. The eldest daughter of King Edward has been declared duchess of York. There are persistent rumours that the king is about to marry her, a thing which all consider will be most beneficial for the kingdom. The king himself is considered most prudent and also very merciful: all things seem disposed towards peace if only men's minds remain constant. For there is nothing more harmful to this kingdom than ambition and insatiable greed, the mother of all faithlessness and inconstancy: and if God will preserve us from

this, the condition of this kingdom will be peaceful [...]'

Henry's marriage to Elizabeth of York was a powerful means of legitimising his claim to the throne in both Lancastrian and Yorkist eyes. The marriage had been proposed by Henry's shrewd mother, Margaret Beaufort, back in 1483. Elizabeth was the eldest daughter of Edward IV and Henry publicly promised in a ceremony at Rennes Cathedral, while in exile, that he would make her his queen should he succeed in wresting the throne from Richard. In so doing he could rely on the support of those disaffected Yorkists who loathed Richard III's usurpation. They were finally married on 18 January 1486, having secured special dispensation from the pope since, as descendants of Edward III, they were distant cousins.

The significance of this marriage was not lost on Polydore Vergil in *Anglica historia* (1537):

'It is legitimate to attribute this to divine intervention, for plainly by it all things which nourished the most ruinous factions were utterly removed, by it the two houses of Lancaster and York were united, and from this union the true and established. royal line emerged which now reigns.'

In March 1486 Henry VII's claim to the throne was confirmed by a papal bull 'by reason of his highest and undoubted title of successor as by the right of his most noble victory, and by election of the lords spiritual and temporal and other nobles of this realm, and by the act, ordinance, and authority of Parliament'. For his and his queen's personal security he surrounded himself with a troop of hand-picked men, including a number of good archers, whom he named the 'Yeomen of his Guard'. In so doing he adopted a French custom and a wise defence against court intrigue.

Rebellions and pretenders to the throne

Throughout this period Henry was troubled by challenges to his authority. These included risings led by Yorkist lords (Lord Lovell in Yorkshire, Thomas and Humphrey Stafford in the west in 1486 and Sir

John Egremont in Yorkshire in 1489), a popular protest against taxes for a war on Scotland (the Cornish rebellion of 1497), and the phenomenon of 'pretenders', conspiracies in support of fake claimants to the throne (Lambert Simnel during 1486 and 1487, and Perkin Warbeck between 1491 and 1499).

Richard Grafton, a mid-sixteenth-century chronicler, wrote that, in 1486, having settled his affairs in London, Henry set out on a 'progress' of his realm 'so that he might weed and root out and purge the minds of men tainted and defiled with the contagious smoke of dissension and privy factions, especially in the county of York, which were secret favourers and comforters of his opponents'. Shortly after Easter, Henry arrived in York, only to be warned of an impending assault on the city by Francis, Lord Lovell, which was to coincide with an attack in the Midlands on the city of Worcester, launched by Humphrey Stafford. The king promptly instructed the Duke of Bedford and other magnates to organise armies with which to confront any encamped rebels. They were to offer free pardons to all who would submit and to take every measure necessary to avoid bloodshed. The rebellion was successfully pre-empted: Lovell deserted his army in the middle of the night and fled to Lancashire and from thence to Flanders. Hearing this news, Humphrey Stafford also took fright and moved east towards Oxford, near where he was taken prisoner, conveyed to London and executed at Tyburn. However, his brother and co-conspirator was forgiven for having made the mistake of following an evil older brother's malignant advice.

The crisis passed, the king returned to London. Shortly afterwards, in September, his queen, Elizabeth of York, gave birth to their first child - a boy, destined, they hoped, to become the future King of England. He was named Arthur. Henry Tudor thus set a Tudor precedent at this point by associating the dynasty with England's most revered and ancient of kings.

Arguably Lovell's and Stafford's was a lost cause. Without a legitimate Yorkist claimant to the throne, their gesture had been an empty one, destined to be defeated by a 'rightful' king who, furthermore, had reunited the houses of Lancaster and York. History now took a surprising turn as Henry's diehard opponents backed the claims of impostor princes.

The first pretender to challenge Henry was a ten-year-old boy from Oxford, the son of an organ maker. His resemblance to Richard of

York, the youngest of Edward IV's sons, the princes presumed to have been murdered in the Tower, caused him to become the pawn of Yorkist supporters around Oxford. When it began to be rumoured that Edward IV's nephew, the Earl of Warwick, also detained in the Tower, had died, Simnel's advocate, an Oxford priest named Richard Symonds, decided to change the boy's supposed identity to that of Warwick. He was subsequently taken to Ireland and, in May 1487, crowned King Edward VI in Dublin, another centre of Yorkist sympathy.

Once more Henry VII tried to pre-empt war by offering those who had supported the impostor king a free pardon if they admitted their mistake. This time, however, he was less successful. Simnel provided the cause that the aborted rebellion of 1486 had lacked. With the backing of such powerful supporters as the Earl of Kildare and the Archbishop of Dublin, the boy's new-found 'aunt', Margaret of Burgundy, sister of Edward IV and Richard III, co-ordinated the insurrection.

Despite Henry's parading of the real Earl of Warwick in London, an invasion led by John de la Pole, the Earl of Lincoln, and Lord Lovell, supported by 2,000 German mercenaries, was staged in the summer of 1487. Landing in Furness, Lancashire, the predominantly Irish army met Henry's at Stoke, near Newark, on 16 June and, outnumbered, was decisively defeated. The Earl of Lincoln had not met with the support of his fellow English nobles he had hoped for but, hoping to defeat the king's larger army, as Henry himself had done at Bosworth, he did not shy from an engagement. Henry, however, had had plenty of time to prepare for the invasion and his well-organised and well-armed force was more than a match for the poorly equipped Irish retainers under the command of Kildare, although the presence of hardened German mercenaries helped prolong the fight.

The battle of Stoke was the last battle of the Wars of the Roses. Lovell was never heard of again and probably died on the battlefield along with Lincoln. The pretender and his creator were both captured but, characteristically, Henry spared them both - partly for purely propagandist reasons but also perhaps because one an innocent child and the other was a priest. Richard Symonds was sentenced to life imprisonment and Simnel was found employment in the king's kitchen.

John Guy declared this to one of the most serious revolts faced by Henry VII since it had 'dynastic intentions'. It was all the more worrying to the security of the new regime since it came so soon after the Battle of Bosworth.

Of the lenient way in which the surviving conspirators were treated, G. R. Elton remarked, 'Henry proved merciful in a politic manner': instead of unleashing bloody vengeance, such as his royal descendants would upon their opponents in the sixteenth century, he proved magnanimous. Simnel eventually became one of the king's falconers. Henry VII successfully played down the Simnel conspiracy whereas a less shrewd statesman would have martyred those responsible.

Henry VII broke with tradition early in his reign by making the same tax demands on northerners as on southerners. Custom appears to have excused the north from raising certain monies for the defence of England and ventures abroad, on the grounds that they tended to foot the bill for defending the border country from the ravages of Scottish raiding parties. When Henry declared in 1489 that every man, including those in the north of the realm, should pay a tenth penny of his goods towards the cost of a campaign in Brittany, people in Yorkshire and in the bishopric of Durham refused. The Earl of Northumberland, entrusted with enforcing payment by any means, was attacked and murdered, together with a number of his household servants. A small army of defiant non-taxpayers and, doubtless, some sympathisers of Richard III, was formed under the leadership of Sir John Egremont. They openly defied the king and declared they would fight if necessary to retain their liberty and rights. Henry VII himself joined the Earl of Surrey in an expedition to the north to impose his will upon the rebels. The ringleader, John Chamber, together with his accomplices, was hanged at York. The majority of those who had resisted paying their dues, however, were spared. Egremont meanwhile had escaped and joined fellow malcontents gathered around Margaret of Burgundy in Flanders.

The other great pretender to challenge Henry VII was the mysterious Perkin Warbeck. He began to cultivate the rumour, started when he was in Cork in Ireland in 1491, that he was in fact Richard, the younger of the murdered princes in the Tower. For the rest of the nineties he would cause trouble for Henry through his habit of making alliances with the king's foreign enemies in Ireland, Scotland and France. He led a forlorn invasion of England in 1497, but survived until the end of November 1499, when he was hanged after being found guilty of plotting to escape from captivity in the Tower of London.

The Henrician chronicler, Edward Hall, catalogued reasons for the considerable support this new pretender attracted:

'many [...] who had fallen into debt and feared to be brought into captivity and bondage assembled together in a company and crossed over the sea to Flanders, to their counterfeit Richard son of King Edward IV, otherwise named Perkin Warbeck. After this many noblemen conspired together, some induced by rashness and temerity, some so earnestly persuaded of their own conceit as if they knew perfectly that this Perkin was undoubtedly the son of King Edward IV [...] Others joined them through indignation, envy and greed, ever judging and thinking they were not suitably rewarded for their pains taken on the king's behalf in his quarrels. Others who it grieved and vexed to see the world stand still in security and all men living in peace and tranquility, desirous for some change, ran headlong into that fury, madness and sedition.'

What motivated this young Fleming from Tournai is uncertain and intriguing, although his own account given on the scaffold 'shortly before his execution in 1499 provides some clues:

'Now when we were there arrived in the town of Cork [there] came unto me an Englishman and said to me [...] that they knew that I was King Richard's bastard son [...] They advised me not to be afeared but that I should take it upon me boldly [...] so that they might be revenged on the King of England, and so against my will made me learn English and taught me what I should do and say. And after this they called me the Duke of York, second son to King Edward IV, because King Richard's bastard son was in the hands of the King of England [...]'

Controversy remains over whether, in J. D. Mackie's words, he was merely 'a conceited, ambitious youth with an engaging address' who stumbled by chance upon Yorkist opportunists in Cork, or whether, as claimed by one of Henry VII's biographers, S. B. Chrimes, this was in fact 'the first overt action in the unfolding of a definite plan'.

Warbeck's most influential ally was the sister of Edward IV and Richard III, Margaret, duchess of Burgundy (1446-1503) - 'this diabolical duchess [...] she always cared nothing for peace and tranquility and desired nothing more than dissension, civil war and the destruction of Henry.'[41] Sister of Edward IV and Richard III, Margaret of Burgundy ruled the Low Countries for the first part of Henry's reign. She was the widow of Charles the Bold, Duke of Burgundy, who died in 1477. She became heavily involved in various conspiracies against Henry during the first half of his reign. Yorkist supporters flocked to her court, including Francis, Lovell Lord and John de la Pole, the Earl of Lincoln. Here too she gave shelter to Lambert Simnel, possibly from as early as 1486. She used her position and wealth to support his campaign by providing him with 2,000 German mercenaries and a fleet to carry them to Ireland.

Following Simnel's defeat she became involved in the activities of Perkin Warbeck. Accepting Warbeck's claims, she publicly named him as her nephew. Once more, she used her wealth to assist a pretender as indicated by a document from 1494, in which Warbeck acknowledged to her a debt of 800,000 florins. In Holinshed's chronicle, published in 1571, he wrote:

> 'Also they sent unto Flanders to the Lady Margaret, sister to King Edward and late wife to Charles, Duke of Burgoyne [Burgundy], to purchase aid and help at her hands. This Lady Margaret bore no small rule in the Low Countries, and in very deed sore grudged in her heart that King Henry (being descended of the house of Lancaster) should reign and govern of the realm of England, and [...] though she well understood that this was but a coloured matter, yet to work her malicious intention against King Henry, she was glad to have so fit an occasion, and promised the messengers all the aid she should be able to make and also to procure all the friends she could [...]'

At one stage Warbeck claimed to be the son of Margaret and the Bishop of Cambrai. (Historians since have been intrigued by the fact that, when visiting London in 1498, the bishop specifically asked to see the pretender.) As Warbeck's fortunes declined, Margaret disassociated herself from him and, in 1498, sent Henry VII a formal apology for her previous involvement.

The highest profile victim, after Warwick, of the Warbeck years was Sir William Stanley. William Stanley, the younger brother of Henry

---

[41] Edward Hall.

VII's stepfather, Thomas Stanley, first Earl of Derby, had played a crucial role at Bosworth where he turned his army of 3,000-8,000 against Richard III. His assistance at Bosworth was amply rewarded for he was appointed chamberlain of the royal household and came to be considered the richest commoner in England.

He was beheaded in 1495 on the grounds that, ostensibly, he was in league with Margaret of Burgundy and her 'puppet', Perkin Warbeck. Allegedly he had remarked, perhaps in a moment of humour, that he would not resist Warbeck if indeed he really was Prince Richard. It is possible that he was in contact and conspiring with Margaret through Sir Robert Clifford, who returned from her court in January 1495. This was Clifford's own claim and, while he was not indicted (was he a 'double agent' working for the king as well as Stanley?), the chamberlain, who had turned coat at a critical hour once before, was found guilty of treason and executed.

Quite likely Stanley, guilty or not, was killed in order to deter anyone from even contemplating lending their support to the pretender, who was expected to launch an invasion in the near future. It seems unlikely that a man as successful as Stanley would see anything to gain in support of such a spurious claimant. Moreover, Henry VII had shown on a number of occasions that he had capacity for mercy even when dealing with the most treasonable of offenders. Cynical realpolitik as opposed to genuine conspiracy or kingly paranoia might well explain Sir William Stanley's fate.

Stanley's motives, if indeed he was guilty, have always mystified historians as this extract from Edward Hall's *The union of the two noble and illustre families of Lancaster and York* (1548) testifies:

> 'What caused the sincere and faithful mind which Sir William Stanley always bore to King Henry to turn into cankered hatred and spite, and why the special favour the king bore him was changed to disdain and displeasure, different men have different explanations. Some say that [...] he remembered more the benefit he had done to the king than the rewards and gifts he received [...] Some say he desired to be Earl of Chester and being denied that began to bear a grudge and to disdain his high friend the king [...] When the king perceived that his stomach began to canker and grow rusty he was not a little displeased with him, and so when both their hearts were inflamed with

melancholy both lost the fruit of their long-continued friendship and favour [...] At this time the king thought it best to use some sharp punishment and correction for the offences of his subjects, so that the lately begun sedition might sooner be oppressed. When knowledge of the slanderous and opprobrious words concerning the expected arrival of the feigned Richard, Duke of York, came to the king's ears, he caused several people to suffer punishment for their heinous offences.'

Even after the executions of Warbeck and Warwick and the start of a new century, Henry VII continued to be plagued by conspirators and would-be rebels. One such was another Yorkist heir, Edmund de la Pole, the Duke of Suffolk, nicknamed 'The White Rose'. Suffolk was the nephew of Edward IV and Richard III, and the brother of the Earl of Lincoln who had been slain in 1487 at the Battle of Stoke for his part in supporting Lambert Simnel's insurrection.

Alarmed no doubt by the fate of Stanley and Warwick, Suffolk fled England in July 1499 and took refuge in France, near Calais. After a brief reconciliation with the king he took flight again, this time joining other Yorkist exiles in Flanders. Suffolk became more of a threat after the deaths of Henry's infant son, Edmund, in 1500 and his heir, Arthur, in 1502, the succession now passing to Arthur's younger brother, ten-year-old Henry.

In 1504 Suffolk's family, together with other associates tarnished by previous Yorkist/Ricardian sympathies, was ruthlessly purged. The chronicler, Richard Grafton, writing around 1550, explained the rationale behind Henry's actions at this time:

> 'King Henry now [1504] growing old, before this time had always been vexed and provoked by the scrupulous stings of sedition and civil commotion, so that he detested and abhorred internal and private war more than death or anything more terrible. Therefore he determined to provide so prudently that all causes of such unquietness and mischief to come should be rooted out and banished [...] remembering the old proverb that men through abundance of riches grow more insolent and headstrong [...]'

Fifty-one men were attainted by parliament, their coffers,

according to the chroniclers, being emptied into the king's purse. Chief among those who carried out Henry's vengeful work, indicting men for transgressing previously neglected penal laws, were Sir Richard Empson and Edmund Dudley. Both of these men would pay dearly for their activities early in the reign of Henry VIII. Some in the process were condemned to death, most famously Sir James Tyrell, who was made to confess that, during his tenure of the office of constable of the Tower, he had murdered Edward's sons at the start of Richard III's reign. In so doing, Henry and his fellow accusers could hope to eliminate the possibility of further pretenders posing as the troublesome princes now grown to adulthood. On the eve of his execution, with nothing personally to gain in so doing, Edmund Dudley admitted that some of what he had been instructed to do by his royal master amounted to extortion. Henry VII himself effectively admitted the dubious nature of his money-raising schemes in the last years of his reign when, in his will, he instructed the setting-up of a committee to investigate claims by individuals who had been wronged under his administration.

In 1506 he finally wrested Suffolk from the protection of Philip of Burgundy on the condition that he spare his life. This he did, but kept Suffolk captive in the Tower until he was executed in 1513 in the reign of Henry VIII. At last, for the first time in more than twenty years, with most of his potential dynastic rivals buried or imprisoned, Henry could feel reasonably secure, but the future of his own dynasty rested precariously with the life of his surviving son, Henry.

The Cornish rebellion, 1497

Described by John Guy as 'the most important revolt in Henry's reign' this rebellion was provoked by the demand for additional taxes needed to raise revenue with which to pay for a projected invasion of Scotland, part of an ages-old conflict that had been made worse by Perkin Warbeck's recent activities. According to Raphael Holinshed's *Chronicle* (1571), the rebel leaders promised 'not to hurt any living creature' but to punish those of the king's ministers, including the Archbishop of Canterbury, who were associated with the imposition of the unwanted tax. The 15,000 Cornish rebels marched on London before being defeated on 17 June 1497. The *Registrum Annalium Collegii Mertonensis* for the year 1497 gives an account of the events:

> 'Memorandum, in this year about the beginning of May, a great rising of the people occurred in the kingdom beginning in Cornwall where the ringleader was a smith named Michael Joseph. A great multitude of people supported him, but there was none of noble blood except Lord Audley. Crossing the counties of Devon, Somerset, Wiltshire, Southampton, they came at length to Blackheath on 16th June, where they pitched their camp for the night. On the morrow, 17th June, Henry VII met them with a great multitude of nobles. He gained the victory without great slaughter on either side and the said captain and Lord Audley with others were captured and committed in chains to the Tower for their deeds. From there on the 27th of the month the said Michael and one Flammok, a lawyer, were drawn through the places of the city to Tyburn and there were hanged. Their bodies were taken down quartered, and by the king's orders were hanged in various cities and places in the kingdom. On the next day, the 28th, the said Lord Audley was drawn from Newgate through the places of the city to the place of punishment near the Tower, and there his head was struck off. His body was, by the king's grace, buried in the Preachers, but his head was fixed on London Bridge.'

According to John Stow in his *Annals of England* (1592), both the king and the rebels lost about 300 men, and about 1,500 were captured following the battle. More recently, it has been estimated that around 1,000 rebels were killed at Blackheath. A number of important families in the south and west were accused of connections with the rebellion and fined accordingly; in Somerset alone the charged included three members of parliament and four sheriffs. Those who rallied around Warbeck later in the year, when he arrived in the south-west, might have done so because of the severity with which the Cornish rebels were treated.

The *Registrum Annalium Collegii Mertonensis* for 1497 stated:

> 'Memorandum, in that year on 7th September, one Perkin, by nationality a Fleming, pretending that he was the second son of Edward IV, and calling himself Richard, Duke of York, landed

at the port of St Ives in Cornwall and proclaimed himself King of England. About 10,000 Cornishmen who hated Henry VII on account of their defeat at Blackheath on the previous 17th June, and who wished to avenge themselves on the king joined him, and they set out towards the east in battle array.'

Henry abandoned the Scottish campaign and, instead, took a conciliatory line with James IV in which he was successful.

Foreign policy

'[...] the English are great lovers of themselves and of everything English. They think there are no other men worth considering and no other part of the world either.'

(Venetian envoy to England, c.1500)

Yorkist and early Tudor foreign policy was determined by the need to secure the throne in England, to safeguard trade interests and to maintain English aspirations in continental Europe. These objectives could be achieved by either diplomacy or war. England's population during the sixteenth century was at best half that of Spain and only one third that of France. The income of English kings was smaller than that of their immediate neighbours and involvement abroad represented the additional cost of transporting armies abroad. Henry VII's fleet was insignificant - a total of seven royal ships on his inheritance and just five by the time he died. In armed diplomacy England was seriously disadvantaged.

Henry's position in 1485 in relation to continental powers was the reverse of his predecessors. The Yorkist policy was anti-French and pro-Burgundian. France, since 1330, had been regarded as a legitimate claim of English kings and Burgundy, the bitter enemy of France ever since she had gained her independence earlier in the century, was an obvious ally. Henry had, however, attained the throne by enlisting French support, and Burgundy, with Margaret of Burgundy sponsoring pretenders to engineer his downfall, was his enemy. After her husband, Charles the Bold, died in 1477, the dukedom was inherited by

Maximilian of Habsburg, who became the Holy Roman Emperor in 1493. He was the husband of Charles the Bold's daughter by a former marriage. Thus England was potentially embroiled in the bitter conflict between the French house of Valois and the Austrian Habsburg dynasty.

Once again, events in Brittany turned things around. English kings had long sought the preservation of Burgundian and Breton independence, a vital counter-balance to the might of France. France of course aspired to a full absorption of these provinces into the kingdom, and when duke Francis of Brittany died in 1488, leaving as heir a minor, his daughter Anne, Charles VIII exerted his feudal right of wardship which, effectively, would place the duchy in French hands.

The Treaty of Redon in 1489 brought England into an alliance with Brittany in defiance of French interests and Henry put further pressure on France by making the Treaty of Medina del Campo with her southern neighbour, Spain. Despite this, Charles had no intention of backing down and proceeded to marry Anne of Brittany in December 1491, thus reuniting Brittany with the French crown.

Henry, troubled by Perkin Warbeck at home, was in no position to wage a major war and, instead, launched a short campaign, reasserting English claims to France, in October of 1492. A short siege of Boulogne was ended by the Treaty of Étaples, from which Henry secured a pension of 50,000 crowns a year, payable until the agreed total of 745,000 crowns had been met. In addition, Charles promised to cease supporting English rebels.

The support Perkin Warbeck received from Burgundy continued until 1496. The damage done to Anglo-Burgundian trade due to the embargo Henry placed on all trade with the Low Countries in 1493, coupled with Emperor Maximilian's desire to enlist English support for his campaign against France, led to a truce. As a result, Margaret of Burgundy, Maximilian's mother-in-law, was obliged to abandon Warbeck and his supporters. Although England joined Maximilian's Holy League, Henry had no intention of being drawn into the Habsburg-Valois conflict and the peace with France remained intact.

At the turn of the century, therefore, Henry's foreign relations could not have been better: he had made his peace with France, he was the ally of Spain, he had the support of the Emperor, and the rapprochement with Burgundy had begun. Just as his victory at Stoke had marked his acceptance as king at home, the Treaty of Medina del Campo represented recognition abroad.

The alliance with Spain, however, guaranteed by the marriage of first Prince Arthur and then Prince Henry to Catherine of Aragon, began to founder after 1504. The relationship with Ferdinand, King of Aragon, turned sour when his wife, Isabella, queen of Castile, died. Instead of supporting Ferdinand's claims to his deceased wife's kingdom, Henry decided to back the claims of Isabella's mad daughter, Joanna, who was married to Emperor Maximilian's son, Philip the Handsome of Burgundy. In October 1505 Ferdinand signed the Treaty of Blois with France and married Louis XII's niece the following March. The ruination of Henry's Spanish policy was amplified when, in 1508, Ferdinand joined France in the League of Cambrai. France and Spain were thus aligned together against Henry and his unreliable allies.

During the fifteenth century, English kings effectively abandoned their claims to overlordship in Scotland. After years of intermittent skirmishes in the border regions and at sea, English kings after 1461 sought an ending to this 'cold war' with Scotland. So long as English interests were threatened by France Scotland was a dangerous enemy, gravitating towards anti-English alliances with France.

In June 1463 Edward IV, fearing a Lancastrian invasion from the north, secured a fifteen-year truce with James III of Scotland. Further Scottish raids across the border in the early 1480s, however, inspired Edward's decision to capitalise on the conflicts between James and his brother, Alexander, the Duke of Albany. Richard of Gloucester organised a campaign headed by Albany in 1482. When Albany regained his former positions, however, he abandoned his claim. Gloucester then released the recently captured James and withdrew his army from Edinburgh. After Albany was charged with treason by the Scottish parliament in 1483, Gloucester, now Richard III, pursued the cause of the duke, now fugitive in England. This led to a second, unsuccessful invasion and Albany was forced to flee to France. In 1484 a three-year truce was agreed between Richard and James. The 'Auld Alliance' between Scotland and France, however, remained and Scottish troops would soon fight with the French-backed invasion that led to Richard's destruction on Bosworth Field.

Henry VII tried to secure a lasting peace with Scotland and made a new truce, with James IV, when he became king in 1488. Despite this, relations deteriorated to such an extent that James married his cousin, Lady Catherine Gordon, to the pretender to the English throne, Perkin Warbeck, in 1495. In the event of Warbeck achieving his objectives, it was agreed that Scotland should take back Berwick, lost to the English in 1482. Warbeck's subsequent invasion from Scotland, in 1496, was a fiasco, his Scottish troops retreating back across the border once it became apparent that the north would not rally to his cause. It was in retaliation to this that Henry attempted to raise the subsidy to wage a war against Scotland that resulted in the Cornish rebellion. The revolt was quelled, though not before the rebels reached Blackheath in their march on London. Meanwhile James IV's troops made another incursion into England but were pushed back by an army under the command of the Earl of Surrey.

Henry reverted to a policy of peace rather than punishment and, in September 1497, signed the Truce of Ayton with James IV, This was extended by the Treaty of Perpetual Peace in 1502, reinforced by the marriage of James to Henry's daughter, Margaret in 1503. This peace proved a lasting one and Henry enjoyed good relations with Scotland for the remaining half-decade of his reign.

James III, who was murdered in 1488, had been a weak and feeble king. His son and heir to the Scottish throne, James IV, was of a different breed. A Spanish visitor to Scotland from 1496 to 1497 wrote that James was:

> '[…] of noble stature, neither tall nor short, and as handsome in complexion and shape as a man can be […] He speaks the following foreign languages: Latin, very well; French, German, Flemish, Italian and Spanish […] He is courageous, even more so than a king should be.'

He promised to be a formidable foe should the new English king endeavour to pursue claims to lordship over Scotland, revived by Henry's Yorkist predecessors, Edward IV and his brother, Richard III. James shared many of those qualities of the archetypal Renaissance prince that some have identified with Henry VII. An extract from Henry VII's funeral oration in 1509 states:

> 'His politic wisdom in governance was singular, his wit was always quick and ready, his reason pithy and substantial, his memory fresh and holding, his experience notable, his counsels fortunate and taken by wise deliberation, his speech gracious in diverse languages, his person goodly and amiable, his natural

complexion of the purest mixture, his issue fair and in good number; leagues and confederacies he had with all Christian princes, his mighty power was dreaded everywhere [...]'

However, in one respect they seem to have been very different. The chronicler, Polydore Vergil, in *Anglica Historia* (1537), declared that Henry was 'constitutionally more inclined to peace than war', and another early commentator, Bernard Andreas, stated, in his *Life of Henry VII*, 'without doubt, he first of all the kings to come in future years, deserves to be crowned with the title of the "peacemaking king."' According to one contemporary observer quoted in the *Calendar of State Papers Venetian, 1202-1509*, his was very much a defensive and cautious policy:

'He garrisons two or three fortresses, contrary to the custom of his predecessors, who garrisoned no place. He has neither ordnance nor munitions of war, and his body guard is supposed not to amount to one hundred men.'

James IV on the other hand was a dedicated and reckless warrior. Given his limited resources, his expenditure on weaponry was remarkable. He was a great enthusiast for artillery and established, at vast cost, a huge and up-to-date arsenal. He deluded himself into believing that he could be a major player in European affairs and the politics of armed diplomacy. Scotland, ultimately, paid the price, with defeat on Flodden Field in 1513. He also, unwisely, took the offensive against England in the 1490s when Henry VII appears to have been content to play down English aspirations beyond the border.

By 1497 Henry VII was assembling the largest army of his reign in order to punish James for lending support to Warbeck. Scotland never felt the full force of Henry VII's retribution; the taxation imposed to raise this army helped spark the Cornish rebellion which diverted Henry from his Scottish campaign and used up some of the resources upon which it relied. According to G. R. Elton it was a lucky escape for James IV:

'The story of Scotland's share in Warbeck's Odyssey has already been told. At one time, in 1497, it looked as though Henry VII would accept the challenge and attempt serious war in the north, but the Cornish rebellion came just in time to save James IV from his ill-regulated combativeness. If one may judge from later events in Henry VIII's reign, the Scottish army would have stood but a poor chance against the forces which the Earl of Surrey was marshalling on the border.'[42]

As it was, Henry VII preserved his peaceful reputation unsullied, to prove once more how well he could exploit difficult situations without precipitating war. Surrey did cross the border once to teach James a sharp lesson, incidentally refusing a typically chivalrous but unrealistic offer of single combat. The end of War beck left James rather at a loss, and his own position in a country where some of whose chief lords were ready to throw in their lot with the enemy was none too comfortable. Henry even hinted that two could play at the game of supporting pretenders and showed signs of adopting the cause of a Stuart claimant, the Duke of Albany, then living in France. All these things working together, and Henry still continuing to offer real peace, an agreement was arrived at in December 1497.

The ensuing Treaty of Ayton of 1497, as we have seen, resulted in harmonious relationships with Scotland for the rest of Henry's reign. Flodden Field James IV's support for Louis XII of France resulted in a disastrous defeat at Flodden at the hands of the Earl of Surrey. James, along with 10,000 other Scots, was killed.

Opposition in Ireland and Poynings' Law

> '[…] if any Parliament be held in the land hereafter, contrary to the form and provision aforesaid, it be deemed void and of no effect in law.'

(Poynings' Law, 1494.)

Though considered a part of the kingdom by English kings, much of Ireland remained in cultural and political isolation throughout the period. As G. R. Elton wrote in *England under the Tudors* (1974): 'The better part of the wild, wooded, boggy, and hilly country of the

---

[42] G. R. Elton, *England under the Tudors* (1974).

north and west had never so much as seen an English soldier or administrator.' No Tudor monarch visited Ireland and, in 1485, only the 80 kilometre strip extending northwards from Dublin, known as the Pale, was securely held by the crown. Elsewhere the greater Anglo-Irish families, notably the Geraldines and Butlers, and the Irish chieftains held sway.

In Ireland rebellions were fermented: Lambert Simnel's invasion of England was launched from Ireland, and Perkin Warbeck first appeared in the southern Irish port of Cork in 1491. Initially, as elsewhere, Henry relied upon local magnates to impose his authority. In 1485 the post of Lord Deputy was held by a Fitzgerald, the Earl of Kildare. When Lambert Simnel was brought to Ireland and, posing as the Earl of Warwick, crowned in Dublin in 1487, Kildare, eager to undermine English authority in Ireland, was among those to recognise him as King Edward VI. Following Simnel's defeat at the Battle of Stoke, Kildare gave himself up, admitted his mistake in supporting the boy's claim, and was forgiven.

In 1491 Kildare expressed support for a second pretender, Perkin Warbeck, and this time Henry was less forgiving. Kildare was dismissed in 1492. In his place in 1494, Henry, breaking with tradition, chose an Englishman, Sir Edward Poynings. Poynings bought off potential rebels in the northern province of Ulster and assembled a parliament, passing laws designed to reduce Irish independence. By the terms of Poynings' Law, no laws could be passed in Ireland without the English king's approval, and any new English legislation would automatically apply to Ireland as well. The first parliament attainted the Earl of Kildare, had him arrested and sent to the Tower of London. This apparent destruction of Ireland's most powerful leader was impressive indeed. In 1495 Perkin Warbeck was driven out of Ireland into a Scottish exile.

The cost of controlling Ireland and trying to impose English Law outside the Pale proved great, and in 1496 Henry reverted to the tradition of relying on the Irish nobility to manage Irish affairs. Characteristically, Henry forgave. Kildare his earlier indiscretions and he was reappointed lord deputy. The show of strength between 1492 and 1496 helped establish the authority of Henry VII. The country furnished no more pretenders and, from this point on, Henry was largely untroubled by Irish affairs. Kildare, now married to the king's cousin, denied Warbeck further support in 1497, and remained in post as deputy until the end of the reign.

Traditionally English kings had administered Ireland through the Anglo-Irish nobility. The lord deputy in Dublin enjoyed a good deal of autonomy and distance from the king's government in England. When Henry VII acquired the throne in 1485, Dublin and its Pale remained staunchly loyal to the Yorkist cause. In 1487 the pretender, Lambert Simnel, was crowned king in Dublin, much to Henry VII's irritation. However, not wishing to jeopardise his position in England by getting embroiled in a conflict in Ireland, Henry proved remarkably lenient in pardoning those involved in promoting Simnel's unsuccessful coup. In return for a mere oath of allegiance the lord deputy, the Earl of Kildare, and the other great Anglo-Irish magnates were left to run Ireland as before.

When, in 1491, a second pretender, Perkin Warbeck, arrived in Ireland, posing as the younger of the princes in the Tower, Richard, Henry VII's patience was stretched too far. Kildare was dismissed, a small English army was landed in Ireland, and Warbeck fled to France. In 1494, to quell continuing Irish troubles and prevent Warbeck using Ireland as a base a second time, Henry sent over another small army and a governor, Sir Edward Poynings. The English governor brought with him a package of proposals, subsequently passed by Ireland's parliament, which undermined Irish autonomy by preventing the Anglo-Irish nobility, likes the Kildares, from holding parliamentary sessions and legislating without the English government's approval. During the brief spell of his governorship (he returned to England in December 1495) he crushed a major rebellion organised by Kildare's brother, captured Kildare and sent him to England as a prisoner, and he once more dispersed another attempt by Perkin Warbeck to gain a footing in Ireland.

In 1496, however, Henry VII reverted to the old policy of governing Ireland through that country's own nobility and he reinstated Kildare as lord deputy. Kildare's son stayed at the English king's court in England: a surety for his father's good behaviour.

Historians are divided over the success of Poynings' governorship and the reasons for Henry VII's reinstatement of Kildare. The lack of support for Warbeck in Ireland compared to that he found in Scotland, and compared to that enjoyed by Simnel in Ireland some years earlier, has been cited as evidence for a generally successful colonial policy. His recall of Poynings and restoration of authority in the hands of Irish nobles, according to some, was the decision of a strong and confident king who had quelled the Irish. Roger Lockyer commented:

> 'By the end of 1495 Ireland had been pacified, and Poynings returned to England. Henry, who needed money and men for operations against Scotland, now disentangled himself from his Irish involvement and returned to the practice of ruling through the Irish magnates. He had been impressed by Kildare, and when it was pointed out to him that 'All England cannot rule yonder gentleman', he replied 'No? Then it is mete to rule all Ireland'. Kildare was therefore reinstated as Deputy, having abandoned his Yorkist inclinations, and Ireland ceased to be a major problem for Henry.'[43]

Other historians have been less generous to Henry VII and have questioned the success of his Irish policy:

> 'In effect Henry despaired of the success of the measures initiated in 1494 when [...] he recalled Poynings and restored Kildare to favour [...] The problem of Ireland had turned out to be too big for solution; the return of Kildare meant the end of effective English control, despite the operation of Poynings' laws [...] There were no claimants about to disturb the peace from Ireland; why, then, waste good money on a probably futile policy of direct rule? Henry VII was lucky to die before the Irish problem revived, but revive it did - and largely because he gave up the fight.'[44]

According to S. J. Gunn, Henry, like his predecessors and successors, was dogged by old problems in Ireland that Poynings' Law manifestly had failed to resolve:

> 'In the years 1470-1534, the Fitzgeralds [Earls of Kildare] were repeatedly appointed as governors, removed for misgovernance or political disloyalty, and then reappointed, often when the local followers through whom they ruled refused to co-operate with any alternative regime. Only when they overstepped the mark

---

[43] Roger Lockyer, *Henry VII* (1983).

[44] G. R. Elton *England under the Tudors* (1974).

totally in the revolt of 1534 did Henry VIII turn to direct rule by an English governor with a subsidised garrison.'[45]

Edward Hall, the early Tudor historian, implied Henry's Irish policy in the mid-1490s was only ever intended as a temporary measure, 'to purge all the towns and places where Perkin was received, relieved or favoured'. Certainly Poynings succeeded in quelling the pro-Warbeck movement in Ireland through negotiation with the Irish lords and swift retribution where treason was encountered. His recall coincides exactly with Warbeck's arrival in Scotland in November 1495. Henry VII's policy in Ireland should only be considered a failure if he had any genuine intention of achieving more than the assertion of his authority in the face of Warbeck's posturing.

Government

The length of Henry VII's reign (twenty-four years) and the fact that the dynasty he founded would occupy the throne for the whole of the sixteenth century are testimony to his adept handling of the day-to-day business of government. John Guy has described him as the most able businessman ever to wear England's crown. Like a good businessman, he knew how to deal with people, how to raise capital, how to save and how to spend wisely. He was very wary of imposing additional or increased taxes on his subjects, however, and preferred to resort to the Yorkist device of benevolences where possible. His interest in the crown's financial affairs is shown by his signature which appears on a daily basis in the royal accounts. He probably did not leave a great hoard of treasure to his heir but he did stay solvent and, despite a reputation for avarice, maintained one of the most conspicuously wealthy courts in Europe. Between December 1491 and his death in April 1509, he spent over £128,000 on jewels, and foreign dignitaries visiting Windsor Castle slept under throws of woven cloth of gold.

Henry VII sought to make his kingdom richer, too, by promoting trade abroad, although his hands often were tied by more pressing

---

[45] S. J. Gunn, *Early Tudor Government* (1995).

political considerations. To this end, he supported the voyages of John and Sebastian Cabot. He made a number of trade treaties with various countries, including the *Magnus Intercursus* (Great Commercial Exchange) with Maximilian I, the Holy Roman Emperor, in 1496. This confirmed favourable trade arrangements with Holland and, perhaps more importantly for Henry, secured the Emperor's promise to stop aiding Yorkist rivals. His support of merchants through the Navigation Acts of 1485 and 1489, which were designed to prevent the carriage of certain goods in non-English vessels, also had a political as well as economic objective. He could rely on the support of merchants when he wished to hire their ships in order to form a fleet for defensive or offensive purposes.

Henry Tudor surrounded himself with a number of able councillors, around seventy at any one time. While he promoted those who had supported him during the period of his exile abroad, he also forgave and then promoted former enemies. Thomas Howard, son of the Duke of Norfolk, fought against him at Bosworth in 1485, where his father was killed. By 1501, however, he had been made Lord Treasurer.

In many ways Henry VII's was a traditional, even medieval, approach to kingship and government. Although he took initiatives, notably in the setting up of two new, although fairly short-lived, tribunals in Star Chamber for handling particular types of legal cases, he was more concerned with making an old system work effectively than replacing it with a new.

The conventional view of Henry's skill in government was that he was very competent but miserly. He certainly was accomplished in the art of government but he was no miser, as he kept a magnificent and lavish court. His miserly reputation is founded on the fact that, despite his spending, he managed his financial affairs well, he was unerringly efficient in claiming his dues, and he died leaving a full treasury. The contemporary historian, Polydore Vergil, declared in his *Anglica historia* (1537) that avarice was his only failing, and one to which he only succumbed in the latter part of his reign as he tried to safeguard his son's inheritance:

> 'This avarice is surely a bad enough vice in a private individual, whom it forever torments; in a monarch indeed it may be considered the worst vice, since it is harmful to everyone, and distorts those qualities of trustfulness, justice and integrity by

which the state must be governed.'

Henry followed in the footsteps of Edward IV in trying to extend his personal control over financial matters. His closest servants, members of the Privy Chamber, took on important treasury roles as the royal household was transformed into a government department. The highest office, treasurer of the chamber, was filled by two men during the reign, Sir Thomas Lovell (1485-92) and Sir John Heron (1492-1521). The king also relied heavily on the advice of Sir Reginald Bray, chancellor of the duchy of Lancaster, who was instrumental in increasing the revenue raised on royal estates, and who assisted Heron in the chamber.

The king's ordinary revenue was largely raised from the land owned by the crown. The king's estates were vast, much having been gained through the extinction of family titles on the battlefields of the recent wars, or confiscation following acts of attainder. He inherited all the Yorkist and Lancastrian lands on becoming king and, unlike Edward IV, he proved reluctant to give them to his supporters. He had comparatively few family obligations in this respect, having no brothers and a single son after the death of Prince Arthur in 1502. He outlived both his mother and his wife and their lands too became his when they died. Under the guidance of Bray his estates were managed more profitably from the early 1490s, and the annual income from crown land increased from £29,000 in 1485 to £42,000 in 1509.

The tenants-in-chief, those who had received land from the crown, were expected to fulfil certain feudal obligations. If an estate was inherited by a minor it was placed under the control of the king in his capacity as guardian, until his ward was old enough to take full possession. The ending of this wardship would be marked by another feudal obligation called 'livery', in which a payment had to be made before the lands were returned. A kind of death duty known as 'relief' had to be paid as lands were passed on, and the crown could even profit from the marriage of heiresses by selling suitors the right to marry them or, if an heiress wished to be free to choose, selling her the right instead.

The care Henry took over the collection of feudal dues is revealed in his establishment of special commissions to identify ways of increasing such revenues. New positions, surveyor of the king's wards (1503) and surveyor of the king's prerogative (1508), were created for the same purpose.

Initially the revenue collected from customs duties was even greater than that gathered from the crown lands. Like Edward IV before him, Henry took measures to identify ways in which such revenue could be increased, such as introducing the book of rates, which clarified valuations of particular goods and rates to be paid, and placing a greater emphasis on the need for documentary evidence recording transactions between merchants. Corrupt officials and smugglers were dragged before the courts in large numbers where they could expect to receive severe fines. The amount of income from this source was of course mainly reliant upon the health of the economy and the scale of its import and export trade. In this Henry was fortunate in that his reign coincided with a trade boom based upon greatly increased cloth exports. As S. J. Gunn pointed out, 'Henry was not merely lucky, he had in part made his own luck' by adopting a foreign policy which, whenever possible, encouraged trade.[46]

A significant part of Henry's revenue was made up of fines paid by those found guilty in the law courts. For many offences, fining became the norm, even for quite serious crimes that might, technically, have warranted lengthy prison terms or execution. In addition, enormous fines were imposed upon those who fell out of favour and became attainted.

An important function of parliament was to grant the king extraordinary means of raising money. In times of national crisis, Henry turned to parliament for financial assistance, as in 1496 in the face of threats from Perkin Warbeck and Scotland. The emergency taxes levied in these situations sometimes proved deeply unpopular. This was especially true when the projected wars for which the taxes were raised were never fought. Resentment over parliamentary taxation was a key element in the risings of 1489 and 1492 in Yorkshire and 1497 in Cornwall. For this reason, and because of the opportunity it gave parliament to make demands of the king in return, Henry was reluctant to rely on such sources and tried instead to 'live of his own'.

A less dangerous extraordinary means of raising cash was by asking the wealthiest families for loans. These were both granted and paid back because of the king's and his subjects' mutual interests: to refuse the request would imply an absence of loyalty and this might well result in the imposition of bonds and recognisances. The crown's failure to repay the loan might justify a noble's support for some pretender or

---

[46] S. J. Gunn, *Early Tudor Government* (1995).

other challenger to the throne.

Forced loans or gifts, known as benevolences, were less welcome. These were introduced by Edward IV to finance an invasion of France in 1475. It was assumed that this obligatory 'loan', paid by the rich and for which there was no recompense, was made willingly as a token of loyalty to, and affection for, the king. No wonder then that Polydore Vergil, when he came to write about the subject, suggested a payment of this kind might more appropriately be called a 'malevolence' than a 'benevolence'.

It was customary for monarchs in the period to squeeze money out of the church, too, and Henry was no exception. Like parliament, the church was also expected to raise revenue by taxation in times of crisis. The sale of clerical offices (simony), by which the crown profited, was normal practice. Bishoprics might be left vacant for up to twelve months, while the crown received the revenue from the see before a new appointment was made. The vacancies might arise through the death of an incumbent or because bishops were moved from see to see by royal instruction. Inevitably, appointment to a new bishopric would be accompanied by a 'fine', payable to the crown.

Henry's income was further supplemented by the 'pension' paid by the King of France. This had been negotiated by Edward IV in 1475 and was renewed by Henry in 1492. In return for the pension (around £5,000 per annum) Henry agreed to remove his troops from France and not interfere with French dynastic interests.

Estimates of Henry VII's annual revenue from the main sources:

Crown lands	£40,000 (average 1502-5)
Customs	£37,000 (average 1485-1509)
Parliamentary taxation	£12,000 (average 1485-1509)
Wards and liveries	£9,400 (average 1504-6)
Total revenue	£104,800 (average 1502-5)

The king and the nobility

Henry would have known, when he seized the crown from Richard III at Bosworth, that his own survival as king depended upon his dealings with the other great noble families. His success in containing noble aspirations caused early commentators to identify Henry with an 'anti-noble' policy but this is now considered inaccurate. Henry certainly did restrict the extension of aristocratic influence in a number of cases and, as the history of opposition to his reign reveals, some of the more rebellious lords were destroyed by Acts of Attainder, imprisonment or execution. However, he also promoted the interests of loyal men, noble and non-noble alike, as demonstrated by his generosity in the weeks and months following Bosworth.

There are a number of reasons for supposing, at first sight, that Henry was anti–aristocratic. He was a great deal more reluctant to create new peers than other monarchs such as Edward IV and Henry VIII, and during his reign the nobility diminished in size whereas under Edward it had expanded. Sometimes the king promoted the interests of commoners, over and above those of peers. He relied heavily on two lawyers of non-noble birth, Edmund Dudley and Richard Empson, who did much of the work of collecting noble debts in the form of bonds and recognisances. Dudley and Empson were impeached and executed, accused of challenging Henry VIII's accession, in 1510. Furthermore Henry curbed the might of the nobility by passing, in 1485, 1487 and 1504, laws restricting the keeping of retainers, potential armies of servants and supporters identified by the wearing of their lord's livery. Over half of the peerage in Henry's reign was obliged to give recognisances to the crown, many nobles giving more than one. In most cases these recognisances were not collected in, but peers lived under the threat of having to make possibly crippling payments should they offend the king. This carefully organised use of recognisances in order to guarantee good behaviour was very different to the haphazard approach of Henry's predecessors.

However, as his leniency towards many of those who opposed him demonstrates, Henry could be generous in his dealings with the nobility. The creation of new peerages certainly was limited – Henry VII created one new earl and five new barons in his reign compared to nine and thirteen in Edward IV's. Between the start and end of Edward's reign the total number of nobles had risen from forty-two to forty-six, whereas in Henry's it shrank from fifty to just thirty-five. However, this was compensated to an extent by his bestowing the order of the garter on thirty-seven loyal subjects. This was a cheaper alternative for the crown since, unlike the creation of a new peer, it was not traditionally accompanied by a gift of land. Thus, much of the land received by the crown through the extinction of noble families was retained. Henry's ability to forgive and then reward is most strikingly demonstrated by the career of Thomas Howard, the Earl of Surrey. Despite fighting on the other side at Bosworth, being attainted (hence having all his estates confiscated) and ending up in the Tower, his good behaviour resulted in a gradual restoration. His loyal service to the crown, particularly in containing threats from the north and Scotland, enabled him to regain the greater part of his inheritance and to secure the office of Lord Chancellor. Henry VII was not the first monarch to attempt limiting the military capacity of the nobility, however, his acts against retaining reinforced, and made more effective, Edward IV's of 1468. Retaining was not totally prohibited and the private armies of loyal families were employed in royal campaigns.

The nobility remained important and powerful in the reign of Henry VII. However, circumstances and royal policy enabled the king to keep noble aspirations in check more effectively than had been the case in previous reigns.

Acts of Attainder, bonds and recognisances

Henry VII's dealings with the nobility remain a controversial subject. Although the 'anti-aristocratic' tradition is inaccurate, a case can be made for claiming that Henry's treatment of noble families was more rigorous and interventionist than that of his Yorkist predecessors. His dealings with the nobility continue to be seen by some historians as part of a general revolution in government, initiated by Henry VII and completed in the reign of his son, Henry VIII.

The king certainly relied heavily on the sanction of attainder: 140 Acts of Attainder were passed in Edward IV's reign, 100 in Richard III's, and 138 in Henry VII's, ninety-nine of which were passed directly after the battle of Bosworth. However, as John Guy has explained: 'It used to be argued that Edward IV and Henry VII launched calculated attacks on the power of the nobility after 1461, but this view is refuted by the fact that 84 per cent of noble attainders were reversed.'[47] Forty-two

---

[47] John Guy, *Tudor England* (1988), pp. 7-8.

of Edward's 140 were reversed compared to forty-six of Henry's; just one of Richard's 100 were reversed in his short reign.

A less drastic means of controlling the nobility was through the imposition of bonds and recognizances. David Grossell has eloquently stated the subtle distinction between these concepts:

> 'In their most basic form, bonds are simply written obligations to pay some kind of penalty if certain conditions are not met. Recognizances were a form of bond, which referred to some previous action or misconduct and would impose penalties if good behaviour were not maintained in the future. It was a system not dissimilar to the modern procedure of being bound over to keep the peace.'[48]

The number of peers placed under bond in the reign of Edward IV amounted to just seven compared to thirty-six noble families, out of a total of sixty-two, during the reign of Henry VII.[49]

The King's Council

Fifteenth-century government was centred upon the king and his immediate circle of advisers: members of the king's council. Henry's council, it has been suggested, differed from those of his predecessors in that councillors were selected according to merit and, once chosen, were expected to provide real service. Many of Henry's leading councillors had participated in previous governments. No doubt their experience helped shape the new king's policies as he tried to avoid the mistakes of previous monarchs. It is clear, however, that Henry himself was very much in control of his council and the other institutions through which he governed the realm.

The composition of the king's council helped create the

---

[48] David Grossel, 'The Reign of Henry VII', in John Lotherington (ed.), *The Tudor Years*, (London, 1994), p. 48.

[49] John Guy, *Tudor England* (1988), p. 8.

traditional image of Henry as the monarch who distrusted, and undermined, the nobility. In fact, nobles continued to fill important posts on the council - the Earl of Oxford, for example, was appointed lord great chamberlain and his former opponent at Bosworth, the Earl of Surrey, later became lord treasurer. Of Henry's councillors, thirty had also served in the councils of Edward IV and/or Richard III. In addition to these, however, a number of non-noble men (though several had aristocratic connections), such as Edmund Dudley and Thomas Lovell, received high office on the basis of their ability, not birth. The experience of estate management offered by those born into gentry families was invaluable to a king anxious to extract the greatest profits from crown lands, and so too was the legal training of some of his councillors.

The council was both an advisory and administrative body. Of the total 227 councillors recorded for Henry's reign, no more than forty at anyone time were likely to be sitting in council and most of its work was done by rather smaller groups numbering seven or eight. In this inner circle of regular councils, more councillors than previously were trained lawyers. The most prominent of these, until his death in 1500, was Cardinal Morton who attended nearly all recorded meetings of the council. However, more than forty of Henry's councillors never attended a single meeting.

Different types of business, issues related to maintenance and livery for example, were handled by sub-councils and committees, some of which emerged under Henry.

The Central Common Law Courts, located at Westminster, each headed by a chief justice or equivalent, were divided into three further parts: the King's Bench, the Court of Common Pleas, and the Exchequer. A separate court, The Court of Requests, heard poor men's requests regarding trade and landholding. Chancery was the chancellor's court of equity, for issuing writs and dealing with cases unresolved, or not satisfactorily resolved, in the common law courts.

The Court of General Surveyors was concerned with auditing revenue from crown lands. The Council Learned in Law was created in Henry's reign and was concerned at first with feudal dues and the enforcement of bonds and recognisances, and eventually all aspects of financial policy-making. As a debt-collecting agency it was deeply unpopular. It was presided over by Sir Reginald Bray until 1503 and then by Sir Richard Empson in association with fellow lawyer, Sir Edmund

Dudley, until 1509. Resentment resulted in their impeachment and execution (1510).

Between four and forty councillors met in the Star Chamber in Westminster Palace, so called because of its decorated ceiling. Concerns of the Council in Star Chamber included internal security, defence of the realm, foreign affairs. Financial policy was dealt with elsewhere by a select group of councillors that originally included Chancellor, Archbishop Morton, and Secretary, Bishop Fox. Star Chamber, dominated by clerics, was managed by the Lord Chancellor (John Morton, Archbishop of Canterbury, 1487-1500, William Warham, Archbishop of Canterbury, 1504-15), supported by the king's Secretary of State, the Keeper of the Privy Seal and the Treasurer. The work of the council was dealt with by various, often overlapping, courts and committees.

Established by the Star Chamber Act of 1487, yet another court, the Tribunal for Law Enforcement, was once, mistakenly, identified as the original Court of Star Chamber. Mainly concerned with internal security, it dealt with such matters as maintenance and livery, and riots.

Ancillary provincial courts managed affairs elsewhere in the kingdom. The Council for the North, serving similar functions to the council at Westminster, with a particular interest in maintaining law and order and preventing foreign invasion, met intermittently during the reign. Initially Henry VII pursued a policy of placing it in the hands of the Marcher lords, heads of powerful local families such as the Percys and Dacres. Following the murder of royal tax collector, the Earl of Northumberland, in 1489, Henry modified this policy by dividing responsibility for the council between Lord Dacre and a southern aristocrat, Thomas Howard, the Earl of Surrey. Established in 1471, the Council of Wales and the Marches, was restored, following its termination in 1483, when Prince Arthur Tudor was made Warden of all the Marches in 1490.. This council was based at Ludlow in Shropshire. The Council in the Marches, created in 1499 was an unofficial council in the Midlands established and presided over by the queen mother; Margaret Beaufort, from her seat near Stamford, Lincolnshire.

Parliament

'Since Henry VII governed England as his private estate through his council and household, parliament played no role at all in policymaking but acted as a working instrument of government underpinned by feudal notions [...]'

(John Guy, *Tudor England*, Oxford, 1988, p. 58)

Parliament met seven times under Henry VII: in 1485, 1487, 1489, 1491, 1495, 1497 and 1504. Its sessions totalled a mere twenty-one months in a reign of over twenty-three years. The two parliaments after 1495 sat for just 120 days. During this time it was mostly concerned with financial matters and issues concerning law and order. Acts were passed, for example, to protect the English cloth industry, to clarify the responsibilities of justices of the peace, to regulate wages, and to prevent the keeping of retainers. Every part of every act was signed by the king; Henry kept the same tight control over parliamentary affairs as he did with the council. The franchise was restricted to the elite among burgesses in borough elections and those who held freehold land worth at least forty shillings per annum in county elections. Prospective MPs had to be knights or men of similar standing.

Henry did not launch major campaigns abroad and he, like Edward IV, was granted the customs on wool and woollen cloth exports by his first parliament. This freed him from some of the financial constraints that necessitated the summoning of parliaments in order to impose extraordinary taxes.

Parliament in Henry VII's reign, to paraphrase Roger Lockyer, was not yet a regular or integral part of the machinery of government. Although its 'revolution', in terms of an extended role in government, did not come until after 1529, parliament had an undeniably important role in early Tudor government. It brought together peers, prelates, gentry and urban dignitaries and in so doing provided a sounding board for how proposed royal initiatives might be received. It's backing, while technically not essential, was of great value as the institution which most realistically could claim to represent national public opinion. Although Henry could, and often did, rule by proclamation, statute law made by parliament was the highest law in the land and even kings were subject to the common law. Parliament, therefore, was a crucial means of extending royal authority. Attainders were imposed by Act of parliament and more were passed by his last parliament of 1504 than any before. Parliament's recognition of Henry's right to rule and its legalising of his methods for dealing with troublesome members of the nobility and gentry were highly important to a king trying to establish the credibility and strength of a new dynasty.

The Church

> 'The overall picture of the *Ecclesia Anglicana* [the English church] in Henry VII's reign is that of an institution which, despite its obvious flaws, commanded the voluntary allegiance of the great majority of the English people, from the king downwards.'

(Roger Lockyer, *Henry VII*, 2nd edn, Harlow, 1983, p. 57)

With a council dominated by clerics, the influence of the church in secular affairs was considerable. Clerical skill in legal matters (fifteen of the thirty-three bishops appointed by Henry had degrees in law) was as influential in shaping careers as spirituality or theological knowledge. The appointment of such men to ecclesiastical sees enhanced the management of the church, although the demands of council affairs restricted the time that men such as Archbishop Morton could spend on church matters and amplified the old problem of non-residence. The other 'flaws' mentioned above included pluralism, the widening gulf between the highly paid clerical elite and lesser clergy, and a general decline in monastic standards. The background in a rigorous theological training for bishops further declined (38 per cent of all bishops in Edward IV's reign to just 21 per cent in Henry's), whereas those with a background in Law increased from 50 per cent under Edward IV to 57 per cent under Henry VII.

Through Archbishop Morton, Henry secured good relations between the state and the church and he was also careful to retain the pope's support. This he did by maintaining an entirely orthodox approach to ecclesiastical affairs. He tried to gain the pope's ear by appointing a cardinal protector - a cardinal who agreed to pay particular attention to all papal business that affected England. In line with the general concern for improving the quality of English law, an Act concerning church law was passed in 1489. This addressed the loopholes in the current system whereby the accused might evade common law justice by exercising the privileges of those in holy orders. To demonstrate basic literacy by reading a verse of scripture might be enough, even for a layman, to gain access to the more lenient ecclesiastical courts rather than the ordinary courts under benefit of clergy. Moreover, the taking of refuge (sanctuary) in a religious building could save even those accused of treason from arrest. Sanctuary was now restricted, a papal bull having been secured to make an exemption for traitors, and an Act in 1489 limited the benefit of clergy. Those seeking the privilege a second time had to prove they were in holy orders.

John Colet was prominent in the movement to reform the most glaring abuses of the church. He was much admired by the great humanist, Erasmus, when Erasmus first came to England in 1499. Despite the fact that comparatively little was done to improve matters in the reign of Henry VII, Colet and his circle, which included Thomas More, were supported by the establishment. He found supporters in such influential clerics as John Fisher and Richard Fox, and the king was sufficiently impressed to make him dean of St Paul's in 1504.

While willing to take on board the new humanism, Henry did not tolerate heresy and, during his reign, seventy-three suspected heretics were brought to trial, of whom eleven were burned.

Henry VII, in his religious devotions, was inspired by both political and pious intentions. The sense of divinity in late medieval / early modern kingship prompted kings to assert their role as defenders of the faith, particularly if the nature of their accession was of dubious legitimacy. Henry VII founded new Franciscan houses and ordered prayers to be said throughout the country in support of the King of Spain's crusade against the Moors. His instruction for the completion of Henry IV's chapel at King's College, Cambridge, and Edward IV's chapel at Windsor strengthened his claim to be the one who had managed to reconcile the houses of York and Lancaster.

Early Tudor kingship

For some time now, the sixteenth and seventeenth centuries in England have been termed the 'early modern' period. 1485 has been described as a 'watershed' year, after which things were very different. The Tudors, therefore, Henry VII included, have been regarded as monarchs with a 'modern' approach to government. Recent work in this area, however, questions the extent to which the transition from the medieval to the modern can be clearly seen and pinned down to any particular events or period in the past.

Arguments can be made which support both the 'medievalist' and 'modernist' interpretations of Henry's rule. For example, one might stress his interest in regal mythology: how he, or at least his propagandists, traced his dynasty back beyond 'history' to supposed reigns of such enigmatic figures as King Arthur as described in the influential work of Geoffrey of Monmouth in the early twelfth century, the *History of the Kings of Britain*. On the other hand, Henry commissioned an Italian, Polydore Vergil, to write a new, more trust-worthy, history of the English monarchy.

Medieval monarchs ruled by 'divine right' - a powerful myth that a monarch would not give up lightly. Henry was careful to endorse the myth, to express the institution's divinity through lavish and awe-inspiring display. J. D. Mackie, in *The Earlier Tudors* (1952), wrote of his sense of the 'sacrosanctity' and 'superstition' surrounding the concept of kingship, and commented on the spectacular funerary arrangements he devised for himself in his declining years:

> 'For some years foreign observers had noted his failing health, and on 21 April he died at the age of 52 in his Palace of Richmond. A few days later, after magnificent obsequies, his body was buried in the great chapel which he had begun to build in 1503 and for which he had designed the tomb which to this day attests his good taste and the skill of Torrigiano [...] Chapel [and] tomb [...] are eloquent of Henry's mind. It was essentially a medieval mind.'

In terms of ostentation, G. R. Elton, in *England under the Tudors* (1974), maintained that Henry was even more of a 'medieval' monarch than those who came before him:

> 'The most obvious way in which Henry's kingship differed from that of his predecessors was in the greater stress he laid upon it. Even this far from impressive-looking man fostered the visible dignity of the office and took good care that the greatest of his subjects should appear small by his side. The Tudor court, with its red-coated guard and its vast expenditure on silks, satins, and velvets was always a gorgeous affair, and ceremonial was one thing on which Henry invariably spent in a prodigal manner. The feasts and joustings and displays which attended the visits of foreign potentates, the coronations and weddings of the reign, were things to marvel at, impressive even to the cynical eyes of Venetian and Milanese ambassadors [...] Henry VII built up the formal and ceremonial element in medieval kingship to new heights, even as in other ways he greatly developed its practical attributes.'

The real debate, however, revolves not around the trappings of kingship but the nature of its administration. A 'modern' approach would imply centralised control and a professional and efficient bureaucracy. Compared to his namesake, Henry VI, Henry was very much more in control of his people. The handing over of power into the hands of over-mighty magnates was very much less evident. However, more recent commentators like J. A. F. Thomson in *The Transformation of Medieval England, 1320-1529* (1983) have seen Henry VI's reign and the chaotic, anarchic era of the Wars of the Roses as an unusual rather than a typical profile of medieval styles of kingship:

> 'It is fair to say that Henry VII's approach to government was strongly traditional, and that parallels to it, notably in his reliance on professional administrators, can be traced in the fourteenth century. It was the reign of Henry VI, when magnate influence was excessive, which in fact deviated from customary practice. The search of historians for a 'new monarchy' or a 'more modern' form of kingship, whether of the Yorkists or the Tudors, is in that sense the pursuit of a myth. In political terms, however, there is some justification in regarding Henry VII's accession as the start of a new epoch, because the dynastic change brought

with it in the long run a more securely based royal authority than had previously existed.'

This argument is shared by another 'post-revisionist' historian, Alexander Grant, who in *Henry VII* (1985) endeavoured to prove that 'the contrasts between Henry VII's reign and Edward IV's are more important than the continuities':

> 'the level and extent of Henry's personal control was much greater than his predecessors [...] Moreover, Henry VII's personal government [...] was very different from that of his predecessors [...] The most important revolution in government of the [early Tudor] period was surely the restoration of a high degree of peace and stability throughout most of the country, and its architect was Henry VII. For this reason, his victory over Richard III in August 1485 deserves to be re-established as a major turning point in English history.'

Circumstances more than any conscious plan enabled Henry and his Tudor successors to develop aspects of their government. Factors such as the destruction of actual and potential opposition, and the general weariness of war in the noble families blighted by decades of conflict, provided the dynasty with the right conditions in which to extend its authority and might. In this sense, Henry did pave the way for a 'new', more confident monarchy, and the staggering achievements of his illustrious son - the supreme autocrat, King Henry VIII.

The history of Richard III's reign was originally written almost exclusively by his critics. Henry's early chroniclers were his supporters. Often, they unashamedly, in the case of Edward Hall, for example, produced gushing Tudor propaganda to enhance the reputation of the living monarchs they served and thus promote their own interests. Although Henry VII comes across as a less colourful and attractive character than, say, Edward IV, it remains hard to deny the conclusions of his first biographers. In Hall's view, he was a peculiarly shrewd and consistent monarch, and one hard to fault in either personality or policy:

> 'And so the king, living all his time in the favour of fortune, in high honour, riches and glory, and, for his noble acts and prudent policies, worthy to be registered in the book of fame, gave up his

spirit at the last, which is undoubtedly ascended into the celestial mansion where he has the sure fruition of the godhead, and the joy that is prepared for such as shall sit on the right hand of our saviour, for ever world without end.'

SOURCES

Henry VII's policy after the battle of Bosworth

(Vergil, *Anglica Historia*)

In the previous book we have recounted Richard's actions after the death of Edward, the defection of the nobles, and, further, his own death. Now we shall set out at length what followed afterwards. Henry, the master of events, determined from the beginning of his reign to wipe out sedition. So, before he left Leicester, he sent Robert Willoughby into Yorkshire to bring in Edward, Earl of Warwick, the only surviving son of George, Duke of Clarence, a lad of fifteen, whom Richard had up to then detained in a fortress called Sheriff Hutton. For, indeed, Henry feared that if this lad were to escape, at some time or another, owing to a change in circumstances he might stir up other troubles, for he was not unaware of the habits of the mob, which is always keen for change. Reaching the fortress without delay, Robert received the lad from the governor of the place and brought him to London, where the wretched boy, born to trouble, remained in the Tower until his death, as will be told elsewhere. In the same fortress was the lady Elizabeth, the eldest daughter of King Edward, whom Richard had kept safely with the idea of making her his wife. This the young woman utterly loathed, and for this reason weighed down by her sorrow she daily mourned saying, "I will not be thus married, but miserable creature that I am, I will rather endure the torments which, so they say, St. Catherine bore for love of Christ, than be joined to a man who is the enemy of my family." This young woman, too, was brought to her mother in London, attended by noblewomen. Meanwhile, Henry set out for London, like an emperor on triumph, receiving wherever he went the greatest rejoicing from everyone. For everywhere the people lined the roads to greet him as king, and filled his journey all the way with groaning tables and overflowing cups, so that the weary conquerors might refresh themselves. And when he drew near to the capital, the chief magistrate, known as the "Mayor", and all the citizens came out to meet him and ceremoniously accompanied him as he entered the city, trumpeters leading the way with the spoils of the enemy and sounding martial airs. Thus Henry came into his kingdom after his labours, welcomed by everyone. And afterwards, he called a parliament, according to custom, in which he might receive the crown of the kingdom by popular assent. His first care was to arrange affairs of the state well, and in order that the English people should not be further torn by rival parties, he publicly proclaimed that (as he had already promised) he would take to wife Elizabeth, the daughter of King Edward, and that he would give complete pardon and forgiveness to all who swore obedience to his name. And so, at last, having won the goodwill of all men, he was made King by the will of the nobles and the people, on the 31 October, at Westminster, and he was called Henry, the seventh of that name. These things took place in the year 1486 after the birth of our Saviour.

[…] When he had done these things the king straightway granted his pardon for all past offences to all regardless of party provided they swore allegiance to him, thus deserving well both of friends and enemies. Then he took to wife Elizabeth, the daughter of Edward, a woman shrewd indeed above all others, and at the same time, beautiful this must be regarded as the work of providence, for by this union all the causes of the two most deadly factions were completely destroyed, whereby the two houses of Lancaster and York became one, and from it sprang the true and established royal line which now reigns.

Lambert Simnel's rebellion, 1487

(Vergil, *Anglica Historia*)

Latest among such adventurers was a lowborn priest called Richard, whose surname was Simons, a man as cunning as he was corrupt. He evolved a villainous deed of this sort, by which he might trouble the country's tranquillity. At Oxford, where he devoted himself to scholarship, he brought up a certain youth who was called Lambert Simnel. He first taught the boy courtly manners, so that if ever he should pretend the lad to be of royal descent (as he had planned to do) people would the more readily believe it and have absolute trust in the bold deceit. Some time having elapsed since Henry VII had (as soon as he had gained power) flung Edward, the only son of the Duke of Clarence, into the Tower of London, and since it was popularly rumoured that Edward had been murdered in that place, the priest Richard decided that the time had arrived when he might profitably execute the villainy he had projected. He changed the boy's name and called him Edward, by which name the Duke of Clarence's son was known, and forthwith departed with him to Ireland. There he secretly summoned a meeting of a considerable number of Irish nobles whom he understood by popular report to be ill-disposed to Henry. Having secured their trust, he described to them how he had saved from death the Duke of Clarence's son, and how he had brought him to that land, where (so he had heard) the name and family of King Edward were always cherished. The story was readily believed by the nobles and was soon communicated to others. It was accepted without dispute to such an extent that Thomas Fitzgerald, the Irish-born chancellor of King Henry in the island, was among the first to entertain the boy as if he were of royal descent and to begin to give him all his support. Fitzgerald first called together all his own followers, informed them of the boy's arrival and how the Kingdom of England was his by right as the only male of royal descent, and exhorted them on that account to support him in an attempt to restore the boy to the throne. He then communicated the project to other nobles who, having heard his plan, promised all the help in their power. Thus it quickly came about that the news spread to all Irish cities, which spontaneously transferred their allegiance to the youth and called him king. Then the leaders of the conspiracy sent secret messengers to those in England whom they knew had been of King Richard's party, to implore them to remain loyal and decide upon supporting the boy. Other messengers were dispatched to Edward's sister Margaret in Flanders, the widow of Charles Duke of Burgundy, to demand her assistance also [...] The woman Margaret was not indeed unaware that the House of York had been almost utterly destroyed by her brother Richard, but she was not satisfied with the hatred which had almost obliterated the family of Henry VI, nor mindful of the marriage which, as we have shown, finally united the two Houses of York and Lancaster. She pursued Henry with insatiable hatred and with fiery wrath never desisted from employing every scheme which might harm him as a representative of the hostile faction. Consequently, when she learnt of the new party which had recently arisen against Henry, although she considered the basis of it to be false (as indeed it was), she not only promised assistance to the envoys, but took it upon herself to ally certain other English nobles to those already active in the new conspiracy. Furthermore, Francis Lord Lovell, who had crossed to Flanders at this time, encouraged the woman to undertake more ambitious plans [...]

Lord Lovell's invasion

(Vergil, *Anglica Historia*)

Meanwhile John Earl of Lincoln and Francis Lovell, having received from Margaret an army of about two thousand Germans, whose commander was that most martial man Martin Schwartz, crossed over to Ireland and in the city of Dublin crowned as king the lad Lambert, of ignoble origin and, having changed his name, called Edward, whom falsely (as they very well knew) they called the Duke of Clarence's son. After this, having assembled a great number of the destitute and almost unarmed Irish under the leadership of Thomas Geraldine, they sailed to England with their new king. They landed according to plan on the west coast not far from Lancaster, putting their trust in the wealth and assistance of Thomas Broughton, who was of great authority in that part and who (as was explained above) was one of the conspirators.

King Henry indeed had anticipated what actually happened, and had a little prior to the arrival of the enemy dispatched Christopher Urswick to find out whether the ports on the Lancashire coast were capable of handling large ships; so that if they proved likely to be useful to his enemies he could at once so place his soldiers as to deny them the coast. Christopher carried out these orders and, after he had learnt from the depth of the bed of the sea that the ports were deep, returned to the king. But on his way he was informed of the sudden landing of the enemy, sent ahead a messenger to tell the king of the approach of his enemies and, following on the heels of the messenger, himself gave a fuller account of the whole matter. The king was at Coventry when he received the messenger, and, abandoning all other business, he judged he must set out forthwith against the foe wherever he might betake himself, lest time should be given him for assembling greater forces. He marched to Nottingham and encamped not far from the town in a wood which is called Banrys in the vernacular. Accompanied by a great number of armed men, George Talbot Earl of Shrewsbury, George Lord Strange, and John Cheyney, all outstanding captains, with many others well versed in military affairs, came to him there [...]

The battle of Stoke

(Vergil, *Anglica Historia*)

[...] it was only then, when the battle was over, that it was fully apparent how rash had been the spirit inspiring the enemy soldiers: for of their leaders John Earl of Lincoln, Francis Lord Lovell, Thomas Broughton, and the most bold Martin Schwartz and the Irish captain Thomas Geraldine were slain in that place [...]. Lambert the false boy king was indeed captured, with his mentor Richard: but each was granted his life - the innocent lad because he was too young to have himself committed any offence, the tutor because he was a priest. Lambert is still alive to this very day, having been promoted trainer of the king's hawks; before that for some time he was a turnspit and did other menial jobs in the royal kitchen.

The Treaty of Medina del Campo, 1489

The terms of this treaty included:

1 A true friendship and alliance shall be observed henceforth between Ferdinand and Isabella, their heirs and subjects, on the one part, and Henry, his heirs and subjects, on the other part. They promise to assist one another in defending their present and future dominions against any enemy whatsoever.

2 Neither party shall in any way favour the rebels of the other party, nor permit them to be favoured or stay in his dominions.

5 Henry is not to conclude peace, alliance, or treaties with France without the sanction of Ferdinand and Isabella, who, on their side, bind themselves to the same effect with respect to Henry.

6 As often as and whenever Ferdinand and Isabella make war with France, Henry shall do the same, and conversely.

17 In order to strengthen this alliance the Princess Catherine is to marry Prince Arthur [...]

A letter from Perkin Warbeck to Isabella of Castile, 1493

Most serene and most excellent princess, most honoured Lady and cousin, I commend me entirely to your Majesty. When the Prince of Wales, eldest son of Edward formerly King of England [...] my dearest lord and father, was miserably put to death, and I myself, then nearly nine years old, was also delivered to a certain lord to be killed, it pleased the Divine Mercy that the lord [...] should preserve me alive and unhurt. First, however, he caused me to swear on the holy sacrament that I would not disclose my name, origin or family to anyone until a certain number of years had elapsed. He sent me abroad therefore, with two persons to watch over and take charge of me. Thus I, an orphan, bereaved of my royal father and brother, an exile from my kingdom, and deprived of my country, inheritance, and fortune, a fugitive in the midst of extreme perils, led my wretched life in fear and grief and weeping, and for nearly eight years lay hidden in various provinces. At length, when one of those who had charge of me was dead and the other had returned to his country [...] I remained a while, scarcely emerged from childhood, alone and without means in the kingdom of Portugal. From there I sailed to Ireland where I was recognised by the illustrious lords, the Earls of Desmond and Kildare [...] and by other noblemen of the island, and was received with great joy and honour. When the King of France invited me with many ships and attendants and promised me aid against Henry of Richmond, the wicked usurper of the kingdom of England, I came here to the aforesaid King of France, who received me honourably as a kinsman and friend. Since the promised assistance was not forthcoming, I went to the illustrious Princess, the lady Duchess of Burgundy, my father's sister and my very dear aunt, who [...] welcomed me [...] I promise if the Divine Grace should restore to me my hereditary kingdom that I shall continue with both Your Majesties in closer alliance and friendship.

Perkin Warbeck and Margaret, duchess of Burgundy

(Vergil, *Anglica Historia*)

[...] Charles [VIII of France] summoned Peter [i.e. Perkin] to him in order to arm him against Henry, who was then attacking him. Peter was most agreeably surprised by this message, for now he had begun to number kings among his friends, and he at once betook himself to Charles, by whom he was kindly received honoured with a retinue and all the other dignities which were fitting for a man of royal descent. Soon after this, however, peace having been made with the English [...] Charles dismissed the man, who returned his hopes dashed, to Margaret in Flanders. Margaret received Peter on his return as though he had been raised from the dead and as if (so she dissembled) she had never cast eyes on him before; so great was her pleasure that her happiness seemed to have disturbed the balance of her mind. So that her rejoicing should be noted by all, she publicly congratulated her nephew on his preservation and took pleasure in hearing him repeat the tale of how, having been saved by a ruse from death, he had wandered among many peoples, in order by this means that she might convince all that he was indeed Richard the son of her brother Edward. Thereafter she started to treat the youth with great respect and for her sake the Flemings likewise all exalted him. The more the deceit was given an appearance of truth, the more people professed that they believed the youth had escaped the hand of King Richard by divine intervention and had been led safely to his aunt.

The rumour of so miraculous an occurrence rapidly spread to neighbouring countries and even more quickly crossed into England, where the story was not merely believed by the common people, but where there were many important men who considered the matter as genuine. As a result, when it began to be rumoured that Richard, King Edward's son, was alive and that among the Flemings he was held in great esteem, conspiracies immediately began to multiply, just as in spring the trees always clothe themselves in a multitude of flowers. On the one hand there were the desperadoes who, on account of the various crimes they had committed, were taking refuge in sanctuaries; these were induced by poverty or bribes to break forth and flock to Peter in Flanders. On the other hand, many among the nobility turned to conspiracy; some were actuated by mere foolhardiness; others, believing Peter to be Edward's son Richard, supported the claim of the Yorkist party; others again, considering themselves ill-rewarded by King Henry for the services they had zealously rendered on his behalf, were moved partly by resentment and partly by greed; lastly, there were others whose desire for a revolution flung them headlong into this conspiracy. But all this happened somewhat later [...]

Meanwhile the rumour of Richard, the resuscitated Duke of York, had divided nearly all England into factions, filling the minds of men with hope or fear. For there was no one who was not deeply concerned over such an affair. Each, according to his disposition, anticipated either peril or profit. The king indeed and his friends marvelled that anyone could have fabricated such a fiction as to make a transparent untruth gain such currency as truth, and to make many of his magnates (for already he perceived plainly that this had happened) consider it as established fact. Hence Henry feared that, unless the deception was quickly recognised as such by all, some great upheaval would occur. There were some who were pleased by the new situation and considered the facts to be true and not false, hoping thereby to benefit themselves; the conspirators in particular were confident that it would come about. And since this type of crime is always more dangerous actually to attempt than merely to plot, it was accordingly decided by the conspirators to send some of their number to Margaret in Flanders, who should learn when Richard Duke of York would be ready to make his way to England; and who should promptly inform them so that, when he did arrive, they could come forward with timely support. With general consent Sir Robert Clifford was sent to Flanders, with William Barley, and he revealed to Margaret all the plans of the conspirators. Margaret was exceedingly pleased by Robert's arrival and easily persuaded him that all which had been rumoured concerning Duke Richard was true. Later she showed him her Peter, who had assumed the part of Richard with great skill. Having seen the youth, Robert forthwith believed him to be of royal descent and reported in this sense to the conspirators. Having received Robert's message, the conspirators, in order to rouse up a popular upheaval, everywhere asserted that to be true which had previously been spoken of publicly concerning the Duke of York. But they did this with such artfulness, that none who heard could be certain as to who was responsible for the rumour.

When the king saw the pernicious tale gather authority among the people, he suspected what was in fact the case, that some members of the nobility were conspiring against him (indeed evidence of this was the sudden departure of Robert Clifford); and he at once sent some knights with carefully picked troops to guard the coast and ports. They were to prevent anyone being able to sail, so that no one should be able to cross to the continent or land in the island; and to guard diligently all roads and footpaths lest anyone should approach the shore, and lest anywhere there should be gatherings of many men [...]

During this time the king sent spies into Flanders, some indeed who, pretending they fled to the rediscovered Duke of York, were to find out the conspirators' plans and their names; and yet others who, with an offer of forgiveness, were to persuade Robert Clifford and William Barley to return. These emissaries performed both their duties well, they learnt the names of some of the conspirators and persuaded Robert Clifford to return. William Barley, indeed, would hear nothing of returning then, but two years later, having been forgiven by Henry, he came to his senses and returned home. In this fashion the spies secretly left the false duke one at a time and coming back to Henry carefully reported all that they had found out. Several of them remained in order to accompany Robert when he returned. All the conspirators identified by the spies were ordered by the king to be arrested and brought to him at London. Among the nobles arrested were John Ratcliffe Lord Fitzwalter, Sir Simon Mountford, Sir Thomas Thwaites, William Daubeney, Robert Ratcliffe, Richard Lacy and many more. There were also several priests, who were more sound in body than in mind, to wit brother William Richford, provincial of the English Dominicans, and William Sutton, both learned men and distinguished preachers, William Worsley Dean of St Paul's, Robert Layborne and Thomas Powys, Prior of Langley and a Dominican. The other conspirators, when they heard that the conspiracy had been found out, fled to various sanctuaries. They were all taken and condemned for treason; from their number Simon Mountford, Robert Ratcliffe and William Daubeney were executed as the leaders and instigators of the plot. The remainder, including the priests (out of reverence for their cloth), were spared. The penalty was remitted for John Lord Fitzwalter, but he was sent to Calais; because, while imprisoned there, he had bribed the guards and tried to escape, he also was soon beheaded [...]

Warbeck's invasion of Kent, 1495

(*The Great Chronicle of London*)

Also upon the third day of July arrived at a place or haven in Kent named the Deal, a certain persons to the number of five hundred or more, the which were of the adherents of that ungracious mawmet in Flanders, that had deceived so many men by th'aid and comfort of a few lewd persons as after will appear. This now being accompanied with fourteen small sails, and thinking that by the commons of Kent that he should have been aided, caused the said number to land, and himself with other rascal hoved still upon the water fast by. And when those other had been a certain season upon land, and saw no comfort of people drawing to them ward, but rather tokens of discomfort, they withdrew little and little toward their ships. Whereof the Mayor of Sandwich being ware, with such a company as tofore he had provided, came so fast upon them that some were compelled to fight, while the other fled to their ships. In the which fight a few were slain, and upon an hundred and sixty taken on live among the which were four named captains called Mountford, Corbet, White and Belt, which Mountford was the son of Sir Simon Mountford before beheaded. And when the chief rebel with the residue of his lewd company saw his men thus slain and taken, seeing well that there was no tarrying to his profit, in all haste hoisted up his sails and after drew westward, and the other thus taken, were led unto Sandwich, and so forth toward London, that upon the 12th day of July foresaid, Sir John Pecche then Sheriff of Kent brought them railed in cart ropes as horses been traced to draw in a cart and some in carts unto London bridge foot where the Sheriffs of London being ready received of the said rebels by tale an hundred and fifty-nine, of the which forty-two were sent unto Newgate, and the remnant were had to the Tower. These were most Flemings and other outlandish men as gunners and other such as lived by theft and ravine.

Perkin Warbeck's assault on Exeter, 1497

(*The Great Chronicle of London*)

And in this month of September landed in an haven of Cornwall, Perkin Warbeck, with three small ships only, as it was reported, and with him to the number of six score [i.e. 120] persons or fewer, which rode unto a village named Bodmin whereas then drew unto him more people, so that, shortly after, his company was numbered at 3000 or above, whereof the most part were naked men and rascals, the whole flock. Then he, thus being accompanied, made his proclamations, and named himself King Richard the 4th, and second son unto Edward IV, late King, and so, being established with three noble captains and his chief counsellors, that is to mean John Heron, mercer, of London, which before days had fled the city of London for debt, Richard Skelton and John Asteley, a scrivener, of like authority, and dishonest, sped him towards Exeter, and upon the 17th day of September assaulted the said town in two places, that is to wit, at the East and North gates. But by the manly knighthood of the Earl of Devonshire, and the help of the citizens, he was there put off, and upon 200 of his men there slain. Then, upon the morrow, they made another assault and then fired the gates and fought sharply for the while, but by the prowess of the forenamed earl, and good assistance of the said citizens, they were again beaten off, to their more shame and damage, at which said second assault the said earl was hurt in the arm with an arrow, and so were divers others, but few or none, thanked be God, slain. When Perkin with his rebels saw the mighty defence that of the city of Exeter was made, and the peril of him and his, if he there longer rested, he, as dismayed, considering the loss and hurt of his adherents, departed thence, and took his way toward Taunton where, upon the Wednesday following, being the 20th day of September he, in the fields adjoining, mustered and counted the number of his adherents, the which he found diminished and somewhat decreased, for when the poor and needy people saw the rescue and defence made against him at the city of Exeter, and that no men of honour, nor yet of honesty, drew unto him as they before were put in comfort by him and by his lewd counsellors, anon they withdrew by sundry and secret companies from him, in providing their own safeguard. The which, he then perceiving, as a man comfortless, passed forth that day with dissembled countenance, and at night with 60 horsemen in a company, in the dead of the night, departed from that place and secretly came unto a sanctuary town besides Southampton, named Beaulieu, where he, with certain of his accomplices, were registered as John Heron and other for sanctuary men, upon the Friday after his foresaid departure from the poor commons, his adherents. Anon, as this was known, my lord chamberlain being sent towards him with a company of Dears and others, sent in all possible wise then toward the seaside [...] to keep him from the sea, and to search the country, if they might hear of him, the which shortly after were informed that he was in the forenamed sanctuary town, whither forthwith were sent certain persons to see that he and his accomplices were surely kept till the King's pleasure were further known. And in the time of the rage of this Perkin, a rebel and rover named James [and his retinue] met and took the provost of Penrhyn, and so brought him unto the foresaid town of Taunton, and there tyrannously dismembered him in the market place, and after shewed unto the people that he was one of the chief procurers and occasioners of the rebellion of the Cornish men by reason that he, being admitted for a commissioner in those parts, levied of them much more money than came unto the King's use, which caused great murmur and grudge among the commons towards the King, and lastly rebellion as after ensued. [...] Upon the Sunday following came a messenger from the King unto the mayor ascertaining him that Perkin was taken, wherefore the mayor assembled his brethren at Saint Paul's and there caused *Te Deum* to be sung in most solemn wise. And upon the Wednesday following was tidings brought to the said mayor that the said Perkin, with certain of his accomplices as John Heron and others, were brought to the King's presence at Taunton [...]

Perkin Warbeck's confession, 1496

First it is to be known that I was born in the town of Tournai, and my father's name is called John Osbek; which said John Osbeck was controller of the town of Tournai. And my mother's name is Kateryn de Faro. And one of my grandsires upon my father's side was called Deryk Osbeck, which died; after whose death my grandmother was married unto [...] Peter Flamme; and that other of my grandsires was called Peter Flam, which was receiver of the foresaid town of Tournai and dean of the boatmen that be upon the water or river of Leystave. And my grandsire upon my mother's side was called Peter Faro, the which had in his keeping the keys of the gate of St. John's, within the above-named town of Tournai. Also I had an uncle named Master John Stalyn dwelling in the parish of St Pyas within the same town, which had married my father's sister, whose name was Johane or Jane, with whom I dwelled a certain season; and afterward I was led by my mother to Antwerp for to learn Flemish in an house of a cousin of mine, officer of the said town, called John Stienbek, with whom I was the space of half a year. And after that I returned again unto Tournai by reason of the wars that were in Flanders. And within a year following I was sent with a merchant of the said town of Tournai named Berlo, and his master's name Alex, to the mart of Antwerp, where as I fell sick, which sickness continued upon me five months; and the said Berlo set me to board in a skinner's house, that dwelt beside the house of the English nation. And by him I was brought from thence to the Barowe Mart, and lodged at the Sign of th'Old Man, where I abode the space of two months. And after this the said Berlo set me with a merchant in Middleburgh to service for to learn the language, whose name was John Strewe, with whom I dwelled from Christmas unto Easter; and then I went into Portugal in the company of Sir Edward Brampton's wife in a ship which was called the Queen's ship. And when I was comen thither I was put in service to a knight that dwelled in Lisbon, which was called Peter Vacz de Cogna, with whom I dwelled an whole year, which said knight had but one eye; and then because I desired to see other countries I took licence of him. And then I put myself in service with a Breton, called Pregent Meno, the which brought me with him into Ireland. And when we were there arrived in the town of Cork, they of the town, because I was arrayed with some clothes of silk of my said master's, came unto me and threped upon me [asserted] that I should be the Duke of Clarence son, that was before time at Dublin. And for as much as I denied it there was brought unto me the Holy Evangelist and the Cross by the mayor of the town, which was called John Lewelyn; and there in the presence of him and other I took mine oath as truth was that I was not the fore said duke's son, nother of none of his blood. After this came unto me an English man, whose name was Steffe Poytron, with one John Water, and said to me in swearing great oaths, that they knew well I was King Richard's bastard son; to whom I answered with high oaths that I were not. And then they advised me not to be a-feared but that I should take it upon me boldly, and if I would so do they would aid and assist me with all their power again the King of England; and not only they, but they were well assured that the Earls of Desmond and Kildare should do the same, for they forsid [cared] not what party so that they might be revenged upon the King of England; and so against my will made me to learn English, and taught me what I should do and say. And after this they called me Duke of York, the second son of King Edward the fourth, because King Richard's bastard son was in the hands of the King of England. And upon this the said John Water, Steffe Poytron, John Tiler, Hubert Bourgh, with many other, as the foresaid earls, entered into this false quarrel. And within short time after this the French king sent unto me an embassy into Ireland, whose names was Loyte Lucas and Master Steffes Frion, to advertise me to come into France; and thence I went into France, and from thence into Flanders, and from Flanders into Ireland, and from Ireland into Scotland and so into England.

The Cornish rebellion, 1497

(Holinshed's chronicle)

These unruly people, the Cornishmen, inhabiting in a barren country and unfruitful, at the first sore repined that they should be so grievously taxed and burdened by the king's council [...] And thus being in a rave, two persons [...] the one called Thomas Flammock, a gentleman learned in the laws of the realm, and the other Michael Joseph, a smith, men of stout stomachs and high courage, took upon themselves to be captains of this seditious company. They laid the fault and cause of this exaction unto John Morton, Archbishop of Canterbury, and to Sir Reginald Bray, because they were chief of the King's council [...] Flammock and Joseph exhorted the common people to put on harness and not be afeared to follow them in that quarrel, promising not to hurt any creature, but only to see them punish that procured such exactions to be laid on the people, without any reasonable cause, as under the colour of a little trouble with the Scots, which (since they were withdrawn home) they took to be well quieted and appeased. So these captains, bent on mischief [...] persuaded a great number of people to assemble together and [...] do as their captains would [...] appoint. Then these captains [...] set forth with their army and came to Taunton, where they slew the Provost of Perin, which was one of the commissioners of the subsidy, and from thence came to Wells, so intending to go to London [...] When the King was advertised of these doings, he was somewhat astonished [...] being thus troubled with the war against the Scots and this civil commotion of his subjects at one instant. But first meaning to subdue his rebellious subjects and after to proceed against the Scots, as occasion would serve; he revoked the Lord Daubeney which [...] was going against the Scots, and increased his army with many chosen and picked warriors. Also mistrusting that the Scots might now (having such opportunity) invade the realm again, he appointed the Lord Thomas Howard, Earl of Surrey (which after the death of the Lord Dinham was made high treasurer of England) to gather a band of men in the county of Palatine of Durham, that they, with the aid of the inhabitants adjoining and the borderers, might keep back the Scots if they chanced to make any invasion. The nobles of the realm, hearing of the rebellion of the Cornishmen, came to London every man with as many men of war as they could put in a readiness to aid the King if need should be [...]

In the meantime, James Twitchet, Lord Audley being confederate with the rebels of Cornwall [...] being come to Wells, and took it upon him as their chief captain to lead them against the natural lord and king [...] The captains of the rebels [...] brought their people to Blackheath, a four miles distant from London, and there in a plain on top of an hill they ordered their battles, either ready to fight with the King if he would assail them, or else assault the city of London; for they thought the King durst not have encountered with them [...]

The city was in a great fear [...] the rebels were encamped so near the city, every man getting himself to harness and placing themselves some at the gates some on the walls, so that no part was undefended.

The defeat of the Cornish rebels, 1495

(John Stowe, *Annals of England*)

From Wells they went to Salisbury and from thence to Winchester, and so into Kent, where they hoped to have great aid, but they were deceived: for the Earl of Kent, George Bergaveny, John Brooke, Lord Cobham, Sir Edward Poynings, Sir Richard Guilford, Sir Thomas Bourchier, John Peche, William Scott, and a great number of people were ready to defend the country, which thing marvellously dismayed the Cornishmen, so that many of them fled the company. The captains brought their people to Blackheath, and there ordered their battles, either ready to fight with the king if he would assail them, or else assault the City of London. The king sent John, Earl of Oxford, Henry Bourchier, Earl of Essex, Edmond de la Pole, Earl of Suffolk, Sir Rise ap Thomas, and Sir Humphrey Stanley, noble warriors, with a great company of archers and horsemen, to environ the hill on either side, to the intent that all by ways being stopped, all hope of flight should be taken from them, and incontintently he himself being furnished with a great army, set forward out of the city, encamped himself in St. George's Field where he lodged that night, and on the next morning sent the Lord Daubney with a great company to set upon them early in the morning, which first got the bridge at Deptforde Strande, while the earls set on them on every side, the Lord Oaubney came into the field with his company, and without long fighting on the 22nd of June, the Cornishmen were overcome [...] there were slain of the rebels about 300, and taken of them, about 1,500 [...] the king wanted of all his number but 300 men, which were slain [...] The Lord Audley was drawn from Newgate to the Tower Hill in a coat of his own arms painted upon paper, reversed and torn and there beheaded [...] Flamocke and Joseph the blacksmith were drawn, headed and quartered at Tilburn, and their heads and quarters set up at London and other places, and at London Bridge foot.

War and diplomacy

(Vergil, *Anglica Historia*)

While the English were taken up with these affairs [the Cornish rebellion] news reached James, King of Scots, that no English army had been prepared against him, and that king Henry and some nobles with the men of Cornwall were waging civil war amongst themselves. James, thinking a splendid chance had been provided for a successful operation, once again hurriedly invaded the English border territory, laying waste everything with slaughter, fire, and pillage. While part of his forces laid waste the county of Durham James himself, with the rest of his forces began a siege of the strongest castle on the Anglo-Scottish border, called locally Norham, which belongs to the Bishop of Durham. Shortly before the Scottish attack Richard Fox, Bishop of Durham, had provided the castle with a strong guard, for he had anticipated that once the Scottish king heard of the rising in England he would break through the English borders on a sudden raid. This same Richard, whom we mentioned above as Bishop of Exeter was later, on account of his great loyalty, honesty, and discretion called to the see of Bath and Wells, and was afterwards translated from that see to Durham. He at once, by frequent messengers, informed the king (who was then in London) of everything that had happened. Other messengers he sent to summon as quickly as possible Thomas, Earl of Surrey, who had collected a strong force in Yorkshire, to come by forced marches to the relief of Norham. Thomas, realizing the urgency, went quickly, as did the other magnates of the region, each of them collecting, according to his resources, a small or large band of troops.

In the meantime the Scots, after spending many days besieging the castle and incurring great losses without breaching the fortifications, decided of their own will to withdraw. When, shortly afterwards, they discovered that Earl Thomas was drawing near with his troops, and that the English were gathering around in various places, they raised the siege and withdrew into Scotland, taking with them as much loot as they could. When Thomas heard of the flight of the enemy he invaded Scotland in pursuit, and laid waste the land. Since, however, he could nowhere come upon the enemy, and owing to the speed with which he had made his pursuit, he had not taken with him provisions for more than a few days, he was forced, as a result, to return in haste to Durham county. Pitching his camp there he decided to await a more favourable chance to get to grips with the enemy.

In the middle of these events Pedro de Ayala, a man not learned, but very clever, and extremely discreet, came to Scotland, sent by Ferdinand, King of Spain to king James, to negotiate a peace between the kings of England and Scotland. For Ferdinand and his wife Isabella, a most remarkable woman of our time, whose virtues will ever be the admiration of posterity, had the most friendly feelings towards king Henry, wishing him well, and anxious to make a marriage alliance with him. They had in their family a marriageable daughter Catherine, whom they sought to marry to Henry's elder son, Arthur, shortly before this created Prince of Wales. Ferdinand therefore was all the more willing to put himself forward to each king as a peacemaker. Pedro at once began to discuss peace terms with king James: and when he discovered that the king was not unfavourably inclined, he wrote at once to king Henry suggesting that he should entrust the task of making peace to one of his subjects, with whom he might negotiate the terms for a treaty with the Scottish king. Henry was a lover of peace so long as it could be gained without disadvantage to himself, and he particularly wanted it at this time when he was troubled by sedition amongst his subjects. He at once entrusted the negotiations to Richard, Bishop of Durham, to whom he usually left the conduct of all his affairs. So Richard and Pedro as an impartial mediator met the Scottish envoys and proceeded to discuss the business of a treaty. After long discussions it was found impossible to agree upon any peace terms. This was because King Henry insisted that Peter Warbeck should be handed over to him. On the other hand, king James specially urged that he could not hand Peter over into the hands of his enemy: although James was at last beginning to be aware of Margaret's deceit, but because he was related to the young man by marriage he deemed it dishonourable to deliver him up to his death. At last, after many days of discussion, a treaty of lasting friendship was agreed, which they preferred to call a truce for a period of years. Among other clauses in this treaty or truce the most important clause was that James should expel Peter Warbeck from his kingdom. And so peace was established between the two kings.

While these negotiations were being carried on in the north Henry in the meantime received in London the ambassadors of king Charles whom we have described above as being deliberately held up at Dover lest the upheaval in the country should reach their ears. Henry congratulated them on the safe return of Charles, and shortly afterwards dismissed them, giving them rich gifts. Henry also received with courtesy the ambassadors of the archduke Philip sent to him at the same time, or a little earlier or later, to negotiate a treaty, and after long discussions with them a treaty of perpetual friendship was made with Philip. Having thus established friendly relations with neighbouring princes Henry then wrote to king Ferdinand, sending him his most sincere thanks for acting as intermediary for peace between him and the Scottish king. Pedro de Ayala, Ferdinand's envoy, was indeed considered so deserving that he was not presented with many gifts, and then promoted to several valuable ecclesiastical preferments in England. These agreements between the kings were arrived at in that year which was 1498, after the birth of our Saviour, and the twelfth from the beginning of Henry's reign.

Ralph Wulford's pretence, 1499

(*The Great Chronicle of London*)

In this passing of time in the borders of Norfolk and Suffolk was a new mawmet areared which named himself to be the forenamed Earl of Warwick, the which by sly and covert means essayed to win to him some adherents. But all in vain. In conclusion he was brought before the Earl of Oxford, to whom at length he confessed that he was born in London, and that he was son unto a cordyner [cordwainer] dwelling at the Black Bull in Bishopsgate Street, after which confession he was sent up to the king and from him to prison, and upon that arraigned and convict of treason, and finally upon Shrove Tuesday hanged at St Thomas Watering in his shirt, where he so hung still till the Saturday following, and then

[...] he was taken down and buried, being of the age of nineteen years or twenty. And as it was of him after reported, he confessed that being at Cambridge at school he was sundry times stirred in his sleep that he should name himself to be the Duke of Clarence's son and he should in process obtain such power that he should be king.

A description of Henry VII

(Vergil, *Anglica Historia*)

His body was slender but well built and strong; his height above the average. His appearance was remarkably attractive and his face was cheerful, especially when speaking; his eyes were small and blue, his teeth few, poor and blackish; his hair was thin and white; his complexion sallow. His spirit was distinguished, wise and prudent; his mind was brave and resolute, and never, even at moments of the greatest danger, deserted him. He had a most pertinacious memory. Withal he was not devoid of scholarship. In government he was shrewd and prudent, so that no one dared to get the better of him through deceit or guile. He was gracious and kind and was as attentive to his visitors as he was easy of access. His hospitality was splendidly generous; he was fond of having foreigners at his court and he freely conferred favours on them. But those of his subjects who were indebted to him and who did not pay him due honour or who were generous only with promises, he treated with harsh severity. He well knew how to maintain his royal majesty and all which appertains to kingship at every time and in every place. He was most fortunate in war, although he was constitutionally more inclined to peace than to war. He cherished justice above all things; as a result he vigorously punished violence, manslaughter and every other kind of wickedness whatsoever. Consequently he was greatly regretted on that account by all his subjects, who had been able to conduct their lives peaceably, far removed from the assaults and evil doing of scoundrels. He was the most ardent supporter of our faith, and daily participated with great piety in religious services. To those whom he considered to be worthy priests, he often secretly gave alms so that they should pray for his salvation. He was particularly fond of those Franciscan friars whom they call Observants, for whom he founded many convents, so that with his help their rule should continually flourish in his kingdom. But all these virtues were obscured latterly only by avarice, from which [...] he suffered. This avarice is surely a bad enough vice in a private individual, whom it forever torments; in a monarch indeed it may be considered the worst vice, since it is harmful to everyone, and distorts those qualities of trustfulness, justice and integrity by which the state must be governed.

The kingdom of Henry VII

(*Calendar of State Papers Venetian I 1202-1509*)

[...] this kingdom is perfectly stable, by reason, first, of the King's wisdom, whereof everyone stands in awe; and, secondly, on account of the King's wealth, for I am informed that he has upwards of six millions of gold, and it is said that he puts by annually five hundred thousand ducats, which is of easy accomplishment, for his revenue is great and real, not a written schedule, nor does he spend anything. He garrisons two or three fortresses, contrary to the custom of his predecessors, who garrisoned no place. He has neither ordnance nor munitions of war, and his body guard is supposed not to amount to one hundred men [...] He well knows how to temporise, as demonstrated by him before my arrival in this kingdom, when the French ambassadors wanted to go to Scotland under pretence of mediating for the peace, but he entertained them magnificently, made them presents, and sent them home without seeing Scotland; and now he sends one of his own gentlemen in waiting to France. The Pope is entitled to much praise, for he loves the King cordially, and strengthens his power by ecclesiastical censures, so that at all times rebels are excommunicated.

An Act of Attainder, 1491

Forasmuch as Sir Robert Chamberleyn [...] knight, and Richard White gentleman [...] traitorously imagined and compassed the death and destruction of our said sovereign lord, and also the subversion of all this realm, then and there traitorously levied war against our said sovereign lord and adhered them traitorously to Charles the French king, ancient enemy to our said sovereign lord and this realm, against their duty and liegance; Be it therefore ordained and enacted by authority of this present parliament that the said Robert and Richard stand and be attainted of high treason, and forfeit all manors, lands, tenements, rents, reversions and all other hereditaments […]

Bonds and recognisances

24 December 1507

Indenture between the King and the same George, Lord Burgavenny: whereas George is indebted to the King in £100,000 or thereabouts for unlawful receivers done, retained and made by him in Kent contrary to certain laws and statutes, as was found by inquisitions certified into the King's Bench and adjudged after free confession by him in the said court in Michaelmas term last; and whereas for execution and levy of this debt, being clearly due both in law and conscience, the King may attach his body and keep him in prison and take all the issues of his lands till the whole sum be paid; the King is graciously contented, at his suit for avoiding the extremity of the law, to accept as parcel of the debt the sum of £5,000 payable over ten years at Candlemas and the Purification; for which payments, as well as the residue of the debt, George binds himself and his heirs.

Given 24 December, 23 Henry VII. Cancelled by warrant, 1 Henry VIII.

A licence to retain

Henry, by the grace of God, King of England and of France and lord of Ireland - greeting […] WE […] by the advice of our Council, intending to provide a good, substantial and competent number of captains and able men of our subjects to be in a readiness to serve us at our pleasure when the case shall require, and trusting in your faith and truth, will and desire you, and […] by these presents give unto your full power and authority from henceforth during our pleasure to take, appoint and retain by indenture or covenant in form or manner as hereafter ensueth, and none otherwise, such persons our subjects as by your discretion shall be thought and seemeth to you to be able men to do us service in the war in your company under you and at your leading at all times and places and as often as it shall please us to command or assign you, to the number of - persons, whose names be contained in a certificate by you made in a bill of parchment indented betwixt us and you and interchangeably signed by us and subscribed with your hand and to our secretary delivered [...] PROVIDED always that you retain not above the said number which you shall indent for in form and manner hereafter ensuing. PROVIDED also the same able persons shall not be chosen, taken nor retained but only of your own tenants or of the inhabitants within any office that you have of our grant [...] And these our present letters shall be unto you, and all and every the persons by you to be retained in form above specified and indented for with us, and such other as you shall retain in the place of any of them died, avoided or discharged as above is specified, sufficient discharge in this behalf at all times hereafter, any act, statute, prohibition or other ordinance in the time of us or any of our noble progenitors or predecessors, by authority of parliament or otherwise, heretofore made, enacted, passed or ordained to the contrary notwithstanding. PROVIDED always that you, under colour hereof or by virtue of these our letters of placard, retain no more in number by word, promise or otherwise than is contained in your said certificate indented and indented for with us as above, under the pains specified in our statutes made and ordained in that behalf.

The king's bodyguards

(Vergil, *Anglica Historia*)

Henry, moreover, was the first English king to appoint retainers, to the number of about two hundred, to be a bodyguard [Yeomen of the Guard]: these he incorporated in his household so that they should never leave his side; in this he imitated the French kings so that he might thereafter be better protected from treachery.

Tonnage and poundage, 1485

To the worship of God. We, your poor Commons, by your high commandment come to this your present Parliament assembled, grant by this present indenture to you, our sovereign lord, for the defence of this your said realm, and in especial for the safeguard and keeping of the sea, a subsidy called Tonnage, to be taken in manner and form following: that is to say, iiis. of every Ton of wine coming into this your said realm, and of every Ton of sweet wine coming into the same your realm; by every merchant alien, as well by the merchants of Hansa and of Almain as of any other merchant aliens, iiis. over the said iiis. afore granted: to have and to perceive yearly the said subsidy, from the first day of this present Parliament, for term of your life natural. And over that, we your said Commons, by the assent aforesaid, grant to you, our said sovereign lord, for the safeguard and keeping of the sea, another subsidy called Poundage.

Benevolences

(Vergil, *Anglica Historia*)

The king - lest the poorer sort should be burdened with the charge of paying the troops for the war - levied money from the rich only, each contributing to the pay of the troops according to his means. Since it was the responsibility of each individual to contribute a great or a small sum, this type of tax was called a 'benevolence'. Henry in this copied King Edward IV, who first [...] raised money from the people under the name of loving kindness. In this process it could be perceived precisely how much each person cherished the king - something which it had not before been possible to observe for the man who paid most was presumed to be most dutiful; many none the less secretly grudged their contribution, so that this method of taxation might more appropriately be termed a 'malevolence' rather than a 'benevolence'. However, since no one would have it said he was less dutiful, all competed to pay the required money.

PART TWO: REFORMATIONS

Timeline of significant events

1491 Birth of Henry VIII

1501 Marriage of Prince Arthur and Catherine of Aragon

1502 Death of Prince Arthur

1509 Death of Henry VII; start of reign of Henry VIII; marriage of Catherine of Aragon and Henry VIII

1510 Execution of Empson and Dudley; Thomas Wolsey became a member of the Council

1511 England became the ally of the Pope and the Holy League

1512 England entered war with France

1513 Henry VIII led an army into France and secured victory in the Battle of the Spurs; England defeated the Scots at the Battle of Flodden

1514 Death of Richard Hunne

1515 Wolsey made Lord Chancellor

1516 Birth of Mary I; Thomas More's *Utopia* published

1517 Establishment of the Royal Commission of Inquiry into Enclosures

1518 Wolsey appointed as Papal Legate

1520 Henry VIII and Francis I met at the Field of Cloth of Gold in France

1521 Henry VIII rewarded by the Pope with the title 'Defender of the Faith' following his publication in the same year of anti-Lutheran *The*

Assertion of the Seven Sacraments

1523 England at war with France

1524 Imposition by Wolsey of the Amicable Grant

1525 Rebellion in East Anglia against the Amicable Grant; printing in Cologne of William Tyndale's English Bible

1526 England entered alliance with France and other powers against former ally, the Holy Roman Emperor, Charles V

1527 Start of Henry VIII's divorce proceedings against Catherine of Aragon

1528 Thomas More replaced Wolsey as Lord Chancellor

1530 Arrest and death of Wolsey; Thomas Cromwell joined the Council

1532 Act of Annates; Commons' Supplication against the Ordinaries; the Clergy submitted to the authority of the Crown; More resigned as Lord Chancellor; Henry VIII's marriage to Catherine of Aragon annulled by Archbishop Cranmer

1533 Marriage (23 January) of Henry VIII and Anne Boleyn; Act in Restraint of Appeals; Thomas Cromwell appointed Chancellor of the Exchequer; birth (7 September) of Elizabeth I

1534 Act of Supremacy; Earl of Kildare's rebellion in Ireland

1535 Executions of Bishop John Fisher and Sir Thomas More

1536 Anne Boleyn beheaded; marriage of Henry VIII and Jane Seymour; the Ten Articles; Princesses Mary and Elizabeth made illegitimate by Act of Parliament; start of the Pilgrimage of Grace

1537 Execution of the Earl of Kildare; execution of Robert Aske, leader of the Pilgrimage of Grace; birth of Edward VI; death of Jane Seymour

1538 Excommunication of Henry VIII; shrines destroyed and 'superstitious worship' suppressed by royal injunction

1539 Act of Six Articles

1540 Marriage of Henry VIII and Anne of Cleves; Statute of Wills; Henry VIII's marriage to Anne of Cleves annulled; marriage of Henry VIII and Catherine Howard; execution of Thomas Cromwell; English Bible to be made available in every church

1542 Execution of Catherine Howard; English army defeated the Scots at the Battle of Solway Moss; birth of Mary Queen of Scots

1543 Marriage of Henry VIII and Catherine Parr

1544 English liturgy made compulsory in church services; Henry VIII participated in an invasion of France in alliance with Charles V; debasement of the coinage

1545 English army defeated by the Scots at the battle of Anerum Moor; French attempted invasion of England – loss of the *Mary Rose* and French occupation of the Isle of Wight

1546 English Army defeated by French at Boulogne

1547 Death of Henry VIII; start of reign of Edward VI; start of protectorship of Edward Seymour; Seymour made Duke of Somerset; Scots defeated by English at the Battle of Pinkie; dissolution of chantries by Act of Parliament

1548 Commission of inquiry into enclosures

1549 Act of Uniformity; the Prayer Book Rebellion in the South West; Kett's Rebellion; imprisonment of Somerset

1550 John Dudley, Earl of Warwick became President of the Council and master of the King's Household

1551 Warwick made Duke of Northumberland

1551 Execution of the Duke of Somerset; second new prayer book in Edward's reign published

1553 Death of Edward VI; Lady Jane Grey proclaimed Queen prior to her arrest; start of reign of Mary I; arrest of Archbishop Cranmer; Mary I's Act of Repeal designed to restore the Church to its pre-Reformation position; Queen's proposal to marry Philip II of Spain announced

1554 Wyatt's rebellion; execution of Jane Grey; marriage of Mary I and Philip II; reunification of English and Roman Churches approved by Parliament

1555 Bishops Ridley and Latimer burnt at the stake in Oxford; Philip II became ruler of the Netherlands; Cardinal Pole replaced Thomas Cranmer as Archbishop of Canterbury

1556 Philip II became King of Spain; Cranmer burnt at the stake in Oxford

1558 Death of Mary I; death of Cardinal Pole; publication of John Knox's pamphlet attacking Mary I, *First Blast of the Trumpet against the Monstrous Regiment of Women*; start of reign of Elizabeth I; William Cecil reappointed as Chief Secretary of State

1559 Elizabeth I's coronation; the Elizabethan Religious Settlement (the Acts of Supremacy and Uniformity); Treaty of Cateau-Cambrésis; Matthew Parker enthroned as new Archbishop of Canterbury

1560 Treaty of Edinburgh; Mary, Queen of Scots, abandoned claim to English throne; marriage looked very likely between the Queen and Robert Dudley; Scotland becomes a Protestant realm

1562 (October) Elizabeth I seemed likely to die of smallpox; Elizabeth aided Protestant rebels in France

1563 'Puritanical' six articles presented to the Convocation of Canterbury; Spain closed Antwerp to English merchants; Statute of Artificers; Act for the Relief of the Poor; plague epidemic

1565 Netherlands trade was resumed through Emden; bubonic plague; Mary, Queen of Scots married Henry, Lord Darnley

1566 Refusal of London clergymen to wear vestments led to their suspension; murder of David Rizzio; enclosure commissions; assertion of Spanish authority in the Netherlands resulted in rebellion (the revolt would continue until 1648)

1567 Murder of Lord Darnley; abdication of Mary, Queen of Scots

1568-9 Genoese Bullion Crisis (ended 1569); Mary, Queen of Scots, fled to England and the incriminating 'Casket Letters' appeared

1569 The Rebellion of the Northern Earls

1570 Excommunication of Elizabeth I; the Ridolfi Plot

1571 William Cecil received the title Lord Burghley; negotiations designed to lead to the marriage of Elizabeth I and Henry, Duke of Anjou; Treasons Act; William Strickland was removed from the House of Commons for proposing a bill in to reform the Prayer Book - reinstated following protests in the Commons; Duke of Norfolk (Thomas Howard) imprisoned for involvement in the Ridolfi Plot

1572 Execution of the Duke of Norfolk; Treaty of Blois; St. Bartholomew's Day Massacre; vagabonds punished with whipping and mutilation: the burning of a hole through the right ear; Sir Francis Drake captured Spanish treasure in the West Indies

1573 The Nymegen Convention reopened trade between England and Spain; radical Protestant, Sir Francis Walsingham, appointed as a Secretary of State

1574 Missionary priests, trained abroad, began to arrive in England

1575 Elizabeth backed a rising against the new French king, Henry of Anjou; Archbishop Parker died, replaced by Edmund Grindal

1576 Accession Day added to the calendar of Church festivals;

imprisonment of outspoken MP, Peter Wentworth

1577 Archbishop Grindal was placed under house-arrest following dispute with the Queen over religious matters

1579 Marriage negotiations led to Francis of Anjou's meeting with the Queen in Greenwich; pamphleteer, John Stubbs, and his publisher, William Page, had their right hands cut off in lieu of execution for daring to challenge the marriage proposal

1580 Jesuit priests began to arrive in England

1581 New act imposed £200 fine and a year's imprisonment as the penalty for saying Mass, and making attempts to convert others to Catholicism a treasonable offence; execution of Jesuit priest, Edmund Campion

1583 Confession of Francis Throckmorton, under torture, to his plot to place Mary on the throne; Archbishop Grindal died (still under house-arrest), replaced by John Whitgift; three 'separatists' executed for implying the Queen was a 'jezebel'

1584 Execution of Throckmorton; expulsion of Spanish ambassador on charge of complicity in the Throckmorton Plot; Bond of Association established by Cecil and Walsingham

1585 Treaty of Nonsuch; Act against Jesuits and Seminary Priests

1586 Babington Plot; the 'Enterprise of England' was devised by the Spanish to force English troops out of the Netherlands

1587 Arrest of five Puritan MPs; execution of Mary, Queen of Scots; Sir Francis Drake attacked the Spanish fleet in harbour at Cadiz

1588 Armada launched against England; Battle of Gravelines

1589 Elizabeth I sent men and money to the new Huguenot King Henry IV in his struggle against the Spanish backed Catholic League; a Spanish army was defeated in the Netherlands the troops of Sir Francis Vere

REBELLIONS AND REFORMATIONS

1589-91 Anti-Puritan persecution conducted by Richard Bancroft; seven Catholics executed in December 1591

1592 Apprentices, servants and 'masterless men', caused serious disturbances in London

1593 First severe outbreak of plague; Sir Peter Wentworth and Sir John Bromley imprisoned after petitioning Queen to name her successor; execution of radical Protestants, Henry Barrow and John Greenwood

1594 Bad harvest

1595 Armada set sail for Ireland but was lost at sea; apprentices, servants and 'masterless men', caused serious disturbances in London; hunger sparked off food riots throughout the south of England

1596 Another armada sailed towards Ireland but was also wrecked at sea; hunger sparked off food riots in Kent; sack of Cadiz

1596-1597 Bad harvests provoked the severest famine in Tudor history

1597 Yet another armada sailed for Ireland but was wrecked in the Bay of Biscay

1598 Revival of the position of an ancient post, the 'Archpriest', to govern the Catholic Church in England; vagrancy punishable by whipping 'until his or her body be bloody' and forcible return to place of settlement, to be held in a secure place until suitable employment be found; death of Philip II of Spain

1599 Armada destined for Ireland was defeated off Brittany

1600 Execution of two Catholic priests

1601 The last attempted coup against a Tudor monarch was hatched by Robert Devereux, Earl of Essex; introduction of the Elizabethan Poor Law; elimination of the more offensive monopolies

1603 Plague killed 30,000 people in London alone; James VI of Scotland named by Queen on her deathbed as her successor; death of Elizabeth I (March)

The House of Tudor

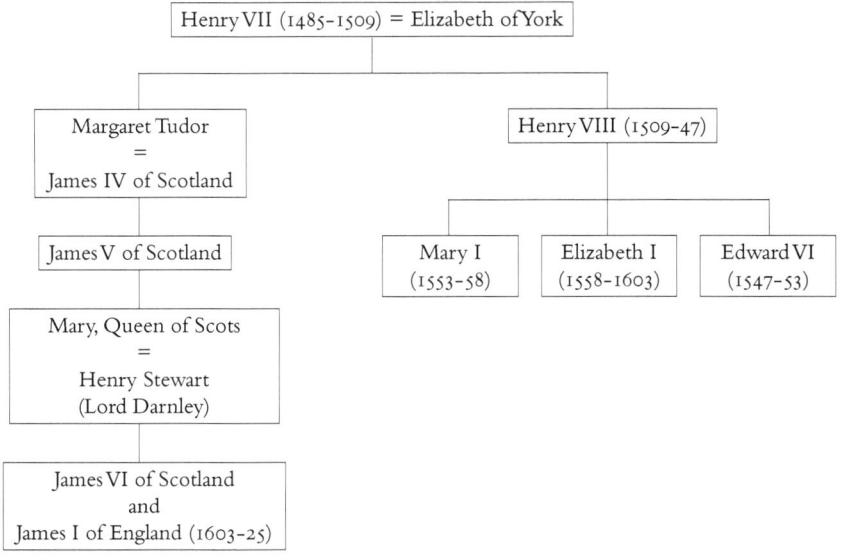

Chapter 6: The Reign of Henry VIII

The new king

> 'The king was young and lusty, disposed all to mirth and pleasure, and to follow his desire and appetite, nothing minding to travail in the busy affairs of this realm.'

(George Cavendish, c.1554)

Views on Henry VIII's personality have divided historians and other commentators for centuries. Perceptions have ranged from that of Bluff King Hal – 'a cross between Father Christmas and John Bull'[50] – to that of a monster – a "disgrace to human nature, and a blot of blood and grease upon the history of England' in the opinion of Charles Dickens[51]. In J. D. Mackie's opinion he was 'brutal, crafty, selfish, and ungenerous' and what little magnanimity he might have possessed 'was eaten up by his all-devouring egoism'. However, even Mackie had some positive thoughts regarding this cruel, fearsome pragmatist, this 'utter realist': 'His high courage - highest when things went ill - his commanding intellect, his appreciation of fact, and his instinct for rule carried his country through a perilous time of change, and his very arrogance saved his people from the wars which afflicted other lands [...] the people of England knew that in Henry they had a great king.'[52] Lacey Baldwin-Smith searched for the man behind 'the mask of royalty' and concluded:

> '[...] the King was a baffling composite of shifting silhouettes. As a sovereign filled with the spirit of divine duty modelling his royal

---

[50] Keith Randell, *Henry VIII and the Government of England* (1991).

[51] Cited in Lacey Baldwin Smith, *Henry VIII; the Mask of Royalty* (1971), p. 14.

[52] J. D. Mackie, *The Earlier Tudors 1485 – 1558* (1952), pp. 442-3.

stance on the actions of Old Testament kings, he appears with one face. As a Christian of excessively tender conscience, who knows he must eventually make a very special reckoning with God, he reveals another image. As a man of honour, a warrior knight and noble gentleman who lived a dream drawn from Arthurian legend and shared by every sovereign and nobleman of Europe, he is something else again. Finally, as a ruler and manipulator of men, for whom power was not so much a tool of political life as a mantle in which to wrap his own private fears and inadequacies, he presents still another mask.'[53]

Henry was almost eighteen years old when his father died in 1509 and he was already accomplished in a variety of physical and intellectual pursuits. Young and capable, the legitimacy of his right to rule was unassailable, and his cautious father had produced a Crown so solvent he had not needed to ask a Parliament for funds for the last five years of his reign. The young king seemed possessed of a fitting respect for the Catholic Church and a fitting disrespect for the French while also having a keen interest in the culture of the Renaissance and the ideas of the great continental humanists. That he failed to match his father in personally overseeing day-to-day matters of government mattered little when he entrusted the work to talented administrators like Cardinal Wolsey and spent his time in such laudable royal pursuits as jousting, hunting and war-mongering.

The seeds of future discord, however, were sown early in his reign. Just seven weeks after his accession, despite his initial reservations, he married his brother's widow, Catherine of Aragon, by special dispensation from the pope. Catherine and Prince Arthur had been married for just five months when her fifteen-year old husband died in 1502. It is likely that the marriage was never consummated. Henry and his Queen's coronation was spectacular. Just a few days later the Queen Mother, Henry VII's remarkable wife, Margaret of Beaufort, died. Henry had already made clear his decision not to rely exclusively on his father's councillors: Henry VII's two most unpopular ministers, Dudley and Empson, were arrested three days after their master's death on a trumped

---

[53] Lacey Baldwin Smith, *Henry VIII: the Mask of Royalty* (1971), p. 25.

up treason charge and their execution followed in 1510. The Council Learned in Law with which they were associated was abolished as the young king curried favour with his subjects. The figurehead of the new regime would become Thomas Wolsey, the Dean of Lincoln, who was invited onto the King's Council in June 1510.

The Venetian ambassador, on the first day of Henry's reign, described the new sovereign as 'Magnificent, liberal, and a great enemy of the French.' From that first day Henry committed himself to waging war against France, to reopening the old quarrel regarding England's right to a French kingdom. At best Henry could have hoped to dissuade the French king from challenging the English presence at Calais and her Pale, at worst an aggressive policy towards France could lead to cripplingly expensive campaigns and humiliating defeats. His inspiration was more to do with such concepts as 'honour' and 'chivalry' than the rationale of best-serving English interests abroad. Energetic and ambitious, determined to make a grand entry on the European stage, an aggressive foreign policy appealed not just to his ego but also to those nobles who sought their own moments of glory, the prestige of a military office and sundry other profits of war.

The war he helped start in 1512 was fought, ostensibly, as a papal crusade. Fighting in the Holy League, England was allied to Spain, the Papal States, Venice and Switzerland in a campaign designed to prevent French interference in Italy. The largest English army to enter France since Agincourt was impressive and succeeded in routing a French army outside Therouanne following the 'Battle of the Spurs' in August 1513. After Therouanne, Tournai fell into English hands and remained there for five years. The strategic advantage to England of acquiring additional territory scarcely compensated for the immense cost of Henry's (and Wolsey's) French campaign. The need to refortify and defend the towns further drained the royal coffers. On the other hand the king's prowess and the nation's martial pride were assured and Henry's greatest victory was more in the field of public relations at home than on the battlefield abroad. A favourable peace settlement in 1515 restored the French pension granted to Henry VII by the Treaty of Étaples and Henry's sister was betrothed to the French king, Louis XII.

The rise of Cardinal Wolsey

'The king's Council in short attended not on the king, but on the king's minister.'

(David Starkey. 'Privy Secrets: Henry VIII and the Lords of the Council', *History Today*, vol. 37, August 1987.)

Cardinal Wolsey, as Lord Chancellor and legate *a latere*, dominated English politics from 1515 to 1529. While the young king indulged himself in the chase, music, astronomy and theology, the business of governing was left largely in the capable hands of his first minister. The extraordinary position of influence in which Wolsey was placed literally enabled the cardinal to live like a king, making a personal court of Star Chamber, and dwelling with his entourage in palaces that rivalled Henry's in splendour. A contemporary poet, John Skelton, wrote:

'Why come ye nat to court? To which court?
To the king's court? Or to Hampton Court?'

Hampton Court was Wolsey's palatial home on the river Thames. In 1519 the Venetian ambassador remarked, 'This cardinal is the person who rules both the king and the entire kingdom.' The near totality of his power would eventually confirm his downfall, blamed and scapegoated for the failings in foreign policy and Henry's marital problems. After years of enjoying the royal confidence and administering affairs in line with the king's wishes, Wolsey would be the first of Henry's great ministers to be discarded on the grounds that, as the King later declared, 'Those who had the reins of government in their hands deceived me'.

Thomas Wolsey had humble beginnings. Born around 1473, he was the son of an Ipswich butcher. A career that started in training for the priesthood at Magdalen College, Oxford, eventually led to his becoming chaplain to Henry VII in 1507. By the time Henry VIII succeeded to the throne in 1509 this energetic, able and ambitious priest was Royal Almoner and he became a member of the King's Council in 1511. Already recognised for his considerable diplomatic ability, Wolsey's chance to demonstrate his greater potential came in 1512 with the royal plan to send an expeditionary force to France. Entrusted with the organisation of a major campaign, his exceptional efficiency was rewarded with, first, the newly acquired bishopric of Tournai, then, in 1514, the archbishopric of York. Enjoying by now full royal support, he was made Cardinal by Pope Leo X in 1515 and in the same year won the chancellorship following the resignation of William Warham, Archbishop of Canterbury. Wolsey's temporal and ecclesiastical control was made complete in 1518 when the Pope was persuaded to make him legate *a latere*, an appointment that gave him an authority even higher than that of Archbishop Warham.

As first minister Wolsey had four main areas of interest: the Church, the Law, finance, and foreign affairs. As legate *a latere*, Wolsey had accepted responsibility for reforming abuses within the Church. Despite his avowed interest in the principle of reform, he achieved nothing of worth in this area. Indeed, as a cleric holding a clutch of religious offices, including never less than two bishoprics, he was perpetually guilty of the abuse of pluralism. His other moral indiscretions were seen in his extravagant lifestyle, his acceptance of bribes and a number of illegitimate children. Historians have even suggested that Wolsey, by embodying all that was wrong with the unreformed Church, personally precipitated the crisis that destroyed it. This view has been vigorously rejected by Wolsey's biographer, Peter Gwyn, and in his defence it should be noted that he made plans for the closure of the most decadent monasteries and the appointment of new bishops. However, little was achieved other than the founding of new colleges at Oxford and Ipswich.

Wolsey's main interest in Church affairs appears to have been the extent to which he could use his authority to strengthen his own position. This was achieved by filling vacant posts with men he trusted (or those offering sufficiently generous bribes!), and by intervening in the Church courts, imposing what amounted to a ten per cent inheritance tax on the estates of the deceased. However, as G. R. Elton concluded, perhaps his prime objective in Church affairs was never achieved: 'the English Church had no single head or organization except the king - though Wolsey, as legate, had tried to provide one - and therefore no existence at all without the monarch.'[54]

Wolsey made greater efforts in his attention to the reform of the Law. As Lord Chancellor he extended the activities of the Court of

---

[54] G. R. Elton, *The Tudor Constitution* (1982), p.333.

Chancery, an institution providing equitable justice for those involved in cases in such complex areas as trade and the inheritance of property. He became deeply involved in the affairs of the prerogative court of Star Chamber, an institution that, in part, acted as an extraordinary criminal court. Star Chamber became Wolsey's personal court, not merely a place for meeting out justice where it was said 'he spared neither high nor low', but also the place where policy was proclaimed and enforced. By Wolsey's reckoning at least, his recognition of the central role of the Law and justice in good government meant 'the realm was in such good peace and order as has not been known before'.

Wolsey' s achievements in the field included some success in preventing the illegal seizure of common land (1515 enclosure act), and the speeding up of cases handled by Chancery and Star Chamber. For many the reality of Wolsey's intervention in legal matters, above all, represented the possibility of public humiliation or financial ruin should they dare to cross the Cardinal. It is interesting that Wolsey ruled, not through the Common Law courts, but those of equity and prerogative power. In this respect his legal reforms were limited even if financially effective.

Wolsey's ability to fund an extravagant foreign policy between 1513 and 1520 without any extraordinary devices for increasing revenue, such as the later dissolution of the monasteries, is certainly mysterious. Henry VII, it seems, found it hard to make ends meet, yet Wolsey, operating within similar financial constraints, had no qualms about blowing £20,000 in one day on the Field of Cloth of Gold. Peter Gwyn concluded that Wolsey was enjoying the fruits of careful budgeting in the last years of Henry VII's reign; other commentators find some credibility in the ancient notion of an early Tudor treasure trove that somehow fell into Wolsey's hands.

As Royal Almoner with particular responsibilities concerning charitable bequests in the king's will, he was privy to information regarding funds for the late king's 'good works'. These were not considered the business of the Chamber, unlike other accounts of the king's income and expenditure; perhaps some 'insider' knowledge of how the new king might afford a spectacular reign helped him in his meteoric rise to power. According to Francis Bacon in his *History of King Henry VII*, written over 350 years ago, it was 'reported by tradition' that a secret reserve did exist, amounting to a staggering £1,800,000. Modern historians however generally reject the traditional concealed treasure theory on the grounds that, according to the Chamber accounts, the king never had more than £200,000 disposable income. The idea though is still an attractive one and one that has enjoyed a flurry of recent interest.

Whether or not Wolsey ever had access to hidden monies hoarded by Henry VII is not known, but it is certain that he was running into financial difficulties by the early 1520s. An enormously expensive foreign policy had impoverished the Crown. Wolsey's need to levy additional taxes to cover royal costs resulted in a personal conflict with Parliament. Following the announcement of a forced loan known as the 'Amicable Grant' of 1525, a major civil disturbance was threatened when 20,000 men in East Anglia gathered to resist its introduction. The levy was withdrawn and Henry's 'Great Enterprise' in France, that it was designed to pay for, was abandoned.

Wolsey's main interest lay in foreign affairs. Of all his activities this is the hardest to comprehend fully since it is difficult to establish when the inspiration was his and when it was that of the king he served. Historians now agree that in the past Wolsey's influence over foreign policy has been exaggerated. Wolsey had to balance the need for preserving England's presence in continental Europe with that of the young king's desire for glory in battle and his own duties to the Church as the Pope's legate. His biographers have differed in their opinions as to the main objective of his foreign policy. Traditionally he was depicted as the great peacemaker, determined to maintain the existing balance of power in Europe, then, in Pollard's 1920s biography, he became the committed supporter of papal policy, a view since rejected by J. J. Scarisbrick who found plenty of evidence for turbulent relations between the Pope and the Cardinal.

Initially Wolsey and Henry adopted various strategies for containing the other great powers of France and Spain, including the signing of alliances, notably the Treaty of London in 1518, signed by over twenty countries. The most lavish gesture of friendship was the meeting between Henry and Francis I at the Field of Cloth of Gold, outside Calais in 1520, co-ordinated by Wolsey. The focus of the two-week event was a series of tournaments; the objective was the securing of lasting good relations between the ancient rivals. The cost of providing pavilions and provisions for the three thousand people who attended Henry's temporary court was enormous, equivalent to a year's normal income, and nothing of lasting value was achieved; the following year England agreed to support Spain against France.

Wolsey's attempts to maintain the existing *status quo* proved incapable of containing the rivalry between Habsburg Spain and Valois France. By 1523 England was embroiled, mainly as a result of Henry's ambitions, in a new war between the two powers, fighting with Spain against the aggressor, France. Francis I's defeat at the battle of Pavia and imprisonment in 1525 fuelled Henry's desire for securing the French crown. The necessary invasion of a temporarily leaderless France never came as a result of Wolsey's failure to secure his Amicable Grant in 1525 from sources in England already exhausted by the previous campaign. The Spanish king and Holy Roman Emperor, Charles V, turned his back on Henry's claim and reinstated Francis. Henry and Wolsey now aligned themselves with the imperial opposition and, in 1528, declared war on Charles. The declaration was mere display and no fighting incurred; when that series of hostilities between France and Spain ended a year later with the Treaty of Cambrai, England took a token role in the drawing up of the settlement, just as she had played a token role in the hostilities. The illusion that England had a primary place in European affairs, so impressively cultivated by Wolsey a decade earlier, had been shattered.

How powerful was Thomas Wolsey? Events demonstrate that his authority rested entirely upon the goodwill of the king and once the king's displeasure was incurred his fall was certain and rapid. It is harder to determine how total his authority was while he enjoyed the king's confidence. Some historians have maintained that Wolsey was given a free hand to do as he pleased as the acting head of government, a fun-loving Henry happy to delegate the tedious tasks of administration, law-making and diplomacy to his trusted servant. Others see his work overshadowed, and often shaped by, the king's imperial, religious and marital plans. J. D. Mackie concluded that:

> 'It is part of his genius that he was able to bring Henry to his own way of thinking and so, whilst seeming to obey, to carry out his own designs. His task was the easier because he and his master were, in fact, like-minded. Each valued greatness and prestige and each identified his own glory with that of England.'[55]

---

[55] J. D. Mackie, *The Earlier Tudors* (1952), p.302.

Elton was also of the opinion that 'Though Henry never surrendered ultimate control over affairs, it was Wolsey who ruled'[56]. John Guy identified a more independent king in the relationship, noting that 'he kept a much tighter rein on patronage [...] than is sometimes supposed' and that he was 'attentive to Wolsey's letters: he read them carefully, [...] and enjoyed catching out Wolsey's sources from time to time'[57].

The fall of Cardinal Wolsey

It has been estimated that Wolsey was ten times richer than anyone in the kingdom other than the king, and that he had more spending power than even the king himself. He owned several palaces and kept a court that rivaled Henry's and the pope's in size and splendour. By the 1520s he surrounded himself with more than 500 low and high born retainers. His celebrations were extravagant, his gifts lavish. Contemporary accounts reveal that when he rode out to Star Chamber or Chancery 'on a mule trapped with crimson velvet and his stirrups of copper and gilt', he travelled in style. surrounded by his most noble retainers dressed in livery, 'the most part of them with great chains of gold about their necks'. His procession was led by servants carrying 'his two great crosses of silver', marking his status as Archbishop of York and legate *a latere*.

By the late 1520s the king's chief concerns lay nearer home than the affairs abroad in which Wolsey had played such a central role. His wife Catherine had not yet produced a male heir to the throne and, as she entered her mid-forties, was unlikely ever to do so. The absence of a male heir threatened a disputed succession on Henry's death and the terrible danger of civil war that that might entail. Furthermore Henry had fallen in love with Anne Boleyn, the beautiful daughter of an influential London gentleman with powerful connections at Henry's court through her sister's marriage to the Duke of Norfolk. Henry wanted a divorce and

---

[56] G. R. Elton, *England Under the Tudors* (1974), p.75.

[57] John Guy, *Tudor England* (1988).

his grounds for getting one would be the fact that he had broken biblical law by marrying his deceased brother's wife. Wolsey, the papal legate, would be his means of persuading the pope to grant the dispensation.

John Guy has considered how far Wolsey was compromised by accepting the position the pope had offered him:

> '[...] Wolsey's position was constitutionally anomalous. Legates *a latere* were supposed to be papal diplomats, but Wolsey was the subject and lord chancellor of Henry VIII. When Henry Beaufort had received a cardinalate and legatine commission during Henry VI's minority, his opponent Humphrey, duke of Gloucester, had him charged with praemunire, even though he had resigned the chancellorship before accepting the appointments. Wolsey must have realized that his own legatine commission rendered him vulnerable given the different values of the common lawyers. He may have accepted it only because he believed he enjoyed Henry VIII's total confidence [...] When accused in the court of the king's bench, England's 'vice-pope' bowed before the Statutes of Provisors and Praemunire. He confessed that, on the authority of bulls obtained by him from Rome which he had published contrary to the statutes, he had illegally vexed the realm, thereby incurring the penalties of praemunire.'[58]

Wolsey's failure to secure papal support for Henry's divorce, coupled with, for Wolsey, disastrous developments in foreign affairs, and the development of an anti-Wolsey faction in Henry's court, brought about the Cardinal's destruction. The pope, so long as he was in Charles' custody was disinclined to defy him and Charles was Catherine's nephew. Meanwhile Anne Boleyn's brother-in-law, Norfolk, and the Duke of Suffolk, jealous for the power and influence that Wolsey had wielded for the past fourteen years, conspired to blacken the butcher's son's name and restore themselves and their aristocratic clique.

Accused of challenging the king's authority, the cardinal was stripped of the chancellorship and most of his health in 1529. For a time his relations with the king were cordial. and his enemies began to fear his reinstatement; then, in 1530, letters bound for home were intercepted in

---

[58] John Guy, *Tudor England* (1988), pp. 114-5.

which Wolsey implored the pope to threaten Henry with excommunication. He was at once arrested and charged with treason. He escaped execution by falling ill, and subsequently dying, at Leicester, on his way from York to London to face his accusers.

It has been argued that Wolsey's destruction was assured by his failure to resist the powerful faction of noble courtiers that had gathered around the cardinal's latest, and most formidable opponent, Anne Boleyn. This faction included the Duke of Norfolk and her father, Lord Hochford. Other interpretations deny the very existence of an identifiable Boleyn faction.

According to historian David Starkey, with the new king came a new style of government that amounted to a political revolution. Under Henry VIII a new intimacy between king and courtiers was developed with a greater willingness on the monarch's part to hand over business to a small executive council - a hotbed of political intrigue. Even closer to the king were those members of the Privy Chamber. Henry's 'minions' and 'pretty boys' (some just fifteen years old), jostling for favour with the young king they partnered on the jousting field.

Starkey depicted Wolsey as the counter-revolutionary, restoring government to the way it was in Henry's father's day by concentrating authority and influence in one man's hands - his own. To this end he destroyed the Council's executive role, drove out the earl of Surrey and other over-ambitious courtiers, and, in May 1519, found most of Henry's closest minions employment, as virtual exiles, at Calais, a fate they considered 'sore displeasant'. Wolsey's position was secure until 1527 when Anne Boleyn began to break his monopoly of influence over the king. Boleyn's arrival opened the floodgates as her own supporters and others besides returned to Court. Starkey has concluded:

> 'in the late 1520s (and not before) faction became the principal element in politics. The fact was a symptom of Wolsey's decline; its first result was to complete his ruin. This was effected by a general alliance of opposites – Boleyns, Aragonese, and aristocrats - against the Cardinal.'[59]

This opinion certainly seems to be confirmed by the observations of George Cavendish in his *Life of Cardinal Wolsey* published in around

---

[59] David Starkey, 'From Feud to Faction', *History Today*, vol. 32, November 1982.

1554. Peter Gwyn in *The King's Cardinal: The Rise and Fall of Thomas Wolsey* (1991) argued that the politics of faction had nothing to do with it and that Henry alone engineered Wolsey's downfall: 'It was Henry who had made Wolsey and it was Henry who destroyed him'. Gwyn found no evidence of a deep-rooted enmity for Wolsey felt by the nobility as a group and portrayed his destruction as an impassionate and shrewd political move by a king who had reached an impasse in the divorce proceedings.

Gwyn's interpretation was at once challenged by Eric Ives who defended Starkey's conviction that faction is of central importance:

> 'indeed, debunking 'faction' is something of an *idee fixe* with him. His method is first to caricature it and then to rubbish the caricature [...] But what he does not do is to offer any plausible alternative [...]'[60]

Instead of a cold and ruthless king fully in control, as depicted by Gwyn, and reminiscent of Holbein's paintings, Ives and Starkey envisaged a far less self-assured Henry in 1529, one seemingly ambivalent in his feelings towards Wolsey, at once robbing him of his authority while at the same time sending him tokens and messages of friendship. Ives concluded:

> 'It was [...] faction which destroyed the great cardinal, though only after an intense struggle. By the end of 1528 Anne had decided that Wolsey's exhortations to trust him disguised a bankruptcy of ideas or, worse, a deliberate attempt to frustrate her marriage to Henry VIII, and she had allied her faction with that of the disgruntled nobles who had been vainly sniping at Wolsey for years. In July 1529 their carefully prepared plan to have Wolsey arrested was blocked by the intended victim, despite the failure of his legatine court at Blackfriars to annul the king's marriage to Katherine of Aragon, and it was only the control which Anne and her faction were able to establish over the court during August and September which finally persuaded the king to abandon his servant.'[61]

---

[60] Eric Ives in *History Today*, June 1991.

[61] Eric Ives, *Faction in Tudor England*, (1986), p. 16.

Heresy and popular Protestantism

'If a lion knew his strength it were hard for any man to rule him.'

(Thomas More to Thomas Cromwell - a reflection on the King c.1532)

Between 1529 and the king's death in 1547, papal control over the English Church was eliminated, and many of its greatest institutions were demolished; prelates remaining loyal to the pope were executed and both the Bible and liturgy were read in English. Although A. G. Dickens made a strong case for the spread of popular Protestantism in the decades preceding the English Reformation, most historians, including Elton, Scarisbrick and Haigh, subscribed to the concept of a Protestant Reformation imposed from above. They maintained that the assault on Roman Catholicism in the 1530s was not generally popular, that the great majority was content with their Church.

The intolerance of the regime to heresy in the decades before the Henrician Reformation is evident in the record of heresy trials in the century between 1423 and 1522. There were at least 544 trials in the period that led to a range of punishments including at least twenty-nine, possibly thirty-four, burnings.[62]

The Richard Hunne affair was one of the more widely publicized heresy indictments in the early part of Henry's reign. Richard Hunne was a merchant tailor from London who, in 1511, found himself engaged in a heated dispute with the Church. First he had refused to pay a mortuary fee on the death of his baby son, in this case the child's own christening gown, and a few months later he was mixed up in a legal wrangle with a local rector regarding title to a tenement. The mortuary case, that might otherwise have been dropped, was brought to court by a Church at this time anxious to reassert its authority over would-be lay challengers. Both the priest and the rector involved in the dispute served the parish of St. Mary Matfellon and when Hunne attended Vespers there in December 1512 he was declared excommunicate, 'Hunne, thou art accursed and standest accursed!' This was tantamount to an accusation of heresy and

---

[62] John Guy, *Tudor England* (1988).

Hunne, in retaliation, commenced proceedings against several named clergy, seeking to sue them on the grounds of a public defamation that had affected both his social and business standing.

Hunne was invoking the ancient laws of 'praemunire', designed to keep ecclesiastical and lay matters apart. The details of Hunne's case are not known but certainly he was challenging the right of Church courts to intervene in what he considered secular affairs.

In early 1514 he was charged with heresy and locked up in the Lollard's Tower at St. Paul's. Without doubt the Church wanted to silence him because he had raised the praemunire issue that threatened to erode the status of its courts. It seems likely that he did hold 'heretical' views; a Wycliffite Bible and 'divers English books prohibited and damned by law' were found in his house at the time of his arrest. Thomas More later conjectured he started the praemunire proceedings to forestall the heresy action.

On 4 December 1514, he was found hanging in his cell. Evidence of a struggle supported the claims of those that supposed he had been murdered in order to terminate the praemunire case, while a posthumous declaration of certain heresy added weight to claims that he had committed suicide in anticipation of conviction. Four bishops found him guilty of heresy and his body was burned on 20 December. The following February however a secular coroner's jury declared he had been murdered by his gaolers, Joseph and Spalding, possibly while following instructions to 'soften him up' before his trial for heresy.

King Henry's 'Great Matter'

> 'The divorce was the spark which ignited the flame, but the combustible materials had long been existent, the divorce, in fact, was the occasion and not the cause of the Reformation.'

(A. F. Pollard, *Henry VIII*, 1902)

Traditionally it was assumed that the break with Rome was a simple matter of necessity following Henry's infatuation with Anne Boleyn and subsequent need for a divorce that the pope refused to grant. This explanation no longer seems satisfactory - why should Henry destroy so much to gain in marriage the woman who probably first became his mistress, like her sister before her, back in 1529?

Henry's grounds for divorcing Catherine of Aragon lay in the 'illegality' of the marriage in the first place: she was previously married to his older brother, Arthur.

> 'And if a man shall take his brother's wife, it is an unclean thing: he hath uncovered his brother's nakedness; they shall be childless.'

(Leviticus 20:21)

Divine disapproval of their union could be seen in Catherine's failure to produce for Henry a suitable heir - of the seven children she bore, only one, a girl, Mary, survived infancy. Concern regarding the succession, according to Pollard, was what motivated Henry, not his passion for Anne. This view was shared by Richard Rex who commented in 1993, 'The primary motivation for the divorce lay not [...] in Henry's wanton lust, nor purely, as he himself maintained, in scruples of conscience. The problem was the lack of a legitimate male heir to inherit the crown.'[63]

Henry began, publicly, to question the legality of his marriage in 1527, inspired by his growing interest in Anne since 1526. By 1528 Henry was committed to marrying her. Since his marriage to Catherine in 1509 had been granted by special papal dispensation he challenged the infallibility of popes by suggesting it should never have been allowed. At a time when the influence of Rome was being so successfully challenged by the new Zwinglian and Lutheran doctrines, it is not surprising that a theologically and politically oppressed papacy should choose to make a stand over such an issue. The position adopted by Rome when first approached for a divorce was reinforced by Catherine's persistent declaration that her marriage to Arthur was not consummated.

The case was opened in September 1528 in a court in London, presided over by the pope's legates, Cardinals Campeggio and Wolsey. In July 1529 Campeggio instructed the Legatine Court to adjourn and subsequently the case was called to Rome on the instruction of Pope Clement VII. Henry's lawyers challenged the legitimacy of transferring

---

[63] Richard Rex, *Henry VIII and the English Reformation* (1993).

proceedings opened in England to another province and found precedents by which he might reasonably demand its continuation on English soil where he might be more likely to secure a favourable verdict. The dispute had reawakened the spirit of the praemunire acts of the fourteenth century which protected the Crown's dealings in ecclesiastical matters from foreign and papal interference.

As early as 1530 Henry's lawyers were presenting him with arguments by which he might claim complete authority within his kingdom. Since the tenth century English kings periodically claimed they ruled empires, and emperors were answerable to none but God. The device, ultimately, was used to justify Henry's break with the Rome.

The death of Archbishop William Warham in 1532 enabled Henry to appoint in his place Thomas Cranmer, a prelate less committed to the notion that Henry's marriage could not be annulled without the papal authority. In January 1533 Henry was secretly married to Anne Boleyn who was now pregnant with the baby Elizabeth, born the following September.

Richard Rex commented on popular reactions to the proposed divorces:

> 'Henry's pursuit of a divorce was almost universally unpopular, and Catherine was soon cast as the wronged wife. Women in particular sympathised with her - when two royal emissaries came to Oxford in 1530 to elicit an opinion on the marriage, they were pelted with rubbish by the women of the town - and she had many friends among the higher clergy. She was on good terms with some prominent noble families, such as the Poles and Courtenays.'[64]

The break with Rome

The 'Reformation Parliament', as it has come to be known, was convened in the autumn of 1529 and sat intermittently until its dissolution in 1536. It has been suggested that the anticlericalism of

---

[64] Richard Rex, *Henry VIII and the English Reformation* (1993).

certain MPs was condoned and encouraged by the Crown as a means of putting pressure on the pope.

Acts were passed in 1529 designed to reduce clerical abuses such as pluralism, and to restrict privileges such as Benefit of Clergy. Charges of praemunire (illegal ecclesiastical interference in lay affairs) were brought against several bishops in 1530 and the whole clergy in 1531. A subsequent pardon, the Act for the Pardon of the Clergy (1531) covering the province of Canterbury and an additional act for the province of York, was passed in exchange for an enormous fine amounting to £119,000.

In 1532 a further assault was made - a parliamentary petition ('supplication') against the alleged abuse of legal powers by bishops (also known as 'ordinaries'). This Supplication against the Ordinaries, first drawn up in 1529, resulted in legislation that broke the Church's legal independence by making canon law subject to the Crown's authority. The Submission of the Clergy (1532) was signed by eight bishops who accepted the right of the Crown to supervise clerical proceedings:

> '[…] we will never from henceforth enact […] or execute any new canons or constitutions provincial, or any other new ordinance, provincial or synodal, in our Convocation or Synod in time coming, which Convocation is, alway hath been, and must be, assembled only by your Highness's commandment of writ […] '

The decision to break with Rome was taken in 1532. Henry was persuaded by his councillors, particularly Thomas Cromwell and Thomas Cranmer, that the divorce depended upon it and, in any case, the pope had no legitimate right to claim jurisdiction over English affairs. In that year the Act in Restraint of Annates deprived the pope of most of his English revenue by restricting the papal tax on senior prelates incomes from around one third to a mere 5 per cent. In March 1533 the Act in Restraint of Appeals severed links between English Church courts and the papacy. Henceforth the highest authority to which an appeal might be made was the Crown. The papal bull excommunicating Henry VIII took effect in September 1533.

In May 1533 Archbishop Cranmer declared Henry's marriage to Catherine of Aragon void and his marriage to Anne Boleyn, the previous January, valid. On May 31 Anne was crowned Queen. The Treason Act and the Act of Succession, both drawn up in 1534, were designed to prevent any of the King's subjects from challenging the legality of his actions. In August 1534 all six religious houses of the Observant Franciscan order were closed down and the friars themselves were either sent to the Tower, placed in the custody of Franciscans, or forced to flee the country. Up to thirty of the 200 concerned probably died in captivity. In May 1535 three Carthusian priors were executed and three Carthusian monks were executed in the following month. Several more subsequently starved to death in captivity.

Some historians believe Henry might have endeavoured to restore relations with Rome at this late stage had the pope backed down in the face of such determination. However, shortly before he died in 1534, Pope Clement VII once again insisted on the legitimacy of Henry's first marriage and Thomas Cromwell, on the basis of the claims enshrined in the Act of Supremacy (1534), was allowed to complete his work of destroying papal authority in England.

The Act of First Fruits and Tenths (1534) obliged all clerics on appointment to offices to make a one-off payment to the Crown equivalent to a year's income, followed by an annual tax of one tenth of their subsequent earnings. As a result royal revenue was increased by around 40 per cent. The Act forbidding Papal Dispensations and Payment of Peter's Pence (1534) abolished the right, by papal consent, to commit certain clerical 'abuses' such as pluralism, and it also ended a small but ancient papal tax worth about £200 a year. By 1536 all payments previously intended for Rome were diverted into the royal coffers, clerical appointments were made internally on the king's authority, and the Crown determined official beliefs and practices. The break with Rome was concluded in 1536 with a final act - the act extinguishing the authority of the Bishop of Rome.

This Reformation combined with unprecedented royal pretensions and a cult of monarchy, described here by Richard Rex:

> 'The claim to imperial status was a claim to full sovereignty, the denial of any superior jurisdiction on earth. It was not an entirely original claim on the part of the English monarchy. The 'crown imperial' had appeared on English coinage since the reign of Henry VII, and references to the "imperial crown" pepper early Tudor English documents. But the Act against Appeals was, as Professor Elton argues, the first claim of imperial status for the

realm as such rather than the crown, and imperial pretensions were undoubtedly advanced with a greater sense of purpose from this time. This can be seen even in the king's favoured style of address. "Highness", "grace", or "sovereign lord" had long sufficed as descriptions of the king in statutes, proclamations, and similar official documents. But in 1534 the more grandiose term "majesty" (already current unofficially) appeared for the first time in both statutes and proclamations [...] as a translation of the Latin "majestas", the property of the emperor under Roman law, it had obvious imperial connotations. The growing imperial pretensions of the king were part and parcel of the cult of monarchy which accompanied the extension of royal power under the early Tudors. This cult was expressed in a host of media, such as coinage - Henry VII was the first English king to adopt the Renaissance fashion of issuing coins bearing his own image - and royal portraiture as such - Henry VIII is the first English king of whom we have full-length portraits. The royal supremacy was part of this cult, making a return to earlier medieval traditions of sacral or theocratic kingship.'[65]

Thomas Cromwell and the break with Rome

'the most remarkable revolutionary in English history'

(G. R. Elton on Thomas Cromwell)

Thomas Cromwell's role in the English Reformation remains a subject of vigorous historical debate. A. F. Pollard described a Reformation masterminded by the king himself (*Henry VIII*, 1905), a view upheld by more recent historians including J. J. Scarisbrick (*Henry VIII*, 1968). G. R. Elton however, emphasised the role of Cromwell as the instigator of royal policy. Both the Reformation of the English Church and the 'revolution' in government in the 1530s are now commonly regarded as being primarily the work of Henry's first minister.

---

[65] Richard Rex, *Henry VIII and the English Reformation* (1993).

Cromwell was typical of the new breed of first ministers employed by early Tudor monarchs. Of humble birth, and, by his own admission, a 'ruffian' in his youth, Cromwell served France as either a soldier or page at the battle of the Garigliano in 1503. He became immersed in the world of banking and trade in the great merchant cities of Europe before embarking on a legal and, ultimately, political career. His breadth of experience, natural intelligence, eloquence and determination, combined with a capacity for ruthlessness, a vital ingredient for success in Tudor politics, resulted in his remarkable rise to power during the 1520s. Having offered his services he entered Wolsey's household in 1516 and enjoyed the Cardinal's patronage until the latter's fall in 1529. His first foray into the reformation of religious houses was in 1525 when he was instructed by Wolsey to investigate the smaller monasteries, an exercise resulting in the dissolution of twenty-nine establishments.

Cromwell stayed loyal to Wolsey to the last but did not fall with him. Although he shared Wolsey's interest in a general reform of the English Church, he was not, unlike his master, bound to uphold the papal line over the divorce issue. By the early 1530s he had aligned himself with the new radical faction in the Privy Council (which Cromwell entered in 1531) led by Bishop Cranmer. The king recognised Cromwell as a talented and astute ally who was permitted to shape a policy that promoted Henry's interests. According to Rosemary O'Day (*The Tudor Age*, 1995), he was 'instrumental' in persuading Henry VIII to make himself head of the English Church and subsequently became 'the moving spirit' in the dissolution of the monasteries. Again, it was on Cromwell's initiative that the Reformation of the 1530s happened both piecemeal and by parliamentary act. By so doing the full extent of the changes were made more palatable to both king and commoners. This, arguably, was Cromwell's masterstroke: no longer were the people's representatives in the Commons, at least those of the gentry and merchant classes, merely colluding in the granting of extraordinary taxes, they were now equally culpable in the Henrician revolution in the relationship between Church and State.

Elton suggested Cromwell was motivated primarily, not by religious conviction (although he certainly had Protestant leanings), but by a commitment to constitutional monarchy - the king ruling through Parliament: 'To Cromwell, the reformed church was to serve the purposes of the reformed commonwealth.'[66] Such claims have been disputed and no absolutely watertight case has been made in support of either the notion that Cromwell was Elton's 'man behind the Henrician Reformation' or that he had some master plan for establishing a genuine parliamentary monarchy. Subsequent developments revealed a monarchical power untrammeled by a parliamentary involvement that, essentially, legitimised tyranny. Historians such as J. Hurstfield subscribe to the idea that Cromwell was in fact dedicated to the promotion of Henry's absolute authority, not fledgling parliamentary democracy.

According to Richard Rex the origins of the Reformation in England cannot be precisely identified:

> 'It had roots in the conflict between common law and canon law; it drew on fourteenth-century conflicts between papacy and temporal princes; it owed something to Roman law concepts of imperial authority; it gained strength from the focussing of moral and spiritual aspirations on the monarchy; and this diverse material was integrated in an image of kingship modelled on that found in the Old Testament. It is hardly worth asking, and certainly impossible to answer, in precisely whose mind these various skeins first came together in what was to become the English royal supremacy, or at precisely what stage the "turning point" came.'[67]

The dissolution of the monasteries

The official dissolution of religious houses was not uncommon before the 1530s. Wolsey's attempts at reform in the 1520s, including Cromwell's closure of twenty-nine small establishments, received the papal blessing. Dissolution of 'decayed' houses was regarded as a legitimate and necessary part of the process of ecclesiastic

---

[66] G. R. Elton, *Reform and Reformation: England 1509-1558* (1977).

[67] Richard Rex, *Henry VIII and the English Reformation* (1993).

rationalisation. Formal 'visitations' of religious houses to ensure standards were maintained was an established procedure and Cromwell's visitation of a number of monasteries in 1535 was unexceptional. More remarkable was the *Valor Ecclesiasticus*, an attempt to survey and record all of the property held by the Church. This collosal undertaking has been compared to the Domesday survey, although the speed at which it was conducted made it a record of questionable reliability. Soon rumours were circulating of government plans to confiscate church lands, amounting to between one fifth and one third of all the land in England.

Although some monasteries obstinately rejected the king's claim of supremacy, and were duly closed down, the majority of establishments, like the majority of bishops, accepted the changes. The reason why these subservient monasteries also were all dissolved by 1540 is another subject of considerable debate. Although it is commonly claimed that the break with Rome did not necessitate the dissolution of the monasteries, the presence of international holy orders, with continental brethren that upheld the papal supremacy, was an anomaly that very likely was intolerable to Henry and Cromwell. The financial might of the Church and dubious loyalty of its members, represented a considerable security risk at a time when calls for an imperial crusade against England could be heard at home and abroad. If, as so many historians believe, Cromwell was the moving spirit behind the Reformation, then his personal religious opinions might explain the assault on monasticism during his period of office. Elton, who subsequently modified his view of Cromwell, once commented:

> 'His temper was secular, sympathetic to the prevailing anti-clericalism of the time; dislike of the priesthood may have been magnified into contempt for the papacy by what he saw in Italy. But he appears to have been utterly devoid of passion, even in his anticlericalism: he did not hate priests as such, or as purveyors of bad religion, but simply objected to them as obstacles to his plans.'

Elton in fact considered financial considerations a primary factor in the dissolution of the monasteries. Under Wolsey government expenditure had exceeded income, revenue from customs on wool exports was in decline, a 'pension' from the French king was terminated in 1534, a rebellion in Ireland in 1534 had to be suppressed, and

Cromwell needed to improve England's defences against a possible attack from Spain. 'Thus', Elton wrote, 'Cromwell turned to the Church' in the same way that both he and the king knew that continental reformers had done before them.

Elton considered the monasteries ripe for closure since they no longer served an important function and were generally unpopular; monasticism might have ended in England at this time regardless of other events. Christopher Haigh vehemently disagreed, but he too identified financial gain as the prime motive:

> 'The cost of the Irish rebellion of 1534 had produced a draft plan for the confiscation of Church property, including a dissolution of smaller monasteries, and had given good reason for the new taxes of first fruits and tenths.'[68]

The official explanation was that of clerical vice identified by the visitations of 1535: monks were accused of homosexuality and masturbation, nuns were found guilty of breaking their vows of chastity. A picture of clerical immorality, largely unfounded, was painted by government propagandists. In 1536 the Act for the Dissolution of the Lesser Monasteries was passed. This brought about the closure of all houses with an income of less than £200 with the exception of those exempted by the king. In the preamble to the act these were described as wasteful and generally corrupt, the inhabitants accused of 'carnal and abominable living' and 'slander of good religion', all 'to the high displeasure of Almighty God' and 'to the great infamy of the King's Highness and the realm'.

The dissolving of ecclesiastical houses no doubt was perceived by many at a local level as a disaster without mitigation. In the north of England this provoked open rebellion. This rebellion, dubbed the Pilgrimage of Grace, began on October 1, 1536, at Louth in Lincolnshire. Within a fortnight the first rising had collapsed but further unrest now surfaced in Yorkshire, led by a lawyer named Robert Aske. In December, following negotiations with the Duke of Norfolk, Aske was persuaded to disperse, without recrimination, his force of 30,000. After further troubles in January and February, 1537 the pardon was revoked and 216 of the rebels, including Aske, were executed. The rebellion had lasted

---

[68] Christopher Haigh, *English Reformations* (1993).

many months and received widespread support that included that of aristocrats and ecclesiastical magnates.

Between 1536 and 1539 pressure was put on the larger monasteries and a number went into voluntary dissolution. Those remaining were formally closed by the Act for the Dissolution of the Greater Monasteries (1539). Three abbots, Richard Whiting of Glastonbury, Thomas Beche of Colchester and Hugh Cook of Reading, were executed for treason in the same year.

Christopher Haigh argued, convincingly, that the king did not share the views of his more radical servants:

> 'For Cromwell, Cranmer, and the preachers they patronised, the attack on the monasteries was another step in their evangelical programme. Monasticism was a pious fraud, founded upon the false doctrine of purgatory; monks were no more useful than images, relics, and prayers to saints. For Henry it was different. He might concede the practical need for negotiation with Lutherans or seizure of monastic endowments, but he had not abandoned belief in the sacramental system or the efficacy of masses satisfactory for suffering souls.'[69]

Nevertheless he had begun a revolution that could not be easily stopped and he seems to have recognized the direction in which his kingdom was inexorably headed. Despite Cromwell's fall Archbishop Cranmer kept his office, the Act of Six Articles was not enforced, his Bible, the first authorised English version, continued to be read, and the Six Articles, designed to halt the march of Protestantism, were not enforced. Most significantly, Henry's son was educated by Protestants.[70]

The last decade

The Reformed Church

---

[69] Christopher Haigh, *English Reformations* (1993).

[70] Rosemary O'Day, *The Debate on the English Reformation* (1986).

In July 1540 Henry ordered the execution of Thomas Cromwell and the almost simultaneous execution of three Protestants for heresy and three Catholics for treason. These facts have often been interpreted by historians as a blatant statement of intent for the future of the English Church: an absolute refusal to tolerate full-blown Lutheranism while maintaining a stand against Roman Catholicism. The king's reaction against radical Protestantism can be traced to the fall of Anne Boleyn.

Anne's role in the English Reformation is a subject of considerable debate but it seems likely that the original radicalism of the mid-1530s was influenced by her religious convictions. She helped convince the king of the necessity for Bible reading in the vernacular, she patronised supporters of Lutheran doctrines, and it is likely she had some say in the appointment of radical bishops, including Cranmer and Latimer.

When Anne miscarried in January 1536, three weeks after the death of Catherine of Aragon, amid rumours of infant deformities, Henry read this as a sign of divine wrath regarding their marriage. At the same time he was becoming infatuated with another member of his court, Jane Seymour. The Aragonese faction, supporting the birthright of Catherine's Catholic daughter Mary, endeavoured to undermine further Anne's position. Cromwell, no doubt afraid of further association with the queen, with whom he had recently differed over such matters as foreign policy, cynically transferred his allegiance to Boleyn's enemies. Under Cromwell's orders, in March 1536, a court musician, Mark Smeaton, was arrested and accused of adultery with Anne Boleyn. Under interrogation he confessed and a day later the Groom of the Stool, Henry Norris, was arrested on the same charge as, subsequently, were two other members of the Privy Chamber. Anne's brother, Lord Rochford, was found guilty of incest and, together with the other men, he was executed on 17 May. On 19 May Anne was beheaded, a last kindness befitting a royal execution. A little over a week later Henry was married to Jane Seymour.

Anne Boleyn's rise coincided with, and perhaps contributed to, a slide towards Protestantism; her fall, according to Richard Rex, 'heralded a dramatic shift in policy':

> 'The elimination of the two women who posed the greatest obstacles to Anglo-Imperial friendship opened the way to rapprochement, and Cromwell's new-found warmth to Chapuys (the Imperial Ambassador] shows how readily he appreciated

this. The shift is best illustrated once more by episcopal appointments. The strongly Catholic Richard Sampson, long a favourite of the King, played a crucial role in putting together the case for annulling Henry's marriage to Anne. His reward was the bishopric of Chichester [...] For the rest of Henry's reign episcopal nominations were dominated by conservatives [...]'[71]

The Ten Articles of July 1536 fell far short of Protestant objectives but neither these nor the execution of the widely disliked Anne Boleyn were sufficiently reassuring to prevent the most serious revolt ever faced by a Tudor monarch, the Pilgrimage of Grace, which began in October. Disaster was averted by a truce negotiated between the rebels and the Duke of Norfolk, the commander of the royal forces. By its terms Norfolk promised to support the rebels' demands for the undoing of the worst excesses of the Reformation and the removal of the bishops and ministers responsible, the 'king's evil councillors'.

In 1537 legislation was passed obliging every parish, within two years, to acquire a copy of the Bible in English – the first authorized version prepared by Miles Coverdale for Cromwell. It was to be made freely available to the entire congregation. However, further legislation in 1543 restricted public access, stipulating that 'no women nor artificers, prentices, journeymen, serving men of the degrees of yeomen or under, husbandmen, nor labourers', in other words, ninety per cent of the population, should be permitted to read it. A month in prison faced those who ignored this dictate. Women of noble birth and those of gentry families were permitted to read it in private.

A fuller account of post-Reformation doctrine than that provided by the Ten Articles was drawn up by Cromwell and the reformist bishops in 1537. When this statement was published it was attributed to the bishops and not the king since he had been too busy to scrutinise its contents. This Bishop's Book therefore was never an official royal proclamation and by the time such a thing appeared in the form of the King's Book in 1543 any gesture towards Lutheran doctrine during Cromwell's period in office had been stifled.

The Act of Six Articles, 1539, clarified any ambiguities in the Ten Articles and upheld certain Catholic doctrines, including transubstantiation, and principles such as the celibacy of priests. This

---

[71] Richard Rex, *Henry VIII and the English Reformation* (1993).

coincided with the fear of a papal inspired crusade against England. Shortly afterwards a substantial public mourning was arranged in London on the death of Charles V's empress, Isabella. Masses and prayers for her soul helped convince foreign ambassadors that, despite the continued persecution of papists, the English Church in other respects remained a Catholic Church.

The Six Articles represented the resounding defeat of the Protestants and the victory of the conservative faction led by Stephen Gardiner, Bishop of Winchester. In alliance with the reformed Boleyn faction, led by her uncle, the Duke of Norfolk, the conservatives brought about the fall of the architect of the Reformation, Thomas Cromwell.

Following the death of Jane Seymour in October 1537, shortly after producing for Henry the long-awaited son, Edward, the king, prompted by Cromwell, sought a new marriage that would secure a German alliance in the face of a threatening new accord between Charles V and Francis I. On the basis of a flattering portrait by Hans Holbein, Henry married Anne of Cleves, sister of the Duke of Cleeves, in 1540. The King disliked his 'Flemish mare' from the first and the arrangement was concluded for purely political reasons. Henry's minister had let him down and at the first opportunity he would seek a release from his latest, unconsummated, marriage.

Cromwell's opponents, banking on Henry's supposed theological orthodoxy, and capitalising on his marital discontent, endeavoured to 'expose' Cromwell's alleged Lutheranism and brought to the king's attention another desirable niece of Norfolk, the nineteen year old Catherine Howard. The rapidity of Cromwell's fall from grace was startling: still in favour after the arrival of Anne of Cleves, not least for his securing of an important parliamentary loan. he was made Earl of Essex and Lord Chamberlain in April 1540; in July, accused first of treason, and ultimately found guilty of the Lutheran heresy, he was beheaded. Ironically. in the same month, legislation was passed whereby the English Bible was to be made available in every English church.

Cromwell's influence in religious affairs continued to be felt after his death through the preservation of the close relationship between the King and Cromwell's ally, Archbishop Cranmer. Cranmer, in the privacy of the royal mass revealed to Henry in the winter of 1541 details of the adulterous behaviour of his new queen. Enraged, Henry uncharacteristically burst into tears before the Privy Council and called for a sword to slay Catherine. She and her two accused lovers, together with a female accomplice, were executed, and her relations in the Privy Council were removed. Cranmer's friendship with the king survived a further conservative counter-attack when Gardiner accused the archbishop of heresy.

Henry's last wife, Catherine Parr, to whom he was married in 1543, rekindled hope among the reformers since she was manifestly sympathetic to new religious ideas. Gardiner and the conservatives endeavoured to indict her and, in 1546, Henry granted permission for an investigation into her affairs. But for her success in convincing him of her loyalty as his wife and subject in religious and other matters it is likely she would have been arrested. The scheme had backfired on the conservatives and largely accounted for the exclusion of Gardiner from the Council in November 1546.

When King Henry died on 27 January 1547, the official position of the Church in theological matters had not shifted from the relatively orthodox stance of the Six Articles. The struggle between reformers and conservatives however was not abated and the factional strife in the closing years of Henry's reign did not cease with his passing.

Foreign affairs, fortress-England

> 'What a realm will England be, when his grace has set walls according to the ditches, that run round about us. England will then be more like a castle than a realm.'
>
> (Richard Morison, *Exhortation to stir all Englishmen to the defence of their country*, 1539)

The Reformation further isolated England from the other great powers. The rejection of papal authority and the abandonment of his aunt, Catherine, severely damaged Henry's relationship with the Holy Roman Emperor, Charles V. The French king, Francis I, valued an alliance with the pope above any agreement with England, and the German Lutherans, the Schmalkaldic League, were too far removed from Henry in religious matters for him to combine in a united anti-papal front. When Jane Seymour died in 1537 Henry investigated the possibility of marriage to either a Habsburg or Valois subject, optimistic that the one or the other would welcome an alliance now that the ghost of his past marital indiscretions had been laid with the deaths of Catherine of Aragon and Anne Boleyn. Such ambitions were shattered when the Pope brought Charles and Francis together in a ten-year truce in June 1538. This pact united them in a common crusade against the enemies of Roman Catholicism. On 17 December Henry was excommunicated and England was faced with the likelihood of imminent invasion.

Over the next two years England's coastal defences were massively improved. The sale of monastic lands helped pay the cost and the very fabric of dissolved monasteries was used in building fortresses. Henry's marriage to Anne of Cleves in January 1540 provided an alliance with the Pope's enemies elsewhere in Europe. By the spring of 1540 it was apparent that the old differences between Charles and Francis remained and a united action against the English king no longer seemed likely. On 12 July Henry's marriage to Anne of Cleves was annulled.

The resurgence of hostilities between Francis and Charles reopened the possibility of a Habsburg or Valois alliance. Approached first by the French, Henry eventually allied with Charles in June 1542, promising to join him in an invasion of France in the following year. The war began prematurely although Henry's great and costly army of 40,000 soldiers, including many hired mercenaries, was not dispatched against France until 1544. Henry followed, the warrior king leading his men to battle, albeit carried in a litter and not astride a warhorse. Boulogne was captured on the day Charles made peace with Francis and for a time England fought France alone. The Treaty of Campe in June 1546 left Boulogne in English hands for eight years, its subsequent return to be compensated by a fee of £600,000 and an annual 'pension' of £35,000. Francis thus guaranteed for France the return of a newly fortified town that had cost a fortune to capture and a further fortune to re-defend against French counterattacks. Susan Doran arrived at the following conclusions:

> 'According to the most reliable figures which have been compiled, the capture of Boulogne cost nearly £600,000 and its fortifications another £400,000. The war could not be financed by taxation alone; hence the heavy sale of Crown lands and feudal rights after 1540, the debasements of the coinage (1541-46) and the borrowing of large sums on the Antwerp money market from 1544. But not only Crown finance suffered. The

wars resulted in a contraction of trade and contributed to the decay of old established industries by starving them of capital investment. The increase in the pace of inflation in the mid-Tudor years also owed much to the war; both the debasement of the currency and increase in government expenditure worked to raise prices.'[72]

G. R. Elton was equally critical:

'[...] in exchange for immediate gain to himself, swallowed up by the insatiable war, Henry damaged the economic life of the country so seriously that even twenty years of various efforts could barely retrieve the situation. The sum total of Henry's last years of direct personal rule was therefore to undo the good work of his father and of Thomas Cromwell. In order to pursue his futile and ill-conducted wars, the king destroyed the financial independence of the crown and undermined the prosperity of his country.'[73]

In 1545 Francis launched a naval attack against England, intending to isolate Boulogne by preventing supplies from leaving the Southern ports. To this end Portsmouth was targeted and the Isle of Wight was identified as a desirable acquisition from which the French might intercept further excursions. Outnumbered by between two and three to one, the threat of the French armada to Henry's navy was a serious one indeed. The conflict in the Solent started badly for the English: one of the two greatest ships, *Great Harry*, bore the brunt of the French cannon for an hour, and the other, *Mary Rose*, turned turtle in the confusion, her opened gunports admitting the flood that sank her.

'From such a hard beginning there can only be a better ending' Henry stoically remarked after witnessing this sinking of his flagship with more than 400 hands trapped below the gundecks. The following day French troops were landed on the Isle of Wight where they met a fierce and effective resistance; over 1500 more subsequently came ashore at Seaford in Sussex but they too were driven back by the English

---

[72] Susan Doran, *England and Europe 1485-1603* (1986).

[73] G. R. Elton, *England under the Tudors* (1974).

archers. The French armada remained in English waters for a further three weeks, fighting the occasional skirmish, before abandoning the invasion.

The fate of the *Mary Rose*, according to the French admiral, D'Annebault, was no accident:

> 'Fortune favoured our fleet [...] for above an hour during which time among other damages the English received, the *Mary Rose*, one of their principal ships, was sunk by our cannon and of 5 or 600 men which were on board only five and thirty escaped.'

Contemporary English versions of events told a different story. Another witness, Sir Peter Carew, brother to Vice Admiral, Sir George Carew, who captained the *Mary Rose* and perished with his crew, recorded this description of the disaster:

> 'Sir George Carew being entered into his ship commanded every man to take his place and the sails to be hoist but as the same no sooner done than the *Mary Rose* began to heel, that is to lean to one side. Sir George Carew being in his own ship and seeing the same called for the master of his ship and told him thereof and asked him what it meant who answered that if she does heel she is like to be cast away. Then the said Sir Gawain [Sir George Carew's uncle, Sir Gawain Carew] passing by the *Mary Rose* called out to Sir George Carew asking him how he did, who answered he had the sort of knaves whom he could not rule and it was not long after that the said *Mary Rose* thus heeling more and more was drowned with 700 men which were in her with very few escaped. He had in the ship a hundred mariners the worst of them being able to master in the best ship within the realm, and those so maligned and distained one another that refusing to do that which they should do were careless to do that which they ought to do and so contending in envy perished in forwardness.'

Tudor efforts to salvage the wreck failed and it remained undisturbed until the 1830s when developments in diving technology made the retrieval of several guns and other objects possible. Using sonar equipment the wreck mound was rediscovered in the 1960s and in 1970 another cannon was raised. In 1979 the *Mary Rose* Trust was founded to carry out a major excavation of the mound and, ultimately, the retrieval of her hull. The anaerobic conditions of the silted site had preserved items made of organic materials, including wood, leather, bone and vegetable matter. A classic 'time capsule', where catastrophe brought the life of the great vessel to a sudden end, the excavation of the *Mary Rose* in the early 1980s has provided an unprecedented insight into aspects of the Tudor past. Finds included over 120 longbows and 2000 arrows; only one Tudor arrow was known before the excavation of the *Mary Rose*. Rigging, compasses, medical tools, musical instruments, meat, vegetables, fruit and the pewter plates off which they were eaten were all recovered. Among the many human bones found were also those of a dog, found next to the skeleton of the rat it was chasing the moment the ship 'heeled' over.

Scotland, Ireland and Wales.

War with Scotland

The 'auld alliance' between France and Scotland represented a major security threat for King Henry as he contemplated invading the French. In 1539, when an anti-English crusade was threatened, the Scottish king, Henry's nephew, James V, was ready to support the pope's cause. In 1542 Scotland was given a taste of things to come should James ever contemplate an invasion of England while Henry's troops were preoccupied with a French campaign.

Under the Duke of Norfolk a number of Scottish towns and villages were attacked, looted and torched by the English. Undeterred James counter-attacked and suffered a disastrous defeat at the Battle of Solway Moss in November 1542 in which the Scottish army of some 10,000 men was routed by 3000 English soldiers. Three weeks later James died leaving as heir an infant daughter, Mary.

The capture of a great number of Scottish notables, a minor as monarch, combined with glaring evidence of military ineptitude, presented Henry with an unprecedented opportunity for asserting England's authority over the Scottish crown. His failure to do so can be accounted for by his primary interest in the French campaign and a series of ill-judged decisions in his negotiations with the Scots. The hostage nobles were returned in the hope that they would further Henry's interests. Mary was permitted to remain in Scotland until she was ten years old when, by the terms of the Treaties of Greenwich (July 1543) she was to come to England to be married to Edward, Henry's son and heir. Scotland's treaty obligations to the French however were not forcibly revoked and within months the terms of the treaties were rejected by the Scottish parliament. By the time it was apparent the Scots would resist further attempts at securing the Scottish crown, having restored their defences, it was too late to achieve Henry's objectives by a show of strength. A ten-day campaign in May 1544, resulting in the sacking of Edinburgh, Leith and St Andrews, helped weld together the Scottish magnates in the anti-English cause. The only positive outcome of this and a subsequent raid in 1545 was that it helped protect England against a Scottish rearguard action in the course of Henry's conflict with France.

When Henry died in 1547 Scotland was as steadfast as ever in its hostility towards the English. Although A. F. Pollard was mistaken in claiming Henry's principal foreign policy objective in the 1540s was the acquisition of Scotland in which the war against France was a necessity in order to weaken the 'auld alliance', his failure to subdue Scotland and to eliminate any pretensions the Scottish crown might have to the English, was great indeed.

Henry, King of Ireland

Ireland, effectively, reverted to rule by local lords, first the Butlers and then the Geraldines, after the withdrawal of the Earl of Surrey in 1521, sent over with an inadequate army to subdue Irish incursions upon the Pale around Dublin in 1520. The Reformation of the 1530s necessitated a firmer hold over Ireland, a potential base for any counter-Reformation force. In 1533 the Earl of Kildare, Henry's deputy in Ireland, was called to London, accused of 'manifold enormities', and imprisoned in the Tower where he later died, of natural causes, in 1534. His son 'Silken' Thomas Fitzgerald, renounced his allegiance to England, called for papal and imperial support against Henry and rose, with the other Geraldine notables, in revolt. A large army under Sir William Skeffington, the new Deputy, was sent over by Cromwell and, with the support of the Butlers, succeeded in crushing the rebellion in 1533.

Silken Thomas and five of his Geraldine uncles subsequently were executed at Tyburn in 1537. Direct rule now replaced indirect rule through the great families. An act of 1537 endeavoured to prohibit the wearing of Irish dress and the use of the Gaelic language. The Irish Parliament was persuaded to repudiate the pope and in June 1541 Henry assumed the title of King of Ireland and Head of the Irish Church. The suppression of the Irish abbeys that followed provided the means by which the Irish magnates could be bribed into accepting English rule and, for the time being, the troubles in Ireland subsided although Roman Catholicism, in reality, was far from eliminated.

The Union with Wales

The north-west of Wales comprised six counties conquered by Edward I in the thirteenth century. The remainder was made up of 'marcher lordships' which retained a relatively autonomous status, areas which, like the larger part of Ireland, were subject only to the indirect rule of the English Crown and as such represented a refuge for criminals from other areas and had some potential as a nest for those in opposition to royal policy. Furthermore, as Henry's own father had demonstrated in 1485 when he landed at Milford Haven, the Welsh coast might provide a foothold for potential invaders. In 1534 Cromwell appointed Rowland Lee, Bishop of Coventry, Lord President of the Council of Wales and the Marches with the express purpose of breaking the partial independence of the marcher estates. Under his jurisdiction thousands of 'evildoers' in the later 1530s were hanged in the assault on lawlessness in the marches. In a letter to Cromwell at this time he wrote: 'Although the thieves [...] have hanged me in their imaginations I am confident that I shall be equal to them soon in all acts.'

He hunted down the most notorious 'thieves', particularly those of higher social rank for, as he explained in 1536, 'to hang one of that kind would cause forty to fear for their lives.' He proudly proclaimed the execution of 5000 in the first six years of his administration in Wales. These terror tactics paid dividends and soon the marches were pacified - ready to be anglicised.

The Acts of Union (1536-1543) abolished the marcher lordships which were replaced by seven new shires, thus establishing the foundation of modern Wales. The acts enabled the shires to send MPs to Parliament, to appoint JPs to maintain English (as opposed to Welsh) law and order, and to admit the king's judges who hitherto had not travelled in Wales beyond the Principality. English became the language of administration. While confrontation continued to characterise English rule in Ireland, Wales was successfully assimilated. However, not all historians are united in the assumption that the Acts undermined the 'Welshness' of the people they directly affected:

> 'It may be that historians have adopted too narrow and preconceived a view of the Acts of Union, believing that they were designed to destroy all that was considered worthy in the Welsh cultural tradition [...] What is the significance of the Act of Union and its aftermath in any interpretation of the early modern period in Welsh history? It was an effective catalyst and created a new territorial entity within the realm in an era that led to individual Welshmen achieving prominence in various fields of activity. The Tudor settlement established political cohesion [...] improved economic opportunities, imposed upon Wales the Elizabethan Protestant Church and, regardless of its official policy, provided the conditions that led to the translation of the scriptures into Welsh and the consolidation of the Protestant faith. The period also gave Welsh gentry and parliamentary representatives - already deeply involved in local affairs - a conspicuous role to play in governmental circles [...]'[74]

While on the one hand the Acts of Union promoted the enforcement of English law they also presented the Welsh elite with considerable new political opportunities.

The death of King Harry

Henry VIII died on 28 January 1547. The cause of his death, like so many other aspects of his reign, is a subject of historical controversy. For historians who assume he played the key role in the dramatic policy making of the 1530s and 1540s his physical and mental state in the last

---

[74] J. Gwynfor Jones, *Early Modern Wales, c.1525-1640* (1994).

REBELLIONS AND REFORMATIONS

fifteen years or so of his reign is a matter of considerable importance. It might be that the drama of these years had a connection with the various illnesses from which he suffered, illnesses that might have contributed to his cantankerous and erratic behaviour.

Surviving documents make possible a chronology of Henry's physical decline:

February and March 1514: reports that Henry had smallpox or the measles.
March 1516: Henry suffered an 'indisposition'.
May 1521: the king had a fever and 'paroxysms'; he suffers 'pains "in his head'.
April 1527: the king's foot, allegedly, is damaged in a game of tennis.
May 1527: Henry's foot is protected by a black velvet slipper.
March 1529; the king is reported to have 'wrenched' his foot.
January 1531: Henry is restless and cannot sleep at night.
November 1532: he experiences 'a sudden catarrh and toothache'
September 1532: the king takes pills to relieve gout.
February 1535: 'hoarseness and ill health prevent Henry from receiving guests.
Spring 1537: the first reports of the king's ulcerated legs.
March 1538: Henry has a cold and is further troubled with leg ulcers.
April 1538: the king's legs are bandaged, his pain is so great that at times he is unable to talk and he is 'black in the face'.
November 1538: Sir Geoffrey Pole is heard to say he 'had a sore leg that no poor man would be glad of, and that he should not live long for all his authority next to God'.
September 1539: Henry receives one of several enemas to relieve constipation.
Spring 1540: Henry makes a 'very laborious and painful journey towards the sea coast'.
February 1541: the French ambassador reports Henry had 'a slight tertian fever, which should have profited than hurt him, for he is very stout, but one of his legs, opened and kept open to maintain his health, formerly suddenly closed, to his great alarm, for, five or six years ago, in like case, he thought to have died'. Despite this he was 'marvellously excessive in drinking and eating'. He finds him moody and cantankerous, 'often of a different opinion in the morning than after dinner'.
February 1542: the French ambassador comments on the king's extreme

lethargy, melancholia and stoutness. Henry begins to use a staff to support himself.

April 1543: fevers and a 'humour descending to his leg'. According to the imperial ambassador, he has 'the worst legs in the world, so that those that have not seen them are astonished that he does not stay continually in bed'.

March 1545: a 'rheum and a cough'.

March 1546: bad legs and acute melancholia. He is carried around in a sedan chair, unable to walk.

December 1546: legs cauterised with hot irons to stem fungoid growths.

Susan Maclean Kybett used this and related evidence, such as a study of the growth in the king's girth through an analysis of suits of armour made for Henry, to challenge the traditional assumption that his chief illness was syphilis.[75] The syphilis claim was first made by A. S. Currie in 1888 but firm evidence for his suffering from the 'French disease' is missing. Foreign ambassadors made no comment when contemporary rumours of such a condition would have been something of a 'scoop', and he does not appear to have received the mercury treatment that the royal surgeons doubtless would have prescribed as a cure.

Kybett instead suggested Henry might have suffered from 'land scurvy' - a less-pronounced and more gradual version of the disease associated with sailors deprived of fresh fruit and vegetables. Not only did Henry suffer from a number of the conditions common to scurvy but they appeared in the appropriate progression for the scurvy-sufferer. The onset of scurvy was heralded by red, itching spots across the body, easily mistaken for measles or smallpox; sore, puffed up gums and loose teeth would follow; an ulcer would later form, probably on a foot or ankle; tissue would swell, walking would become painful, constipation would be likely, the complexion of the victim would become sallow and the patient would be prone to melancholia and irritability. Surprisingly a healthy appetite was sustained throughout. Symptoms would usually be most severe in the late winter when the sufferer was most deprived of Vitamin C. Towards the end the face of the person affected would would be puffy and the nose would appear to have collapsed because of the

---

[75] Susan Maclean Kybett, 'Henry VIII - a Malnourished King?', *History Today*, September 1989.

damaging effect of scurvy upon the collagen by which the nose, below the bridge, is supported.

That a king might be malnourished is explained by the fact that fruit and vegetables were not preserved for winter consumption and food grown in the lowly earth was considered fit for peasants but not royalty. The eating of fruit was widely considered unhealthy, described by physician Sir Thomas Elyot in his *Castel of Helth*, published in 1539, as 'harmful to man and do engender ill humours, and are often the cause of putrified fevers, if they be much and continually eaten'.

Although the king's medical record is far from complete it would be extremely difficult to suggest an alternative disease that fits the whole. Kybett identified some of the symptoms of scurvy in the medical case histories of some of Henry's contemporaries, including Cardinal Wolsey, as well as future monarchs - Mary I, Elizabeth I and James I. She concluded that 'Although the king's medical record is far from complete, every item fits in with a scurbotic condition, and it would be extremely difficult to suggest an alternative disease that fits the whole.'

SOURCES

Resistance to the Amicable Grant, 1525

(Report from the Duke of Norfolk to Wolsey, 11 May 1525)

Please it your grace to be advertised that this day at 10 o'clock we the Duke of Norfolk and Suffolk met together at a place chosen two miles on this side of Bury with all the company of both the shires which was a right goodly company to look upon - at the least three thousand who were gathered since Tuesday morning. And unto us came a great number of people from the towns of Lavenham and Ely. They came all in their shirts and kneeling before us, crying for pity, and insisting they were the king's most humble and faithful subjects and so would continue during their lives saying that this offence they had committed [failing to pay the Amicable Grant] was only for lack of work so that they knew not how to get their living. And for their offence they most humbly requested us to seek the king's pardon. In response we did our best to make them fully aware theirs was a heinous offence, declaring it amounted to high treason [...] Finally we took custody of three of the principal offenders [...], intending to give them as sharp and severe a lesson as we could devise, and gave all the rest leave to depart.

In defence of Wolsey

(George Cavendish, *The Life of Cardinal Wolsey*, c. 1554)

Forsooth this cardinal was my lord and master, whom in his life I served, and so remained with him, after his fall, continually, during the term of all his trouble, until he died [...] And since his death I have heard diverse sundry surmises and imagined tales, made of his proceedings and doings which I myself have perfectly known to be most untrue [...] in my judgement I never saw this realm in better order, quietness, and obedience, than it was in the time of his authority and rule, nor justice better ministered with indifference [...]

Anne Boleyn – victim of faction

(George Cavendish, *The Life of Cardinal Wolsey*, c. 1554)

The king waxed so far in amours with this gentlewoman [Anne Boleyn] that he knew not how much he might advance her. This perceiving, the great lords of the council, bearing a secret grudge against the cardinal because that they could not rule in the scene well for him as they would, who kept them low, and ruled them as well as other mean subjects, whereat they caught an occasion to invent a mean to bring him out of the king's high favour, and them into more authority of rule and civil governance. Themselves.

[...] perceiving the great affection that the king bore lovingly unto Mistress Anne Boleyn, fantasying in their heads that she should be for them a sufficient and an apt instrument to bring their malicious purpose to pass, with her they often consulted in this matter. And she having both a very good wit, and also an inward desire to be revenged of the cardinal, was as agreeable to their requests as they were themselves.

The Lutheran heresy, 1526

(Cuthbert Tunstall, Bishop of London, 1526)

By the duty of our pastoral office, we are bound diligently, with all our power, to foresee, provide for, root out, and put away all those things which seem to tend to the peril and danger of our subjects, and especially to the destruction of their souls. Wherefore we, having understanding by the report of divers credible persons, and also by the evident appearance of the matter, that many children of iniquity, maintainers of Luther's sect, blinded through extreme wickedness, wandering from the way of truth and the catholic faith, craftily have translated the New Testament into our English tongue, intermeddling therewith many heretical articles and erroneous opinions, pernicious and offensive, seducing the simple people; attempting by their wicked and perverse interpretations to profanate the majesty of the Scripture which hitherto hath remained undefiled, and craftily to abuse the most holy word of God, and the true sense of the same; of which translation there are many books imprinted, some with glosses and some without, containing in the English tongue that pestiferous and most pernicious poison, dispersed throughout all our diocese of London in great numbers; which truly, without it be speedily foreseen, without doubt will contaminate and infect the flock committed unto us with most deadly poison and heresy, to the grievous peril and danger of the souls committed to our charge, and offence of God's divine majesty.

Henry to Anne, 1527

(Henry VIII to Anne Boleyn, 1527)

[...] you will expressly certify me of your whole mind concerning the love between us two. For of necessity I must ensure me of this answer, having been now above one whole year struck with the dart of love, not being assured either of failure, or of finding place in your heart and grounded affection. Which last point has kept me for some time from calling you my mistress, since if you love me in none other sort save that of common affection, that name in no wise belongs to you, for it denotes singular love, far removed from the common. But if it shall please you to do me the office of a true loyal mistress and friend, and to give yourself up, body and soul, to me [...] I will take you for my only mistress, rejecting from thought and affection all others save yourself, to serve you only.

Anne to Henry, 1527

(Henry VIII to Anne Boleyn, 1527)

The warrant of maid of honour to the Queen induces me to think that your Majesty has some regard for me, since it gives me the means of seeing you oftener, and of assuring you, by my own lips (which I shall do on the first opportunity), that I am

Your Majesty's very obliged and very obedient Servant, without any reserve, Anne Boleyn.

The Act in Restraint of Appeals, 1533

(Extract from the preamble)

Where by divers sundry old authentic histories and chronicles, it is manifestly declared and expressed, that this realm of England is an empire, and so hath been accepted in the world, governed by one Supreme Head and King [...] unto whom a body politic, compact of all sorts and degrees of people, divided in terms, and by names of spiritualty and temporalty, be bounden and owe to bear, next to God, a natural and humble obedience: he being also institute and furnished, by the goodness and sufferance of almighty God, with plenary, whole, and entire power [...] and final determination in all causes, matters, debates, and contentions without restraint or provocation to any foreign princes or potentates of the world [...]

The Act of Supremacy, 1534

(Extracts from The Act of Supremacy, 1534)

Albeit the King's Majesty justly and rightfully is and oweth to be the Supreme Head of the Church of England, and so is recognised by the clergy of this realm in their Convocations [...]
    […] be it enacted by authority of this present Parliament, that the King our Sovereign Lord, his heirs and successors, kings of this realm, shall be taken, accepted, and reputed the only Supreme Head in earth of the Church of England, called *Anglicana Ecclesia*, and shall have and enjoy, annexed and united to the imperial Crown of this realm [...] all honours, dignities (etc.).
    [...] kings of this realm, shall have full power and authority from time to time to visit, repress, redress, reform, order, correct, restrain, and amend all such errors, heresies, abuses, offences, contempts, and enormities, whatsoever they be, which by any manner spiritual authority or jurisdiction ought or may lawfully be reformed, repressed, ordered, redressed, corrected, restrained, or amended, most to the pleasure of Almighty God, the increase of virtue in Christ's religion, and for the conservation of the peace, unity and tranquility of this realm; any usage, custom, foreign laws, foreign authority, prescription, or any other thing

or things to the contrary hereof notwithstanding.

Sir Thomas More, 1535

(Words attributed to Sir Thomas More at his trial prior to his execution on 6 July 1535)

[...] this indictment is grounded upon an Act of Parliament directly repugnant to the laws of God and his Holy Church, the supreme government of which [...] may no temporal prince presume by any law to take upon him, as rightfully belonging to the see of Rome [...]

[...] I nothing doubt but that, though not in this realm, yet in Christendom about, of these well-learned bishops and virtuous men that are still alive, they be not the fewer part that are of my mind therein. But if I should speak of those that are already dead, of whom many be now holy saints in heaven, I am very sure it is the far greater part of them that, all the while they lived, thought in this case that way I think now; and therefore am I not bounden, my lord, to conform my conscience to the Council of one realm against the general Council of Christendom. For of the foresaid holy bishops I have, for every bishop of yours, above one hundred. And for one Councilor Parliament of yours (God knoweth what manner of one), I have all the Councils made these thousand years. And for this one Kingdom, I have all other Christian realms.

Report on a visitation, 1535

(St. Edmund's Monastery at Bury)

As touching the convent, we could get little or no reports among them, although we did use much diligence in our examination, and thereby, with some other arguments gathered of their examinations, I firmly believe and suppose that they had conferred and compacted before our coming that they should disclose nothing [...] Amongst the relics we found much vanity and superstition, as the coals that saint Laurence was toasted with all, the paring of S. Edmund's nails, S. Thomas of Canterbury's penknife and his boots and divers skulls for the headache; pieces of the holy cross able to make a whole cross of; other relics for rain and certain other superstitious usages, for avoiding of weeds growing in corn, with such other.

The Ten Articles, 1536

(Extracts)

IV As touching the sacrament of the altar [...] our people [...] must constantly believe that under the form and figure of bread and wine [...] is verily, substantially and really contained and comprehended the very selfsame body and blood of our Saviour Jesus Christ [which] is corporally, really and in the very substance exhibited, distributed and received [...] whosoever eateth it or drinketh it unworthily, he eateth it and drinketh it to his own damnation; because he putteth no difference between the very body of Christ and other kinds of meat.

VI As touching images [...] especially the images of Christ and Our Lady [...] it is meet that they should stand in the churches [...] As for kneeling and offering unto them [...] the people ought to be diligently taught that they in no wise do it, nor think it meet to be done to the same images, but only to be done to God, and in his honour, although it be done before images [...]

X [...] it is much necessary that such abuses be clearly put away, which under the name of purgatory hath been advanced, as to make men believe that through the Bishop of Rome's pardons souls might clearly be delivered out of purgatory and all the pains of it, or that masses might be said [...] might likewise deliver them from all their pain, and send them straight to heaven; and other like abuses.

The Pilgrim's oath, 1536

(Robert Aske, 1536)

Ye shall not enter into this our Pilgrimage of Grace for the Commonwealth, but only for the love that ye do bear unto Almighty God his faith, and the Holy Church militant and the maintenance thereof, to the preservation of the King's person and his issue, to the purifying of the nobility, and to expulse all villein blood and evil councillors against the commonwealth from his Grace and his Privy Council of the same. And that ye shall not enter into our said Pilgrimage for no particular profit to yourself, nor to do any displeasure to any private person, but by counsel of the commonwealth, nor slay nor murder for no envy, but in your hearts cut away fear and dread, and take afore you the Cross of Christ, and in your hearts His faith, the Restitution of the Church, the suppression of those Heretics and their opinions, by all the holy contents of this book.

The Pilgrims' ballad, 1536

Alack! Alack!
For the church sake
Poor commons wake,
And no marvel!
For clear it is
The decay of this
How the poor shall miss
No tongue can tell.

The Pontefract Articles, 1536

(Extracts from the Pontefract Articles delivered by the Yorkshire Pilgrims, December 1536)

I. Touching our faith, to have the heresies of Luther, Wyclif [and others], the works of Tyndale [and others], and such other heresies of Anabaptists, clearly within this realm to be annulled and destroyed.

II. To have the supreme head [...] to be reserved unto the see of Rome, as before it was accustomed.

III. We humbly beseech our most dread sovereign lord that the Lady Mary be made legitimate and the former statute therein be annulled [...]

IV. To have the abbeys suppressed to be restored - houses, lands and goods.

VII. To have the heretics [...] and their sect to have condign punishment by fire [...]

VIII. To have the Lord Cromwell, the Lord Chancellor, and Sir Richard Rich to have condign punishment as subverters of the good laws of this realm and maintainers of the false sect of these heretics and first inventors and bringers in of them.

XIII. Statutes for enclosures and intacks [intakes from wastes or commons] to be put in execution, and that all intacks and enclosures since the fourth year of King Henry VII be pulled down, except on mountains, forests, or parks.

XV. To have the parliament in a convenient place at Nottingham or York, and the same shortly summoned.

XVIII. That the privileges and rights of the Church be confirmed by act of Parliament.

XX. To have the Statute of Uses repealed.

XXI. To have the statutes of treasons for words [...] be in likewise repealed.

Hugh Latimer on the Pilgrimage of Grace, 1536

(A sermon delivered by Hugh Latimer, 29 October 1536)

These men in the north country, they make pretence as though they were armed in God's armour, girt in truth, and clothed in righteousness. I hear say they wear the cross and the wounds before and behind, and they pretend much truth to the king's grace and to the commonwealth, when they intend nothing less; and deceive the poor ignorant people, and bring them to fight against both the king, the church and the commonwealth. They arm them with the sign of the cross and of the wounds, and go clean contrary to him that bare the cross and suffered those wounds. They rise with the king, and fight against the king in his ministers and officers; they rise with the church, and fight against the church, which is the congregation of faithful men; they rise for the commonwealth and fight against it, and go about to make the commons each to kill the other, and to destroy the commonwealth. Lo, what false pretence can the devil send among us! It is one of his most crafty and subtle assaults, to send his warriors forth under the badge of God, as though they were armed in righteousness and justice.

Robert Aske's defence, 1537

(Extracts from Aske's statement following his arrest, March 1537)

The said Aske says:

(1) That he against the statue of suppressions, and so did all the country, because the abbeys in the North gave great alms to poor men and laudably served God [...] And by the said suppression to service of God is much minished, great number of masses unsaid and consecration of the sacrament now not used in those parts, to the decrease of the Faith and spiritual comfort to man's soul [...] Also several of the abbeys were in mountains and desert places, where the people be rude of conditions and not well taught by the law of God, and when the abbeys stood the people not only had worldly refreshing in their bodies but spiritual refuge [...] by preaching, and many of their tenants were their fee'd servants, who now want refreshing both by meat, clothes and wages, and know not however have any living [...]

(2) To the statute of illegitimacy of the lady Mary the said Aske says that [...] she ought to be favoured in this realm rather than otherwise, considering that her mother's ancestors have long been friends of the common wealth of this realm. Moreover it was thought that the divorce made by the Archbishop of Canterbury was not lawful pending the appeal, and some even doubted the authority of his consecretion [...]

As to the statue of Supremacy he says all men murmured at it and said it could not stand with God's law [...]

Not only he but in manner all men that rebelled blamed much divers bishops and preachers for division in preaching and variance in the Church of England, and thought that much of this insurrection arose by them. Also they blamed divers of the King's Council for the Statute of Suppression [...]

Retribution, 1537

(Henry VIII to the Duke of Norfolk)

Before you close up our said banner again you shall in any wise cause such a dreadful execution to be done upon a good number of every town, village and hamlet that have offended in this rebellion, as well by the hanging them up in trees, as by the quartering them, and the setting up of their heads and quarters in every town, great and small, and in all such other places, as they may be a fearful spectacle to all other hereafter that would practise in any like manner.

A royal injunction concerning the Great Bible, 1538

(Extract from the Second Royal Injunctions of Henry VIII, 1538)

[...] you shall provide on this side the feast of Easter next coming, one book of the whole Bible of the largest volume, in English, and the same set up in some convenient place within the said church that you have cure of, whereas your parishioners may most commodiously resort to the same and read it; the charges of which book shall be rateably borne between you, the parson, and the parishioners aforesaid, that is to say, the one half by you, and the other half by them.

The Bishops' Book, 1537

(Extracts from the Bishops' Book, 1537, drawn up at the King's command)

[...] this holy Church is catholic, that is to say, that it cannot be [...] restrained within the limits or bonds of anyone town, city, province, region, or country; but that it is dispersed and spread universally throughout all the whole world. Insomuch that in what part soever of the world, be it in Africa, Asia, or Europe, there may be found any number of people, of what sort, state, or condition soever they be, which do believe in one God the Father, creator of all things, and in one Lord Jesu Christ his Son, and in one Holy Ghost [...]

[...] all the particular churches in the world, which be members of this catholic Church, may be called apostolic churches, as well as the church of Rome, or any other church, wherein the apostles themselves were sometime resident; forasmuch as they have received and be all founded upon the same faith and doctrine that the true apostles of Christ did teach and profess.

[the] pretended monarchy of the Bishop of Rome is not founded upon the gospel, but it is repugnant thereto.

The Act of Six Articles, 1539

(Extract from the Act of Six Articles, 1539)

[...] after the consecration there remaineth no substance of bread or wine, nor any other substance but the substance of Christ, God and man.

[...] priests [...] as afore, may not marry by the law of God.

War with France, 1527

(Henry's instructions to his ambassadors on what to say to the Emperor following his defeat and capture of Francis I, March 1527)

[...] who should succeed in the realm of France, the French King and his line removed? The King's Highness verily trusteth that, his just title and right thereunto remembered and considered, the Emperor, since the treaties and alliances passed between the King's Grace and him, was never [...] of other mind but firmly to join with His Highness for recovery of the said crown [...] one of the chief and principal things intended [...] by their confederation hath always been to expel the French King from his usurped occupation of the crown of France, and to conduce the King's Highness, as right requireth, unto the same [...]

Solway Moss and the Treaties of Greenwich, 1543

(A letter to Henry VIII from his ambassador in Scotland, dated 20 March 1543, in which he reported a conversation with Sir George Douglas, a Scottish nobleman who was sent back to Scotland shortly after the battle of Solway Moss)

'Well,' I said, 'Mr Douglas, the king's majesty has had large offers, as you know, both for the government of the realm, and to have the child brought into his hands, with also the strongholds, according to your promises; and if your ambassadors should now come with mean things, not agreeable to his highness, you are a wise man, you know what may ensue as a consequence.'

'Why', said he, 'his majesty shall have the marriage offered [...] and having that first, the rest of what he desires may follow in time. But for my part I made no such promise that you speak of; and they that made such promises are not able to perform them. For surely,' he said, 'the noblemen will not agree to have her out of the realm, because she is their mistress; but they are content that the king's majesty shall appoint some gentlemen of England, and some English ladies, to be here about her person, for her better tuition, at his majesty's pleasure [...] but I tell you [...] if there be any motion now [...] to bring the government of this realm to the king of England, I assure you it is impossible to be done at this time. For', said he, 'there is not so little a boy but he will hurl stones against it, and the wives will handle their distaffs, and the people universally will rather die in it, yea, and many noblemen and all the clergy be fully against it [...]'

Chapter 7: The Reign of Edward VI

Edward VI and Protector Somerset, 1547-49

When Henry VIII died in January 1547, his heir, Edward, was nine. The Henrician legacy was not an auspicious one: the massive changes of the 1530s and the belligerent foreign policy of the 1540s placed the Crown in a dangerous position. The religious differences that had threatened to tear the country apart in the later 1530s had been contained but not eliminated and the Court continued to be riddled with the struggles of opposing factions, defined by both religious and political aspirations. The wars of the 1540s had swallowed up much of the financial gain of the Reformation and they had done nothing towards improving relations with England's troublesome neighbours, Scotland, France and Spain. Memories of the civil wars of the previous century cast an ominous shadow over the minority reign of Edward VI.

Edward Somerset, Earl of Hertford, the Duke of Somerset

'the same day the death of his father was proclaimed in London. where was great lamentation and weeping; and suddenly he proclaimed King. The next day [...] he was brought to the Tower of London where he tarried the space of three weeks; and in the mean season the Council sat every day for the performance of the will and at length thought it best that the Earl of Hertford should be made Duke of Somerset, Sir Thomas Seymour Lord Sudeley [...] Also they thought best to choose the Duke of Somerset to be Protector of the realm and Governor of the King's person during his minority, to which all the gentlemen and lords did agree, because he was the King's uncle on his mother's side.'

(*The Chronicle of Edward VI*)

Henry left the kingdom in the hands of a sixteen member Privy Council, more or less evenly balanced between the conservative and reformist factions. Contrary to Henry's evident intent, but in the tradition of the fifteenth century, personal rule was assumed by the heir's uncle, on the advice of other councillors, to act as regent until the boy came of age. Edward Seymour, leader of the moderate Protestant party, was appointed Lord Protector by the King's Council on 31 January and in February he arranged to have himself made the Duke of Somerset, three days before Edward's coronation at Westminster. Somerset had not been named by Henry as his successor, thus making the possibility of a factional struggle for power all the more likely.

In a bid to win public support, and as preparation for subsequent religious legislation, Somerset's government, through Parliament, passed a new Treason Act in November 1547. The laws regarding heresy and censorship were relaxed and Protestant literature and ideas could now circulate more freely. The act greatly strengthened the Protestant cause and in London there were riots, some that resulted in the destruction of statues and other sacred ornaments in the churches. The new act also abolished the Proclamation Act of 1539 which had guaranteed the king's right to legislate without Parliament so long as he kept within the confines of existing laws. The repeal of the act was no more than an empty gesture in recognition of Parliament's place in the constitution: Somerset issued seventy-seven proclamations in his short tenure, clocking up a considerably higher annual average than the 'tyrant' King Henry. Rulers throughout history have resorted to their 'emergency' powers in times of crisis and this habit of ruling by decree might be a measure of the fragility of England's government in the middle years of the sixteenth century. Although Cromwell's reforms of the 1530s had made the Tudor state more powerful, it was no longer rich now that most of what he stripped from the monasteries had been sold off or given away. The debasement of the coinage in the 1540s speeded up inflation by reducing their content of precious metal and so diminishing their value. While economic and social problems at home were a major concern so too were threats from Catholic Europe. Somerset offended others who expected to share in government by adopting quasi-regal powers and ruling largely independently of the Council. He in preference through members of his own household, his 'new council', only one of whom, Sir Thomas Smith, was a privy councillor. He possessed a 'dry stamp' of Edward's signature enabling him to legislate by royal decree.

He later commanded that nothing signed by Edward himself should be acted upon without his counter-signature. It was this autocratic arrogance as much as his actual policies that fermented the opposition to his rule that would finally overthrow him.

Another early piece of legislation was the new Vagrancy Act of 1547. This too addressed the threat of public disorder by passing draconian punishments for those found guilty of vagrancy. The unemployed, able-bodied vagrants now ran the risk of being branded with a V and enslaved for two years - all for wandering about, in search of work, for a mere three days.

Somerset could be ruthless too on a much more personal level. Thomas Seymour was ambitious like his brother and had secured the hand in marriage of King Henry's last queen, Catherine Parr. Following her death in 1548, shortly after giving birth to a daughter, rumours spread of Thomas Seymour's attempts to gain Elizabeth, the fifteen year-old daughter of Henry and Anne Boleyn. At the same time he was probably defrauding the royal mint and involved in plots against the brother who had decided not to appoint him to the regency council. The Earl of Warwick encouraged Thomas Seymour to consider laying claim to the regency: he was, after all, another of the young king's uncles. On March 20, 1549 Edward Seymour, threatened, and perhaps shamed by Thomas' behaviour (it was rumoured that the princess Elizabeth was pregnant by him), took an unpopular step in having him executed for high treason. Historians have identified in all this a crafty conspiracy by Somerset's opponents who drove a wedge between the two brothers by first encouraging the one to plot against the other then advertising his disloyalty to the protector. In so doing they had presented Somerset with the dilemma of being seen either to condone treason, by excusing his brother, or committing fratricide.

The continuing inflation, exacerbated by bad harvests, prompted the government in 1548 to adopt reformist as well as repressive measures to reduce the risk of rebellion. Erroneously identifying enclosure as the cause of economic hardship, action was taken to prevent landholders from enclosing their property. New taxes were imposed upon sheep farmers and woollen cloth in order to discourage enclosures. The landowners resented intervention and the lot of the masses was unchanged.

In desperation the government went on to ban unlawful assemblies, the spreading of rumours, and even football, already associated with sporadic outbreaks of rioting and general disorder. Despite all these attempts to keep law and order the country plunged into the chaos of two major rebellions in 1549 - the Western Rebellion, and Kett's rebellion in the East. Only one of these, the Western Rebellion, was primarily concerned with religion; general social and economic grievances however were causes of both. Although Edward VI survived this crisis, Somerset did not; his protectorate was dissolved on October 13 and he and his family were imprisoned in the Tower of London.

Somerset's reputation as the 'Good Duke' has been explored by many historians including Michael Bush:

> 'Somerset's social concern was basically political and personal. In this respect his consideration for poverty cannot be described as a genuine concern for the plight of the poor. Poverty was appreciated as a cause of military insufficiency and peasant insurrection, and as a means of earning virtue by remedial acts of justice and charity [...] Somerset had some concern for the lower orders but because he subscribed to common aristocratic feelings, not because of an unusual compassion. As a ruler he acted conventionally for the preservation of the state; as a person he sought for a virtuous reputation [...] Somerset succeeded only to the extent of acquiring a reputation for goodness in spite of his activities as a builder of a sumptuous house, as a sheep master, as an encloser and a rack-renter; but by the time of his fall even his reputation was not what he would have wished, having become entangled with a reputation for radicalism, largely because of his behaviour to peasant rebels [...]'[76]

John Guy found him 'vacillating but self-willed, high-minded yet prone to *idees fixes*', all the while courting popularity 'while sugar-coating his natural severity with talk of clemency and justice'[77].

---

[76] M. L. Bush, *The Government Policy of Protector Somerset* (1975).

[77] John Guy, *Tudor England* (1988).

Reform and compromise: Somerset's religious policies

Although economic issues were paramount, religious concerns helped provoke the rebellions of 1549. The fall of Norfolk and Gardiner in the last years of Henry's reign had severely damaged the Catholic faction and Somerset's acquisition of a protectorship was a Protestant triumph. Protestant exiles began to return to England together with continental reformers, seeking refuge after Charles V's destruction of the Protestant Schmalkaldic League.

That the accession of Edward, educated by Protestants, and the protectorship of the Duke of Somerset heralded a new drive towards Protestantism could not be doubted after Henry's reactionary Act of Six Articles was revoked by Parliament in November 1547. The Lutheran idea of justification by faith, as opposed to deeds, was encouraged - a challenge to the common assumption that the giving of gifts to the Church and the doing of good works, such as the undertaking of pilgrimages, might guarantee and hasten one's entrance into Heaven. The restriction of Bible reading in the vernacular to men of the higher orders was repudiated by the re-introduction of Cromwell's Injunctions of 1538:

> 'you shall discourage no man secretly or openly from the reading or hearing of the said Bible, but shall expressly provoke, stir, and exhort every person to read the same [...]'

The iconoclasm of Cromwell's first set of Injunctions issued in 1536 was also encouraged and many new books and pamphlets appeared urging the destruction of statues, church murals and the like. The government largely ignored the subsequent riots, destruction and looting of church property in a number of eastern counties. All parishes in 1547 were ordered to keep copies of two 'classic' Protestant texts: Erasmus' *Paraphrases* and Cranmer's *Book of Homilies*. Bishops were instructed to remove from their churches any images, including statues, associated with superstitious practices. At the same time the great Catholic tenet of transubstantiation received official support and certain Catholic feast-days and Lent were defended.

The dissolution of ecclesiastical houses continued into Edward's reign with the Chantries Act of 1547. Chantries were small establishments, usually comprising a chapel and enough land to support the priest whose job it was to chant masses for the soul of its deceased benefactor. Their dissolution certainly satisfied reformers, opposed to the notion of Purgatory, but the motive behind the closures was more to do with financial gain and the funding of an expensive foreign policy. The gold and silver plate confiscated was melted down to make more coins.

The ambiguity of official doctrine, all the greater for the repeal of the Six Articles, needed sorting out and in January 1549 the First Edwardian Act of Uniformity was passed. Once more this proved to be a compromise: services were to be conducted in English, the clergy once more could marry, the chanting of masses for the souls of the dead was discouraged. On the other hand the form of the English communion service followed closely that of the Catholic Latin mass and priests continued to be set apart from the laity by wearing the traditional rich vestments. The doctrine of transubstantiation was affirmed and no specific statement was made regarding the truth of Purgatory. Priests were obliged to deliver services according to the conditions of the act but the laity were not subject to compulsory attendance. No-one was especially pleased with the outcome apart from the conservative Bishop Gardiner, and his endorsement made the new service even less acceptable to Protestants.

Foreign Affairs 1547-49

The threat of a Catholic crusade against England remained an uncomfortably real possibility after Henry's death. Henry's great opponent, the French king, Francis I, also died in 1547, to be replaced by the more vigorous and belligerent Henry II. In June 1547 the Franco-Scottish alliance was renewed and 4000 French troops were landed in Scotland. Somerset made a pre-emptive strike in the form of a combined naval and overland invasion of Scotland in September 1547. The Scots were badly defeated at the battle of Pinkie, outside Edinburgh on September 10. Having secured the border Somerset withdrew with the bulk of his victorious army on September 18. Rather than embark upon conquest Somerset's plan for Scotland was one of containment and new English garrisons were established at key strategic locations in the east, including the Firth of Forth, the mouth of the River Tay, along the Tweed and, to the west, at Dumfries, beside the Solway Firth. At the same time attempts were made to win the Scots over to the English and protestant cause with propaganda, preaching and the distribution of bibles.

Hostilities between England and France continued into 1548. Shipping from both countries was attacked in the Channel and Somerset reinforced his troops around the port of Boulogne, seized by Henry VIII in his invasion of 1544. Hopes of an Anglo-Scottish alliance were receding fast as the Scottish Council responded favourably to French overtures regarding the possibility of the Mary Queen of Scots marrying Henry II's eldest son instead of Edward VI as previously arranged in 1543 by the terms of the treaties of Greenwich. Somerset pleaded with the Scots to reconsider where their natural allegiance lay - surely, he wrote in January 1548, their commonality of language, character and culture, 'the two bretheren of one island of Great Britain', made it 'unmeet, unnatural, and unchristian that there should be between us so mortal war'. His appeal was to no avail - Mary was sent to France to be educated while the French and Scottish prepared a counter-attack on the border garrisons. Haddington Castle was beseiged and relieved, at great cost to the English purse, by a substantial army under the leadership of the Earl of Shrewsbury. As soon as Shrewsbury withdrew the Franco-Scottish force returned but they too abandoned the assault, because of the expense, towards the end of 1548.

Most of the gains in Scotland following the campaign of 1547 were finally relinquished in 1549 when the popular risings in the south and the continued threat of French invasion obliged Somerset to recall his troops from the Scottish strongholds. Henry II capitalised on England's misfortunes by renewing the pressure on Boulogne. The crisis on all fronts by the autumn of 1549 assured Somerset's fall. In just two years Somerset had spent £351,000 on foreign affairs, almost twice as much Henry VIII's five year war with Scotland. His legacy to his successor, the Duke of Norfolk, was to be the loss of Boulogne and the enforced abandonment of the remaining Scottish garrisons according to the terms of the Treaty of Boulogne, 28 March 1550, 'the most ignominious treaty signed by England during the century'.[78]

Susan Doran has identified some degree of success in Somerset's

---

[78] W. K. Jordan, *Edward VI: The Threshold of Power* (1970).

foreign policy nevertheless:

> 'At the same time Somerset was trying to keep Charles V's friendship, since his goodwill was needed for the supply of foreign mercenaries from Flanders. Furthermore, should France aid the Scots, Somerset wanted to ensure that French ships should be able to ensure that the French ships would be unable to use the Netherlands' ports. With these ends in view, Somerset tried to present himself to the Imperial ambassador as a religious conservative and delayed the introduction of religious reform. Here his policy was more successful; Charles V was inclined to be friendly, and Anglo-Imperial amity deterred Henry II from declaring war on England immediately and sending a very large army to Scotland.'[79]

The Duke of Northumberland, King Edward and Queen Jane

'Dudley had an immensely strong and indeed almost terrifying personality.'

(Christopher Morris, *The Tudors*, 1955)

John Dudley had made a name for himself long before he became the Duke of Northumberland, towards the end of his career, in October 1551. His previous titles during the reign of Henry VIII included Deputy-Governor of Calais, Warden of the Scottish Marches, Great Admiral, and Governor of Boulogne, seized from the French by an army under his command in 1544. He played a leading role in assuring Somerset's domination over the more reactionary elements in the Privy Council in 1547. Only when Somerset made himself Lord Protector did Dudley begin to challenge his supremacy. He promoted the interests of Somerset's brother, Thomas Seymour, which resulted in the latter's execution for treason in 1549. Thus began a fierce factional struggle between the camps of Northumberland and Somerset which continued

---

[79] Susan Doran, *England and Europe 1485-1603* (1986).

until the former protector was brought to the block in 1552.

The unpopularity of Somerset's religious policies, the cost of war, the anarchy and rebellion of 1549, all contributed to the abandonment of his cause and to his arrest in October 1549. The accomplished Dudley had the upper hand as commander of the main army in England that had been mustered to defeat Robert Kett and the eastern rebels. During the assault on Somerset Dudley had secured a temporary alliance with the conservative Lords Wriothesley and Arundel by assuring them that he had no interest in further religious reform and would even countenance the regency of the Catholic princess Mary for the remainder of Edward's minority following the protector's fall. Once Somerset was out of the way however he aligned himself unreservedly to Archbishop Cranmer and the Protestant king, determined not to be ousted himself by his conservative allies. With the backing of Cranmer, who feared a Catholic reaction after the fall of Somerset, he became, on 21 February 1550, Lord President of the Council and Master of the King's Household. Wriothesley and Arundel, accused of plotting a second coup, were banished from Court. For a time Somerset was reinstated on the Council only to be re-arrested in October 1551 and beheaded the following January for allegedly conspiring to bring down Dudley, now the Duke of Northumberland.

Henry VIII's last Council, designed to share the duty of government during the minority of Edward VI, comprised sixteen tried and tested men drawn, more or less evenly, from the conservative and reformist parties. Fatally, Somerset's virtual personal rule alienated the majority while his excessive reliance on proclamations rather than Parliament increased his unpopularity. Northumberland revitalised and considerably enlarged the Council to around forty members, filling it with both loyal and competent advisors, including several with military expertise who could be relied upon to quell any further rebellions. At the same time the Council was purged of further conservatives including Tunstall, the Bishop of Durham and also of Somerset's former right-hand man, William Paget. Where possible he steered legislation through Parliament rather than ruling by decree. Effectively Northumberland's became a personal rule like Somerset's but he took care to give the impression that he followed the inclinations and instructions of the king as opposed to ruling in his place. In February 1551 twelve trained bands, constituting 850 cavalrymen, were established to act as the king's, and his, personal bodyguard. This initiative has been described by John Guy as representing 'the first step towards the formation of a standing army in England'.[80]

Government and religion under the Duke of Northumberland

The problems facing Northumberland and the Council in 1550 were manifold. The French war was ended by the Treaty of Boulogne in March, 1550, but the abandonment of the city was widely regarded as a national disgrace. Relations with the Holy Roman Empire continued to deteriorate as the Protestant reform of the English Church gathered pace. In April English merchants were compromised by Charles V's edict permitting the Inquisition to arrest heretics in the Netherlands. Scotland remained a considerable risk to national security; in 1551 further troops and supplies were sent over from France. The war between Henry II and Charles V that broke out in 1552 reduced the threat of further conflict with either power and Northumberland, resisting imperial efforts to embroil England in another French war, stayed staunchly neutral.

The cost of Somerset's wars had bankrupted England. To redeem matters money was raised on the sale of chantry and Crown lands, and in 1552 inflation, encouraged by the successive debasements of currency up to 1551, was addressed by the recall of all coins which were then reissued with a silver content equal to that of coins in 1527. Northumberland placed such matters in the capable hands of William Cecil and Thomas Gresham whose wise investments and efforts to cut costs by improving the efficiency of government departments helped resolve the crisis by 1553. Cost saving devices included, perhaps fatally for Northumberland, the dissolution of the palace guard, and plans were made, to be realised in the reign of Mary I, for the streamlining of the revenue courts connected to the Exchequer.

The depression, exacerbated by poor harvests, caused widespread unemployment and high prices. Measures were taken to prevent economic hardship and general distress from fermenting into political discontent. The draconian Vagrancy Act of 1547 and the sheep tax of 1548 were repealed, and a new Treason Act, strengthening the arm

---

[80] John Guy, *Tudor England* (1988).

of local authorities, was passed. Action against enclosure and the introduction of a more generous poor law for those unfit to work helped prevent further rebellions in Edward's brief reign.

Under Northumberland the Church was subjected to radical Protestant reform. This was probably begun, not as a result of any deep religious conviction of his own, but as a political expedient in order to deflate the conservative faction with which Northumberland had allied himself in the destruction of Somerset but which subsequently posed a threat to his own ascendancy. Furthermore Edward himself was increasingly inclined towards Protestantism and the reformist faction gathered around Nicholas Ridley, Bishop of London. Northumberland's opportunism in religious matters, and his willingness to accept the religious beliefs of his monarch, was most evident in his astonishing 'conversion' to Queen Mary's Catholicism shortly before his execution. Although he may have been swayed by the arguments of the reformers once in power, most historians agree that he was not a deeply spiritual man.

Ridley launched a campaign in 1550 to tear down altars and rood screens and replace them with simple communion tables; the bishops' injunctions were later affirmed by order of the Council, issued in November. In 1551, providing a further means of raising money to pay off the national debt, the Council ordered the removal of gold and silver plate from parish churches. The concept of purgatory and the efficacy of prayers for the dead were effectively rejected by the terms of the 1552 Act of Uniformity. It now became an offence for clergy and laity to abstain on Sundays from the reformed Church services 'having no lawful or reasonable excuse to be absent'. Edward's Second Book of Common Prayer in the same year abolished the Mass. The Catholic belief in transubstantiation in the Eucharist was unequivocally replaced by the belief in consubstantiation, the Lutheran doctrine that the bread and wine did not miraculously transform into the flesh and blood of Christ when consecrated. Those found attending services that did not conform to the doctrines of the new Prayer Book were to be severely punished: '[...] for the first offence suffer imprisonment for six months, without bail [...] and for the second offence [...] imprisonment for the whole year; and for the third offence [...] imprisonment during his or their lives.' Although 'superstitious' practices such as kneeling when taking communion were maintained, regarded as idolatrous by radical reformers, the Church of England became truly Protestant during the reign of Edward VI.

In considering and contrasting the personalities and achievements of Somerset and Northumberland, G. R. Elton found them both wanting:

> 'Thus Somerset, noble-minded and generous, but also ambitious, high-handed, and incompetent, made way for a man for whom no one has ever had a good word [...] Unquestionably Northumberland was exceedingly ambitious of power and very greedy. He represented, at its worst, the type of man who was speculating in monastic property and the exploitation of land, and the businesslike landowning gentry looked to him to save them from Somerset's predeliction for the peasants [...] Where Somerset was attractive as a man but disastrous as a ruler, Northumberland displayed every unpleasant personal characteristic but seems to have shown skill and penetration in public affairs. It is difficult to say who did more harm to the country they were supposed to govern.'[81]

Dale Hoak went some way towards salvaging Northumberland's poor reputation:

> '[Northumberland] preferred to do business secretly, which created the impression that his government's policies promoted his private gain. Thus, when the Council laid up gold and silver coin in the Tower, it was thought that Northumberland was robbing the King. In fact, such hoarding crudely served Thomas Gresham's officially sponsored attempts to raise the price of English money on the Antwerp exchange. It would be inaccurate to claim that Northumberland did not use the King's money either for his own gain or for his political ends, but, rather than assuming him to have been the slave of an unbridled greed or a gangster bent on throttling the King, one should try to fit the pattern of his actions into a context which explains him historically.
> Pride, hypocrisy and an insatiable greed: every writer has cited these to explain how Northumberland brought about his own end. In fact, since his alleged traits can be explained circumstantially, it is more likely that accident felled him.

---

[81] G. R. Elton, *England Under the Tudors* (1974).

Allegations of avarice are irrelevant here. Was there anyone at court in Edward's last hour who had not benefited materially by the Reformation? If Northumberland is to be judged on this count, a whole generation of courtiers and Crown servants must be condemned. Given the conditions of a royal minority, rate at which he acquired property was unusual only the by Tudor standards, and even that was not unique. The duke of Somerset appears to have been more avaricious, more ostentatious, more wealthy at the height of his power, more shamelessly proud. By 1551 Northumberland's power required a pre-eminence (a dukedom) and an income appropriate to his rank. Essentially without salary, he rewarded himself in the acceptable manner of the age.

Reluctantly [...] he chose to destroy Somerset [in 1551] [...] he had to fabricate the case against Somerset and it weighed heavily on his conscience thereafter. Nevertheless, his calculated action probably saved England the spectacle of a bloody counter-coup and the administrative chaos of a revived protectorate.

Fearing a "Catholic" counter-coup, he adopted Protestantism in order to test the conservatives' political loyalties. The introduction of the reformed faith into England thus came as a by-product of the intrigues of October 1549 to February 1550. Northumberland's true objective was [...] to provide for the government's stability, and this could be achieved only by neutralising political strife at court and reordering the King's finances [...] given the circumstances which he inherited in 1549, the duke of Northumberland appears to have been one of the most remarkably able governors of any European state during the sixteenth century.'[82]

The 'Device for the Succession': Jane Grey, the Nine Day Queen

'And though I liked not the religion

---

[82] Extracts from: Dale Hoak, 'Rehabilitating the Duke of Northumberland: Politics and Political Control, 1549-53'. in Jennifer Loach and Robert Tittler, *The Mid-Tudor Polity c.1540- 1560* (1980).

Which all her life Queen Mary had professed,
Yet in my mind that wicked notion
Right heirs for to displace, I did detest.'

(Sir Nicholas Throckmorton)

Northumberland's position was reliant upon the King's good health. In the event of Edward's death it had been ordained by Henry's will that Mary and her heirs should inherit the Crown. Mary's Catholicism would make her intolerant of the minister who had so recently brought about the full-blown Protestant reform of the English Church.

Having survived the crisis of 1550, Northumberland's future looked bright. He had secured the friendship of the young king and, contrary to popular belief, Edward's health seemed unimpaired. He was below average height and short-sighted and had suffered a couple of potentially fatal childhood illnesses, yet he enjoyed such pastimes as riding, hunting and archery. When, in January 1553, he began to show symptoms of what was probably acute pulmonary tuberculosis, Northumberland was greatly alarmed. His condition rapidly declined. John Banister, a young medical student, recorded the prognosis in May:

'He does not sleep except he be stuffed with drugs [...] The sputum which he brings up is livid, black, fetid and full of carbon; it smells beyond all measure [...] His feet are swollen all over. To the doctors all these things portend death, and that within three months.'

Northumberland acted swiftly. Desperate circumstances called for desperate measures and Edward was persuaded to write a will that disinherited his sisters on the grounds of their illegitimacy. In their place he named Jane Grey, the elder daughter of Henry's sister Mary who had been named successor in Henry's will after Mary and Elizabeth. Once intended for Edward she was now promptly married to Northumberland's own son, Sir Guildford Dudley. Three days after Edward's death on 6 July she was proclaimed Queen.

Northumberland's gamble might well have paid off; he had some support in Protestant circles, his reputation as a military commander was formidable, and he enjoyed the clandestine support of the French who feared the closer relations with Spain that the half-Spanish Mary's ascendency seemed likely to promote. However he had many enemies even among confirmed Protestants. The blatant conspiracy to wed his personal fortunes to the issue of succession was offensive in the extreme and, in any case, the country at large was more sympathetic to the Henrician Catholicism Mary was considered to represent than the fanatical Lutheranism associated with Northumberland. Caught off guard by the suddenness of Edward's illness he had taken no adequate measures to protect his interests in military terms having paid off the mercenaries employed to suppress the riots and rebellions of 1549 and disengaged the standing army established in 1551.

Supported by key figures among the English nobility and many of the gentry and commoners of East Anglia, Mary was proclaimed Queen at Bury St Edmunds. Members of the Privy Council began to switch their loyalty to Mary. Northumberland, abandoned and unable to raise more than 2000 troops, who also soon deserted him, was arrested at Cambridge on 24 July. On 3 August Mary was acclaimed Queen at London and Jane Grey's short 'reign' was over. Northumberland's execution for treason followed on 22 August but Lady Jane survived until Sir Thomas Wyatt's rebellion in January 1554 prompted the Marian government into eliminating other contenders for the throne. Princess Elizabeth was imprisoned in the Tower and, on 12 February, her sixteen year old cousin was beheaded. Robert Tittler has described hers as 'the only successful English revolt of the entire century'.[83]

---

[83] Robert Tittler, The Reign of Mary I, 1991

SOURCES

The 'Good Duke'

(William Paget, Privy Councillor and friend, in a letter to the Duke of Somerset, 7 July 1549)

I told your Grace the truth, and was not believed: well, now your Grace sees it, what says your Grace? Marry, the King's subjects out of all discipline, out of obedience, caring neither for Protector or King, and much less for any other mean officer. And what is the cause? Your own levity, your own softness, your opinion to be good to the poor. I know, I say, your good meaning and honest nature. But I say, sir, it is a great pity (as the common proverb goes) in a warm summer that ever fair weather should do harm. It is a pity that your so much gentleness should be an occasion of so great an evil as is now chanced in England by these rebels […]

Rebellion in Somerset, 1549

(Somerset and his councillors' instruction to Lord Russell, commander of the King's army in the county of Somerset, July 27 1549)

[If necessary] Ye shall hang two or three of them, and cause them to be executed like traitors […] sharp justice must be executed on those sundry traitors which will learn by nothing but the sword.

The Prayer Book Rebellion, 1549

(Religious demands of the western rebels, 1549)

1. First we will have the general counsel and holy decrees of our forefathers observed, kept and performed, and who so ever shall speak against them, we hold as heretics.

2. Item we will have the Laws of our Sovereign Lord King Henry the VIII concerning the Six Articles. to be used as they were in his time.

3. Item we will have the mass in Latin, as was before, and celebrated by the priest without any man or woman communicating with him.

7 [...] Images to be set up again in every church, and all other ancient olde Ceremonies used as heretofore, by our mother the holy Church.

8. Item we will not receive the new service because it is like a Christmas game, but we will have our old service of Matin, mass, Evensong and procession in Latin not in English, as it was before. And we the Cornishmen (whereof certain of us understand no English) utterly refuse this new English.

9. Item we will have every preacher in his sermon, and every priest at his mass, pray specially by name for the souls in purgatory, as our forefathers did.

10. Item we will have the whole Bible and all books of scripture in English to be called in again [...]

14. Item we will that the halfe part of the abbey lands and Chantry lands, in every man's possession, howsoever he came by them, be given again to two places, where two of the chief Abbeys used to be in every County [...]

Kett's Rebellion, 1549

(Robert Kett's religious demands, 1549)

4. We pray that priests from henceforth shall purchase no lands neither free nor bonded, and the lands that they have in possession may be let to temporal men, as they were in the first year of the reign of King Henry VII.

8. We pray that priests or vicars that be not able to preach and set forth the word of God to His parishioners may be thereby put from his

benefice, and the parishioners there to choose another or else the patron or lord of the town.

15. [We pray that no] priest [shall be a chaplain] nor no other officer to any man of honour or worship but only to be resident upon the benefice whereby the parishioners may be instructed with the laws of God.

20. We pray that every proprietary parson or vicar having a benefice of £10 or more per year shall [...] teach poor men's children of their parish the book called the catechism and the primer.

England and Scotland 1547-49

(William Paget's advice to Somerset, 28 April 1549)

When Boulogne was won the victory seemed honourable at the first and so did our entry into war on the death of the king upon Scotland. But now having felt the charges of both to have been so great [...] diverse wise men wish that we had lived in [peace] with Scotland. When Boulogne was won it was said we should never have good peace with France til it were restored. And when we began war first with Scotland the French king said he would rather lose his realm than leave them [...] Wherefore without peace in Scotland I believe that the French king will never be at peace with England. Then if war with Scotland brings war with France, it is good to consider whether we be able to maintain war with France so many years as we shall make them weary to take part with Scotland. And if we be, then may we be the bolder to continue our conquest and fortifications in Scotland. But if we be not I think we are not then to take more and fortify more and in the end to be obliged to leave it over to your enemy, albeit the first part *viz.* taking, has a look of honour: yet the other part *viz.* after waste of much time, expense of much money, loss of your people, to leave to your enemy that which you have taken, and to the king, his own realm in misery and beggary when he shall enter himself to government, is a certain and inevitable dishonour in the judgement of the world [...]

The usurpation of Mary Tudor, 1553

(Reply of the Privy Council to Mary Tudor, 9 July 1553, regarding her claim to the throne)

To my Lady Mary,

Madame, we have received your letter [...] declaring your supposed title which you judge yourself to have: the Imperial Crown of this Realm and all the domains thereunto belonging. Our answer is to advise [you that] our Sovereign Lady Queen Jane is after the death of our Sovereign Lord King Edward VI a prince of most noble memory, invested and possessed with right and just title in the Imperial Crown of the Realm, not only by good order of old ancient laws of this realm, but also by your late Sovereign Lord's letters patent signed with his own hand and sealed with the Great Seal of England in the presence of the most part of the nobles and councillors, judges, and diverse other grown and sage persons assenting and subscribing unto the same.

The Nine Day Queen, 1553

(Baptisa Spinola, a Genoese merchant)

Today I saw Lady Jane Grey walking in a grand procession to the Tower. She is now called queen, but it is not popular for the hearts of the people are with Mary, the Spanish Queen's daughter.

This Jane is very short and thin, but prettily shaped and graceful. She has small features and a well-made nose, the mouth flexible and the lips red. The eyebrows are arched and darker than her hair, which is nearly red. Her eyes are sparkling and reddish brown in colour. I stood so near her grace that I noticed her colour was good but freckled. When she smiled she showed her teeth, which are white and sharp. In all a gracious and animated figure. She wore a dress of green velvet stamped with gold, with large sleeves. Her headdress was a white coif with many jewels [...] The new queen was mounted on very high chopines [shoes with very thick soles] to make her look much taller, which were concealed by her robes, as she is very small and short. Many ladies followed, with noblemen, but this lady is very heretical and has never heard Mass, and some great people did not come into the procession for that reason.

Jane Grey and the Duke of Norfolk

(Jane Grey to Mary I, 1553)

The Duke then added that I was the heir named by His Majesty to succeed to the Crown [...] how I was beside myself stupified and troubled, I will leave it to those Lords who were present to testify, who saw me, overcome by sudden and unexpected grief, fall on the ground, weeping very bitterly [...] I was conducted to the Tower, and [...] afterwards were presented to me by the Marquis of Winchester, Lord High Treasurer, the jewels, with which he brought me also the Crown, although it had never been demanded from him by me [...] and he further wished me to place it on my head, to try whether it really became me well or no. The which, although with many excuses, I refused to do, he nevertheless added I might take it without fear, and that another also should be made to crown my husband with me. Which thing I [...] heard truly with a troubled mind, and with ill will, even with greater grief and displeasure of heart [...] but afterwards I sent for the Earls of Arundel and Pembroke, and said to them that, if the Crown belonged to me, I should be content to make my husband a Duke, but would never consent to make him a King.

Chapter 8: The Reign of Mary I, 1553-58

Queen Mary

Born in 1516, Mary was Henry VIII's third but only surviving child from his marriage to Catherine of Aragon. Despite becoming the Princess of Wales in 1525 her claim to the throne was jeopardised by the declaration of her illegitimacy in 1533 following Henry's marriage to Anne Boleyn. Although she was not being redeemed to a state of legitimacy, Mary was partially reconciled to Henry after Anne's execution in 1536 and, in 1544, her place in the succession, after Henry's legitimate heirs, was formally recognised. Her childhood experience was that of a period of public adoration as the charming and talented princess followed by years of public rejection by her father and the privation and humiliation that entailed. As her mother lay dying she was forbidden to see her: she was not even permitted to inherit her furs.

The young princess, able to read six different languages, a graceful dancer and player of several musical instruments, began to suffer a physical and emotional decline in the later 1530s. For the rest of her life she suffered chronic bouts of illness: headaches, occasional hysteria, palpitations of the heart and dreadful toothache necessitating many extractions. By the time she ascended to the throne at the age of thirty-seven she was very thin and pale, childless and embittered.

Although given a humanist classical education Mary was a devout Catholic throughout her life. Long before Edward's death she had become a symbol of the Catholic struggle in England, practising Catholic rites in her home, her freedom to do so 'defended' by her cousin, the Holy Roman Emperor, Charles V. The rise of Northumberland was deeply threatening to Mary and, having failed to maintain her right to practice the Catholic religion in the privacy of her household, she contemplated fleeing to more conducive surroundings in Spain.

Edward's death provoked a crisis of succession that, at one level, represented a desperate and deadly struggle between reformers and reactionaries for control over the English Church and government. For both sides it was a dangerous gamble, where flight or compromise would have been the safer options. On the face of it the prospects of the unmarried, middle-aged, bastardised, half-Spanish, Catholic princess defeating the empowered warlord Northumberland, champion of the Henrician and Edwardian reformations, seemed slight. Even Charles V felt her chances of survival were small when she was first proclaimed Queen. Her insecurity, both before and after her accession, in part explains her endeavours to establish alliances with the Habsburgs. Despite Northumberland's advantages, Mary's daring in putting to the test the popular commitment to the legitimacy of Henry's will prevailed.

Mary's claim doubtless was supported by the fact that all the other potential claimants to the throne were female: her younger, also 'illegitimate' sister Elizabeth, and her cousins Jane Grey and Mary, Queen of Scots. Discounting Jane Grey, Mary was England's first female monarch since the disputed reign of Empress Matilda in the twelfth century. So great were public doubts regarding rule by queens that in 1554 Mary's Parliament passed an Act Concerning Regal Power asserting the right of women to rule with the same authority as men:

> '[...] be it declared and enacted by the authority of this present Parliament, that the law of this realm is and ever hath been and ought to be understood, that the kingly or regal office of the realm, and all dignities, prerogative, royal power, pre-eminences, privileges, authorities, and jurisdictions thereunto annexed, united, or belonging, being invested either in male or female, are and be and ought to be taken in the one as the other [...]'

A Spanish Marriage and an English Rebellion

Now queen and, by proclamation, legitimate, Mary was highly eligible for marriage despite her age. At thirty-seven she could still hope to bear a child and wrest the succession from her half-sister Elizabeth who did not uphold the Catholic faith. The daughter of a Spanish queen of England with a commitment to Roman Catholicism, Mary gravitated towards the prospect of a Spanish marriage with none other than prince Philip, Charles V's son and heir. The suit was proposed in October 1553 by the imperial ambassador, Simon Renard, and Mary, much to the offence of her councillors who were not consulted on the matter, accepted. Only one Privy Councillor, William Paget, approved of the match; others, led by Chancellor Gardiner, and including a majority within the House of Commons, favoured an English marriage as a less provocative arrangement in the wake of Henry's and Edward's Reformations. Some advanced the hand of Edward Courtenay, the great-grandson of Edward IV and, at twenty-seven, marginally older than Philip and ten years younger than Mary.

By December 1553 the Council was persuaded to accept the forthcoming marriage on the understanding that Spaniards would not hold English offices and that, in the event of Mary's earlier death, Philip would make no claims to the English throne. Furthermore the marriage should not be the basis upon which England might become embroiled in any of Philip's continental wars. In return any child of the marriage should inherit the whole of Spain's empire in the event of Philip's son by his first marriage, Don Carlos, dying childless.

Such qualifications were insufficient to appease those who opposed the marriage on religious, national or commercial grounds. The threat of Catholic Spain's intervention in English affairs was greeted with dismay, and led to plotting and, ultimately, armed resistance. A conspiracy to overthrow Mary and restore a Protestant monarchy under Elizabeth fermented throughout the last months of 1553. A simultaneous rising across several southern counties planned for March 1554 erupted in some areas prematurely in January, following the discovery by Renard and the government of the conspiracy. The biggest disturbances were in Kent where the two week long rebellion was inspired and co-ordinated by Sir Thomas Wyatt.

Wyatt's rebel army of around 3000 reached London and crossed the Thames before surrendering in February when the defending army commanded by Pembroke proved constant in its loyalty and London failed to rise. The curious decision of the rebels to besiege Cooling Castle instead of marching directly to London had given the queen and her Council time to prepare London's defences. The imperial ambassador, Renard, advocated the executions of both Courtenay and the princess Elizabeth; they were spared but Wyatt and other rebels were not. Among the hundred put to death were Lady Jane Grey and her husband Guildford Dudley. To most however leniency was shown and most of Wyatt's captive supporters were set free.

In April, during the month of Wyatt's execution, the 1554

Parliament reluctantly agreed to the Spanish marriage and Mary and Philip were wed on 24 July. The coronation of Philip however was postponed and Philip returned to Spain at the earliest opportunity. Mary's ministers were united in their determination to restrict Philip's influence in England and, despite Philip's wishes, Mary gave in to parliamentary pressure. He never became a crowned king of England.

David Loades has challenged the notion that this was, essentially, a religiously-motivated rebellion:

> 'The original leader of this plot seems to have been William Thomas, a protestant and one-time clerk to Edward's Privy Council. Some of the others involved, such as Sir James Croft and Sir Edward Warner, had also been closely associated with the previous regime [...] Apart from Thomas, whose leadership was short-lived, none of these men were inspired by religious motives.'[84]

In Anthony Fletcher's opinion 'The rising sprang much more from fears and exaggerated rumours of what Philip might do than any firm evidence of his intentions when he became Mary's husband'[85]. These included fears that Philip would take the country into foreign wars it could ill-afford. Robert Tittler has identified social and economic grievances underpinning the unrest: 'it is clear that Kent as a whole had experienced a precipitous and very troubling decline in its cloth industry; had a tradition of popular protest both of long-standing duration and frequent expression; and had recently undergone a considerable shake-up in office-holding among the gentry who comprised the governing structure'[86].

The leadership of the rebellion suggests religion was an important factor: of the twenty-three leaders seventeen were certainly Protestants, including all nine clergymen involved at this level. None of the lay leaders is recorded as being a practicing Roman Catholic.

Protestant fears of future English involvement in Spain's conflict

---

[84] D. M. Loades, *Politics and the Nation, 1450-1660* (1979).

[85] Anthony Fletcher, *Tudor Rebellions* (1983).

[86] Robert Tittler, *The Reign of Mary I*, (1991).

with France were not misjudged: between 1557 and 1559 Mary joined Philip in war with the French king, Henry II. War with France was by no means the certain outcome of Mary's marriage, but Philip did use his title as King of England to win English assistance. The Anglo-French war, financially, was a calamity with no gain to justify the expense.

English economic interests dictated the logic of neutrality in the struggle between Spain and France over control of Italy and the papal states. English merchants traded in France, exporting wool and cloth and importing salt, sailcloth and wine; the port of Calais, though in decline, remained a mercantile as well as an imperial foothold on the continent. In the mid-fifties England was especially reliant on France as a supplier of grain when bad harvests at home had resulted in a famine. Political considerations also made hostilities with France undesirable because of continuing French influence in Ireland and Scotland. Even Catholic loyalty at first could be no justification for involvement - the pope, Paul IV, was staunchly anti-Spanish and deeply affronted by Philip's invasion of the Papal States in September 1556.

The activities of the French government helped to provoke Mary and her Council into supporting Philip by providing English Protestant exiles with a safe haven from which to plan further plots against Mary and her Catholic counter-Reformation. The Spanish marriage inevitably increased French interest in English domestic affairs and the great conspiracy of 1554 included in its design the support of the French navy which would secure the Channel from Spanish intervention. The conspirators had negotiated with Antoine de Noailles, the French ambassador, and de Noailles appears to have been an initiator of a further scheme in the spring of 1556. Having secured support among a number of lesser gentry in the South and West, Sir Henry Dudley, with French backing, planned an invasion from France with a view to placing Elizabeth on the throne. The plot was soon uncovered and de Noailles recalled to France. It is likely that Dudley would never have received the French support he would have needed since Henry II was anxious not to draw England into full-scale war.

A further plot in 1557 however helped push England into the conflict Henry was so keen to avoid. In April 1557 an exiled Protestant, Thomas Stafford, sailed from France to Scarborough in a ship loaded with French arms. This self-appointed 'Protector of England' hoped to raise a spontaneous rebellion against Mary; he was rapidly suppressed but English suspicions of the French were confirmed. Within two months

England and France were at war.

Ironically the war provided the opportunity for those dishonoured by their association with Wyatt, such as Sir James Croft and Sir Peter Carew, and Northumberland's 'device', including his three sons, to prove their loyalty. Such men shouldered arms with their Catholic counterparts and fought for Mary in France. The high proportion of ex-rebels in Mary's new army has been explained by C. S. L. Davies:

> 'This was partly because soldiers and sailors had been drawn into an opposition stance, through their association with the duke of Northumberland's regime, which had a strongly military colouring. Moreover, as Dr Loades observes, many of the conspirators were small gentlemen or younger sons whose only hope of a career lay with the sword - if necessary, in French service, but preferably in that of their Queen. On its side, Mary's government could not afford to waste military talent and experience. The war provided an opportunity, therefore, to reunite a deeply divided ruling class.'[87]

A massive naval refurbishment was initiated. Henry VIII's great navy had been allowed to decline from twenty-one sea-worthy and equipped men-of-war in 1557 to just three. By 1557 the fleet was fully restored. At a cost of between £14000 and £20000 per annum England soon boasted the finest fleet in her maritime history. The government's expenses were met largely by ordinary means including a highly lucrative, and long overdue, reassessment of customs duties. The army, hitherto reliant upon local quasi-feudal recruitment, began to be reorganised on a national basis with stricter, more uniform musters and levies, administered after 1588 by local officials and ten new Lord-Lieutenants, each responsible for one of the lieutenancies into which the country was now divided.

Despite a promising start with the English domination of the Channel and Spanish acquisitions, aided by English troops, in northern France, the campaign, for England, proved disastrous. In January 1558 the French, in revenge, seized Calais after 200 years of English occupation. In April English insecurity was heightened by the marriage

---

[87] C. S. L. Davies, 'England and the French War, 1557-9' in Jennifer Loach and Robert Tittler, *The Mid-Tudor Polity c.1540-1560* (1980).

of the Dauphin to fifteen year-old Mary, Queen of Scots, necessitating further expense in reinforcing the English-Scottish border. By the time Mary died on 17 November 1558 the tables had been turned in Anglo-French relations: England's ancient foothold in France was relinquished while the French presence in Britain was much enhanced.

The English Counter-Reformation

The Protestant Reformation was driven by the printed word in a more literate world using, for the first time, the printing press. As early as 1520 in England an index of prohibited books was published to stem the spread of Protestant ideas. An Index drawn up by Pope Paul IV in 1559 still informs Roman Catholics as to what reading matter should be avoided. In 1542, to identify and eliminate heresy, a Roman Inquisition, modelled on the Spanish Inquisition, was established in Italy.

In the vanguard of Counter-Reformation was the Society of Jesus founded in 1540. These 'Jesuits' exercised a fanatical, Jesus Reformation disciplined and soldierly commitment to orthodoxy. The absolute devotion of the Jesuit to papal instruction was summed up by the order's founder, Ignatius Loyola:

> 'I will believe that the white object is black if that should be the decision of the hierarchical church.'

A Spaniard, of Basque and noble origin, Loyola, before becoming a mystic, was a soldier. His conversion came through his reading of devotional works while convalescing after having his leg shattered by a cannonball. In 1548 his manual for appropriate religious observances, *The Spiritual Exercises*, was first published. The Society of Jesus, obedient to the General (Loyola) and the pope over and above any secular ruler, made it a truly international movement. By the middle of the century at least one ruler, Philip II, had come to resent the Jesuits and their missionary zeal. Between 1542 and 1565 the Council of Trent, in which the Jesuit Diego Lainez was highly influential, redefined Catholic doctrine and, by clarifying belief, produced a Church that was unremittingly intolerant even of the slightest deviation from its official code.

The Counter-Reformation combined the assault on Protestantism, with a continuation of attacks on malpractice within the Catholic Church. A society of priests known as the Oratory of Divine Love, established in 1517, was called upon by Pope Paul III to lead the way in ridding the Church of its own abuses. Six members, including Mary I's archbishop, Reginald Pole, were made cardinals and, in 1538, called upon to produce a report, the *Consilium de emendanda ecclesia*, concerning the present condition of the Church. Their findings, including the shortcomings of previous popes, clerical vice in Rome, widespread simony and non-attendance, were so shocking that Paul suppressed the report's publication.

The mid-century Catholic revival is evident in the triumphalism of its architecture, literature and music. The character of Counter-Reformation popes was strikingly different to those of the Renaissance; the cardinals began to elect men who were highly educated, dedicated and hardworking. Many new orders were founded and, often under the influence of Jesuits, great advances were made in the field of religious and secular education. Whole countries including Poland and, for a time, England were returned to the Catholic faith through force and propaganda. Those already officially orthodox, particularly Italy, were purged of heresy.

Meanwhile the Protestant camp was split between Calvinists and Lutherans, and other sects too such as the Hussites and Utraquists. For a time Roman Catholicism seemed to have the upper hand and its champion was Philip II, Mary I's husband and Elizabeth I's implacable opponent. Religious enthusiasm, often masking political ambition, brought in its wake civil and international conflict and war.

Reformation and propaganda

> 'simple folk [...] are more easily moved by pictures and images to recall divine history than through mere words and doctrines'

> 'without images we neither think nor understand anything'

> (Martin Luther)

When Mary's first Parliament in 1553 began to undo the Protestant reforms of Edward's reign it is unlikely that anyone was much surprised. Whatever little else her subjects knew of her, her adherence to the old faith was well known. What many would have expected however was simply a return to the way things were at the end of Henry's reign and not the full-blown restoration of papal authority that Mary embarked upon. Re-Catholicisation by force was not necessarily anticipated, and Mary's hopes for a spontaneous popular restoration looked as if they might be fulfilled as her subjects celebrated her accession, parishioners began to refurbish their churches and traditional activities banned by the Protestants such as the May games and morris dancing reappeared. Stephen Duffy's *The Stripping of the Altars* (1992) challenged old assumptions by demonstrating the very considerable popularity of the old religion on Mary's accession. He estimated that eight or nine congregations out of ten were resolutely Catholic (Anglo-Catholic, if not Roman Catholic) during her reign.

Repealing the recent legislation was easy enough - a single statute at the end of 1553 swept away the several Edwardian acts that had eliminated the Mass, abolished images, abandoned certain holy days and fasting days and permitted clerical marriages. Harder to achieve was the restoration of the Church in England to its pre-Reformation scale. Massively diminished in terms of both financial resources, establishments and personnel, Mary tried to rebuild the Church. She refounded a number of houses around London, including Westminster Abbey and, in 1555, reintroduced the clerical tax of First Fruits and Tenths.

The Counter-Reformation in England was stalled for a time by the political crisis provoked, chiefly, by Mary's decision to marry Philip II. The restoration of the late Henrician Church in 1553 was followed after the suppression of Wyatt's revolt by an assault on leading Protestants. Hundreds of priests were already living abroad, forced into exile for refusing to give up the wives they had married in Edward's reign. Robert Tittler estimated that perhaps as many as 2000 clerics were removed from their offices and some, including a number of bishops, were imprisoned.

When Archbishop Pole, now a Cardinal, finally returned to England from his own Henrician and Edwardian exile, the stage was set for the repeal of the keystone of the Henrician Reformation - the Act of Supremacy. Although the dismantling of Edward's reforms had been, by and largely tolerated, even welcomed in many quarters, the royal supremacy was championed by the great majority of men of influence and its repeal would be resented for the same nationalistic reasons as the Spanish marriage.

Mary's second Statute of Repeal, the formal reconciliation with Rome, was passed in November 1554 but only after those that owned ex-Church lands were given an assurance that their property rights would not be violated:

> '[...] all persons having sufficient conveyance of the said lands and hereditaments, goods and chattels, as is aforesaid by the common laws, acts, or statutes of this realm, may without scruple of conscience enjoy them, without impeachment or trouble by pretence of any General Council, canons, or ecclesiastical laws, and clear from all dangers of the censures of the Church.'

This clause has been characterised by A. G. Dickens as 'a bargain between Queen Mary and the governing classes'. While on the one hand clearing the path for the abandonment of the royal supremacy it confirmed the irrevocability of the dissolution; short of the landed elite giving up their lands voluntarily, the dream of a complete restoration of the pre-Reformation Church would never be realised. What little remained in the possession of the Church was restored - a rather pitiful gesture that deprived the Crown, on the eve of the great famine and just a couple of years before the French war, of an annual income of some £60,000. However there were some voluntary gifts to the Church of its former property - Christopher Haigh has estimated that around a fifth of all churches for this time benefited from the return of church-plate, bells, books, vestments and the like.

The re-introduction of the medieval heresy laws at this time anticipated the religious persecution of the mid-fifties that provided Mary with a nickname - 'Bloody Mary'. The first Marian burning for heresy was in February 1555. The most celebrated executions were those of bishops Nicholas Ridley and Hugh Latimer, burned together on 16 October 1555 in the centre of Oxford, where they are commemorated by the famous Martyrs' Memorial. Shortly before they died Latimer cried out to his fellow martyr:

'Be of Good Comfort, Master Ridley, and play the man: we shall this day light such a candle by God's grace in England as, I trust, shall never be put out!'

The scale of persecution increased after the death of Stephen Gardiner, Bishop of Winchester, a month later. Despite having played a prominent role in initiating the campaign, he had begun to advise moderation, acutely aware of the regime's growing unpopularity and the strength that martyrdom lent to the Protestant cause at home and abroad. The continued persecution has been attributed by David Loades to the desire for personal revenge shared by Mary and Cardinal Pole, both of whom had suffered greatly in the past because of the spread of Protestantism. Robert Tittler perceived a significant Spanish influence upon these cruel English affairs:

> 'it is difficult to imagine that their role was entirely ceremonial [one] the Bishop of Cuenca, Alfonso de Castro, a Friar Observant, was one of the Church's acknowledged authorities on the theory and practice of persecuting heretics, and the author of several works on the subject. De Castro accompanied Philip to England for his wedding, heard his confession, offered mass in his presence the day after, and urged him to more zealous persecution of heresy in England in 1556.'[88]

Despite recanting many of his beliefs, Henry VIII's Archbishop, Thomas Cranmer, was one of 300 burned at the stake before Mary died in 1558. The great majority of those executed were men of the 'middling' and labouring sorts. The executions were preserved in the English consciousness by the publication in 1563 of John Foxe's hugely popular *Acts and Monuments*, more commonly known as *The Book of Martyrs*, in which virtually every victim is commemorated. Several hundred equally committed but usually wealthier contemporaries fled with their families to the Continent rather than renounce their beliefs or face the flames. However, shocking though these executions were, most people's lives were little changed by the Marian Counter-Reformation. Haigh has argued that for the majority days of Mary's reign were no darker than those that had gone before:

---

[88] Robert Tittler, *The Reign of Mary I* (1991).

'The unattractive disciplinary side of things - the hounding of heretics and married clergy [...] must be kept in perspective [...] Marian England was not merry England - but it was pretty cheerful England, at least until the dearth, defeat, and disease of the last years. Civic festivities on the great feasts of the Church, curtailed under Edward, were commonly restored.'[89]

Deaths by burning in the forty-six months between the first (20 January 1555) and the last (2 August 1557) amounted to at least 280 individuals of whom at least fifty-one were women and 229 were men. Of the 135 recorded by Foxe there were five bishops, sixteen priests, nine drawn from the gentry, four were tradesmen, twenty-six were skilled cloth-workers, and seventy-five were humble labourers. The great majority was resident in the south-east of England.

It is impossible to say whether a lasting restoration of Roman Catholicism was prevented only by Mary's death and the accession of Elizabeth. Suffice to say the elite relinquished the royal supremacy in return for economic security just as they gave in to the Spanish marriage in the interests of political stability. The failure of the 1554 revolt, and the absence of rebellion even at the height of religious persecution in a time of famine and military disaster, implies that the majority were either broadly in support of Marian religious policies, indifferent, or too afraid of the consequences to dare resist. Eamon Duffy's research confirms the case for widespread religious conservatism and the enduring appeal of the old religion. Without doubt thousands continued to practice, in secret or in exile, the Protestant religion but those in authority, with a handful of celebrated exceptions, had acquiesced. Those empowered were genuine in their loyalty to Mary despite not always agreeing with her policies and the Church hierarchy was staunchly Roman Catholic. In an age when men appointed to high ecclesiastical office often proved extremely flexible in theology, the refusal of all but one of Mary's bishops to accept in 1559 Elizabeth's Act of Supremacy is striking.

In the past historians have questioned the potential for Marian style Catholicism to survive at all in the post-Reformation world, regardless of other factors; it was accused of an anachronistic medieval obsession with ceremony and ritual, of being unintellectual. A. G.

---

[89] Christopher Haigh, *English Reformations* (1993).

Dickens' classic picture of the Marian Church is one of abject failure - unreformed and unpopular. More recently the English Catholic revival in the hands of such academics as Pole and Bonner has come to be seen as innovative and reformist. In a recent article Jennifer Loach identified their enthusiasm for such initiatives as the translation of scriptures and prayers into the vernacular and the establishment of 'seminaries' to provide an education for non-graduate priests. Even the burning of heretics is now being reassessed - such persecution happened in other places where a lasting re-Catholicisation was achieved and there is scarcely any evidence of it being counter-productive in turning spectators, by revulsion, to Protestantism; even Foxe records just one such conversion. The Catholic restoration was not necessarily as reactionary and uncreative as Protestant historians since Foxe have implied:

> 'The Marian authorities had hit, it would seem, upon exactly those methods of re-Catholicisation that were to prove so successful later in the century in other parts of Europe - an emphasis on the pastoral role of the bishops, an insistence on a high standard of clerical education, achieved in part by the establishment of seminaries, a stress on preaching and catechising. There is no reason to doubt that, given time, they would have achieved a similar success.
>
> The Marian Church, in some, mainly rural, areas was flourishing well into the 1580s, a living rebuke to Foxe's judgement on ' the unfortunate event of all [Mary's] purposes, who never seemed to purpose anything that luckily came to pass'[90].

Colonial Rule and the Counter-Reformation in Ireland

'ambitious but ill-conceived experiments'

(S. G. Ellis, *Tudor Ireland*, 1985)

---

[90] Jennifer Loach, 'Mary Tudor and the Re-Catholicisation of England', in *History Today*, vol. 44, November 1994.

Ireland posed particular problems for the English government in its campaign to reinstate Roman Catholicism. On the one hand the native population was already largely sympathetic to the old religion, on the other the imposition of English 'protestantism' had represented the subjugation of a potentially disloyal population. The Marian government wished to promote Catholicism while at the time it sought to contain Irish nationalism. For these reasons the re-Catholicisation of Ireland was pursued with significantly less fervour than on the mainland. Some leading Protestant clergy such as Bishop Bale went into voluntary exile, some married priests were deprived of their livings and St Patrick's Cathedral was reconsecrated. In 1557 the Henrician and Edwardian religious statutes were repealed. However the restitution of First Fruits and Tenths did not occur until a few months before Mary's death.

The assertion of English rule over the Irish was not promoted by religious proclamation but by what has been seen as a first experiment in colonial rule. Mary's government implemented the idea of Somerset's for the establishment of loyal 'plantations'. Confiscated lands were sold to English settlers and subjected to English common law. The new landowners were obliged to pay for the upkeep of roads and bridges and to provide military service. Under the able and firm administration of Sir Thomas Ratcliffe two new colonies, the Queen's and King's counties, were established between 1556 and 1563. The experiment however proved costly in military terms, provoking further Gaelic unrest against the English overlords in the Pale. Somerset's reliance on a strong English military presence was maintained with a permanent (and expensive) garrison of rarely less than 1500 men. In the verdict of one historian, A. G. R. Smith, the garrisoning and 'planting' of English settlers 'was a very clear sign that conciliation had been replaced by aggression' and thus marked a profound development of Anglo-Irish affairs. English colonialism, far from reducing the danger of Irish revolt, and of providing a haven for would-be continental invaders of England, exacerbated the problem. The Elizabethan English chauvinism that defined the 'land of saints' as a land of barbarians was in place.

SOURCES

Queen Mary's proclamation in York, 1553

(Robert Parkyn, curate of Adwick-le-Street near Doncaster)

And so the said Queen Mary was proclaimed there [York] on the xxi day of July, and at Pontefract, Doncaster, Rotherham and many other market towns on the 22 July (*viz.* Saint Mary Magdalen's day), she to be right inheritor and Queen of England and Ireland [...] whereat the whole commonalty in all places in the North parts greatly rejoiced, making great fires, drinking wine and ale, praising God. But all such as were of heretical opinions, with bishops and priests having wives, did nothing rejoice, but began to be ashamed of themselves, for the common people would point [at] them with fingers in places when they saw them [...]

Celebrations in London, 1553

(Eye-witness account of the celebrations in London, July 1553)

The Earl of Pembroke threw away his cap full of angelots. I saw myself money was thrown out at windows for joy. The bonfires were without number, and what with shouting and crying of the people, and ringing of bells, there could no man hear what another said.

Treason Act, 1553

(First Treason Act of Mary, 1553)

[...] the Queen's most excellent Majesty, calling to remembrance that many, as well honourable and noble persons as other of good reputation within this her Grace's realm of England, have of late, for words only without other opinion, fact or deed, suffered shameful death not accostomed to nobles; her Highness therefore, of her accostomed clemency and mercy, minding to avoid and put away the occasion and cause of like chances hereafter to ensue, trusting her loving subjects will, for her clemency to them shewed, love, serve and obey her Grace the more heartily and faithfully than for dread or fear of pains of body, is contented and pleased that the severity of suchlike extreme dangerous and painful laws shall be abolished, annulled and made frustrate and void.

The legitimisation of Mary I, 1553

(Act declaring Mary I legitimate, 1553)

[...] in any other act or acts of Parliament, as whereby your Highness is named or declared to be illegitimate, or the said marriage between [...] your father and [...] your mother is declared to be against the word of God or by any other means unlawful, shall be repealed [...]

The Queen to her subjects, 1554

(Mary I, January 1554)

Now, loving subjects, what I am ye right well know. I am your Queen, to whom at my coronation when I was wedded to the realm and laws of the same [...] you promised your allegiance and obedience unto me [...] And I say to you, on the word of a prince, I cannot tell how naturally the mother loveth the child, for I was never the mother of any, but certainly if a prince and governor may as naturally and earnestly love her subjects as the mother doth love the child, then assure yourselves that I, being your lady and mistress, do as earnestly and tenderly love and favour you.

Wyatt's Rebellion, 1554

(Words attributed, by G. Nichols in *The Chronicle of Queen Jane and of two years of Queen Mary*, to Bret, captain of 500 troops raised in London and sent by the Duke of Norfolk to Kent to break the rebellion. They deserted to the rebels at Rochester.)

'Masters, we go about to fight against our native countrymen of England

and our friends in a quarrel unrightful and partly wicked, for they, considering the great and manifold mysteries which are like to fall upon us if we shall be under the rule of the proud Spaniards or strangers, are here assembled to make resistance of the coming in of him or his favourers; and for that they know right well, that if we should be under their subjection they would, as slaves and villains, spoil us of our goods and lands, ravish our wives before our faces, and deflower our daughters in our presence, have now, for the avoiding of so great mischiefs and inconveniences likely to light not only upon themselves but on everyone of us and the whole realm, have taken upon them now, in time before his coming, this their enterprise, against which I think no English heart ought to say, much less by fighting, to withstand them.'

Wyatt's proclamation, 1554

(Wyatt's proclamation to his supporters recorded by John Proctor in *The Historie of Wyattes Rebellion*, 1554)

For [...] manifest proof of this intended purpose, ten, now, even at hand, spaniards be now already arrived at Dover at one passage, to the number of an hundred, passing upward to London in companies of ten, four and six, with harness, arquebuses [guns] and morians [moors], with match light, the foremost company whereof be already at Rochester. We shall require you therefore to repair to such places as the bearers hereof shall pronounce unto you, there to assemble and determine what may be best for the advancement of liberty and commonwealth in this behalf, and to bring with you such aid as you may.

Foxe's martyrs, 1557

(John Foxe's account of the execution of George Eagles in 1557)

With him were cast certain Thieves also, and the next day, when they were brought out to be executed with him, there happened a thing that did much set forth and declare the innocency and godlyness of this man. For being led between two Thieves to the place where he should suffer [...] one William Swallow [...] did hackle off his head, and sometime hit his neck, and sometime his Chin, and did fowly mangle him, and so opened him. Notwithstanding this blessed Martyr of Christ abode steadfast and constant in the very midst of his torments [...]

His head was set up at Chelmsford on the Market Cross on a long Pole, and there stood till the Wind did blow it down, and lying certain days in the street tumbled about, one caused it to buried in the Church yard in the night. Also a wonderful work of God was it that he shewed on this wicked Bayliff Swallow, who within short space after this was so punished, that all the hair went well near off his head, his eyes were as it were closed up, and could scantly see, the nails of his fingers and toes went clean off.

War with France, 1557

(Mary I's proclamation of war, June 1557)

Although we, the Queen, when we first came to the throne, understood that the Duke of Northumberland's abominable treason had been abetted by Henry, the French King, and that since then his ministers had secretly favoured Wyatt's rebellion [...] we attributed these doings to the French King's ministers rather than to his own will, hoping thus patiently to induce him to adopt a truly friendly attitude toward us [...] Lately, when Badely and Seaton started a new conspiracy, the King's ambassador was not only cognizant of it but received them in his house and supported them in their diabolical undertaking [...] He has also favoured pirates, enemies of Christendom, who have despoiled our subjects [...] The other day he sent Stafford with ships and supplies to seize our castle of Scarborough, not content with having intrigued so long with a view to getting possession of Calais and other places belonging to us across the seas [...] We therefore command all Englishmen to regard Henry, the French King, and his vassals as public enemies of this kingdom and to harm them wherever possible, abstaining from trading or any other business with them.

The fall of Calais, 1558

(Report of the Venetian Ambassador at Brussels, January 1558)

Today, at noon, news arrived of the entry into Calais of the French, which in like manner as it is of greater importance than any other intelligence that could be heard at this present time, so has it very greatly troubled everybody here, both on account of the actual loss and the subsequent detriment; the French, on the other hand, having made the greatest possible acquisition in these parts, well nigh expelling the English from Flanders, and depriving them of that port which rendered them masters of the Channel, and of a fortress which they held in such great account, and giving them such vast repute, they being thus able to harass France and Flanders and all these states at any time.

Chapter 9: The Reign of Elizabeth I

Princess Elizabeth

> 'To promote a woman to bear rule, superiority, dominion or empire above any realm, nation or city is repugnant to nature [...] the subversion of good order, of all equity and justice.'
>
> (John Knox, *First Blast of the Trumpet against the Monstrous Regiment of Women*)

The reign of Mary I had done little to remove the popular prejudice regarding female rulers. This other bastardised daughter of Henry VIII, Elizabeth, likely to marry some foreign prince, quite possibly her half-sister's husband, Philip of Spain, did not seem ideal monarchical material. As with Mary's accession however the other potential candidates were also female: Lady Jane Grey's younger sister Catherine, and Mary, Queen of Scots. After years of danger during Mary's reign, when Elizabeth's life was threatened by association with Wyatt's and other attempted rebellions, so much so that for a time she was even incarcerated in the Tower of London, Mary's death in 1558 guaranteed Elizabeth's succession. The terms of Henry VIII's will, which had named Elizabeth after Edward and Mary, the conditions on which Philip married Queen Mary, and the childlessness of that marriage, prevented any dispute and she was crowned with the customary pageant in January 1559.

Born to Anne Boleyn in 1533 and largely brought up among those of a Protestant persuasion, Elizabeth, unlike Mary, had no desire to restore Roman Catholicism in England, and this religious position largely determined the history of her reign.

The religious settlement, 1559

> 'The new reign was greeted by the English Protestant community as a divine deliverance; Elizabeth was to be the English Deborah, sent to save God's Englishmen.'

(Wallace MacCaffrey, *Elizabeth I*, 1993)

> 'If the Israelites might joy in their Deborah, how much more we English in our Elizabeth.'

(The Duchess of Suffolk, 1559)

The Act of Repeal, passed by Parliament in the reign of Mary I in 1553, in principle, restored the Church to its pre-Reformation position. As the daughter of Anne Boleyn with a humanist education, it was to be expected that Elizabeth, despite her compliance with Mary's Catholicism during the 1550s, would share her father's, perhaps even her brother's, religious stance. Protestants hoped for a structural and spiritual reformation while the Marian bishops braced themselves to uphold the recent counter-reformation.

Elizabeth had acquired the humanist's antipathy towards the 'superstitions' of the 'old religion' but she had none of her sister's doctrinal zeal. So long as she could be assured of their allegiance to her, to 'show themselves quiet and not manifestly repugnant to the laws of the realm', she preferred not to make enemies of her subjects by condemning their personal convictions and practices. Her brother, Edward VI, had been troubled by a violent uprising in in Cornwall and Devon in 1549, a reaction to the introduction of his overtly Protestant prayer book for compulsory use in every English church; likewise, Mary I faced possibly the most threatening of all Tudor rebellions, when Sir Thomas Wyatt in 1554 raised an army in Kent and marched to London to force her to abandon her proposed marriage to Philip II of Spain and, almost certainly, to abandon her endeavours to restore Roman Catholicism in England. In any case Elizabeth seems not to have been a religious radical and she shared the common affection for some of the ceremony of the old religion, offending the purists by retaining the crucifix and candles in her own chapel.

Her desire to place the English Church firmly in royal hands without causing more offence than necessary was evident in the title she took in 1559 as 'Supreme Governor' rather than 'Supreme Head', the more provocative title assumed by Henry VIII. Catholics could thus take the necessary oath acknowledging the Queen's 'Supremacy' without repudiating the ultimate supremacy of the Pope. The Act also removed Mary I's heresy laws.

The other key piece of religious legislation in 1559 was the Act of Uniformity. A new prayer book was introduced for compulsory use in every parish which was essentially the radical Edwardian version of 1552 but with a couple of important concessions. The ambiguities concerning transubstantiation of the more moderate prayer book of 1549 were used in place of the outright rejection of that doctrine in the 1552 Prayer Book and condemnation of the Pope 'and all his detestable enormities' was dropped from its pages entirely.

Even so J. E. Neale suggested in 1950 that this virtual reinstatement of the Edwardian liturgy, started life as an initiative of the House of Commons and not the Crown and thus represents an early victory for the radical Protestants over a moderate government. Certainly the raising of the issue of doctrine in this first session of Parliament inevitably created unhelpful friction at a time when the smooth passage of the Supremacy Bill was of paramount importance. Was the restoration of Edwardian style Protestantism instead of Henrician style 'Catholicism without a Pope' wrested from the Crown by an increasingly assertive House of Commons? Norman Jones in 1982, and most other historians since, rejected this, claiming that the Bill was a part of the Crown's planned programme. On the other hand some, such as P. Haugaard, argue that she sought a settlement based on the 1549 Prayer Book but was pushed into one based on the 1552 version. However the number of radical *'emigre'* Protestants in Parliament at this time has been exaggerated in the past and recent research suggests they scarcely outnumbered committed Catholics, let alone moderate conservatives. Yet another interpretation identifies a staunchly Protestant Queen pushed into moderation:

> 'These amendments had emphasised continuity with the Catholic past: a compromise settlement had been forced on a reformist

queen by the resistance of conservatives in the Lords.'[91]

The absence of contemporary evidence suggests this controversy over such a key event in English history will never be fully resolved.

The continued use of vestments and ornaments in churches, to the great disappointment of the radicals, was not abolished. Subsequent injunctions in 1559 enforced the wearing of Edwardian style clerical dress. Clerical marriage was neither condoned nor condemned but priests were discouraged from marrying by obliging them to secure permission to do so from their bishop and two JPs.

The Uniformity Bill, having passed through the Commons, met with difficulties in the Upper House. The Lords were split evenly between those for and against, despite measures taken including new appointments and arrests of two bishops to ensure success. In a remarkable gesture of defiance the Marian bishops and nine conservative peers voted against the government and the bill was passed by a margin of three out of a total thirty-nine. With one exception Mary's bishops refused to take the oath of loyalty and thus forfeited their sees, to be awarded over the coming months to Protestants. This demonstration neither proved successful in provoking a general outcry (the vast majority of lesser clergy took the oath) nor did it prevent the reintroduction of Protestant worship. It revealed the devotion of certain great families to the Catholic cause and possibly helped guide Elizabeth down a more moderate Protestant line and away from that of the continental reformers and English puritans.

The religious settlement of 1559 brought with it financial as well as political gains. The Act of Supremacy enabled the Crown to divert the lucrative tax on First Fruits and Tenths from the papal to the royal coffers. Mary's restored monasteries and other foundations were dissolved and an Act of Exchange gave the Queen the right to swap the Church lands of the newly vacated episcopal sees for Crown lands of the same value. Invariably these in fact would be exchanged for inferior lands and further profit was made by unnecessarily delaying the replacement of some of the Catholic bishops thus enabling the Crown to claim several months' worth of ecclesiastical revenue.

By 1560 the framework of the Elizabethan Church was in place and the Catholic opposition removed; doctrinal clarification by the

---

[91] Christopher Haigh, *Elizabeth I* (1988).

bishops was still needed and in the following months and years a vigorous struggle ensued between radical Protestant reformers and the moderates more conducive to the Queen's way of thinking. The settlement of 1559, seen by some contemporaries (and some historians since) as a compromise, was greeted with dismay by many conservatives as well as reformers. However, it was broadly acceptable to the vast majority of ordinary priests and churchgoers after the years of intolerance of the two previous reigns.

For the future Bishop of Salisbury, John Jewel, the *via media* was a dismal compromise, 'a leaden mediocrity' as he described it in a letter to a friend in Zurich in 1559. For eminent politicians such as Sir Nicholas Bacon, Lord Keeper of the Privy Seal, this 'mediocrity' was an essential principle – his own motto was *Mediocria firma*. However, in the opinion of Susan Doran, the *via media* was not in fact the outcome of political principle: 'In reality, the nature of the Church was greatly influenced by pragmatic political considerations, and its shape was formed as a result of serious tensions between the queen and her divines, which were never completely settled.' Thus recent historians have avoided using the nineteenth century concept of 'Anglicanism' in describing England's Church in this period since it endows it with a doctrinal cohesion and direction it lacked.[92]

The Puritan movement

In the previous section reference was made to the English 'puritans'. This term began life as a description of radical Calvinistic Protestants before the mid-1560s when the word appears to have been first coined, as a term of abuse, by the Catholic opposition. The more extreme ('hotter') Puritans, also sometimes nicknamed 'precisionists', questioned the authority of bishops and other external bodies in the running of a community's churches, and all placed the word of God as written down in the Bible above that of any temporal ruler. Their leaders were the newly returned exiles of the 1550s, fired by their firsthand experience of the continental reformation and the Calvinism of Geneva.

---

[92] Susan Doran, *Elizabeth I and Religion 1558-1603* (1994).

Elizabeth's *via media* of 1559, with its adulteration of the 1552 Prayer Book and concessions on such matters as vestments, was, for them, anything but a satisfactory settlement. A Puritan 'movement' sought to purify the Church at grassroots level, with priests abandoning such 'popish' practices as making the sign of the cross. Some bishops and other leading clerics supported the 'puritanical' six articles presented in 1563 to the Convocation of Canterbury, a body summoned to clarify the doctrine of the Church of England. Convocation elected, by a tiny majority, to retain the tenor of forms of worship as directed in 1559 and rejected the Calvinistic belief in 'double- predestination' confirming that although salvation for some was preordained by God, He did not predestine others to Hell. For hard-liners, fully committed to the concept of predestination, this was an unacceptable compromise.

Puritan ministers were not necessarily at loggerheads with their bishops - many were prepared to conform with the terms of the settlement while others, unmolested, ignored it. Many bishops themselves hoped for further reforms, some shared the Puritan distaste for religious vestments while others upheld Calvinist doctrines. However the extremism of certain Puritan MPs and the emergence, from 1570, of a 'Presbyterian' movement, drove a wedge between the episcopate and 'hot' Puritanism. The Presbyterians hoped to restructure the English Church by dispensing with bishops, relics of the pre-Reformation, altogether and placing control, locally, in the hands of ministers and lay 'elders' and, nationally, through the gathering of local representatives into a 'synod'. In retaliation the bishops began to enforce the wearing of surplices and appropriate use of the new Prayer Book and to withhold licenses to preach from the non-conformists, While the Puritan movement as a whole did not endorse the radicalism of the Presbyterians and their demands for the complete separation of Church and State, they found a few powerful allies including the Queen's favourite, the Earl of Leicester and William Cecil. Motivated by political reasons as much as religious, such men were inclined in the 1570s to defend all Protestant zealots at the height of the continental Catholic counter-attack on the English Reformation. This patronage helped save the fledgling Presbyterian movement from a concerted attempt by the bishops under Archbishop Parker in the early 1570s to suppress its propaganda and arrest its leaders. However, when William Strickland introduced a House of Commons bill in 1571 proposing the reform of the prayer book to eradicate old Catholic practices such as the exchange of wedding rings, the wearing of vestments, and kneeling at the communion table, he was arrested.

Puritan causes seemed likely to make some headway when the moderate Archbishop Parker died to be replaced, in 1575, by the more radical Edmund Grindal. Even before his appointment a somewhat unholy alliance against Catholicism was forged between Grindal and the chief spokesman for the Presbyterians, John Field, the one attacking vestments, the other suspending his assault on the Church hierarchy. The growing intolerance of the Establishment, even to moderate 'conformist' Puritans, was most evident in the remarkable conflict between the Queen and her Archbishop. It was an uneven conflict in which Grindal's conscience was no match for Elizabeth's determination to impose her authority. The Archbishop was suspended and placed under house arrest for condoning, along with ten of his fifteen bishops, 'prophesyings' , discussion and prayer meetings that he believed improved the quality of his priests but that she thought encouraged dissent. Hopes of a puritanical 'reform from within' were shattered.

When Grindal died in 1583 he was replaced by the less sympathetic John Whitgift, a Calvinist but no friend to the Presbyterians, unconcerned by the *adiaphora* - 'matters indifferent' such as Church government and vestments on which there was no biblical ruling. Whitgift demanded that all ministers acknowledge three key principles ('articles'). These were the acceptance of the royal supremacy, the 1559 Prayer Book, and the Thirty-nine Articles.

The suspension of over 300 'Godly ministers' for failing to implement official doctrine and forms of worship inspired a parliamentary campaign to win Puritan / Presbyterian concessions. Radical bills concerning Church administration and the Prayer Book were introduced by Puritan MPs in spite of the Queen's ruling that such matters were not the concern of Parliament. Sir Anthony Cope took the opportunity in 1687 to promote a radical Protestant overhaul of the religious settlement by introducing his 'Bill and Book' when a Parliament was summoned to carry out proceedings against Mary, Queen of Scots. This led to the arrest of five Puritan MPs, including Peter Wentworth who asserted the freedom of speech for MPs. The death of John Field and his great supporter, the Earl of Leicester, in 1588, together with the decline of the Catholic threat following the execution of Mary, Queen of Scots in 1587 and the defeat of the Spanish Armada in 1588, combined to further undermine radical Puritanism and those few

MPs sympathetic to Presbyterianism. It did not re-emerge as a political force during the remainder of Elizabeth's reign. Further attempts to spread radical Puritanism from the bottom up with further propaganda and meetings were the focus of an anti-Puritan persecution between 1589 and 1591, conducted by Richard Bancroft, a future Archbishop in the early years of the reign of James I. A series of anonymous pamphlets, known as the 'Martin Marprelate tracts' were distributed towards the end of the reign that targeted "profane, proud, paltry, popish, pestilent, pernicious, presumptuous prelates [i.e. bishops]'. The authors of the tracts were not identified but a puritan preacher, John Penry, was executed in 1593 for their distribution.

Extremist sects such as the Barrowists and Brownists, collectively known as the 'Separatists' (also sometimes called 'sectaries') because of their aim to separate from the Church of England, were outlawed in the 1590s and their exponents faced the prospect of a traitor's death. As early as 1583 three separatists were executed for implying the Queen was a 'jezebel'. In 1593 the radical Protestants, Henry Barrow and John Greenwood, were executed. These two men, together with Penry, were the first puritans to be dispatched for their beliefs.

The decline of the 'Old Religion'

Although some historians, notably Christopher Haigh, regard the Elizabethan Religious Settlement as nonsense in doctrinal terms, a heap of contradictions and ambiguities, it did offer some scope for both moderate Protestants and Catholics to outwardly conform. It is now broadly accepted that Elizabeth did have deep religious convictions yet it is also recognised that her sense of political expediency permitted men and women to believe what they liked so long as they behaved as they were told. Her intolerance of prophesyings, even of preaching as opposed to the reciting of prayers and Bible passages, underlines her commitment to unquestioning institutional obedience.

There was a good deal in the Settlement to commend it to followers of the 'old religion'. Although draconian laws existed for the suppression of Roman practices they were rarely enforced. Up until 1582, Elizabeth was relatively soft on Catholics. Most Catholics chose conformity ('Church Papistry') rather than recusancy, finding opportunities to pursue their preferred rituals in private.

By the late 1560s the situation was much changed. Relations with Catholic Spain had deteriorated and a new climate of religious crusade emerged with its Catholic figureheads - Mary, Queen of Scots, Pope Pius V, and Philip II. In 1570, too late to assist the cause of the Northern Earls who rebelled partly for religious reasons in the previous year, Pius excommunicated the Queen, making disobedience to her a religious obligation for English Catholics.

Although the subsequent Treasons Act of 1571 increased the discomfort of English Catholics, Elizabeth continued to resist the demands of certain MPs to root out Catholicism, and the majority of its exponents maintained a low, conformist and loyal profile. Despite having the backing of Parliament, a bill to increase the penalties for recusancy was vetoed by the Queen. Another bill she rejected would have turned the saying of Mass into a capital offence. Nevertheless, an Act of 1581 imposed a £200 fine and a year's imprisonment as the penalty for saying Mass and a 100 mark fine for others in attendance. Attempts to convert others to Catholicism became a treasonable offence and in December of that year Edmund Campion, a Jesuit priest, was executed.

Missionary priests, trained abroad, began to arrive in England from 1574. With a brief to provide the true religion for their host Catholic gentry families, and to convert others, hostility towards indigenous Catholicism increased. The involvement of William Allen - who had founded the seminary at Douai, France in 1568, and which furnished England with many of its evangelising priests - together with two Jesuits, in the Throckmorton Plot of 1583, confirmed Protestant suspicions. The arrest of Francis Throckmorton exposed plans for an invasion of England by Catholic France with the support of Spain and the Pope. The Act against Jesuits and Seminary Priests of 1585 which expelled all Catholic priests in England and punished, by death, any that harboured them resulted in 123 executions by the end of the reign. Dozens more were condemned on other charges.

The contribution to English Catholicism by these missionary priests, has been much debated. When investigating historical controversies it is helpful to start with the opinions of those originally involved. Certainly there was a good deal of resentment among conformist Catholics for the uncompromising activities of the missionaries, particularly the Jesuits who began to arrive from 1580. The priests themselves were not necessarily united in their common cause - the seminary priests or 'seculars', so-called because they belonged to no particular order, sometimes clashed with the hardline Jesuit 'Soldiers of the Faith'. A major row between the Jesuits and other Catholics erupted in the late 1590s. It concerned the revival, in 1598, of the position of an ancient post, the 'Archpriest', to govern the Catholic Church in England in the absence of a Catholic episcopate. Traditionalists felt uneasy about this arbitrary invention of, effectively, a new ecclesiastical office. Worse still it was awarded to a pro-Jesuit priest, George Blackwell. A campaign to unseat Blackwell was launched. Appeals were made to Rome, the 'Appellants' highlighting the damaging effect the Jesuit mission was having on tolerance of Catholicism in England. In 1602 Blackwell was instructed by the Pope to consult with Appellants and to avoid affiliating himself with the Jesuits.

According to Christopher Hill in *The English Reformation* (1964): 'English Catholicism was recreated during the last three decades of the reign by the adventurous labours of the Seminarists and Jesuits.' In more recent years this view has been challenged by historians such as Christopher Haigh. Such revisionists accept the fact that the missionary priests helped preserve, even revive, the faith in the homes of the gentry (but not in the wider community) in some areas. However English Catholicism was not defunct before their arrival and the contribution of the missionaries has been exaggerated. Many places were untouched by the missions whether they were or were not Catholic footholds before 1580. Both the 'discontinuity' and 'continuity' theses however agree on one essential truth:

> 'At the end of Mary's reign, Catholicism had been the religion of a large majority of English people; by the end of Elizabeth's it was the faith of a small sect [...] Within two generations, the Catholics had dwindled to numerical insignificance.'[93]

After decades of sometimes ferocious conflict between opposing religious views, religion was still a divisive factor in the 1590s. The assault on Presbyterianism among parliamentarians in the late 1580s succeeded in undermining the Puritan movement. At a local level dissent in some places, particularly in the Midlands and the East Anglia, thrived,

---

[93] Christopher Haigh, *English Reformations* (1993).

largely unmolested. Most Puritans after all were regular attenders of parish services. Those that were not, the Separatists, remained active until the early 1590s, particularly in London, The execution of three of their leaders however, Henry Barrow, John Greenwood and John Penry, effectively destroyed the fledgling Elizabethan movement.

    The arrival of missionary priests in the 1580s and 90s had a limited impact and the clashes between the Jesuit order and other Catholics were unhelpful in the great endeavour to re-Catholicise England. At the height of the Anglo-Spanish war, under more or less continuous threat of invasion and facing a Catholic 'crusade' levelled against the English Protestant presence in Ireland, it is hardly surprising that the government and the majority of the population were unsympathetic even to those Catholics who pledged their loyalty to the Crown. The Appellants, Catholics who had appealed to the Pope concerning the damaging effects of the Jesuit mission, for a time earned some government backing, but once the Irish rebellion was suppressed and Anglo-Spanish relations were on the mend, they were declared in 1602, by royal proclamation, disloyal and disobedient. However, although all priests found subscribing to the Pope's authority were exiled, those denying it were allowed to remain so long as they abandoned their vocations. Although higher levels of recusancy were recorded in some places in the 1590s, notably around London, Catholicism over all continued its rapid decline, virtually disappearing in more remote areas such as North Wales, Cumberland and Cornwall.

The 'auld alliance'

    The restoration of Protestantism after 1559 revived the old fear of a great alliance of European powers in a crusade against England and heresy. Survival depended on continued hostilities between Spain and France - English military and economic resources would be hard pressed to fend off a concerted attack from the combined Catholic houses of Europe. The preservation of good relations with Spain was of paramount importance and, with this end in sight, Elizabeth's councillors would be likely to urge moderation in religious affairs and even a marriage alliance with the Habsburg dynasty.

    In some respects the 1559 settlement was a compromise and the 'hotter' reformers were to be frustrated in their pursuit of a Puritan revolution. For a time, at the start of the reign, a marriage to an Austrian Habsburg prince, the Archduke Charles, seemed a real possibility. The reservations of some councillors however, and Elizabeth's evident infatuation with Robert Dudley soon eliminated Charles' candidature. At the same time Philip II himself contemplated marriage to his sister-in-law Elizabeth and relations between the two powers were, at first, cordial.

The greater threat to English security remained France. French influence in Scotland was consolidated in the person of Mary, Queen of Scots and daughter-in-law to Henry II of France. The relatively conciliatory approach of Henry II towards the English in the closing years of his reign was replaced by the more provocative stance of his son and Mary's husband, Francis II, after Henry's death in July 1559. Mary assumed the title 'Queen of England' and adopted the English royal arms in addition to those of France and Scotland. For Catholics in all three countries, those who had never accepted the legitimacy of Henry VIII'S marriage to Anne Boleyn, a simple case could be made for disputing the legitimacy of the reign of Boleyn's daughter, Elizabeth. It could be argued that by right Mary, Queen of Scots, the direct descendant of Henry VIII's older sister, Margaret, should have inherited the English throne on the death of Mary I. In practice most English Catholics accepted the legitimacy of Elizabeth, and not all Scots were united in support of Mary Stuart's claim: many, particularly among the Protestant community, resented the growing French and Catholic influence in Scottish affairs.

Antagonism between the Scottish Protestant nobility (the 'Lords of the Congregation') and the Catholic Franco-Scottish party, centred around Mary of Guise, Mary Stuart's mother and regent of Scotland, erupted in rebellion in the spring of 1559. The posturing of the new French king, Francis, in the summer of that year convinced William Cecil, Elizabeth's principal secretary, that a campaign for the unseating of the English Queen was underway. A pre-emptive strike therefore was planned in support of the Protestant rebels, despite Elizabeth's distrust of Scottish Calvinism and her deep-rooted respect for the sanctity of legitimate monarchy, be it Protestant or Catholic. Arms, money and, later, an army and a fleet were dispatched to Scotland and, for the time being, French aggression was stifled. By the terms of the Treaty of Edinburgh of 1560 the French and English military presence in Scotland was withdrawn and Mary Stuart's use of the English royal arms abandoned. Neither the English nor the Scottish queen was satisfied however, Elizabeth wanted more from the French, including the return of Calais, and Mary personally refused to be bound by the settlement. Even so the treaty was a triumph for Cecil and a convincing demonstration of English resilience in the face of Franco-Scottish presumptions. A new relationship had been forged between Protestant England and Protestants in Scotland, who now provided Scotland with a provisional government. By the time Scotland turned Protestant in August 1560 the 'auld alliance' between Scotland and France, dating back to 1295, was shattered.

The Francis / Mary partnership was cut short by his death in December 1560. On the one hand Mary was less threatening now that she could not command the authority of the French crown: this had passed into the hands of the Queen Mother, Catherine de Medici, regent to her ten year old son, King Charles IX. On the other hand Francis' death created a new problem by raising once again the matter of Mary's marriage. The implications of Mary's own pursuit of marriage to Philip of Spain's son were serious indeed and Elizabeth endeavoured to steer her into a more conducive wedding to an English Protestant - none other than her own favourite', Robert Dudley. In the event, in 1565, Mary married another cousin, Henry Stewart, Lord Darnley. Darnley shared Mary's religious sympathies as well as her royal lineage, and Protestant hopes for a Protestant succession in Scotland, perhaps even England, were jeopardised. This marriage heightened tensions within Scotland and provoked further civil war. The following year she bore her son and heir, James, later James VI of Scotland and James I of England.

The success of the Scottish campaign helped inspire an expedition to France in 1562. The *raison d'etre* for intervention was the massacre of French Protestant 'Huguenots' at Vassy on the command of the Duke of Guise. Politically the recovery of Calais provided a further motive, as did the egotistical ambitions of key individuals, most notably Robert Dudley. Fairly rapidly it became clear to French Catholics and Huguenots alike that English political ambitions took precedent over religious considerations and as relations between the two faiths in France improved they combined to force the English armies out of France. Le Havre, recently captured, was relinquished and the war was terminated, ingloriously, by the Peace of Troyes in 1564.

Mary, murder and mayhem: Scotland c.1565-70

Mary's arrogance in marrying her pro-Catholic kinsman Henry Stewart, the Earl of Darnley, infuriated Elizabeth. Without the certain backing of the French crown and faced by a hostile, rebellious Protestant nobility Mary would have been wise to err on the side of caution and to establish a rapport with England. Although her half-brother the Earl of Moray's rebellion immediately after the marriage in 1565 failed, within two years Mary, Queen of Scots, had been deposed. The sordid events that followed in the wake of Mary's marriage to Lord Darnely precipitated catastrophe.

Mary did most of the running in their brief courtship during 1565. Although Mary's was, first and foremost, a marriage for dynastic and perhaps religious reasons, she was genuinely attracted to her handsome, ambitious cousin. Relations between them however soon turned sour, not least because Mary seemed determined not to relinquish her political authority to her husband, and Darnley began to show his resentment towards Mary's close relationship with David Rizzio, an Italian musician who first came to Scotland with the Savoy ambassador and later became Mary's own ambassador, friend and advisor. Darnley was lured into a plot to kill the Italian. In a remarkably unsubtle and brutal act on March 9, 1566, Rizzio was dragged by a gang from the Queen's presence and murdered in the royal apartments of Holyrood Palace.

If Darnley had expected to secure greater influence over his Queen and the Scottish nobles by asserting himself in the Rizzio affair he was to be disappointed. Mary now loathed him while his fellow assassins showed no further interest in promoting his personal interests. A period of separation, during which Darnley missed the last great Papal celebration in Scotland, the baptism of Prince James, on 17 December, was followed by an apparent reconciliation late in 1566. However before being restored to Holyrood Palace Darnley was obliged to live away from his wife and son in a house at Kirk-o'-Field until he recovered from a disease - smallpox according to some but now commonly assumed to have been virulent syphilis. Here on 10 February he died: the house was blown up and his strangled body was found in the garden.

The degree of Mary's involvement in the murder of the man she so wished to be rid of, at least for the better part of 1566, has been disputed ever since. Popular rumour immediately associated James Hepburn, the Earl of Bothwell with Darnley's murder and some even spoke of his intent to marry the Queen. When she did exactly that on 15 May, having been abducted by Bothwell and held in his castle at Dunbar on 24 April, her complicity, for many, seemed beyond doubt. Her defenders have argued variously that she was 'ravished' by Bothwell and forced into marriage in a Protestant ceremony, that her senses were disordered by the shock of Darnley's murder, or that she felt genuinely grateful to Bothwell for, allegedly, preventing the coup against Rizzio from becoming a regicidal bloodbath in which she would also have been victim. On the other hand a French ambassador reported that in the aftermath of her mariiage she wept continuously and even contemplated suicide.

Whatever the truth of the matter the outcome is certain. A Protestant army led by the Earl of Moray captured the Queen and forced Bothwell into exile in June 1567. In the same month, while being held at Loch Leven Castle, she miscarried twins fathered by Bothwell. Moray obliged Mary to abdicate and he set himself up as regent to the new infant king, James VI. Meanwhile Bothwell fled Scotland and died, ultimately, in Denmark. Elizabeth, despite her differences regarding Mary and her conviction that Mary's new husband was a murderer deserving the severest retribution, was appalled. Her feeling for the sanctity of a crowned ruler came close to provoking war between England and the new regime in Scotland. When Mary escaped from her island prison in May 1568 civil war again afflicted Scotland. The Marian force was defeated at Langside and Mary fled to England and Elizabeth's protection. This 'protection' proved to be custody, imprisonment and, ultimately, almost twenty years later, execution.

The struggle in Scotland between the pro-English Protestant usurpers and Mary's pro-French Catholic supporters continued until the final Protestant triumph in 1573. Not wishing to be seen as the advocate of rebel causes and anxious not to be drawn into full-scale war in Scotland, particularly at a time of deteriorating relations with Spain, Elizabeth's intervention in support of James VI was minimal.

The rebellion of the Northern Earls, 1569

Within two years of Mary's arrival in England, Elizabeth was challenged by the largest rebellion of her reign. This rising, led by the Catholic earls of Northumberland and Westmorland, was the one among many plots associated with Mary Queen of Scots that resulted in rebellion. In the year of Elizabeth I's excommunication and set in the context of courtly intrigues concerning Mary's claims to the succession and attempts to undermine Lord Cecil by his Catholic and Protestant enemies, the rebellion was the result of months of planning by the northern lords. They planned to capitalise on court faction fighting and the unpopularity of its first minister. Eager to champion the cause of the now captive Mary, and optimistic of the chances of a Catholic restoration by relying on feudal loyalties and popular support, they intended to raise armies in the north to defeat, and perhaps overthrow, Elizabeth. In the event the rebels were anything but confident of success and rose out of preference to flight, only after being summoned to explain themselves before their Queen.

After a few weeks spanning the winter of 1569/70, a few skirmishes and one minor battle, the rebellion was over, the ill-conceived rising being denied sufficient support at home and none from abroad. Despite its rapid defeat the combination of religious discontent in the north, the possibility of foreign intervention, aristocratic rivalry at court and the dubious loyalty even of high profile Protestant peers, including Leicester, had made the rebellion 'extremely dangerous' (Haigh, 1988). In the same year the foremost peer in the kingdom, and suitor for the hand in marriage of Mary, Queen of Scots, Thomas Howard, the Duke of Norfolk, was also arrested.

For Lord Cecil, the principle architect of Elizabeth's religious settlement, the successful suppression of the rebellion appears to have restored and reinforced the Queen's confidence in her foremost royal servant. In the same year as the rebellion he granted Sir Francis Walsingham the role of establishing a 'secret service', the establishment of a network of unofficial spies searching for evidence of treasonous activities. The Duke of Norfolk was executed in 1572 having been found guilty of involvement in various plots, despite his professed Protestantism, and the Queen's reluctance and prevarication in condemning her close relation and the highest peer of the realm. These plots included the Ridolfi Plot, named after the Florentine banker who, in 1570, planned to depose the Queen with the help of a Spanish invasion. Mary, unwisely, allowed herself to become embroiled in the plot. She wrote to Norfolk as a potential ally, hinting that she might even be willing to marry him.

Elizabeth responded to her Council's demands for Mary's execution by protesting: 'Can I put to death the bird that, to escape the pursuit of the hawk, has fled to my feet for protection? Honour and conscience forbid!' Another plot was hatched by Francis Throckmorton who was executed in 1584 having played his part in the irretrievable collapse of diplomatic relations between Spain and England. Even so Elizabeth continued to protect Mary.

Walsingham's unearthing of the Babington Plot in 1586, a conspiracy by a friend to the Jesuits and supporter of Mary, Anthony Babington, to assassinate Elizabeth sealed the fate of the former Queen of Scots. Having unearthed Babington's plans, Walsingham appears to have exploited the conspiracy to satisfy his and Cecil's own political objectives. Walsingham wrote to the Earl of Leicester as he uncovered Babington's conspiracy, 'If the matter be well handled, it will break the neck of all dangerous practices during her Majesty's reign.' A defecting Catholic refugee, Gilbert Gifford, was Walsingham's chief informant in his interception of illicit letters exchanged between Mary and the French ambassador, hidden in a watertight container smuggled into a cask of beer. Mary's endorsement of the plan to assassinate the Queen in a letter she seems to have dictated on 7 February, 1586, ultimately sealed her fate.

Following Mary's trial, Elizabeth, very reluctantly signed her death warrant. After years of royal prevarication and fearing the Queen would change her mind, Cecil called a Privy Council meeting, without the Queen's knowledge, to make the arrangements for Mary's prompt execution. She was beheaded at Fotheringhay Castle in Northamptonshire on 7 February 1587. Elizabeth, after years of procrastination, went into mourning for Mary, and had her own secretary, William Davison, imprisoned for drawing up her death warrant.

The struggle with Spain

As well as becoming King of Spain in 1556, Philip Habsburg was also King of Naples, King of Sicily, the Duke of Milan, the Duke of Burgundy (with control of the Netherlands), ruler of Franché Comte, and, from 1580, King of Portugal. Dying in 1598, he thus dominated European affairs for most of the second half of the sixteenth century and virtually all of Elizabeth's reign.

During the 1560s, while using the Spanish Inquisition to crush Protestantism in Spain, Philip remained on friendly terms with Elizabeth for political and economic reasons. On two occasions, in 1561 and 1563, he prevented the Pope from excommunicating her, and tried to do the same, unsuccessfully, in 1570. Furthermore he did not lend his support to Mary, Queen of Scots, in this period because of his rivalry with France and his concern that the French royal family, through its marriage alliance with Mary, who had been Queen of France until her husband's death in July 1559, might end up controlling England.

In 1566 attempts to assert Spanish authority in the Netherlands largely provoked the great revolt that continued until 1648. Meanwhile Philip was asserting himself elsewhere – notably through the destruction of the Turkish fleet at the naval battle of Lepanto in 1571. This was followed by a lasting peace between the two countries, continuing until the 1590s. He also used force to subdue Portugal in his assertion of his claim to the Portuguese throne in 1580. By this time the wealth of Spain was rapidly growing - between 1580 and the end of Philip's reign Spanish revenue in the form of imported silver from South America increased four-fold.

Between 1585 and 1589 the threat of France to Spanish security was much reduced by civil war in France (the War of the Three Henrys). This was a struggle between the King (Catholic Henry III), allied with the protestant 'Huguenots' (led by his son, Henry of Navarre, Henry IV from 1589) against the Catholic League (led by Henry, Duke of Guise) in which Philip backed the Catholic League.

The Netherlands, England and Spain

English foreign policy was dictated at least as much by England's economic interests in the Netherlands as by religious ideology. Antwerp and the Netherlands provided England's principal market for the lucrative wool and cloth trade. The Elizabethan economy was founded on textiles and the associated taxes provided the Treasury with most of its assured revenue. The protection of this trade was foremost in Elizabeth's foreign policy making. The Netherlands was a federation of seventeen semi-autonomous provinces held by the Dukes of Burgundy since the beginning of the fifteenth century. For the most part Elizabeth's predecessors had cultivated good relations with the House of Burgundy and supported Burgundian resistance to French *aggrandisement*. The improved relationship between England and France largely derived from the attempts of the latest Burgundian ruler, Philip II of Spain, to extend his control over the Low Countries. The prospect of the Netherlands as a Spanish satellite was worrying indeed - not only might the vital wool trade be stifled but so too might the Netherlands provide a convenient base for a Catholic crusade against England. As early as 1563 Spain's potential for endangering English interests was demonstrated when Philip's regent decided to close Antwerp to English merchants, on the grounds of needing to prevent the spread of the plague taken to England by soldiers returning from the French campaign of the previous year. Catastrophe was averted by the discovery of the port of Emden in Lower Saxony as an alternative market and the Netherlands trade was resumed in 1565.

The assertion of Spanish authority in the Netherlands resulted in rebellion in 1566. In 1567 the formidable Duke of Alva was sent with a Spanish army to crush the revolt and eliminate heresy. In 1562 Elizabeth had aided Protestant rebels in France against their legitimate rulers and achieved nothing for them or England. Intervention in the Netherlands might prevent the establishment of a Spanish dominated Catholic hegemony throughout northern Europe but it would be immensely expensive and likely to fail given the resources available to Alva.

An opportunity to help the rebel cause without openly opposing Spain arose in November 1568. Spanish ships carrying a substantial Genoese loan for the payment of Alva's troops were forced into harbour in Devon and Cornwall by bad weather and French privateers. After some procrastination Elizabeth decided to confiscate the bullion. Even before she had made up her mind the Spanish ambassador, Don Guerau de Spes, advised Alva to arrest English merchants in the Netherlands and seize their ships and goods. Spaniards in England received reciprocal treatment. Trade between England and the Netherlands did not recommence for the best part of five years. The old Anglo-Burgundian alliance was shattered and the need to woo France (and her princes) paramount. By 1571 Philip was prepared to endorse rebellion against the newly excommunicated Elizabeth and he instructed Alva to prepare an invasion by 10,000 men to assist the abortive Ridolfi plot. Meanwhile Elizabeth encouraged the activities of the English privateers preying on Spanish ships. However this was not open warfare and by 1573 the Nymegen Convention agreement between Elizabeth and Alva restored the old relationship in part by reopening trade between England and Spain.

After years of hesitation Elizabeth finally committed England to uninhibited participation in the Dutch revolt. Despite having recently declined the Dutch offer of sovereignty over the Netherlands, by the terms of the Treaty of Nonsuch in 1585 she pledged 5000 footsoldiers and 1000 horse under the command of Leicester, fearing that plans for a Spanish invasion of England were already underway. Her justification for this action was Philip's alleged support of the plots against her associated with Mary, Queen of Scots. Even after Mary's execution it was feared that Philip harboured dynastic ambitions for England. In her will drawn up in 1577 Mary bequeathed her claim to the English throne to Philip II should her son, James VI of Scotland, remain a heretic.

Leicester's Netherlands expedition was expensive and ineffective and quite possibly persuaded Philip to launch the Armada of 1588 which had as its main political objective the forcing of the English out of the Netherlands.

Spain and Spanish armadas

Elizabeth intervened in the Netherlands in support of the Dutch rebels because Henry III of France, preoccupied with his struggle against the Catholic League, could not be induced to do so, and because she intended to demonstrate English strength and so deter Philip from a presumed invasion attempt. English intervention in fact stirred Philip into the action against England it was intended to prevent. Although the tide of the Netherlands war was not turned by the poorly provisioned English forces under Leicester's inept command, Philip believed their timely arrival boosted Dutch morale and protracted the resistance. Furthermore the activities of English privateers in Spanish colonial waters, designed to secure treasure in order to finance the continental war, were an irritation and affront to Spanish pride. The 'Enterprise of England' was devised in 1586 to end English hostilities and force English troops out of the Netherlands. While it was envisaged that English territory might be held for a time while negotiations took place, this was no wholesale invasion programme, nor was it, first and foremost, a Catholic 'crusade', although a pro-Spanish Anglo-Catholic uprising unseating the Protestant Queen would have been a welcome bonus.

The first of the great Spanish fleets ('armadas') launched against England in Elizabeth's reign set sail from Lisbon in May 1588, having been delayed after Sir Francis Drake had attacked the fleet in harbour at Cadiz a year earlier, 'singeing the king of Spain's beard', and then menaced treasure ships in the Azores. Its aim was to clear the Channel of English warships and so enable a safe passage for the Duke of Parma's 17,000 strong army ferried in barges from the Netherlands to England's south-east coast. A unified assault was prevented by the fact that, partly because of English intervention in 1586, Spain held no deep harbour port in the Netherlands.

It was an ill-conceived plan. The military invasion depended upon the successful outcome of an engagement with an English navy better armed (though short of ammunition) than the Spanish. The Spanish fleet had twenty-one long-range guns, the English 153, their superior four-wheeled truck carriages enabling rapid reloading. Even if the armada had succeeded Parma's army still had to survive the harrying by the well-prepared Dutch in shallow waters before it could gain the safety of the armada's protection. Parma himself was doubtful as to whether 'these little, low, flat boats, built for these rivers and not for the sea' could cross the Channel even if they eluded English or Dutch shipping. Parma's troop barges in fact never attempted the crossing, for the armada, temporarily thrown into confusion by English 'fireships', burning hulks cast into the enemy fleet, and then subjected to heavy artillery fire at close quarters, was scattered and routed, many ships subsequently wrecked off the Scottish and Irish coasts. In his report to

Philip II, the Spanish admiral, the Duke of Medina Sidonia, commented on the aftermath of the confusion caused by the English fireships: 'Ammunition and the best of our vessels were lacking [some having been carried by a strong current towards Dunkirk], and we could depend little upon the ships that remained, the Queen's fleet being so superior to ours in this sort of fighting in consequence of the strength of their artillery and the fast sailing of their ships.'

However, as Simon Adams has noted, England's preparations for the invasion were far from complete:

'[...] lost in both legend and historical orthodoxy is a major and under-appreciated fact: the English were taken by surprise by the Armada. By July 29th they had reached the conclusion that it would not sail so late in the summer. They were preparing to depart for the Azores to intercept the annual silver fleet from the Spanish Americas. Not only did the surprise cause many English ships to leave Plymouth hastily before they could load adequate supplies of food and ammunition, but they had never intended to fight the Armada where they did in the first place. The running battle up the Channel was both unplanned and unexpected.'[94]

Geoffrey Parker placed responsibility for the Spanish defeat squarely on the shoulders of Philip II:

'[Philip] was not only an armchair strategist, but an armchair tactician too [...] he never summoned his senior commanders for a face-to-face meeting to discuss how best to carry out the grand design [...] he did everything he could to stifle their criticisms [...] the lion's share of the blame should go neither to Parma nor to Medina Sidonia, but to Philip II.'[95]

What might have happened had the Armada defeated the English fleet is a subject of some debate: some historians claim Parma's experienced and professional army would have overwhelmed the far bigger force it would have encountered on English soil, while others share Parma's own

---

[94] Simon Adams, 'The Lurch into War' in *History Today*, vol. 38, May 1988.

[95] Geoffrey Parker, 'Why the Armada Failed' in History Today, vol. 38, May 1988.

pessimism regarding the prospect of a Spanish victory on land. Had he succeeded, according to Felix Barker:

> 'We know that the country was to be occupied, from the scheme outlined by the Grand Commander of Castile at Philip's instigation in 1585. Philip would either have appointed a viceroy to rule or would have nominated a King of England from his own family. His nephew, the victorious Parma, would have been the most likely choice [...] [Elizabeth's] chance of being allowed to live would have been slim.'[96]

Other writers however envisage a temporary Spanish presence in England and a Queen unmolested once she agreed to Philip's terms regarding English troops in the Netherlands, toleration of Catholics and reparations for the cost of invasion. The outcome in fact was anything but decisive: English soldiers continued to assist the Dutch rebels throughout the rest of Elizabeth's reign, the war dragged on between Spain and the Netherlands until the independence of the northern provinces was recognised by the Spanish in 1648, Cadiz was raided a second time with great success in 1596, and Philip launched three more armadas against England in 1595, 1596 and 1599, all of which failed because of bad weather. The historian Garrett Mattingley, considering the mentality of the times, wrote eloquently of the way in which news of Spain's failure may have been perceived by Protestants and Catholics in other parts of Europe:

> 'When the Armada challenged the ancient lords of the English Channel on their own grounds the impending conflict took on the aspect of a judicial duel in which, as was expected in such duels, God would defend the right [...] So, when the two fleets approached their appointed battleground, all Europe watched.
>
> For the spectators of both parties the outcome, reinforced as everyone believed by an extraordinary tempest, was indeed decisive. The Protestants of France and the Netherlands, Germany and Scandanavia saw with relief that God was in truth, as they had always supposed, on their side. The Catholics of

---

[96] Felix Barker (1988).

France and Italy and Germany saw with almost equal relief that Spain was not, after all, God's chosen champion.'[97]

The balance of power in Europe that Elizabeth had been so eager to retain was preserved; the success of the Dutch rebellion prevented the total domination of the Netherlands by either Spain or France, while the Spanish presence in the southern provinces and civil strife at home kept French expansion in check. Elizabeth's mostly cautious (some would say indecisive) foreign policy was unspectacular but effective in averting the disasters that might well have been incurred had she gambled security for glory.

Foreign affairs after 1588

The triumph of 1588, 'Armada year', was followed in 1589 by further victory in the continuing war against Spain when, in December a Spanish army was defeated in the Netherlands by the troops of Sir Francis Vere. However, earlier in the year the feted Drake was less successful in an *attempt to* destroy the remains of the Spanish fleet, waiting to be re-equipped in Portuguese ports. The expedition was badly organized and poorly planned, the lure of Spanish treasure ships in the Azores proved a stronger attraction to the privateers than the immediate object of sinking the armada. Bad weather wrecked many English vessels, none reached the Azores, and the survivors limped back to England with nothing to show for the £100,000 invested in them by the Queen and private sponsors.

Lack of resources and her desire to maintain the continental balance of power, which necessitated the survival of Spain, explains the relatively modest contributions Elizabeth made to the Huguenot French and Dutch war efforts. Privateering was a cheaper, if less reliable, alternative to campaigns paid for by unpopular royal levies. Nevertheless, she sent to France £30,000 and 20,000 troops between 1589 and 1595. Some of this was invested in the force led by Robert Devereux, Earl of Essex, in 1591. Essex proved a foolhardy commander.

---

[97] Garrett Mattingley, *The Defeat of the Spanish Armada* (1959).

Desirous of proving his military prowess he marched his army 100 miles across enemy territory and finally abandoned it, much depleted, in a fruitless siege of Rouen, 'he touched nothing that did not decay', Elton has commented. This fiasco clearly demonstrated the limitations of even comparatively large English armies campaigning on foreign soil.

The English presence in Brittany and Normandy helped preserve the French king, Henry IV, in his war with the Spanish backed Catholic League but, combined with attacks on Spanish shipping and the sack of Cadiz in 1596, it also provoked Philip II into endeavouring to launch new armadas against Elizabeth. In the later 1590s their objective was not a direct assault upon England but an invasion of Ireland in support of the Earl of Tyrone's papal backed rebellion. Spanish fleets sailed for Ireland in 1595, 1596, 1597, 1599 and 1601. The first three were all scattered and wrecked at sea and the fourth was defeated off Brittany; only the fifth succeeded in landing troops in Ireland. Despite the presence of 3400 Spanish soldiers however Tyrone suffered a resounding defeat at the battle of Kinsdale on Christmas Eve 1601.

When Elizabeth died the Irish rebellion was over but Tyrone was still at large. Less than a week after her death he submitted but only after his supremacy in Ulster was guaranteed by the English government. The war with Spain was not concluded until the following year. The king who signed the treaty, James VI of Scotland and James I of England, indirectly had played a role in preventing a successful Catholic crusade against Elizabeth in the closing years of her reign. Despite the fate of his mother, Mary, Queen of Scots, the Protestant James, as next in line to the English throne, had no quarrel with the English queen who, obligingly, had chosen not to marry and so jeopardise his succession. Although on occasions James had flirted with Elizabeth's enemies - the Pope, Spain and the Irish rebels - perhaps in the hope of prompting Elizabeth to commit herself in his favour, a less compliant government in Scotland might have turned a crisis, such as that of 1601, into a disaster.

Privateering and piracy

Piracy and privateering were the ancient practices of British seamen long before the emergence of the Tudor dynasty. Both terms imply assault and robbery at sea but 'privateering' has the distinction of being piracy licensed by the state. There were two types of license, both issued by the Lord High Admiral: 'letters of reprisal' permitted assaults on foreign ships as compensation for some injury done to the privateer by that nation, and 'letters of marque' allowing general war against the ships of any foreign power with which England was presently at war.

The navies of the earlier Tudors certainly relied to a considerable extent on private vessels but these were formally indentured from their owners and then armed and manned by captains in the direct employ of the Crown. Extensive privateering in Tudor England began early in the reign of Elizabeth. The disastrous outcome of Hawkins' third expedition promoting the new trade in slaves of 1567 provoked him and Hawkins into acts of piracy in the Americas, vengeance for the recent destruction of their vessels by Spanish warships in Mexico. By the late 1570s this dangerous, but potentially highly profitable, ransacking of Spanish treasure ships had won the backing of the Queen and her government. Drake's great expedition of 1577-80, which combined exploration, trade and piracy, was commissioned by Elizabeth.

Privateering of course made a certain amount of economic sense: the privateer was furnished at his own expense and by private investors (possibly a court syndicate), seeking a substantial return; the profit motive very likely made the privateer a more committed captain, in some circumstances, than the paid professional captain. At the same time the often ambiguous relationship between state and privateer enabled the government to distance itself from their activities and not find itself embroiled in open war with another power. However, once war was openly declared reliance on privateers could have its drawbacks. In 1589 Elizabeth sponsored Drake and Sir John Norris to the tune of £49,000 to help pay for a fleet of 150 ships and over 20,000 personnel, assembled to destroy the rest of Philip II's storm battered armada at harbour in Santander and San Sebastian, to provoke an anti-Spanish revolt in Portugal and then to seize Spanish treasure ships in the Azores. As far as the privateers and their other investors were concerned the most profitable part of the plan was the interception of the treasure convoys in the Indies. They ignored the instructions to attack the armada entirely, attempted but failed to provoke a Portuguese rebellion and then set sail for the Azores! Bad weather prevented them and forced them back to Plymouth to explain themselves before the Privy Council and an angry Queen.

Although hundreds of Spanish ships fell victim to the English

Navy and its privateers in the Anglo-Spanish war they were ineffective in preventing the flow of silver into Spain which peaked in the early 1590s. Philip's growing expenditure on protecting the convoys made the piracy ever more perilous for English sailors. Raleigh's cousin, Sir Richard Grenville, colonist, Armada veteran and privateer, was killed in action seeking the treasure fleet in the Azores in 1591 when he recklessly engaged his ship, the *Revenge* (commanded by Drake in 1588), in a fight with fifteen Spanish warships carrying 5000 men. Drake and Hawkins launched further attacks on the Spanish and perished in an attack on Panama in 1595, also commissioned by the Queen. Meanwhile Hawkins' son, Sir Richard, languished in a Spanish gaol after attempting to emulate Drake's exploits in the Pacific and being captured with his ship, the *Dainty*, in the process.

The privateers did not cow the Spanish but they did inflict consider- able damage, notably when the Earl of Cumberland sacked Puerto Rico in 1598.Their contribution to the English economy lay in part in the luxuries they brought into England through trade and seizure, but most significantly they helped co-ordinate investors into the overseas trading concerns such as the East India Company, founded in 1600, which flourished during the seventeenth century.

Marriage and diplomacy

The 'personality cult' associated with Elizabeth, endorsed by the poets and painters of her reign, was not particularly evident before the 1570s. The celebration of her virginity in particular was not a feature of royal propaganda while it was still assumed in the 1560s that her marriage was inevitable. The issues of greatest public concern at the beginning of Elizabeth's reign were much the same as those of Mary's: royal marriage and the succession, and the government's religious policy.

Hopes of a royal marriage were never entirely abandoned but Elizabeth quite possibly was committed to staying single as early as 1565. In the Autumn of 1560 however a marriage looked very likely between the Queen and her 'favourite' Robert Dudley. His first wife had recently died - a convenience that, probably unfairly, aroused suspicions of foul play. Although some councillors at this stage favoured a match with a foreign prince, and many, including Secretary Cecil, bitterly opposed marriage to this son of Northumberland who had engineered the Jane Grey coup and married Dudley's older brother to the 'nine-day Queen' all were agreed that a marriage of some kind was vital. After Elizabeth there were no surviving children of Henry VIII; the various claims of Jane Grey's sister Catherine, of Mary Stuart, now Queen of France and Scotland, of Mary Stuart's half-sister Lady Margaret Douglas, and of a number of Yorkist heirs made civil war, or worse, a distinct possibility. Lord Cecil, the Secretary of State, suggested an interesting contingency plan in 1563 when Elizabeth seemed, likely to die of smallpox - a (Protestant) successor could be elected by Parliament!

On the first day of the first session of Elizabeth's first Parliament, which sat on the 25 January 1559, she was presented with a petition from the House of Commons urging her to marry. Elizabeth did not dismiss the idea of marriage but clarified matters by stating that she was not yet ready to make a choice. Her early suitors included the King Eric of Sweden, Philip of Spain and the Holy Roman Emperor's son, Archduke Charles II of Austria.

These purely political alliances were overshadowed by Elizabeth's evident infatuation with Robert Dudley. The hostility to Dudley expressed in Court and Council alike helped prevent Elizabeth from giving her hand to this physically attractive but intellectually unsophisticated man. By the summer of 1561 the 'crisis' (some foresaw a major rebellion in the event of such a marriage) had passed although her fondness for Dudley remained; he was disappointed in failing to win the greatest prize but compensated by her continued and generous patronage. Dudley was granted lands, the valuable license to export 80,000 undressed white cloths each year, and Kenilworth Castle. His brother Ambrose was also rewarded and given Warwick Castle, lost to the family after their father and brother's disgrace in 1553. The Dudley family, having been attainted by Mary I, and its principal members beheaded for treason, ten years earlier for its role in the Lady Jane Grey affair, designed to keep Mary off the throne, had been fabulously restored, ready to play once more a major role in national affairs.

Elizabeth's known preference for Robert Dudley helped keep other suitors at bay in the early 1560s. However in 1564 he was being preened by Elizabeth with a view to marrying him off to the newly widowed Mary, Queen of Scots. To enhance his appeal Elizabeth had him raised to the earldom of Leicester. Neither party was impressed in the least by Elizabeth's match-making and Leicester's hand, to Leicester's relief, was rejected.

When Mary did remarry it was to another British noble, one untainted by his ancestry, Lord Darnley. The arrival of a son in 1566 greatly strengthened Mary's position regarding the succession and demands for Elizabeth's marriage became even more anxious. Talk of an Austrian marriage was revived and, from the spring of 1565, the thirty-two year old Queen was urged by some, including Leicester, to consider the fifteen year old Charles IX of Prance. As hopes of Elizabeth naming a partner receded the matter developed into a struggle of will with Elizabeth on one side and Council, Court and Parliament on the other. Petitions for her marriage, encouragement of foreign suitors through contact with their ambassadors, and attempts to withhold a subsidy until the Queen made a decision, were met with fierce indignation, accusations of treachery and conspiracy, self-interestedness and blackmail. She acknowledged the difficulties of an unnamed succession but insisted, probably correctly, that, for the time being, it was the lesser of two evils. Her decision not to marry was as personal as it was political - she shared the abhorrence of many of her subjects for the notion of her marriage to a foreign prince, she had no desire to support the cause of one English faction against another which marriage to Dudley would have represented, and, above all, she was not yet ready to hand over the business of ruling her kingdom.

The French dukes

Elizabeth's 1562 campaign in France had been costly and entirely unsuccessful. The Huguenots she claimed she wanted to help had themselves turned against the English invaders, and Le Havre, which might have been used as a bargaining tool in subsequent negotiations to win back Calais, was ignominiously abandoned because of French resistance and a bout of the plague which was then carried back to England by returning soldiers.

During the 1560s England's relations with Spain began to deteriorate. A French initiative to forge a new alliance between the two powers through Elizabeth's marriage to one of the sons of Catherine de Medici was greeted with some enthusiasm in the English court. These opened in 1571 with negotiations designed to lead to a marriage with Henry, Duke of Anjou, who ruled France as Henry III between 1575 and 1589. They were revived in the later in 1578 with his younger brother, the Duke of Alençon, and successor to his duchy of Anjou, Francis, taking on the role as French suitor. They even met in 1579 when Francis visited the queen at Greenwich, and the queen wrote a poem, 'On Monsieur's Departure', seemingly expressing her love and unhappiness when he left. For a time it looked like they would be wed despite the disparity between them in age and strong opposition in the council and court. An official position paper written in 1579 declared:

> 'The Queen's Majesty by this marriage shall be a peace maker over all Christendom; shall by her greatness keep a hand over France, the Low Countries, Spain and Scotland, and all her own dominions [and] shall have more fame than ever king was in Europe a thousand years past, shall live happily upon the earth and shall be blessed in the sight of God.'

The negotiations continued until Francis died in 1584. The 'natural' enmity between England and France after a phase of traditional hostilities in Scotland and France at the beginning of the reign was on the wane.

In 1572 the Treaty of Blois reflected the new *entente* and the common interest in resisting Spanish aggression. By its terms both countries promised to aid each other in the event of attack by some third party. It did not however commit England to supporting a French offensive against the Spanish, a vital provision given England's interest in patching up Anglo-Spanish relations at the first opportunity. Furthermore Elizabeth had no intention of encouraging French territorial ambitions in the Netherlands nor did she relish the expense of having to garrison a portion of the Netherlands should they be carved up between France and her allies as Charles IX had proposed in 1571. The absence of reference to Mary Stuart and the English succession issue in the treaty negotiations amounted to a tacit declaration that her cause no longer enjoyed French backing.

In the same year the new understanding was seriously jeopardised when Catherine de Medici's assassination of the French Protestant leader Admiral Coligny was seen as an invitation for the Paris mob and Catholics elsewhere to kill Huguenots. The thousands killed on

St. Bartholomew's Day, 24 August, 1572, and during the weeks that followed, placed Elizabeth in a quandary. As the Protestant Queen of England the defence of French Huguenots was a matter of religious principle; as a crowned head in Europe her support of other legitimate monarchs against potential rebels was an equally valid presumption.

Negotiations were undertaken with both sides, but, ultimately non-intervention was perhaps the wisest course and the one taken - Elizabeth had no intention of playing figurehead for some monumental religious crusade in Europe. This policy contravened the advice of her leading ministers, including Walsingham and Leicester, who supported intervention in this and the concurrent Dutch revolt, both for ideological reasons and because they rightly feared the consolidation of Catholicism across continental Europe. However in 1575 Elizabeth was willing to back a rising against the new French king, Henry III, a fanatical Catholic. According to Susan Doran, had his opponents risen 'she might well have been drawn into the French civil wars'.[98]

During the early 1580s Elizabeth helped fund French intervention in the Netherlands against the Spanish, and in 1589 she sent men and money to the new Huguenot King Henry IV in his struggle against the Spanish backed Catholic League, continuing to do so even after Henry converted to Catholicism in 1593. Henry himself had no doubt regarding the primary motive behind England's involvement - English security demanded intervention as more of France fell into Spanish hands. Henry's conversion helped unite France and civil war turned into a national war against the Spanish, ending in 1598 with a settlement that restored the territorial arrangements of 1559's Treaty of Cateau-Cambrésis.

The Court

Elizabeth's Court was both intimate and exhibitionist. The personal contact it represented for Queen and courtiers was a vital element in Elizabeth's control over principal subjects, while the Court's spectacular pageants addressed a wider audience. The royal progresses

---

[98] Susan Doran, *England and Europe, 1485-1603* (1986).

continued under Elizabeth at considerable expense to the Crown; they were suspended as an economy during the difficult years of the 1580s. Indeed, compared to the court kept by her father, Elizabeth's was economical: menus were less lavish, lesser members were no longer admitted to the formal breakfast, patronage in both cash and land was withheld from all except the most favoured, and she spent far less on palace building work.

The Court also played a part in the forming of royal policy, sometimes in association and sometimes in conflict with the Council. Courtiers such as Sir Walter Raleigh were permitted to advise the Queen on such matters as the war against Spain and councillors such as Sir William Cecil were expected to be in attendance at Court and participate in the lighter aspects of courtly life. Both political power and patronage emanated from the Court and courtly contacts were desirable for those on the outside. Christopher Haigh estimates around two-thirds of the nobility in the early years of Elizabeth's reign were at least part-time courtiers and many were 'resident courtiers', thus 'Roughly one in five of the political heavyweights of England were thus under the regular influence of the Queen'.[99]

The Court provided the centre of a great web of patronage. William Cecil (Lord Burghley after 1571) became Master of the Court of Wards in 1562 and Lord High Treasurer in 1572 placing him in control of most areas of royal patronage. Applications for royal favour were mostly directed towards him although other favourites, notably the Earl of Leicester, offered alternative routes. What Simon Adams has described as Burghley's 'monopolistic tendencies' created tensions between him and Leicester, exacerbated by their differences over foreign policy.

The ultimate triumph at Court was that of securing the Queen's affection. Love: mostly feigned, bound together the coquettish Queen and her courtly admirers. Perhaps the truest indicator of success for the courtier was the acquisition of a pet-name: Leicester became Elizabeth's 'Eyes' and Raleigh she nicknamed 'Water'. Christopher 'Lids' Hatton was exemplary as the triumphant courtier who courted his Queen. Joining the court in 1564, emerging as a favourite by about 1570, he was finally rewarded in 1578 with the highly lucrative office of Receiver of First Fruits *and* Tenths, becoming in the process a font of the highest

---

[99] Christopher Haigh, *Elizabeth I* (1988).

patronage himself.

Courtly love in Elizabeth's Court became more ritualised, more artificial, as Gloriana aged and her alleged beauty faded. At sixty she was still fêted by Raleigh as a goddess - a warrior Diana, a gorgeous Venus of mythological proportion. Lavish gifts at New Year, together with lavish praise, helped preserve her favour and might win even more spectacular presents from her in return. Bold exaggeration and continuous play-acting were deceptions designed to trick Elizabeth's courtiers, and perhaps herself, into believing at least some of what was said. By the final decade of her reign however her young suitors gestures of courtly love were still welcome but no longer likely to win political favour. As Elizabeth grew old and more withdrawn the once glittering Court was tarnished by jealousies and factionalism, culminating in the Earl of Essex' disastrous attempted coup of 1601.

Elizabeth did not greatly change either the structure or the membership of the Tudor Court other than initiating a purge of some senior (Marian) personnel on her accession, and to distinguishing the Royal Bedchamber from the Privy Chamber. Younger men and women continued throughout the reign to fill vacant posts but those already established, by and large, were permitted to remain at Court into old age. Although arguments raged over foreign affairs and marriage proposals the Court, after the religious struggles of the 1650s and '60s, was relatively united although political jealousies continued to engender factionalism. The Puritan sympathies of the great patrons Leicester, Burghley and Walsingham contributed to this courtly cohesiveness. There was religious diversity at Court but the rising of the Northern Earls had compromised the great conservative families and confirmed the Protestant ascendency. Most courtiers were members of established families and they were linked by blood and marriage to one another. Only two members of Elizabeth's inner ring were outsiders who, despite their relatively humble origins, secured the Queen's special favour; they were Sir Christopher Hatton, the charming 'dancing Chancellor', and Sir Walter Raleigh.

Christopher Haigh has made some interesting observations on the heightened political influence of women in the court of this female monarch:

'Certainly Elizabeth used her ladies as sources of political gossip. In 1569 she heard of the plot to marry Queen Mary of

Scots to Norfolk from 'some babbling women', as Leicester complained [...] It is also clear that the women could be used to provide essential information on the Queen's thoughts, and even to influence her views [...] In 1581, after the Queen had announced that she would marry Alençon, Hatton and Leicester got the ladies to weep and wail through the night about the horrors of marriage, to frighten her off.

The role of the ladies of the Chamber in the distribution of patronage was especially clear. In 1566, when Leicester was in mild disfavour, he was advised to pursue a request for lands through Blanche Parry. In 1592, the Countess of Warwick put a suit to the Queen for John Dee, the astrologer, and Ladies Warwick and Huntingdon were active patrons in the late 1590s [...] In 1601, Joan Thynne told her husband rather shortly that, if he could not get a knighthood through the influence of Court politicians, he had better make use of his friendships with the ladies!'[100]

The Queen's Council

Just over a quarter of Elizabeth's first Privy Council comprised great provincial magnates: leaders of the most powerful families in the kingdom. As her reign progressed Elizabeth relied less heavily on the landed aristocracy, surrounding herself all the more with her talented relations and friends. By 1597 there were no territorial magnates on the Council, it was now dominated by officials and the newly ennobled, appointed as reliable administrators and entirely dependent upon their Queen's favour. Furthermore Elizabeth, working on the premise 'a multitude doth make rather discord and confusion than good counsel', had shrunk the Council to a mere eleven members, about half its original size, and it was decidedly Protestant. Scarcely any clerics, Archbishop Whitgift a notable exception, sat on the Council: a mark of emergent lay talent and the decline of the Church hierarchy in high politics. The filial intimacy of Elizabeth's Council is striking: eighteen of her twenty-five

---

[100] Christopher Haigh, *Elizabeth I* (1988).

privy councillors between 1568 and 1582 were related to the Queen. In the tradition of family businesses, sons followed fathers: Robert Cecil, for example, became Secretary of State in 1596, a couple of years before his father, William, once Secretary himself, died. Such exclusivity provoked those alienated from the charmed circle, and it accounts, in part at least, for Essex' rebellion in 1601 – arguably the only time in her reign when personal rivalries within the *inner sanctum* got out of hand, although Christopher Haigh has suggested that the rivalry between the Dudley and Howard (i.e. that of the Earls of Norfolk and Sussex) factions came close to open conflict in the period 1565-66. In the opinion of Haigh this lean, trustworthy Council was 'dangerously narrow and weak in its membership'.

The ideal of a dedicated Council reflecting the monarch's interests and implementing, without contradiction, her policies, does not describe Elizabeth's Privy Council. Elizabeth clashed with councillors over both marriage proposals and foreign affairs. Her Secretary, William Cecil, contrived to control the Queen by restricting the amount of sensitive political information reaching her. The Queen's courtiers and councillors alike grew adept at fathoming her mood and acting accordingly. Cecil's ultimate sanction in forcing the Queen's hand was to threaten resignation. This he did in order to strengthen his hand in persuading the Queen to intervene in Scotland on behalf of the Protestants during the war of 1559, and again in 1560 when he prevented her marriage to Robert Dudley. 'Dirty tricks' campaigns were waged by councillors against their enemies; Secretary Walsingham set up the 'Stafford Plot', allegedly a conspiracy to murder the Queen by igniting gunpowder placed under her bed, the last of several exploded conspiracies that finally persuaded Elizabeth to execute Mary, Queen of Scots. She immediately regretted her decision however and William Davison, the second secretary of state, was sent to the Tower for acting so speedily on her warrant. Elizabeth's vacillation in taking such major decisions exacerbated her ministers. For much of the 1570s she kept them waiting on her decision whether or not to marry the Duke of Anjou. When she finally decided in favour of the match (at least that's what she declared to the Council late in 1579), Leicester led a conciliar and popular campaign against the marriage and Elizabeth, for the time being, abandoned her proposal.

Elizabeth was not over-reliant on the advice of her Council as a whole. As the reign progressed she chose, particularly in matters of foreign affairs, to act independently in conjunction with individual advisers, drawn from the Court as well as the Council. Leicester commented in 1578, 'Our conference with her Majesty is both seldom and slender'. Although the Council did influence certain key decisions most of its work was to do with the mundane and day-to-day routine administration. Such activities ranged from hearing petty disputes concerning land ownership to the huge task of organising the war against Spain. By the end of the reign it met most days, including Sundays, as the burden of work increased. Councillors who crossed her might be threatened with execution but hers, compared to her father's and half-sister's, was not a bloody regime. Instead of a beheading they ran the risk of a slap in the face or, in the celebrated case of Walsingham, the sting of a royal slipper hurled by the royal hand! Such passionate outbursts of violence were balanced by the affection she lavished on her favourites at other times, particularly during their real or feigned illness, perhaps brought on by a regal reprimand.

The Earl of Essex

In 1601 the last attempted coup against a Tudor monarch was hatched by Robert Devereux, Earl of Essex. His mother had married Robert Dudley, Earl of Leicester, who brought the young earl to court and found a place for him in the Netherlands campaign of 1586. His charming manner and appearance, as opposed to talent, made him a favourite of the Queen. He was involved in other campaigns abroad, advocating the maintenance of hostilities against Spain when William Cecil (Lord Burghley) and his son, Essex's arch rival, Robert were looking for peace. In 1598 Burghley, quoting from the Bible, warned him 'Men of blood shall not live out half their days.' In the same year he deeply offended his great patron, the Queen, by turning his back on her when she rejected his proposal that Sir George Carew be made the next Deputy in Ireland. Robert Cecil reported that Elizabeth boxed his ears in her fury.

Following a reconciliation with the Queen he led the 1599 expedition to Ireland against the Earl of Tyrone, who was once more in open rebellion. The campaign was a disaster; after suffering a defeat at Deputy's Pass in County Wicklow in May he finally made a truce with

Tyrone in September and returned to England without royal authorisation. Elizabeth was incensed and placed Essex under house arrest. In January 1600, she spurned his customary New Year gift and that June he was tried for desertion of his post in Ireland and other irresponsible acts. Stripped of most of his offices and deprived of the monopoly he held on the duties on sweet wines, his main source of income (at a time when he was £16,000 in debt), he began plotting his rebellion in the winter of 1600-1. He had some powerful allies including the Earl of Southampton and several lesser nobles, a couple of whom were eminent Catholics. Their objectives were to purge the Queen's Council of Robert Cecil and his supporters, to summon Parliament, and to persuade the Queen to name James VI of Scotland as her successor.

When his conspiracy was discovered in February 1601 he captured the privy councillors sent to bring him before the council. His subsequent attempt to raise London against his accusers was a total failure – just 200 to 300 men marched with him and they were swiftly overwhelmed and taken into custody by the London trained bands. A few days later he was tried and dispatched on the headsman's block. Four more of his followers were executed in March. The Earl of Southampton was heavily fined but spared his life.

Not until the last year of Elizabeth's reign was the relative calm of former years restored. In January 1602 the Spanish army in Ireland surrendered and in October Tyrone himself submitted. Inflation had peaked and despite continuing hunger there were no major civil disturbances. Although the last Parliament in 1601 had once more challenged the government on financial matters, notably over the unpopular granting of monopolies to the privileged few, the divisive faction struggles among her courtiers and councillors that also focused on royal favours had been eliminated. She had survived the crises of the 1590s and, after more than forty years on the throne, she remained active and alert. The Queen's decline in the winter of 1602-3 was sudden and unexpected. By the time she died on March 24 1603, however her last great minister, and Essex's chief rival, Robert Cecil, had completed the necessary arrangements for James VI of Scotland's peaceful succession. He would inherit a Crown that was a mere £350,000 out of pocket, and a kingdom with greater internal stability than his own and one no longer facing the threat of imminent invasion from abroad.

Elizabethan parliaments

Christopher Haigh extravagantly defined Elizabethan England as the ultimate 'nanny-state'. This is how he paraphrased her rebuke to Parliament in 1566 for concerning itself with her private affairs: 'I told you *off* rather than spanked you, and let that be enough - don't misbehave again! But there's no need to be upset, I shall forgive you if you're good boys from now on - and never forget, Nanny loves you really.' This supposedly representative assembly that she summoned thirteen times in forty-five years was, according to Haigh, an irritation to the Queen and something she treated with unrelenting condescension: 'For Elizabeth, parliamentarians were little boys - sometimes unruly, usually a nuisance, and always a waste of an intelligent woman's time.'[101] Certainly she called Parliament irregularly compared to her predecessors and her relationship with Parliament was often strained. Was this all symptomatic of confident 'Tudor despotism' or evidence for a Queen provoked an increasingly assertive and oppositionist House of Commons?

Elizabeth needed Parliament to authorise aspects of her rule: the raising of revenue by extraordinary means, the sanctioning of her religious settlement, the creation of reformed treason acts. Parliament also provided a 'sounding board' for the Queen and her ministers, contact with those who handled much of the routine business of enforcing law and order, administering the localities and collecting taxes.

Throughout her reign Elizabeth experienced a measure of conflict with the so-called 'Puritan choir', those MPs seeking a more fundamental Protestant Settlement. The argument between Queen and Commons in this instance revolved around the right of Parliament to initiate reform, to open the debate on such matters. As far as the Queen was concerned this was her prerogative and attempts to place new bills before Parliament on religious matters might result in arrest and exclusion. Support in Parliament however might save such offenders - when William Strickland was removed from the House of Commons for proposing a bill in 1571 to reform the Prayer Book the outcry this caused persuaded the Queen to have him reinstated. Similar bad feeling

---

[101] Christopher Haigh, *Elizabeth I* (1988).

surrounded discussion of Elizabeth's marital intentions. The deadlock between Queen and Commons of 1566, with demands being made regarding free speech and threats to suspend a subsidy until she declared her intentions in matters relating to the succession, resulted in the premature dissolution of Parliament and much of the legislative work, for which it was intended, remained undone. Arguments regarding both religion and the succession dogged Elizabeth and her Parliament into the 1590s.

While Elizabeth expected Parliament to leave alone matters of 'state' such as religion, the succession and foreign policy, it was permitted to take initiatives regarding matters of 'commonweal', the social and economic lives of her subjects. Thus the Statute of Artificers of 1563 and the Poor Law of 1601 were born in Parliament. Sometimes matters of commonweal directly concerned the Queen. During the 1590s grievances were lodged regarding the granting of monopolies to favoured royal servants. By eliminating competition they tended to raise prices. The Queen's need for parliamentary subsidies eventually, in 1601, resulted in her elimination of the more offensive monopolies.

Such episodes in the history of Elizabeth I's dealings with Parliament substantiated historian J. E. Neale's claim in 1950s that the parliamentary opposition, which plagued the Stuarts in the next century, was forged in her reign. In fact, for the most part, Parliament was co-operative. The Queen continued to be granted the subsidies she required, not just in wartime but also in times of peace. While it might concern itself with matters of state there is little evidence that it actually shaped relevant legislation. Historians are no longer convinced by Neale's argument that the Religious Settlement of 1559 emanated from the Commons as opposed to the Crown. The notion of an emergent oppositionist Puritan party is no longer tenable; there was never, in Elizabeth's reign, a substantial and organised opposition in Parliament. There were outspoken individuals, notably Peter Wentworth, but the vast majority of members were conformist, deferential and accommodating. Parliament challenged neither the Queen nor her councillors' right to govern; most MPs were preoccupied with local issues and they shared their Queen's view of the role of Parliament. When parliamentary pressure was placed on Elizabeth, very often, the campaign for Mary Queen of Scots' execution for example. It was co-ordinated and led by her own appointed privy councillors rather than elected parliamentarians. The exclusivity of the suffrage and the abundance of tiny boroughs provided magnates and councillors the opportunity with filling Parliament with their own men. The reliance on patronage in Elizabethan politics was a powerful force in assuring cohesion and consent. In the last resort the Queen's right to veto bills (the Royal Assent employed by Elizabeth on over sixty occasions) and dissolve parliaments helped eliminate potential opposition. In the Lords the bishops, councillors and others, were dependent upon the Queen's favour and acted accordingly.

Parliament under Elizabeth was far less significant than it had been in the second half of the reign of Henry VIII. During the 1530s the role of Parliament had been greatly advanced as the organ by which changes in statute law were made. After passing the Religious Settlement in 1559 its most important work was completed during the long reign of a cautious Queen. The relative infrequency of its sittings (meeting usually for just a few weeks every three years on average) marks a Parliamentary development that at best was stagnating, at worst, in decline.

Gloriana

In October 1562, when Elizabeth seemed likely to die of smallpox, her reign threatened to be remarkably short; in fact it was remarkably long. The second half of the great 'Tudor' century would be dominated by Elizabeth, a towering figure cultivating her own legend, a myth of queenship, long before she, and with her a dynasty, died in 1603.

Elizabeth's was very much a personal rule in which her ministers were denied the might of Wolsey and Cromwell, and, unlike her sister, Mary, she never came to share power through marriage. It has been suggested that the cult of the unmarried Virgin Elizabeth filled a vacuum created by the assaults on the cult of the Virgin Mary. The longevity of her reign and Elizabeth's powdered public face, enshrined by fabulous costumes and youthful red wigs, created an impression of immortality. The illusion was reinforced by strict guidelines issued to her official portrait painters. In reality the aging, pock-marked Queen grew arthritic and bony, her teeth were rotten and she suffered bouts of melancholia.

Elizabeth's theatricality combined with great learning and an astute grasp of political skills. Elizabeth was a genuine Renaissance princess with something of her father's intellectual and physical prowess.

Like Henry she was a capable musician, proficient in playing the virginals and the lute. She is said to have been the mistress of no less than nine languages including the ancient Celtic tongues of Wales, Ireland and Cornwall; fluent in the key languages of sixteenth century diplomacy, Italian, Latin, Spanish and French, she could be her own ambassador. She enjoyed hunting, dancing, singing, card playing and chess. On the eve of her seventieth birthday she rode ten miles in a single day and also hunted, and just weeks before her death in March 1603 she danced a coranto! Her autograph in an Italian style, perhaps the most famous example of English handwriting, was a product of her rigorous humanist education, directed by Cambridge scholars William Grindall and Roger Ascham. Her tutors provided her with a thorough grounding in the Classics and, in addition, she was instructed in the principles of statecraft and Protestant theology. According to Ascham she was a brilliant and industrious student: 'I am inventing nothing [...] there is no need.'

Circumstances, pride and self-reliance kept Elizabeth centre-stage throughout her reign. Her decision not to marry maintained her supremacy in a political world designed by and for men. In her most celebrated speech, allegedly that delivered to her army on the eve of the expected Spanish invasion of August 1588, it is evident that Elizabeth shared some of the gender assumptions of her age, but she proved irrevocably that a woman could rule as effectively as any man:

> 'I know I have the body of a weak and feeble woman, but I have the heart and stomach of a king, and a king of England too, and think foul scorn that Parma or Spain, or any prince of Europe should dare to invade the borders of my realm; to which, rather than any dishonour shall grow by me, I myself will take up arms, I myself will be your general, judge, and rewarder of every one of your virtues in the field.'

The Virgin Queen

> 'This Maiden-Queen Elizabeth came into this world, the Eve of the Nativity of the blessed virgin Mary; and died on the Eve of the Annunciation of the virgin Mary. 160[3]. She was, she is

(what more can be said?) In earth the first, in heaven the second Maid.'

(Inscription on an early seventeenth century engraved stone.)

Not only have historians considered Elizabeth a psychological substitute for the Virgin Mary, some have translated the cult of Elizabeth and its attendant pageant into compensation for the lost ceremony of the Catholic Church. In common with autocrats and dictators of more recent times Elizabeth provided her subjects with a new holiday commemorating her acquisition of power. This rival to the traditional Saints' Days and other Holy Days fell on November 17, Accession Day. Combining the traditional elements of religiosity and merriment it also reasserted the unity of Church and State by marking both the new reign and the restoration of the true faith.

Accession Day was first celebrated in 1567 with the ringing of bells in the Archbishop's parish church at Lambeth. The event grew each year: by the late seventies special services, bonfires, dances and even fireworks were commonplace; in the words of Christopher Haigh, '17 November became an excuse for a booze-up.' After the defeat of the Spanish Armada in 1588 celebrations on the Queen's Day were more or less universal.

Although it rapidly received official sanction, added to the calendar of Church festivals in 1576, Accession Day, like many aspects of Elizabethan propaganda began spontaneously among a people with genuine affection for a popular queen. By the 1590s however this popularity had waned and this annual 'booze-up' was nothing more than an excuse to party. The vision of queenship built up over the first three decades of the reign had passed and the Golden Age of Elizabeth celebrated on Accession Day had proved illusory.

In the early 1570s the Accession Day tilts became a highlight of the festival. This was an elaborate ceremonial tournament in which the medieval chivalric traditions were revived. The Queen had her champion and other knights participating could show their loyalty by choosing her as the lady to whom their lives were devoted. It both flattered a vain queen and made good political sense for Elizabeth to use her gender to her advantage by encouraging her courtiers to become Lancelots. Where Lancelot and his Queen, Guinevere, failed, Elizabeth would succeed - she was after all the Virgin Queen and ultimately unattainable even to her most devoted knights.

Part of the essence of medieval romance is the tension between chaste love and sexual desire and on this the Elizabethan court thrived. The Queen's chastity, her purity, was expected to be emulated by those about her. She had a very low opinion of extramarital sex and courtiers and ladies-in-waiting could expect severe retribution if discovered. Walter Raleigh's prompt marriage to Elizabeth Throckmorton on discovering she was pregnant did not save them from being sent to the Tower in 1592. The Queen had reservations regarding marriage in any case and deeply resented her courtiers' wishes to wed. Requests were sometimes refused and one poor applicant, Mary Shelton, received a beating and a broken finger for her troubles!

Her intolerance did not lessen with age. She continued to expect the devotion of, preferably, celibate courtiers and continued to cultivate her image of ageless youth, beauty and purity. At the age of sixty-four she troubled the French ambassador by continually pulling open her dressing-gown that he might gaze admiringly on her charms. Whatever she or anyone else thought, all were required to endorse publicly the myth. Once she had tried to retain her youth by 'science', establishing a secret laboratory in Somerset House for a Dutch alchemist seeking the elixir of life, she now sought to retain it by persuasion and propaganda.

While poets and playwrights could (and did) proclaim her beauty to the end of her life, the great romance could only last if it was seen to be true. She took great care over her personal appearance, and, to quote Christopher Haigh again, 'Elizabeth I was a show-off, and she dressed to kill.' Her wardrobe was spectacular and quite as magnificent and outlandish as the costumes in which she was portrayed by contemporary painters. When she met the Venetian envoy in 1603 after nearly half a century on the throne she dressed in silver and white taffeta trimmed with gold, she wore a crown and was generously bedecked with jewels. Her hair he reported was 'of a light colour not made by nature'. At nearly seventy Elizabeth still looked impressive. The hair in fact was probably a wig and the ambassador perhaps also noted her emaciated face and irregular yellow teeth. However she did enjoy remarkably good health and very likely benefited from regular exercise, walking or riding, and a natural aversion towards quack medicines. One foreign visitor in 1592 generously commented: 'She need not indeed, to judge both from her person and appearance, yield much to a young girl of sixteen'. According to one of her biographers, J. E. Neale, 'Age enhanced rather than diminished her remarkable dignity.'

In her portraits she ceased aging entirely. A 'mask of youth' developed by the miniaturist Nicholas Hilliard, became the conventional depiction of the Queen for all likenesses. Portraits that did not conform were recalled and destroyed by the Sergeant Painter in 1596 and the Privy Council from 1600. Her vanity was inflated by her ministers, anxious to preserve the image of English stability and vigour, while many privately looked forward to rule by a younger and male monarch.

The closing years of Elizabeth's long reign were at least as turbulent as any since her accession back in 1558. The struggle with Spain continued and defences were maintained against further invasion attempts. Anglo-Irish relations deteriorated further still and open rebellion against the English presence spanned the last seven years of the reign. The activities of religious extremists, Puritans and Jesuits, still troubled Elizabeth's government, and a new obsession with identifying the perpetrators of diabolical deeds gave rise to witch-hunts towards the end of the century. The pressures of population growth and inflation, as people adapted to the new order of post-Reformation England, created social tension, paranoia even, as the century lurched, uncomfortably, to a close. Plague and atrocious harvests contributed to the general malaise and helped spark off the many popular riots of the 1590s. Plots on the life of the Queen continued to be uncovered and one final attempted English rebellion was foiled and its leaders executed. She kept her councillors on tenterhooks regarding the succession, only naming James VI of Scotland with her dying breath in 1603.

Despite all her endeavours to maintain the illusion of Gloriana, according to Christopher Haigh, 'Elizabeth died unloved and almost unlamented, and it was partly her own fault.'[102]

---

[102] Christopher Haigh, *Elizabeth I* (1988).

SOURCES

Princess Elizabeth, c.1550

(Roger Ascham, tutor to Elizabeth, in a letter to his friend and fellow humanist Johannes Sturm, c.1550)

It is difficult to say whether the gifts of nature or of fortune are most to be admired in my distinguished mistress. The praise which Aristotle gives, wholly centres in her; beauty, stature, prudence, and industry. She has just passed her sixteenth birthday and shows such dignity and gentleness as are wonderful at her age and in her rank. Her study of true religion and learning is most eager. Her mind has no womanly weakness, her perseverance is equal to that of a man, and her memory long keeps what it quickly picks up. She talks French and Italian as well as she does English, and has often talked to me readily and well in Latin, moderately in Greek. When she writes Greek and Latin, nothing is more beautiful than her handwriting. She delights as much in music as she is skillful in it. In adornment she is elegant rather than showy.

Queen Elizabeth, 1558

(Report of the Spanish ambassador to Philip II, 14 November 1558)

Although it is difficult to judge a person one has known for as short a time as I have this woman, I shall tell your Majesty what I have been able to gather. She is a very vain and clever woman. She must have been thoroughly schooled in the manner in which her father conducted his affairs, and I am very much afraid that she will not be well-disposed in matters of religion, for I see her inclined to govern through men who are believed to be heretics and I am told that all the women around her definitely are. Apart from this she is highly indignant about what has been done to her during the Queen's lifetime.

Elizabeth I and Edmund Grindal, 1576

(Archbishop Grindal's letter to Elizabeth I, 20 December 1576)

These orders following are […] observed in the said exercise (prophesying), First, two or three of the gravest and best learned pastors are appointed of the bishop to moderate in every assembly. No man may speak unless he be first allowed to by the bishop, with this proviso that no layman be suffered to speak at any time. No controversy at this present time and state shall be moved or dealt withal. If any attempt the contrary, he is put to silence by the moderator […] If any man utter a wrong sense of the Scripture, he is privately admonished thereof and better instructed by the moderators and other his fellow-ministers. If any man use immodest speech or irreverent gesture or behaviour, or otherwise be suspected in life, he is likewise admonished as before. If any wilfully do break these orders, he is presented to the bishop to be by him corrected.

Howsoever report hath been made to your Majesty concerning these exercises, yet I and others of your bishops whose names are noted in the margin thereof, as they have testified unto me by their letters, having found by experience that these profits and commodities following have ensued of them: 1. The ministers of the Church are more skilful and ready in the Scriptures, and apter to teach their flocks. 2. It withdraweth them from idleness, wandering, gaming, etc. 3. Some afore suspected in doctrine are hereby brought to open confession of the truth. 4. Ignorant ministers are driven to study, if not for conscience yet for shame and fear of discipline. 5. The opinion of laymen touching the idleness of the clergy is hereby removed. 6. Nothing by experience beateth down popery more than that ministers (as some of my brethren do certify) grow to such a good knowledge by means of these exercises that where afore were not three able preachers, now are thirty meet to preach at St. Paul's Cross […] Only backward men in religion and contemners of learning in the countries abroad do fret against it; which in truth doth the more commend it.

Pray you to consider these two short petitions […] The first is that you would refer all these ecclesiastical matters which touch religion, or the doctrine and discipline of the church, unto the bishops and divines of your realm […] For indeed they are things to be judged […] in the church, or a synod, not in a palace.

The second petition [...] is this: that, when you deal in matters of faith and religion [...] you would not use to pronounce so resolutely and peremptorily, as from authority [...] but always remember that in God's causes the will of God, and not the will of any earthly creature, is to take place. It is the antichristian voice of the pope, 'So I will have it; so I command; let my will stand for a reason'.

Remember, madam, that you are a mortal creature [...]

Via Media, 1564

(Summary of the returns from the dioceses submitted to William Cecil in 1564)

Some say the service in the chancel, others in the body of the church, some in the pulpit with their faces to the people; some keep precisely the order of the book, others intermeddle psalms in metre; some say in a surplice, others without a surplis; the table standeth in the body of the church in some places, in others it Standeth in the chancel; in some places the table standeth altarwise, distant from the wall a yard, in some others in the middle of the chancel, north and south; in some places the table is joined; in others it standeth upon trestles; in some places the table hath a carpet, in others it hath not; administration of the Communion is done by some with surplis and cap, some with surplis alone, others with none; some with chalice, others with a Communion cup, others with a common cup; some with unleavened bread, some with leavened; some receive kneeling, others standing, others sitting; some baptise in a font, some in a basin; some sign with the sign of the cross, others sign not. Apparel - some with a square cap, some with a round cap, some with a button cap, some with a hat.

Mary, Queen of Scots, and the succession, 1559

(Elizabeth I to the House of Commons, 1559, in response to the request of the Scottish ambassador to name Mary, Queen of Scots, her successor)

I will be Queen of England so long as I live; after my death let them succeed to whom in right it shall appertain if that be your Queen [Mary,

Queen of Scots] (as I know not who should be before her), I will not be against it [...] you assume [...] that, upon this declaration, the friendship would be more firm between us. I fear you are deceived; I fear it would be rather an origin of hatred [...] I am well acquainted with the nature of this people; I know how easily they dislike the present state of affairs; I know what nimble eyes they bear to the next succession [...] I have learned this from experience of mine own times. When my sister Mary was Queen, what prayers were made by many to see me placed in her seat. Assuredly, if my successor were known to the world, I would never esteem my state to be safe.

Mary, Queen of Scots, 1568

(Sir Francis Knollys to Sir William Cecil, 1568)

[...] this Lady and princess is a notable woman [...] She shows a disposition to speak much, to be bold, to be pleasant, and to be very familiar. She shows a great desire to be avenged of her enemies; she shows a readiness to expose herself to all perils in hope of victory. She delights much to hear of hardiness and valiance [...] The thing she most thirsts after is victory, and it seems to be indifferent to her to have her enemies diminished either by the sword of her friends, or by the liberal promises and rewards of her purse, or by the division and quarrels raised among themselves; so that for victory's sake pain and peril seem pleasant to her [...] Now what is to be done with such a Lady and Princess [...] whether such a princess and lady [should be] nourished in one's bosom, or whether it be good to halt and dissemble with such a lady I refer to your judgement.

The rebellion of the northern earls, 1569

(Proclamation of the Northern Earls, 16 November 1569)

Thomas, Earl of Northumberland and Charles, Earl of Westmoreland, the Queen's most true and lawful subjects, and to all Her Highness' people, send greetings:- Whereas diverse new set up nobles about the Queen's Majesty, have and do daily, not only go about to overthrow and put down the ancient nobility of this realm, but also have misused the Queen's Majesty's own person, and also have by the space of twelve years now past, set up, and maintained a new found religion and heresy, contrary to God's word. For the amending and redressing whereof, diverse foreign powers do purpose shortly to invade these realms, which will be to our utter destruction, if we do not ourselves speedily forfend the same. Wherefore we are now constrained at this time to go about to amend and redress it ourselves, which if we should not do and foreigners enter upon us we should be all made slaves and bondmen to them. These are therefore to will and require you, and every of you, being above the age of sixteen years and not sixty, as your duty to Cod doth bind you, for the setting forth of his true and Catholic religion; and as you tender the commonwealth of your country, to come and resort unto us with good speed, with all such armour and furniture as you, or any of you have. This fail you not herein, as you will answer the contrary at your perils. God save the Queen.

Causes of rebellion, 1569

(From a report sent by Sir Ralph Sadler from York to Sir William Cecil, 6 December 1569)

I perceive Her Majesty is to believe that the force of her subjects of this country should not increase, and be able to match with the rebels; but it is easy to find the cause. There are not ten gentlemen in all this country that favour her proceedings in the cause of religion. The common people are ignorant, superstitious, and altogether blinded with the old popish doctrine, and therefore so favour the cause which the rebels make the colour of their rebellion, that, though their persons be here with us, their hearts are with them.

The confession of the Earl of Northumberland, 1572

(The Earl of Northumberland shortly before his execution in August 1572)

Our first object in assembling was the reformation of religion and preservation of the person of the Queen of Scots, as next heir, failing issue of Her Majesty, which causes I believed were greatly favoured by most of the noblemen of the Realm.

The excommunication of Elizabeth I, 1570

(Extracts from the Papal Bull, *Regnans in Excelsis*, excommunicating Elizabeth I, February 1570)

[...] Elizabeth, the pretended queen of England, the servant of wickedness [...] monstrously usurped the place of supreme head of the church in all England, and the chief authority and jurisdiction thereof, hath again reduced the said kingdom into a miserable and ruinous condition, which was so lately reclaimed to the Catholic faith and a thriving condition [...] we seeing that impieties and wicked actions are multiplied one upon the other, as also that the persecution of the faithful and affliction of religion groweth every day heavier and heavier, through the instigation and by the means of the said Elizabeth, and since we understand her heart to be so hardened and obdurate [...] we do, out of fulness of our apostolic power, declare the aforesaid Elizabeth, as being an heretic and favourer of heretics, and her adherents in the matters aforesaid, to have incurred the sentence of excommunication, and to be cut off from the unity of the body of Christ. And moreover we do declare her to be deprived of her pretended title to the kingdom aforesaid, and of all dominion, dignity, and privilege whatsoever [...] And we do command and charge all and every the noblemen, subjects, people, and others aforesaid, that they presume not to obey her, or her orders, mandates and laws: those which shall do the contrary, we do include them in the like sentence of anathema.

The Genoese Bullion Crisis, 1568-9

(Ambassador de Spes to the Duke of Alva, 22 December 1568)

Cecil was very grave about it, as also was the earl of Leicester. Sometimes they said they were guarding it for his Majesty, and sometimes that it belonged to other persons; but they would not say whether they had sent similar orders to Plymouth and Falmouth. Their refusal to declare themselves on this point, however, proves that they have done so. They consulted the Queen and then said that the money was in safe keeping and no other answer could then be given. I pressed for an audience and they told me to ask again after dinner, they in the meantime being closeted with the ambassador of the prince of Conde, so that I could get no reply from them [...] The affair is thus in a very bad way and these people are determined to do any wickedness, so this money will not be recovered. I pray Your Excellency do not fail to seize all English property and send word to Spain for them to do the same there.

Spain: 'that wicked nation', 1568

(Sir Arthur Champerpoun and letters received from Secretary Cecil, December 1568)

I have of late received from your honour a couple of letters both tending to one end, which was that I should under cover of friendship use all policy to recover such treasure of the King of Spain as is presently within our western ports [...] anything taken from that wicked nation is both necessary and profitable to our commonwealth.

Retaliation in Antwerp, 1568

(Elizabeth I, 1568)

Her Majesty has heard that the Duke of Alva, governor of the States of Flanders for her brother the King of Spain, had suddenly ordered the detention of all merchants and other subjects of Her Majesty in the city of Antwerp, and had placed guards of soldiers over them, and had sequestrated all their property [...] which is a strange and unheard of thing for the House of Burgundy to do the Crown of England [...] her Majesty thinks fit to declare briefly the facts of the case.

    An officer of Her Majesty in a port in the west of England advised the arrival from Spain of three or four small boats called cutters bringing in a quantity of money belonging to certain Italian merchants

[...] on the coast there were many armed French ships of war on watch for these cutters [...] The Spanish ambassador [...] asked that orders should be given for the defence of these vessels and the treasure against the French [...] At this time the Queen learnt that the money was the property of certain merchants and decided that it was not unreasonable nor opposed to the bonos mores of sovereigns in their own country that she should negotiate with the owners thereof with their full consent [...] for borrowing from them all or part of it [...]

Before she saw the ambassador [...] she learned that all the ships, goods and merchandize of her subjects were embargoed and seized in Antwerp on the 29th December.

The 'Enterprise of England', 1587

(The Marquis de Santa Cruz to Philip II, 1587)

If it really be decided to go to England itself I would only observe that this Armada, even when united with the troops of the Duke of Parma, which would at this season be embarked and carried over the straits with no small difficulty, does not seem to me sufficient to attempt this enterprise in the very heart of the winter.

[...] It is my opinion that the sailing of the Armada should be delayed, if not till March, at least till the middle of February, to allow the weather to grow milder. And your majesty must remember that should any misfortune befall the fleet, which God forbid, it would be impossible to put together another such Armada for a long time to come. To me it seems that a sovereign with such a reputation in the world would not allow himself to be swept away by a thirst for vengeance.

Spanish landing craft, 1588

(The Duke of Parma to Philip II, January 1588)

These craft are so light and small that four warships could sink every boat we have.

Spanish troops, 1588

(The Duke of Parma to Philip II, March 1588)

Even if the Armada supplies us with the 6,000 Spaniards as agreed - and they are the sinews of the undertaking - I shall still have too few troops... If I set foot on shore, it will be necessary for us to fight battle after battle. I shall, of course, lose men by wounds and sickness. I must leave the port and town garrisons strongly defended, to keep open my lines of communications: and in a very short time my force will thus be so much reduced as to be quite inadequate to cope with the great multitude of enemies.

English artillery, 1588

(Philip II's advice to his admirals)

The enemy's objective will be to fight at long distance, to get the advantage of his artillery and shot (said to be in great quantity) [...] the objective of our fleet must be to attack and close with them, ready for hand-to-hand combat.

Spain and the Earl of Tyrone's Rebellion, 1595

(The Earl of Tyrone to Philip II, 27 September 1595)

Our only hope of re-establishing the Catholic religion rests on your assistance. Now or never our Church must be succoured. By the timidity or negligence of the messengers our former letters have not reached you. We therefore again beseech you to send us 2,000 or 3,000 soldiers, with money and arms [...] With such aid we hope to restore the faith of the Church, and to secure you a kingdom.

Spanish aspirations, 1596

(The Spanish Council of State to Philip II, c.1596)

Your Majesty would gain enormously in prestige by conquering a kingdom thus unexpectedly. The bridle which the possession of Ireland by your Majesty would put upon England and the northern powers, would enable you to divert them from all other points of attack, and prevent them from molesting Spain, the Indies, etc. It would enable you to make good terms of peace and recover the Flemish fortresses held by the English for the rebels.

In the event of the Queen's death, your Majesty, as master of Ireland, would be in a greatly improved position to nominate a successor to the English crown.

Ireland, Spain and England, 1598

(The Council of Ireland to Elizabeth I's Privy Council, 1598)

We have daily advertisements of Tyrone's treacherous practices to extend his rebellion and treason into all parts of the Realm [...] and to introduce Papistry, which he begins now to make a more firm ground of his rebellion than he did before, insinuating that he is borne up and maintained therein by the Spanish King, by which course he has wrought dangerous impressions in the hearts of the people [...] yet we are of the opinion that it is not religion [...] that carries him, but that it is the alteration of the government and state that he aims at, as by his letters, of which we have previously informed you Lordships, he has promised to the Spaniards, and is still countenanced and encouraged therein by them.

Privateers, 1603

(Report of the Venetian Ambassador to England, 1603)

While on this topic I must not omit to say that the English through their rapacity and cruelty have become odious to all nations. With Spain they are at open war and are already plundering her and upsetting the India trade; they are continually robbing with violence the French, whom they encounter on the long stretches of the open sea [...]

Hence both those who command, and those who execute here in

England, see quite clearly how great, how universal, and how just is the hatred which all nations, nay all peoples we might say, bear to the English, for they are the disturbers of the whole world. And yet with all this they not only do not take any steps to remedy the mischief, but in a certain sense they glory that the English name should become formidable just in this way. For whereas the kings of England, down to Henry VII and Henry VIII, were wont to keep up a fleet of one hundred ships in full pay as a defence, now the Queen's ships do not amount to more than fifteen or sixteen, as her revenue cannot support a greater charge; and so the whole of the strength and the repute of the nation rests on the vast number of small privateers, which are supported and increased to that dangerous extent which everyone recognises; and to ensure this support, the privateers make the ministers partners in the profits, without the risk of a penny in the fitting out, but only a share in the prizes which are adjudged by judges placed there by the ministers themselves.

Elizabeth I on marriage, 1565

(Elizabeth I to the Spanish ambassador, 1565)

If I could appoint such a successor to the crown as would please me and the country, I would not marry, as it is a thing for which I have no inclination. My subjects, however, press me so that I cannot help myself or take the other course which is a very difficult one. There is strong idea in the world that a woman cannot live unless she is married or at all events if she refrains from marriage she does so for some bad reason.

Elizabeth I's early suitors

(William Camden, *The History of the Most Renowned and Victorious Princess Elizabeth*, 1630)

1560: She, out of singular love to her country, was all this while so attentive to the public good, that in the meantime she almost quite put out of her mind the love of potent princes. For at the same time there sought to her for marriage, Charles, Archduke of Austria, a younger son of the Emperor Ferdinand [...] James, Earl of Arran, commended by the

Protestants of Scotland, with purpose to unite by him the divided kingdoms of England and Scotland [...] Eric, King of Sweden [...] this great and singular love she acknowledged and commended; she answered, 'he should be welcome, but she could not yet persuade herself to change her single life, most pleasing to her, for a married life '

[...] But Charles of Austria hoped and expected that the House of Austria, which had been most fortunate by matching with the greatest princesses, should be greatened by the addition of England; and also that by him the old religion should be, if not restored, then at the least wise tolerated. Neither did Queen Elizabeth at the first dash cut off his hope. For she made show openly [...] and by many letters to the Emperor, 'that amongst many most honourable matches propounded none was more honourable than this with Charles of Austria.

[...] And at home also there were not lacking some which (as lovers use to do) feigned unto themselves vain dreams of marrying with her: namely Sir William Pickering, Knight, who had some nobility of birth, a mean estate, but some honour by his studies of good arts, elegancy of life, and embassies in France and Germany [...]

Henry, Earl of Arundel, a man of very ancient nobility, great wealth, but of declining age, and Robert Dudley, the Duke of Northumberland's younger son, who was restored in blood by Queen Mary, a man of flourishing age and comely feature of body and limbs, whose father and grandfather were not so much hated of the people but as he was much favoured by Queen Elizabeth [...]

The court of Queen Elizabeth, 1598

(Description of a Court dinner in Paul Hentzner, *Travels in England*, 1598)

When they had waited there a little while, the yeomen of the guard entered, bareheaded, clothed in scarlet, with a golden rose upon their backs, bringing in at each turn a course of twenty-four dishes, served in silver most of it gilt; these dishes were received by a gentleman in the same order as they were brought and placed upon the table, while the lady-taster gave to each of the guard a mouthful to eat of the particular dish he had brought, for fear of any poison [...] At the end of all this ceremonial, a number of unmarried ladies appeared, who with particular solemnity lifted the meat off the table, and conveyed it into the Queen's inner and more private chamber, where after she had chosen for herself, the rest goes to the ladies of the court. The Queen dines and sups alone with very few attendants; and it is very seldom that anybody, foreigner or native, is admitted at that time, and then only at the intercession of some distinguished personage.

Faction, c.1598

(The Earl of Essex's threat to Secretary Robert Cecil concerning Francis Bacon's appointment to the Attorney-Generalship, c.1598)

The attorneyship for Francis is that I must have; and in that I will spend all my power, might, authority and amity, and with tooth and nail defend and procure the same for him against whom whatsoever, and that whosoever getteth this office out of my hands for any other, before he shall have it, it shall cost him the coming by.

The rebellion of the Earl of Essex, 1601

(Proclamation against Essex, 1601)

February 9th 1601: Proclamation that whereas the Earl of Essex, with the Earls of Rutland and Southampton and other gentlemen, their accomplices, being discovered in treason in Ireland with Tyrone and also in England, did, on 8th February, imprison the Lord Keeper, Lord Chief Justice and others of the Council, sent to persuade him to disperse his disordered company, and lay open his just complaints for redress, threatening to murder them if they stirred, and traitorously issued into London, breaking into open rebellion and pretending their lives were threatened and continued in arms, killing diverse subjects, after proclamation of rebellion read by the heralds.

Peter Wentworth, 1576

(Extract from Peter Wentworth's speech in the House of Commons,

1576)

Amongst other, Mr. Speaker, two things do great hurt in this place, of the which I do mean to speak: the one is a rumour which runneth about the house and this it is, 'Take heed what you do, the queen's majesty liketh not such a matter. Whosoever prefereth it, she will be offended with him'. Or the contrary, 'her majesty liketh of such a matter. Whosoever speaketh against it, she will be much offended with him'.

  The other: sometimes a message is brought into the house, either of commanding or inhibiting, very injurious to the freedom of speech and consultation, I would to God, Mr. Speaker, that these two were buried in hell, I mean rumours and messages, for wicked they undoubtedly are. The reason is, the devil was the first author of them, from whom proceedeth nothing but wickedness [...]

Queen of the Amazons, 1695

(Edmund Bohun, *The Character of Elizabeth*, 1695)

But how the Queen indeed stood affected to wedlock may be partly understood by Roger Ascham, who read to her, and was frequently with her. For when Sturmius, the learned man of Strasburg, had in his correspondence with Ascham, anno 1562, inquired into that affair [...] he answered, 'That in all the course of her life she resembled Hyppolite, and not Phaedra.' These were the two wives of Theseus; Hyppolite was the Queen of the Amazons, and a warrior; Phaedra, on the other hand, was very amorous. Ascham told him that he had adventured to shew his letter to the Queen [...] which the Queen read thrice smiling, but very bashfully and modestly, and said nothing. Then he added that for her disposition towards wedding, he nor none else could know anything certain, nor tell what to say. And it was not without reason he had told him, that all her life she was more like to Hyppolite than Phaedra; which, he said, he meant in regard of the chastity of her mind; and that of her own nature, not by the council of any, she was so strange and averse from marriage.

Chapter 10: Society and the State

Anti- clericalism and the Authority of the Church.

> '[...] charity and peace is almost extinct, faith dispersed, hope dissolved, virtue and pity outlawed, sanctity annulled, priesthood distained, religion decayed.'

(Richard Whitford, *The Pomander of Prayer*, 1528)

    The cry of the cleric that religion is in decline was nothing new in 1528 and would continue to be heard to the present day. Ironically, the books of Richard Whitford were bestsellers, running into several editions as the public clamoured for his latest work. The massive sales of his books on the eve of Reformation suggests that orthodox Catholicism, as championed in his writing, was firmly rooted in the lives of the majority of literate laymen and women. The churches were filled and prohibition from attending services was regarded as a severe penalty for minor misdemeanors brought before the Church courts. Such punishment might be imposed on a defendant who failed to appear at court and this sanction would usually be enough to secure co-operation. Those who persisted in ignoring the demands of the court, such as William Bankes of Loughborough who publicly tore up his summons, ran the risk of excommunication and imprisonment.
    For many cases lay-people would seek a church hearing since the Church courts tended to deal with business relatively swiftly and at less cost than the secular courts. The ecclesiastical courts were under attack from one quarter though - lawyers tried hard to wrest from the Church some of its valuable legal business. Demands were made for a clarification of what should and should not constitute a case suitable for hearing in Church courts. The activities of ecclesiastical and secular courts overlapped and the Church was accused of meddling in matters such as trade and finance in which it had no legitimate interest or expertise. Increasingly slander suits and cases involving debt became the

business of common law.

In a political as well as legal sense the authority of the Church was restricted during the reign of Henry VII. After his death the Church endeavoured to reassert its ancient rights, including that of clerical immunity from trial in secular courts. Although the Church made little headway in such matters, Henry VIII, before the fall of Cardinal Wolsey, made no move to further erode ecclesiastical privileges and the status of the Church. Indeed, contrary to the opinions of Richard Whitford and some modern historians, the Church was on the offensive with a new dynamism that can be detected in its rigorous pursuit of heresy.

Furthermore, under such men as Bishop Fisher and Cardinal Wolsey, it appeared committed to its own reform. For whatever reason, genuine or otherwise, Wolsey advocated the elimination of certain abuses and endeavoured in the 1520s to rationalise and reform the monasteries. The irony of this was not lost on Archbishop Warham's chaplain, Henry Gold, who suggested in 1528 that it was not those in religious orders most in need of reform but the cleric-politicians themselves.

In addition to claims that clerics were abusing their rights regarding the collection of tithes and mortuary fees, complaints were made against pluralism, non-residence, nepotism, and simony. The Church did not officially condone such abuses but they were not uncommon. On the other hand recent studies indicate that in most instances clergymen were competent and committed in their vocation and complaints against them were comparatively rare. Bishops too, for the most part, fulfilled their religious duties to an acceptable standard, endeavouring to take time out from their secular activities to attend to ecclesiastical affairs in their dioceses. Pluralism and non-residence could be compensated by the appointment of suitable clerics to deputise for absent incumbents and the claim that simony and nepotism resulted in an inept clergy can be challenged by the fact that a higher proportion were university graduates (though not necessarily in Theology) than ever before: 32 per cent in the period 1450 to 1499 and 42 per cent from 1500 to 1532.

The writings of the German reformer, Martin Luther, had started to arrive in England by 1518. By 1520 his books were banned in London and Cambridge. seized and burned. Persuaded by Cardinal Wolsey. Henry VIII published in 1521, in his name, a repudiation of Luther entitled *Assertio Septem Sacramentorum*. Lutheranism was not widespread but certainly taking root in the East where commercial activity necessitated contact with Germany. Luther's ideas were regularly discussed by a group of academics, including Hugh Latimer and Stephen Gardiner, at the White Horse tavern in Cambridge. Lutherans were in contact with Lollards and shared similar views, particularly the emphasis on biblical authority and the right of the laity to read the Bible in the vernacular. A new English translation, printed by William Tyndale in Germany, began to be shipped into England, hundreds of copies at a time, after its completion at Worms in 1526.

Tyndale's Bible was quickly suppressed, as Wycliffe's had been back in 1410, and all copies had to be handed in to the ecclesiastical authorities on pain of excommunication. By 1530 the booksellers and readers were being burned as well as the books. These included Thomas Hitton, burned at Maidstone in Kent for returning from the Continent to England in possession of two 'heretical' works, one of which was Tyndale's Bible. Tyndale himself was arrested near Brussels in 1535 and executed the following year.

Despite all of this activity and the increasingly intolerant stance of the Church, neither Lollardy nor Lutheranism was extensively practised. Indeed, the victims of official persecution were not popularly lamented, on the contrary, the wearers of the faggot badge were ostracized and unable to gain employment, and the fires for the condemned were further fuelled by the men, women and children who came to abuse them in their agony and delight in seeing them burned. Christopher Haigh has concluded: 'The Lutheran call remained a lonely voice in a hostile wilderness.'

Famine, hunger and rebellion

Although plenty of potentially arable land remained to be exploited, the growth in population, in bad years, created a demand that outstripped the supply of basic foodstuffs. The early years of Elizabeth's reign revealed an agricultural economy able to feed this growing population when climatic conditions were favourable but the dearth years of the 1590s revealed its vulnerability. In the short term the supply from year to year was relatively inelastic and bad weather could produce localised famines; however, in the long-term the country was quite capable of adapting to supply the growing number of mouths that needed feeding. Despite this contemporaries expressed a fear that the population was facing what would later be termed, after the late eighteenth century demographic alarmist, Thomas Malthus, the 'Malthusian trap' - the predicament of a society having so large a population that its continued sustenance is no longer possible. Thus Robert Gray, shortly after Elizabeth I's death advocated emigration to Virginia:

> 'Our multitudes, like too much blood in the body, do infect our country with plague and poverty. Our land hath brought forth but it hath not milk sufficient in the breast thereof to nourish all those children which it hath brought forth.'

The potato was unheard of until Elizabeth's reign and not widely eaten until long afterwards; the masses, for the most part, lived on bread. The lack of fodder crops for winter-feed meant that herds of livestock had to be small and consequently meat and dairy products were not abundant. Meat dishes were as likely to contain rabbit or sparrow as they were mutton or pork. Coastal communities of course enjoyed a diet rich in fish and a good deal more coarse fish, such as pike and carp, were eaten in Tudor times than our own. The absence of refrigeration necessitated other means of preserving food or keeping it fresh: meat was smoked and salted, vegetables were preserved in vinegar, dairy produce was stored in caves or underground in purpose built boxes. Archaeologists occasionally unearth 'bog butter' buried in boxes long ago but still in a good state of preservation due to its immersion in peat. Spices helped disguise the taste of rotten food. Honey provided a natural sweetener.

In the 1590s men, women and children in parts of England, notably the north, starved to death. The bad harvests between 1594 and 1597 were disastrous. By 1596 it was deemed necessary to pass legislation that forbade the export of grain and other foodstuffs. The main cause of the significant increase in mortality during those years in Cumbria, Westmorland, parts of Durham and Yorkshire, appears to have been starvation. Between 1596 and 1597 the death rate rose by 21 per cent and by a further 5 per cent in 1597-8.

The bouts of famine coincided with visitations of the plague. The first severe epidemic in Elizabeth's reign occurred in 1593 and concluded with the great plague of 1603 which killed 30,000 people in

London alone. There was no known cure, though doctors advocated as cures the use of tobacco, dried toads, arsenic, even the placing of a live chicken against the plague sores until the afflicted person or the chicken died.

The 1590s were years of privation, riots and rebellions. In the summers of 1592 and 1595 apprentices, servants and 'masterless men', impoverished youths mostly, caused serious disturbances in London, and hunger sparked off food riots throughout the south of England in 1595 and in Kent in 1596. Average agricultural prices were higher in real terms than at any time before 1615 and real wages were lower than at any point between 1260 and 1950. Malnutrition was widespread and possibly as much as two-fifths of the population fell below the subsistence level, putting a colossal demand on the providers of poor relief.

John Guy painted a sorry picture of turn of the century England: 'Although Elizabethan government worked well until 1595, thereafter the strains of war, taxation, and economic distress proved corrosive.'[103]

Population

The population of England had begun to recover from the ravages of the Black Death by the middle of the fifteenth century. When Henry VII secured the throne the population numbered just over two million; when Elizabeth died in 1603 it was approaching four million. Since there was no mass immigration from abroad in the period this must be accounted for by either greater fertility or less mortality, or a combination of both. Population growth does not necessarily imply improved health - evidence for increased fertility in the period has at least as much to do with earlier marriages as it does with improved diets of women of child-bearing age. Although there were no epidemics on the scale of the Black Death in the period, the bubonic plague and other diseases struck frequently and arbitrarily. Their effects were exacerbated by the inadequate living conditions and poor nutrition of the masses in both town and country.

---

[103] John Guy, *Tudor England* (1988).

Life expectancy for the second half of the sixteenth century fluctuated between around thirty-five and forty, peaking at just below forty-eight years in 1581. It varied considerably from place to place and was significantly lower for the urban population. Towns in the southeast, including London, Norwich, Ipswich and Colchester, were densely populated and dirty, the filth in the streets encouraging rat infestation and outbreaks of bubonic plague. Other prevalent diseases included smallpox, typhus and the English sweat, a new killer arriving in the country in the same year as Henry VII's accession. Urban mortality was compensated for by a steady migration of people from demographically more stable rural areas (where 90 per cent of the population lived) in which the number of baptisms continued, overall, to outstrip the number of burials.

By the mid-sixteenth century the population was growing rapidly, about 1 per cent per annum. The Black Death, arriving in England in 1348, reduced its population from between 5 and 6 million to about 3 million. Subsequent plagues and a reduced fertility continued the downward trend and by the mid-fifteenth century the population had fallen to around 1.5 million. By the 1520s however recovery was well under way and the population is estimated at 2.3 million. For reasons still not fully understood by historians the rate of recovery greatly increased in the 1540s. Such factors as disease and poor harvests undermined potential growth in the half-century before. The same factors are thought to help explain the slowing down of growth after 1550: nevertheless, in the reign of Elizabeth the population rose by around 25 per cent.

Annual population estimates in millions:

1526 2.3	**1571** 3.3
1541 2.8	**1576** 3.4
1546 2.9	**1581** 3.6
1551 3.0	**1586** 3.8
1556 3.2	**1591** 3.9
1561 3.0	**1596** 4.0
1566 3.1	**1601** 4.1

(Source: E. A. Wrigley and R. S. Schofield, *The Population History of*

England 1541-1871, 1981)

Work

Many people, whether they lived in town or country, had a 'dual economy' in which their main occupation was supplemented by one or more other kinds of work. The lowliest kind of work, 'honest' labour that saved people from begging, included that of gathering fuel from the common land for the poor man's more prosperous neighbours. The common land sustained growing numbers of those living on the poverty line. The increasing population forced young people to look beyond the villages of their birth for work as labourers elsewhere, migrating perhaps to new centres of rural industry and setting up home on common land. These communities eventually became known as 'squatters' villages' and can be identified today by their ironic names such as 'Ireland' and 'Scotland'.

During the period more and more people became reliant on the wages they received for their unskilled labour. Day labourers, so-called because they were employed by the day, were highly vulnerable to fluctuations in their local economy and to seasonal requirements. When farmwork was plentiful, such as at harvest-time, the whole family might find employment; when it was scarce the labourer might turn his hand to work in a local rural industry such as brewing or cloth work. More secure were those engaged on a yearly basis at the annual hiring fairs. Increasing numbers entered some form of domestic service and all were likely to receive a measure of support by way of food, shelter and even clothing, in addition to, or in place of, money wages. Such non-monetary factors often determined the 'standard of living' of a 'waged' labourer and hence generalisations of experience are of very limited value.

The Statute of Artificers of 1563 sought to regulate wages and to oblige the unemployed to become engaged as waged labourers - young men to do farmwork, unattached young women to go into domestic service. In places where the act was enforced (it often was not) young people might find themselves restricted in their pursuit of more lucrative work or frustrated in an ambition to become apprenticed to a skilled craftsman.

All work was influenced by natural rhythms: the seasons, day and night, climate. The Statute of Artificers, personal choice and religious observances, also played a part in determining the extent of an individual's work. Among other clauses the Statute of Artificers limited the working day to twelve hours in the summer and the hours of daylight in the winter, it stated that all servants should be hired for a full year or more and that apprenticeships should be of seven years duration. This was in line with common practice in many areas and was intended in part to reduce beggary and vagabondage. Such 'idleness' however was rarely a matter of choice and certainly represented no 'life of leisure'; no amount of law-making of this kind could guarantee full and productive employment, plus a decent wage, for all.

The traditional peasant farmer was not subject to the demands of an employer although he did have certain feudal obligations to fulfil. Except for those days when he was required by feudal law to do work on his lord's land he was pretty much free to choose when to start and finish his routine daily tasks. He was forced into 'idleness' for a considerable number of days out of respect for the religious calendar, Saints' Days and the Sabbath. The fifteenth century peasant enjoyed a good many more holidays (holy days) than many modern factory workers. The 'proletarianisation' of the workforce, bringing with it more 'disciplined' modes of modern employment, has been identified by socialist historians as formative in the making of the 'wageslaves' of modern capitalist societies.

Although life for most was precarious and extremely 'tough', some of the horrors that would confront the labouring population as Britain became industrialised in the late eighteenth and early nineteenth centuries were unknown to their Tudor ancestors. Work was largely unmechanised and the industrial accidents of the 'Industrial Revolution' involving unfenced machinery were very rare, although work in flour and fulling mills entailed a certain degree of risk. Most mining was either open cast or in shallow pits; death by asphyxiation or drowning was unlikely. Very young children were employed but usually in light agricultural work such as bird-scaring, stone clearing and minding sheep; unlike those employed in the itinerant agricultural 'gangs' of the nineteenth century, they would return home each evening. For older children 'home' might not be the parental home but the accommodation provided for them having commenced a life of domestic or husbandary service. The cottages and hovels they lived in lacked creature comforts but even those living in the stinking towns probably were better off than the tenement and cellar dwellers of industrial towns in the first half of the nineteenth century, While the finer distinctions between male and female 'spheres', so clearly delineated in Victorian Britain, were yet to be clarified, many activities and occupations were gender orientated. In the woollen cloth trade for example spinning was the domain of unmarried women ('spinsters') while men were employed as weavers ('websters'). Heavy farmwork such as ploughing, carting and hedging was done by men and boys, and highly skilled craftsmen made wheels, barrels and shoes, and thatched roofs. Dairying, baking, brewing, looking after cattle and taking fruit to the market were principally female occupations. Bereavement might cause women to become active in traditionally male spheres - women for example might be found running iron mongering businesses or apprenticing young cloth or leather workers. When it came to the months of the summer harvest all distinctions, 'class' as well as gender, were eroded as everyone rolled up his or her sleeves to bring the harvest home.

Enclosures

The sixteenth century was an age of inflation with prices rising most dramatically in the middle years of the century and in the last decade. Population growth and inflation caused the land to be farmed more intensively and more efficiently. Economic historians have suggested the seeds of the eighteenth century 'revolution' in agriculture were sown in the sixteenth and seventeenth centuries. One, Eric Kerridge (*The Agricultural Revolution*, 1967), considered developments in sixteenth century agriculture amounted to a revolution in their own right. Agricultural revolution can be defined as a relatively short period of time in which monumental changes occur in agrarian affairs. If we are to consider the Tudor age an age of agricultural revolution we can expect to find evidence of new technology in farming methods, new ways of managing the land, new crops, increased output, specialisation and bigger farms.

Most people living in England in Tudor times made a living through farming. As the sixteenth century progressed subsistence farming increasingly gave way to commercial farming in which peasant smallholdings were absorbed into larger concerns and the peasants themselves became waged farm labourers. This was particularly evident in the more populous south-eastern counties.

Traditional farming methods in some predominantly arable areas, as exemplified by the 'fielden' villages of the south-east, divided the land into, typically, three open fields. These were farmed in 'strips', each proprietor probably holding a number of strips in each of the fields. Alternating between 'spring corn' (oats or barley) and 'winter corn' (wheat, rye or mixed grain), one field each year would be left unsown ('fallow'). This was rarely long enough to renew the vitality of the land, not least because of inadequate supplies of manure, and fields became progressively less productive. The growing demand for a diminishing supply was met, principally, by a more efficient use of existing farmland and the exploitation of land previously uncultivated.

In the fourteenth century roughly half the population of rural England was bound in servitude to a lord. These serfs or 'villeins' held small-holdings in return for rent and agreed amounts of work for the lord. Although serfdom continued into the Tudor period (and has never been formally abolished) it had begun to decline since the fourteenth century when the decline in population gave labourers more bargaining power and created opportunities for those wanting to flee from their feudal lords and start a new and free life elsewhere. This increased social mobility, with serfs claiming or buying their freedom, produced a social environment conducive to the establishment of a modern market economy.

Prosperous yeomen began to forge larger farms by purchasing or renting available land, encroaching upon marginal common land and enclosing areas hitherto unfarmed. Enclosure, as with other developments such as the increased incidence of waged labour, was not a new phenomenon. However extensive new enclosures were created from the late fifteenth century providing pasture for the sheep on whose backs vast profits in the wool trade were made. Enclosure also represented the opportunity for more profitable arable farming by freeing landholders from the tyranny of the open field system which dictated to them how their land should be used, and wasted land with the furrows that separated one strip from another. Enclosure, 'engrossing' (the buying out of one farmer by another), and 'assarting' (the clearance and cultivation of common woodland), however were condemned by many for allegedly depopulating villages and forcing peasants into lives of vagrancy and beggary. M. W. Beresford in a pioneering study, *The Lost Villages of England* (1954) identified 359 villages deserted in the Tudor age, mostly small and less able to withstand the pressure of enclosing landlords and the bigger engrossing farmers. Of particular offence was the privatising of the land held in common and with it the ancient rights to forage for fuel, berries and other wild foods, and graze livestock.

A general disapproval of enclosure was shared by successive governments. Two acts in 1489 ordered the maintaining of present housing in the face of 'pulling-down and wilful waste' and a royal commission set up in 1517 by Cardinal Wolsey investigated the impact of subsequent enclosures. In 1526, 1528 and 1529 he ordered the opening of past enclosures but, as the need to proclaim his will in this matter three times in as many years indicates, his instructions were largely ignored. Further commissions followed in 1545 and 1566. These commissions were a direct response to complaints, particularly from the Midlands, and enclosure was a common grievance of many who rioted or rebelled in the period. Some governments, for example the Duke of Somerset's in the reign of Edward VI, shared the common inclination to scapegoat enclosure for all economic and social problems. Laws introduced to restrict further enclosure were rarely enforced - they simply provided further cause for complaint when they were seen to be abused.

Agriculture and rural society were certainly changing in England under the Tudors; the decline of the open field system (although this was neither as typical nor as universal as once supposed), and the 'commercialisation' of farming encouraged efficiency and specialisation. Enclosures provided greater opportunities for selective breeding and helped reduce the spread of disease among animals. More land was devoted to the production of fodder crops such as clover and 'industrial' crops such as hops for brewing and flax for linen. Wetlands in some places were drained and water-meadows were used to irrigate dry fields. 'Ley farming' became more common - the custom of using land for arable purposes for several years and then for pastoral for some years afterwards before reverting to arable. This crop rotation was more likely to enable soil to recover than was possible with reliance on a fallow year.

Few historians would share Kerridge's view that this all amounted to a revolution in farming; although there was some progress, such developments are best described by the word 'evolution'. Studies into developments in farming in the early modern period have been most significant not for providing new dates for England's 'agricultural revolution' but in causing historians to doubt whether there ever was a revolution in farming.

The woollen cloth trade

During the fourteenth century woven cloth took over from raw wool as the country's main export. The population growth of the sixteenth century greatly increased demand and the industry expanded. By the 1520s over 40 per cent of all urban workers worked in the cloth trade although it was by no means exclusively an urban industry. Production in some areas was based on a 'putting-out' approach whereby consignments of raw wool or unfinished cloth were delivered to the workers at their own homes or small workshops in which were set up spinning wheels, looms and dye vats. This system represented a major advance on traditional forms of production. Before the fourteenth century the woollen cloth industry had been a 'domestic industry' in which workers purchased their own materials and sold their own products. The putting-out system relied on entrepreneurs, clothiers who coordinated all stages of production, including the provision of equipment as well as materials. and sold the finished cloth. Some historians refer to this development as 'proto-industrialisation' - the phase in which a traditional 'cottage industry' adopts capitalist modes of production and the work of individuals is absorbed into a comparatively large-scale business.

Just as modern historians have challenged the notion of a spectacular agricultural revolution in the second half of the eighteenth century by highlighting the more gradual evolution of approaches to farming, many of which can be traced to the Tudor age, so too has the late eighteenth / early nineteenth century 'industrial revolution' come to be seen as less of a watershed period in Britain's history. Some apologists have toned the claim down by focusing on the novelty of factory production at that time, but even the 'dark satanic mills' of the eighteenth century had a much earlier, medieval precedent in the shape of the water-powered fulling mills where the cloth was cleaned and thickened.

Work associated with woollen cloth provided a useful supplementary income to families mainly employed in agriculture. All could contribute - children prepared the woollen fibres, carding them for spinning which was mostly done by older females while weaving on a hired loom was commonly the preserve of men. The 'spinsters' working on the old medieval distaffs or newer spinning wheels greatly outnumbered the weavers; typically a small village would have a single 'webster' to several spinsters. After being soaked, pounded by hammers, scoured with fuller's earth, stretched on tenter-hooks and dried in the fulling mill, the nap of the cloth was then raised ('teased') by teasle combs and cropped by shearmen to leave a smooth surface. The main areas for such work were East Anglia, the West Country and the West Riding. Although some towns such as Lavenham in Suffolk were great centres of the cloth industry, increasingly the work was done in the countryside. Ironically, while the towns mostly continued to house small-scale craft industries and markets, rural communities provided the context in which 'modern' modes of industrial production could flourish. Clothiers setting up in the countryside had the advantages of cheap labour and lower living costs. In addition they operated free of the traditional restrictions imposed by urban guilds which stifled growth and kept up standards (and prices and wages) by insisting on long apprenticeships.

The cloth produced by the less skilled rural workforce was of poorer quality than that associated with urban guild manufacture. It was sold at Antwerp as 'unfinished' cloth. The complaints of the guilds at a time of decline in sales of English cloth abroad because of continental preference for the lighter 'new draperies' to the heavy 'old draperies' still dominating English production, contributed to legislation designed, in part, to raise standards. The Statute of Artificers of 1563 insisted on the apprenticeship principle stating in Clause 24 that:

> 'it shall not be lawful [...] to set up, occupy, use or exercise any craft [...] except that he shall have been brought up therein seven years at the least as apprentice [...]'

During Elizabeth's reign English clothiers began to produce the 'new draperies' learning how to make a lighter weave by combining wool with lighter textiles such as cotton and silk from foreign weavers settled in England, many of whom arrived as Flemish and French Protestant refugees. Much of the woollen cloth exported remained inferior however and England's turbulent relationship with the continental powers continued to disrupt trade and necessitate the finding of new markets. Despite this, the woolllen industry continued to thrive, some clothiers became fabulously wealthy and woollen cloth retained its place as England's primary export. When clothier Peter Blundell of Devon died in 1601 he left £40,000 to charity. Thomas Spring, a clothier from Lavenham, in 1522 was the third richest man in the kingdom, outside London.

Other industries

Timber and coal were important elements in the production of iron goods. Timber provided the charcoal that was used in the smelting process and coal fuelled the blacksmiths' forges. Water-power was harnassed from the fourteenth century onwards at 'bloomeries' to power tilt-hammers and bellows in the vital process of removing slag from the melted ore. The great 'hammer ponds' of the Sussex Weald are relics of a once flourishing iron industry. The other centre of production was the Forest of Dean and these two were joined by South Wales in the second half of the sixteenth century. Foundries were sited where timber supplies were still abundant; coal was carried by sea from shallow coastal pits, located in the north-east, for example at Glamorgan and Tyneside, to London and markets abroad.

By the mid-sixteenth century blast furnaces located in the Weald were taking the place of the less productive bloomeries, and casting the cannon that fortified Henry VIII's coastal forts and strengthened his navy. The blast furnace was introduced into England in 1496 and was widespread throughout the country by the end of Elizabeth's reign. As with the 'new draperies' in the English textile industry, in Elizabeth's reign blast furnace technology was learned from continental ironworkers living in England. Industrial villages emerged specialising in lesser and domestic items such as chains, nails, locks and knives. The industry accounted for a good deal of internal migration during the period as displaced peasants sought waged work. Many however in this and other industries, including coal, continued to rely on a dual economy of industrial work combined with farm labouring or the maintaining of their own allotments.

Just as claims have been made for a Tudor revolution in agriculture so too has a revolution in industry been suggested. J. U. Nef noted in the 1930s a major expansion of the north-eastern coal industry in the second half of the sixteenth century associated with a perceived timber crisis and the exploitation of hitherto untapped coal reserves following the dissolution of the monasteries. This coal was used increasingly in a number of industrial capacities such as salt extraction and brick making. Animal powered machines for pumping water out of mines, combined with improvements in transport organisation promoted coal as an affordable and available domestic fuel. Between 1560 and 1690 national output may have increased fourfold. In turn this expansion of the coal industry stimulated ship-building and coastal trade. As such it could possibly be considered the 'leading sector' in this supposed revolution.

Subsequent historians have rejected this thesis finding insufficient evidence to prove particularly significant growth in the coal industry before the seventeenth century. Most mining was still open cast and what was recovered was largely used locally. Both the coal and the iron industries were hampered by poor roads and un-navigable rivers - pack animals and sledges in many areas were the principal means of carrying industrial and agricultural produce until well into the eighteenth century.

Other industries expanded in the period including leather working and building. W. G. Hoskins, a great pioneer in the field of local history, in an influential article, 'The Rebuilding of Rural England, 1570-1640' (1953), identified a 'great rebuilding' of English vernacular houses beginning in Elizabeth's reign and continuing until the Civil War. This involved new building and improvements of existing buildings by, for example, introducing chimneys and ceilings, and replacing wattle and daub walls with bricks. The houses belonged to the yeomen and merchants benefiting from the profits of their enterprises. Subsequent studies have toned down Hoskins' claims, particularly for Scotland, Ireland, Wales and the northern counties of England which had their 'great rebuilding' somewhat later, but certainly major developments took place in housing in the southern counties at this time.

The leather trades had always had an important place in the economy of the Middle Ages. By Tudor times much of the work was concentrated in towns such as Northampton. Production was on a small scale and craftsmen working in leather, particularly in rural locations, were mostly independent artisan specialists, such as shoemakers, or less skilled workers complementing their agricultural work with simpler kinds of leather work. Some worked in well-established family concerns such as tanning businesses. Like those involved in the building trade they produced for a local market. Like urban cloth workers they protected their interests by organising themselves into guilds.

Many other forms of light industry flourished in the later fifteenth and sixteenth centuries as a result of population growth and increasing consumerism. Brewing, haberdashery, the manufacture of dyes were among the many concerns offering at least partial employment for thousands of men and women.

Families, Sex and Marriage

> 'As widely held as the assumption about child marriage [...] is the supposition that our ancestors lived in large familial groups.'

(Peter Laslett, *The World We Have Lost - further explored*, 1983)

It was once assumed by many historians that the English peasantry most commonly lived in extended family units, that is, families comprising three or more generations, with brothers and sisters often living in the same house well into adulthood. This notion has been successfully challenged and it is now generally agreed that in fact households, typically, were of a nuclear character - parents and their children living apart from other family members.

Despite Sir Francis Bacon's warning that marriage and children represented 'impediments to great enterprises', marriage was the norm and intended to be a permanent arrangement; divorces were almost impossible to secure although separations in cases of adultery were tolerated. A major factor determining the age at which a couple married is likely to have been the availability of a home into which they might move. Peter Laslett identifies for early modern society an unwritten 'rule' that two married couples did not exist together in one family. Since property is not infinite this meant that couples wishing to be married had to wait until a niche, probably through deaths in their parents' generation, presented them with the opportunity for establishing their own household.

Surprisingly few married partners originated from the same village. The size of the village, typically of around 200, restricted the chance of finding a suitable partner in the immediate neighbourhood, and strict incest rules regarding the marrying of blood relatives, particularly after Henry VIII's divorce from Catherine of Aragon, further narrowed the field. Courtship frequently began at the local fair or in service, servants meeting in their employer's house. Gifts were central in any courtship, coins, rings and gloves being the most likely tokens of affection. Once both partners consented to marriage this promise, ritualised by the 'handfast' (a declaration of intent while holding hands, usually in the presence of witnesses) was considered, according to canon law to be absolutely binding. Sometimes the permission to marry was requested of and given by the young person's employer rather than a parent. This was particularly the case among domestic servants and reinforces the notion that the household in which the young employee worked became his/her surrogate family. An engagement could last a long time: every sensible couple would resist engaging in sexual intercourse until they had a sufficiently secure financial base upon which to start a family. For example in the 1577 Jane Blitte and William Emberton of Cambridgeshire had been betrothed for six years without marrying due to 'the want and lack of things necessary'.

The most reckless behaviour for a young woman was forming a sexual relationship before securing an engagement. In so doing she not only ran the risk of becoming a single parent but also of jeopardising her good name, possibly the most important attribute she had in arranging for herself a prosperous future. In this account from York in 1381, a somewhat irresponsible young woman is defended by the witness to her impropriety:

> 'On Monday night before the feast of the Ascension last she came to a certain high room located inside the dwelling-house of the said witness where she found, as she says, Robert and Agnes lying alone together in one bed. The witness asked Robert, "What are you doing here, Robert? To this Robert replied, "I'm already here". The witness said to him, "Take Agnes by the hand in order to betroth her". Robert said to the witness, "I beg you wait until the morning". The witness said to him in reply, "By God, no. You'll do it now". Then Robert took Agnes by the hand and said, "I will take you as my wife". The witness said to him, "You will speak in this manner: I take you Agnes to my wife and to this I plight you my troth", and Robert, thus instructed by the

witness, took Agnes by the right hand and contracted with her using the words just recited [...] Asked how Agnes replied to Robert, she said that Agnes replied to him that she considered herself satisfied. She did not depose further save that she went away and left them alone.'

Unfortunately for Agnes this declaration might not have secured a marriage with Robert since, according to church law, two witnesses were needed to prove the betrothal. After betrothal couples would be likely to live as man and wife, the actual marriage being deferred in many cases until pregnancy.

Prostitution was rife throughout the Tudor period. Until 1546 it was a perfectly legitimate business, brothels were licensed (there were twelve in London) and their activities regulated by the Crown. The women in the brothels took their rooms at the official rent of 14d. a week or less and they were allowed to come and go as they chose. They were expected to be unmarried and clear of venereal disease, they were not meant to solicit as such but to serve those men that came to them on their own volition.

This perhaps seems surprising considering the religiosity of the age and the fact that all non-marital sexual relations were regarded as a mortal sin. It appears that prostitution was frowned upon but tolerated in the belief that it could never be entirely suppressed and that it reduced the incidence of other immoral behaviour including seduction, rape, and sodomy. Contemporary arguments for permissiveness in this matter are almost as ancient as the profession itself. The inherent contradiction in all of this is reflected in the fact that on Holy Days these licensed courtesans were obliged to leave the areas in which they worked (invariably the less respectable parts of town) and the brothels in which they worked were compelled to shut. While tolerated in the secular world they were banished from the ecclesiastical, as indicated by the Elizabethan antiquary, John Stow:

> 'I have heard ancient men of good credit report that these single women were forbidden the rites of the Church, so long as they continued that sinful life, and were excluded from Christian burial if they were not reconciled before their death. And therefore there was a plot of ground, called the single women's churchyard, appointed for them, far from the parish church.'

A dramatic shift in attitude came in the middle years of the sixteenth century. The combination of Reformation and Counter-Reformation religious enthusiasm and the emergence in Western Europe of the potentially fatal venereal disease, syphilis, caused continental and English authorities to crack down on prostitution. Brothels in London were closed by royal proclamation in 1546:

> '[...] toleration of such dissolute and miserable persons as, putting away the fear of Almighty God and the shame of the world, have been suffered to dwell beside London and elsewhere, in common open places called the stews, and there without punishment or correction to exercise their abominable and detestable sin.'

From this point on prostitution was punishable by imprisonment and whipping.

Most cases of sexual misconduct were brought before the archdeacon's court, the lowest of the spiritual courts, and here fines and public penances would be the penalty for the misdemeanour. The court was popularly known as the 'Bawdy Court' because of its pre-occupation with relatively minor sexual offences. Really serious deviations, 'things fearful to name', were the business of the high courts. Acts of homosexuality or bestiality were capital offences. Sexual intercourse with animals was particularly abhorred, not least because it was commonly assumed that animals and humans were capable of cross-breeding; consequently, following a conviction, the participating cow or sheep would also be put to death.

A 'want of affection'? Children's lives in Tudor times

The experience of children living in Britain during the fifteenth and sixteenth centuries is difficult to define. Obviously gender, class and regional differences make it almost impossible to draw any general conclusions. The evidence for examining children's lives is scanty and very few children left their own documentary record. Inevitably the history of childhood is riddled with myth and generalisation.

Lawrence Stone in *The Family, Sex and Marriage in England*

1500- 1800, painted a picture of family life in the Tudor period that tended to lack affection between its members and included comparatively weak emotional bonds between parents and children. This claim has been challenged by many historians since Stone's book was published in 1977 and it is commonly accepted now that Tudor emotional life was rather more healthy and relations were rather more 'modern' than Stone suggested.

Jeremy Goldberg outlined some of the traditional assumptions regarding this issue:

> 'We are told that children were born into a hostile or at least uncaring world. Numbers of girl babies were disposed of at birth as a burden to their parents. There was little bond between mother and child as many children passed their infancy suckled by a wet-nurse. As an infant the child was constrained in swaddling bands and left unattended and unchanged for many hours on end. Until the child reached her fifth birthday, she was treated with indifference because high rates of infant and child mortality warned parents against investing emotionally in such fragile lives. Parents regularly brutalised their children by beating them.
>
> From the age of about seven to nine a girl might be sent into hard service. There she might be ill-treated or sexually abused by masters or other males within the household. By the time she reached her twelfth birthday a girl was of age to be married. This would be a business transaction in which the girl was merely a chattel transferred from the patriarchal authority of her father to that of a husband and father-in-law. She would pass from a childhood largely devoid of nurturing, of play, or of what we would recognise as education, to the role of wife and mother whilst still a teenager.'[104]

Most cases of infanticide have been left out of the historical record. Without doubt many, probably the majority, 'got away with it' and, for obvious reasons, took great care to keep the secret to themselves. Some though were discovered such as this young mother from the early

---

[104] Jeremy Goldberg, 'Girls Growing Up in Later Medieval England' in *History Today*, June 1995.

sixteenth century:

> 'Alice Ridyng, unmarried, the daughter of Eton in the diocese of Lincoln appeared in person and confessed that she conceived a boy child by one Thomas Denys, then chaplain to Master Geoffrey Wren, and gave birth to him at her father's home at Eton one Sunday last month and immediately after giving birth, that is within four hours of the birth, killed the child by putting her hand in the baby's mouth and suffocating him. After she had killed the child she buried it in a dung heap in her father's orchard. At the time of the delivery she had no midwife and nobody was ever told as such that she was pregnant, but some women of Windsor and Eton had suspected and said she was pregnant, but Alice always denied this saying that something was wrong with her belly. On the Tuesday after the delivery of the child, however, the women and honest wives of Windsor and Eton took her and inspected her belly and her breasts by which they knew for certain that she had given birth.'

The stigma attached to, and punishment associated with, the birth of an illegitimate child probably inspired most cases of infanticide and not some cold-blooded decision to be rid of the child (particularly the female child) for purely economic reasons.

That the bearing of an illegitimate child was considered a most serious offence is clearly revealed in this JP's record from 1583:

> 'William Lewyn and I took order that Margaret Dutton should be first whipped at Gravesend and then sent to the house of correction for a bastard woman child there born and begotten on her by Robert Cole, as it is thought, whom also we committed till he give sureties to appear at the Easter sessions [...] The same day he and I also took like order for the whipping of Abigail Sherwood for a bastard man child born by her at Chatham and for her like sending to the house of correction.'

According to some historians parents during the period were emotionally indifferent to their babies, not forming particularly close bonds because of the high incidence of infant mortality (probably around 50 per cent by the late sixteenth century). Edward Shorter in *The Making of the Modern*

Family claimed that mothers simply 'did not care'. Supporters of the counter-argument have used the findings of anthropologists to prove that poverty, deprivation and ignorance do not necessarily lead to bad parenting. After all the human baby is an utterly dependent creature and without a considerable amount of care and attention, perhaps even love, it will not survive - those who grew to adulthood are testimony to a measure of parental kindness at least.

Although some infants were raised by wet-nurses the practice received much contemporary criticism and was not employed by the great majority of mothers. It was not exclusive however to the upper classes; for some it was a necessity due to the mother's inability to breastfeed or her death in childbirth. Some city dwellers engaged wet-nurses living in healthier rural districts and sometimes they nourished the weak and elderly as well as the juvenile.

Babies were dressed in tight swaddling bands. The half-comatose state this could induce doubtless diminished the demands an infant might make on a working mother but the custom had more to do with the assumption that such restrictive binding was necessary for the development of straight limbs than with parental neglect.

Peasant sons and daughters were expected to work from around the age of six. Their work would involve assistance in cultivating the family smallholding and/or tasks linked to spinning and other domestic handicrafts. Older children were likely to find work in industry or husbandry, girls typically becoming dairymaids. Many older teenage girls going into some form of service or working on a farm would leave home and begin their own largely independent lives, trained, clothed, fed, boarded and paid by their employers.

According to this late sixteenth century Venetian visitor to London, children were obliged to work very hard indeed:

> 'The want of affection in the English, is strongly manifested towards their children, for after having kept them at home until they arrive at the age of seven or nine years at the utmost, they put them out, both males and females, to hard service in the houses of other people, binding them generally for seven or nine years. And these are called apprentices, and during that time they perform all the most menial offices, and few are born who are exempted from this fate, for everyone, however rich he may be, sends away his children into the houses of others, whilst he, in

return, receives those of strangers into his own. And on inquiring their reason for this severity, they answered that they did it in order that their children might better learn manners. But I, for my part, believe that they do it because they like to enjoy all their comforts themselves, and that they are better served by strangers than they would be by their own children [...]'

Without doubt some girls and young women had bad experiences in service but for many it represented security and a widening of horizons including the making of new friends and possibly the meeting of a future husband. Legally girls could marry very much earlier than they are permitted to today. That they did so in large numbers is open to question.

The sixteenth century price rise

The most striking economic development of the Tudor age is the so-called price 'revolution', the inflation of the sixteenth century. Across the century, prices of essential consumables rose by around 400 per cent. After more than a hundred years of stability in prices the opening years of the sixteenth century was a period of moderate inflation becoming rapid after about 1510. By the 1550s grain and meat prices had risen by 250 per cent. For most of the second half of the century the inflation slowed before a return to hyper-inflation in the closing decade.

Historians have long debated the causes of this revolution in prices and the solution would seem to lie in a combination of a greater supply of gold and silver throughout western Europe brought from the Americas in Spanish galleons to Andalusia (the main 'traditional' explanation), the melting down of Church plate following the Dissolution (the major cause of the hyper-inflation of the 1540s), debasements of the real value of coins by reductions in their gold and silver content and, perhaps most significant, the simultaneous growth in population. A larger population represented a greater demand which, so long as there was not a corresponding increase in supply, would have the effect of pushing up the prices of food and other basic necessities. Although it has been suggested that the triumphs of the agricultural 'revolution' of the eighteenth century can be traced back to an earlier Tudor 'revolution' the increased productivity of English farming did not keep up with increased demand for its products nor was there any 'revolution' in industry. Just as the growing number of mouths to feed forced food prices up, so did the increased supply of labour depress manufacturers' wages in the later sixteenth century. As the prices of grain and meat rose, doubling in some urban markets between 1510 and 1530, so too did land rents.

Sixteenth century inflation was subject to considerable regional variation. The highest food prices were likely to be in towns in the South East and land commanded the highest rents around London. A host of historical events, in addition to the underlying causes outlined above, affected, at least in the short term, the scale of the inflation. Epidemics such as the English sweat slowed population growth, wars interrupted trade and provoked debasements, the falling demand for English wool in foreign markets in the 1550s caused unemployment and reduced wages while a simultaneous run of bad harvests pushed up grain prices. In 1552 inflation was slowed after the hyper-inflation of the 1540s by a combination of a reduced population because of disease and the reminting of the debased coinage, restoring its former silver content.

The people most vulnerable to market forces were those who paid rents and received wages. The growing numbers of vagrants, most of whom were young men and women, is evidence that the able-bodied of the lower orders, reliant on selling their labour, were hard hit and no longer enjoyed the opportunities of previous generations in the fifteenth century. Many migrated to the towns. This was a period of rapid urbanisation and by the end of Elizabeth's reign about 25 per cent of the population was living in towns. Although far less than half the population was entirely dependent on a wage, the majority experience was that of a decline in living standards, in financial terms at least, with over half the population by the end of the Tudor period living on or below the poverty line. Landowners and the urban elite on the other hand tended to get richer and a polarisation of English society into two 'nations', the rich and the poor, has been identified for the sixteenth century.

Mortality and economic stress

Research has forged direct links between increased mortality and periods of economic stress. For example in the late 1550s a devastating influenza epidemic coincided with bad harvests. This was the greatest mortality crisis of the age and the population dropped by 6 per cent; it also coincided with some of the most troubled years of the century in political terms - the reign of Mary I. On the other hand outbreaks of plague are also recorded during periods of low bread prices. The disastrous harvests of 1596 and 1597 provoked the severest famine in Tudor history. Ironically periods of high mortality could stimulate subsequent fertility: deaths provided economic opportunities for the survivors who might as a consequence be induced to marry earlier; infant deaths terminated lactation which might in turn hasten the next pregnancy.

Starvation and epidemic disease then were the great killers of the sixteenth century. It is often difficult to attribute death to any specific cause since surviving records are imprecise and the words 'plague' and 'pestilence' were used indiscriminately by contemporary physicians. Climate was the crucial factor in both instances: a wet late summer and autumn could ruin the harvest while a mild winter would fail to eliminate plague-bearing fleas.

Different parts of the community were more susceptible to different ailments. Bouts of famine hit hardest the very young and the economically vulnerable, beggars and widows for example. The plague primarily struck the towns. Although the impact of epidemic disease did not equal that of 1348 in some towns it was just as disastrous; Stratford-on-Avon for example lost nearly one third of its population in 1564, the year its most famous son, William Shakespeare, was born. In 1592-3 bubonic plague, particularly virulent in the dockland slums, carried off 18,000 Londoners. Poverty reduced life expectancy just as riches improved fertility; a healthy, well-fed woman, able to afford a wet-nurse and so restore her fertility soon after childbirth, might well achieve twenty pregnancies! The wealthy were not in danger of starvation but none was immune from disease. Elizabeth I was almost killed by smallpox and she lived in constant fear of bubonic plague; when it returned in 1563, the worst outbreak since the Black Death, the Queen fled from London to Windsor and ordered a gallows to be erected from which she could hang anyone who dared follow her from the infected capital!

Poverty and the Elizabethan Poor Law

As the sixteenth century progressed more and more people faced the appalling prospect of homelessness and hunger as employment opportunities contracted and prices rose. The extent of poverty in Tudor England was unprecedented. By the end of Elizabeth's reign the old reliance on independent charity and self-help was superseded by a growing acceptance of the need for extensive state intervention.

From this time until comparatively recently investigations into contemporary poverty identified two types of pauper: the 'able-bodied' and 'impotent' *deserving* poor, and the *undeserving* poor. Unemployment, under-employment, age and ill-health were factors that pauperised the deserving poor. Indolence and an inclination to crime were considered characteristics of undeserving vagabonds and beggars.

During the fourteenth and fifteenth centuries the itinerant homeless poor were routinely punished because of their condition. Until 1495 this might well have been imprisonment but increasingly after the legislation of 1495 this was transmuted to the less expensive punishment in stocks in which a vagrant could expect to languish for three days and nights with a diet of bread and water. Only the disabled were permitted to beg, and only if they were beggars in their own parishes. The 1531 Act concerning Punishment of Beggars and Vagabonds provided for the whipping of the able-bodied and the Act for Punishment of Sturdy Vagabonds and Beggars threatened offenders with hard labour. While the impotent poor continued to be treated with some leniency, licensed begging in their own parishes being permitted and the provision of alms permitted, the legislation regarding the able-bodied became ever more draconian. In 1547 'sturdy' vagrants, anyone unable to sustain him/herself after three days of unemployment, could be enslaved for two years and branded with a 'V' on the chest. The slave became the property of the informant and any attempt to run away was rewarded with enslavement for life and an 'S' branded on the face. A second attempt was punishable by hanging. Such terror tactics it soon became evident would not eliminate begging and vagrancy in an era of dearth exacerbated by successive bad harvests and the legislation was revoked in 1549. The simpler expedient of 'impressing' thousands of vagabonds and beggars into the army was employed in Mary and Elizabeth's reigns although this could only ever provide short-term relief with survivors returning to life on the streets once their services were no longer required. They returned too of course as trained fighters - not a comforting thought for governments fearful of popular disturbances, riots and rebellions.

Increasingly acts regarding the poor concentrated on wresting from the better-off poor relief contributions. The 1563 Act for the Relief of the Poor detailed substantial fines for parish officials such as churchwardens who failed in their duties to collect their dues. An act of 1572 invoked the spirit of the dread 1547 act by punishing vagabonds with whipping and mutilation: the burning of a hole through the right ear. Houses of Correction ('bridewells'), the original workhouses, effectively imprisoning the destitute and putting them to work, were to be established in every county according to the terms of an act of 1576. Many cities had already established bridewells, the first, London's, having been chartered in 1533. In 1598 a new post was created, that of the 'overseer'. Each parish was to nominate its overseers who accepted responsibility for administering relief and finding useful employment for the able- bodied poor. In the same year the Act for the Punishment of Rogues, Vagabonds and Sturdy Beggars replaced all existing legislation and reinforced the principles of Houses of Correction and punishment by whipping. In addition the concept of exile abroad for incorrigible beggars was introduced.

The sixteenth century witnessed the transition from the principle of purely voluntary relief to that of obligatory almsgiving starting with the introduction of compulsory poor rates in some cities, including London, Norwich and York, in the late 1540s and early 1550s. Fines for failing to attend Anglican church services were accumulated into funds for the poor following the Act of Uniformity of 1559. The poverty of the able-bodied unemployed began to be tolerated in the 1570s when certain categories, including demobilised soldiers, were allowed to receive licences to beg in their home parishes by the terms of the 1572 legislation. By the end of Elizabeth's reign the duty of parishes to provide for their poor with alms, occupations and Houses of Correction removed, in theory, any necessity for begging.

Changing attitudes regarding poverty in the sixteenth century are linked by historians to two key themes: the scale of the problem and the Protestant 'work ethic'. With half the population in a state of abject poverty and vast numbers of vagrants, mostly 'lusty' and 'sturdy' young men, roaming the countryside, forced to beg and thieve when no other means of sustaining themselves was available, the poor represented a serious threat to the stability of the realm. No wonder then that governments became increasingly anxious to contain their poor by whatever means. Their intolerance in the case of the 'idle' poor may have reflected the Puritan's conviction that, while 'good deeds' were no guarantee of salvation, 'idleness' was a sure sign of the damned.

It would be too generous to describe the spate of legislation clarified by the acts of 1598 and 1601 as marking the beginning the modern welfare state. This Elizabethan Poor Law however does represent a major break with earlier traditions since it combined two great new principles: statutory taxation and the secular administration of parish affairs.

Elementary Education

There were four main types of elementary schools in the early fifteenth century, endowed secular grammar schools, monastic schools, cathedral ('king's') schools, and the hundreds of small parish church 'petty' or 'alphabet' schools. These schools provided a rudimentary education for those that could afford the small fees or, in the case of 'free' schools, the charge for educational materials, candles and heating. At the heart of the curriculum lay the learning of Latin, usually achieved through the liberal use of corporal punishment.
The growth of education generally can be accounted for by a number of factors which include the spread of Renaissance values, the Protestant concern for Bible reading in the vernacular, developments in printing, and the requirements of an increasingly complex and competitive economy. The most striking evidence for interest in the promotion of schooling lies in the number of new grammar schools that were established during the sixteenth century, of which there were 124 by 1530. The endowments enabling the foundation of new schools more than compensated for the closure of a number of ecclesiastic schools following the dissolution of the monasteries. Schools within walking distance became available for most parents with the means and inclination to provide an elementary education for their children.

New schools founded by private endowment:

1520s	13	1560s	42
1530s	8	1570s	30
1540s	39	1580s	20
1550s	47	1590s	24

Universities and Inns of Court

'Be directed in your studies by some learned judicial man of the university, logic, and philosophy, methinks cosmography especially histories yield excellent matter of instruction and judgement.'

(Advice given by William Wentworth to his son in 1604)

Although many had humbler backgrounds, it is estimated that between one-third and two-fifths of students at the two universities of Oxford and Cambridge during Elizabeth's reign were sons of the nobility and gentry. Students in Scotland had a choice of four universities: St Andrews (founded 1410), Glasgow (1451), Aberdeen (1494), and Edinburgh (1582). Trinity College in Dublin was founded in 1591. Jesus College in Oxford, after its foundation in 1571, provided higher education for many Welsh students. Not all took a degree and many devised, in conjunction with their tutors, their own programmes of learning. Until the passing of the Elizabethan matriculation statutes it was possible to be a student without any formal registration and so it is difficult to estimate the extent to which the universities were expanding. By the 1590s an average of 721 'freshmen' were being admitted each year.

Higher education could be extended at the 'third university', the four Inns of Court that provided, in addition to the continued study of astronomy, history, theology, mathematics and suchlike, a grounding in the Law.

'[...] there is in these greater Inns, yea and in the lesser too,

> beside the study of the laws as it were in a university or school of all commendable qualities requisite for Noblemen. There they learn to sing themselves in all kinds of harmony and to exercise. There they also practise dancing and other Noblemen's pastimes as they do who are brought up in the king's house. On the working days most of them apply themselves to the study of Holy Scripture; and out of the time of Divine Service to the reading of Chronicles. For there indeed are virtues studied and vices exiled.'

(Sir John Fortescue, c.1468)

Principally the concern of the gentry, the Inns of Court expanded during the period as a further London education became more fashionable and the future owners of property required a greater understanding of ever more complicated legal processes. The number of legally educated MPs rose considerably during Elizabeth's reign, from 140 in 1563 to 253 in 1601. Increasingly government officials of all kinds were drawn from this secular 'third university' instead of the Church.

Many of the sons of the nobility circumvented the grammar schools, universities and Inns of Court entirely, receiving instead a traditional tuition at home. A knowledge of the Law was less essential to the larger landowners who were in a position to employ lawyers and other professionals to manage their affairs.

Yeomen and the better off husbandmen and craftsmen sent their sons to grammar schools, university, even Inns of Court. The expansion of government offices and the growth of the professions provided considerable career opportunities. As the second sons of the gentry established themselves in secular careers, ecclesiastical offices were filled by the offspring of yeomen.

Rosemary O'Day considered the question, 'Why did young men go to university?':

> 'It seems clear that most students who intended to enter the church had plebeian or, after 1600, clerical origins. At some colleges over 40 per cent of students were clerical recruits. The remaining plebeian students probably made their livelihoods as teachers or entered the ranks of attorneys, scriviners, estate agents and clerks for whom there was now increasing demand.

Few students of higher social rank entered the church - those that did tended to land plum positions which conferred considerable social status [...]

Future clergy and minor bureaucrats were certainly being educated alongside future Justices of the Peace, Members of Parliament, Earls and Ministers of the Crown. Does not this prove that the university experience was a socially unifying one? No.

The evidence against such an assumption is overwhelming [...] Undergraduates were ordered to mix with their own kind and to ostracise men of inferior rank.'[105]

The flowering of the arts

The Tudor monarchs themselves spearheaded the cultural revolution that some historians associate with their age. The young Henry VIII epitomised the Renaissance prince - the physical and intellectual all-rounder as accomplished in philosophy as he was in jousting. His daughter Elizabeth hunted, flirted and danced, spoke fluently a number of languages, and played the lute. In their reigns, particularly, high learning was a highly regarded quality among their courtiers. Meanwhile an increasingly well educated gentry and merchant class invested in the establishment of grammar schools, notably Thomas Sutton who purchased the London Charterhouse and founded its famous school.

Henry's Reformation combined with Caxton's printing press to break the clerical monopoly on such learning. Protestant propaganda and a Bible in the vernacular stimulated literacy and helped demolish some the mystique that once surrounded the written word. Henry VIII also provided a haven for the continental humanist Erasmus. Erasmus and his English followers, notably Thomas More and John Colet, advocated a classical education as the foundation for a religious life. Such Renaissance values emanating from Italy were further encouraged by the

---

[105] Rosemary O'Day, 'Room at the Top: Oxford and Cambridge in the Tudor and Stuart Age' in *History Today*, February 1984.

presence of Italians in the Tudor court, notably Polydore Vergil during the reign of Henry VIII. By the time Elizabeth became queen the full impact of the Italian Renaissance (c.1400-1600) was finally felt in England.

Elizabeth was provided with an education by humanists William Grindall and Roger Ascham. Her stepsister, Mary, received an equally rigorous education under the instruction of the Spanish humanist Juan Luis Vivés. Literature, notably Vergil's history, completed in 1512, celebrated the dynasty and created its myth as a golden age after a dark age of violence, immorality and ignorance. Writers too, from More and Sir Thomas Wyatt in Henry VIII's reign to Sir Walter Raleigh and Sir Philip Sidney in Elizabeth's, sometimes played a central role in affairs of state. Court painters, notably Hans Holbein in Henry VIII's reign and Nicholas Hilliard in Elizabeth's, were quite as important as the poets, playwrights and historians, in turning their sovereigns into public icons, revered in cheap copies hanging on the walls of hundreds of homes of their wealthier subjects. The relative cheapness of glass enabled the building of fabulous new mansions such as Hardwick Hall which soon gained a reputation for having more glass than wall.

Elizabeth was patron also to the mathematician-philosopher, occultist, antiquarian and geographer, John Dee. His activities early on earned him a reputation for sorcery and landed him in Star Chamber facing prosecution in 1553 during Mary I's reign. His supposed magic resulted in the destruction by a mob of much of his scientific equipment and many books at his house in Mortlake while he was abroad in 1583. Certainly his esoteric interests included alchemy, he was an astrologer as well as an astronomer, and he communicated with spirits and apparitions through his associate and medium, Edward Kelley, while resident in Prague. For Dee and his acolytes the 'mystic' and the 'scientific' were complementary pursuits. Despite their futile attempts at turning base metals into gold, alchemists invented many of the chemical processes in use today while working in a state of spiritual elevation achieved through prayer. Dee's astrology for example, by which he ascertained for Elizabeth the most appropriate day for her coronation, was rooted in strict 'scientific' principles and procedures.

Dee attracted the attention of the most influential men and women wherever he travelled. Back in England Philip Sidney and Edmund Spenser were his friends and students and Queen Elizabeth visited his fine library at Mortlake in 1575 and 1580. Frances A. Yates in

The Occult Philosophy in the Elizabethan Age (1979) dubbed him 'The Leader of the Elizabethan Renaissance'. Robert Dudley, later Earl of Leicester and favourite of the Queen, was his pupil as a child. His association with many great political figures of his time encouraged his enthusiasm for applying his learning to the greater advantage of his countrymen and the Tudor monarchy. In *General and Rare Memorials Pertaining to the Perfect Art of Navigation* (1577) he advocated expansion of the navy and further exploration as part of the realisation of the Tudors 'imperial' destiny, the creation of what he described as a 'British Empire'. His contribution to navigational knowledge was of some considerable benefit to English sailors and merchants.

His interest in the occult, which might have had him burned in counter-Reformation Italy, was not taboo in the places to which he decided to travel. Historians suspect his visits to the court of the occultist Emperor Rudolf II were engineered by the government in the hope of securing some kind of rapport with a potential ally. However by the time he returned in 1589 his influence was already in decline: his champions, Sidney and Leicester, had both died, Elizabeth's interest had diminished and when she died he found himself completely isolated. As further waves of witchcraft 'mania' broke on English shores in the 1590s he was in danger of the proverbial witch-hunt. Ironically he seems to have survived *because* he was considered an expert in the field of demonology, and one that might be consulted in witchcraft trials. He survived the early years of the reign of witch-finder James I but died in great poverty at Mortlake in 1608. Dee's life story has been seen as a metaphor for the whole history of the Elizabethan Renaissance he led and helped to inspire:

> '[His real] significance, as I see it, is the presentation in the life and work of one man of the phenomenon of the disappearance of the Renaissance in the late sixteenth century in clouds of demonic rumour. What happened in Dee's lifetime [...] was happening all over Europe as the renaissance went down in the darkness of the witch-hunts.'[106]

Elizabeth's passion for the arts ensured their promotion in courtly circles. Her annual 'progresses' to other parts of the kingdom

---

[106] Frances A. Yates, *The Occult Philosophy in the Elizabethan Age* (1979).

sponsored their development elsewhere as the court went on the road.

Ian Mortimer identified a Tudor 'revolution in reading'. Where the original printed books had been in Latin, produced in short runs to the highest standards, and very expensive, by the time of Elizabeth's reign numerous titles in English were being printed for ordinary people. These included self-help books such as collections of remedies, cookery books, and, of course, the Bible. More people *wanted* to read and, for occupational reasons in an increasingly bureaucratic age, more people *had* to read than ever before. Male literacy in England rose from about 10 per cent at the start of the sixteenth century to about 25 per cent by the end. Female literacy in the same period increased from about 1 per cent to around 10 per cent. In the first year of Elizabeth's reign 113 new titles were published in England; in the last year 456 new titles appeared.

Popular culture

Although developments in officially sanctioned and monitored theatre might be considered a high-jacking of the common culture, Elizabethan drama transcended both the elite and the popular. Although professional companies toured the provinces (Shakespeare very likely made his way to London when the Queen's Men and Leicester's Men visited Stratford in 1587), the main developments in theatre had a London focus. All communities however had their own, sometimes unique, cultural traditions and festivities.

In the weeks before the forty days fasting that defines Lent, the world was turned upside down in the extravagant Carnival celebrations. Here the spirit of the Lord of Misrule endorsed several days of indulgence - Carnival plays, cross-dressing, drunkenness, over-eating and other licentious behaviour. In some places at Christmas a Lord of Misrule would be elected as the figurehead of a further twelve days of ritual chaos. Shakespeare's *Twelfth Night*, a comedy of role reversals, was born of such popular festivities. A Puritan critic recorded in some detail the character of Christmas Revels:

> 'First, all the wild heads of the parish [choose a] Lord of Misrule, and him they crown with great solemnity and adopt for their king. This king annointed, chooseth forth twenty, forty,

three-score, or a hundred lusty guts like to himself to wait upon his lordly majesty, and to guard his noble person [...] They bedeck themselves with scarves, ribbons and laces, hanged all over with gold rings, precious stones and other jewels: this done, they tie about either leg twenty or forty bells, with rich handkerchieves in their hand [...] Then they have their hobby horses, dragons and other antiques, together with their bawdy pipers and thundering drummers, to strike up the devil's dance withal: then march these heathen company towards the church and churchyard, their pipers piping, their drummers thundering, their stumps dancing, their bells jingling, their handkerchieves swinging about their heads like madmen, their hobby horses and other monsters skirmishing amongst the throng like devils incarnate, with such a confused noise, that no man can hear his own voice.'

Pagan tradition provided reasons for celebrations linked to the changing seasons, Mayday for example, and Christian icons were revered on ninety or more Saints' Days. At least up until the Reformation the number of Holy Days, which of course included the Sabbath, greatly outnumbered the holidays of modern workers in full-time employment. The modern distinction between work and play, for many, was less clearly defined. Holidays were times for serious religious observances, although these might be commuted into celebrations of bodily pleasure. Various points of the yearly work cycle were marked with celebrations - harvest festivals and the great annual fairs for example. The hiring fairs, or 'Mop' fairs, where people advertised their labour and their skills, brought communities together, and the customary 'hiring penny' that an employer paid to seal the bargain, put money in people's pockets which might then be spent at the various stalls set up by local traders.

Although Carnival and the Lord of Misrule seemed to undermine authority and mystery plays might lampoon religious figures like Noah, the great institutions of Elizabethan England were at times themselves the cause of celebration. The Church Ales at Whitsun were communal booze-ups provided by the church-wardens who sold, for the benefit of the Church, their own strong beer to the revellers. In some places in the week after Easter, 'Hocktide' men held women ransom and women held men ransom and the money that released them was donated to the Church fund. By the 1580s a new celebration had been established -

Accession Day (November 17), when jousting contests, fireworks, bonfires, bell-ringing, sermons and pageants commemorated the beginning of Elizabeth's reign. Also in November Londoners enjoyed their Lord Mayor's Show.

Military considerations had long encouraged certain 'sporting' activities. 'Running at the quintain' was an ancient exercise of mounted pages and squires aiming their lances at a swinging target. By Elizabethan times this had degenerated into a popular pastime commonly engaged in at country wedding celebrations. All able-bodied men between the ages of seventeen and sixty were required by law to undertake practice archery on holy days in a specially designated field known as the butts. By the second half of the sixteenth century however the great age of the longbow was passed and the law, still on the statute book, was no longer observed.

Primitive (and violent) forms of football, bowls and a version of fives were popular ball games. To the dismay of Puritans, fives was often played against the church wall; churches and churchyards of course provided a focus for all manner of indoor and outdoor leisure pursuits. Tennis, a particular passion of Henry VIII, like the 'higher' forms of hunting, such as stag hunting and falconry, was very much the province of the elite. Popular blood-sports were often confined to the cockpit, the dog-pit, the bear-garden, and places of human execution.

'Popular culture' in Tudor England is defined by its communality. Be it dancing around a Maypole, crowding into an enclosed space to watch a cudgel fight, or joining with other parishioners to follow the priest around circumference of the parish ('beating the bounds'), these more or less essential activities were communal. As government became more centralised, more people received the rudiments of Renaissance learning, and individuals had more cause to leave the parishes into which they were born, old traditions and customs were undermined. Some historians identify with the period the emergence of a cultural gulf between the common folk and the educated secular elite.

The Law

The legal system during the Tudor period was extremely

complex. There were four major types of law: common law, equity, statute law and canon law. In addition each locality had its own customary law. These laws were enforced by a great number of different courts such as the Common Law Courts, the Privy Council and the Ecclesiastical Courts. The courts tended to specialise in particular areas but a considerable amount of doubling up occurred with different courts concerning themselves with the same kind of cases. Across the period there was a great expansion of legal activity and, while the system remained confused, co-ordination from the centre developed. The sixteenth century was the first great age of lawyers and many of the most powerful political figures had a legal background.

Common Law was also known as the King's Law, so-called because it applied to everybody in the kingdom. This covered such issues as the use of common land, trading standards and minor cases of debt and assault. A tenant might be brought before his lord's manor court while townsfolk could have a hearing in the borough court. At local level the King's courts was the county court which held its assizes, presided over by judges from London, twice a year. This heard the more serious criminal cases such as treason and forgery. Lesser criminal cases were heard by the local justices of the peace (JPs) at their county court quarter sessions. If the local courts failed to settle disputes or the accused wished to appeal against verdicts, such matters might be taken up by the higher common law courts which included the Court of King's Bench, the Court of Common Pleas and the Court of Exchequer.

Additional 'prerogative' law was associated with the courts of the Chancery, the Privy Council and other central bodies. The Council sat as a court in Star Chamber, and in the courts of Requests and the Council Learned. Justice in these 'equity' courts was not so bound by common law and here verdicts might be reached that provided a 'fairer' judgement in particular cases that because of some anomaly might have received a less equitable outcome in a common law court. The Councils of the North and Welsh Marches operated in much the same way.

The Ecclesiastical Courts were concerned with any misdemeanour related to Church matters. Consequently they handled cases as varied as the non-payment of tithes, sexual immorality, and heresy. They also acted as a supervisory institution regarding marriages, wills and the conduct of the clergy. The system was overseen by the bishop who would make regular visitations around his diocese to ensure the maintenance of church laws (canons).

Ecclesiastical and secular matters were also the concern of the prerogative courts. The Court of High Commission emerged during the sixteenth century to enforce the supremacy of the Crown in Church affairs.

Crime and Punishment

As with so many aspects of social history, assumptions concerning crime until comparatively recently were based upon anecdotal or literary evidence. The 'archival revolution' in historical research into Tudor society has produced more informed accounts that rely heavily on court records. These records are rarely 'complete' making it difficult to reconstruct a profile of crime and punishment for the country as a whole. Where records have survived they are hard to interpret, giving little indication of which cases were settled out of court or merely abandoned. The legal jargon of the time is often imprecise however - 'assault' for example might indicate a minor scuffle or a near murder.

There is no way of telling how many crimes and disputes never received a court hearing. At best the records provide a crude indication of how many people appeared before the judges and for what crimes. They do offer some indication of variations across time and place. Archives for the assizes are limited to the south-east but large numbers of quarter sessions and manorial courts archives exist for many areas.

Recent research suggests the majority of crimes dealt with by the courts fall into the 'victimless' category, such as drunkenness, blasphemy and receiving stolen goods, as opposed to those associated with assaults on the person or property. Attacks on people appear to have been the least common type of offence. The vast majority of offenders in all places were male although certain crimes, those of witchcraft and infanticide for example, were most commonly associated with women. Significant numbers of women also received retribution for riot. Offenders' ages unfortunately were rarely recorded. Since the majority of people in England at this time lived on or below the 'subsistence line' it is to be expected that most cases of crime recorded by the courts, particularly that involving property, was committed by the poor. However this can remain little more than a broad assumption. The status of the accused was usually listed though not necessarily with any great accuracy or precision. The better-off were more likely to find means of settling their disputes out of court.

The extent to which theft was perpetrated by organised gangs, 'professional' thieves, is open to question. The local records reveal little solid evidence and public proclamations, such as John Stow's 1598 account of melodramatic pamphlets, London, tend to reflect contemporary fears more than reality. Such propagandist sources have been misread in the past as reliable evidence for urban criminal gangs. Organised crime and racketeering probably was a characteristic of criminality in London but even there, and certainly elsewhere, criminals mostly acted independently and spontaneously.

For a wide variety of crimes the punishment was death. By the end of the sixteenth century the number of annual executions averaged about 800. Those convicted of felony (crimes such as murder, arson and rape, for which death might be the penalty), as opposed to a lesser offence or 'misdemeanour', stood a one in four chance of being hanged in the second half of the sixteenth century. The 'benefit of clergy' exempted clerics from being tried in secular courts for felonies and the normal punishments might be waived or lessened - a clergyman murderer for example might be branded with an 'M' on the left thumb instead of being executed. Where originally membership of a minor order was the condition, the ability to read a Latin passage in the sixteenth century might entitle anyone to such benefit, an echo from the past when reading was almost exclusively a clerical skill. Many categories of offence, such as theft from a church, ceased to be subject to benefit during the period although the tradition was preserved in part until 1827. For those unable to claim benefit punishments could be very severe indeed: mutilation, whipping and confinement in foul prisons for, by modern standards, minor offences.

The demographic and economic pressures of the age probably contrived to increase the incidence of crime, particularly that against property. By the end of the Tudor period the Protestant emphasis on the fallibility of humanity and the post-Reformation focus on the unity of Church and State, increased central and parochial concern for the godliness and orderliness of the masses. Proportionately more crimes may have been committed and certainly greater efforts were made by the authorities to identify and punish offenders.

Law and order in the localities was maintained by the justices of the peace. Across the period the number of JPs increased considerably, between twenty and thirty-five per county in 1509 to between forty and ninety in 1603. JPs were unpaid officials answerable to the Council. The job represented an enhancement of personal status and, invariably, was one filled by local gentlemen of some standing. They administered the law through the four annual quarter sessions and smaller petty sessions in the interim. More serious cases could be referred by the JPs to the assize judges, the twelve judges of the central courts who visited the counties once (in the north) or twice (in the south) each year to convene their assize courts. JPs were not permitted to try the most serious felonies of treason and forgery. They were assisted in their work in the parishes by the parish constables, further unpaid officials, responsible for basic policing at ground level. The appointment was for one year and the post was filled by the better-off members of the community such as yeoman farmers and the richer tradesmen. The constable maintained the stocks, pillory and village lock-up, collected various parish dues, dealt with disturbances, raised the local militia and supervised the alehouses. Done well, the job was arduous and immensely time-consuming. Inevitably in many parishes even the conscientious constable, and many doubtless were not, was unable to fulfill all of his duties.

If the much maligned parish constable was the sixteenth century equivalent of the village bobby, Sir Francis Walsingham's intelligence service in Elizabeth's reign was the precursor of MI5. As Royal Secretary after 1573 he established a network of agents and informants in England and the great courts of Europe. His intelligence service sought out conspiracies against the Queen including those connected with Mary, Queen of Scots. He had probably fewer than a dozen full-time spies in his employ at any one time and at first it seems he provided their wages out of his own pocket. In the early 1580s he began to receive an annual budget for the service which rose to £2000 in 1588, 'Armada year'. \

Witchcraft

Starting in the early 1400s and more or less over by the 1770s, the great age of witch-hunting in Western Europe was that of the sixteenth and seventeenth centuries. Historians' estimates of the total number of people executed for witchcraft presently fall within the range of 40,000-100,000 with, perhaps, something in the region of double that number facing charges. Of these, less than 1000, perhaps as few as 500, were English 'witches'

Witchcraft trials were extremely rare in England even after the first statute to deal specifically with witchcraft was passed in 1542, during the reign of Henry VIII. The act made no reference to pacts with the Devil, although it did comment on 'the conjuration of Spirits'. It demanded harsh penalties for alchemists and witches who aimed to perform *maleficia* through black magic, including the use of waxen images ('poppets'). Witchcraft itself, however, was still no ground for a case - and, as things turned out, only one suspect (later pardoned) was arrested under the act before it was repealed by Edward VI in 1547. A new act was prepared in 1559 but failed to become law and, for a few years, there was no statute prohibiting witchcraft in English law.

The climate changed significantly in 1563 when new legislation designed to control witches was issued under Elizabeth I. The queen herself had supposedly been the target of several witchcraft plots, and she evidently appreciated that allegations by fortune-telling sorcerers that the monarch had little time to live could easily provoke a rebellion led by those concerned with the succession. Several of Elizabeth's Protestant bishops had been influenced by witch burnings that they had witnessed in other countries, and pressed repeatedly for sterner measures to be taken at home. Bishop John Jewel, preaching before the queen at Oxford around 1560, broke from his prepared text to deliver an alarmist warning about the activities of witches throughout the realm, claiming that because of witches 'Your Grace's subjects pine away even unto death, their colour fadeth, their flesh rotteth, their speech is benumbed, their senses are bereft.'

The 1563 act was rooted in the key concept that witchcraft involved the 'conjurations of evil and wicked spirits' and that it was 'contrary to the laws of Almighty God'. Murder by witchcraft was punishable by death, and for those found guilty of using witchcraft to cause the 'wasting', 'laming', or 'consuming' of a person, or equivalent damage to his goods and chattels, the statute imposed a year's imprisonment and life for re-offenders and the death penalty if convicted on the same charges a second time. The method of execution was hanging 'by the neck until he or she be dead'.

A year's imprisonment was stipulated for any attempt to injure, kill, provoke a person 'to unlawful love', or to use witchcraft to find lost or hidden objects. A second offence of this kind was punishable by life imprisonment and the confiscation by the Crown of the individual's property. During the year of imprisonment the convicted witch was be pilloried in a public place in the local market town for the duration of six hours, once in each quarter of the year. Any substantial length of time in a squalid Tudor prison was likely to be fatal for those so punished.

The reasons for the re-identification of witchcraft as a crime at the start of Elizabeth's reign are subject to debate. Historians in their explanations have paid particular attention to the context in which the legislation was passed, which included the passing of the throne from the overtly Roman Catholic Queen, Mary I, to her Protestant sister, Elizabeth. Some have also highlighted the significance of developments on the Continent in this period, including the enthusiasm for witch-hunting abroad in an age of confessional conflict. English Protestant theologians at the start of Elizabeth I's reign, some of whom had been exiled to continental Europe during Mary I's Counter-Reformation, considered both witchcraft and Catholicism dangerous superstitions. It has long been thought that the phrase 'Hocus Pocus', used to mimic a magic incantation, is derived from the sacred words *hoc est corpus* ('Here is the body') as stated by Catholic priests in the Eucharist ceremony, the sacred Holy Communion that focused on the miracle of transubstantiation: the transformation of bread to flesh and wine to blood. Real and imagined Catholic plots in Elizabeth's reign, and also at the start of James I's, may have contributed to the stiffening of witchcraft legislation and helped to heighten the anxieties that encouraged persecution.

Popular Protest

Every Tudor monarch experienced at least one major 'rebellion' during his or her reign. These rebellions covered the length and breadth of the land, from Northumberland to Cornwall, the western shires to Norfolk and Lincolnshire. They can be divided into two broad categories - popular protest in which large numbers of people rose with particular social, economic grievances, and political rebellions already mighty sought an extension of their religious or in which the influence by challenging the authority of other powerful figures such as the King or his first ministers. These political rebellions, such as Wyatt's Rebellion against Mary Tudor (1554) and the Northern Rising against Elizabeth I (1569), are dealt with elsewhere in this book.

Under Henry VII and during the first half of Henry VIII's reign the prime motive for revolt was taxation. In 1489 the northern shires were required to raise £100,000, a contribution to the cost of Henry VII's foreign policy. The burden of an additional tax, in the spring following a particularly bad harvest, brought about the Yorkshire Rebellion. A decade later Perkin Warbeck's attempt to seize the throne necessitated a further subsidy and provoked the more serious Cornish Rebellion of 1497. Henry VIII's foreign policy, conducted by Cardinal Wolsey in the early 1520s again called for a raising of additional revenue by extraordinary means, this time with the imposition of the Amicable Grant. A combination of poverty and opposition to Wolsey resulted in a widespread refusal to pay in the eastern counties.

The Henrician Reformation heralded a series of protests linked to religious grievances. The Lincolnshire Rising of 1536 was initiated by the clergy with their demands for an ending of the dissolution and the dismissal of bishops Latimer and Cranmer. In the same year the greatest all these demonstrations of public dissatisfaction occurred: the Pilgrimage of Grace. Although the exact motives for this are hard to identify, religious complaints played a significant role. Once again the fate of the great abbeys was an issue at stake as was resentment towards the erosion of church traditions and the removal of cherished ornaments and ritualistic treasures. In 1549 Protector Somerset's endeavours to introduce the new Prayer Book inspired the Western Rebellion. The list of complaints on this occasion also concerned the fate of the monasteries in including a clause that demanded their partial restoration.

A further cause of complaint was that of enclosure. This was the inspiration for Robert Kett's Rebellion of 1549, resulting in the bloody suppression at Dussindale near Norwich where around 3000 of Kett's followers were killed.

These popular protests were essentially conservative and reactionary in character. Those in revolt tended to take great care in expressing their loyalty to the Crown. Invariably the monarch's chief councillors were targetted - Wolsey, Cromwell, Somerset. A direct assault on the King after all was treasonable and punishable by death. Although these revolts caused remarkably little damage to life and property considering the scale of the risings they were often prone to the most draconian punishment. Hundreds and sometimes thousands of people were killed as the risings were crushed and many more were subsequently hanged for treason.

Overall these popular revolts achieved very little. Wolsey was forced to back down on the Amicable Grant in 1525 and opposition to the Statute of Uses (affecting the freedom of landowners to leave their property to whom and as they chose) in the 1530s resulted in the more tolerable Statute of Wills of 1540; but, by and large, these provincial, localised protests stood little chance of significantly diverting government policy.

Overseas trade

Overseas trade during the years of civil war in the fifteenth century was mostly in the hands of foreign merchants. They provided the majority of the ships that carried English goods abroad. Henry VII determined to secure the vast profits accumulated by foreign merchants, particularly those of the German towns affiliated into the Hanseatic League, on the sale and transportation of English products. The Navigation Acts of 1486 and 1489 obliged merchants to use English ships whenever possible and an act in 1489 prevented the sale of wool to foreigners before English buyers had bought all they required. Despite his interest in 'commercial diplomacy', Henry VII's negotiations and trade agreements with France, Spain, Denmark, Venice and Florence did not result in a great flowering in English overseas trade. The Navigation Acts however, although they provoked retaliation abroad, placed merchant shipping firmly in English hands and laid the foundations of the Tudor maritime strength associated with Henry VIII and Elizabeth I.

Throughout the period England's chief export was woollen cloth. The principal centre for this was Antwerp and a virtual monopoly on the trade was in the hands of the Merchant Adventurers. The Merchant Adventurers were London merchants who had organised themselves into a company in the fifteenth century. In return for a substantial entry fee merchants entered a body, effectively a guild, that fixed prices, provided the protection of sailing in convoy to the Netherlands, and negotiated trading arrangements with governments at home and abroad. The domination of the cloth trade by London merchants (by the 1550s 90 per cent of overseas trade went through London) was deeply resented by merchants elsewhere and hastened the decline of competitor ports such as Boston and Beverley.

In addition to undyed cloth the Merchant Adventurers exported other 'unfinished' goods and raw materials including wool (though in much smaller quantities than before), tin and lead. A vast array of luxuries was imported, ranging from wine and spices to playing cards and tennis balls, and some essentials such as iron, saltpeter and grain. All could be purchased, at the most competitive prices, at Antwerp.

Fluctuations in the Netherlands cloth trade, particularly when relations with the Habsburgs deteriorated during the reign of Elizabeth I, obliged English merchants to broaden their horizons and seek markets elsewhere. Political crises made temporary centres, for the trade in cloth, of Calais (1493-6) in Henry VII's reign and Emden (1563-5) in Elizabeth's. In addition to expanding markets in the Mediterranean and the Levant, after 1550 Protestant England openly challenged the Spanish and Portuguese monopolies on trade in the Far East and America which had been guaranteed by the Pope according to the terms of the 1494 Treaty of Tordesillas.

While John Cabot and his son, Sebastian, can be seen as the first of the great Tudor explorers, William Hawkins and his son, John, are foremost in the advent of Tudor long-distance trade. William Hawkins was a Plymouth merchant who between the 1520s and 1550s was trading cloth and iron for spices, ivory, saltpeter and sugar along the African and Brazilian coasts. His ground-breaking voyages provided valuable information for merchants in Elizabeth's reign. In 1562 John Hawkins began to exchange English goods in Africa for a human cargo to be traded for gold and other goods in the Americas, thus laying the keystone for the lucrative Bristol 'triangular' slave trade of the seventeenth century. His second voyage in 1564 was backed by the Queen and members of her Privy Council and, like the first, proved a great success. He sailed in one of the Queen's own ships, the Jesus. In 1567, sailing with Francis Drake, his third expedition was abandoned after all but two of his vessels fell victim to a Spanish armada, determined to eliminate English pretensions at trading in a Portuguese-Spanish domain. He lost £100,000 of treasure but subsequently was recompensed with £40,000 when he persuaded the Spanish he was a devout Catholic, and one prepared to desert with the Queen's ships to Spain.

The most important contribution of the Cabots' expeditions

during Henry VII's reign, in economic terms, had been the discovery of the Newfoundland cod fisheries. The fishing industry increasingly was seen as a surety in the face of a faltering London-Antwerp wool trade. In 1563, the year that Philip II's regent in the Netherlands closed Antwerp to English merchants, William Cecil passed the extraordinary legislation that made Wednesdays and Fridays 'fish days' when it was illegal to eat meat. This, it was hoped, would both expand fishing and increase nautical understanding at a time when it became apparent that England was set on becoming increasingly reliant on long-distance markets. The growth of the off-shore fishing industry provided some incentive for colonisation in America, providing safe havens for fishing vessels far from home.

By the end of Elizabeth's reign English long-distance trade was still very much in its infancy. Only 10 per cent of English imports came from America and the Far East although important markets for English cloth had been set up in Africa and elsewhere. The traditional Iberian monopolies had been successfully challenged in the second half of the sixteenth century and important lessons in financing, navigation and shipping had been learned. The quantity as well as the quality of English merchant shipping increased dramatically: between 1560 and 1582 the number of ships between 100 and 199 tonnes more than doubled to a total 155 while there was a threefold increase in shipping of 200 or more tonnes to a total of eighteen. Trade and colonisation overseas that had been dominated by the Portuguese and the Spanish in the sixteenth century was set to become the province of the English, French and Dutch in the seventeenth.

Exploration

Tudor monarchs supported explorers mainly for economic gain. Henry VII was a patron of John Cabot after learning of the success of Christopher Columbus in finding the New World under the patronage of the king of Spain. Columbus might have sailed from England had Henry's Council decided it was worth supporting his enterprise, although it is likely that had he done so he would have been steered by the winds towards Nova Scotia rather than the more desirable Caribbean. Cabot sought a shorter passage to Asia, popular belief at the time being that this could be achieved by sailing westwards across the Atlantic. Henry's sponsorship helped carry Cabot in 1497 to North America, probably Newfoundland. Probably convinced by now that Columbus had discovered a previously unknown continent Cabot was in no doubt that he had located Asia. When he returned he was given a pension by the king and won the adulation of an admiring London public. In return for his patronage, which included exemption from custom duties on any goods the adventurer brought back and a monopoly on future trade in the newly discovered lands, the Crown was to receive a fifth of all profits accruing from this and subsequent voyages by Cabot or his heirs.

In 1498 Cabot sailed west from Bristol on a second voyage, this time with five ships, four hired and one the gift of the King. He never returned but may have reached Ameriqa. The fate of just one vessel, which went into harbour in Ireland after a storm on the way out, is known. Many other expeditions across the north Atlantic, including that of Cabot's son, Sebastian, received Henry's backing and merchants and other travellers that returned from the 'New Found Lands' were rewarded with gifts from the King's purse. Henry's interest in the exotic was well rewarded with New World curiosities brought back to England including three 'savages' exhibited at court in 1502. Although the Newfoundland cod fisheries provided a valuable commodity in his reign, Henry VIII's preoccupation with wars in Europe effectively diminished royal patronage of explorers.

Sebastian Cabot, like Columbus before him, left England for the more lucrative Spanish court. The reign however was not totally devoid of explorers and adventurers, the most enterprising being William Hawkins who broke the Portuguese monopoly on trade with Brazil and the Guinea Coast of West Africa. Such voyages were very costly and likely to end in disaster: by the 1540s those that had the capital to spare were more likely to invest their money in Church lands following the Dissolution than the schemes of would-be explorers.

New government initiatives were taken during the regency of the Duke of Northumberland. Cabot had returned to England in 1547 and Northumberland subsequently employed his expertise in seeking new markets for English cloth at a time of decline in the Antwerp trade. In 1551 he became the first governor of the new Company of Merchant Venturers for the Discovery of Lands Unknown. New expeditions established trade links with Morocco and the Gold Coast. The old search for a short passage to the Orient was also revived, this time, on Cabot's advice taking a north-eastern route. The expedition comprised three ships under Richard Chancellor and Sir Hugh Willoughby. They failed in achieving their objective and Willoughby and his crew died that winter, marooned in Lapland. Chancellor however reached Russia, had an audience with Tsar Ivan the Terrible and established the trade that was launched in 1555 with the formation of the Muscovy Company.

Although the Northumberland era should not be overlooked in the history of England's overseas trade and the first steps towards the founding of a colonial empire, the great age of Tudor exploration was that of Elizabeth's reign. Unlike Mary I, who had withdrawn her sponsorship of explorers and merchants in Guinea at the request of her husband Philip II of Spain, Elizabeth had no qualms about challenging the monopolies of Portuguese and Spanish traders.

With the government's blessing Martin Frobisher in 1576 sailed in search of a north-west passage. When he arrived at what is now called Frobisher Bay at the southern tip of Greenland he thought he had found its entrance and returned home triumphant. Further expeditions were funded by London merchants but Frobisher disappointed them in their hope of finding gold. John Davis made three similar voyages in the 1580s and greatly contributed to the cartographer's understanding of Greenland by identifying the strait, the Davis Strait, that divides it from America.

Failed attempts at finding a north-east passage led the newly formed Levant Company, which had revived the fifteenth century trade with the Ottoman Empire, to seek an overland route to India through Syria. Ralph Fitch's perilous journey subsequently lasted eight years and took him through India to Malaya but failed to provide a practical alternative to the Portuguese monopoly on Indo-European trade.

Exploration provided a cover for Francis Drake when, ostensibly he sought the lost continent of Terra Australis, but in fact seems to have been briefed by the government to plunder Spanish vessels in the Pacific. Setting sail in 1577 he was the second man to circumnavigate the globe, seizing in the process a fortune in Spanish silver and gold and claiming what became California (his 'New Albion') for Elizabeth and England. Drake, now a national hero, was knighted on his return by the Queen on the deck of the ship he had sailed in, now renamed the *Golden Hind*. Unlike many other ventures, including Drake's previous disastrous expedition to America in 1567, the Queen and the court syndicate that had backed him were well rewarded for their investment.

In 1584 Sir Walter Raleigh attempted to establish an English colony in what he named Virginia. The first colonists fled back to England when Drake visited in 1586, the next 'colony' comprising fifteen men was wiped out by native Americans, and the third settlement of men, women and children left their stockade for some unknown reason and apparently perished, leaving no trace.

Perhaps the most romantic of all journeys made by Elizabethan explorers was Raleigh's search in 1595 for the legendary South American city of gold, Eldorado. He never found such a place or the gold mines thought to furnish it, his way up the Orinoco being barred by waterfalls. However he wrote down his experiences and convictions concerning what remained to be discovered in *The Discovery of Guiana* and thus earned himself a considerable amount of popular acclaim at a time when he was out of favour with the Queen having secretly married Bess Throckmorton, one of her maids of honour.

Tudor Government – Court, Council and Parliament

'No serious student can any longer ignore the court any more than the council or the parliament can be ignored.'

(David Loades, *The Tudor Court*, 1989)

Until the late 1970s, following an influential lecture by G. R. Elton and the publication of writings by David Starkey, the role of the Tudor Court in government was both little understood and underestimated. It is now recognised as a crucial channel through which Tudor monarchs made contact with their subjects and promoted the mystique of their rule.

Kings had always had a 'court'. When Harold Godwinson was slain in the field at Hastings he fell in the company of his greatest warriors and most trusted servants, kinsmen and liegemen. By the time of Henry VIII's reign martial prowess was just one attribute among many that might be deemed desirable in a courtier, and his glittering court was intended to be a model of Renaissance sophistication and taste.

The Court describes all those who were gathered around and in attendance upon king. It was a highly fluid assemblage, literally changing from day to day as the king received people, foreign ambassadors for example, into his household. The two hundred and fifty or so staff employed in routine domestic tasks however were rarely changed and it was not uncommon for servants to be replaced by near relatives on their retirement. On the occasion of the most fabulous display of the Tudor Court, Henry VIII's meeting with Francis I at the Field of Cloth of Gold, the Court numbered 5000 and included most of the most powerful men in the kingdom.

The Court was divided into two parts - the upper household and the lower household. From the smallest gentry hall-houses to the greatest palaces high status individuals in medieval buildings were physically raised above those of lower status. The owner of the hall ate at a dais a step above floor level and the upper household in a king's palace met upstairs. The Lord Chamberlain presided over the Upper Household or 'Chamber' and the Lower Household was controlled by the Lord Steward.

Closest to the king in Henry VIII's reign were the Gentlemen of the Privy Chamber. These were particularly trusted servants, the king's personal friends, who were granted access to the king's private chambers. Henry VII usually allowed only humble servants access to his most private chambers but his son, perhaps emulating the French king, created a court within a court by appointing high status courtiers to the most intimate posts.

Consequently the somewhat menial sounding position, Groom of the Stool, was highly prized as one of the most influential offices in the kingdom. Henry's queens likewise had their own 'consort's Privy Chamber'. Mary I and Elizabeth I of course restricted the access of powerful male councillors to their private chambers and during the second half of the sixteenth century appointments to the Privy Chamber had less political significance.

The Court was a highly competitive environment with courtiers struggling to gain the King's or Queen's ear and patronage. Bitter rivalries were commonplace and, at worst, sometimes resulted in violence. In 1573, for example, John Fortescue was beaten up in a London street by twelve servants of the Earl of Oxford. Jousting prowess, a striking costume and a pleasing wit were all means by which courtiers might secure a ruler's attention. Ann Boleyn and Robert Dudley were just two of the many courtiers who were triumphant by virtue of their attractiveness to a monarch of the opposite sex. David Loades related how Nicholas Carew won Henry VIII's favour in showing off his equestrian and jousting skills while balancing a heavy beam on his head, and Sir Jacques Granado was killed 'when he tried too hard to impress Philip and Mary in the exercising of a mettlesome stallion'. Competition among courtiers reflected the competition between kings that was such) a distinctive feature of the age.

The tone of the Tudor Court was set in the reign of Henry VIII. Like his father, who named his first son Arthur, he exploited the dynasty's claim to descent from King Arthur and set about creating a court that reverberated with echoes of the Arthurian romance. He led the way in reviving the courtly love tradition, pledging himself to a lady of the court, wearing her colours on the jousting field and celebrating her beauty love-songs and lovesick letters. Perhaps the greatest exponent however was not Henry but his daughter Elizabeth who used the device to devastating effect in securing the devotion of her male courtier-suitors.

Play-acting in Court was not restricted to the extravagences of courtly love. From the 1530s a Master of Revels co-ordinated members of the Court in the production of plays for the monarch's and their own entertainment. By Shakespeare's time the Revels were more usually provided by outside, professional agencies benefitting from the Queen's patronage. Music had a high profile in the Tudor court - both Henry VIII and Elizabeth were accomplished musicians. A fine singing voice could be a ticket into Henry's inner sanctum, the Privy Chamber. Culture was complemented by learning; Henry's children, Edward and Elizabeth received humanist educations and Elizabeth's own court was peopled by some of England's foremost scholars.

The need to clear cess pits rather than any potential saving on domestic costs encouraged the monarch and his / her entourage to take to the road periodically. These costly 'progresses' brought court culture to the provinces, the unstated obligation of the localities to receive the monarch in appropriate style compensating for the cost of hiring horses and other transport expenses. The 'country' similarly was expected to be in attendance at Court in London periodically; the heads of noble families and even those of the leading gentry made routine visits and endeavoured to find a court post for a family member.

Life at Court could be ruinously expensive. The cost of living and dressing in style, coupled with the gambling that helped while away hours of waiting on the king, bankrupted some. The giving of gifts to those of influence in the hope of securing their recommendation was common and normal practice. The potential gains were considerable, monopolies, pensions, the repudiation of debts owed to the Crown, the acquisition of lucrative posts were all possibilities. The hey-day years of the 1540s presented courtiers with the opportunity to buy monastic lands at bargain prices. For some the Court provided a career and the prospect of enoblement.

Lord Burghley understood the councillor's role (in 1596) clearly: it was his function to advise the Queen and to act upon her instructions:

> 'I do hold, and will always, this course in such matters as 1 differ in opinion from her Majesty; as long as I may be allowed to give advice I will not change my opinion by affirming the contrary, for that were to offend God, to whom I am sworn first; but as a servant I will obey her Majesty's commandment and no wise contrary the same, presuming that she being God's chief minister here, it shall be God's will to have her commandments obeyed, after that I have performed my duty as a councillor.'

In addition to its advisory and administrative role the Council had adjudicatory responsibilities with the power to interrogate, torture and condemn, or pardon. offenders. Every aspect of government was the concern of the Council - religion, the economy, law and order, foreign affairs.

The principle of having a permanent Council, an institution as opposed to an *ad hoc* and temporary gathering of advisors around the king, was developed by the Yorkist kings. The Tudors maintained and further refined the practice. Henry VII's Council was large, comprising about 150 magnates and officials of the royal household and met at Court. About half of its members were clerics and included bishops such as John Morton, Archbishop of Canterbury and Chancellor, and Richard Fox, Bishop of Winchester and King's Secretary. Around 1498 a new subcommittee emerged, peopled by lawyers and responsible for legal affairs - the Council Learned in the Law. This, together with other subcommittees, increased the Council's efficiency and promoted the place of specialists in its affairs. Although Henry's Council contained numerous men of noble blood, his closest advisers, Dudley and Poynings for example, were often men of humbler origins but with expertise in areas such as the law and estate management. His successors followed his example: when Elizabeth I died scarcely more than one third of her councillors were peers.

Further steps towards the rationalisation of the King's Council were taken during Henry VIII's reign. After 1516 its judicial role was formalised by Cardinal Wolsey in the Court of Star Chamber. In 1526 he attempted, unsuccessfully, to reduce its membership. Such streamlining occurred in the years after his death when an inner council, the Privy Council, emerged, probably set up by Cromwell in 1536, comprising around twenty members. This Privy Council did not become a formal body until 1540 by which time it had its own clerk with the duty of recording its business. Such exclusivity encouraged efficient government but also provoked rivalries and the formation of factions, sometimes with dire consequences. Star Chamber and the Privy Council were now, theoretically at least, separate bodies although the privy councillors were also the Star Chamber judges. The Council's financial business was dealt with by a number (eventually six) of different courts specialising in different areas.

Thomas Cromwell's initiatives in the 1530s amounted to what G. R. Elton considered the Tudor revolution in government which became the title of his massively influential book, first published in 1953. In this he argued that Cromwell undermined the influence of the royal household in government and promoted the role of a leaner, more bureaucratic and efficient Council. 'Revolution' is one of the strongest words in the historian's vocabulary and it is to be used with great caution. Elton's critics have pointed to the bureaucratic sophistication of medieval monarchs and the initiatives of Cromwell's predecessors, including Wolsey, and thus find the concept of evolution more satisfactory. Others have emphasised the very personalised nature of Tudor government at particular times after this so called 'revolution' and David Starkey has asserted the continued importance of the Court which in any case encompassed the Council. While the 1530s are widely regarded as watershed years in the history of English government the role of the Court was not superceded so much as augmented by developments in conciliar administration.

The Council increased in size under Edward VI and Mary I but contracted again in Elizabeth's reign. By the end of her reign her privy councillors numbered a mere fourteen. As the main executive body in the kingdom it co-ordinated campaigns abroad, the defence of the country when threatened by invasion, it supervised local government and reviewed cases brought before it by those claiming they had not received justice in the regular courts. In such instances it not only carried out the sovereign's instructions but legislated in the sovereign's name. Its work from the second half of Henry VIII's reign was organised by the Secretary of State - Thomas Cromwell in the 1530s, William Cecil, Francis Walsingham and Robert Cecil during the reign of Elizabeth I. Elton described the post as 'the centre and driving force of the administration'. Of this uniquely powerful position Robert Cecil wrote:

> 'All officers and counsellors of princes have a prescribed authority by patent, by custom or by oath, the secretary alone excepted.'

Monarchs were not answerable to Parliament, only to God. Parliament existed as a sounding-board, a representative body that might be consulted in the governing process. Its members did not have a creative role; it was not the font of government.

Members of Parliament included the great landowners and representatives of the shires and boroughs. From the 1330s onwards they met as separate 'Houses', the Lords and the Commons. Late medieval sovereigns increasingly relied on the House of Commons to sanction new taxes and, in return, they heard petitions presented by MPs.

The comparative wealth of Tudor monarchs and the political stability of the late fifteenth and early sixteenth century after the turbulence of the civil war reduced royal dependency on Parliament and it met less frequently. At crucial moments however, the era of royal divorce and monastic dissolution particularly, it played a major role in legitimising acts of government. Between 1529 and 1559 it met every year before reverting to infrequent meetings throughout the reigns of Elizabeth I and James I.

The reliance on Parliament during the 1530s reveals Henry VIII's recognition that, while the royal prerogative was indisputable in theory, in practice he was bound by custom and precedent and the cataclysmic reforms of that decade required parliamentary approval. statute law could only be made through the parliamentary process and, since the late fourteenth century, the levying of taxes required parliamentary consent. Foreign policy on the other hand remained a royal prerogative but the taxes that funded it were raised via Parliament.

Kings chose when to call Parliament. In Henry VII's reign it met seven times but just once during the whole of the last twelve years. In total it sat for just over a year and a half in a reign that lasted almost twenty-four. This marked the king's growing financial security and his ability to raise capital by non-parliamentary means. It would be foolish however to belittle the place of Parliament in Henry's reign since the new dynasty was affirmed in 1486 'by authority of this present Parliament'. Parliament also passed the acts of attainder that punished disloyal magnates.

It was once supposed that the accession of Henry VII signified a dramatic break with past traditions of government, so much so that his approach and that of his immediate successors amounted to no less than a 'New Monarchy'. More recent studies emphasize continuity and evolution in practice across the fifteenth century. A 'New Monarchy' has been identified as the consequence of the Tudor 'revolution' in government during the 1530s which was discussed in the previous section. Although Elton's original Cromwellian revolution in government 1950s thesis has been modified, chiefly regarding Cromwell's intentions and personal contribution, many historians remain comfortable with the essential concept. How far the relationship between Crown and Parliament was 'revolutionised' is open to question. Certainly Parliament played a crucial role in the Henrician Reformation. In the opinion of Rosemary O'Day:

> 'The Reformation Parliament of 1529-1536 signalled enormous changes in the nature and function of parliament both because the monarch chose to implement a revolution through it and also because the legislation it produced incorporated parliament fully into the system of government of church and state.'[107]

The role of Parliament in the Reformation reaffirmed the place of Parliament in the constitution, as the only place where statute legislation could be made, yet it remained an intermittent institution. The Reformation Parliament, comprising seven sessions and spanning seven years, was exceptionally long; most lasted for just a few months, even weeks. For substantial periods, the four years between January 1567 and April 1571 in Elizabeth I's reign for example, following the offence caused by parliamentarians requesting the Queen's marriage or

---

[107] Rosemary O'Day, *The Tudor Age* (1995), p. 119.

nomination of a successor, no Parliament was summoned. Although it expanded in size, grew more assertive and became increasingly preoccupied with national as well as local issues, Parliamentary opposition to government policy was rare. The great exception to this general rule was the refusal of certain prelates in the House of Lords to endorse the 1559 religious settlement as England lurched from the Catholicism of Mary's reign to the Protestantism of Elizabeth's. The claim that in the sixteenth century organised parliamentary opposition emerged, pointing the way to the calamitous relations between King and Commons in the seventeenth century, is no longer tenable. Under the Tudors the concept of King-in-Parliament was greatly strengthened but the prerogative of kings (and queens) was fiercely upheld and parliamentary subservience successfully maintained.

The Tudor Age

The Tudor 'Age' has been distinguished by historians and other commentators as a mostly glorious era of transition from late medieval chaos to ordered and rational modernity. This volume has endeavoured to explore and question this reputation by considering continuity as well as change, catastrophe as well as triumph.

Without doubt the kingdom of 1485 was very different to that of 1603. Perhaps it is appropriate to talk of demographic, cultural, economic, political and religious revolutions in the twelve decades of Tudor control. A new sense of nationhood emerged with a more cohesive and centralised diffusion of authority and power. The peripheral territories of the North, Wales and even Ireland by 1603 were subordinated under the English Crown and London government. The sixteenth was the century of England's Reformation and although Roman Catholicism had held on with limpet tenacity in many parts of the realm long after the monasteries were dissolved, by the time of Elizabeth's death Protestantism was dominant in English consciousness and culture.

Revolutions have ends as well as beginnings. The great Trotskyist credo of 'permanent revolution' is an inspirational metaphor but a contradiction in terms. Historians have begun to write of English Reformations that span four reigns, not just Henry VIII's. The accession of James I likewise marked no abrupt conclusion. His was a less 'heroic' reign than his predecessor's but his less dignified reputation is more to do with his (and his courtiers) less dignified behaviour and personality than with any shift in approaches to government. He inherited the Elizabethan system which, in turn, she had inherited from her forbears. If there was a 'revolution in government' in Tudor times it came in the 1530s and 40s when Thomas Cromwell further bureaucratised the administration. Then again, England had a more sophisticated bureaucracy than rival states under medieval kings, and the monarch's personal touch in finance and policy making, particularly in the reigns of the early Stuarts, remained a fundamental characteristic of government for one hundred years. For similar reasons it is no longer fashionable to identify the emergence of a 'New Monarchy' in Henry VII's time; true, the face of monarchy and the character of monarchs did change with the Tudors but the conventional image of Tudor monarchy - a posturing, proud, learned Henry VIII; the all-seeing, ageless Gloriana Elizabeth - is not that of Henry VII.

The period of British history in which the Tudors occupied the English throne was not a glorious one. It was born of ambitions which had more to do with greed for political power than any sense of the divine right of legitimate kings, the Reformation was a cynical, pragmatic response to circumstances that had little to do with religious belief, and campaigns abroad proved time and again that England was no great player in continental affairs. Regimes survive through propaganda, coercion or force. The Tudors deal t out all three in good measure. The genuine popularity of 'Bluff King Hal' and 'Good Queen Bess' is as hard to measure as the alleged unpopularity of 'Bloody Mary'. Certainly the thousands brutalised and persecuted in their names had little cause to respect the dynasty. The widespread affection for Elizabeth is probably as mythical as the tradition of a Protestant England's near universal loathing for Catholic Mary.

For ordinary people life was hard and, in the closing years of Elizabeth's reign, getting a good deal harder still. However, their lives had been touched by the literary, scientific and architectural breakthroughs of their era: more people than ever before could read, they were witnesses to a great flowering of learning and literature, and in ordinary homes chimneys burned coal. The legacy of the Tudors has as much to do with the first printed books, Shakespeare's plays and Elizabethan mansions, as it does with ruined abbeys, a ramshackle legal system, and tales of heroic seadogs and their larger-than-life kings and queens.

SOURCES

Luther's sect

(Cuthbert Tunstall, Bishop of London, 1526)

By the duty of our pastoral office, we are bound diligently, with all our power, to foresee, provide for, root out, and put away all those things which seem to tend to the peril and danger of our subjects, and especially to the destruction of their souls. Wherefore we, having understanding by the report of divers credible persons, and also by the evident appearance of the matter, that many children of iniquity, maintainers of Luther's sect, blinded through extreme wickedness, wandering from the way of truth and the catholic faith, craftily have translated the New Testament into our English tongue, intermeddling therewith many heretical articles and erroneous opinions, pernicious and offensive, seducing the simple people; attempting by their wicked and perverse interpretations to profanate the majesty of the Scripture which hitherto hath remained undefiled, and craftily to abuse the most holy word of God, and the true sense of the same; of which translation there are many books imprinted, some with glosses and some without, containing in the English tongue that pestiferous and most pernicious poison, dispersed throughout all our diocese of London in great numbers; which truly, without it be speedily foreseen, without doubt will contaminate and infect the flock committed unto us with most deadly poison and heresy, to the grievous peril and danger of the souls committed to our charge, and offence of God's divine majesty.

Scripture in the mother tongue

(William Tyndale, *Obedience of a Christian man and how Christian Rulers ought to govern*, 1528)

'If the Scripture were in the mother tongue,' they will say, 'each lay person would understand it in his own way.' What function serves the curate but to teach them the right way? Why were the holidays made but that the people should come and learn? Are you not abominable schoolmasters if you take great wages but you will not teach? If you would teach, how could you do it so well and with so great profit as when the lay people have the Scripture before them in their mother tongue'? For then they should see, by the order of the text, whether you juggle meanings or not. And they would believe it because it is the Scripture of God [...] But alas, the curates themselves (for the most part) know no more what the New or Old Testaments mean than do the Turks. Neither do they know any more than that which they read at mass, matins and evensong, which they also don't understand [...] they will not let the lay-man have the word of God in his mother tongue, yet let priests have it who mostly understand no Latin at all, who sing and mutter things all day which, in their hearts, they do not understand.

A Supplication for the Beggars, 1528

(Simon Fish, *A Supplication for the Beggars*, 1528)

Here, if it be please your grace to mark, ye shall see a thing far out of joint. There are within your realm of England 52 thousand parish churches. And this standing, that there be but ten households in every parish, yet are there five hundred thousand and twenty thousand household. And of every of these households hath every of the five orders of friars a penny a quarter for every order, that is for all the five orders, five pence a quarter for every house [...] Oh! grievous and painful exactions thus yearly to be paid! from which the people of your noble predecessors, the kings of the ancient Britons, ever stood free. And this they will have, or else they will procure him that will not give it them to be taken as a heretic [...]

Poverty and the dissolution of the monasteries, 1546

(*A Supplication of the Poor Commons*, 1546)

For, although the sturdy beggars (the monks) got all the devotion of the good charitable people from them, yet had the poor impotent creatures some relief of their scraps, where now they have nothing. Then had they hospitals, and alms houses to be lodged in, but now they lie and starve in the streets. Then their number was great, but now much greater.

The Statute for Artificers, 1563

(Extract from the Statute of Artificers, 1563)

And be it further enacted by the authority aforesaid, That all artificers and labourers being hired for wages by the day or week shall, betwixt the midst of the months of March and September, be and continue at their work, at or before five of the clock in the morning, and continue at work, and not depart until between seven and eight of the clock at night (except it be in the time of breakfast, dinner or drinking, the which times at most shall not exceed two and a half hours in a day, that is to say, at every drinking one half-hour, for his dinner one hour, and for his sleep, when he is allowed to sleep, the which is from the midst of May, to the midst of August, half an hour at the most, and at every breakfast one half-hour). And all the said artificers and labourers, between the midst of September, and the midst of March, shall be and continue at their work from the spring of the day in the morning, until the night of the same day, except it be in time afore appointed to breakfast and dinner.

Vagabonds, 1567

(Thomas Harman, *A Caveat or Warning for Common Cursetors, vulgarly called Vagabonds*, 1567)

Of those ranging rabblement of rascals, some be serving men, artificers, and labouring men, traded up in husbandry. These not minding to get their living with the sweat of their face, but casting off all pain, will wander after their wicked manner through the most shires of this realm [...] These unruly rascals [...] disperse themselves into several companies, as occasion serveth, sometime more and sometime less. As, if they repair to a poor husbandman's house, he will go alone, or one with him, and stoutly demand his charity, either showing how he hath served in the wars and there maimed, [or] that he seeketh service, and saith he would be glad to take pain for his living (although he meaneth nothing less). If he be offered any meat or drink, he utterly refuseth scornfully, and will

[have] nought but money. And if he espy young pigs or poultry, he will noteth the place, and then, the next night or shortly after, he will be sure to have some of them [...] If any search be made, or they suspected for pilfering clothes off hedges, or breaking of houses - which they commonly do when the owners be either at the market, church, or otherwise occupied about their business - [or] rob some silly [simple] man or woman by the highway, as many times they do, then they hie them into woods, great thickets, and other rough corners, where they lie lurking three or four days together [...]

Plague, 1574

(Dr Perne, the Vice-Chancellor of Cambridge University to Chancellor Lord Burghley, 1574)

Although I must confess that sin is the principal cause of this and of all other plagues sent by almighty God, yet the secondary cause and means is [...] so far as I understand, is not the corruption of the air as the physicians claim at present, but partly to do with the apparel of one that came from London to the midsummer fair and died of the plague in Barnwell, where the plague has been and remains most vehement. The other cause I conjecture is the corruption of the King's ditch which goes through Cambridge; I will arrange to have it cleaned, especially those places where there is the most infection, as soon as we have a hard frost.

Sickness and mortality, Plymouth, 1588

(Lord Howard of Effingham to Lord Burghley, 10 August 1588)

My good Lord:- sickness and mortality begins wonderfully to grow amongst us; and it is a most pitiful sight to see, here at Margate, how the men, having no place to receive them into here, die in the streets [...] It would grieve any man's heart to see them that have served so valiantly to die so miserably.
    The *Elizabeth Jonas*, which hath done as well as ever any ship did in any service, hath had a great infection in her from the beginning, so as of the 500 men which she carried out, by the time we had been in

Plymouth three weeks or a month there were dead of them 200 and above; so as I was driven to set all the rest of her men ashore, to take out her ballast, and to make fires in her of wet broom, three or four days together; and so hoped thereby to have cleansed her of her infection; and thereupon got new men, very tall and able as ever I saw, and put them into her. Now the infection is broken out in greater extremity than ever it did before, and the men die and sicken faster than ever they did […]

It is like enough that the like infection will grow throughout the most part of our fleet; for they have been so long at sea and have so little shift of apparel and so few places to provide them of such wants and no money wherewith to buy it, for some have been - yea the most part these eight months at sea […] Good my Lord, let mariners be pressed and sent down as soon as may be; and money to discharge those that be sick here; and so in haste I bid your Lordship farewell.

Thomas More on enclosure, 1516

(Thomas More, *Utopia*, 1516)

These placid creatures (sheep), which used to require so little food, have now apparently developed a raging appetite, and turned into man-eaters. Fields, houses, towns, everything goes down their throats. To put it more plainly, in those parts of the kingdom where the finest, and so the most expensive wool is produced, the nobles and gentlemen, not to mention several saintly abbots, have grown dissatisfied with the income that their predecessors got out of their estates. They're no longer content to lead lazy, comfortable lives, which do no good to society - they must actively do it harm, by enclosing all the land they can for pasture, and leaving none for cultivation. They're even tearing down houses and demolishing whole towns - except, of course, for the churches, which they preserve for use as sheepfolds. As though they didn't waste enough of your soil already on their coverts and game-preserves, these kind souls have started destroying all trace of human habitation, and turning every scrap of farmland into a wilderness.

So what happens? Each greedy individual preys on his native land like a malignant growth, absorbing field after field, and enclosing thousands of acres with a single fence. Result: hundreds of farmers evicted. They're either cheated or bullied into giving up their property, or systematically ill-treated until they're finally forced to sell. Whichever way it's done, out the poor creatures have to go, men and women, husbands and wives, widows and orphans, mothers and tiny children, together with all their employees [...] Of course, they can always become tramps and beggars, but even then they're liable to be arrested as vagrants, and put in prison for being idle - when nobody will give them a job, however much they want one. For farm-work is what they're used to, and when there's no arable land, there's no farm-work to be done. After all, it only takes one shepherd or cowherd to graze animals over an area that would need any amount of labour to make it fit for corn production.

For the same reason corn is much dearer in many districts [...] Thus a few greedy people have converted one of England's greatest national advantages into a national disaster. For it's the high price of food that makes employers turn off so many of their servants - which inevitably means turning them into beggars or thieves. And theft comes easier to a man of spirit.

Robert Kett on enclosure, 1549

(Three of Robert Kett's twenty-nine demands, issued by the Norfolk rebels in 1549)

1. We pray your grace that where it is enacted for enclosing that it be not hurtful to such as have enclosed saffron grounds, for they be greatly chargeable to them, and that henceforth no man shall enclose any more.

3. We pray your grace that no lord of any manor shall common [i.e. graze his own livestock] on the Commons.

11. We pray that all freeholders and copyholders may take the profits of all commons, and there to common, and the lords not to common nor take profits of the same.

Good husbandry, 1557

(Thomas Tusser, *Five Hundred Points of Good Husbandry*, 1557)

The country enclosed I praise,
The t'other delighteth not me;
For nothing the wealth it doth raise,
To such as inferior be.
More plenty of mutton and beef,
Corn, butter, and cheese of the best,
More wealth anywhere, to be brief,
More people, more handsome and prest [alert].
Where find ye? (go search any coast)
Than there where enclosures are most.
More work for the labouring man,
As well in the town as the field;
Or whereof (devise if ye can)
More profit, what countries do yield?
More seldom, where see ye the poor,
Go begging from door to door?

Act against vagabonds and beggars, 1495

(*An Act against Vagabonds and Beggars*, 1495)

For as much as the King's grace most entirely desireth amongst all earthly things the prosperity and restfulness of this his land and his subjects of the same, to live quietly and surefully to the pleasure of God and according to his laws [...] his Highness will [that] by the authority of this present Parliament it be ordained and enacted that [...] constables and petty constables and all other governors and officers of cities, burghs, towns, townships, villages and other places, within three days of the Act proclaimed, make due search, and take or cause to be taken all such vagabonds, idle and suspect persons living suspiciously, and them so taken to set in stocks, there to remain by the space of three days and three nights and there to have none other sustenance but bread and water; and after the said three days and three nights to be had out and set at large, and then to be commanded to avoid the town [...] And if any person or persons give any other meat or drink to the said misdoers being in stocks in form aforesaid, or the same prisoners favour in their misdoing, that then they forfeit for every time so doing twelve pence.

Poverty in Somerset, 1596

(Edward Hext, Justice of the Peace in Somerset, 1596)

I do not see how it is possible for the poor countryman to bear the burdens laid upon him and the rapines of the infinite numbers of the wicked, wandering, idle people of the land [...] And this year there assembled eighty in a company and took a whole cartload of cheese from one driving it to a fair and dispersed it amongst them for which some of them have endured long imprisonment and fine by the judgement of the good Lord Chief Justice, at our last Christmas Sessions; which may grow dangerous by the aid of such numbers as are abroad, especially in this time of dearth, who no doubt animate them all to contempt both of noblemen and, gentlemen continually buzzing into their ears that the rich men have got all into their hands and will starve the poor. And I may justly say that the infinite numbers of the idle, wandering people and robbers of the land are the chiefest cause of the dearth, for though they labour not and yet they spend doubly as much as the labourer doth, for they lie idly in the ale houses day and night eating and drinking excessively.

Gypsies, 1597

(Extract from *An Act for Punishment of Rogues, Vagabonds and Sturdy Beggars*, 1597)

[...] all such persons, not being felons, wandering and pretending themselves to be Egyptions, or wandering in the habit, form or attire of counterfeit Egyptions; shall be taken, adjudged and deemed rogues, vagabonds and sturdy beggars, and shall sustain such pain and punishment as by this act is in that behalf appointed.

Bear baiting, 1599

(Account of bear-baiting, 1599)

Every Sunday and Wednesday in London there are bear baitings. The bear pit is circular with stands around the top for spectators. The ground space down below is empty. Here a large bear on a rope was tied to a stake. Then a number of great English Mastiff dogs were brought in and shown to the bear. After this they baited the bear, one after the other. Although the dogs were struck and mauled by the bear they did not give in. They had to be pulled off by sheer force and their mouths forced open with long sticks. The bear's teeth were not sharp and they could not injure the dogs; they have them broken short. When the mastiffs tired, fresh ones were brought in to bait the bear. When the bear was tired a powerful white bull was then brought in. One dog at a time was set on him. He speared these with his horns and tossed them so they could not get the better of him.

On arranged marriages, c.1562

(Thomas Becon, *Boke of Matrimony*, c.1562)

This kind of marrying hath ever been detested. And not without a cause. For when they come into the perfection of age, and see other whom they could find in their heart to fancy and love better, then many of them begin to hate one another and curse their parents even unto the pit of hell for the coupling of them together. Then they seek all possible means to be divorced one from another. But if it be so that they remain still together, what frowning, overwharting, scolding and chiding is there between them, so that the whole house is filled full of those tragedies even unto the top. What a wicked and hell-like life is this! [...] What is the original cause of all these tragical and bloody dissensions but only the covetous affection of those parents which for lucre's sake so wickedly bestow their children in their youth, and yoke them with such as they cannot favour in their age.

Star Chamber, 1565

(Sir Thomas Smith, *De Republica Anglorum*, 1565)

There is yet in England another court, of the which that I can understand there is not the like in any other country [...] which is called the Star Chamber, either because it is full of windows or because at the first all the roof thereof was decked with images of stars gilded [...][The effect of this court is] to bridle such stout noblemen or gentlemen which would offer wrong by force to any manner men and cannot be content to demand or defend the right by order of law. This court began long before, but took great augmentation and authority at that time that Cardinal Wolsey, Archbishop of York, was chancellor of England, who of some was thought to have first devised the court because that he, after some intermission by negligence of time, augmented the authority of it, which was at that time marvellous necessary to do, to repress the insolency of the noblemen and gentlemen of the north parts of England, who being far from the King and the seat of justice made almost as it were an ordinary war among themselves and made their force their law [...]

Star Chamber, c.1600

(Sir Edward Coke, *Fourth Institute*, c.1600)

It is the most honourable court (our Parliament excepted) that is in the Christian world, both in respect of the judges of the Court and of their honourable proceeding according to their just jurisdiction and the ancient and just orders of the court. For the judges of the same are (as you have heard) the grandees of the realm, the lord chancellor, the lord treasurer, the lord president of the King's Council, lords spiritual, temporal and the lord privy seal, all the others of the King's most honourable Privy Council and the principal judges of the realm, and such other lords of Parliament as the King shall name [...] This Court [...] doth keep all England in quiet.

A bill in Star Chamber, 1500

(A bill in Star Chamber, 1500)

TO THE KING OUR SOVEREIGN LORD
In humble wise complain to your most noble grace your faithful subjects and true liegemen Richard Joyfull, John Mercer of Warcop in your county of Westmorland, yeomen, Gabriel Warcoppe, Thomas Mosse the

elder, Robert Gibson and Robert Mosse, of the same, yeomen. That where your said beseechers were in God's peace and yours, one Robert Warcoppe the elder, of Warcop, Robert Warcoppe the younger, and other riotous and misruled people, to the number of fifty three persons and more, the forteenth day of the month of October last past, with force of arms, that is to say with bows, arrows, bills, swords and bucklers, at Warcop forsaid in the county of Westmorland riotously assembled, made assault upon your said beseechers and there beat, wounded and put in jeopardy of their lives without occasion on their part giving, to the great peril of your said beseechers and to the worst example of other like offending unless due punishment be had for reformation of the premises. In consideration whereof, and that your said poor subjects might there live in God's peace and yours, sovereign lord, that it might please your most noble grace to grant to your said beseechers your gracious letters of privy seal to be directed to the said misdoers, commanding them by the same to appear before your highness and your honourable Council at a day by your grace to be limited, and to bring with them such other of the said offenders as shall like your grace; to answer to the premises and therein further to do and receive after their demerits, as shall accord with right and good conscience. And your said beseechers shall pray to God for the preservation of your most noble estate in joy long to endure.

War and trade, 1586

(A Spanish report, 1586)

They [the English] are much troubled with this war they have entered into with against Spain, as the whole country is without trade, and knows not how to recover it; the shipping and commerce here having mainly depended upon the communication with Spain and Portugal. They feel the deprivation all the more now, with the loss of the cloth trade with Germany, which they formally carried on through Holland and up the Rhine, but have now been deprived of by the capture of Nutz on that river. If Berck be taken also, which please God it will be now that the neighbouring places have been taken, they will not be able to send any cloth at all, and this is causing much dissatisfaction allover the country [...] The rest of their trade with the other German ports and Muscovy is a mere trifle, as all they brought from those places was sent by them to

Spain, and their Spanish trade being now gone the other is of no use to them, as they do not know what to do with the merchandise they bring hither. All that is left to them is the Levant trade, which is with Turkey and Italy, and that with Barbary. If these two are taken from them, which can be easily done, they will be driven into a corner, without any commerce or navigation at all. Their French trade is very insignificant, and is carried on by a few small vessels only.

The start of England's trade in African slaves, 1564

(John Hawkins' account of his voyage to Guinea and the Indies in 1564, recorded in Richard Hakluyt, *The Principal Navigations, Voyages; Traffiques and Discoveries of the English Nation*, 1598-1600)

The captain was advertised by the Portuguese of a town of the negroes, where there was not only great quantity of gold, but also that there were not above forty men, and an hundred women and children in the town, so that he might get an hundred slaves [...] and thereupon prepared his men in armour and weapon together, to the number of forty men well appointed, having to their guides certain Portuguese: we landing boat after boat, and diverse of our men scatrtering themselves, contrary to the captain's will, by one or two in a company, for the hope that they had to find gold in their houses, ransacking the same, in the meantime the negroes came upon them, and hurt many being thus scattered [...]

We departed with all our ships from Sierra Leone, towards the West Indies, and for the space of eighteen days, we were becalmed, having now and then contrary winds, which happened to us very ill, being but reasonably watered, for so great a company of negroes, and ourselves, which pinched us all, and that which was worst, put us in such fear that many never thought to have reached the Indies, wi thout great death of negroes and of themselves: but the Almighty God, who never suffereth his elect to perish, sent us the sixteenth of February, the ordinary breeze, which is the northwest wind, which never left us, till we came to an island of the cannibals, called Dominica [...]

We came to a place the main called Cumana [in Venezuala] [...] Near about this place, inhabited certain Indians, who the next day after we came thither, came down to us, presenting mill and cakes of bread, which they had made of a kind of corn called maize, in bigness of a pease, the ear whereof is much like to a teasel, but a span in length, having thereon a number of grains. Also they brought down to us hens, potatoes and pines, which we bought for beads, pewter whistles, glasses, knives, and other trifles.

These potatoes be the most delicate roots that may be eaten, and do far exceed our parsnips or carrots.

Raleigh's Search for El Dorado

(Sir Walter Raleigh, 'The Discovery of Guiana' in Richard Hakluyt, *The Principal Navigations, Voyages; Traffiques and Discoveries of the English Nation*, 1598-1600)

I sent Captain Whiddon the year before to get what knowledge he could of Guiana, but my intelligence was far from truth, for the country is situated above 600 English miles further from the sea, than I was made to believe it had been [...] I passed 400 leaving my ships so far from me at anchor in the sea [...] and in one barge, two wherries [small boats] and a ship boat of the Lion's Whelp, we carried 100 persons and their victuals for a month, being all driven to lie in the rain and weather, in the open air, in the burning sun, and upon the hard boards, and to dress our meat, and to carryall manner of furniture in them, wherewith they were so pestered and unsavoury, that what with victuals being most fish, with wet clothes of so many men thrust together, and the heat of the sun, I will undertake there was never any prison in England, that could be found more unsavoury and loathsome, especially to myself, who had for many years been dieted and cared for in a sort far more differing.

[...] The empire of Guiana is directly east from Peru towards the sea, and lieth under the equinoctial line, and it hath more abundance of gold than any part of Peru, and as many or more great cities than ever Peru had when it flourished most: I have been assured by such of the Spa~iards as have seen Manoa the imperial city of Guiana, which the Spaniards call El Dorado, that for the greatness, for the riches, and for the excellent seat, it far exceedeth any of the world.

Although these reports may seem strange, yet if we consider the many millions which are daily brought out of Peru into Spain, we may easily believe the same: for we find that by the abundant treasure of that country the Spanish King vexeth all the princes of Europe, and is become, in a few years, from a poor King of Castille, the greatest monarch of this part of the world.

How all these rivers cross and encounter, how the country lieth and is bordered mine own discovery, and the way that I entered, with all the rest, your lordship shall receive in a large chart or map, which I have not yet finished, and which I shall most humbly pray your lordship to secrete and not to suffer it to pass your own hands; for by a draught thereof all may prevented by other nations: for I know it is this very year sought by the French.

[...] Nothing got us more love amongst them [the Arawak people] than this usage: for I suffered not any man to take from any of the nations so much as a pina, or a potato root, without giving them contentment, nor any man so much as to offer to touch any of their wives or daughters: which course so contrary to the Spaniards drew them to admire Her Majesty, whose commandment I told them it was, and also to wonderfully honour our nation.

[...] There was nothing whereof I was more curious, than to find out the true remedy of these poisoned arrows [used by the Aroras nation]: for besides the mortality of the wound they make, the party shot endureth the most insufferable torment in the world and abideth a most ugly and lamentable death, sometimes dying stark mad, sometimes their bowels breaking out of their bellies.

It is more strange to know, that in all this time there was never Spaniard either by gift or torment that could attain to the true knowledge of the cure, although they have martyred and put to invented torture I know not how many of them.

[...] I made him [the king of Aromaia] know the cause of my coming thither, whose servant I was, and that the Queen's pleasure was, I should undertake the voyage for their defence, and to deliver them from the tyranny of the Spaniards, dilating at large Her Majesty's greatness, her justice, her charity to all oppressed nations, with as many as the rest of her beauties and virtues, as either I could express, or they conceive: I began to sound the old man as touching Guiana, and the state thereof, what sort of common wealth it was, how governed, of what strength and policy, how far it extended, and what nations were friends or enemies adjoining.

[...] Next unto Aro there are two rivers Atoica and Caura, and on that branch which is called Caura, are a nation of people, whose heads appear not above their shoulders: which though it may be thought a mere fable, yet for mine own part I am resolved it is true, because every child in Arromaia and Canuri affirm the same: they are reported to have their eyes in their shoulders, and their mouths in the middle of their breasts, and that a long train of hair groweth backward between their shoulders. Such a nation was written of by Mandeville, whose reports were held for fables for many years, and yet since the East Indies were discovered, we find his relations true of such things as heretofore were held incredible: for mine own part I saw them not, but I am resolved that so many people did not all combine, or forethink to make the report.

[...] I will promise these things that follow [...] The common soldier shall here fight for gold, and pay himself instead of pence, with plates of half a foot broad [...] There is no country which yieldeth more pleasure to its inhabitants, either for the common delights of hunting, hawking, fishing, fowling, or the rest. [...] Both for health, good air, pleasure, and riches I am resolved it cannot be equalled [...] It hath [...] great quantities of brazil-wood, and diverse berries that dye a most perfect crimson and carnation.

All places yield abundance of cotton, of silk, of balsam [...] The soil besides is so excellent and so full of rivers, as it will commodities, which the carry sugar, ginger, and all those other West Indies have [...] The navigation is short, for it may be sailed with an ordinary wind in six weeks [...] It is besides so defensible [...] whatsoever prince shall possess it, shall be greatest, and if the King of Spain shall enjoy it, he will become irresistible [...]

[...] I trust in God, this being true, will suffice, and that he which is King of Kings and Lord of Lords, will put it into heart which is Lady of Ladies to possess it.

The court of Henry VIII

(George Cavendish, *The Life of Cardinal Wolsey*, 1558)

After the return of these strangers [French ambassadors] from Windsor, which place with the goodly order thereof they much commended, the day approached that they were invited to the court at Greenwich; where first they dined, and after long consultation of the sagest with our counsellors, and dancing of the rest and other pastimes, the time of supper carne on. Then was the banqueting chamber in the tilt yard furnished for the entertainment of these strangers, to the which place they were conveyed by the noblest persons being then in the court, where they both supped and banqueted. But to describe the dishes, the subtleties, the many strange devices and order in the same, I do both lack wit in my gross old head, and cunning in my bowels to declare the wonderful and curious imaginations in the same invented and devised [...] In the midst of this banquet there was tourneying at the barriers (even in the chamber), with lusty gentlemen in gorgeous complete harness, on foot; then there was the most goodliest disguising or interlude, made in Latin and French, whose apparel was of such exceeding riches that it passeth my capacity to expound.

This done, then came in such a number of the fair ladies and gentlewomen that bare any bruit or fame of beauty in this realm, in the richest apparel, and devised in divers goodly fashions that all the cunningest tailors could devise to shape or cut, to set forth their hauty, gesture, and the goodly proportion of their bodies [...] with whom these gentlemen of France danced [...]

Thus was this night occupied and consumed from five of the clock until two or three after midnight [...]

Royal patronage

(George Cavendish, *The Life of Cardinal Wolsey*, 1558)

[...] Mistress Anne Boleyn was revoked unto the court, where she flourished after in great estimation and favour [...] after she knew the king's pleasure, and the great love that he bare in the bottom of his stomach then she began to look very hault [haughty] and stout [bold], having all manner of jewels, or rich apparel, that might be gotten with money. It was therefore judged by-and-bye through all the court of every man, that she being in such favour, might work masteries with the king, and obtain any suit of him for her friend.

Henry VIII's Privy Council, 1540

(Proceedings of the Privy Council, 1540)

The 10th day of August in the 32nd year of the reign of our sovereign lord King Henry VIII [...] an order was taken and determined by his Majesty by the advice of his Highness' Privy Council [...] That there should be a clerk attendant upon the said Council to write, enter and register all such decrees, determinations, letters and other such things as he should be appointed to enter in a book. to remain always as a ledger, as well for the discharge of the said councillors touching such things as they should pass from time to time, as also for a memorial unto them of their own proceedings; unto the which office William Paget, late the Queen's secretary, was appointed by the King's Highness and sworn in the presence of the said Council the day and year abovesaid.

HISTORICAL SOURCES

The main chronicles and other historical texts referred to in this book are:

The Crowland chronicle
(1459-86)
Pronay, N. and Cox, J. (eds.), *The Crowland Chronicle Continuations 1459-86* (London, 1986).

The Great Chronicle of London
(unknown author, written in the fifteenth century, covers English history from 1089 to 1483)
Thomas, A. H., and Thornley, I. D. (eds.), *The Great Chronicle of London* (London, 1938).

Historical notes of a London citizen
(1483-88)
Green, R. F. (ed.), 'Historical notes of a London citizen', 1483-88, in *English Historical Review*, vol. 96, 1981.

Historie of the arrival of King Edward in England
(early 1470s, unknown author, supporter of Edward IV, claims to have witnessed some of the events described)
Bruce, J. (ed.), *Historie of the Arrivall of King Edward in England* (Camden Society, 1838).

The Paston letters
(1422-1509)
Gairdner, J. (ed.), *The Paston Letters* (Chatto and Windus, 1904).

An English Chronicle of the Reigns of Richard II, Henry IV, Henry V and Henry VI
(c. 1465)
Davies, J. S. (ed.), *An English Chronicle of the Reigns of Richard II, Henry IV, Henry V and Henry VI* (Camden Society, 1856).

Robert Bale's chronicle
(a London lawyer, part of the text was written within days of the

first battle of St Albans, 1461)
R. Flenley (ed.), *Six Town Chronicles* (Clarendon Press, 1911).

John Benet's chronicle
(probably written in Oxford, 1440-41, and London, 1447-62)
G. L. Harriss and M. A. Harriss (eds.), *Camden Miscellany, XXIV* (Camden 4th Series vol. 9, Royal Historical Society, 1973).

Jean Chartier's chronicle
(c. 1480, probably commissioned by Edward IV)
de Viriville, V. (ed.), *Chronique Française du Roi de France Charles VII* (France, 1858).

Robert Fabyan's *Great Chronicle of London*
(London-based draper, sheriff and alderman, died c.1512
Ellis, H. (ed.), *The New Chronicles of England and France in Two Parts* (London, 1811).

Gregory's Chronicle
(c. 1450-61)
J. Gairdner, J. (ed.), *The Historical Colleections of a London Citizen in the Fifteenth Century* (London, 1876).

Edward Hall, *The union of the two noble and illustre families of Lancaster and York*
(Hall was born in 1497 and died in 1547; his history was first published in 1542)
Whitby, C. (ed.) *The Union of the Two Noble and Illustre Families of Lancaster and York* (London, 1904).

Raphael Holinshed's chronicles
(Holinshed was born in 1529 and died in 1580; his chronicles were first published in 1577)
Snow, V. F. (ed.), *Holinshed's Chronicles of England, Scotland and Ireland* (New York, 1965).

Dominico Mancini, *The Usurpation of Richard III*
(Italian visitor to England and observer of events, 1482-3)
C. A. J. Armstrong (ed.), *The Usurpation of Richard III* (Oxford, 1969).

Sir Thomas More, *The History of King Richard III*
(written c.1513-18; Privy Councillor to Henry VIII; executed 1535)
R. S. Sylvester, R. S. (ed.), *The History of King Richard III* (New York, 1963).

John Rous, *Historia Regum Angliae*
(completed in 1486)
Hearne, T. (ed.), *Historia Regum Angliae* (Oxford University Press, 1745).

The Rous Roll
(1480s)
Ross, C. (ed.), *John Rous and the Warwick Roll* (Alan Sutton, 1980).

Polydor Vergil, *Anglica Historia*
(Italian diplomat located mostly in England between 1502 and 1553; first published in 1534 but largely written 1512-13)
D. Hay (ed. and trans.), *Anglica Historia, 1485-1537* (Camden Series, 1950).

John Warkworth, *A Chronicle of the First Thirteen Years of the Reign of King Edward the Fourth*
(authorship and date uncertain; probably c.1480)
Halliwell, J. O. (ed.), *A Chronicle of the First Thirteen Years of the Reign of King Edward the Fourth* (Camden Society, 1839).

Jean de Waurin, *Recueil des Croniques*
(compilation of sources by a Burgundian soldier and pro-Yorkist historian; completed version first published in 1469 with subsequent additions up to 1471)
Hardy, W., Hardy, E. L. C. P. (eds.), *Recueil des Croniques* (Rolls Series, 1872-1873).

John Stow's memoranda
(Elizabethan chronicler, born c.1525, died 1605)
Gairdner, J. (ed.), *Three Fifteenth Century Chronicles with Historical Memoranda by John Stow* (London, 1880).

The 'Sources' sections at the end of Chapters 2-4 comprise sources derived from Myers, A. R. (ed.), *English Historical Documents, 1327-1485* (Routledge, 1969).

The 'Sources' section at the end of Chapter 1 and 5 and those that appear elsewhere in the book have been selected and adapted from modernized versions in a range of secondary sources including:

Cook, D., *Lancastrians and Yorkists: the Wars of the Roses* (Longman, 1984).
Barry Coward, *Social Change in Early Modern England 1550-1750* (Longman, 1988).
Doran, S., *England and Europe, 1485-1603* (Longman, 1986).
Anthony Fletcher, *Tudor Rebellions* (Longman, 1983).
Michael A. R. Graves, *Elizabethan Parliaments 1559-1601* (Longman, 1987).
Michael A. R. Graves, *Early Tudor Parliaments 1485-1558* (Longman, 1990).
Christopher Harper-Bill, *The Pre-Reformation Church in England, 1400-1530* (Longman, 1989).
Lander, J. R., *The Wars of the Roses* (Stroud, 1965).
Lockyer, R., *Henry VII* (Longman, 1968).
Newman, S., *Yorkists and Tudors, 1450-1603* (Oxford, 1989).
O'Sullivan, D., Lockyer, R., *Tudor England, 1485-1603* (Longman, 1993).
Geoffrey Regan, *Elizabeth I* (Cambridge University Press, 1988).
Robert Tittler, *The Reign of Mary I* (Longman, 1991).
Williams, C. H. (ed.), *English Historical Documents, 1485-1558* (Routledge, 1967).

Index

Agincourt, 54, 57, 59, 79

agriculture, 27

Albany, Duke of, 15, 126, 211, 213

Alnwick Castle, 108, 109, 133, 134

Amicable Grant, 256, 268, 297, 298, 436

Antwerp, 16, 25, 243

Aragon, Catherine of, 15, 17, 210, 255, 256, 264, 276, 278, 285, 289, 328, 413

Arras, treaty of, 15, 60, 123, 126, 127

Arthur, Prince, 17, 255, 264

Aske, Robert, 256, 284, 303, 305, 306

Audley family, 98, 140, 208, 245, 246

Ayton, treaty of, 211, 213

Bamborough Castle, 133, 134

Barnet, battle of, 14, 42, 104, 118, 147, 148, 149, 151

Bath and Wells, bishop of, 138

Battle of the Spurs, 255, 265

Beaufort, 60, 61, 63, 64, 66, 108, 133, 135, 180, 181, 196, 199, 226

beggars, 36, 48, 49, 50

Berkeley Castle, 118

Berwick upon Tweed, 15, 123

Berwick-upon-Tweed, 126

Black Death, 18, 22, 23, 24, 27

Blois, treaty of, 210

Blore Heath, battle of, 13, 74, 97, 98, 120

Boleyn, Anne, 29, 256, 271, 272, 276, 277, 278, 285, 286, 289, 298, 299, 300, 312, 328, 345, 346, 355, 464

Bosworth, battle of, 15, 21, 43, 72, 162, 166, 170, 171, 172, 174, 180, 181, 182, 183, 193, 196, 197, 198, 202, 205, 211, 218, 221, 222, 224, 232

Brittany, 14, 15, 62, 123, 124, 139, 166, 167, 172, 173, 180, 189, 190, 191, 196, 202, 209, 210

Buckingham, Duke of, 15, 19, 38, 68, 70, 71, 72, 74, 75, 85, 90, 93, 94, 95, 104, 111, 120, 163, 164, 165, 166, 167, 171, 177, 178, 179, 181, 182, 185, 186, 187, 188, 189, 191

Burgundy, 14, 15, 16, 17, 27, 42, 60, 64, 94, 106, 112, 113, 115, 116, 123, 124, 126, 127, 136, 137, 139, 140, 144, 146, 157, 159, 201, 203, 204, 205, 207, 209, 210, 234, 237

Butler, Eleanor, 163, 164

Cabot, John, 16, 218

Cade's rebellion, 13, 65, 66, 83, 85, 87

Calais, 52, 54, 56, 59, 67, 68, 70, 72, 73, 74, 82, 89, 98, 109, 110, 113, 124, 125, 136, 146, 159, 206, 240

Cambrai, bishop of, 205

Canterbury, archbishop of, 70, 75, 90, 99, 104, 148, 207, 225, 244

Caxton, William, 15, 41, 42

Cerne Abbey, 118

Charles the Bold, Duke of Burgundy, 204

Charles V, 61, 256, 257, 269, 287, 288, 313, 316, 318, 328, 329

Charles VIII, King of France, 16, 180, 210

Christ's College, Cambridge, 17

Clarence, Duke of, 15, 20, 44, 111, 112, 113, 114, 115, 116, 117, 120, 121, 122, 131, 132, 136, 137, 138, 140, 142, 143, 144, 146, 148, 156, 161, 165, 184, 191, 232, 233, 234, 235, 243, 248

Cleves, Anne of, 257, 287, 289

Clifford, Lord, 77, 90, 93, 95, 100, 101, 147, 205, 239

cloth industry, 25, 27, 45, 226

Colet, John, 32, 33, 228

Conyers, Sir John, 113

Cornish rebellion, 16, 200, 207, 211, 213, 244, 246

Coventry, 44, 45, 47, 74, 76, 98, 100, 114, 117, 142, 235

Cranmer, Archbishop, 256, 257, 258, 277, 278, 281, 284, 285, 288, 314, 317, 337, 436

Cromwell, Thomas, 149, 256, 257, 274, 278, 279, 280, 281, 282, 283, 284, 285, 286, 287,

INDEX

288, 290, 293, 294, 304, 311, 314, 381, 436, 445, 447, 448

Crowland chronicle, 36, 106, 112, 125, 129, 161, 162, 165, 166, 167, 168, 169, 172, 173, 465

Dacre, Lord, 226

Dartford, 68, 87

de la Pole family, 60, 201, 204, 206, 245

Denmark, 16, 139, 159

Dublin, 53, 65, 73, 201, 214, 215, 235, 243

Dudley, Edmund, 93, 207, 222, 224, 225

Duke of Gloucester, Duke of, 14, 15, 20, 42, 59, 60, 62, 64, 80, 84, 88, 111, 119, 121, 132, 153, 155, 156, 161, 162, 163, 164, 184, 185, 186

Durham, bishop of, 246, 247

Edgecote, battle of, 14, 113

Edward IV, 14, 15, 16, 20, 22, 26, 27, 38, 39, 42, 44, 63, 75, 77, 80, 103, 105, 106, 107, 108, 110, 112, 114, 116, 118, 119, 120, 121, 122, 127, 128, 129, 130, 131, 132, 133, 135, 136, 138, 142, 150, 154, 160, 161, 162, 163, 164, 165, 166, 167, 168, 169, 170, 172, 174, 177, 178, 180, 181, 184, 185, 191, 196, 199, 201, 203, 204, 206, 208, 211, 212, 219, 220, 221, 222, 223, 224, 226, 228, 231, 241, 253, 465, 466

Edward V, 15, 49, 162, 163, 164, 165, 175, 177, 178, 179, 186, 192

Edward, prince of Wales, 13

Egremont, Sir John, 90, 200, 202, 203

Ely, bishop of, 164, 172, 188, 189, 190

Empingham, battle of, 14, 114

Empson, Sir Richard, 207, 222, 225

enclosure, 46, 267, 407, 408

Erasmus, Desiderius, 32, 228

Etaples, treaty of, 16, 210

Exeter, bishop of, 104, 135, 190, 246

Exeter, Duke of, 44, 85, 100, 148, 149

feudalism, 21, 22, 24, 28, 38, 53, 120, 127, 210, 219, 225, 226

Field of Cloth of Gold, 255, 268, 269, 442

517

first battle St Albans, first battle of, 13, 92, 466

Fisher, Bishop, 228, 256, 400

Flanders, 16, 134, 136, 140, 147, 150, 201, 203, 204, 206, 234, 237, 238, 239, 240, 243

Flodden, battle of, 213, 214, 255

Fotheringay, 13

Fougères, 62

France, 13, 14, 15, 16, 26, 40, 44, 54, 56, 57, 58, 59, 60, 61, 62, 63, 65, 67, 72, 73, 79, 80, 81, 84, 88, 89, 104, 106, 109, 110, 112, 113, 114, 115, 116, 119, 120, 122, 123, 124, 125, 126, 127, 128, 133, 135, 137, 138, 139, 140, 144, 147, 156, 157, 158, 159, 160, 172, 173, 176, 180, 197, 203, 206, 209, 210, 211, 213, 214, 215, 221, 236, 237, 244, 250, 251, 255, 256, 257, 258, 265, 266, 268, 269, 280, 289, 292, 293, 308, 310, 315, 316, 318, 326, 331, 332, 333, 344, 353, 355, 356, 360, 361, 362, 363, 366, 370, 371, 372, 373, 396, 437, 464, 466, 471

Glendower, Owen, 57

Grey family, 185, 191

Grey, Sir John, 110

Hall, Edward, 136, 175, 176, 198, 203, 204, 205, 217, 231, 466

Hanseatic League, 14, 26, 27

Hastings, Lord, 104, 110, 137, 147, 163, 164, 165, 178, 186, 187, 188

Hedgeley Moor, battle of, 108, 109, 133, 135

Henry V, 13, 20, 26, 39, 48, 54, 57, 59, 60, 62, 63, 74, 79, 80, 85, 92, 97, 120, 124, 166, 465

Henry VI, 13, 14, 26, 30, 38, 39, 40, 43, 53, 54, 58, 59, 60, 62, 65, 67, 68, 74, 76, 77, 78, 79, 80, 85, 92, 95, 97, 100, 102, 106, 109, 115, 116, 117, 119, 121, 123, 124, 130, 131, 136, 141, 154, 155, 166, 173, 174, 176, 180, 193, 196, 198, 230, 234, 465

Henry VII, 15, 16, 17, 19, 20, 21, 22, 25, 26, 27, 29, 30, 34, 39, 119, 128, 130, 132, 162, 178, 179, 196, 198, 200, 201, 202, 203, 204, 205, 206, 207, 208, 209, 211, 212, 213, 215, 216, 217, 218, 221, 223, 224, 226, 227, 228, 229, 230, 231, 232, 233, 248, 249, 251, 468

INDEX

Henry VIII, 27, 28, 29, 175, 198, 207, 213, 217, 222, 223, 231, 251, 255, 256, 257, 263, 264, 265, 266, 271, 272, 273, 275, 276, 277, 278, 280, 281, 282, 286, 295, 296, 300, 306, 307, 308, 310, 315, 316, 317, 328, 333, 337, 345, 346, 355, 370, 381, 394, 400, 411, 413, 427, 431, 435, 437, 439, 442, 443, 445, 446, 448, 463, 464, 466

Herbert, Lord, 111, 131

heresy, 13, 34, 51, 228

Hexham, battle of, 14, 109, 133, 135

Historie of the Arrivall of King Edward in England, 107

Holinshed's chronicle, 204, 244

Holland, 113, 115, 144, 218

Holy League, 210, 255, 265

Holy Roman Emperor, 209, 218

Howard, Catherine, 257, 287

Hundred Years' War, 35, 54, 62, 68

Hunne, Richard, 255, 274

Ireland, 13, 16, 46, 52, 53, 57, 62, 63, 66, 74, 75, 89, 98, 136, 176, 201, 203, 204, 214, 215, 216, 217, 233, 235, 237, 243, 251, 466

James III, King of Scotland, 15, 123, 126, 127, 211, 212

James IV, King of Scotland, 16, 17, 209, 211, 212, 213, 214

Joan of Arc, 59

John of Gaunt, 34, 56, 64

Kildare, Earl of, 201, 202, 214, 215, 216, 217, 237, 243, 256, 293

Lancaster, Duke of, 56, 58, 64, 78

Lancastrians, 14, 27, 55, 74, 75, 76, 77, 78, 109, 110, 120, 124, 127, 130, 152, 468

League of Cambrai, 210

Lincoln, Earl of, 198, 201, 204, 206, 234, 235

Lincolnshire rising, 14

literacy, 18, 40, 228

livery and maintenance, 44

Lollards, 34, 57

London, 13, 22, 23, 26, 27, 29, 36, 42, 50, 51, 57, 60, 64,

519

65, 66, 67, 69, 70, 71, 74, 75, 76, 77, 82, 85, 86, 87, 88, 90, 91, 92, 93, 94, 100, 101, 102, 104, 105, 109, 112, 114, 117, 118, 119, 122, 127, 128, 130, 132, 134, 136, 137, 138, 142, 143, 146, 147, 148, 149, 151, 154, 155, 156, 158, 159, 162, 163, 164, 167, 168, 170, 171, 177, 178, 180, 184, 185, 187, 188, 189, 195, 200, 201, 205, 207, 208, 211, 224, 232, 239, 240, 241, 244, 245, 246, 248, 465, 466, 467

Louis XI, King of France, 15, 27, 36, 109, 112, 114, 116, 123, 124, 126, 127, 135, 146, 159, 160

Loveday, 73

Lovell, Lord, 170, 200, 201, 202, 204, 219, 224, 234, 235

Low Countries, 16, 25, 29, 204, 210

Ludford, battle of, 98

Ludlow, 47, 62, 67, 68, 74, 89, 97, 163, 165, 226

Maine, 60, 61, 62

Malory, Thomas, 14, 37, 38, 41

Mancini, Dominico, 107, 110, 111, 121, 127, 128, 163, 164, 165, 178, 184, 466

March, Earl of, 57, 74, 77, 91, 98, 101, 102, 226

Marcher lords, 54, 226

Margaret of Anjou, 13, 37, 60, 61, 63, 68, 72, 73, 74, 115, 118, 120, 123, 144

Margaret of Burgundy, 209, 210

Mary I, 59, 255, 257, 258, 297, 319, 323, 327, 328, 331, 334, 335, 337, 342, 344, 345, 346, 347, 355, 370, 421, 427, 440, 442, 445

Maximilian, Emperor, 15, 16, 17, 123, 209, 210, 218

Medina del Campo, treaty of, 15, 210, 236

Melton, William, 32, 33

Middleham Castle, 114, 168

Montague, Marquess of, 115

More, Sir Thomas, 29, 33, 41, 167, 172, 175, 176, 177, 208, 228, 466

More, Thomas, 255, 256, 274, 275, 301, 302, 427, 453, 454

mortality, 23, 25, 40

INDEX

Mortimer's Cross, battle of, 14, 77, 102, 107

Morton, John, 172, 188, 199, 225, 227, 228, 244

Navigation Act, 15

Navigation Acts, 26, 218

Neville, 15, 20, 63, 69, 100, 101, 104, 109, 112, 113, 115, 117, 121, 140, 146, 154, 156, 161, 162

Norfolk, Duchess of, 111

Norfolk, Duke of, 85, 88, 90, 103, 104, 105, 170, 181, 193, 218

Normandy, 13, 59, 62, 63, 64, 68, 80, 81, 88, 89, 109, 124, 138, 139, 144, 157, 158, 159

Northampton, 67, 75, 100, 120, 192

Northampton, battle of, 14, 100

Northumberland, Duke of, 198

Northumberland, Earl of, 93, 95, 101, 147, 170, 180, 181, 194, 199, 202, 226

Oxford, Earl of, 56, 147, 148, 149, 193, 194, 224, 245, 248

papal bull, 15, 31, 200, 228

Parliament of Devils, 74, 75

patronage, 19, 21, 39, 53, 56, 59, 73, 80, 110, 180

Pecock, bishop, 13, 34, 40

Pembroke, Earl of, 91, 93, 100, 102, 113, 114, 140, 196

Percy family, 57, 108, 133, 134, 135

Perpendicular architecture, 29, 31, 37, 39

Perpetual Peace, treaty of, 17, 211

Picquigny, treaty of, 14, 123, 124, 128, 157, 159

Pilgrimage of Grace, 256, 284, 286, 303, 305, 436

Plantagenet, 15, 56, 78, 121

Pope, the, 35, 250

population, 28

Poynings, Sir Edward, 214, 215, 245

Poynings' Law, 16, 214, 217

Prince Arthur, 15, 17, 210, 219, 226, 236

Princes in the Tower, 15, 161, 165, 170, 174, 175, 177, 180, 196, 203, 215

printing press, 15, 41

readeption, 14, 115, 116, 121

Redon, treaty of, 15, 210

Renaissance, the, 35, 197, 212

Richard II, 54, 55, 56, 57, 74, 77, 78, 80, 85, 92, 97, 141, 465

Richard III, 13, 15, 18, 20, 42, 63, 119, 128, 131, 132, 161, 162, 163, 164, 166, 167, 168, 170, 172, 173, 174, 175, 176, 177, 179, 180, 181, 182, 183, 184, 188, 191, 192, 196, 201, 202, 204, 205, 206, 211, 212, 221, 224, 231, 466, 467

Richard Ill, 15, 165, 180, 181, 196, 199, 207

Richard, Duke of York, 16, 59, 62, 64, 106, 177, 178, 206, 208

Richmond, Earl of, 91, 166, 172, 182, 189, 190, 196, 229, 237

Rivers, Earl of, 14, 110, 111, 114, 119, 135, 137, 138, 140, 163, 185

Robin of Redesdale, 14, 113

Rous, John, 46, 166, 174, 176, 181, 182, 183, 184, 192, 467

Rutland, Earl of, 56, 76, 98, 101, 161

Salisbury, bishop of, 64, 66, 80, 111

Salisbury, Earl of, 74, 91, 92, 93, 97, 98, 101

Sandal, 76, 101

Scales, Lord, 86, 137, 140

Scotland, 14, 15, 17, 53, 77, 101, 105, 106, 108, 109, 120, 122, 123, 126, 127, 133, 139, 159, 162, 171, 172, 200, 203, 207, 211, 212, 213, 216, 217, 220, 222, 244, 247, 250, 466

Seymour, Jane, 256, 285, 286, 287, 289

Shaa, Dr Ralph, 188

Simnel, Lambert, 15, 179, 200, 201, 202, 204, 206, 214, 215, 216, 233

Somerset, Duke of, 60, 63, 64, 67, 69, 70, 71, 72, 88, 89, 90, 91, 92, 93, 94, 95, 100, 101, 105, 108, 109, 133, 134, 135, 150, 153

St Albans, 43, 71, 72, 73, 76, 92, 93, 95, 102, 103, 104, 110

St Albans, second battle of, 14, 43, 102

INDEX

St Paul's Cathedral, 68, 73, 116, 118

Stafford family, 86, 93, 119, 140, 163, 190, 200, 201

Stanley family, 16, 147, 180, 181, 182, 183, 193, 194, 195, 198, 205, 206, 245

Statute of Treasons, 16

Stoke, battle of, 15, 201, 202, 206, 210, 214, 235

Strange, Lord, 180, 183, 187, 235

Suffolk, Duke of, 13, 59, 60, 62, 63, 64, 65, 66, 82, 84, 85, 92, 206, 207, 245, 248

Sumptuary laws, 14, 21

Surrey, Earl of, 194, 198, 199, 202, 211, 213, 214, 222, 224, 226, 244, 246

sweating sickness, 23, 182

Tewkesbury, battle of, 14, 118, 150, 152, 155, 156, 161, 174, 196

The Paston Letters, 82, 90, 92, 465

Tower of London, 14, 15, 16, 57, 64, 65, 66, 67, 69, 70, 75, 82, 83, 90, 106, 109, 116, 117, 119, 121, 131, 136, 149, 154, 155, 161, 162, 163, 164, 177, 178, 186, 187, 188, 189, 197, 198, 201, 203, 207, 208, 215, 222, 232, 233, 240, 246

Towton, battle of, 14, 43, 44, 77, 105, 107, 108, 119, 135

trade, 16, 17, 18, 22, 25, 26, 27, 28, 29, 46, 47, 107, 116, 125, 129, 130, 136, 209, 210, 218, 220, 225

Tours, treaty of, 13

Troyes, treaty of, 58, 59

Tudor, 15, 17, 56, 78, 91, 102, 108, 118, 119, 129, 130, 162, 166, 167, 170, 171, 172, 173, 174, 175, 179, 180, 181, 182, 183, 196, 198, 201, 209, 214, 217, 218, 220, 223, 224, 226, 227, 229, 230, 231, 468

Tudor, Jasper, 180, 196

Tyndale, William, 256, 304, 401, 450

universities, 35, 40

Utrecht, treaty of, 14, 27

vagabonds, 45, 49, 50

Vergil, Polydore, 108, 174, 183, 193, 199, 212, 218, 221, 229, 232, 233, 234, 235, 237, 246, 249, 252, 467

wages, 24, 28, 46, 64, 80, 123, 226

Wakefield, battle of, 14, 36, 37, 76, 101, 161

Warbeck, Perkin, 16, 179, 200, 203, 204, 205, 206, 207, 208, 210, 211, 213, 214, 215, 216, 217, 220, 236, 237, 240, 241, 242, 247

warfare, 18, 27, 37, 42, 60, 81, 184

Warkworth, John, 110, 114, 116, 119, 135, 136, 147, 155, 467

Wars of the Roses, 13, 19, 20, 35, 36, 37, 38, 39, 42, 56, 58, 60, 61, 68, 72, 76, 77, 78, 79, 132, 202, 230, 468

Warwick, earl of, 14, 16, 19, 20, 47, 69, 70, 71, 72, 73, 74, 75, 76, 88, 91, 92, 93, 95, 97, 98, 101, 103, 104, 105, 108, 109, 110, 111, 112, 113, 114, 115, 116, 117, 118, 119, 120, 121, 131, 134, 135, 136, 137, 138, 140, 142, 143, 144, 145, 146, 147, 148, 149, 150, 156, 161, 162, 165, 166, 169, 174, 193, 198, 201, 205, 206, 214, 232, 248, 467

Waurin, Jean de, 63, 64, 77, 112, 137, 139, 142, 467

Westminster Abbey, 17, 31, 45, 55, 75, 85, 86, 88, 93, 95, 97, 99, 104, 116, 128, 133, 137, 149, 185, 189, 191, 192, 225, 226, 233

Winchester, bishop of, 39, 67, 116, 245

witchcraft, 15, 31, 114, 121, 191

Wolsey, Thomas, 255, 265, 266, 270, 273

Woodville family, 20, 111, 113, 114, 137, 140, 162, 163, 165, 168, 173, 185

Woodville, Elizabeth, 14, 22, 106, 110, 112, 121, 163, 164, 168, 173

wool, 18, 25, 26, 28, 29, 30, 39, 41, 116, 126, 129, 226

Wycliffe, John, 19, 33, 40

York, archbishop of, 68, 112, 117, 137, 142, 148, 188

York, Duke of, 13, 19, 57, 63, 64, 65, 67, 70, 71, 72, 78, 84, 88, 90, 91, 92, 93, 94, 95, 96, 97, 98, 99, 100, 101, 102, 104, 111, 188, 203, 238, 239, 243

York, Elizabeth of, 166, 169, 199, 201

York, Richard, Duke of, 59, 66, 69, 72, 161, 201

York's first protectorate, 13

York's second protectorate, 13

Yorkists, 14, 16, 27, 43, 65, 72, 74, 75, 77, 98, 107, 110, 118, 130, 133, 196, 199, 230, 468

Made in the USA
Charleston, SC
01 August 2015